Warfare in the WESTERN ★ WORLD

D1100803

VOLUME I

Military Operations From 1600 to 1871

Robert A. Doughty
United States Military Academy

Ira D. Gruber
Rice University

Roy K. Flint
United States Military Academy

Mark Grimsley
The Ohio State University

George C. Herring
University of Kentucky

Donald D. Horward
Florida State University

John A. Lynn
University of Illinois

Williamson Murray
The Ohio State University

HOUGHTON MIFFLIN COMPANY
Boston • New York

Custom Publishing Editor: Martin Lew
Custom Publishing Production Manager: Kathleen McCourt
Custom Publishing Project Coordinator: Katie Finn
Acquisitions: James Miller
Development: Pat Wakeley
Editorial Production: Melissa Ray
Design: Alwyn R. Velásquez
Art Editing: Diane Grossman
Production Coordination: Richard Tonachel
Photo Research: Picture Research Consultants, Inc
               Sandi Rygiel & Pembroke Herbert

Cover Designer: Joel Gendron
Cover Photograph: Photodisc, Inc.

The views expressed herein are those of the authors and do not purport to reflect the position of the United States Military Academy, the Department of the Army, or the Department of Defense.

For permission to use copyrighted materials, grateful acknowledgement is made to the copyright holders listed on page A-1, which is hereby considered an extension of this copyright page.

Copyright © 1996 by D.C. Heath and Company.
Copyright © 2001 by Houghton Mifflin Company.

No part of this work may be reproduced or transmitted in any form or by any means, electronic or mechanical, including photocopying and recording, or by any information storage or retrieval system without the prior written permission of Houghton Mifflin Company unless such copying is expressly permitted by federal copyright law. Address inquiries to College Permissions, Houghton Mifflin Company, 222 Berkeley Street, Boston, MA 02116-3764.

Printed in the United States of America.

ISBN: 13 - 978-0-618-17993-0
ISBN: 10 - 0-618-17993-3
N00202

7 8 9 – KP – 04

Houghton Mifflin
           Custom Publishing

222 Berkeley Street • Boston, MA 02116

Address all correspondence and order information to the above address.

PREFACE

We first talked of writing a history of warfare in the Western world during the spring of 1985. We knew that a number of books dealt broadly with the history of war, usually emphasizing the relationships between war and society. We also knew that there were several multi-volume histories of military operations as well as a multitude of books treating particular wars and campaigns. But we could not find a general history of military operations in the Western world that was both comprehensive and coherent. We decided, therefore, to write such a book. We intended that our book should be sound and readable and that it should appeal to students, to general readers, and to anyone seeking an authoritative reference on warfare.

To give our book the depth and breadth we thought essential to understanding four centuries of warfare, we planned a work of two volumes and six parts. The first volume, which begins with Gustavus Adolphus's synthesis of early seventeenth-century European warfare, analyzes the development of limited warfare in seventeenth and eighteenth-century Europe; the emergence of the citizen soldier and mobile, decisive warfare in the era of the French Revolution and Napoleon; and the adoption of near total warfare in the United States Civil War and the application of Prussian organizational skills to European warfare of the mid-nineteenth century. The second volume, which begins with the small wars of the late nineteenth century, considers successively the systematic harnessing of human and material resources for the total warfare of the First World War, the continuation of total warfare in an even more virulent form during the Second World War, and the resort to varieties of limited warfare since 1945, since the creation of atomic and nuclear weapons.

Because each of the parts of our history is self-sufficient and because several deal with topics that are of special interest to readers, those parts are published separately. Three are available as individual volumes: *The American Civil War: The Emergence of Total Warfare*; *World War II: Total Warfare Around the Globe*; and *Limited Warfare in the Nuclear Age*. A fourth volume, drawn broadly from *Warfare in the Western World*, is titled *American Military History and the Evolution of Warfare in the Western World*. Each of these derivative volumes, like its parent, is profusely illustrated; indeed *Warfare in the Western World* contains more than 150 photographs and an equal number of maps drawn especially for the work.

In undertaking a book on such an extensive and often fragmented subject as four centuries of warfare in the West, we knew that we would need the help of other scholars. Our work, then, has been a cooperative effort from its inception. Ira Gruber wrote chapters 1–5; John Lynn, chapter 6; Donald Horward, chapters 7–9; Mark Grimsley, chapters 10–14; Williamson Murray, chapters 15 and 21–26; Robert Doughty, chapters 16–20, 27, and 30–31; Roy Flint, chapter 28; and George Herring, chapter 29. Doughty and

Gruber contributed the Introduction and Conclusion and helped each other and the other authors to develop unifying themes.

Each of us has, of course, drawn upon the work of scores of other scholars; and each has benefited from the comments of specialists, colleagues, and students who have read portions of this history. We are particularly indebted to Richard Kohn and John Shy, who read carefully an entire draft of the text and drew upon their remarkable understanding of military history and sharp critical judgment to suggest ways for improving the whole. We, and our fellow authors, are grateful to all who have had a part in creating this book. We do not imagine that we will have satisfied our critics; we do hope that they and other readers will continue to share their knowledge of warfare with us.

R. A. D. and I. D. G.

CONTENTS IN BRIEF

CONTENTS

MAP SYMBOLS

The symbols shown below are used on the maps in this volume. Most of the symbols suggest the organization of units in particular campaigns or battles. The reader should understand that the organization of military units has changed over time and has varied from army to army or even within armies. For example, the composition and size of Napoleon's corps varied within his own army and differed from those of his opponents; they also differed dramatically from those of armies later in the nineteenth century. The symbols thus indicate the organization of a unit at a particular time and do not indicate its precise composition or size.

Division	x x ☐
Corps	x x x ☐
Army	xx xx ☐
Army Group	x x x x x ☐
Cavalry Screen	● ● ●
Armor	▭
Airborne	☂
Fort	¤
Mine	○—○—○—○
Bridge	⌣⌢
Boundary between Units	——xxxxx——

LIST OF MAPS

INTRODUCTION

Warfare in the Western World is a history of military operations in the West from the seventeenth century to the present; it is not a comprehensive history of warfare or of wars. It concentrates on selected campaigns in major wars and explains how political and military leaders have used armies to wage war effectively—to defeat the enemy's army, occupy his territory, or break the will of his people. It considers war aims and strategy, the overall goals of a war and the use of military forces to achieve those goals. It also considers tactics, the particular measures taken by a commander to defeat enemy forces engaged in battle with his own. But it focuses on operations, the employment of relatively large forces within a specific theater of war. To make its analysis of operations meaningful, it touches on the history of warfare at sea and in the air and on joint actions involving land, sea, and air forces; and it sometimes discusses warfare throughout the world. But this is primarily a history of military operations in Europe and North America, an explanation of how armies have been used and how the waging of war has changed over the past four centuries.

We emphasize warfare in the Western world in part because the West has had its own separate and remarkably successful way of waging war and in part because this book is intended primarily for readers in the United States, whose military institutions and practices are clearly Western in their origins. Europeans have not always been able to generate superior military power, but from the beginning of the seventeenth until the end of the nineteenth century they were more successful in waging war than any other people on earth. Their experience in warfare has had a global influence, and their methods, somewhat modified, have helped the United States preserve its union and become one of the greatest military powers of the twentieth century. So it is that a book intended for readers in the United States concentrates on the remarkable history of warfare in the Western world.

Our story begins in the early seventeenth century when European warfare was becoming decidedly modern. Improvements in firearms had already rendered medieval fortifications obsolete, given musketeers a marked advantage over soldiers equipped with pikes or swords, and driven the most affluent states of western Europe to invest in ever-larger armies and more elaborate fortresses. But not until the beginning of the seventeenth century were commanders able to take full advantage of firearms in their operations, and no one was more successful than King Gustavus Adolphus of Sweden in exploiting and improving upon contemporary practices. He showed not only how handguns and artillery might be combined to generate devastating firepower and make an army formidable offensively and defensively but also how one small state might draw upon its own resources and those of other states to wage war on an unprecedented scale. This book begins, then, with a principal figure in one of the most significant episodes in the history of warfare—the prolonged European adjustment to improvements in firearms that marked the transition from medieval to modern warfare.

In the nearly four centuries since the death of Gustavus Adolphus, warfare in the West has undergone further dramatic changes, and this book attempts to identify and explain them. From the sprawling campaigns of Gustavus Adolphus to the sieges and skirmishes of the age of limited war; from the sustained marches and decisive battles of Napoleon to the even more rapid deployments, larger forces, and costlier battles that came with railroads and rifled weapons in the mid-nineteenth century; and from the land, sea, and air battles that destroyed soldiers and civilians alike in the world wars of the twentieth century to the geographically and militarily more limited operations of the nuclear age; warfare has undergone substantial and unpredictable changes. In the past four centuries operations have increased fundamentally in scale, speed, complexity, and destructiveness. Those increases, however, have at times been interrupted or even reversed, and they have not made warfare progressively more decisive. To what extent have changes in warfare been affected by underlying developments in the population, food supply, industry, and technology of the Western world? To what extent have changes in warfare been the result of deliberate alterations in the ways that leaders have chosen to organize, train, equip, and employ their forces? We hope that this history will suggest answers to these and other fundamental questions about warfare in the Western world.

I

★ ★ ★ ★

The Age of Limited War

1

GUSTAVUS ADOLPHUS AND THE MILITARY REVOLUTION

The Military Revolution

Gustavus Adolphus and the Military Revolution

Gustavus Adolphus in the Thirty Years' War

From the late fifteenth until the mid-seventeenth century, Europeans suffered through a succession of unusually long and destructive wars. Intense dynastic rivalries kept France and Spain at war from 1494 to 1559—at first in Italy and then along the frontiers of France. Spain, Austria, and other smaller states fought intermittently throughout the sixteenth and early seventeenth century to keep the Ottoman Turks from conquering the central Mediterranean and advancing up the Danube to Vienna. Denmark, Sweden, and Russia disrupted the Baltic in contests over territory and trade; and the Dutch fought for nearly eighty years to gain their independence from Spain (1567–1648)—to preserve their Protestant faith, commerce, and separate government. All these wars disrupted ordinary life and brought much suffering. But none was as destructive as the Thirty Years' War (1618–1648), which engulfed Germany and eleven other states in a complex struggle over religion, dynastic claims, local autonomy, and prestige—in the greatest European war before the French Revolution.

So many wars over so long a time gave Europeans the incentive and the opportunity to make comprehensive changes in the way they fought—in the way they raised, equipped, and employed armies and organized states for war. Considered together, these changes frequently have been described as revolutionary—indeed, as the "military revolution" of early modern Europe.

In essence, this military revolution was a sustained European effort to adjust warfare to improvements in firearms. The development of more

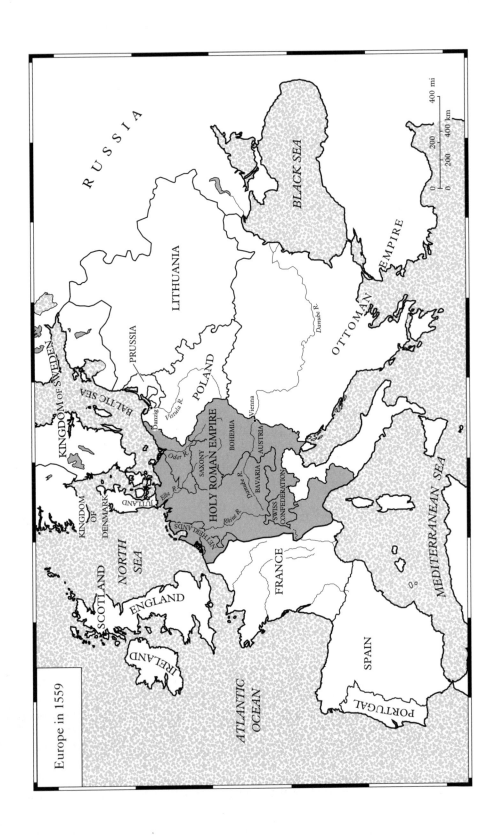

Europe in 1559

effective handguns and artillery in the fifteenth century led Europeans to change the composition of their armies and the design of their fortresses: to rely increasingly on infantry using handguns and on lower, thick-walled fortifications protected by angled bastions. These changes gave such an advantage to the army on the defensive as to discourage general engagements and to encourage long, indecisive, and destructive wars of siegecraft and maneuver. Waging war required ever larger armies and ever greater expense. States sought more effective methods not merely of raising men and revenue but also of training, equipping, and employing armies so as to use firepower decisively. Thus, in adjusting to improvements in handguns and artillery, Europeans worked a military revolution that significantly increased the power of their governments and armed forces. As a result, kings gained greater control over armies, economies, and individual subjects; and European forces came to dominate a third of the earth's landmass by the end of the eighteenth century.

Although the military revolution began in the late fifteenth century in the most affluent parts of western Europe, it reached fruition more than a century later in a relatively small and backward state—in Sweden during the reign of King Gustavus Adolphus (1611–1632). In the intervening years soldiers of France, Spain, Italy, and the Netherlands had taken the lead in the art of war. But it remained for Gustavus Adolphus to give the military revolution its fullest expression. To provide security for his small state at a time when war was becoming increasingly complex and costly, he drew comprehensively on European military practices. He began by strengthening Sweden's government and economy so as to have the means for waging war—the men, money, and munitions. He then trained and equipped his army to exploit the latest improvements in firearms, to act offensively as well as defensively. With his small Swedish army he not only defeated his Baltic rivals but also raised money enough to enter the Thirty Years' War on the side of Protestant German states, hire tens of thousands of mercenaries, and campaign from the Baltic to the Danube. In doing all these things and in waging war on an unprecedented scale, Gustavus Adolphus came to personify the military revolution.

The Military Revolution

Improvements in Firearms

The military revolution began in the fifteenth century with improvements in handguns and cannon. Europeans had firearms as early as 1326, but until the end of the fifteenth century, handguns were not powerful or accurate enough to be primary weapons of war. Early handguns remained light and inaccurate because they were fired by a slow match applied with one hand to a touch hole while the stock of the weapon was supported by the other hand

and braced against the center of a soldier's chest. With the development of the matchlock firing mechanism around 1500, handguns could be fired by pulling a trigger mounted under the stock, thereby allowing a soldier to support his gun with both hands while bracing it against his shoulder and sighting along the barrel. The matchlock made it possible to increase the weight, power, and accuracy of handguns. The ten-pound arquebus, firing a half-ounce lead ball, and the eighteen-pound musket, firing a two-ounce ball, soon became important weapons for sixteenth-century armies. Although the musket was too heavy for all except the strongest men, and although it had to be supported with a forked rest when fired, its ball could stop a heavily armored cavalryman. Matchlocks were particularly valuable in defending fieldworks and fortifications.

Mid-fifteenth-century changes in cannon were no less important than those in handguns. Until about 1450, Europeans made cannon from wrought-iron wedges banded together with iron hoops. These breechloaders, firing stone balls, were mounted on planks and used mainly to attack or defend fortresses. Then, in the middle of the fifteenth century, Europeans developed cannon that were more powerful and more mobile. These new cannon were the product of three technological developments: cast-iron shot, cast-bronze barrels, and corned gunpowder. Cast-iron shot, with greater penetrating power than stone cannonballs, permitted reduction in the size of both shot and cannon without reducing their effectiveness (and cast-iron shot was cheaper to make and easier to standardize than stone). Cast-bronze muzzleloaders, having stronger and better sealed breeches, took more powerful charges and gave projectiles higher velocity. And corned powder, which burned more rapidly than earlier gunpowder, provided a more effective propellant. When the new bronze cannon were equipped with trunnions and carriages, Europeans had lighter, more powerful, and cheaper guns that were also easier to move and aim. These guns could be used not merely in sieges but also with infantry and cavalry in open field battle.

The Italian Wars

Improved artillery and handguns gradually became important to European armies during the Italian Wars of 1494–1530. Although these wars were fought primarily by France and Spain, they included forces from various Italian states, Switzerland, and Germany. Thus commanders could draw from a variety of military traditions and experiment with new weapons and tactics. In the first two decades of the Italian Wars, armies continued to rely mainly on cavalry and infantry armed with lance, javelin, sword, shield, and pike. Arquebuses and bronze field pieces were more important in sieges than in battles; and Swiss pikemen were still able to dominate all other forces as late as 1513. But by then the new cannon and handguns were becoming increasingly important. In 1515 at Marignano, cavalry and artillery were able to check the Swiss pike. In 1522 at Bicocca, Spanish infantry who were armed with arquebuses and pike, supported by artillery, and formed behind a sunken road were able to defeat 8,000 Swiss pikemen attacking in columns. Spanish gunfire and pike killed nearly 3,000 Swiss soldiers in thirty minutes. Three years later at Pavia, in the last great battle of the Italian Wars, arquebusiers again played a prominent part in defeating pikemen and cavalry. The new handguns and cannon were firmly established on the battlefields of Europe.

Bronze cannon firing cast-iron shot had an even earlier and more dramatic effect on sieges and fortifications. At the beginning of the Italian Wars, the French used their new, lighter, and more powerful cannon to take one medieval Italian fortress after another. Cast-iron shot demolished the high stone walls and crenellated superstructures of the medieval works, leaving fortresses and towns defenseless. But Italian architects were already working on fortifications that would withstand the latest artillery and besieging techniques. These new works, appearing in central Italy in the middle of the fifteenth century and throughout the Italian states by 1525, were distinguished by lower, thicker walls and angled bastions faced with brick. These bastions were sharply angled platforms projecting from fortified walls. Defenders on the bastions were able to sweep every foot of the adjacent curtain walls and bastions with artillery and small-arms fire. To these angled bastions and thick, low walls, architects added huge dry moats and exterior earthworks to prevent mining and to protect the main fortifications from direct incoming fire. More elaborate fortifications also included tiered gunrooms in the bastions, countermine shafts and listening posts, and detached fortified chambers or casemates in the dry moats. These new fortifications, developed in late fifteenth-century Italy and known as the *trace italienne*, were very expensive; but when well equipped with modern weapons and adequately garrisoned and supplied, they were able to withstand a determined siege for many months.

By the time of the Italian Wars, improvements in cannon were also affecting war at sea. Mediterranean galleys of the sixteenth century regularly carried bronze muzzle-loading cannon, and those cannon helped Christians defeat a Turkish fleet at Lepanto in 1571. Galleys were well suited to warfare in the confined waters of the Mediterranean. But the large number of oars and oarsmen that gave these vessels superior maneuverability also limited the number of cannon they could carry and the length of time that they could remain at sea. By 1500 the French had begun to place bronze muzzle-loading cannon on sailing ships—on ships that could mount far more guns along their sides than galleys and could venture into the rough waters of the Atlantic. The cannon on these sailing ships were, moreover, powerful enough to sink enemy ships. The English used such ships and guns to defeat the Spanish Armada in 1588. Soon thereafter, the Dutch began building square-rigged sailing ships called frigates that could fight in heavy seas and undertake prolonged ocean voyages. In the seventeenth and eighteenth centuries frigates would help Europeans project power to America, Africa, India, and Indonesia, enabling them to dominate a third of the land on earth by 1800.

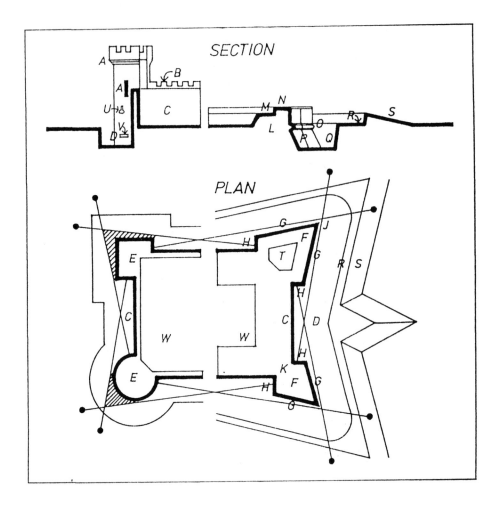

Fig. 1. Medieval and Early Modern Fortification. Diagram contrasts medieval wall and tower defenses (left) with the bastion and rampart system (right). Lines of fire illustrate how the triangular trace avoids blind spots. A: Machicolations or machicoulis gallery, bracketed upper-level works allowing defenders to drop heavy objects to the foot of the wall. B: *Merli* (Italian) or merlons (English), solid protective components between embrasures. C: Curtain, section of wall or rampart between towers or bastions. D: Ditch. E: Towers, with hatching indicating blind spots. F: Bastions, solid gun platforms projecting from the curtains. G: Face of the bastion. H: Flank of the bastion. J: Salient or pointed tip of the bastion. K: Gorge or throat of the bastion. L: Rampart. M: Terreplein or gun platform. N: Parapet. O: Cordon, moulding dividing vertical and battered sections of a rampart or bastion. P: Scarp, battered (sloping) lower section of rampart/bastion. Q: Counterscarp, outer wall of ditch. R: Covered way, protected infantry position outside the ditch. S: Glacis, gently sloping earth bank concealing the covered way and all but the uppermost defensive works. T: Cavalier, raised gun platform on rampart or bastion. U: Keyhole gunport. V: Letterbox gunport. W: Enceinte, area enclosed (literally "belted") by a fortification.

As Simon Pepper and Nicholas Adams's section and plan make clear, the new angled-bastion fortresses of the sixteenth century were designed to offset and exploit improvements in firearms. Even with more powerful artillery and better handguns, Europeans found it difficult to breach the walls of the new angled-bastion fortress.

Stagnation of War

While muzzle-loading cannon were giving sixteenth-century European sailors victories at sea, those same new weapons were working against decisive action ashore. For nearly a century after the Italian Wars, men in western Europe used firearms and fortifications to make warfare inconclusive, protracted, and expensive. The battles of Bicocca and Pavia had left commanders with a keen appreciation of the effectiveness of handguns and artillery used in defense of earthworks. Generals were, with good reasons, reluctant to attack a well-placed enemy or even to maneuver in his presence. No one arm—not pikemen or arquebusiers or heavy cavalry—could be expected to attack successfully; and it was very difficult to decide how to use the various arms together in an offensive action—how pikemen and arquebusiers might cooperate without obstructing one another, how lumbering and slow-firing artillery might be brought into an attack, or what part cavalry should play. Much of the difficulty lay in deciding how to persuade mercenaries to risk their lives against firearms or accept the discipline necessary to make them effective when attacking. Deploying mercenaries for battle took so much time that there was little prospect of surprising an enemy. Even when given new weapons, commanders had trouble using them offensively. The invention of the wheellock firing mechanism (c. 1520) made it possible to use a pistol on horseback and to imagine cavalry blasting a hole in opposing infantry. But cavalrymen tended to use their pistols in desultory firing that was only a substitute for charging with a lance or saber. Similarly, gradually replacing arquebuses with longer-range and more powerful muskets after the mid-sixteenth century seemed mainly to encourage longer-range and inconclusive exchanges of fire. The most celebrated tactical unit of the sixteenth century was the Spanish *tercio*, a dense formation of about 3,000 pikemen and arquebusiers that was best suited to defensive action and remained so even after 1584, when it was reduced to 1,500 men and given as many musketeers as pikemen. Considering, then, the advantages that firearms had given to the defense and the difficulties of deciding how to use various arms and mercenaries in an attack, it is understandable that commanders thought defensively and that there were almost no decisive battles for a century after the Italian Wars.

Without decisive battles, wars in western Europe dragged on in expensive sieges and skirmishes. After the Italian Wars, the angled bastion made its way to those parts of Germany, France, and the Low Countries that were prosperous enough to afford the massive works; and those works shaped the long wars between Spain and France (1530–1559) and between Spain and her rebellious subjects in the Low Countries (1567–1607). The development of cast-iron cannon in the 1540s lowered the cost and increased the availability of siege guns. But cannon remained in short supply throughout the sixteenth century and were not powerful enough to reduce the new fortifications easily or quickly. Conducting a siege required men, equipment, money, and time; conducting many sieges and holding many fortresses required increasingly larger armies. As wars dragged on from one decade to another, monarchs found it ever more difficult to pay and supply their mercenary armies. (The Spanish maintained 13,000 to 15,000 troops in the Low Countries in peacetime and 65,000 to 85,000 in wartime.) And when pay or food failed, mercenaries mutinied. Indeed, the Spanish Army of Flanders—the most famous army of its day—mutinied forty-five times between 1572 and 1607. No wonder the Spanish had trouble waging war decisively against the Dutch.

Dutch Reforms: Maurice of Orange

The success of the Dutch in their struggle for independence depended in no small measure on their creative contributions to the art of war—contributions that played an important part in the military revolution. Maurice of Orange, commander-in-chief of Dutch forces from 1588 to 1609, was one of the first European soldiers to seek a comprehensive system for employing handguns. Since the Italian Wars of the early sixteenth century, arquebuses and muskets had gradually proved their worth, particularly when used with other arms to defend a fortress or fieldwork. But arquebuses and muskets still had technical limitations. They were inaccurate, slow firing (no more than one shot every three minutes), and short ranged (even the musket was ineffective beyond 150 yards). Because of these limitations, handguns did not fit easily into tactics. They were most effective when fired in volleys by men deployed in line. But once a line of arquebusiers or musketeers had fired a volley, it was virtually defenseless while reloading. Arquebusiers and musketeers did not yet have bayonets, and their swords were of little use against enemy pike or cavalry. Commanders tried placing musketeers both on the periphery of and within dense formations of pike, and the pike were able to keep cavalry at bay while the shot were reloading. But firepower was much diminished when musketeers were mixed with columns of pike.

So it was that Maurice of Orange took comprehensive measures to improve the use of handguns. Knowing the frustrations of waging war with mercenaries and militiamen and inspired by the history of Republican Rome, Maurice began by trying to create a professional army that would put service to the state before its own selfish interests and that would submit to a discipline worthy of the Romans. He insisted that his army be well and regularly paid and that it be drilled incessantly by well-educated officers and noncommissioned officers. It would take such an army and such hard, repetitive training, he thought, to develop the firepower and mobility needed to defeat the Army of Flanders. Men who were accustomed to the security of large, densely ordered tactical units like the *tercio* would have to be organized into smaller, more manageable companies of 120 men and into battalions of 580. They would have to learn to fight in thin, extended lines that would make the best use of their muskets, minimize the effects of the enemy's fire, and permit musketeers and pikemen to act together without obstructing each other. And, they would have to master the countermarch so as to sustain a succession of volleys. (In the countermarch, the first rank of musketeers would fire together and then retire to the rear of the files to reload and follow the other ranks in stepping forward to fire another volley in

Pictorial section: Seventeenth century musket drill

Seventeenth-century musket drill, from an English drill book of 1642.

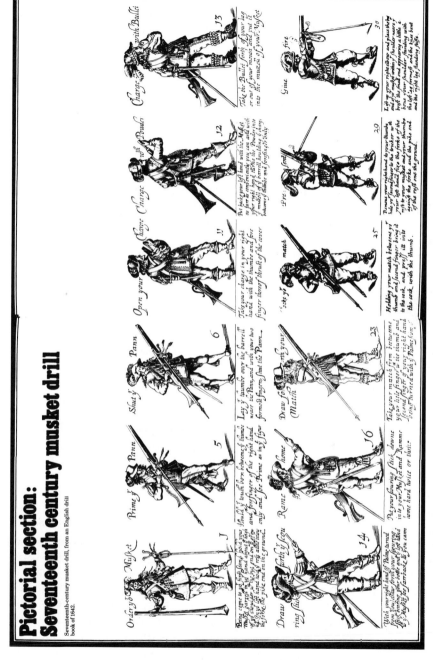

Here are twelve of the thirty-two steps required to load and fire a matchlock musket in 1642. They show how much discipline and training were required to use handguns effectively in combat.

turn.) Although Maurice did not succeed in reforming his cavalry or in coordinating artillery and cavalry with infantry, and although he was conventionally defensive in both tactics and strategy, he did defeat the Spanish in the only battles of his era—at Tournhout in 1597 and Nieupoort in 1600. With disciplined professional soldiers and increased firepower and mobility, he helped win Dutch independence.

After Maurice had demonstrated the value of his military reforms by his victories over the Army of Flanders, other European soldiers began to study and adopt his methods. Protestant states quickly employed the Dutch as military advisors or sent their own officers to serve with the Dutch, read their books, and study their methods (after 1619, by attending the military academy established at Siegen by Maurice's cousin, John of Nassau). No country was more interested in what the Dutch had done than Sweden. Swedish kings hired the Dutch to modernize their army, and Swedish officers studied in the Netherlands and read Dutch books. But it was Gustavus Adolphus who most systematically exploited Dutch practices in recruiting, training, organizing, and employing his army.

Gustavus Adolphus and the Military Revolution

The King and the Military State

Although only seventeen when he came to the throne of Sweden in 1611, Gustavus Adolphus was even then remarkably well suited to be king. His formal education had been broad: in addition to reading in the classics, history, politics, theology, and law, he had made intensive studies of languages (he would come to know nine), warfare, and rhetoric. He had also served a full apprenticeship in government, attending council meetings from the age of ten, hearing complaints from his subjects, receiving ambassadors, addressing the legislature, and traveling throughout Sweden. As he matured, he proved to be energetic and highly intelligent. He was not merely an eloquent and moving speaker who could give a legislature or an army a sense of destiny but also a formidable debater who was willing to test his policies in rough exchanges with his legislature or with leaders of the Lutheran Church. If he was sometimes abusive, and if under increasing responsibilities he lost his sense of moderation and compromise, he ever retained his humility, simple habits, and high sense of duty to Sweden and his Protestant God. He was an inspiring and commanding presence, a man capable of shaping the history of a country or an era.

Among his many talents, none was to be more fully developed than that for leading men in war. As a boy, he read the leading ancient and modern authorities on the art of war, including Polybius, Vegetius, and Machiavelli. From them he learned to admire the citizen soldier who put service to the state before private interest, who depended on discipline and skill to

Gustavus Adolphus was, as this portrait suggests, a commanding and inspiring personality. He synthesized early seventeenth-century European military practices to give the military revolution its fullest operational expression.

defeat more numerous enemies, and who waged war with prudence and perseverance. He also became thoroughly familiar with the best military practices of the early seventeenth century: he studied tactics with a Swedish general trained in the Netherlands, and he lost no opportunity in his travels to observe other armies or to discuss tactics and strategy. To these studies, Gustavus Adolphus added a comprehensive experience of war. On becoming king, he accompanied and led his forces in Sweden's wars with Denmark (1611–1613), Russia (1613–1617), and Poland (1617–1629). Campaign after campaign, war after war, he deepened his understanding of the importance of recruiting and training, of technology and logistics, and of the tactics and strategy best suited to different kinds of war. In resisting the Danes in the rough, wooded terrain of Sweden, he learned the value of fieldworks; in conquering the Baltic provinces of Russia, he came to appreciate the way in which devastating a countryside could deny the enemy food, fuel, and shelter; and in his Polish campaigns he mastered siegecraft and discovered how effective cavalry could be as a shock force. In short, training and experience combined with curiosity and intelligence to give him an extraordinary knowledge of war; and he applied that knowledge with such skill and courage as to become a truly great commander.

While Gustavus Adolphus was learning the art of war in relatively small conflicts with his Baltic neighbors, he was also systematically reforming the government and economy of Sweden. He knew that such reforms would be necessary if Sweden, a relatively small and poor country, were to be secure at a time when war was becoming ever more expensive. To gain the support of leading men, he expanded the role of the representative assembly in making laws and considering foreign policy, and he enlisted members of the nobility to staff his central administration. Then, to gain greater control over his people and to increase revenues and conscription, he not only reorganized his bureaucracy and opened careers to men of talent but also won approval for many new taxes, took control of basic industries (timber and mining), and encouraged other industries, such as munitions, with grants of monopolies. Although these measures did not do all that the king hoped, they did provide the resources needed to bring order and security to Sweden and to provide a foundation for even more ambitious military adventures overseas.

Recruiting

Once he had strengthened his government and economy and ended his wars with Denmark and Russia, Gustavus Adolphus began a comprehensive reform of his army. He turned first to the interrelated problems of recruiting and paying soldiers. To get enough men to defend Sweden and support wars overseas, Gustavus Adolphus had to employ conscripts and mercenaries as well as volunteers. Having found mercenaries to be expensive and unreliable (they required payment in cash, refused to dig trenches, cheated on allowances, and mutinied when dissatisfied), he decided in 1620 to develop a system of conscription that would make him less dependent on mercenaries and that would require fewer cash payments. He had already tried to make the army more attractive—to encourage volunteers and reduce desertions—by associating each unit in the army with a particular recruiting district. In 1620 he organized the adult male population into groups of ten and required each group to furnish and equip one soldier per year, one able-bodied man between eighteen and forty years of age. This system, administered by soldiers and civilians, did meet some opposition—particularly when exemptions were eliminated to meet an increasing demand for men. But the system worked.

So too did Gustavus Adolphus's plan for paying conscripts and volunteers succeed. To reduce the need for cash in a country that was chronically short of cash, he gave conscripts and volunteers the use of or proceeds from land. In peacetime, officers were given farms and common soldiers were billeted with peasants. In wartime, officers and men were paid, respectively, from the rents on farms and taxes on peasants' homesteads. This plan required much land and occasioned some complaints, but it worked. It did not provide cash for mercenaries, for the tens of thousands of men needed for Gustavus Adolphus's campaigns in Prussia and Germany. For that cash, he relied increasingly on contributions, tolls, and subsidies extracted from foreigners.

Handguns and Artillery

While providing for recruits and pay, Gustavus Adolphus also equipped his army with modern weapons. His father and John of Nassau had been unable to persuade Swedes to give up arquebuses for muskets and pikes. But after the arquebus had proved ineffective against both Polish cavalry and Danish infantry, Gustavus Adolphus insisted upon better, if more burdensome, weapons. The matchlock musket that he adopted was more uniform in caliber and slightly lighter than those used by the Dutch and Spanish. Although it weighed more than an arquebus—it still had to be fired from a rest—it was far more powerful. Gustavus Adolphus also reintroduced the pike into the Swedish army. Believing that pikemen would be essential both in protecting musketeers from cavalry and in pressing an attack on infantry, he equipped nearly half of his infantry with pike, helmet, and body armor. The pike itself, somewhat shorter than those of other armies, was sheathed in iron to withstand the hacking of sabers; and its butt was sharpened so that it might be driven into the ground to form a hedge against cavalry. Finally, Gustavus Adolphus equipped his cavalry with wheellock pistols and sabers, intending that the cavalry would both fire and charge into the enemy. He did not use the wheellock firing mechanism in his standard musket because the wheellock was less dependable than the matchlock; and he did not use rifled muskets because they had an even slower rate of fire than smoothbores. By 1632 Sweden was self-sufficient in muskets and pike, if not in match and powder.

Although Gustavus Adolphus found his artillery better equipped than his infantry, he made far more significant improvements in cannon than in muskets or pike—improvements that would revolutionize the role of artillery in battle. Swedish artillery in 1611 was conventionally cumbersome, slow firing, and inaccurate; it was better suited to a siege or defense of an earthwork than to an attack in a general engagement. Gustavus Adolphus determined to make his artillery light and powerful and accurate enough to join decisively with infantry and cavalry in almost any action, offensive or defensive. He began by reducing the artillery in his army to three basic types (those firing 24-, 12-, and 3-pound shot). He then directed his founders to develop a truly mobile 3-pounder. Their experiments of 1627–1629 with thin copper barrels sheathed in rope, mastic, and leather were not a success: these leather guns lacked the strength to receive an adequate charge. But by 1630 his founders had cast a bronze 3-pounder that was light enough to be drawn by one horse or by two or three men. It could be loaded rapidly with a cartridge (powder and shot packaged together) and could fire canister or grapeshot that were lethal at three hundred yards. Here was a weapon that had the mobility, rate of fire, range, and accuracy to be used effectively with other arms, offensively as well as defensively. Gustavus Adolphus promptly assigned one or two of these 3-pounders to every Swedish infantry squadron (about 400 men), giving his army more firepower, temporarily, than any other in Europe. Other countries would soon follow his lead, but Sweden, with its large deposits of copper and its skilled workmen, would continue to produce all the high-quality field artillery that its forces could use.

Discipline and Tactics

Having taken measures to raise, pay, and equip his army, Gustavus Adolphus concentrated on preparing it for war. He knew that his men would have to be thoroughly disciplined to fight as he expected: to form in relatively thin lines before the enemy, to deliver controlled musket and artillery fire while standing under enemy fire, to charge into an enemy with pike or saber (or to receive a charge), and to remain under control of his commands amid the confusion, noise, and terror of close combat. In creating such discipline he began with several advantages. He could expect that each regiment or squadron, having been recruited in a particular part of Sweden, would be strengthened by regional if not family or community ties; he could also expect that regular pay and provisions would free his troops to concentrate on learning and doing their duty and would remove some of the temptation for mutiny, desertion, and plundering. Moreover, he could rely on Protestantism, patriotism, and personal loyalty to him to promote order and common purpose. He was not only a gifted orator and linguist who knew how to bind men together with words. He was also a leader who shared the drudgery and dangers of war—who dug and fought beside his rank and file. But above all Gustavus Adolphus relied on constant training to create and sustain discipline. In peace or war, in garrison or on campaign, even on the eve of battle, he drilled his men in the use of their arms and in maneuvering to the tap of a drum. Thus he created a coherent, disciplined army. Although this army sometimes plundered, and although it had to absorb huge numbers of German mercenaries after 1630, its discipline remained remarkably firm.

On such discipline Gustavus Adolphus built his innovative and highly successful tactics, tactics that required close cooperation of infantry, cavalry, and artillery, that exploited both firepower and shock, and that were as well suited to offense as to defense. Like other commanders of his day, he arranged his army for battle in a line with infantry in the center, cavalry on the wings, and heavy artillery in front of the infantry. But unlike others, he put a second line behind the first and reserves behind both; and he intermixed light artillery with infantry and both light artillery and infantry with his cavalry. So placed, his infantry, artillery, and cavalry could cooperate in using firepower or shock as circumstances required.

His infantry, organized like that of the Dutch in relatively small units with a high proportion of officers, was deployed so that pikemen and musketeers could act without obstructing each other. Gustavus Adolphus's basic infantry unit, the squadron, went into battle in a line six ranks deep, with 216 pikemen in the center, 96 musketeers on each flank, and two 3-pound cannon in close support. On defense, this squadron fought much as the Dutch did: the musketeers used the countermarch to fire a succession of volleys, while the pikemen stood ready to repel an assault by enemy cavalry or infantry. But here the similarity between Maurice's and Gustavus Adolphus's infantry tactics ended. Gustavus Adolphus not only added field artillery to increase the firepower of his infantry but also taught his infantry to act offensively. By employing the countermarch in reverse, his musketeers were able to provide a rolling barrage of fire sustained by 3-pound cannon and exploited at the right moment by a push of the pike. Since the success of these tactics depended upon the coordination of musketeers, pikemen, artillery, and cavalry in many squadrons, Gustavus Adolphus had to have a high proportion of officers and noncommissioned officers (58 to a squadron) and a very well-disciplined rank and file.

In reforming his army, Gustavus Adolphus freely borrowed ideas and practices from others. It is not clear how much he learned from Swedish history; but his grandfather and uncle had experimented with conscripting a national army, with blending handguns and pike in small tactical units, and with the countermarch. His debt to Maurice and the Dutch is much more obvious. Maurice showed him the value of discipline and training, of small tactical units deployed in a thin line, of pike in support of musketeers, and of the countermarch to create sustained fire. Moreover, the Dutch engineers he employed not only built his angled-bastion fortresses but also taught him how to conduct a siege and use earthworks. And he relied on his founders and craftsmen to create the cannon, muskets, and pike that he needed to increase the power of his troops. Gustavus Adolphus even learned from his enemies: from the Russians and Poles, to appreciate devastation as a defensive strategy and cavalry as a shock force; and from the Spanish, to value territorial recruiting as well as the blending of infantry and cavalry and of light artillery and infantry.

But if few of his reforms were his own, he so refined and so synthesized what others had done as to achieve an original and superior expression of the early seventeenth-century art of war and to make his own special contribution to the military revolution. He mobilized the resources of a poor, primitive country to create the most powerful army of its day. He developed the tactics to exploit firepower offensively as well as defensively, and he undertook to wage war on an unprecedented scale. Just how much he accomplished would become clear after 1630, when he intervened in the Thirty Years' War.

Gustavus Adolphus
in the Thirty Years' War

Swedish Intervention

By 1630 the Thirty Years' War had been in progress a dozen years. While Gustavus Adolphus fought Russia and Poland along the Baltic and prepared for war on a larger scale, most of central Europe had been involved in a complex struggle over religion, dynastic claims, and local autonomy. Ferdinand of Styria, hereditary ruler of Habsburg lands in central Europe and elected head of the Holy Roman Empire, had done much to start and sustain the war. A zealous Catholic, he sought to crush Protestants in his own lands and to extend his power and the influence of the Roman Catholic Church to the more than 1,000 other semiautonomous states that made up the Holy Roman Empire. For at least a decade after 1618, he seemed to be succeeding. With the help of Spanish, Bavarian, and papal forces, he was able to defeat a Protestant army at White Mountain, near Prague, in November 1620 and end a revolt in Bohemia. He subsequently deposed the rebellious Protestant elector of the Palatinate and sent armies to subdue Protestant states in central and north Germany. In 1626 his forces defeated the Danes, checking the most serious effort before 1630 at foreign intervention on behalf of Protestants within the Empire; and by late 1627, his armies were in control of much of the Baltic coastline from the Jutland peninsula to the Oder River.

But when Ferdinand tried to exploit his victories, he met increasing opposition within and without the Empire. Germans resented paying taxes and making contributions to support his rapacious mercenary armies. They also resented his growing power and his use of that power to support the Roman Catholic Church. In March 1629 he issued an Edict of Restitution restoring to the Catholic Church all lands it had lost within the Empire since 1552, giving ecclesiastical rulers the same rights as secular rulers to enforce religious conformity, and banishing from the Empire all Protestants except Lutherans. This edict, which threatened many Protestants and jeopardized boundaries, estates, and commercial arrangements throughout central and north Germany, roused fierce opposition. German rulers met at Regensburg in the summer of 1630 to demand that Ferdinand revoke the edict, dismiss his most successful general, reduce his forces, and renounce new wars without the consent of the Empire. Although Ferdinand agreed to give up his general and reduce his forces, he kept the Edict of Restitution—thereby stimulating further opposition among German Protestant rulers. Even before that time, his victories had created jealousies outside the Empire, not just in Protestant countries but also in the largest Catholic nation in Europe, France. Thus, when Gustavus Adolphus was ready to enter the Thirty Years' War, Ferdinand's power had begun to ebb.

The timing was fortuitous for Gustavus Adolphus, who had been considering an invasion of Germany for nearly seven years. As early as 1623, he thought of intervening in the Empire to relieve beleaguered Protestants and to forestall further Imperial conquests. He was not then able to raise the forces he needed: he was at war with Poland; he had not yet completed the reforms of his army or rebuilt his navy; and he was unable to attract allies in or out of Germany. He concentrated, therefore, on the war with Poland, invading East Prussia in the summer of 1626 and establishing himself along the Vistula. But he could not ignore the advance of Imperial forces who reached the Baltic in 1626 and occupied most German ports from the Oder to the Ems by the end of 1627. In June 1628, he joined Denmark in relieving the besieged Pomeranian port of Stralsund; and when in April 1629, 12,000 Imperial troops intervened against him in Poland, he decided to end the war on the Vistula and attack the Imperialists in Germany. The Truce of Altmark of September 1629 not only released some of his troops from Poland but also allowed him to keep possession of all the most important

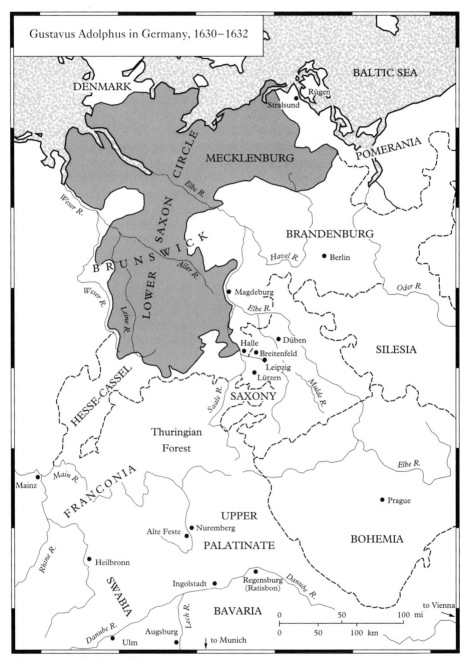

Gustavus Adolphus in Germany, 1630–1632

ports in East Prussia, except Danzig, and to collect the tolls at those ports. Although he remained without allies, he was now ready to wage a larger war in north Germany. In June 1630 he embarked for Pomerania to drive the Imperialists from the Baltic, liberate Protestants in the Empire, provide security for Sweden, and, perhaps, add Stralsund to his kingdom.

For more than a year, Gustavus Adolphus struggled to create and support an army capable of challenging the Imperialists in north Germany.

Although he disembarked in Pomerania with only 14,000 men, he was soon able to establish himself securely along the Oder. The 30,000 Imperial troops then in north Germany could not easily be assembled or reinforced. Even so, shortages of shipping and money made it difficult for Gustavus Adolphus to build up and supply his army from Sweden and other Baltic lands. Nor was he successful at first in drawing support from Protestant German states. Pomerania, which was willing to help, had little to offer. Other German princes preferred to remain independent of both Gustavus Adolphus and Emperor Ferdinand. Without strong support from Germany, the Swedish army in Pomerania grew slowly, perhaps to 50,000 men by the end of 1630. That number was far too small both to garrison posts along the Oder and the Baltic coast and to provide Gustavus Adolphus with enough troops to engage the Imperial army now assembling against him.

Not until the late summer of 1631 would he have enough troops for a major battle. In his plans for 1631, Gustavus Adolphus hoped to raise an additional 80,000 men—to secure Pomerania, mount offensives through Silesia and Saxony toward Vienna, and block any Catholic forces moving north from Bavaria. As it was, he could not even relieve Magdeburg, which fell to the Imperialists in May 1631. But with subsidies from France and Brandenburg, he was able by July to assemble a substantial army on the Elbe and to begin to attract German allies. In August William V of Hesse-Cassel put 10,000 men under Gustavus Adolphus's command; and in September, John George of Saxony joined him with 18,000 men in a desperate effort to save Saxony from an Imperial army led by John Tserclaes von Tilly, an aging but capable commander. Only then, on the eve of the first great battle of his German war, was Gustavus Adolphus able to patch together an army equal in size to the Imperialists.

Breitenfeld

That the two armies should have fought at last in Saxony in September 1631 was the result as much of political and logistical as of tactical considerations. Throughout the summer of 1631, Tilly and the emperor had been pressing the elector of Saxony to join the Imperial cause. It was not just that they wanted to be sure of his allegiance; they were particularly eager to draw supplies and men from his unspoiled lands and to have free passage through Saxony to north Germany. John George would have preferred to remain neutral, but in response to Tilly's increasingly sharp demands, he began recruiting his army and asked Gustavus Adolphus for help. Gustavus Adolphus, having no intention of letting Tilly crush John George, put his army on the road from Brandenburg to Saxony. But he also insisted on an alliance— a formal agreement with John George—as the price of his support. When in late August Tilly invaded Saxony and proceeded to Leipzig, Gustavus Adolphus was able to join forces with John George some twenty miles to the north of Leipzig at Düben.

By then, September 5, each of the commanders wanted a battle. There would be no wearying and vain maneuvers. Gustavus Adolphus had taken care to secure a line of retreat to the north. He was confident in his own 24,000 experienced and well-equipped troops; and he believed that they, with the support of 18,000 Saxons, were well matched against Tilly's army of 35,000. Here was the chance that Gustavus Adolphus had sought, the chance to destroy an Imperial army and turn the war decidedly in his favor. John George did not share Gustavus Adolphus's vision; he was simply provoked enough by the invasion and plundering of his lands and ignorant enough of war to favor battle. Tilly, for his part, had been maneuvering for months to bring Gustavus Adolphus to action. He was confident that he would be able to defeat the Swedes and their new allies in the open rolling country north of Leipzig, in terrain ideally suited to his massive *tercios* and cavalry. Thus the three commanders brought their armies together five miles north of Leipzig, near Breitenfeld. It was September 7, 1631, a fine, warm autumn day.

Although the allies had about 7,000 more men than the Imperialists, the Battle of Breitenfeld was decided not by numbers but by discipline, firepower, and tactical flexibility. The opposing forces deployed and fought very differently. The Imperialists attacked, after a preliminary bombardment by their heavy artillery, in a single, deep line: eighteen *tercios* of infantry in the center with cavalry on the wings and in the rear. Their arms were not combined. The allies received the attack in line, Swedes on the right, Saxons on the left. But while the Saxons were deployed in a dense formation, the Swedes (one-fourth natives, three-fourths foreign mercenaries) were in two thin lines: heavy artillery and infantry in the center, cavalry on the wings and in reserve. Swedish arms were also combined, infantry with light artillery and cavalry with infantry, so that every unit could meet the Imperialists with both firepower and shock.

The Imperialists first attacked the allied flanks: the left of the Saxons and the right of the Swedes. Although they made little headway against the Swedes, the Imperialists soon broke the Saxons, putting the whole of the Saxon army to flight and threatening to envelop the Swedish left. A less experienced army than the Swedes'—or even an experienced army with less discipline, firepower, and tactical flexibility—might have collapsed at this point in the battle. But Gustav Horn, commanding the Swedish left, realigned his units to protect his flank and deliver devastating combined-arms fire into the dense *tercios* and milling cavalry. Here was the advantage of having squadrons of infantry, six ranks deep, that could change front and produce volley after volley of musketry; of light 3-pounders that could be redirected to support the infantry with sheets of canister; and of cavalry mixed with infantry that could sweep away horsemen relying mainly on wheellock pistols. Indeed, as the battle progressed, it was the Swedes who rallied to turn the Imperial flanks and destroy their army. By dusk, after five hours of fighting, only the remnants of the *tercios* remained. The Swedes slept on the field. The next morning they counted 7,600 Imperialist dead and 6,000 prisoners. Altogether, at a cost of 2,100 casualties, the Swedes had killed, wounded, or captured nearly 20,000 of Tilly's men. Gustavus Adolphus and his small disciplined army had used firepower and tactical flexibility to win a great victory.

War on an Unprecedented Scale

However impressive his victory, Gustavus Adolphus soon realized that he would need to do more than win a battle to break Ferdinand's hold on the Empire, that he would need to wage war on an unprecedented scale. Before Breitenfeld, he had kept close to his Pomeranian base, gradually expanding along the Oder, Havel, and Elbe rivers and drawing his supplies from the Baltic and north Germany. But confined as he was, he had great trouble raising and sustaining forces large enough to evict the Imperialists even from Protestant lands. Thus, after Breitenfeld, he decided to shift his army to the southwest and to draw men and supplies from diverse parts of the Empire: he would make Catholics as well as Protestants pay for his war against Ferdinand.

Ignoring the remnants of Tilly's army and leaving John George to secure Silesia, Gustavus Adolphus proceeded to Franconia and then along the Main to the Rhine. By December 1631, he was at Mainz, whence he could block reinforcements en route to Austria from Italy, Spain, or the Low Countries; strike at Bavaria, a center of Imperialist strength; or launch an offensive along the Danube toward Vienna. Just as important, at Mainz he was well placed to coordinate the raising of men and supplies for his armies, particularly in the rich lands of southwest Germany. Because plundering alienated the population and jeopardized the security of his forces, he arranged to work through local German officials to collect taxes and recruit men. He was less successful in negotiating alliances with German princes and in getting further subsidies from European powers.

Gustavus Adolphus took such trouble in recruiting his forces because he was planning an extraordinarily large and complex campaign to end the war in 1632. Although he had raised only about 100,000 men in 1631, including the armies of Saxony and Hesse-Cassel, he intended to have 210,000 men in 1632. The additional men would be used to create the seven armies and one hundred garrisons that he thought essential to defeat Ferdinand. Two of the armies would go along the Danube to Vienna; two would hold the Thuringian Forest to be available as needed in northwest Germany or Saxony; two would cooperate in driving Imperialists from the Lower Saxon Circle (lands along the lower Elbe River); and one would hold the Bohemian frontier and the Oder valley. These armies would be dispersed not merely to engage and destroy Imperial forces in various parts of the Empire but also to decentralize recruitment and supply. If these seven armies were successful in defeating the Imperialists and in establishing garrisons throughout the Empire, and if Gustavus Adolphus were able to reach Vienna—if his strategy were successful—the war might be won in 1632. At least, Gustavus Adolphus hoped that victories might lead to a settlement that would restore Protestant lands, provide security for Protestant German states and Sweden, and compensate Sweden with Pomerania or other territories.

The campaign of 1632 fell far short of what Gustavus Adolphus planned. He could not raise the forces he needed; his allies and his Swedish generals proved less cooperative and less competent than he had hoped; and his enemies were numerous and well led. By March 1632 he had been able to increase his armies to about 140,000 men, mainly by recruiting German mercenaries. But the supply of mercenaries was nearly exhausted because Swedish and Imperial agents were competing in the same limited labor market. Gustavus Adolphus was probably unable to increase the total number of his men much beyond 140,000—70,000 fewer than he had hoped to have. Nor could he depend on his allies or subordinates to make up with inspired leadership what they lacked in numbers. The Saxons, having advanced too far into Bohemia in late 1631, were in danger of being cut off there. Gustavus Adolphus's own Swedish generals, assigned to clear Imperial forces from the Lower Saxon Circle, fared little better; they proved unable to cooperate long enough to defeat the small, imaginatively led Imperial army that had assembled there. Repeatedly during the campaign, unsettling reports from Saxony or the Lower Saxon Circle kept Gustavus Adolphus from advancing toward Vienna.

But it was not just threats to Saxony and the Lower Saxon Circle that spoiled Gustavus Adolphus's campaign of 1632 on the Danube; it was also the intervention of powerful Imperial forces. Even at the beginning of the campaign when he left Mainz to advance toward Vienna, he met tenacious opposition. Although he succeeded in forcing his way across the river Lech, killing General Tilly and dispersing his army, and although he subsequently exacted heavy contributions from Augsburg and plundered Bavaria, he found his passage of the Danube blocked by another Imperial force under Maximilian, Duke of Bavaria, and by angled-bastion fortresses at Ingolstadt and Regensburg. Unable to take these works by storm and unwilling to become entangled in a siege, he returned to Munich and Swabia, apparently hoping to lure Imperial forces from Bohemia to the Danube—to reduce pressure on Saxony and to precipitate a decisive battle. But when on May 26 he learned that the Imperialists had recaptured Prague and were threatening Saxony, Gustavus Adolphus decided to send reinforcements to the Rhine and Lower Saxon Circle and to go himself with 18,500 men to relieve Saxony.

This decision would soon bring Gustavus Adolphus face to face with the most talented of Imperial generals, Albrecht von Wallenstein. Wallenstein was more than a sound tactician and an able strategist; he was also a remarkably skilled logistician. Born into a Protestant Bohemian family in 1583, he converted to the Catholic faith and made a career in the Imperial army, serving against the Turks and helping Ferdinand secure his claim to the thrones of Bohemia and the Empire. Wallenstein became commander-in-chief of all Imperial forces in 1625. By using income from his own estates, subsidies from Spain, and, especially, contributions from occupied territories, he was able to raise and supply armies of 50,000 men without drawing heavily on the Imperial treasury. Moreover, because he was so adept at creating and sustaining armies, he was able to pursue strategies of attrition: to take up strong defensive positions, use his cavalry to protect his supplies while disrupting those of the enemy, and wait for hunger and disease to force the enemy either to attack or withdraw. He was criticized for his slow, expensive methods; but those methods brought success in

Germany. They might also have provided peace and security for the Empire had not Ferdinand been such a zealous Catholic. In August 1630 Ferdinand dismissed Wallenstein in an attempt to appease German leaders angered by the heavy costs of war and the Edict of Restitution. He recalled him to command in the autumn of 1631 after the Battle of Breitenfeld. Now in the late spring of 1632, Wallenstein and Gustavus Adolphus were marching toward each other.

On June 18 while passing through Nuremberg, Gustavus Adolphus discovered that Wallenstein was coming south from Bohemia to meet him. He decided, therefore, to fortify a camp outside Nuremberg and assemble his forces for a climactic battle. Wallenstein arrived at the end of June with 48,000 men, saw the strength of Gustavus Adolphus's fieldworks, and settled down to starve him into submission. The blockade was not entirely effective: Gustavus Adolphus continued to receive supplies and, on August 17, a reinforcement of 30,000 men. Perhaps because he expected trouble in feeding such an army, perhaps because he thought a victory the most promising way to end the war, Gustavus Adolphus decided to attack. Acting on poor intelligence—a report that the Imperialists were withdrawing—he threw his army against their strongly fortified camp. He soon saw his mistake and broke off the action, but not before suffering disproportionate casualties (2,400 of his own killed and wounded to the enemy's 600). In the weeks after this battle of Alte Feste, his supplies failed and his army began to melt away: 10,000 men deserted; 6,000 horses died. By early September he was on the road to Swabia to feed and rest his army and to begin preparations for a new offensive toward Vienna in 1633.

Lützen

The campaign of 1632 might have ended at that point if Gustavus Adolphus had been content to go on with his preparations for 1633. But both he and Wallenstein still sought battle, and they contrived eventually to have one. On September 28 Wallenstein, learning that Gustavus Adolphus had retired to the Danube, decided to take his own army north to subjugate Saxony and try to lure Gustavus Adolphus into another ill-conceived attack. Gustavus Adolphus was at first disposed to remain on the Danube. But when he was sure that Wallenstein was bound for Saxony, he decided to follow and fight him there—to keep him from conquering north Germany and thereby cutting off Gustavus Adolphus's communications with Sweden. By October 5 both the king and Wallenstein were marching for Saxony, each hoping to gain the advantage of the other in a decisive battle: Gustavus Adolphus by surprising Wallenstein before he could gather his army together; Wallenstein by forcing Gustavus Adolphus to attack him in a fortified camp as at Nuremberg. Neither would succeed to the extent he wished. Gustavus Adolphus did not surprise Wallenstein, but he did attack him at Lützen on November 6 before he had gathered all his forces together and completed his defensive works.

The opposing forces at Lützen would be remarkably similar in composition, equipment, tactics, and size. Since Breitenfeld, the Imperialists had, by studying and adopting Gustavus Adolphus's methods, significantly increased the firepower and flexibility of their arms. Wallenstein now deployed his army in three thin lines with arms combined: light artillery with his infantry and musketeers with his cavalry. He also placed his arms with particular regard to the ground, anticipating that Gustavus Adolphus would concentrate his forces against just one wing of the Imperial army—probably the stronger one as at Nuremberg. At Lützen Wallenstein's right or stronger flank was secured by the town, a cluster of windmills, and fourteen pieces of heavy artillery; his center, by the Lützen-Leipzig road and adjacent ditches; and his left, by his cavalry (some absent when the battle began) and a drainage ditch. Gustavus Adolphus planned to attack using much the same disposition as at Breitenfeld: thin flexible lines with his best units massed to the right and his arms combined (indeed, his light artillery was mixed with his cavalry as well as his infantry at Lützen). The two armies were, then, much alike in composition, equipment, and tactical arrangement; and they would be very nearly the same size (about 19,000 men) once Wallenstein's detachments had returned. If Wallenstein had more cavalry and heavy artillery, Gustavus Adolphus had more light artillery. And if Wallenstein had the advantage of a prepared position anchored against the town, Gustavus Adolphus would begin with his best forces against the weakest portion of the Imperial line, the left flank.

Because the opposing forces were so similar and so evenly matched, timing, chance, and inspiration played unusually large parts in the Battle of Lützen. Gustavus Adolphus, knowing that many of Wallenstein's men were scattered about the Saxon countryside, hoped to attack before all could return—that is, as early as possible on November 6. He also planned to attack the Imperial left, which would be lightly held until 3,000 cavalrymen under Gottfried Heinrich Count Pappenheim arrived from Halle, sometime after noon. But a very heavy fog kept Gustavus Adolphus from deploying his troops until nearly eight in the morning, and all were not in place for the attack until ten. Then the fog returned and forced another delay. Finally, at eleven the fog dissipated and the attack began. Swedish forces soon turned the Imperial left flank, driving it in upon the center of Wallenstein's line and threatening to destroy his army. Just then—about noon—Pappenheim appeared with his 3,000 cavalrymen to check the Swedish attack and restore the Imperial line. But when Pappenheim was killed, Wallenstein's left flank again gave way and might have carried the army with it had not fog intervened, stopping the battle once more.

The fog that preserved the Imperialists also saved the Swedish army. In concentrating his forces for the attack, Gustavus Adolphus had weakened his own left flank. He hoped to break the Imperial line before the Imperialists could exploit his weakness. But delayed by fog and by Pappenheim's arrival, Gustavus Adolphus was unable to roll up the enemy before his own left began to give way. To repair the damage, he rode across the battlefield and joined in the fighting. It was the kind of impulsive action that had so often inspired his troops and made him such a charismatic leader. It was also the kind of action that had brought him dangerous wounds and jeopardized his command in more than one battle. Now, at last, his luck ran out; and when he fell, mortally wounded, his troops retreated, shielded only by the fog that was also saving the Imperialists.

When the fog lifted, both armies had been restored to order; but the Imperialists, inspired by news of the Swedish king's death, seemed to be gaining control of the battle. In desperation, Bernard of Saxe-Weimar, who had succeeded to Gustavus Adolphus's command, launched an attack on what had seemed the strongest part of the Imperial line, the right flank where it joined the town. The attack not only carried the windmills and the fourteen cannon posted there but also broke Wallenstein's will to continue the battle. Knowing that his men were exhausted and their ammunition was gone, and fearing he might be trapped by fresh Saxon troops, Wallenstein retreated through Leipzig and, eventually, to Bohemia. The battle had ended in the narrowest of victories for the Swedes. They had killed or wounded more than a third of Wallenstein's men, taken his cannon, and forced him to leave Saxony. But they had lost their king and about a third of their army.

Within two and a half years of the Battle of Lützen, the Thirty Years' War lost much of its religious character. The Swedes were eager, following the death of their king, to withdraw from the war in central Germany. To encourage Germans to take an ever greater part in fighting the Emperor, the Swedes organized southwest German states in the Heilbronn League and let the Elector of Saxony shape strategy in central Germany. But these new measures proved disastrous for Sweden and its allies, because they could no longer raise the forces that they needed or match the skill of Imperial commanders. As a result of defeats in the campaigns of 1633 and 1634, the Heilbronn League appealed to Catholic France to intervene against the Habsburgs; Sweden withdrew from the League; and Saxony, Brandenburg, and other Protestant states made peace with the emperor. The Peace of Prague in May 1635 not only modified the Edict of Restitution, confirming many Protestant holdings in north Germany, but it also created an army of Saxons, Bavarians, and Imperialists to impose peace on those Protestant German states that refused reconciliation with the emperor. Thereafter, opposing sides in the Thirty Years' War were not clearly associated with Catholics and Protestants; the war was fought for the advantage and prestige of states rather than for Protestant or German liberties.

Indeed, following the Peace of Prague, the Thirty Years' War in central Europe was waged mainly by France and Sweden against the emperor and his allies—Spain, Bavaria, Saxony, and Brandenburg. France, which entered the war in 1635 to preserve Sweden, had greater resources than Spain or the emperor; but French armies achieved little until after 1640. Sweden, which remained at war to provide for her own security, continued to lead opposition to the emperor in Germany. To support their armies, the Swedes made alliances with France, took French subsidies, and attacked south from Pomerania into more abundant parts of Germany. Gradually after 1640, France and Sweden prevailed: forcing the emperor to abandon entirely the Edict of Restitution, driving Brandenburg from the war, and defeating the Imperialists in Bavaria and Bohemia. Finally, in October 1648, France and Sweden won a favorable and general peace, the Peace of Westphalia. Thus they ended the greatest of European wars before the French Revolution, a war that had affected Germany unevenly but that had reduced the population by at least 15 percent and damaged the economy of nearly every state.

☆   ☆   ☆   ☆

At its height, the Thirty Years' War marked a culminating moment in the military revolution—in a prolonged European effort to adapt warfare to improvements in firearms. By the beginning of the seventeenth century, Europeans had come to rely on ever larger armies of mercenaries, equipped with muskets and cannon, to garrison their fortresses, conduct their sieges, and fight their battles. Because such armies were best suited to defensive actions, and because the wealthiest parts of Europe were protected by angled-bastion fortresses, battles were rare and wars long, indecisive, and expensive. Maurice of Orange developed a system for using handguns more effectively, a system in which small, disciplined infantry units could sustain nearly continuous defensive fire. But it remained for Gustavus Adolphus to make a truly comprehensive synthesis of the seventeenth-century art of war, to give the military revolution its fullest expression. He mobilized the resources of his primitive state to provide the men, money, and munitions for a fine national army. He then disciplined and trained that army to exploit firepower offensively as well as defensively, creating tactical units that combined infantry, cavalry, and artillery so as to deliver sustained musket and artillery fire without sacrificing the benefits of pike and saber. And he used his small, national army to subdue his neighbors and generate the money he needed to wage war on an unprecedented scale: to hire tens of thousands of mercenaries and to campaign from the Baltic to the Danube. If he did not raise all the men he intended, he raised more than he could sometimes support. And if he did not defeat his enemies decisively—if he failed in his efforts to destroy their armies in battle—he taught them to use firepower with devastating effect. Indeed, in showing what might be done to increase the size and power of an army, he also showed what could not be done until a larger and more powerful state had created a bureaucracy to support war on the scale that he envisioned it.

SUGGESTED READINGS

Barker, Thomas M. *The Military Intellectual and Battle: Raimondo Montecuccoli and the Thirty Years War* (Albany: State University of New York Press, 1975).

Duffy, Christopher. *Siege Warfare: The Fortress in the Early Modern World, 1494–1660* (London: Routledge & Kegan Paul, 1979).

Duffy, M. *The Military Revolution and the State, 1500–1800* (Exeter: University of Exeter, 1980).

Hale, J. R. *War and Society in Renaissance Europe, 1450–1620* (Leicester: Leicester University Press, 1985).

Lindegren, J. "The Swedish 'Military State,' 1560–1720," *Scandinavian Journal of History*, X (1985), 305–335.

Lynn, John A. "The Growth of the French Army During the Seventeenth Century," *Armed Forces and Society*, VI (1980), 568–585.

———. "Tactical Evolution in the French Army, 1560–1660," *French Historical Studies*, XIV (1985), 176–191.

Machiavelli, N. *The Art of War* (Indianapolis: Bobbs-Merrill Co., 1965).

McNeill, William H. *The Pursuit of Power* (Chicago: University of Chicago Press, 1984).

Mork, Gordon R. "Flint and Steel: A Study in Military Technology and Tactics in 17th-Century Europe," *Smithsonian Journal of History* II (1967), 25–52.

Oman, Charles. *A History of the Art of War in the Sixteenth Century* (London: Methuen, 1937).

Parker, Geoffrey. *The Army of Flanders and the Spanish Road, 1567–1659* (Cambridge: Cambridge University Press, 1972).

———. "The Military Revolution, 1560–1660—A Myth?" *Journal of Modern History*, XLVII (1976), 195–214.

———. *The Military Revolution: Military Innovation and the Rise of the West, 1500–1800* (Cambridge: Cambridge University Press, 1988).

———. *The Thirty Years' War* (London: Routledge & Kegan Paul, 1984).

Parrott, D. A. "Strategy and Tactics in the Thirty Years' War: 'the Military Revolution,'" *Militärgeschichtliche Mitteilungen* XVIII, 2 (1985), 7–25.

Pepper, S., and Adams, N. *Firearms and Fortifications: Military Architecture and Siege Warfare in Sixteenth-Century Siena* (Chicago: University of Chicago Press, 1986).

Roberts, Michael. *Essays in Swedish History* (Minneapolis: University of Minnesota Press, 1967).

———. *Gustavus Adolphus: A History of Sweden 1611–1632*, 2 vols. (London: Longmans, Green and Co., 1953–1958).

Rothenberg, Gunther E. "Maurice of Nassau, Gustavus Adolphus, Raimondo Montecuccoli, and the 'Military Revolution' of the Seventeenth Century," in Peter Paret, ed., *Makers of Modern Strategy: from Machiavelli to the Nuclear Age* (Princeton: Princeton University Press, 1986), 32–63.

Wedgwood, C. V. *The Thirty Years War* (London: Jonathan Cape Ltd., 1938).

2

TOWARD LIMITED WAR IN EUROPE, 1648–1714

The Growth of Standing Armies

Standing Armies and the Art of War

Marlborough and Eugene: Testing the Limits of Limited War

The Limits of Limited War

The Peace of Westphalia ended one of Europe's most destructive wars, but it did not bring a lasting peace. For nearly three-quarters of a century after 1648, Europeans fought to preserve the Westphalian settlement against France and other aggressive states. Under Louis XIV (1643–1715), France threatened not only to extend its boundaries to the Rhine, Alps, and Pyrenees but also to become the dominant power in Europe. In wars with Spain (1648–1659, 1667–1668) and with the Dutch Republic, Spain, and their allies (1672–1678, 1683–1684), France gained parts of the Spanish Netherlands as well as Luxembourg and lands along the Rhine, the Swiss frontier, and the Pyrenees. But when in 1688 Louis XIV attacked the Palatinate and supported a Catholic king in England, he found Europe temporarily united against him. In the War of the League of Augsburg (1688–1697), the principal German states joined Austria, England, Holland, Spain, Savoy, and Sweden to defeat Louis and force him to give up some of his conquests in the Low Countries and Rhineland. And in late 1700, when he placed his grandson on the throne of Spain and sent troops to occupy the Spanish Netherlands, much of Europe again joined against him in the War of the Spanish Succession (1701–1714). By 1714 Austria, England, Holland, Savoy, and leading German states had worked together well enough to check Louis's aspirations for a universal monarchy and to restore the European balance of power.

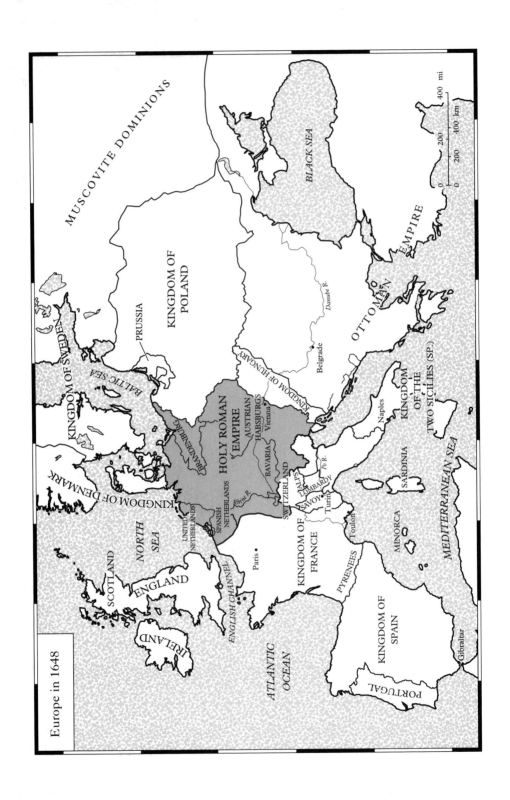

Europe in 1648

MUSCOVITE DOMINIONS

KINGDOM OF SWEDEN

BALTIC SEA

PRUSSIA

KINGDOM OF POLAND

BLACK SEA

OTTOMAN EMPIRE

Danube R.

Belgrade

KINGDOM OF HUNGARY

KINGDOM OF DENMARK

NORTH SEA

SCOTLAND

IRELAND

ENGLAND

ENGLISH CHANNEL

ATLANTIC OCEAN

UNITED NETHERLANDS

SPANISH NETHERLANDS

BRANDENBURG

HOLY ROMAN EMPIRE

AUSTRIAN HABSBURGS

Vienna

BAVARIA

Rhine R.

SWITZERLAND

ALPS

SAVOY

Turin

LOMBARDY

Po R.

Paris

KINGDOM OF FRANCE

PYRENEES

Toulon

MINORCA

SARDINIA

Naples

KINGDOM OF THE TWO SICILIES (SP.)

MEDITERRANEAN SEA

KINGDOM OF SPAIN

PORTUGAL

Gibraltar

0   200   400 mi

0   200   400 km

The wars of Louis XIV produced important changes in the conduct of war. Armies became national standing armies of unprecedented size and power. Unlike the mercenary forces supported by contributions and subsidies that fought the Thirty Years' War, the armies of 1700 were permanent organizations raised, trained, equipped, and sustained by state bureaucracies and regular taxation. These armies were far larger and carried on much more extensive operations than any of their European predecessors. French forces during the War of the Spanish Succession more than doubled those of any state in the Thirty Years' War; they served not only in Europe, as had the Swedish and Imperial forces in the 1630s, but also in North America, the West Indies, and India. Moreover, the armies of 1700 had far more firepower than those of 1632. The adoption of the socket bayonet, flintlock musket, and cartridge at the end of the seventeenth century made it possible to eliminate the pike and, by equipping every infantryman with a flintlock and cartridges, to increase substantially the volume and rate of fire. So too did improvements in the quality and quantity of field artillery.

Europeans invested in these larger, more powerful armies to reduce the risks and costs of war. Kings and ministers were eager to avoid a repetition of the anarchy and destruction that had plagued Europe during the Thirty Years' War. Because they depended on standing armies to maintain domestic order and the international balance of power, few were willing to risk losing an army in a single battle. Most preferred to build ever more elaborate fortifications to protect their frontiers and relied increasingly on earthworks and entrenchments to cover their armies in the field. Even aggressive commanders found that the larger and more powerful their forces became, the more difficult it was to move them and their supplies rapidly enough to impose battle on an unwilling enemy. Most commanders came to prefer or to accept wars of attrition. Sieges and maneuvers might in time destroy more lives and property than a general action, but a siege rarely destroyed an entire army; and losses suffered could be made up in winter when fighting was usually suspended. No wonder that under these circumstances even the most aggressive commanders—the Duke of Marlborough, Prince Eugene of Savoy, and Marshal Villars—were rarely able to precipitate a general action or to exploit a victory. Europe was entering an age of "limited warfare."

The Growth of Standing Armies

Origins

In the half-century following the Thirty Years' War, France and other European states invested heavily in standing armies—permanent professional forces supported by regular taxes and controlled by central bureaucracies. The Thirty Years' War had shown how unreliable and destructive mercenary forces had become: how difficult it was to raise, train, and control troops hired for limited periods and sustained by contributions and plundering. The Dutch Republic and Sweden had also shown how manageable and effective a long-serving, national conscript army could be—an army supported by taxes that was thoroughly disciplined, trained with uniform weapons and tactics, and inspired by loyalty to the state. So it was that after 1648 European rulers relied increasingly on standing armies to provide them with security and power, at home and abroad. Disciplined professional soldiers who owed their allegiance to the crown could crush opposition to the central government, enforce the law, and help collect taxes. Peace and prosperity together with improved tax collection would, in turn, make it possible for the government to increase the size of its army. And a larger, more powerful army would give the state not just greater security from aggressive foreign powers but also increased support for its own foreign policy.

Louis XIV took the lead in creating such a powerful standing army. Since the 1630s, when Gustavus Adolphus and Wallenstein had struggled to raise and support mercenary forces of no more than 140,000 men, the French had significantly improved their military administration—their capacity to raise, support, and control large forces. The French also had the largest population in Europe (roughly 20 million in 1700) and the resources to shape that population into a standing army of unprecedented size. But what fueled the remarkable expansion of the French army in the last half of the seventeenth century were the ambitions of Louis XIV and his ministers. To seize, fortify, and hold lands belonging to his neighbors from the Low Countries to the Rhine and the Pyrenees and to support dynastic claims to other territories, Louis XIV needed ever larger land forces, particularly infantrymen to take and defend fortresses. During the Thirty Years' War and France's war with Spain (to 1659), the French had an army of 150,000 men. That force, reduced to 72,000 in the early 1660s, was increased to 134,000 for the War of the Devolution with Spain (1667–1668), to 279,000 for the Dutch War (1672–1678), and to more than 390,000 for the War of the League of Augsburg (1688–1697) and the War of the Spanish Succession (1701–1713). Altogether, from the beginning of the Thirty Years' War to the end of Louis XIV's wars, the French increased their land forces by more than 240,000 men.

No other European monarch had the resources or the ambition of Louis XIV, and no other state raised a standing army to rival that of France. But other countries did create their own regular forces in the last half of the seventeenth century, not only to counter French aggression but also to strengthen their governments against other threats, domestic and foreign. Prussia, having experienced the humiliation and expense of being unable to defend its territory during the Thirty Years' War, invested in a small regular army in the 1650s. By the War of the Spanish Succession, that army had grown to 40,000 well-trained men who contributed to the defeat of France. The Austrian army, begun in 1679, gained size and strength during the War of the Holy League, reached 100,000 by 1710, and made Austria a principal member of the alliances against Louis XIV. Although the English were reluctant to support a standing army in peacetime fearing that such an army would be used to deprive them of their liberties, they did raise regular forces of at least 75,000 during both the War of the League of Augsburg and the War of the Spanish Succession. These English troops, added to a similar number of Dutch soldiers (perhaps 100,000 by 1710), provided the main opposition to the French in the Low Countries. Savoy and a number of German states created smaller regular contingents that joined Austria against the Turks and French on the Danube, Rhine, and Po rivers. Altogether and including large permanent forces in Sweden and Russia, there were more than 1 million men in the standing armies of Europe by 1710.

Officers and Men

The officers and men who served in those standing armies were drawn primarily from the highest and lowest orders of society. Engineering and artillery officers—the technicians who built fortresses, conducted sieges, and served the guns—were the exception: in all armies they were members of the educated middle classes. But in Austria, France, Prussia, Spain, and Sweden most officers of infantry and cavalry were noblemen; and in the Dutch and English forces most had wealth, education, and social standing, if not titles. Monarchs thought it good policy to employ noblemen and others of wealth and influence as officers—to bind them to the crown and to gain their influence in raising and leading men. Noblemen could, in turn, benefit from serving in the army: by buying and selling commissions; by profiting from allowances for equipping, recruiting, and feeding their men; and by gaining the favor of the king and his ministers. The French nobility gradually came to think of the officer corps as their exclusive preserve, and most other officer corps drew apart from society. The small number of men who became generals were almost always titled and wealthy; and if successful, they could sell their services to great advantage on the international market. Understandably, officers on opposing sides sometimes felt stronger ties to each other than to their respective states.

      The rank and file of standing armies at the turn of the eighteenth century were strikingly different, socially and economically, from their officers. They were typically drawn from the lower, if not the lowest, levels of society: young, poor, and unemployed men who were swept into the army by force and persuasion. Some did willingly enlist, attracted by hopes for adventure, by appeals to their religion or nationality, or by attachments to family and prominent men. But most had to be forced to serve. The life of a common soldier was too short and hard to appeal to a young man with a job and even minimal prospects. Combat and disease could carry off 20 percent of an army in a year; and those who survived endured harsh discipline, uncertain food and pay, and long periods of squalid inactivity interrupted by violence and terror. To recruit men under these circumstances, states employed a variety of measures. They offered bounties to volunteers; recruited foreigners and prisoners of war; commissioned local leaders to raise whole units; and when all else failed, they resorted to conscription and impressment. All these measures worked best with those men who were least able to provide for and protect themselves, those at the bottom of society.

To turn such officers and men into an effective army took considerable time, effort, and money. There was not as yet a formal system of training or promoting officers. Yet some officers did study the art of war, and all were expected to learn the rudiments of their duty by serving with a regiment: how to control the fire and movement of their men, how to manage them in camp or on the march, and how to inspire composure and courage during battle. The men, themselves, were subjected to more regular training, particularly in the manual of arms and small-unit drill. Whether equipped with matchlock and pike or with flintlock and bayonet, soldiers of the late seventeenth century worked endlessly to learn to use their weapons effectively—to load, aim, and fire together in a rapid but carefully controlled way. They also worked endlessly at small-unit drill, not merely to move quickly from one tactical disposition to another but especially to acquire the cohesiveness and discipline that were essential to combat at close range and that would discourage desertion and disorder. It took about a year for a small unit (a company of fifty or more men) to learn the basics of firing and maneuvering; it took much longer for a company to learn its role in a regiment or larger tactical unit. In peacetime, armies were usually dispersed in garrisons or in detachments serving as police and as construction corps building roads, bridges, canals, and fortresses. Occasional maneuvers drew only parts of an army together, and there were no standardized tactics before 1714 in even the best armies. It is, therefore, understandable that commanders found it difficult to employ armies effectively, to gain the speed and coordination necessary to force battle on an unwilling enemy.

State Support

To raise and sustain ever larger regular armies, Europeans created powerful central bureaucracies. Beginning during the Thirty Years' War, a succession of able French ministers supported by middle-class officials came to supervise nearly all military matters. This ministry of war was not free of corruption, and it was never quite able to expand rapidly enough to meet all the needs of a growing army, such as maintaining a steady flow of supplies or imposing a uniform system of tactics on its generals. But the ministry did give France a chain of command under the king and a maréchal général des armées; it standardized dress and discipline; and it improved recruiting, housing, and pay. Nor was the ministry of war the only part of the government that became increasingly powerful during the wars of Louis XIV, that took an ever more prominent role in the lives of ordinary Frenchmen. European states that stood against France also had to develop stronger central governments to wage war effectively. Austria, Prussia, Sweden, the United Provinces, and England all relied on bureaus staffed by men loyal to the state to raise, equip, pay, and supply regular forces. Other countries, like Spain and Poland, that failed to develop such a central administration soon slipped from among the principal powers of Europe.

But it took more than effective ministries to make a great power; it took sound public credit as well. The standing armies that fought in the War of the Spanish Succession required greater state funding than the mercenary forces of the Thirty Years' War. Standing armies were larger and more fully equipped and supplied than their mercenary predecessors. Thus the wars of Louis XIV became tests of public credit. States were forced to experiment with a variety of ways of financing their forces: new taxes and improved tax collection, loans, contributions from enemy lands, and currency manipulation. Because the French clergy and aristocracy claimed exemption from property taxes, Louis XIV found it particularly difficult to increase his revenues. When he raised taxes on his peasants, he stifled the French economy and provoked resistance; and when he increased tolls, tariffs, excise and sales taxes, he depressed trade and revenues. In desperation he sold offices and titles, tampered with the value of coins, issued paper money, and imposed new taxes (which the clergy and aristocracy refused to pay). In the last years of his reign, by the end of the War of the Spanish Succession, France was near fiscal collapse. So too were many of Louis's enemies: not just poor countries like Spain but even the once prosperous Dutch Republic. Only England was able to sustain its credit, which was secured by taxes imposed by a representative government, and which provided adequate funds for war without crippling the English economy. Indeed, the economy flourished, and England emerged victorious in the long struggle with Louis XIV.

Standing Armies and the Art of War

Preferences for Moderation

The creation of standing armies of unprecedented size and power did not make war more destructive, in part because Europeans were determined to avoid a return to the disorder that accompanied the Thirty Years' War. Indeed, many rulers raised standing armies and built new fortifications primarily to defend themselves against insurrection and invasion, to maintain order. Having invested heavily in these forces, and being dependent on them for their security, kings and their ministers were reluctant to risk them in offensive action. Furthermore, they were influenced strongly in considering how to use force by a growing international distaste for unrestricted violence. It was not just lawyers and philosophers who argued that war should be waged with moderation. Officers in most European armies agreed that soldiers should be kept from plundering indiscriminately, that noncombatants and prisoners should be treated humanely, and that sieges should be conducted with consideration for lives and property. These concerns worked strongly against bold offensive actions and efforts to destroy the opposing army in battle. Even Louis XIV, who intended to conquer his neighbors, used force with restraint. Knowing the extraordinary costs of recruiting, equipping, and training an army, Louis sought to avoid costly general engagements. He captured territory by surprise, fortified it, and defied his enemies to evict him. His enemies, sharing his reluctance to risk their forces in battle and being particularly concerned with preserving order and restoring the balance of power, resorted to strategies of siegecraft and maneuver to recover the lands he had taken. Thus widely held preferences for reducing the destructiveness of war and keeping order served to encourage cautious strategies and made it difficult for aggressive commanders to find favorable opportunities for battle.

Fortresses and Siegecraft in the Age of Vauban

Preferences for security and order also encouraged states to invest in more elaborate fortifications. These fortifications, in turn, limited war by encouraging defensive thinking, obstructing the movement of armies, confining fighting to relatively well-defined theaters, and frustrating those few commanders who sought decisive results, who wished to gain victory by destroying the enemy's army and taking his capital. By the beginning of the eighteenth century, Louis XIV and his enemies had thoroughly fortified the principal waterways and roads leading across their frontiers. These fortifications could not keep an army from invading a country, but they could keep that army from receiving the supplies needed to sustain an offensive. It was not possible, therefore, to bypass all fortifications; and capturing a large, modern, and well-garrisoned fortification could delay an army for months, particularly if there were an enemy force in the vicinity to harass the besiegers and succor the garrison. Holding fortresses that had been taken further consumed troops and weakened the attacking forces. Indeed, elaborate fortifications, skillfully placed along the frontiers of France, helped make the wars of Louis XIV long, indecisive, and expensive.

What made fortresses so formidable at the end of the seventeenth century were modifications in their size and design that were undertaken by Louis XIV and his chief engineer, Sébastien Le Prestre Vauban (1633–1707). The king provided the authority and the resources to build on an increasingly grand scale; Vauban engineered the subtle changes in design that made the angled-bastion fortress increasingly difficult to capture. Vauban entered the king's service in 1653 at the age of twenty. He spent the ensuing fifty-three years of his life as a military engineer: conducting sieges in wartime, building fortresses in intervals of peace, and developing the talent that gained him a prominent place in the history of warfare. He began as a lieutenant in charge of repairing a single fortress and then served apprenticeships in Flanders fighting the Spanish (1653–1659) and on the frontiers of France improving fortifications (1659–1667). In the War of the Devolution (1667–1668) he established himself as Louis XIV's chief engineer. He was a man of blunt common sense who cared for his men and who valued merit above privilege. He seemed to personify a new scientific and humane approach to war. As Louis's chief engineer, he not only fortified those parts of the Low Countries taken from Spain and conducted sieges in the Dutch War (1672–1678) but also began a comprehensive program of building fortresses for France. He demolished fortifications in the interior, constructed modern works along the frontiers, and built two giant belts of fortifications from the English Channel to the Meuse River. Although he continued to conduct sieges during the War of the League of Augsburg, and although he was now famous and his methods imitated throughout Europe, his influence with Louis XIV began to wane. He was too critical of the king's persecution of Protestants and of tax exemptions for the clergy and nobility to retain favor at court. Vauban managed his last siege in 1703 and died, ignored, four years later. But his fortresses and siegecraft ensured him a place as one of the greatest of all military engineers.

What then distinguished the more than one hundred fortresses that Vauban built? What made them so formidable and established his reputation as a military architect? Primarily, it was his elaboration of the conventional angled-bastion fortress and his shaping of each design to suit peculiarities of the terrain. He did not attempt to change the basic characteristics of the angled-bastion fortress that had been developed in sixteenth-century Italy: the low, massive curtain walls with angled bastions at the corners, the broad, dry moat and outworks that protected the main walls from mining and direct incoming fire, and the arrangement of artillery and small arms so as to sweep all approaches to the bastions and curtains. Accepting these basic features and benefiting from the ideas of other French engineers, he greatly extended the glacis, or outer bank of the moat, and added many low works both in the moat and beyond the glacis. These elaborations significantly strengthened fortresses. By making his works larger, by adding to the size of the garrison, and, above all, by increasing the complexity of the patterns of defensive fire, Vauban made it much more difficult for the attacking force to place artillery close enough to breach the main curtain walls and end the siege. Vauban was particularly adept at shaping his designs to different kinds of terrain. In mountains, where musketry was more important than heavy artillery, he placed towers at the corners of his main walls and put detached bastions in the moat before the corners. But Vauban knew that design alone could not secure a fortress, that no work could long hold out without a spirited garrison, good artillery, a competent commander, and a covering army. The best defense for a country was, he came to believe, an effective army.

Vauban was no less skilled in attacking than in defending a fortress. When he began his service, French armies dug their way toward an enemy fortress in a series of zigzag trenches. Although these trenches could not be enfiladed, they held few men and were vulnerable to sorties by the garrison. To give his men protection while they worked their way forward, Vauban started in 1673 to use a series of much larger trenches parallel to the main curtain wall of the fortress. These successive parallel trenches held enough troops to repel sorties while sappers dug closer to the enemy's works. Once the attackers had secured a lodgement on the glacis or outer wall of the moat, they were able to erect a battery, bring direct fire on the enemy's curtain, and breach his main line of defense. This last stage of a siege—the

This plan of a siege shows how Vauban used a system of parallels, linked by zigzag communication trenches, to capture a fortress without suffering devastating casualties. In each of the parallels, he was able to assemble enough men to withstand attack from the garrison and to protect nearby cannon while they reduced the fortress.

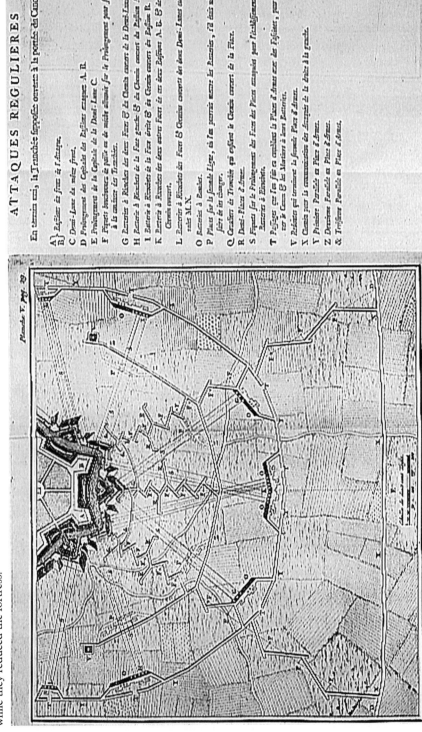

opening of a battery on the glacis—was usually very costly because the attackers were subjected to heavy artillery and musket fire while they prepared and served their guns. Thus Vauban decided in 1684 to cover his final parallel with an earthwork or *cavalier de tranchée*. This innovation, together with his invention of ricochet fire (1688)—the use of low-velocity shot that bounded along the enemy parapets killing defenders and dismounting their guns—further reduced casualties. By 1700 Vauban's parallels, *cavalier de tranchée*, and ricochet fire had become standard European engineering practices. Yet even with these methods, capturing a well-prepared fortress or fortified city took weeks if not months. Fortresses worked against decisive warfare.

Supply: The Magazine System

Just as fortresses made it difficult for commanders to wage war decisively, so too did providing supplies for the increasingly large forces that fought Louis XIV's wars. It was simply not feasible for an army of 60,000 soldiers, with its 40,000 horses and 30,000 camp followers, to carry more than a few days' supply of food, fodder, and ammunition. The supply train needed to do more would have been absurdly cumbersome and vulnerable and would have increased significantly the number of mouths to feed (it took 1,000 carts with horses and teamsters to provide one day's forage for 40,000 horses). Governments expected armies to draw supplies from the enemy's population—by purchase rather than by contributions or plundering as in the Thirty Years' War. But only unspoiled, densely populated regions (like the Low Countries, the Rhineland, and Lombardy where the population exceeded ninety-one people per square mile) could support an army of 60,000 men for any length of time; and the normal progress of a war soon diminished any region's capacity to provide food and fodder. Thus armies that could not carry more than a few days' supplies and that could not live exclusively off the country had to depend on a system of magazines, or storehouses, supplemented by local purchases and requisitions. The government of Louis XIV was among the first to create such magazines, to employ contractors to assemble supplies along a line of march.

This system of supply clearly worked against commanders who sought decisive results, who wished to engage and destroy an enemy's forces and occupy his country. Magazines supplemented by local purchases could not provide enough food to sustain men on long successive marches. Soldiers, consuming an estimated 2,300 calories a day, did not have the energy to march much more than nine miles a day. Nor could magazines furnish all of the fodder needed for horses. Armies were not, therefore, able to campaign except in those months when there was green forage to supplement what had been stored; and regular foraging, which was usually contested by the enemy, further slowed the movement of every army. To circumvent these problems commanders often advanced along waterways. It was far easier to move large quantities of grain and hay on the Meuse, Moselle, Rhine, or Danube rivers than over the roads of Brabant, Lorraine, Alsace, or Bavaria.

But the principal waterways were blocked by fortresses that could be taken only by time-consuming sieges. Thus the magazine system of feeding men and horses slowed the movement of all armies, limited the time available for each campaign, and afforded some months every year for armies to recover from defeats. Even the most aggressive commanders found it difficult under the circumstances to impose battle on their enemies and harder still to exploit a victory, to pursue a beaten enemy for more than a day or two, or to advance far into his country. Not until there were significant improvements in European agriculture and a growth in the population would commanders be able to abandon magazines and live off the country. Only then, only at the beginning of the nineteenth century, would armies gain the mobility that was to give Napoleonic warfare its decisive quality.

Improvements in Weapons and Tactics

Fear of disorder, the proliferation of fortresses, and the difficulty of supplying ever larger armies encouraged cautious strategies in the wars of Louis XIV; so too did improvements in weapons. Consider first the development of the bayonet. Since firearms first proved their value in the Italian Wars of the early sixteenth century, Europeans had equipped their infantry with both handguns and pikes. Although it was difficult to use musketeers and pikemen together, commanders thought each essential: musketeers, to provide firepower; pikemen, to protect musketeers while they reloaded and to exploit advantages gained with fire. As the musket became a better weapon, the proportion of pike to musket declined: from one to one in 1600, to one to two in 1651, to one to four in the French army of 1688. The dwindling proportion of pikemen left the musketeer increasingly vulnerable to cavalry. To restore security without giving up firepower, commanders first equipped their musketeers with stakes that might be planted as a hedge against cavalry. Then, in the middle of the seventeenth century, they experimented with a plug bayonet, a blade that could be inserted in the muzzle of a musket to serve as a pike. The plug bayonet, in regular use by 1671, was not entirely satisfactory because once fixed in the muzzle it could not easily be removed and kept the musket from being fired. Vauban and others solved this problem by developing a bayonet attached to the muzzle of a musket with a socket or sleeve that held the blade to the side of the barrel and allowed both loading and firing of the musket with the bayonet fixed. By the late 1680s the socket or sleeve bayonet had begun to replace the pike in the Austrian, Prussian, and French armies; and by the War of the Spanish Succession, the pike had disappeared from most European armies. Commanders were thus freed from the intricate dispositions and maneuvers required to use musketeers and pikemen together; they were able to increase the firepower of their infantry without increasing its vulnerability to cavalry; and they were able to deploy infantry in relatively simple linear formations that could be used on both offense and defense. The socket bayonet clearly made infantry more maneuverable and more powerful.

Improvements in handguns also increased firepower. For most of the seventeenth century, European infantrymen relied on the matchlock musket. Although very difficult to fire safely and quickly (it used a piece of slowly burning linen rope in its ignition system), the matchlock was long considered more reliable than its principal competitor, the flintlock musket. The flintlock was fired by sparks created when a spring drove a piece of flint against a steel plate; the sparks fell into a small pan of priming powder, igniting the powder which, in turn, flashed through a hole in the barrel, discharging the musket. Until the middle of the seventeenth century the flintlock often failed to fire because springs were poor, flints wore out rapidly, and sparks failed to touch off the powder. But improvements in the springs and in the design of the priming pan gradually made the flintlock more reliable; and since the flintlock was also lighter and could be loaded much more rapidly and safely than the matchlock, the flintlock began to win the support of many soldiers. With cartridges—powder and ball in a paper wrapper that could be loaded rapidly into the muzzle of a handgun—a well-trained infantryman could fire two shots per minute with a flintlock musket (no more than one every minute and a half with a matchlock). The flintlock was more expensive to make and, with its higher rate of fire, was more expensive to operate than the matchlock. Yet by 1690 it had become the standard infantry weapon in the Austrian, Prussian, and English armies, and by 1714, in all European armies except the Russian and Turkish. Indeed the flintlock musket equipped with a socket bayonet would survive, little changed, as the principal military handgun until the 1840s. It added significantly to the firepower of opposing forces in the War of the Spanish Succession and allowed commanders to reduce the depth of their lines of infantry from six to four or even three ranks.

Although the invention of the socket bayonet and improvement of the flintlock musket increased the power and maneuverability of infantry, they did not in general favor the army on the offensive or encourage aggressive tactics. Commanders did find it easier to attack with musketeers deployed in lines than with musketeers and pikemen in separate formations; and musketeers with bayonets were better equipped to deal with the shifting demands of battle and to cooperate with artillery and cavalry than either musketeers without bayonets or pikemen alone. But without cadence, it still took an army of 60,000 men hours to deploy for battle, too long to force an engagement upon an unwilling opponent. Moreover, a general who anticipated battle and who wished to stand on the defensive usually had time to choose a strong position and to improve it with earthworks, trenches, and cannon. The flintlock, a smoothbore, was neither an accurate nor a long-range weapon; but when fired in volleys it was lethal up to 150 yards. And, with its improved rate of fire, it was particularly effective in defense of earthworks. Since earthworks were usually secure against cavalry and field artillery, the commander on the defensive had very great advantages. Thus improved weapons used with field fortifications discouraged engagements. In the War of the Spanish Succession even the most aggressive commanders had trouble finding favorable opportunities for battle.

Marlborough and Eugene: Testing the Limits of Limited War

The War of the Spanish Succession

The War of the Spanish Succession (1701–1714) was caused mainly, but not entirely, by Louis XIV's desire to extend the power of his monarchy. When Charles II of Spain died in November 1700, he left his throne to Louis's grandson, Philip, in an effort to preserve his empire. He believed that making Philip his heir would commit Louis to the defense of Spain and that Louis alone among European kings had the power to keep Spanish lands from being partitioned. Philip accepted, renouncing his claim to the throne of France. Most European rulers would have acquiesced in this settlement had not Louis reserved Philip's claim to the French throne, recognized the Stuart pretender as King James III of England, and, in February 1701, invaded the Spanish Netherlands. Although Louis said he was defending the Spanish Netherlands against Austria, his neighbors suspected that he sought instead to dominate Europe by joining the monarchies of France and Spain. Austria responded by invading Spanish lands in Italy, and England and the United Provinces responded by preparing for war. In September 1701 the English, Dutch, and Austrians revived their Grand Alliance of the War of the League of Augsburg. They would fight not just to prevent a union of France and Spain but also to gain Spanish Italy for Austria and the Spanish Netherlands for the United Provinces. They soon enlisted Denmark and most of the important German states in their cause. Louis, meanwhile, strengthened his position by making alliances with Spain, Portugal, Savoy, Bavaria, and Cologne. Finally, after having raised fleets and armies, England and the United Provinces entered the war in May 1702.

Marlborough and Eugene

The Dutch and English agreed to put their forces under John Churchill, Earl of Marlborough, commander-in-chief of English troops in the Low Countries. Marlborough, an ambitious, energetic man, was a distinguished soldier and an experienced politician. But the ambition and energy that contributed to his success as a soldier marred his career in politics, if not in diplomacy. Born in 1650 into a royalist family, he rose rapidly in the army and society, often with the help of James, Duke of York. Yet when James became king and alienated his subjects with his extreme Catholicism, Marlborough joined in overthrowing James and bringing William of Orange to the English throne. William rewarded Marlborough with an earldom and the command of troops in the Netherlands, England, and Ireland. These distinctions were not enough to satisfy Marlborough who, feeling unappreciated, began a treasonous correspondence with James; and he persisted in that correspondence after being dismissed from the army and imprisoned for his disloyalty. Only gradually was Marlborough able to regain a measure of William's trust. William never doubted Marlborough's ability as a soldier, for he had distinguished himself at every level. As a junior officer serving against the Dutch and the Austrians, he was cited for bravery and aggressive leadership; as a senior officer commanding against English, French, and Irish forces, he proved a bold, innovative tactician and strategist. He took great trouble to care for and discipline his men; he valued controlled uses of firepower; and he was skilled at combining infantry, cavalry, and artillery to win battles. Above all, he was a calm, aggressive leader who preferred a major battle to a campaign of siege and maneuver. For all these reasons Marlborough was well qualified to command the Anglo-Dutch force assembling in the Netherlands in 1702.

Marlborough's authority did not extend to the Imperial army that was fighting the French in Italy. But he soon found that he had much in common with the commander of that army, Prince Eugene of Savoy. Eugene, like Marlborough, was an intensely ambitious man who had found satisfaction and distinction in war. He had been born in Paris in 1663, the son of a French army officer and a favorite courtesan of Louis XIV. He might well have pursued a career in the French army had not his mother fallen from favor and his request for a commission been denied. Fleeing to Vienna, he entered the Austrian army and became a devoted servant of the Habsburgs. He was never an imposing figure: his body was stunted, his shoulders stooped, and his face pockmarked. Yet he was determined to be a soldier. He strengthened his body, studied military history, and showed in Austria's wars with the Turks and the French that he had the will and the talent to become an exceptional officer. His courage and the patronage of his second cousin, the Duke of Savoy, brought him rapid promotion. But he got little satisfaction serving in Italy during the War of the League of Augsburg. He could not persuade his allies, the Spanish and Savoyards, to do more than wage a traditional war of sieges. In 1697 when he had a chance to command an Imperial army against the Turks, he made the most of it. At Zenta, about eighty miles north of Belgrade, he attacked a Turkish army as it was crossing the Theiss River. Using the increased firepower of the flintlock and exploiting the Turks' tactical vulnerability, he destroyed an army of 30,000 men while losing only 400 killed and wounded. In 1701, when Louis XIV occupied the Spanish Netherlands, Eugene was ordered to retaliate—to command Imperial forces attacking Spanish lands in Italy. During the ensuing decade, he and Marlborough would cooperate remarkably well, establishing themselves as the most aggressive and successful commanders of the War of the Spanish Succession and among the greatest captains in the history of warfare.

Opening Campaigns

But the opening campaigns of the War of the Spanish Succession fell far short of what Marlborough and Eugene had hoped. In Italy Eugene's forces were so inferior in numbers and so poorly supplied that he was hard pressed

John Churchill, Duke of Marlborough,
commanded British and Dutch forces in the
War of the Spanish Succession. Although he
won great battles, he was unable to make his
victories decisive in an age of limited war.

to hold his own against even ineffectual French generals. He maneuvered his army skillfully in 1701 and attacked a French detachment in 1702 to check an army that outnumbered his own nearly three to one. Although Marlborough had better opportunities in the Low Countries and enjoyed some success, he was unable to persuade his Dutch allies to take the risks that might have brought much more significant results. He captured and held valuable fortresses on the Meuse and Rhine rivers, securing the southeastern frontiers of the United Provinces, driving a wedge between the French and their allies in Cologne, and opening the Rhine to Anglo-Dutch shipping. But the Dutch repeatedly refused to allow Marlborough to risk battle, and without a victory he was unable to evict the French from Antwerp and Ostend or to mount an offensive toward France. Elsewhere, Anglo-Dutch gains in the Atlantic and Mediterranean (their ships brought Portugal and Savoy into the Grand Alliance) did not offset Imperial defeats on the upper Rhine and on the Danube. By the end of 1703 French and Bavarian forces were threatening Vienna from the west; and Hungarians, who had rebelled against the Emperor in the previous spring, were advanc-

Prince Eugene of Savoy, commander of Austrian
forces in the War of the Spanish Succession,
collaborated successfully with the Duke of
Marlborough. But the two great commanders were
unable to break through the fortresses that protected
France, and Eugene was left to command allied
forces after Britain withdrew from the war.

ing from the east. Marlborough knew that he would have to do more
in 1704 than argue with the Dutch if he were to relieve the beleaguered
Austrians.

The Blenheim Campaign

Marlborough and Eugene agreed, during the winter and spring of 1704, that
they would have to cooperate to save Austria, that Marlborough would have
to take troops from the Low Countries to join Eugene in opposing the
French and Bavarians on the Danube. They also agreed that a decisive battle would be the best way to stop an enemy advance on Vienna. But to take
such bold, unconventional measures, Marlborough and Eugene had to circumvent their friends and surprise their enemies. Knowing that his Dutch
allies were adamantly opposed to a campaign on the Danube and that they
had regularly preferred sieges to battles, Marlborough said he was planning
an offensive on the Moselle River toward Paris and that he would employ
only English and German troops. These deceptive statements served not
only to free him from the Dutch, from the inhibiting presence of their political advisors, but also to mislead the French, force them to shift troops from

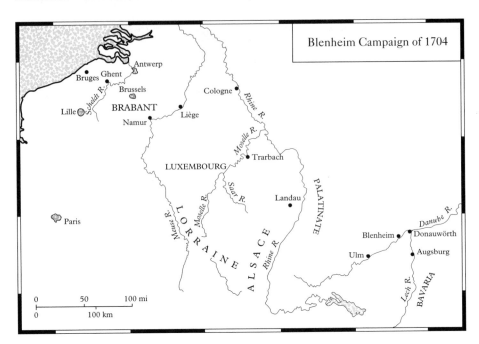

the Low Countries to the Moselle, and keep them there while he moved up the Rhine on his way to the Danube.

After joining forces with Eugene and with the aging Imperial commander, Prince Louis of Baden (between the Rhine and the Danube, June 10–22), Marlborough again had to rely on deception to precipitate battle. Because the cautious Louis insisted on sharing command with Marlborough—on commanding every other day—Marlborough sent Eugene with 30,000 men to watch the French army that was assembling west of the Rhine at Landau. He then took advantage of his day of command to make a forced march of twelve miles and attack the Bavarian garrison at Donauwörth on the Danube, before the garrison could complete its works or receive reinforcements and before Louis could object. Having won a small, impressive victory at Donauwörth on July 2, Marlborough and Louis plundered Bavaria (July 12–August 3) in hopes of forcing the Bavarian army to fight or surrender. But the Bavarians merely retired to the west to await help from a French army that had managed to elude Eugene in late June. By early August the French and Bavarians had joined forces along the Danube and were advancing eastward to maneuver Marlborough and Louis out of Bavaria, to open the way to Vienna.

The French and Bavarians failed to anticipate what Eugene and Marlborough might do. Eugene had already taken part of his army to reinforce Marlborough; and the two had detached Louis to besiege the Bavarian fortress at Ingolstadt, which commanded a crossing of the Danube thirty miles east of Donauwörth, and which in Imperial hands would have proved a formidable obstacle to any French or Bavarian advance on Vienna. Marlborough and Eugene had thus managed to find valuable work for Louis and to free themselves from his cautious influence long enough to seek a decisive

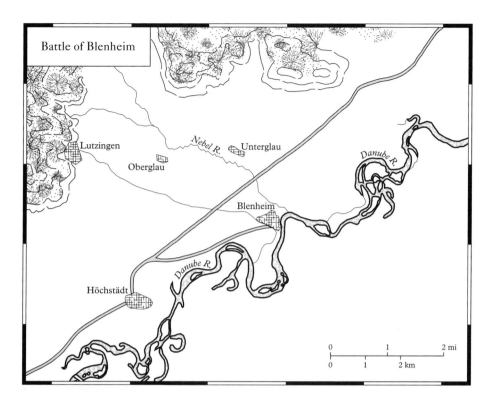

Battle of Blenheim

Lutzingen

Nebel R.

Unterglau

Oberglau

Danube R.

Blenheim

Danube R.

Höchstädt

0   1   2 mi

0   1   2 km

battle. When they learned that the French and Bavarians had crossed to the north bank of the Danube and were approaching Donauwörth from the west, they assembled their own armies (August 10–12) and prepared to attack. The French commanders, Marshals Camille de Tallard and Ferdinand Marsin, and their Bavarian counterpart, Elector Max Emanuel, did not anticipate battle; they believed that their superior numbers and strong position near the village of Blenheim would deter an attack and force Marlborough and Eugene to withdraw from the Danube to secure their line of supply to Germany.

The French and Bavarians were so confident in their advantages at Blenheim that they squandered those advantages, allowing themselves to be surprised in a tactical as well as a strategic sense. On the morning of August 13, 1704, Tallard, Marsin, and Max Emanuel were camped on the north bank of the Danube about twelve miles west of Donauwörth, on a plain four miles wide with their right flank secured by the village of Blenheim and the Danube, their center by a stream (the Nebel) and the village of Oberglau, and their left by wooded hills and another village, Lutzingen. This position had considerable natural strength: the Danube and the wooded hills above Lutzingen protected the French and Bavarians against any wide turning movement; the villages served as redoubts defending their flanks and providing enfilading fire for the center of their line; and the plain in the center afforded a fine, clear downward slope for their artillery and cavalry to engage anyone trying to bridge or cross the Nebel. The French and Bavarians also

had more men (56,000 to 52,000) and artillery (90 to 60) than their opponents if no better handguns (both sides were equipped with flintlocks and
bayonets). Yet they were so sure that they would not be attacked that they
ignored initial reports of Marlborough's advance on the morning of August
13, assuming that he was merely covering his withdrawal toward Germany;
and even when they saw that he was deploying his whole army before them,
they did little to strengthen their lines. They took up arms and fought as
they had been camped: the French on the right with dragoons holding the
ground between Blenheim and the Danube, infantry and artillery in
Blenheim, and cavalry and artillery in the plain from Blenheim to Oberglau;
the Bavarians on the left with infantry and artillery in Oberglau and Lutzingen and with infantry, cavalry, and artillery filling the interval between the
villages on the left wing. There was a reserve of infantry behind Blenheim;
but between Blenheim and Oberglau, a space of more than two miles in
the center of the Franco-Bavarian line, there were only nine battalions
of infantry and no earthworks to support the cavalry and artillery holding
that space.

Marlborough and Eugene saw the potential weakness in the center of
the Franco-Bavarian line and contrived to exploit it with diversions on the
enemy flanks followed by powerful combined-arms attacks on the center.
Having spent the night of August 12 about seven miles east of Blenheim,
they began their march toward the enemy camp around three in the morning
of August 13. By six they had covered four miles and were beginning to
deploy into the plain east of the Nebel. It was then that French scouts
reported their advance and that Marlborough and Eugene confirmed that
the open ground between Blenheim and Oberglau was held primarily by cavalry. Through the remainder of the morning, while Tallard and Marsin belatedly roused their forces, English and Imperial troops deployed and built
bridges across the Nebel—34,000 under Marlborough opposing Blenheim
and the enemy center, and 18,000 with Eugene against Oberglau and
Lutzingen. Shortly after noon, and after an exchange of artillery fire,
Eugene and Marlborough began their diversionary attacks on the Bavarian
and French flanks, respectively. These attacks were not successful, but they
were pressed with such determination that the French committed their
infantry reserve to the defense of Blenheim, and the Bavarians became preoccupied with holding Lutzingen. By two in the afternoon, Marlborough
was ready to make his main attack between Blenheim and Oberglau. Most
of his forces were now across the Nebel and arranged in four lines, two of
cavalry and two of infantry supported by field artillery. But before he
attacked, the French cavalry struck, routing the first line of his cavalry.
Marlborough's infantry used firepower to check the French, and his second
line of cavalry counterattacked, driving the French before them until
checked in turn by infantry advancing from behind Blenheim and by
infantry and cavalry from Oberglau.

At about four in the afternoon, during a lull in the fighting, Marlborough concentrated most of his men for a final assault on the Franco-
Bavarian center, on the open plain between Blenheim and Oberglau that was
held mainly by cavalry weakened in the fighting and by nine battalions of

infantry and some artillery unprotected by earthworks. When Marlborough's men advanced—two lines of cavalry supported by infantry and some light field guns—they were held up for a time by the nine battalions of infantry formed in the plain and by other infantry units advancing from Blenheim and Oberglau. But since the French cavalry was no longer effective, Marlborough's combined arms soon broke through the center of the enemy line, obliterating all in their path and turning left and right to trap the French in Blenheim and to threaten the Bavarians from Oberglau to Lutzingen. Marsin and Max Emanuel succeeded in withdrawing their forces under cover of darkness, but Marlborough and Eugene had nevertheless won a great victory by surprising their enemy, threatening his flanks, and then exploiting the weakness of his center with a powerful combination of shock and firepower—of cavalry, infantry, and artillery. At a cost of 12,000 killed and wounded, they had destroyed nearly three-fifths of the Franco-Bavarian army, killing 14,000, capturing 15,000, and taking in another 3,000 deserters.

Although Marlborough and Eugene did not at once pursue the remnants of the Franco-Bavarian army, they gradually and thoroughly exploited their victory. For nearly a week after the battle of Blenheim, while Marsin and Max Emanuel retired through Ulm toward France, the English and Imperial armies rested, cared for the wounded, and disposed of their prisoners. (They had been too battered in the fighting to do much more temporarily.) Then, calling upon Prince Louis of Baden to give up the siege of Ingolstadt and join them, Marlborough and Eugene followed the enemy through Ulm and across the Rhine. At Louis's insistence they stopped to besiege the French fortress at Landau, which had served as a staging point for French armies invading the Danube and which promised to do the same for Imperial forces advancing into Alsace or the Saar. The ensuing siege lasted more than two months, and before Landau fell, Marlborough went on to capture Trarbach on the Moselle and make preparations for an offensive toward Paris in 1705. By late November it was clear that he, Eugene, and Louis had thoroughly exploited their victory. The French had withdrawn from the Danube and all German soil; the Electress of Bavaria had agreed to disband her husband's army and to surrender his fortresses and conquests; and Anglo-Imperial forces were established well to the west of the Rhine. Vienna and the Empire were secure. Louis XIV was, for the first time, on the defensive.

The Limits of Limited War

Maneuver and Siegecraft, 1705–1708

Despite their success in 1704—their success in risking battle to save the Habsburg empire—Marlborough and Eugene spent most of the ensuing campaigns of 1705 and 1706 maneuvering and conducting sieges. Soon after Blenheim, Marlborough had begun planning an offensive along the Moselle and Saar rivers, an offensive that would have brought English, Dutch, and Imperial forces together for an advance on Paris in 1705. But when the Dutch and Imperialists were slow to assemble, and when the French besieged Liège on the Meuse River, Marlborough was forced to abandon the Moselle River and devote the remainder of 1705 to a frustrating war of maneuver in Brabant. He did skirmish successfully with the French at Wanghe in July and forced them to abandon their line of fortifications in Brabant. Yet he was unable to persuade the Dutch to risk battle; and, without a battle, he could achieve nothing substantial. So disgusted was Marlborough with the Dutch that he would have campaigned with Eugene in Italy in 1706 had the German states been willing to furnish him with troops and had the Austrians been able to keep control of the upper Rhine, to keep open the way to Italy.

As it was, he remained in the Low Countries, and Eugene stayed in Italy. Although each won important battles, each devoted more of the campaign than he wished to sieges and maneuvering. At Ramillies in May 1706, Marlborough found friend and foe willing to fight. Using tactics similar to those that had brought victory at Blenheim, he crushed a French army of 62,000 in little more than two hours. He conducted a feint at one flank of the French army and then struck hard at the other with combinations of cavalry and infantry. Once he had broken through the enemy's line, he turned, took the rest of the enemy in flank, and put the whole to flight. His victory

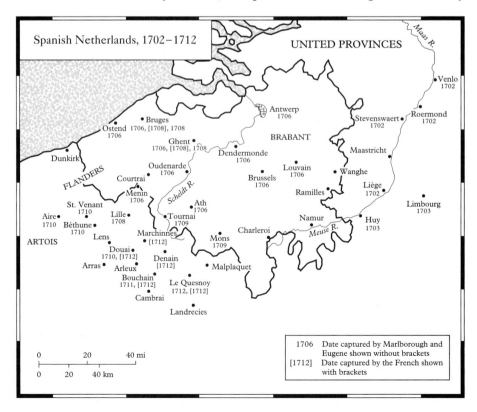

forced the French to abandon the northern portions of the Spanish Netherlands, including Brussels, Antwerp, Ghent, and Bruges. But the French
were determined to hold what they could in the south; and Marlborough
spent the remainder of 1706 recovering Flanders piecemeal, reducing by
siege Ostend, Menin, Dendermonde, and Ath. At the same time, Eugene
was employing a small, mobile army to elude the French in northern Italy,
defeat their forces that were besieging Turin, and preserve Savoy for the
Grand Alliance. By the end of 1706, Marlborough had recovered nearly all
of the Spanish Netherlands, and Eugene, most of Italy.

Paradoxically, their success in 1706 so weakened the Grand Alliance
that Marlborough and Eugene could do little in 1707. Each of the principal
members of the Alliance was encouraged enough by the recovery of the
Spanish Netherlands and Savoy to think of its own interests—the Dutch of
gaining the Spanish Netherlands as a permanent barrier against French
aggression, the Austrians of acquiring Spanish territory in Italy and of placing a Habsburg on the throne of Spain, and the English of expanding their
trade as well as curbing French power. Because they had different interests,
the allies could not agree to prosecute the war as vigorously as Marlborough
and, perhaps, Eugene thought they should. Marlborough proposed to end
the war in 1707 with an offensive in Spain supported by a diversionary
attack on Toulon and holding actions in the Spanish Netherlands and on the
Rhine. But when Austria and France made a separate peace in Italy, a peace
that allowed the French to redeploy 20,000 men from Italy to Spain and the
Spanish Netherlands, and when the Austrians concentrated on occupying
Naples rather than attacking Toulon, Marlborough's plans collapsed. The
French were able to take the offensive in Spain, on the Rhine, and in the
Spanish Netherlands; they were also able to repel Eugene's belated attack
on Toulon. Marlborough, outnumbered and frustrated by the Dutch who
refused repeatedly to risk battle, spent most of the campaign watching the
French in Brabant. Not until late summer and autumn were the allies able
to maneuver the French out of Brabant and out of Germany.

Frustrated by the lack of cooperation among the allies and the ineffectual war they had waged in 1707, Marlborough and Eugene were determined to act decisively in 1708. They agreed to make their principal effort
in the Spanish Netherlands and to seek a general engagement. If they could
win another great battle and shatter the French army, they might be able to
break through Vauban's barrier of fortresses, advance toward Paris, and force
Louis XIV to make peace. But knowing that the Dutch would be reluctant
to engage a French army that was larger than or even equal to their own,
they made plans to gain temporary superiority in numbers. They decided in
April to create three armies for the campaign of 1708: 80,000 under Marlborough in the Spanish Netherlands, 40,000 under Eugene on the Moselle,
and 45,000 under the Elector of Hanover on the upper Rhine. Once these
armies were in the field, the French would be forced to make a similar
deployment, to disperse their own forces. When they did, Eugene would try
to slip away from the Moselle with part of his army and join Marlborough
in the Low Countries. Together they would have enough troops temporarily
to seek a decisive battle. Here was a strategy, like that of 1704, that was

designed to overcome the inertia of siegecraft and maneuver, that depended on surprise and concentration of force to make battle feasible.

Although the execution of their strategy fell short of their expectations, they did succeed in provoking battle and in pushing the war into France. The campaign of 1708 began slowly because the French could not agree on a strategy and because Marlborough and Eugene had difficulty assembling their forces. Then, in early July the French suddenly left their camp near Mons and marched toward the northwest part of the Spanish Netherlands, capturing Ghent and Bruges and threatening Marlborough's lines of supply to England and the United Provinces. Marlborough, still without reinforcements from Eugene, was inferior in numbers to the French (80,000 to 85,000). Yet after stopping to bake bread and after meeting Eugene (who arrived on July 9, four days ahead of his troops), Marlborough set out to overtake and engage the French. By noon of July 11 his advanced units had covered nearly fifty miles and were within sight of the main French army on the west bank of the river Scheldt just north of the town of Oudenarde. The French, who were surprised by this feat of marching, lost little time deciding to attack the Anglo-Dutch army while it was still crossing the Scheldt. The French sought to trap the English and Dutch troops in a confined space against the river; Marlborough and Eugene sought to secure their bridgehead and then turn the enemy's exposed right flank. By early evening, the Anglo-Dutch army had stopped the French attack, encircled their flank, and forced them to retreat toward Ghent. Once again, Marlborough and Eugene had won a substantial victory: they had killed, wounded, and captured nearly 15,000 men and taken in another 5,000 deserters—all at a cost of 3,000 killed and wounded.

The Siege of Lille

Yet Marlborough and Eugene found it difficult to exploit their victory at Oudenarde and nearly impossible to avoid returning to a conventional campaign of maneuvering and sieges. The French army had been defeated but not destroyed; and it retired to the security of Ghent and Bruges. Knowing that he could not profitably attack an army of 65,000 men in fortifications, Marlborough tried to draw them out by invading and plundering the French frontier province of Artois. When the French refused to be drawn from Ghent and Bruges, Marlborough proposed leaving them there and invading France by sea. He would have embarked his army in Flanders, sailed around Vauban's frontier defenses, and landed in the Somme River to establish a base at Abbeville and proceed overland to Paris. This proposal proved too unconventional even for Eugene, who insisted on establishing a secure line of supply through the Spanish Netherlands before striking toward Paris. So it was that he and Marlborough agreed to undertake a siege of Lille, the largest and most important city on the northern frontier of France. Besieging Lille might well force the French to risk battle; taking Lille would give Marlborough and Eugene a large and well-fortified base on the road from Brussels to Paris.

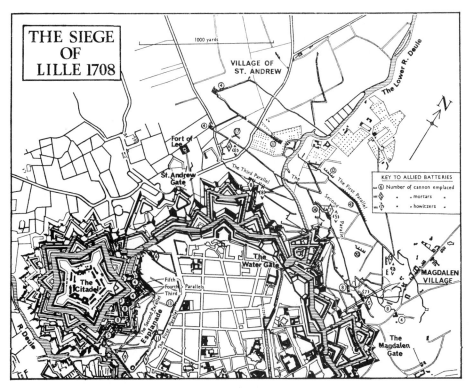

This drawing of the siege of Lille shows the extraordinary depth and complexity of Vauban's fortifications. It also shows the extensive parallels and batteries that Eugene had to build to breach the walls of the town and citadel in a siege that lasted more than three months.

But taking Lille would be far more costly than Marlborough or Eugene expected. The town and citadel were protected by some of the largest and most elaborate of Vauban's fortifications; the garrison of 15,000 was well supplied and skillfully led; and in July 1708 there were still more than 100,000 French troops in the Low Countries to support the garrison. Marlborough and Eugene made very extensive preparations. By mid-August they had assembled 80 pieces of heavy artillery, 20 mortars, 3,000 carts of ammunition, and 95,000 men (40,000 under Eugene to carry on the siege and 55,000 under Marlborough to keep open lines of supply and forestall any relief of the garrison). But they had scarcely begun their trenches (August 22) when a French army of 110,000 men appeared. Marlborough had to suspend the siege briefly and prepare to defend himself. His field-works and trenches discouraged an attack, but he could not keep the French from marching north on September 15 to cut his line of supply to Brussels and forcing him to establish and defend another line through Ostend. Because the French continued to attack his supply trains and depots, and because feeding 95,000 men together with their horses and camp followers was in any case a difficult task, Marlborough had to put his army on short rations and engage in ruthless foraging just to sustain the siege. In late October Eugene at last succeeded in breaching the main walls of Lille and capturing the town. But the citadel held out until December 9; and before the siege ended, Marlborough and Eugene had lost more than three months and 15,000 men, killed and wounded. They had, however, gained a base, deprived France of an important city and fortress, and established the momentum needed to recover Ghent, Bruges, and the remainder of Spanish Flanders by the end of the year.

Villars

These defeats, together with a harsh winter and faltering public credit, seriously damaged the morale of the French army. Troops on the northern frontier mutinied, demanding food, clothes, and pay. In desperation, Louis XIV appointed Marshal Claude Villars to command the Army of Flanders. Although Louis had long recognized Villars as one of his ablest generals, he had found him too independent and impetuous to be trusted with the most important command in the French army. Like his famous opponents, Marlborough and Eugene, Villars was an ambitious, aggressive commander who preferred battles to sieges; but even more than they, he appreciated the value of fieldworks and fortifications. He had entered the French army at seventeen and won rapid promotion for his courage and inspirational leadership: as a junior officer and as a colonel of cavalry in the Dutch War, as a volunteer with the Bavarian army in the War of the Holy League (he led a successful

Marshal Villars was the most talented of French commanders in the War of the Spanish Succession. He rebuilt the Army of Flanders and successfully held the northern frontiers of France against the allied forces of Marlborough and Eugene.

cavalry attack in Eugene's victory over the Turks at Zenta), and as a general officer in the War of the League of Augsburg.

But Villars's preference for battle as well as his habit of quarreling with superiors and disobeying his king kept him in peripheral commands during the first six years of the War of the Spanish Succession. After defeating Prince Louis of Baden at Friedlingen in 1702 and winning his marshal's baton, he was ordered to serve under Max Emanuel of Bavaria. He found Max Emanuel insufferably cautious: unwilling to approve his plan for a campaign against Vienna, to pursue the defeated Imperialists after the battle of Höchstädt, and to authorize an attack on another Imperial army at Augsburg, late in 1703. He remonstrated violently and was removed from command. For the ensuing five years he served successfully in relatively minor, if independent, commands: putting down a rebellion in Languedoc in 1704, holding the Moselle against Marlborough in 1705, making diversionary attacks east of the Rhine in 1705, 1706, and 1707, and organizing the defenses of southeast France in 1708. But not until March 1709 was Louis XIV desperate enough to entrust Villars with the command of French forces in the principal theater of the war.

Malplaquet

Fortunately for Villars and for France, the allies were slow to open the campaign of 1709 and slower still to test his army. Marlborough and Eugene were not ready to take the field until mid-June: they had been late going into winter quarters; the winter had been unusually long and severe, creating shortages of food and fodder and delaying the growth of grass in the spring; and peace negotiations had diminished allied enthusiasm for resuming the war. Villars used the respite to restore his army and improve the defenses of the French frontier. He seized enough grain to begin to feed his men—to prevent mutiny and starvation if not to provide full rations. He was then able to concentrate on building discipline and confidence. He taught his men to march and fire with precision; he sent them in detachments to surprise enemy outposts and convoys and to experience combat and taste success without running large risks; and he said repeatedly how eager he was to engage the main Anglo-Dutch army. By mid-June, when Marlborough and Eugene advanced south from Lille with 110,000 men, Villars was ready to oppose them. He could not match their numbers or stand against them in open combat. But his army of 80,000 men, well dug in from Béthune to Douai, effectively blocked the road to Paris. And when Marlborough and Eugene chose to go around his army and became mired in sieges of Tournai (June 27–September 3) and Mons (begun September 6), they gave him another two months to prepare to engage them. Early in September he set out to relieve Mons. He still did not have an army capable of attacking Marlborough and Eugene; he was ready to offer battle in a position of his own choice, to fight a defensive general engagement.

At Malplaquet, a village nine miles south of Mons, Villars succeeded in provoking battle on his terms. Marlborough and Eugene had not

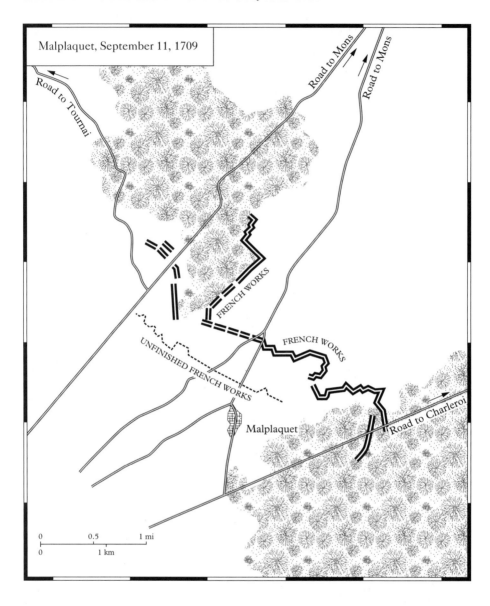

Malplaquet, September 11, 1709

expected him to intervene in the siege of Mons, and their forces were widely scattered when on September 9 they discovered him approaching from the southwest. Although they were able to screen Mons with the forces at hand and might well have remained secure on the defensive (as at Lille in 1708), they decided to gather their troops and attack. They believed they had a chance to win a decisive victory and that such a victory would be more likely to end the war than any number of successful sieges. Yet it would take them nearly two days to assemble the troops they thought essential. In that time Villars was able to place his army in a very strong position just north of Malplaquet where the road to Mons ran through a gap, a mile-and-a-half wide, between large, dense woods. There, on a slight ridge athwart the road, he built a strong line of trenches and redoubts. His flanks were extended forward and tied securely to the adjacent woods, giving his defenses a concave appearance to anyone approaching from Mons. Because these protruding flanks provided converging and enfilading fire against an attack on his center as well as security against an envelopment, Villars put most of his infantry on his flanks. The rest he kept in the center of his line or in reserve, while distributing artillery throughout his works and massing cavalry behind his center. Although inferior in number (perhaps 80,000 against 100,000 on September 11), Villars's army was well disciplined, ready to fight, and very skillfully placed at Malplaquet.

Indeed, Marlborough and Eugene were hard pressed to find or create a weakness in Villars's dispositions. It would be difficult to take or to envelop either of his flanks; and until at least one had been taken and its guns silenced, it would not be feasible to attack his center, to risk advancing through the enfilading fire from his flanks. Nor was an ordinary diversion likely to persuade Villars to weaken any part of his line and make it vulnerable to a surprise attack. His works were too strong and his troops too reliable to be threatened by anything less than a full-scale attack. Thus at Malplaquet, Marlborough and Eugene had to rely less on surprise and more on an initial and obvious concentration of force than in any of their other battles. They had to make their attack much as Villars intended and expected they would. They decided first to try to gain control of the French left flank with a massive infantry attack. They would also make a secondary attack against the French right (to fix the troops there) and look for opportunities that might develop in the center once the left had been taken. But the main effort was to be made from the outset against the left, against one of the most strongly held parts of Villars's line.

This plan eventually succeeded, but at a very high cost. Marlborough and Eugene began the battle of Malplaquet about eight in the morning of September 11 with a bombardment of Villars's works followed by infantry attacks on his flanks. These attacks produced high casualties and few gains against an entrenched and disciplined infantry firing volleys by rank and a well-placed artillery. Fresh allied troops soon tried again on both flanks. Those mounting the main attack on Villars's left gradually took his fortifications and fought their way through the adjoining woods. But on the French right, allied infantry pushed ahead with more courage than discipline, suffered very heavy casualties, and were overwhelmed by a counterattack. As soon as Marlborough had repaired the damage done by this counterattack and prevented his troops from making a third, undisciplined diversionary attack on the French right, he returned to his main offensive which had succeeded by noon in driving the French from the woods that anchored their left flank. By then, Villars had drawn troops from his center to support his left against the overwhelming concentration of allied infantry that threatened to turn or roll up this flank. He was able to check the allies as they emerged from the woods. But before he could organize a full-scale counterattack, a fresh allied detachment arrived from Tournai to fall upon his extreme left flank. Villars was wounded and carried unconscious from the field; his counterattack collapsed; and his left flank began a slow, ordered withdrawal.

Marlborough now acted promptly to exploit this success—to bring infantry, cavalry, and artillery together in a final, decisive drive through the center of the French line. He did so early in the afternoon, after his troops had completely occupied the fortifications on the French left flank and captured the artillery that enfiladed the approaches to their center. As soon as he saw that Villars had withdrawn troops from the center to defend his beleaguered flank, Marlborough sent his infantry to occupy the empty French lines. He then brought up artillery to consolidate his gains and cavalry to carry the attack beyond the trenches. But while his cavalry was passing through the trenches and forming on the Heath of Malplaquet, the French cavalry attacked. Here, as at Blenheim, allied infantry, cavalry, and artillery, acting together, proved superior to French cavalry; and after a series of attacks and counterattacks, the French cavalry joined the rest of Villars's army in a well-ordered retreat. The allies were too weakened and exhausted by the fighting to follow. It was a little after three. The Battle of Malplaquet was over.

Toward Limited War

Malplaquet was a victory so tarnished by the loss of life that it discredited the victors and their aggressive way of war. Marlborough and Eugene had won in a conventional sense: they had driven the enemy from his prepared defenses and forced him to abandon any further effort to relieve Mons, which surrendered on October 20. But they had lost over 24,000 men (nearly one-fourth of their army, killed and wounded) while inflicting no more than 12,000 casualties on the French (about 15 percent of their army). Because the allies had taken such heavy losses and because the French army emerged from the battle with its morale and organization intact, Marlborough and Eugene could not exploit their victory. After Blenheim, Ramillies, and Oudenarde, the allies had been able to gather fortresses and provinces from a demoralized enemy; after Malplaquet, they could do no more than complete the siege of Mons. No wonder that Marlborough's, if not Eugene's, reputation suffered and that Europeans questioned the wisdom of their aggressive tactics. The lethality of Malplaquet, the killing or wounding of 36,000 men in seven hours, shocked contemporaries, making them acutely aware of the destructiveness of increased firepower. Thereafter, kings and generals would be less willing to risk general engagements and be more patient with sieges and maneuvers. This, one of the deadliest battles of the eighteenth century, reaffirmed the limits of limited war.

For four years after Malplaquet, the War of the Spanish Succession continued in campaigns of siege and maneuver. Governments, wary of battle and tired of expensive wars, refused to provide commanders with the authority or the forces for large-scale offensive action. In 1710, while France sought a negotiated peace, Louis XIV ordered Villars to avoid battle and to rely instead on fortifications to contain the allies in Flanders. Marlborough was able to use his superior numbers to capture a line of fortresses from Douai through Béthune to Aire. But in October 1710 a new ministry came to power in England that was more interested in making peace than in prosecuting the war. When Marlborough returned to Flanders for the ensuing campaign, he found that England, Prussia, and Austria had all reduced their forces under his command and that Eugene had been ordered to the Rhine. With fewer men than Villars, Marlborough maneuvered skillfully and took Bouchain by siege in September. But he could not attack Villars or break through the last belt of fortresses protecting the French frontier. By the time he returned home, the ministry had negotiated a separate peace with France and was ready to dismiss him, end its support of the Dutch and Austrians, and consolidate its territorial gains in the Mediterranean and America.

That the British were now in a position to make a separate and favorable peace was primarily the result of allied efforts on the continent—of Marlborough's and Eugene's skill in conducting the war and of the cumulative effects of strong British and weak French public finances. British success in the War of the Spanish Succession was also due to their growing superiority at sea, although to a lesser degree. The British had entered their long wars with Louis XIV with one of the leading navies in Europe—perhaps somewhat weaker than the French and on a par with the Dutch. But because the French and Dutch devoted proportionately more of their resources to the wars on land, and because the British were better able to sustain their public credit, the British gradually surpassed both the French and the Dutch at sea. Yet even as they became the leading maritime power, the British continued to put most of their effort into defeating the French on the continent and continued to find it difficult to use their navy effectively.

The British had trouble exploiting their superiority at sea because, after the opening battles of the War of the League of Augsburg, the French refused to risk their fleet in large-scale engagements. In the century since the English had defeated the Spanish Armada (1588), the navies of western Europe had become significantly larger and more powerful, and warfare at sea, increasingly complex and destructive. As early as 1626 the French had undertaken to create a standing navy, a permanent national force of well-designed warships commanded by trained officers and supported by a central administration—a force that would protect French trade and colonies and enhance French power. Although the French neglected their navy for several decades at mid-century, they began a rebuilding program in 1661 that produced the most formidable navy in Europe by 1688. The English had been slower than the French to develop a standing navy, but during their mid-seventeenth-century wars with the Dutch and the Spanish—wars fought primarily over trade and colonies—they laid the foundation of a permanent national navy. They built or bought hundreds of warships, some larger than 1,000 tons with 100 guns, improved the pay and training of officers and the discipline of seamen, reduced corruption in their administration and adopted standardized tactics that were expressed in Fighting Instructions (1653). They now tried to engage while sailing parallel to their enemy in a line ahead—a formation designed to maximize firepower by allowing each ship to fire broadsides without obstructing the fire of any other friendly ship. Such tactics employed by larger and more powerful ships and increasingly well-disciplined men made battle at sea ever more destructive and—

potentially—decisive. No wonder that after being defeated by the English and Dutch navies in 1692, the French chose to avoid battle and to concentrate on attacking British commerce and colonies.

This French strategy frustrated the English throughout the War of the League of Augsburg and much of the War of the Spanish Succession. Only gradually were the English able to take advantage of their increasing superiority at sea. In the War of the League of Augsburg the English were no match for the French at commerce raiding (losing over 4,000 merchantmen to warships and privateers), or at attacking and defending colonies in North America. Even during the War of the Spanish Succession, when the British were comparatively stronger at sea, they were still ineffective in blockading and raiding French ports in the Atlantic, in protecting their merchant shipping (they lost another 3,250 vessels), and in capturing French colonies in North America. But the British navy was able to establish its superiority in the Mediterranean by taking Gibraltar, Minorca, and Sardinia; encouraging Portugal and Savoy to join the alliance against France; diverting French forces from Flanders; and protecting British trade. And British warships and privateers eventually surpassed the French in commerce raiding, nearly destroying French trade by the end of the war and encouraging France to negotiate a separate peace with Britain.

Only belatedly did the Dutch and Austrians discover that the British government had made a separate peace and had left them vulnerable to France. When Marlborough did not return to the continent, the allies appointed Eugene to command in the Low Countries. But not until the campaign of 1712 had begun did Eugene learn that the British were withdrawing their forces from his command. Thenceforth—from June 1712 until November 1713—he would have to carry on the war with forces that were consistently inferior in numbers to those under Villars. Eugene persisted briefly on the offensive, taking Quesnoy by siege on July 3, 1712. But the French government now authorized Villars to relieve the pressure on its frontiers by capturing fortresses on Eugene's line of supply. Villars did just that, surprising Denain and Marchiennes in late July and forcing Eugene to retire north, toward Brussels. Villars was then able to recover successively Douai, Quesnoy, and Bouchain—nearly half of the French fortresses that Marlborough and Eugene had captured since the summer of 1710. In 1713, after the Dutch had joined the British in making peace with France (leaving Austria alone at war with France), Villars resumed his offensive against Eugene along the Rhine. Although he had far larger forces, Villars proceeded cautiously and ended his campaign with lengthy and successful sieges of Landau and Freiburg.

During the following winter, Villars and Eugene negotiated peace for France and Austria. The terms they agreed to at Rastadt in March 1714, together with the treaties signed at Utrecht in April 1713 by France, Britain, the United Provinces, and other members of the Grand Alliance, ended the War of the Spanish Succession. Above all, the treaties of Utrecht and Rastadt extinguished Louis XIV's hopes for a universal monarchy and restored a European balance of power—separating the crowns of France and Spain, stripping France of conquests east of the Rhine and overseas, reducing

Spanish territories in Europe, and keeping a Habsburg from the Spanish throne. Those treaties also added substantially to British possessions in North America, the West Indies, and the Mediterranean.

✯ ✯ ✯ ✯

The War of the Spanish Succession also confirmed the trend toward limited war in Europe. Since the Peace of Westphalia, Europeans had deliberately sought both to increase the security of their states and to reduce the risks and destructiveness of warfare. As a result they created national standing armies of unprecedented size and power—armies of long-serving professional soldiers supported by regular taxes, state bureaucracies, and magazine systems of supply. They also constructed larger and more complex fortifications to protect their frontiers and internal communications. These measures, taken at a time when armies still lacked the speed and discipline to impose battle on an unwilling opponent, tended to make wars long, expensive, and indecisive. Even commanders as skilled and aggressive as Marlborough and Eugene were hard pressed to engage their enemies and exploit their victories. And when faced with an opponent as able as Villars, they found battle extremely destructive. The outcome of Malplaquet fostered an emerging European preference for limited war—for campaigns in which the risks and potential gains, if not the costs, were substantially reduced. Europeans had had enough of battles that threatened the security of a state; they would be satisfied for some decades to come with campaigns of siegecraft and maneuver that preserved the existing international order.

SUGGESTED READINGS

Atkinson, C. T. *Marlborough and the Rise of the British Army* (New York: G. P. Putnam's Sons, 1921).

Blomfield, Reginald. *Sebastien le Prestre de Vauban, 1633–1707* (New York: Barnes & Noble, Inc., 1971).

Chandler, David G. *The Art of Warfare in the Age of Marlborough* (London: B. T. Batsford, 1976).

———. *Marlborough as Military Commander* (London: Scribner, 1973).

Childs, John. *Armies and Warfare in Europe 1648–1789* (New York: Holmes and Meier, 1982).

Duffy, Christopher. *The Fortress in the Age of Vauban and Frederick the Great, 1660–1789* (London: Routledge & Kegan Paul, 1985).

Graham, Gerald S. *Empire of the North Atlantic: The Maritime Struggle for North America* (Toronto: University of Toronto Press, 1950).

Guerlac, Henry. "Vauban: The Impact of Science on War," in Peter Paret, ed., *Makers of Modern Strategy: from Machiavelli to the Nuclear Age* (Princeton: Princeton University Press, 1986), 64–90.

Henderson, Nicholas. *Prince Eugene of Savoy* (New York: Frederick A. Praeger, 1965).

Kennedy, Paul M. *The Rise and Fall of British Naval Mastery* (London: Allen Lane, 1976).

Lynn, John A. "The Growth of the French Army During the Seventeenth Century," *Armed Forces and Society* VI (1980), 568–585.

McNeill, William H. *The Pursuit of Power: Technology, Armed Force, and Society Since A.D. 1000* (Chicago: University of Chicago Press, 1984).

Mork, Gordon R. "Flint and Steel: A Study in Military Technology and Tactics in 17th–Century Europe," *Smithsonian Journal of History* II (1967), 25–52.

Parker, Geoffrey. *The Military Revolution: Military Innovation and the Rise of the West, 1500–1800* (Cambridge: Cambridge University Press, 1988).

Perjés, Géza. "Army Provisioning, Logistics, and Strategy in the Second Half of the 17th Century," *Acta Historica Academiae Scientiarium Hungaricae* 16 (1970), 1–51.

Sturgill, Claude C. *Marshal Villars and the War of the Spanish Succession* (Lexington: University of Kentucky Press, 1965).

Taylor, Frank. *Wars of Marlborough 1702–09* (Oxford: Basil Blackwell, 1921).

Weygand, Max. *Turenne, Marshal of France* (Boston: Houghton Mifflin, 1930).

Wolfe, John B. *The Emergence of the Great Powers 1685–1715* (New York: Harper, 1951).

3

LIMITED WAR IN WESTERN EUROPE, 1714–1763

The Standing Army and the State

The Art of Limited War

Frederick, Saxe, and the War of the Austrian Succession

Frederick in the Seven Years' War

For a quarter century after the War of the Spanish Succession, Europe enjoyed an era of relative peace—a welcome respite from the long and costly wars of Louis XIV. But in the late 1730s this collective moderation gave way. Separate conflicts—one colonial and commercial, the other European and dynastic—soon flowed together into two world wars, the War of the Austrian Succession (1740–1748) and the Seven Years' War (1756–1763). In the former, a dispute between Britain and Spain over smuggling in America escalated into a world war when in 1740 Prussia seized the Austrian province of Silesia. Eventually Britain, Hanover, and the United Provinces supported Austria; and Spain, France, and Bavaria became allies of Prussia. Intermittent fighting took place in central and western Europe, North America, the West Indies, and India, ending in 1748 without a satisfactory resolution of the basic disputes. Indeed, by 1756 those disputes had again flared into a war. France, supported eventually by Spain, resumed its struggle with Britain for overseas colonies and trade; and Austria resumed its battle with Prussia for Silesia. But the alliances that linked these contests were completely transformed by the diplomatic revolution of 1756. France and Russia now joined Austria against Britain, Hanover, and Prussia. The Seven Years' War, which spread from North America to the West Indies and India and from central to northwest

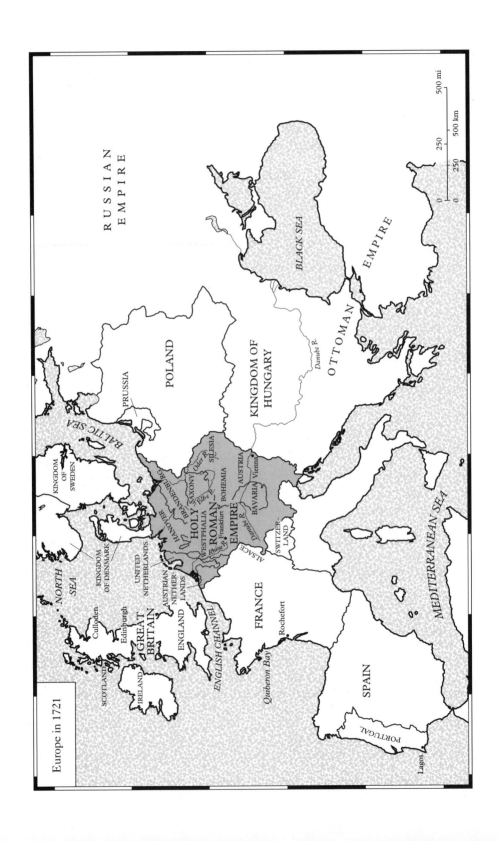

Europe in 1721

RUSSIAN EMPIRE

BLACK SEA

OTTOMAN EMPIRE

Danube R.

POLAND

PRUSSIA

KINGDOM OF HUNGARY

BALTIC SEA

KINGDOM OF SWEDEN

SILESIA

Oder R.

SAXONY

BRANDENBURG

Elbe R.

AUSTRIA

Vienna

BOHEMIA

HOLY

Frankfurt

ROMAN

BAVARIA

Danube R.

KINGDOM OF DENMARK

HANOVER

WESTPHALIA

EMPIRE

Rhine R.

SWITZER-LAND

ALSACE

NORTH SEA

UNITED NETHERLANDS

AUSTRIAN NETHER-LANDS

FRANCE

Rochefort

Culloden

Edinburgh

GREAT BRITAIN

ENGLAND

ENGLISH CHANNEL

Quiberon Bay

SCOTLAND

IRELAND

SPAIN

PORTUGAL

MEDITERRANEAN SEA

Lagos

500 mi

500 km

250

250

0

0

Germany, ended in victories for Britain, Hanover, and Prussia. The Peace of Paris confirmed Prussia's conquest of Silesia and gave Britain the North American continent to the Mississippi River as well as additional territory and influence in the West Indies, Africa, and India.

Paradoxical as it might seem, the world wars of the mid-eighteenth century were limited wars. At least in central and western Europe, those wars were fought for limited ends. British and French colonists might seek to destroy or conquer one another in North America. European governments had no intention of appealing for the broad popular support—of unleashing patriotic or religious feelings—needed for wars of conquest. Valuing political stability above all, they used professional armies to protect and advance their interests with minimal interference in the lives of ordinary subjects and minimal disruption of the international balance of power. In 1740 when Frederick the Great of Prussia seized Silesia, he did so to increase the population, resources, and power of Prussia and to weaken Austria. He did not intend to conquer the Habsburg empire; and he fought subsequently to preserve rather than to enlarge Prussia. Austria, for its part, sought to recover Silesia and to relegate Prussia to its place as a secondary power—not to destroy it or its ruling family. Other states entered the Austro-Prussian wars with similarly limited goals. None wanted to destroy or conquer its enemies, and none systematically attacked the enemy's population or industry. The aims in these wars were indeed limited.

So too were the operations limited. Most commanders sought to avoid general engagements or, at least, to fight in carefully chosen and prepared positions. Knowing how lethal battle had become and how difficult and costly it was to train professional soldiers, commanders usually preferred wars of exhaustion. Rather than attack the enemy's army, they preferred to besiege his fortresses, capture his magazines and supply trains, surprise his detachments, and, occasionally, strip his countryside of food and fodder. Armies were vulnerable to such a strategy because they depended on magazines, field ovens, supply trains, and foraging parties for their regular subsistence. When battle did become necessary or unavoidable, most commanders tried further to limit their risks. On the defensive they anchored their flanks on such impenetrable obstacles as rivers, swamps, or dense forests and covered their front with redoubts and heavy field artillery. On the offensive they maneuvered to surprise the enemy and to concentrate overwhelming force against one part of his army. These strategies and tactics of limited war rarely produced decisive results, but they brought success with few battles and relatively light casualties to those commanders who had the skill, patience, and time to apply them. Even commanders like Frederick the Great of Prussia, who fought more often and took heavier casualties than anyone of his era, came to appreciate and employ the conventionally prudent strategies and tactics of limited war.

The Standing Army and the State

The Rise of Prussia

The European art of war did not change fundamentally in the half-century after the Peace of Utrecht. In 1763 as in 1713, Europeans relied on standing armies to fight their wars—professional forces raised and sustained by central bureaucracies and supported by loans and state-imposed taxes. Kings continued to recruit, equip, and train their armies much as they had at the turn of the century and to expect that they would wage limited wars. The adoption of cadence and improvements in the musket and field artillery increased the speed of deployment and volume of fire, making it easier for one commander to impose battle on another but also easier for an army on the defensive to inflict heavy casualties on an aggressive foe. War was waged slightly differently in different parts of Europe, the density of the population and the presence or absence of fortresses affecting the mobility of armies and the pace of operations. But most commanders continued to prefer sieges and maneuvering to battles, and wars continued to be long and indecisive. The art of war was much the same in 1763 as it had been in 1713.

Yet in the half-century after Utrecht, leadership in the European art of war did change dramatically. During the wars of Louis XIV, France had been the greatest military power on the continent and the model for many military practices. France had shown Europe the advantages of a central administration, a large standing army, and a magazine system of supply. French engineers had taught Europe how to build and to take fortresses, and France had imposed limited war on several generations of European generals. After the War of the Spanish Succession, the French gradually lost their preeminence. They continued to have the largest army in Europe and, until 1750, one of the greatest commanders, Maurice comte de Saxe. But weakened by lax discipline, mounting public debts, and conservative thinking, French forces so declined that by the Seven Years' War they consistently suffered defeats. By then Prussia had emerged as the most admired military power in Europe. Frederick the Great showed Europeans how to harness the wealth and population of a state for war: how to raise, train, equip, and supply the largest army per capita on the continent without ruining his economy or credit. His officers were widely esteemed for their professional competence and devotion to duty; his rank and file, for their disciplined marching and firing; and he, for his innovative tactics and single-minded service to his state. By the late 1750s Frederick and Prussia had won for themselves permanent places in the history of warfare.

Standing Armies

European governments relied for more than half a century after the Peace of Utrecht on standing armies to provide their domestic security, support their foreign policy, and fight their wars. These armies remained, as they had been during the wars of Louis XIV, permanent professional forces raised by a central bureaucracy and supported by regular taxation. But during the Seven Years' War, these armies became significantly larger than they had been at the turn of the eighteenth century, reflecting not just the scope and intensity of warfare in the 1750s but also the capacity of European states to harness the increasing wealth and population of the continent. It is true that the Dutch had allowed their army to decline from 100,000 in 1710 to 40,000 in 1756 and that the French and British armies had increased only slightly: the French from 390,000 to 400,000 and the British from 75,000 to 90,000. But Austrian and Russian forces had grown substantially (from 100,000 to 200,000 and from 220,000 to 330,000, respectively); and Prussian forces increased spectacularly (from 40,000 in 1710 to 140,000 in 1756). Such increases required heavier taxes and the expenditure of ever larger portions of the public revenues on the army (as much as 90 percent of public revenues in Prussia by 1740). The states that had the will and the resources to support such increases grew in power and importance while those that did not, declined. Thus France continued to have the largest army in Europe, but French military dominance was now challenged by the rising strength of Russia, Austria, and especially, Prussia.

These standing armies of mid-eighteenth-century Europe were recruited much as their predecessors of the War of the Spanish Succession. With few exceptions, the general officers of 1750 were high-ranking and wealthy noblemen. Most junior officers, except those in British and Dutch service, were recruited from the lesser nobility. Although commoners were often commissioned as engineers and artillerists and sometimes as infantry and cavalry officers, states continued to rely on noblemen to command their forces, not just because noblemen needed and expected military employment, but especially because they were thought to have the sense of honor and social standing required to lead the rank and file. Those rank and file were still being drawn primarily from the lowest orders of society—the sons of peasants and tenant farmers, unskilled urban laborers, unemployed apprentices, and deserters and prisoners of war. States used such men precisely because they were the least productive members of society and could be enlisted without disrupting the economy and public revenues. But no state seemed to have enough men to keep up its rank and file, to make up for the 15 to 25 percent of its army that was lost each year to disease and desertion. (The French army of the Seven Years' War needed 60,000 recruits each year, exclusive of casualties, to maintain a strength of roughly 400,000.) Thus from 20 to 65 percent of each army was foreign mercenaries, hired to supplement native volunteers and conscripts.

Standing armies of the mid-eighteenth century were, then, remarkably similar in composition. But there were enough differences among them to account for wide disparities in their effectiveness. Compare the armies of France and Prussia. Each drew its officers primarily from the nobility, yet French officers were far less competent. The French government was so eager to favor noblemen that it ruined its officer corps: appointing more officers than it needed and rotating them in and out of assignments before they could learn their duties, promoting and rewarding officers for birth and wealth rather than for merit, granting all too many requests for leave, and tolerating officers who flouted regulations or who refused to accept new tactical instructions. The kings of Prussia, by contrast, did not spare or spoil their officers. They recruited poor rural noblemen who found commissioned service a welcome release from their obscure provincial lives. Although not well educated, these noblemen accepted discipline and became devoted to their duty, to each other, and to the king. Their corporate morale and efficiency survived even the horrendous casualties of the Seven Years' War (more than 4,000 Prussian officers were killed or wounded in a corps that numbered 5,500 at the beginning of the war).

The rank and file of French and Prussian armies appeared quite similar: native volunteers and conscripts were mixed with foreign mercenaries in each army. But the French mixture was not nearly so formidable as the Prussian. Because of their rising standard of living, the French were never able to get enough volunteers for their army; and because they lacked money and recruiters, they were unable to fill their ranks with foreign mercenaries. They had, therefore, to draft militiamen into the standing army; and militiamen, who were conscripts, demanded less severe discipline than volunteers or mercenaries. Like France, Prussia built its army on a combination of mercenaries (two-thirds of the whole in 1740 to one-third by 1763) and conscripts. Although Prussian mercenaries were never thought dependable, they did accept harsh discipline and transmit that discipline to native conscripts who were recruited through a cantonal system. Under that system, introduced in 1727–1733, every regiment in the Prussian army had a recruiting district that was required to keep the regiment up to strength. New recruits were chosen by a regimental officer and a civil official for an indefinite period of service. After a year's basic training, conscripts served with their regiments two months per year in peacetime or continuously in war. The cantonal system worked well, permitting conscripts to work their own lands in times of peace, fostering a sense of cohesion within each unit, and keeping Prussian units up to strength throughout the eighteenth century. Prussia thus maintained an army larger in relation to its total population than any in Europe, an army that survived 160,000 deaths during the Seven Years' War to retain its effectiveness.

That France was less successful than Prussia in recruiting its army was, to no small extent, the result of weaknesses in French military administration. Every eighteenth-century standing army depended on a central bureaucracy for men, money, and supplies. Although France had taught Europe the advantages of such a bureaucracy, the government of King Louis XV (1715–1774) was unable to meet the administrative and fiscal demands of the long wars of mid-century. By the Seven Years' War, the king's failure to provide leadership, the meddling of his favorites, and the independence of royal officials had weakened France's central administration. Moreover, continued resistance of clergymen and nobility to taxation, as well as pervasive corruption, had depleted revenues and made it increasingly difficult for France to manage debts accumulated during the wars of Louis XIV. No wonder that the ministry of war was inadequately staffed, that there were not funds enough for recruiting, that French officers had to use their own money to prevent mutiny among unpaid soldiers, or that because of poor credit France had to spend more per soldier than any European state. These administrative and fiscal weaknesses were not the only causes of French failures in the Seven Years' War, but they contributed substantially to them.

Austria also suffered from a weak central government and poor revenues. But Austria was able to take remedial measures and build a very respectable army for the Seven Years' War. In 1740 the Habsburg monarchy had no common political or military system for its realm and no unified economic policy; its army and civil service had not been paid for two years when Prussia seized Silesia. But, spurred by the loss of this valuable province, the new Habsburg queen, Maria Theresa, and her advisors began creating a central government capable of tapping the resources of the queen's diverse lands. They gradually overcame the opposition of hereditary provincial governments, stripping them of their administrative functions and persuading them to give up their traditional right of granting taxes. That done, they not only sent officials to extract taxes and military service from the peasants but also imposed property and income taxes on the nobility and clergy. By the outbreak of the Seven Years' War, these measures had given the Habsburgs the central administration and revenues they needed to sustain an army of 200,000 men and make an effective response to Prussia's preemptive attack on Saxony.

But no European state of the mid-eighteenth century was as successful as Prussia in creating a central administration to raise and sustain an army. King Frederick William I (1713–1740) combined central and provincial agencies into a single, state administration that substantially increased his revenues. Then, by devoting an ever larger part of those revenues to his army and by raising men through a cantonal system, he expanded the army from 40,000 to 83,000 men. His son, Frederick the Great (1740–1786), went even farther in strengthening the Prussian bureaucracy, revenues, and army. He taught all officials to consider themselves servants of the state and to expect punishments for incompetence as well as rewards for merit. He relied particularly on his nobility to provide the officials needed to mobilize the Prussian people: to combat indolence, encourage trade, collect taxes, and conscript men. These officials were so successful in improving the economy and revenues and in recruiting soldiers that Frederick was able to enter the Seven Years' War with a surplus in his secret military fund and an army of 140,000 men. He subsequently managed, in spite of the wastage of war, to increase and sustain his army without incurring significant debt. He did so by making war pay for itself, by defraying most of his expenses with contributions from other states (especially Saxony), subsidies from Britain, and proceeds from his debasement of Prussian currency.

Discipline and Training

Those who raised and led the standing armies of the mid-eighteenth century agreed that the common soldier had to be well disciplined: that he had to obey and show respect for his superiors, do his duty through the terror and confusion of close combat, kill and plunder only when ordered to do so, and accept the conventions that distinguished him, as a soldier, from civilians. Discipline was thought essential to make soldiers out of the dregs of society. How else were men who were deserters, prisoners of war, mercenaries, or unwilling conscripts to be kept together as an army and made tactically effective? Military leaders of 1756, like those of 1701, agreed on the fundamental importance of discipline. What they did not agree on was how severe discipline ought to be. The French subjected recruits to long and arduous training but not to severe physical punishment or to the sustained supervision of officers. French troops were not thought to be well disciplined: they sometimes performed poorly in combat, plundered, and deserted. The Prussians, conversely, took a more comprehensive and a much harsher approach to discipline. They employed drill, religion, group loyalties, and, above all, a variety of punishments to turn recruits into soldiers. Prussian officers, who regularly supervised their men, were authorized not just to arrest and imprison but also to beat, mutilate, or execute the disobedient. Frederick the Great believed that such harsh punishments gave his army the discipline needed to survive a procession of unusually lethal battles. But harsh punishments also drove more men to desert from the Prussian army than from any other in mid-eighteenth-century Europe (in the course of the Seven Years' War, 1,650 men deserted from one regiment that had an authorized strength of 1,700). It is not astonishing that other states, like Austria and Britain, should have sought a discipline slightly less harsh than Prussia's but not nearly so mild as that of France.

In addition to discipline, it took constant training to make a mid-eighteenth-century army. Waging formal, linear combined-arms warfare in 1759, as in 1709, required large numbers of troops who were trained to march, maneuver, fire, charge, and retire together. Because armies had to replace 15 to 25 percent of their men each year (to offset losses to disease and desertion), and because it took a year to teach an infantryman the basics of using his weapon and marching with his platoon (two years to teach a cavalryman), states were constantly engaged in turning recruits into soldiers. In peacetime, when armies were dispersed in garrisons or serving as policemen and customs agents if not tax collectors, most training was done in platoons or companies (a regiment in the mid-eighteenth-century British army was assembled only 13 percent of the time). Such training was very elementary and very repetitious: learning to march in step, to load and fire a standard flintlock musket (the manual of arms), and to perform platoon or company maneuvers (especially to deploy from column into line and to ploy from line into column). Such training was also very valuable; it gave infantrymen or cavalrymen the basic skills and automatic responses needed in combat at close range. But only at annual reviews or maneuvers did regiments or larger units assemble to practice deploying into line of battle, firing by subdivisions of the line, advancing and retiring, and ploying once more into columns. Since much of each year's maneuvers was devoted to integrating platoons, companies, and regiments into larger units—to imposing uniform procedures on troops that had been dispersed for many months—there was little time for advanced training in combined-arms warfare. Thus although eighteenth-century armies trained constantly, most were not well prepared for the beginning of a war and became effective only after a year or two of regular campaigning.

But in the half-century from 1714 to 1764 European armies did make improvements in training their rank and file. In 1714 Prussia introduced standard drill regulations for its whole army; Britain followed in 1727–1728, and France in 1764. Not all companies and regiments complied at once, but as soon as most were training in the same way, it became easier to assemble those units into an army capable of conducting maneuvers or going to war. Prussia and Britain made other specific changes in training that increased the speed and power of their armies. Frederick William I of Prussia introduced cadence in his army before 1740, and George II of Britain did the same in his by the late 1740s. Marching in step and at a prescribed number of steps per minute increased the pace, predictability, and order in all maneuvers. Similarly, learning to lock ranks to fire and to use a simplified manual of arms, increased the volume and the rate of fire. (In locking, soldiers in the front rank knelt, those in the second stepped slightly to the right, and those in the third moved even farther to the right—about half a pace.) Locking, adopted by the British in the 1720s, increased the volume of fire by permitting more men to fire safely. A simplified, 1756 British manual of arms—using fewer motions to load, point, and fire a musket—increased each man's firing rate. These improvements in training, incorporated in ever larger and more realistic peacetime maneuvers (44,000 Prussians took part in 1753), helped make Prussian and British forces among the most successful of all that took part in the Seven Years' War.

There were also improvements, between 1714 and 1763, in the training of officers. Most officers in the principal armies of Europe received their basic training in a regiment. There they learned the fundamentals of discipline, drill, and tactics and were introduced to the customs and values of the officer corps. Once they had mastered the fundamentals, most officers learned mainly by prolonged service in peace and war. A few men, with ambition as well as money and social standing, supplemented experience with study: reading books on the history and theory of war, corresponding with other officers, traveling abroad to visit battlefields and observe other armies in their annual maneuvers, and, occasionally, serving as volunteers with foreign armies. To these traditional and casual ways of training officers, the kings of Prussia added structure and personal supervision. In 1717, Frederick William I created a cadet school in Berlin. This school, which enrolled thirteen-year-old boys for a three-year course of study, trained about one-third of all Prussian officers from 1717 to 1786. Frederick the Great sought to provide for the remainder by emphasizing the importance of learning basic drill and tactics in their regiments, bringing officers to his headquarters at Potsdam to see his best units perform, keeping promising young men as his adjutants, establishing schools of engineering and topography, and encouraging regimental libraries. For his generals, he drew up detailed, secret instructions. Although Frederick the Great was not uniformly successful in developing generals, he and his father did create the most admired officer corps in Europe. Other states opened their own military academies (Russia after 1731, Austria and France in 1751), established other schools for officers, and allowed, even sometimes encouraged, their officers to visit or serve with the Prussian army.

The Art of Limited War

Refinements in Weapons

Although there was little fundamental change in weapons from 1714 to 1763, there were refinements that increased the rate of fire of handguns as well as the accuracy and mobility of artillery. In making and exploiting these refinements, Prussia usually led most European states. The basic infantry weapon in the Seven Years' War, as in the War of the Spanish Succession, was the .69 or .75 caliber flintlock musket equipped with a socket bayonet. The flintlock remained a muzzle-loading smoothbore weapon that was inaccurate but lethal at 150 yards. It was, however, improved in one important respect after 1714: its rate of fire was increased from about two rounds per minute to nearly three. This increase was the result, in part, of the adoption of an iron ramrod and cartridges, first in Prussia during the wars of Louis XIV and then in other European armies during the 1730s, 1740s, and 1750s. The iron ramrod accelerated the loading of a musket because the iron rod did not easily break. Thus a soldier no longer had to take the time to protect the ramrod while seating a charge or returning the ramrod to its sheath. The adoption of paper cartridges also accelerated loading. Because each cartridge contained the powder and ball needed to load and prime a musket, a soldier needed only to open a cartridge and drop the contents into the pan and muzzle of his weapon; he did not have to measure out powder for a charge and then reach separately for a ball and for priming powder.

Mid-eighteenth-century improvements in European artillery were much like those in handguns: refinements rather than fundamental alterations in design. For more than half a century after 1714, Europeans continued to use muzzle-loading smoothbore cannon that fired a variety of shot and shell. But Prussia and Austria, unlike France, did manage to make their guns more mobile and more accurate. By 1741 the Prussians had created lighter guns by reviving the use of a chambered breech—that is, by casting a gun in which the chamber (where powder burned) was smaller than the interior of the barrel. Thus, for example, they were able to reduce the overall weight of a gun that fired a 3-pound shot from about 1,000 to 472 pounds. This lighter gun, attached to a caisson limber or two-wheeled ammunition cart (1742), had the mobility to serve effectively with infantry. Prussians also increased the accuracy of their guns by developing a backsight and combining it with a wedge driven by a screw that controlled elevation (again reviving an earlier technological achievement). Prussian artillery did have its problems (the chambered breech was not easy to load, and lighter guns lacked the power of conventional pieces); and Prussians did not always use their artillery as effectively as the Austrians. Even so, Prussia had taken the

The flintlock musket, shown here with its sleeve bayonet and ramrod (inserted under the barrel), was the basic infantry weapon in European armies from roughly 1700 until the 1840s. A skilled infantryman could load and fire this weapon three times a minute.

lead in improving the accuracy and mobility of artillery in mid-eighteenth-century Europe. Ironically, France, whose guns were far too heavy to be effective in the Seven Years' War, made the most significant technological advance in the artillery of this era. In the 1750s a Frenchman developed an improved method of boring gun barrels from solid pieces of metal, thereby making cannon that were lighter, safer, and more accurate than any that were cast in the traditional way. Conservative officers delayed the adoption of these new guns until 1776, and they were not distributed until 1788. But they eventually proved their worth, making French artillery supreme in the wars of the French Revolution and Napoleon.

The Magazine System

European armies of the mid-eighteenth century, like their predecessors of the wars of Louis XIV, were bound by the magazine system of supply.

Because only the most densely populated parts of Europe could feed an army for more than a few days, states had to support their forces with magazines or water-borne supplies. Armies were usually expected to remain within about five days' march of an established magazine; and armies on the march usually pushed ahead from one established depot to another. Ministries of war contracted with civilian firms to assemble the most basic food and fodder—to build magazines containing flour, bread, hay, and straw—and to provide transportation for the artillery. The armies themselves were expected to requisition additional transportation and to forage in the theater of operations; and sutlers supplied the rest of the army's food with direct sales to officers and men. This well-established system was designed to preserve an army and to keep it from plundering civilians except in those rare instances when a commander deliberately sought to despoil a particular region, but this system could not support the sustained rapid marching needed to wage war decisively: to impose battle on an unwilling enemy or to exploit a victory. At its best, the magazine system could provide for armies in a limited war.

The system was sometimes quite ineffective. French operations in Germany during the Seven Years' War were frequently impaired by shortages of food, fodder, and transportation. Because of poor public credit, the French were unable to buy supplies in Germany except at exorbitant prices. Thus they had to deal with their own domestic contractors who, dependent on the production of French farms and shops, were unable to maintain magazines in Germany—to provide their forces with regular supplies. Operations were often canceled for want of food or suspended altogether in the winter when fodder ran short and horses were sent home, leaving the army without transportation. These fundamental problems of credit were aggravated by contractors and officials who agreed on fraudulent prices, by army officers who insisted on carrying excessive baggage, by contractors who failed to provide all the horses and wagons they promised, by teamsters who fled during battle taking the artillery with them, and by officials who were too conservative to experiment with portable field ovens. Although the French did keep their forces reasonably well supplied with clothing, arms, and ammunition, they fell so far short with other supplies that they seriously obstructed the army's operations.

The Prussians, conversely, were usually well supplied in the Seven Years' War, in large part because Frederick the Great was able to sustain his credit. In the decade before the war he had relied on the cantonal system to support an increasingly large part of his army, to feed and pay his native troops for up to ten months each year. Spared much of the expense of these troops, he used his peacetime revenues to build up magazines of munitions and food. He had by 1756 all the supplies, equipment, and transportation needed for the opening campaign. With barges on the Oder and Elbe rivers to deliver grain and ammunition, with thousands of horses and carts to link those barges with the army and his portable ovens, and with little excess baggage to encumber his men and animals, he was able to keep his army supplied and preserve its mobility. He did rely on sutlers to supplement the diet of his troops and on the troops themselves to forage for grain, straw, pigs, poultry, and firewood. Eventually his needs outstripped the production of his farms and factories as well as those of occupied lands. Yet through contributions imposed on Saxony, subsidies from Britain, and currency manipulations, he was able to raise the money he needed to buy grain, weapons, and powder on the European market—to supply his armies with British, Dutch, Swedish, and even French products. By the end of the war, his resources were severely strained but not broken. He had sustained his army and Prussia.

Strategy and Tactics

Warfare in mid-eighteenth-century Europe continued to be limited not just by the intentions of the great powers but also by their dependence on standing armies and the magazine system of supply. Yet in conducting these limited wars, commanders were coming to rely less on permanent fortifications and formal sieges and more on battles. The War of the Austrian Succession in Flanders was much like the wars of Louis XIV. The French took the offensive and won by pursuing a cautious war of exhaustion, by relying primarily on sieges and maneuvering to defeat a loose coalition of Austrian, British, Dutch, and Hanoverian forces. The French chose this strategy to exploit their superior numbers, to minimize casualties, and to overcome the web of fortresses that obstructed their advance into Austrian and Dutch territory. In Silesia and Bohemia, the War of the Austrian Succession was fought differently. After seizing Silesia, Frederick the Great relied on his army to hold the Austrians at bay, to defend his conquest in five relatively small but costly battles. Frederick knew that fortresses could be formidable obstacles (he used them to protect his supplies and communications). Yet he never made fortresses or sieges a principal aspect of his strategy, in part because there was a lower concentration of fortresses in Germany than in Flanders, and because he thought his resources were better suited to battles than sieges.

In the Seven Years' War Frederick continued to pursue a strategy that relied heavily on fighting to check the Austrian, French, and Russian armies that converged on him. He initiated or accepted ten unusually lethal battles (casualties on average of 22.5 percent) primarily to exhaust his enemies. He did not have the mobility to make any one of these battles decisive, but he had the will and the resources to make them cumulatively so. Similarly, his brother-in-law, Prince Ferdinand of Brunswick, was able to exhaust larger French forces in Westphalia not only with maneuvering and skirmishing but also with four major if relatively low-cost battles (casualties on average of 6.3 percent). This strategy was well suited to defeat French forces that no longer had the resources or the incentive for a sustained, decisive offensive against British, Hanoverian, and Prussian forces in northwest Germany.

Once battle became more important in their strategies, commanders had to shape their tactics both to exploit and to minimize the effects of increasing firepower. During the War of the Austrian Succession, the Prussians were uniformly successful: they fought and won five major battles with the Austrians, always inflicting more casualties than they received. In all but one battle, the Prussians had superior numbers; and in all, their infantry, if not their cavalry, proved far better equipped and trained. Marching and firing more rapidly and displaying better discipline, the Prussian infantry was able to defeat the Austrians with conventional, processional deployments and frontal attacks. Frederick the Great came to think his infantry could succeed with little more than a menacing advance, bayonets fixed. Yet by the end of the war, he had to fight outnumbered, and he began to look for better ways of deploying and attacking. In 1745 he first tried eliminating a processional deployment. Instead of having his army advance in column, turn in procession, and march parallel to the enemy before wheeling into line, he tried deploying directly from column to line (as units reached the battlefield, they peeled off to right and left and marched obliquely to their places in line). Frederick also began developing an oblique attack. In order to strike successfully at a larger enemy force, he proposed concentrating against one of the enemy's flanks. He would do so by advancing obliquely, or in echelon, so that his own, stronger flank encountered the enemy while his weaker remained unengaged, available either to exploit a victory or to cover a defeat.

The Seven Years' War gave Frederick opportunities to prove the value of rapid deployment and the oblique attack; but to fight outnumbered and win, he also had to increase the firepower of his army and to employ a variety of tactics. In the opening battles of the war he relied too much on the discipline of his troops, made uncoordinated or frontal attacks, and suffered heavy casualties as well as a defeat. He responded to these reverses by emphasizing firepower, training his infantry to fire more rapidly than any other infantry and increasing the number and weight of his field artillery (he doubled the number of cannon in his army between 1756 and 1760). He also worked to make his cavalry a more effective shock force, to teach his troopers to attack at a gallop, sword in hand. He then used his improved infantry, artillery, and cavalry—his increased firepower—together with his oblique order of attack to win great victories over the Austrians and Russians in late 1757 and 1758. But his enemies learned to counter his oblique order. They avoided engaging him in open country and covered their army with skirmishers, earthworks, and heavy artillery firing canister. They also learned to exploit his overconfidence and eagerness for battle. After suffering costly defeats in 1758 and 1759, Frederick again modified his tactics. At Torgau in 1760 he tried dividing his army to attack the Austrians in front and rear. The next year at Bunzelwitz he stood on the defensive against an Austro-Russian army, using earthworks and artillery to offset their greater numbers and to forestall an attack. With these varied tactics but with increasing emphasis on firepower, Frederick survived ten major battles in seven years. Although outnumbered in nine out of ten of these battles, he won seven and inflicted more casualties than he sustained in six. He lacked the mobility to make any of his victories decisive, yet he fought and won often enough to exhaust his more numerous enemies.

Frederick, Saxe, and the War of the Austrian Succession

War in Silesia and Flanders

When Frederick the Great of Prussia seized the Austrian province of Silesia in December 1740, he began a world war. Spain and France were already fighting Britain over trading privileges in the Spanish American empire, and the conflict soon became entangled with Prussia's attack on Silesia. France, Bavaria, and Spain joined Prussia in trying to exploit the inexperience and weakness of the new Habsburg queen; Britain, Hanover, the United Provinces, and various small German states supported Austria out of fear of Prussia and France. These complex rivalries not only brought fighting to many parts of Europe and to European colonies overseas but also linked the progress of the war in one theater with that in another. Prussia and France never joined forces, yet the fortunes of each depended upon the efforts of the other. The principal European conflicts in the War of the Austrian Succession—those between Prussia and Austria in Germany and between France and Britain (supported by Austria, Hanover, and the United Provinces) in Flanders—were inextricably tied together.

Frederick the Great's success in taking and holding Silesia was certainly a triumph of Prussian arms; but it was also, to no small degree, a result of the cumulative pressure brought by French, Bavarian, and Spanish forces against Austria's western frontiers. In the first six months of the War of the Austrian Succession, when Frederick occupied Silesia and survived an Austrian counteroffensive, he had to rely almost entirely on his own resources—on an army and revenues that had been carefully built up by his father. His initial success also kept Britain from intervening on the side of Austria and won him an alliance with France. The French entered the war to serve their own dynastic and territorial ambitions in central Europe. But their invasion of Bohemia in July 1741 forced Austria into a secret armistice with Prussia, an armistice that gave Prussia part of Silesia and left Austria free to concentrate on the war with France. When Austria subsequently recovered Bohemia, Frederick reentered the war to check Austria's resurgence. He invaded Moravia and Bohemia, defeated the Austrians at Chotusitz, and made a separate peace. By the Peace of Breslau, which ended the First Silesian War (December 1740–July 1742), Prussia gained all of Silesia.

For the ensuing two years, while the Austrians fought the French (and their allies) in Italy, on the Rhine, and in Flanders, Frederick rebuilt his army and his finances. In June 1744, after Austria had invaded the French province of Alsace, and after France and Bavaria had threatened to make a peace with Austria that excluded Prussia, Frederick launched another preemptive attack on Austria. He did so to secure Silesia and perhaps to conquer part of Bohemia, but his autumnal offensive in Bohemia became a logistical disaster and he was forced to retire to Silesia. Through the remainder of the Second Silesian War, Frederick had to rely increasingly on his army: Bavaria quit the war; France, preoccupied with Flanders, reduced its subsidy to Prussia; and Austria, having withdrawn from Alsace, invaded Prussia in May 1745. Frederick's well-disciplined troops thrice defeated Austro-Saxon armies and won another favorable peace. The Peace of Dresden (December 1745) confirmed Prussia's conquest of Silesia, the most significant result of the War of the Austrian Succession.

Just as Frederick's success in the War of the Austrian Succession depended in part on French arms, so too did French success depend in part on Frederick's. France entered the war on the continent only after Prussia had shown Austria to be vulnerable to attack. And when the French subsequently suffered reverses against Austria, Frederick twice intervened: in the winter of 1742 after the Austrians had begun to drive the French and Bavarians from Bohemia and in the summer of 1744 after Austria had invaded Alsace. It is true that in each case Frederick had helped to create France's troubles by making a separate armistice or peace with Austria, that he attacked Austria primarily to serve Prussia's interests, and that in December 1745 he left France and Spain to face Austria, Britain, Hanover, and the United Provinces. But his preemptive strikes had helped France in the first years of the war, and by 1745, French armies had taken the offensive in Flanders and enjoyed considerable success under their gifted commander, Maurice de Saxe. Moreover, in the final two-and-one-half years of the war, while Austria devoted much of what remained of its resources to the war in Italy, Frederick remained an unpredictable force on Austria's northern flank. Saxe was thus able to win victories in Flanders that offset French defeats in North America, in India, and at sea.

Frederick the Great

Frederick the Great's rapid success in the War of the Austrian Succession was not entirely a result of his having inherited the fourth largest and best-trained army in Europe. He had come to the throne in May 1740 unusually well prepared to be a king who would serve not only as his own commander-in-chief but also as his own foreign and finance ministers. Much of his training had been as a soldier. He had served for nine of his twenty-eight years as colonel of a regiment—learning the basics of drill, the manual of arms, and small-unit tactics; looking after recruiting and administration; and socializing with other young officers. But he had gone well beyond his fellow officers in studying the art of war. He had visited battlefields, been tutored by the most respected officers in his father's army, accompanied Prince Eugene of Savoy on his last campaign in the War of the Polish Succession, and read widely in the history and theory of warfare. Frederick had also studied political history and politics, developing a strong appreciation for the state. He believed that every man had an obligation to serve his state and that it was the king's particular duty to develop policies that increased the power and standing of the state. This understanding of his duty was intensified by a lust for military glory. Frederick would use force to make Prussia a European power.

Frederick the Great was the most famous
and the most aggressive commander of the
mid-eighteenth century. He regularly sought
battles because he doubted Prussia had the
resources to win a prolonged, conventional
war of siege and maneuver.

Although Frederick would soon become a much celebrated king and commander-in-chief, with his subjects calling him Frederick the Great by the end of the War of the Austrian Succession, he would never be uniformly admired as a leader. His critics found much that was contradictory if not destructive in his leadership. He gained popularity with the rank and file by remembering their names, tolerating their familiarities, and allowing them considerable freedom when off duty. Yet he dispensed rewards whimsically and punishments vindictively, was callously indifferent to disabled or aged veterans, and expended lives more lavishly than any commander of his era. He took much trouble providing instructions for his officers and encouraging them to act independently when on detached service. Yet his zealous supervision and humiliating criticisms stifled initiative, making it difficult for commanders to act imaginatively on their own. He was methodical and confident in planning a campaign or a battle. Yet in combat he sometimes lost his composure, attempting to do the work of junior officers or, alternatively, fleeing an impending defeat. Finally, his presence, his stooped figure on a large English hunting horse, inspired awe and confidence in his army; yet his officers found him unattractive: his clothes were filthy (stained with snuff), his manners revolting, and his behavior unpredictable.

If, then, Frederick was inconsistent as a leader, why was he able to become one of the most celebrated commanders of his age? Because he was an extraordinarily purposeful man with the authority as well as the skill to shape and command an army. Frederick never wavered from his determination to make Prussia a European power. After seizing Silesia, he worked single-mindedly to create the alliances and the army needed to defend Prussia. Subordinates might criticize his methods, but they could not doubt his commitment to serving the state. Nor could they criticize his success in strengthening and employing the army. In war and peace he was tireless in instructing his troops in combined-arms warfare and in developing tactics to repel increasingly numerous and skilled enemies. Contempt for those enemies brought occasional defeats, but he learned from his enemies and his own mistakes; and through two exhausting wars he preserved his army, checked his enemies, and made Prussia a great power.

Frederick's Silesian War

At the beginning of the War of the Austrian Succession, Frederick was an experienced soldier; but he had much to learn about commanding an army. It was indeed fortunate for him that he had inherited an infantry that could defeat the Austrians while he improved the rest of his army and his own skills as a commander-in-chief. In the autumn of 1740 Frederick was able to mobilize and overrun Silesia in less than three months. He did not, however, have the engineers or the equipment to reduce the principal Silesian fortresses; and when in the following spring the Austrians returned to relieve those fortresses and reclaim the province, Frederick barely succeeded in defeating their army. He surprised the Austrians on April 10, 1741, at Mollwitz, twenty-five miles southeast of Breslau. But his cavalry broke and he fled before his infantry salvaged a victory. Frederick used that victory to gain an alliance with France and a secret armistice with Austria that gave him part of Silesia. Even so, he remained a very inexperienced commander when Prussia reentered the war in January 1742. He was forced to abandon a winter offensive in Moravia because he could not protect his communications with Silesia; and after shifting his army to Bohemia, he allowed the Austrians to surprise his camp at Chotusitz, forty miles east of Prague on May 17, 1742. Once again his infantry rallied to defeat the Austrians; and once again he was able to use his victory to make a separate and favorable peace (July 1742), securing his conquest of Silesia and another two years of peace in which to strengthen his army.

By the Second Silesian War, Frederick and his army had improved considerably. He had used autumn maneuvers in 1742 and 1743 to make his cavalry more aggressive and to train his infantry, cavalry, and artillery to work together. But he still had much to learn about strategy. Entering the war in August 1744, he invaded Bohemia—to assist France and, perhaps, to acquire additional territory for Prussia. But after capturing Prague, he advanced into southwest Bohemia where he expected to threaten Austria's communications to the west; instead he nearly lost his army. The Austrians gathered a larger army, cut Frederick's line of supply, and waited in an unassailable position for cold and hunger to force him to retreat. When at last he

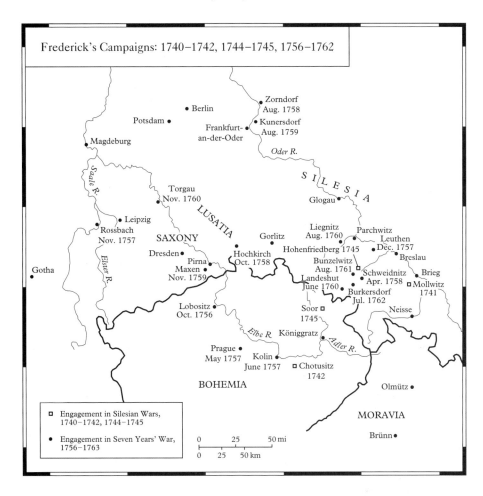

Frederick's Campaigns: 1740–1742, 1744–1745, 1756–1762

□ Engagement in Silesian Wars,
    1740–1742, 1744–1745

• Engagement in Seven Years' War,
    1756–1763

did, he lost large numbers of men to desertion, illness, and Austrian skir-mishers. The Austrians clearly understood a conventional, limited war of maneuver and exhaustion far better than Frederick. With no substantial risks, they had very nearly destroyed one of the best armies of that day.

Such an end to his campaign of 1744 together with mounting debts and enemies (Saxony had joined Austria) persuaded Frederick to stand on the defensive in 1745, to look for a chance to win a battle on Prussian soil. When the Austrians invaded Silesia in the spring of 1745, he was ready for them. Blocking their approach to Breslau, he prepared an oblique attack for the morning of June 4 near the village of Hohenfriedeberg. Although the attack went awry, although fighting began before dawn while his troops were still deploying, his army fought most effectively. His right or advanced flank first dispersed the Saxon infantry and then joined with other Prussian troops coming forward to defeat, in turn, the Austro-Saxon cavalry and the Austrian infantry. However fragmented, this was by far the largest battle of the Sile-sian wars (roughly 60,000 men fought on each side), and it was the first victory for the Prussians in which their arms were well coordinated. Frederick's infantry was as formidable as ever; but his cavalry, his Bayreuth Dragoons, had charged at just the right moment to rout the Austrians.

In the last seven months of the Second Silesian War, Frederick matured considerably as a commander-in-chief. He remained vulnerable to surprise because of his contempt for the Austrians; but to his growing mastery of tactics he added a better sense of the strategy of limited war. During the summer of 1745, he waged a war of attrition. Twice before, shortages of food had driven him from Austria; now he created shortages to defend Silesia. He advanced into Bohemia not just to feed his army at the enemy's expense but primarily to deny the Austrians the food they would need to mount another invasion of Silesia. But Frederick grew careless, and on leaving Bohemia he was surprised once more. At Soor, on September 30, he had to rely again on the superiority of his troops to extricate him from his own complacency. They did, defeating an Austro-Saxon army that outnumbered them two to one. Even then, the campaign and the war did not end until Frederick launched a preemptive attack on Saxony and his forces defeated the Saxons and Austrians once again. The Peace of Dresden confirmed Frederick's conquest of Silesia. He and his army had proved their growing effectiveness against the concerted efforts of Austria and Saxony. Frederick had succeeded in joining cavalry with infantry and artillery; he had experimented for the first time with an oblique attack; and he had shown a willingness to use attrition as well as battle to stop an enemy offensive. The Second Silesian War marked his emergence as a formidable commander-in-chief.

Frederick's wars in Silesia were limited wars. Although he and Maria Theresa threatened at times to violate the conventions of limited war, they adhered ultimately to those conventions. In seizing Silesia, Frederick came close to exceeding acceptable uses of force, to disrupting the European balance of power. He increased his population by nearly 60 percent and added substantially to his revenues, thereby gaining the means to compete with the great powers of Europe. But Frederick did not attempt to destroy Austria. Nor in his operations did he violate conventional limits. His invasions of Moravia and Bohemia were designed mainly to provide relief for France by threatening Vienna or Austrian communications to the west; and except in the summer of 1745 when he stripped food from Bohemia to forestall an Austrian attack on Silesia, he spared the people and the economy of Austria's provinces. He was more willing to risk battle than any of his contemporaries (he was confident in the superiority of his troops and wanted to avoid long, costly wars of exhaustion), and his battles were more lethal. Yet he initiated only three battles in the Silesian wars; those battles were, with the exception of Hohenfriedeberg, comparatively small, and none was tactically decisive (Frederick never pursued a defeated enemy). Maria Theresa, conversely, did consider destroying Prussia in 1745. But her commanders waged a conventional, limited war against Frederick, preferring maneuvering and skirmishing to major battles (they initiated only two general actions), and countering Frederick's invasions by cutting off his supplies, refusing battle, and waiting for shortages to force his withdrawal.

Saxe and Flanders

While Frederick fought for Silesia, his French allies gradually centered their efforts in Flanders. The French had entered the war in July 1741 to exploit Austria's succession crisis. French troops invaded Bohemia to support the Prussians and Bavarians and to encourage the selection of the Elector of Bavaria as Holy Roman Emperor. Even after French and Bavarian forces had been driven from Bohemia and after Britain had sent troops to Flanders in the spring of 1742, the French continued to concentrate their forces on the Rhine. The British and their Austrian, Dutch, and Hanoverian allies were slow to organize an army in the Low Countries; and when at last they did, they decided in early 1743 to use that army on the Rhine, in direct support of the Austrians. Thus the French fought the Allied army at Dettingen (twenty miles east of Frankfurt on the Main) in June 1743 and spent the remainder of the campaign trying to keep the allies from joining an Austrian army on the Rhine. Not until the British and Hanoverian troops had returned to Flanders for the winter of 1743–1744 did the French begin to make their principal effort in the Low Countries. They declared war on Britain in March 1744 and planned an offensive to capture the Channel ports and drive the British from the Continent. That offensive was delayed a year when the Austrians invaded Alsace, forcing the French to divert 36,000 men from Flanders to the Rhine. But by the autumn of 1744 Prussia had reentered the war, the Austrians had withdrawn from Alsace, and the French

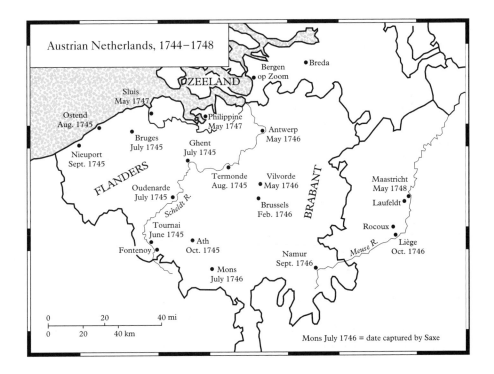

Austrian Netherlands, 1744–1748

Breda
Bergen op Zoom
ZEELAND
Sluis May 1747
Ostend Aug. 1745
Philippine May 1747
Antwerp May 1746
Bruges July 1745
Ghent July 1745
Nieuport Sept. 1745
FLANDERS
Termonde Aug. 1745
Vilvorde May 1746
Maastricht May 1748
Oudenarde July 1745
Scheldt R.
BRABANT
Brussels Feb. 1746
Laufeldt
Tournai June 1745
Rocoux Oct. 1746
Ath Oct. 1745
Meuse R.
Liège Oct. 1746
Fontenoy
Namur Sept. 1746
Mons July 1746

0   20   40 mi
0   20   40 km

Mons July 1746 = date captured by Saxe

were free to concentrate their forces in Flanders for the remainder of the War of the Austrian Succession.

By then, in late 1744, the French had appointed a gifted general to lead their forces in Flanders. Maurice Comte de Saxe was, with the exception of Frederick the Great, the most celebrated commander of the War of the Austrian Succession and the quintessential exponent of limited war. The illegitimate son of an elector of Saxony, he had been a soldier since he was twelve, serving under Marlborough and Eugene at Malplaquet, with Saxon forces against Charles XII in the Great Northern War, with Eugene against the Turks, and with the French army in the wars of the Polish and Austrian Succession. Throughout his service—indeed, since seeing the waste of life at Malplaquet—he had favored wars of exhaustion, of skirmishing and maneuvering rather than engaging the enemy's army. He was capable of acting decisively and boldly and of seeking battle under favorable circumstances. Yet when battle became desirable, he relied on earthworks to preserve lives and discipline. This combination of occasional boldness and usual caution brought Saxe considerable success in the War of the Austrian Succession: he led the night attack that captured Prague during the Bohemian campaign of 1741; he took over the French army that had been defeated at Dettingen, restoring its confidence and using it effectively to keep the allies from joining forces against him on the Rhine in 1743; and he commanded the depleted French Army of Flanders during the summer of 1744, maneuvering skillfully to hold a far more numerous allied army at bay. No wonder that he was chosen to lead the French offensive in Flanders in 1745. He was, at forty-nine, the most accomplished general in the French army, a master of limited war.

When Saxe returned to Flanders in the early spring of 1745, he knew that the French government had concentrated its forces in his hands and expected him to mount a decisive offensive in the Low Countries while other French commanders held their ground on the Rhine. To do what was expected without suffering heavy casualties, Saxe decided to lure the British and their allies into attacking him on ground of his choosing and before their army was fully assembled, that is, while his forces were still numerically

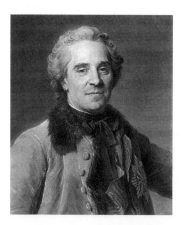

Maurice Comte de Saxe, who commanded the French Army of Flanders during the War of the Austrian Succession, was the quintessential commander of the age of limited war. Even when on the offensive, he sought to minimize the risks and costs of war.

superior. Thus he moved quickly not only to besiege Tournai, a fortified town that guarded the roads leading from France into the western part of the Austrian Netherlands (into West Flanders), but also to feign a siege of Mons, another fortified town twenty-seven miles east of Tournai. Knowing that the allied army was assembling at Brussels, and assuming that it would attempt to relieve any of the frontier posts that were under siege, Saxe made a demonstration toward Mons while besieging Tournai so as to shape the allied army's line of march and force it to proceed from Brussels to Tournai via the roads that led to Mons. This ruse worked perfectly. The allied army ad-vanced on Tournai just as Saxe hoped; and by the evening of May 9, he was preparing to fight a defensive battle about six miles east of Tournai at the village of Fontenoy.

Fontenoy

Saxe had correctly anticipated the allied actions, and he knew the terrain to the east of Tournai. Even so, he could not develop his defensive positions and place his army until reasonably confident that the allies would attack along the road from Mons. His final, tactical preparations were as skillful as his strategic maneuvers. The ground and dispositions he chose were deliber-ately similar to those which Villars had used so effectively at Malplaquet. Saxe put his army on and behind the crest of the ridge that intersected the Mons road at the village of Fontenoy. His right flank was secured by the River Scheldt and the fortified village of Antoing; his center by redoubts and Fontenoy, which was also fortified; and his left by the large, dense Barri Wood that was fringed with two strong redoubts. French infantry and artillery were so disposed along the ridge—in protruding villages, redoubts, and woods—as to provide direct and enfilading fire on any force attacking from the southeast. French cavalry, held in reserve behind the ridge, was to fill breaches in the line and meet any effort to turn Barri Wood. Although Saxe had left troops to continue the siege of Tournai and to cover his own line of retreat across the Scheldt, he was still able to assemble more men at Fontenoy than the allies. By May 11 he had 53,000 to defend a front of 2,100 yards against an allied force of 46,800. All the advantages that careful planning could bestow were with the French at Fontenoy.

What made the French defenses particularly effective were the inex-perience and overconfidence of the allied commander, William Augustus, Duke of Cumberland. A younger son and favorite of King George II of En-gland, Cumberland was twenty-four and in his first command. He knew lit-tle of the history and theory of war, and his only battle experience had been at Dettingen, where French advantages in numbers and position had been overcome by a disciplined British infantry taking advantage of French blunders. At Fontenoy, Cumberland seems to have assumed that discipline would again prevail over superior numbers and position. On May 10 he and his allies agreed to make their principal attack between Fontenoy and Barri Wood, the only place in the French line that was not secured by redoubts or

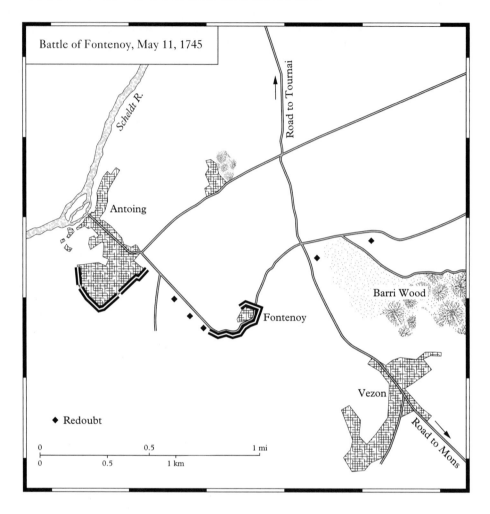

fortified houses. (Saxe had failed to fortify this part of his line because he assumed that no one would choose to attack into a 620-yard gap defended by enfilading fire from Fontenoy and Barri Wood as well as by infantry and artillery posted behind the crest of the ridge.) Allied cavalry would make a secondary attack by riding around Barri Wood to fall upon the French left flank and rear. When these plans were drawn up on May 10, Cumberland did not appreciate the strength of French forces in Barri Wood or the enfilading fire that they could bring to bear on that part of the French line chosen for his main attack. But by dawn on May 11, just before the Battle of Fontenoy was to begin, Cumberland sensed the danger and made one last modification in his plans. He canceled his secondary cavalry attack and ordered detachments to clear the French from Barri Wood and Fontenoy before the main attack began. Even so, Cumberland's plans required frontal assaults on very strongly held positions. Neither he nor his aides seems to have remembered Malplaquet so well as Saxe.

He soon found that he did not have enough disciplined forces to overcome Saxe's numbers, dispositions, and disciplined men. Cumberland's attempts to clear the French from Fontenoy and Barri Wood were complete failures. The brigade ordered to take Barri Wood never attacked (the British officer in command spent more than three hours arguing against the attempt, resisting or misconstruing his orders), and the Dutch detachments sent against Fontenoy twice broke under fire. It was now mid-morning. The 16,000 British and Hanoverian infantrymen who were to make the main allied attack between Fontenoy and Barri Wood had deployed about 400 yards from the French line and were standing under fire. Cumberland had to decide whether to attack without having cleared his flanks or to withdraw and seek a better opportunity for defeating the French and relieving Tournai. Notwithstanding the failures of his detachments, he decided to lead his infantry up the slope and into the converging fire from Fontenoy and Barri Wood. Inexperience and personal courage as well as residual confidence in the superiority of his men seem to have prevailed. He and 16,000 allied infantrymen moved forward in two lines of six ranks each. The lines were compressed by flanking fire; but they kept their discipline, reached the crest of the ridge, shattered the French in front of them with volleys of musketry, and pushed another 300 yards into the enemy's camp. Saxe managed to organize a counterattack that thrust the allies back to the crest. There Cumberland formed his men into a hollow square (to resist attacks coming from all sides) and advanced a second time. The allies threatened briefly to break the French army. But Saxe rallied his men once more. With combinations of infantry, cavalry, and artillery (firing grapeshot), Saxe mounted a final decisive counterattack. The allies withdrew in remarkably good order, turning about from time to time to discourage pursuit but not stopping until they reached Ath, thirteen miles northeast of Fontenoy.

Although Saxe had long advocated vigorous pursuit of a defeated army, he exploited his victory at Fontenoy only gradually. Both armies had suffered many casualties on May 11: the allies, 7,545 killed and wounded (16.1 percent of their army) and the French, about 7,000 (13.2 percent). The French had also become disordered by their desperate counterattacks; and Saxe, who had been ill before the battle, was exhausted by his efforts and in no mood to pursue the enemy more than a few hundred yards beyond the battlefield. Yet in the months that followed his victory, Saxe swept the allies from nearly all of Flanders. He used his superior numbers, rapid marching, and sieges to capture one fortified town after another with a minimum of risks and casualties: Tournai in June; Oudenarde, Bruges, and Ghent in July; Termonde and Ostend in August; and Nieuport in early September. By then, Prince Charles Edward, the pretender to the English throne, had also undertaken to exploit Saxe's victory by quitting his exile in France and raising a rebellion against the Hanoverians in Scotland. So successful was Bonnie Prince Charlie—he captured Edinburgh in September and invaded England in November—that all British troops had to be withdrawn from the Continent in the autumn of 1745 and did not begin returning until late the following spring, until after they had broken the rebel forces at Culloden.

In the interim Saxe finished gathering the fruits of Fontenoy, capturing Ath in October 1745, Brussels in February 1746, and Vilvorde and Antwerp in May. So ended one of the most successful campaigns in the history of limited warfare.

Saxe's Last Campaigns

The final campaigns of the war were far more arduous. Even after the British returned to the Continent in the summer of 1746, Saxe continued to have substantially larger forces than the allies; and the French government continued to expect that he would win the war in the Low Countries. Saxe clearly hoped to build upon his conquest of Flanders by invading the United Provinces, forcing the Dutch to make peace, and driving the British from northwestern Europe. Yet he found it difficult to sustain an offensive against an enemy that no longer attacked rashly, that persisted in skirmishing and maneuvering, and that stubbornly defended those fortresses that blocked his way into the United Provinces. Because Saxe sought to spare lives and remained committed to limited war, it was difficult for him to gain a decisive victory over a wary enemy. He maneuvered boldly; he pressed his sieges. But he refused to mount the kind of determined, full-scale attack needed to destroy the allied army and open the way for a rapid conquest of the United Provinces. His last campaigns went forward successfully but prudently and slowly.

Even with larger forces and great skill it took Saxe two years of limited war to advance fifty miles along the Meuse River toward the United Provinces. He began in the summer of 1746 with an offensive against Namur, the most southern of allied posts on the Meuse. After maneuvering the allied army away from Namur, he opened a siege and kept the allies at bay—without a battle—until the town surrendered in late September. He then followed the Meuse north to Liège, where he found the allied army of 80,000 men camped with its back to the river in an extended line of agricultural villages. Having a superiority of 40,000 men and seeing that the allies were not entrenched, he decided to attack. On October 11 he made a demonstration toward the allied right to fix the Austrians there and then struck hard at the center and left where the Dutch were camped. Battalions of French infantry in dense columns supported by light field artillery soon broke the allied line near the village of Rocoux. The allies fell back across the Meuse covered by their cavalry. At relatively little cost (3,000 killed and wounded or 2.5 percent of his army) Saxe had routed the enemy, inflicted heavier casualties than he took (he killed, wounded, or captured about 7,000 men, or 8.8 percent of the allied army), and captured Liège. Yet because he wanted to minimize his casualties, he did not press the allies as they fell back against the Meuse; he did not take advantage of the best opportunity he would have to shatter the allied army and hasten the end of the war. After the Battle of Rocoux, the allies retreated north to Maastricht and went into winter quarters.

In the final year of the war, Saxe supplemented his offensive on the Meuse with bold strikes against Dutch fortresses in Zeeland, with attacks designed both to draw allied forces from the Meuse and to cut one line of communications between Britain and the United Provinces. His principal effort was, however, against Maastricht, fifteen miles north of Liège on the Meuse; and his principal adversary was the Duke of Cumberland with an army of 90,000 men. Cumberland had been warned against risking battle except on the most favorable terms; and when in early July 1747 Saxe approached Maastricht with 120,000 men, he found Cumberland strongly posted on rising ground two miles south of the town, his left anchored on the Jaar (a tributary of the Meuse), his center on a procession of villages, and his right on a swamp. Although Saxe normally would have declined to attack in such circumstances, he thought the allies were preparing to retire (they were merely improving their defenses) and he knew that Louis XV was impatient for a victory. Thus Saxe decided for once to attack a strongly placed enemy. Using much the same tactics as at Rocoux, he sent his infantry in dense columns against the Dutch who held the center and left of the allied line. In this instance the defenders were far better prepared than at Rocoux, and only after four hours of hard fighting were the French able to break the center of the allied line at the village of Laufeldt. The allies again withdrew in relatively good order, covered by their cavalry. The Battle of Laufeldt was a narrow and costly victory for Saxe. He had forced the allies to retreat, but he had suffered more casualties than they (9,351 killed and wounded to 6,000, or 7.8 percent to 6.7 percent) and had failed to take Maastricht; indeed he would not take Maastricht before an armistice had been signed and the War of the Austrian Succession was over.

Although the War of the Austrian Succession was fought mainly in the Austrian Netherlands and Germany, fighting at sea and overseas had an effect on the outcome that was out of proportion to the resources expended there. After the War of the Spanish Succession, France and Spain had rebuilt their navies in hopes of challenging Britain's superiority at sea. The French concentrated on improving the design of their ships to overcome Britain's numerical advantage. But when war came, the combined fleets of France and Spain were still not ready to risk a major engagement with the British; they concentrated instead on supporting their colonies and attacking British commerce with relatively small detachments of warships. The British, unable to force a decisive battle at sea, employed their fleet primarily in blockading French and Spanish ports and protecting their communications with the Continent. This strategy of containing enemy forces in European waters was largely successful. It gave Britain the advantage in commerce raiding, interrupted the flow of supplies to French colonies, and with one exception, kept French expeditions from reaching North America unopposed. It also allowed the British Leeward Islands squadron to join New England forces in capturing the French base at Louisbourg on Cape Breton in 1745. Louisbourg, which lay on the approaches to the Gulf of St. Lawrence, was important enough to the security and commerce of New France that the British were able to exchange it at the end of the War of the Austrian Succession for Saxe's conquests in the Low Countries.

Frederick in the Seven Years' War

The Diplomatic Revolution of 1756

The Peace of Aix-la-Chapelle did not satisfy the principal antagonists of the War of the Austrian Succession: Britain and France continued to dispute boundaries between their colonies in North America, and Austria did not accept the loss of Silesia to Prussia. These continuing enmities soon brought a reordering of European alliances and, within eight years, another world war, the Seven Years' War (1756–1763). As early as the summer of 1754, British and French colonists were fighting on the frontiers of Virginia, which led both imperial governments to send regulars to the colonies in 1755. Britain hoped that a show of force would forestall war; but fearing that France might respond by attacking Hanover, George II and his ministers began looking for allies on the Continent. They turned first to their friends of previous wars, Austria and the United Provinces. When Austria offered to defend Hanover only if Britain would join in attacking Prussia (recovering Silesia), and when the United Provinces showed no enthusiasm for another war with France, Britain began to consider an alliance with Prussia, its enemy of the War of the Austrian Succession, as the best means of securing Hanover. Austria, in a single-minded effort to recover Silesia, had already made an alliance with Russia and sought another with France, its traditional enemy.

It remained then for Frederick the Great to convert these unconventional overtures into a diplomatic revolution. Fearing that Austria and Russia would join against him, that France would be too preoccupied with its colonies to support Prussia, and that Britain would subsidize Russia—fearing in short that he would be left without a continental ally to defend his conquest of Silesia—Frederick made an alliance with Britain, the Treaty of Westminster of January 16, 1756. He hoped vaguely that this treaty with Britain would not disturb the longstanding friendship between Prussia and France, a friendship that was clearly in the interest of both countries. He was completely mistaken. France, feeling betrayed by Prussia, joined in a defensive alliance with Austria and agreed subsequently to help reconquer Silesia—indeed, to accept a partition of Prussia. Russia too felt betrayed by the Treaty of Westminster, by Britain's support of Prussia; and Russia, with French and secret British subsidies, promised to join in attacking Prussia. This diplomatic revolution of 1756 led directly to a British declaration of war against France and to a Prussian invasion of Saxony and Austria. By the beginning of 1757 the new European system of alliances had ranged France, Austria, Russia, Saxony, Sweden, and various German states against Britain, Prussia, and Hanover in the Seven Years' War.

Frederick's Preemptive Strikes

For more than a decade before he invaded Austria, Frederick had been preparing his country and army for war—for a defense of Silesia and

Prussia's place among the European powers. He strengthened his bureaucracy and economy and drew upon the resources of Silesia so as to expand his revenues. With greater revenues he increased his war chest, gathered supplies, and built fortresses. He also enlarged his army to 143,000 men (it had been 83,000 in 1740), filling his ranks with prisoners from the Silesian Wars and combating desertion with better discipline. Above all, he strove to make his army more effective. Anticipating that he would have to fight against larger enemy forces and wishing to avoid a war of attrition, he trained his officers to attack in oblique order and seek a rapid decision. He not only issued written, secret instructions for his generals but also conducted large-scale reviews and maneuvers (he brought together 44,000 men in 1753). By August 1756—when he launched his preemptive attack on Saxony and Austria—Frederick had a well-prepared army and many experienced and able commanders.

Even so, his army did not achieve decisive results at the beginning of the war. Frederick seems to have hoped that by merely mobilizing he might force Austria to abandon any hostile plans. But when the Austrians were evasive about their intentions, he decided to launch a preemptive attack. He struck at Saxony and Austria because both were hostile to Prussia and because Saxony lay astride the Elbe, the best route south into the Austrian province of Bohemia. He clearly intended to wage a short, decisive, and limited war—to force both states to sue for peace before any other power could intervene. Briefly, in early September 1756, it seemed that he might succeed. His forces needed only two weeks to overrun Saxony and invade Bohemia. But he failed to capture the Saxon army, which retired to a fortified camp at Pirna, twenty miles southeast of Dresden; and on October 1, he fought a battle with the Austrians that was far from decisive. At Lobositz, thirty miles north of Prague, he stumbled into an Austrian army that was slightly larger than his own (34,000 to 28,500) and that fought well. As in his first battle at Mollwitz in 1741, his cavalry was ineffective and he fled before his infantry rallied to drive off the Austrians. Each side suffered about 2,900 casualties. Frederick subsequently captured the Saxon army at Pirna, impressing whole units into his own forces, and levied contributions on the Saxon people. Yet he had clearly failed to defeat the Austrians. He was now faced with what he had sought to avoid—the prospect of a war against a coalition of powerful states.

Nevertheless, throughout the spring of 1757, Frederick persisted in trying to defeat Austria before France or Russia could enter the war. By April he was back in Bohemia, seeking a decisive battle. On May 6 he found an Austrian army of 60,000 men drawn up to receive him just east of Prague. Having slightly more men (64,000) and being confident in their superiority, he attacked at once. The Austrian army was in a strong position and his attack was poorly coordinated. But his troops won a costly victory—the Prussians suffered 14,286 casualties, the Austrians 14,000—and forced the Austrians to retreat to Prague. Frederick invested the city, hoping that its surrender would end the war. In June when another Austrian army approached, Frederick gathered 35,000 men and advanced to attack what he assumed was a relatively small relief force. On June 18 at Kolin, thirty-five

This glimpse of the battle of Lobositz in 1756 shows the ordered ranks and disciplined fire of the Prussian infantry. Here, as at Mollwitz in 1741, Prussian infantry gained a victory after Frederick had left the battle.

miles east of Prague, he encountered an army of 53,000 well-disciplined and skillfully led men. To offset their superior numbers, Frederick planned an oblique attack, concentrating most of his forces against the Austrian right flank and refusing his own right. Yet while deploying across the enemy's front, he changed his mind and improvised a frontal assault on the center of the Austrian line. This hazardous change of plan, reflecting Frederick's contempt for the Austrians as well as his supreme confidence in his own men, led to his first defeat. Prussian discipline and courage were not enough to overcome a larger army that was well placed and had better artillery. Frederick lost 13,768 of his men, killed or wounded (43 percent of his army); the Austrians, 9,000 (20.5 percent).

Rossbach to Leuthen

Soon after his defeat at Kolin, Frederick realized that he could no longer hope to defeat Austria separately, that French and Russian as well as Austrian forces were converging on Prussia, and that he would have to concentrate on preserving his state. At first he merely abandoned the siege of Prague and retired to the northern frontiers of Bohemia—feeding his troops with Austrian stores and waiting. By late July the Austrians had forced him to withdraw into Saxony, and he had begun to develop a defensive strategy. He decided not only to divide his forces to provide some protection for each of his frontiers but also to shift forces from one frontier to another to meet particularly serious threats. Thus by exploiting his central position—using interior lines of communication—he would try to meet his principal enemies separately; he would try to use a series of spoiling attacks to keep his enemies from joining forces against him. If the enemies did not coordinate their efforts, he might be able to keep them at bay with his comparatively meager resources. During the late autumn of 1757, he would prove the value of this strategy in one of the most remarkable campaigns in the history of warfare.

But for three months after Frederick retreated into Saxony, from late July until the end of October 1757, he was hard pressed to parry Austrian, French, and Russian armies on his frontiers. In August when an Austrian army of 100,000 invaded southeast Saxony, he considered attacking. But having only 50,000 men and finding the Austrians unwilling to risk battle outside their fortified camp, he decided instead to leave 41,000 of his men to screen the Austrians while he assembled another army of 25,000 to meet a Franco-German invasion of western Saxony. Although he succeeded in forcing the French and Germans to retire, he did not eliminate their threat. Nor was he able to save Prussian detachments from being defeated by the Russians in East Prussia and by the Austrians in eastern Saxony. By early October he may well have begun to doubt that Prussia could survive. Austrian, French, and Russian armies were on his frontiers; the French had forced his Hanoverian allies to sign a humiliating capitulation that left Brandenburg open to attack; and an Austrian raiding party had taken and held Berlin briefly in October. In response to all of these reverses, he could do little more than shift his army back and forth between Saxony and Brandenburg.

Then, at the end of October, Frederick at last saw an opportunity to arrest his run of corrosive defeats, to strike at one, isolated enemy force. On October 24 he learned that the French and Germans, buoyed by their success in Hanover, were advancing into Saxony and would likely offer battle. He concentrated his forces and set out to meet the enemy. He overtook them on November 4 near Rossbach, about twenty miles to the west of Leipzig. The next day, the French and Germans marched in column as if to turn the Prussian left or eastern flank. Although the enemy outnumbered his forces nearly two to one (41,000 to 22,000), Frederick moved to block their line of march. The French and Germans, assuming that the Prussians who had disappeared behind a low ridge were retreating, pressed forward in column. As they approached the ridge, they encountered Frederick's infantry and artillery deploying directly across their line of march. The Prussians had the advantage not just of surprise and superior firepower but also of a very aggressive and disciplined cavalry. While their infantry and artillery shredded the dense Franco-German columns crowding toward them, Prussian cavalry drove off the French cavalry and then regrouped to fall on the flank of their infantry that had already begun to retreat. In just over an hour the enemy had become a fleeing mob. At a loss of fewer than 500 casualties, the Prussians would kill, wound, or capture more than 10,000 French and German troops. Frederick had little time for a pursuit, but his victory was so decisive that it allowed the Hanoverians to repudiate their recent capitulation, reversing the French gains of the summer and securing the western frontiers of Brandenburg and Saxony. Indeed, after Rossbach, Prince Ferdinand of Brunswick would take command of all allied troops in Hanover and, with British subsidies, keep the French at bay for the remainder of the Seven Years' War.

Frederick did not pursue the French after Rossbach because he was preoccupied with the security of his southeastern frontiers. Fearing that Austria was overrunning Silesia if not eastern Saxony, he assembled his army at Leipzig and, on November 13, marched east through Saxony for Silesia. Even though he allowed every fourth day for rest, he moved along rapidly, drawing food from the countryside and benefiting from unusually mild autumn weather and excellent roads to cover 165 miles in sixteen days. Along the way he gathered enough additional troops to send a detachment into Bohemia, forcing the Austrians to withdraw from Saxony and to leave open his line of march to Silesia. By November 28 when he reached Parchwitz, thirty-five miles northwest of Breslau, he knew that the Austrians had taken Breslau and were threatening to drive his troops from the rest of Silesia. Frederick was determined to save the province. He assembled all available troops at Parchwitz and shaped them into a small but excellent army of 35,000 men, mostly well-disciplined and loyal natives of Brandenburg. On December 4 he set out to strike sharply at the Austrians, to attack them, if necessary, in their entrenched camp at Breslau.

At Neumarkt, about twelve miles from Parchwitz on the road to Breslau, Frederick received excellent news: the Austrians had left their entrenchments and were advancing toward him. He did not know that the Austrians had 65,000 men, but he believed that a decisive battle offered him the best chance of saving Silesia and, perhaps, of bringing his war with Austria to a satisfactory end. He also preferred to engage the Austrians away from their fortified camp and in terrain that he knew well; and there was scarcely any terrain that could have suited him better than the rolling open country southeast of Neumarkt, which had been the site of his peacetime maneuvers. It was with considerable optimism that he continued his advance east of Neumarkt on the morning of December 5; he was ready to attack. But he did not make detailed plans until he met the Austrians and found that they were deployed about the village of Leuthen in a line of battle stretching nearly four miles from north to south. Seeing that the Austrians had significantly larger forces but that their left or southern flank was unsupported, he decided to employ an oblique attack. He would refuse his own left flank and mass to his right against the exposed southern flank of the Austrian army. If he could move a large portion of his army, undetected, behind a range of low hills, he might be able to turn, surprise, and roll up the Austrian left. He might be able to win the kind of decisive victory that would save Silesia and Prussia.

The Battle of Leuthen went almost exactly according to Frederick's plan. He spent the morning of December 5 deploying his forces. By about one in the afternoon he had succeeded not only in creating an effective diversion on his left flank, in drawing Austrian reserves to the northern portion of their line, but also in concentrating his forces against and turning their southern flank. At this point, perhaps remembering the uncoordinated attacks that had spoiled his plans at Prague and Kolin, he made sure that every unit was in position before he began the battle, before he sent his

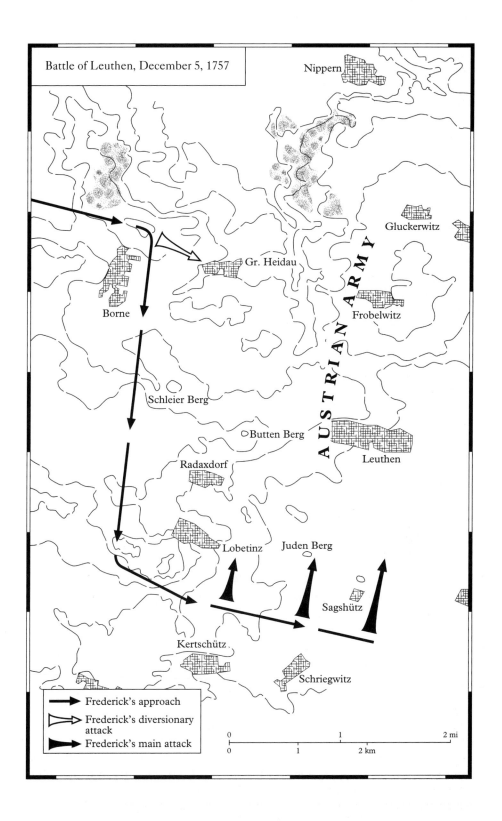

Battle of Leuthen, December 5, 1757

Nippern

Gluckerwitz

Gr. Heidau

Borne

Frobelwitz

AUSTRIAN ARMY

Schleier Berg

Butten Berg

Leuthen

Radaxdorf

Lobetinz

Juden Berg

Sagshütz

Kertschütz

Schriegwitz

Frederick's approach
Frederick's diversionary attack
Frederick's main attack

| 0 | | 1 | | 2 mi |
| 0 | | 1 | 2 km | |

infantry and artillery advancing north against the Austrian flank. This carefully coordinated and paced attack, made in oblique order, soon rolled up the Austrian line. When the Austrian commander wheeled his army to meet the Prussian attack, it seemed that he might succeed in holding the village of Leuthen and in stopping Frederick's advance. But late in the afternoon, the Prussians, showing unusual initiative and determination, used cavalry to repel cavalry charges against their flanks and combinations of infantry and artillery to drive the Austrians from Leuthen. And once they had taken Leuthen, they soon routed the whole Austrian army. Although it was now snowing and becoming dark, Frederick pursued the fleeing Austrians six miles beyond Leuthen to Lissa—to seize the bridge over the Schwednitzer-Wasser and keep the Austrians from making a stand there. Thus he won the greatest victory of his career. He had exploited a thorough knowledge of terrain to make an ordered, well-disciplined attack on the vulnerable portion of the Austrian army. His men had had the initiative and determination to overcome every countermeasure, to defeat a larger and experienced army, killing, wounding or capturing 22,000 men (33.8 percent of the Austrian army) while suffering only 6,382 casualties (18.2 percent).

For once, Frederick exploited his victory. So vigorous was his pursuit of the defeated Austrians that not many more than one-fourth of their troops escaped from Silesia to Bohemia. By Christmas, when the Prussians went into winter quarters, only beleaguered detachments of Austrians remained in Silesia. Frederick had not, as he had hoped, ended the war. But in the last two months of 1757 he had saved Prussia from the converging forces of France and Austria. He had used a small, disciplined army and a central position to win decisive victories, victories that rescued Hanover from the French and Silesia from the Austrians and that enabled him to continue the war. In the brief Rossbach-Leuthen campaign Frederick demonstrated his comprehensive mastery of limited, defensive war. He had proved as skillful a strategist and logistician as he was a tactician; he had won both a defensive and an offensive battle against much larger enemy forces; and he had inspired an army of native troops to exercise initiative in combat as well as discipline in pursuit. The Rossbach-Leuthen campaign is justly remembered as the finest example of Frederican warfare and as one of the greatest achievements in the history of military operations.

Frederick's Last Campaigns

For nearly a year after Leuthen, Frederick's conduct of the war suffered from his contempt for his enemies. He could now rely on Prince Ferdinand of Brunswick to defend Hanover and keep the French away from Prussia's western frontiers. Frederick also had troops enough to garrison Saxony and his northeastern frontiers and to create another army to strike separately at Austria and Russia. He would use that army to keep his enemies from joining against him and, perhaps, to force one or both to make peace. In April 1758 he completed his reconquest of Silesia and invaded the Austrian province of Moravia to besiege the important, fortified town of Olmütz, one hundred miles south of Breslau. The Austrians, refusing to be drawn into battle, cut Frederick's line of supply, maneuvered him aside, and relieved Olmütz. On July 1 he was forced to abandon the siege and retire through Bohemia to Silesia.

Just as Frederick had underestimated his enemies' talent for maneuvering so too would he misjudge their capacity for hard fighting. By mid-August he was marching north from Silesia to intercept a Russian army of 45,000 that was approaching Cüstrin on the Oder, only fifty miles east of Berlin. Rejecting an opportunity to capture the Russian supply train—to win a bloodless victory—he launched an ill-disciplined attack on their army near the village of Zorndorf on August 25. His 37,000 men were tired from forced marching, their oblique attack degenerated into a frontal assault, and the more numerous Russians fought with surprising determination. After eleven hours of close combat, Frederick won a costly victory. (He lost 12,800 men, or 34.6 percent of his army; the Russians, 18,000, or 40 percent of theirs.) As soon as the Russians had started home and his northeast frontier was secure, Frederick went south to confront the Austrians who had invaded Saxony and Silesia. He hoped to force the Austrians to withdraw merely by threatening their communications. Once again he took an enemy too lightly. In mid-October he allowed a portion of his army to be surprised and soundly defeated (9,097 of his 30,000 men were casualties). Although Frederick managed before winter to reassemble his army and regain control over Saxony and Silesia, he had paid a heavy price in officers and men for his incautious conduct of the war in 1758, for his contempt of the Austrians and Russians.

The Prussian army was now reduced in quality and in size—to not much over 110,000 men in 1759. Frederick knew that he would have to remain on the strategic defensive against the larger armies of Austria and Russia. Yet for another two years, through the campaigns of 1759 and 1760, he continued to attack enemy forces invading Prussia and to survive a series of costly battles. He was able to keep an army in the field and to avoid total defeat because he had the money and the will to remain in the war and because his enemies did not cooperate effectively. Indeed, the Austrians and Russians, inhibited by Frederick's reputation and by the conventions of limited war, failed repeatedly in the campaigns of 1759 and 1760 to exploit the advantages they gained and the opportunities they had to win the war.

In the summer of 1759, while the Austrians invaded Saxony and Silesia, the Russians again advanced toward the Oder, defeating a Prussian detachment at Paltzig and threatening Berlin. Frederick chose to deal first with the Russians. By the time he overtook them on August 10 at Kunersdorf, just east of Frankfurt, the Russians had received a reinforcement of Austrian troops and were well entrenched in the low sand hills east of the Oder. Although he had only 49,000 men to oppose a force of 64,000, Frederick decided to attack. He had such poor intelligence that he undertook an exhausting approach march merely to send his men piecemeal against the strongest part of the enemy lines. The Prussians eventually broke before earthworks, cannister, and determined fighting men, losing 19,000 killed and wounded (more than one-third of their army). Even so, the Austrians and Russians did not fully exploit their victory and did not go on to Berlin. Wary of Frederick and fearful that their communications through Saxony would be cut, the Austrians turned away to the south; and the Russians withdrew to the east. In the ensuing three months the Austrians were able to capture two Prussian detachments, a total of 14,500 men, but they were not able to keep Frederick from restoring his army to nearly 100,000 and from recovering parts of Saxony and Silesia.

Nor in 1760 were the Austrian and Russian armies able to use their superior numbers to win the war. In June the Austrians defeated another Prussian detachment at Landeshut in Silesia, killing or capturing 10,000 men. But two months later when they had an advantage of 60,000 men and attempted to trap and crush Frederick's army at Liegnitz, forty miles northwest of Breslau, one wing of their army stumbled into the whole of Frederick's and was defeated. Similarly, 35,000 Austrian and Russian troops captured Berlin in early October but failed to destroy his arsenal and magazines because they feared that he was marching to relieve the city and because they hesitated to destroy Prussian industries, to exceed the usual bounds of limited war. And in November, when Frederick made a poorly coordinated attack on their camp at Torgau, thirty miles northeast of Leipzig, the Austrians were unable fully to exploit his mistakes. They inflicted very heavy casualties on the Prussians (killing or wounding nearly two-fifths of their army). But the chance arrival of uncommitted Prussian troops on an exposed flank forced the Austrians to withdraw, to lose their camp and the advantages they had gained.

Although his resources were severely strained, and although England and France were ready for peace, Frederick insisted on remaining at war for another two years to preserve Prussian territory. He survived those years by relying on foreign contributions and subsidies to support his army, by avoiding battle, and by taking advantage of sudden changes in Russian policy. In the summer of 1761, for the first time in the war, the main armies of Austria and Russia joined forces against Frederick, assembling in Silesia 130,000 men against his 55,000. He was able to avoid battle by taking up a strong defensive position at Bunzelwitz, twenty-five miles south of Breslau. But he could not prevent the Austrians from capturing his magazine at Schweidnitz or from spending the ensuing winter in Silesia and Saxony. Indeed, it was only the fortuitous death of the Tsarina Elizabeth in January 1762 that allowed Frederick to escape the overwhelming force of Austria and Russia. Elizabeth's death brought peace and an alliance between Prussia and Russia in May 1762. Frederick received little help from his new ally (a coup changed Russia's leaders and policy in the summer of 1762). But Russia did withdraw from the war, and Frederick was able to bring pressure enough on Austria in the last months of 1762 to gain a satisfactory, negotiated peace. By giving up Saxony, Frederick was able to keep Silesia—to secure Prussia's boundaries of 1756 and its place among the powers of Europe.

Frederick's success in the Seven Years' War was largely a result of his own and his people's extraordinary efforts. But it was also a result of Britain's economic and naval power, Britain's ability to support Prussia and Hanover while defeating French forces at sea and overseas. Although the

French had rebuilt their navy after the War of the Austrian Succession, they found it increasingly difficult during the Seven Years' War both to contest the British at sea and to maintain an army that could hold its own in Germany and defend colonies from America to Africa to India. By comparison with the French, the British had greater resources and fewer obligations. Flourishing commerce, sound financial institutions, and a strong system of representative government gave the British the credit they needed to build the most powerful fleet and expeditionary forces of the Seven Years' War and to support their allies in Prussia and Hanover. The British could in turn rely on those allies to do most of the fighting on the continent and to tie down much of the French army. Thus the British had the resources—after subsidizing the armies of Prussia and Hanover and contributing nearly 20,000 men to the war in Germany—to bring overwhelming pressure against the French at sea. The British established a blockade of French ports to contain commerce raiders, intercept forces bound for the colonies, and forestall an invasion of England; they raided the French Atlantic coast to destroy shipping and stores and to divert French forces from Germany; they crushed the French navy at Louisbourg, Lagos, and Quiberon Bay; and they sent fleets and armies overseas to conquer French colonies in Canada, the West Indies, West Africa, and India. When in 1761 Spain entered the war on the side of France, the British extended their blockade to the Iberian peninsula and sent expeditions to capture Havana and Manila. With such a vigorous use of their sea power—and their economic resources—Britain contributed substantially to allied victory in the Seven Years' War.

In the Battle of Quiberon Bay the British risked their ships on a lee shore to attack and destroy a French squadron. The victory, won by skillful handling of square-rigged sailing vessels and powerful cannon, contributed substantially to Anglo-Prussian success in the Seven Years' War.

The treaties that ended the Seven Years' War reflected the success of British and Prussian arms. Frederick had suffered heavy casualties in defending his territory against the Austrians, French, and Russians: he had lost 180,000 soldiers, and his population had declined by 500,000. Yet he had also exhausted his enemies, and his persistence and sacrifices were rewarded in the peace he made with Austria. By restoring Saxony's independence and agreeing to support the Austrian candidate for Holy Roman Emperor, Frederick was able to keep all of Silesia—to secure Prussia's boundaries of 1756 and its place among the powers of Europe. So too did Britain's victories at sea and overseas together with Prince Ferdinand's skillful defense of Hanover shape the peace between Britain and France and their respective allies. To hasten a settlement, Britain did return some of its French conquests, principally islands in the West Indies and trading posts in Africa and India. But Britain gained Canada and Florida—indeed, all of North America east of the Mississippi—as well as islands in the West Indies, Senegal, and political concessions in India. The treaties of Hubertusburg and Paris (February 1763) confirmed what had been gained by the economic strength, political will, and military skills of Prussia and Britain.

✳   ✳   ✳   ✳

In the half-century after the War of the Spanish Succession the great powers of Europe sought security in standing armies, a balance of power, and limited war. So strong was their commitment to this system of security that it constrained even the greatest commander of the age. Frederick the Great was more determined than any of his contemporaries to alter the balance of power. To do so with the meager resources of Prussia, he was more willing than any to turn his public revenues and the services of his young men toward war. He was also more willing to risk his army in battle because he believed that conventional wars of exhaustion—of sieges, maneuvers, and skirmishes—would exhaust Prussia. Yet even Frederick found it in his interest to wage limited war. Wary of destroying his own royal authority while making Prussia great, he never tried to destroy his enemies or to call his own people to arms. He relied instead on a professional standing army supported by a magazine system of supply to conquer and hold Silesia. And, for all his willingness to risk battle, he rarely made a battle decisive by pursuing a defeated enemy or by campaigning in winter. Indeed, he learned with experience to appreciate the tactics of more cautious and conventional commanders—to avoid frontal assaults, to deprive his enemies of supplies and, when completely outnumbered, to cover his army with fieldworks and remain on the defensive. Frederick was, in short, the greatest practitioner of limited war.

Prussia was the most admired military power in Europe at the end of the Seven Years' War. But in the last years of Frederick's reign (d. 1786), the Prussian army declined steadily and was woefully unprepared for the wars of the French Revolution and Napoleon. Frederick did much to lower the quality of his forces by relaxing the standards for recruiting his rank and file, purging his officer corps of talented commoners, pursuing false economies in pay and equipment, and favoring harsh over competent officers. The results of these policies were apparent as early as the War of the Bavarian Succession (1778) when his offensive against Austria failed for want of discipline and supplies. Nor were his heirs able to reverse the decline in Prussian arms—to keep pace with the rapid changes in warfare that came with the French Revolution and Napoleon. Frederick William II (1786–1797) lacked the will to exert firm leadership, and his aging officer corps rejected as politically subversive new methods of raising and employing troops. Thus Prussians refused to change until their army was destroyed by Napoleon in the Jena campaign of 1806, when the inspired patriotic forces of France with flexible tactics, improved systems of supply, and talented young leaders overwhelmed the antiquated army of Frederick the Great.

SUGGESTED READINGS

Charteris, Evan. *William Augustus Duke of Cumberland* (London: Edward Arnold, 1913).

Childs, John. *Armies and Warfare in Europe, 1648–1789* (New York: Holmes and Meier, 1982).

Dorn, Walter L. *Competition for Empire, 1740–1763* (New York: Harper & Brothers, 1940).

Duffy, Christopher. *The Army of Frederick the Great* (Newton Abbot: David & Charles, 1974).

———. *The Fortress in the Age of Vauban and Frederick the Great, 1660–1789* (London: Routledge & Kegan Paul, 1985).

———. *Frederick the Great: A Military Life* (London: Routledge & Kegan Paul, 1985).

Graham, Gerald S. *Empire of the North Atlantic: The Maritime Struggle for North America* (Toronto: University of Toronto Press, 1950).

Houlding, J. A. *Fit for Service: The Training of the British Army, 1715–1795* (Oxford: Clarendon Press, 1981).

Kennedy, Paul M. *The Rise and Fall of British Naval Mastery* (London: Allen Lane, 1976).

Kennett, Lee. *The French Armies in the Seven Years' War: A Study in Military Organization and Administration* (Durham: Duke University Press, 1967).

Lynn, John A. "The Growth of the French Army During the Seventeenth Century," *Armed Forces and Society* VI (1980), 568–585.

McNeill, William H. *The Pursuit of Power: Technology, Armed Force, and Society Since A.D. 1000* (Chicago: University of Chicago Press, 1984).

Palmer, R. R. "Frederick the Great, Guibert, Bülow: From Dynastic to National War," in P. Paret, ed., *Makers of Modern Strategy: From Machiavelli to the Nuclear Age* (Princeton: Princeton University Press, 1986), 91–119.

Parker, Geoffrey. *The Military Revolution: Military Innovation and the Rise of the West, 1500–1800* (Cambridge: Cambridge University Press, 1988).

Quimby, Robert S. *The Background of Napoleonic Warfare: The Theory of Military Tactics in Eighteenth-Century France* (New York: Columbia University Press, 1957).

Ritter, Gerhard. *Frederick the Great: A Historical Profile* (Berkeley: University of California Press, 1974).

Roberts, Penfield. *The Quest for Security, 1715–1740* (New York: Harper, 1947).

Robson, Eric. "The Armed Forces and the Art of War," in J. O. Lindsay, ed., *The New Cambridge Modern History* VII (Cambridge, 1957).

Savory, Reginald. *His Britannic Majesty's Army in Germany During the Seven Years' War* (Oxford: Clarendon Press, 1966).

Saxe, Maurice de. *Reveries on the Art of War* (Westport, CT: Greenwood, 1971).

Skrine, Francis Henry. *Fontenoy and Great Britain's Share in the War of the Austrian Succession 1741–48* (Edinburgh: William Blackwood and Sons, 1906).

White, Jon Manchip. *Marshal of France: The Life and Times of Maurice, Comte de Saxe* (Chicago: Rand McNally & Co., 1962).

Whitworth, Rex. *Field Marshal Lord Ligonier: A Story of the British Army, 1702–1770* (Oxford: Clarendon Press, 1958).

4

ANGLO-AMERICAN WARFARE, 1607–1763: THE EMERGENCE OF THE PEOPLE IN ARMS

Anglo-Indian Warfare

The Colonial Wars

The French and Indian War

Just as Europeans of the seventeenth and eighteenth centuries suffered through a succession of wars so too did their colonists in North America. The English, who were far more numerous than other European colonists and more determined to establish permanent settlements, provoked particularly hostile responses from their neighbors in the New World. For more than one-third of their years as colonists (1607–1776), the English were at war. At first—for nearly three-quarters of a century—they fought mainly with American Indians; then, for another seventy-five years, with other European colonists and their Indian allies in wars that were loose extensions of struggles for power in Europe. Finally, in a long, complex war for the conquest of Canada, the French and Indian War (1754–1763), they fought against combinations of European regulars, other colonists, and American Indians.

Except during the last years of the colonial period when British colonists fought with and against regular European forces, warfare in America bore little resemblance to that in Europe. At a time when European states were supporting ever-larger standing armies and waging limited wars, the English colonies in North America were relying on their militia or on expeditionary forces drawn occasionally from the militia to wage nearly unlimited wars of conquest. Colonial forces did use many of the same weapons as regulars, and they sometimes tried to adopt regular methods of marching and firing. Otherwise, colonial forces were raised, trained, and employed very differently than the standing armies of Europe. Neither militia nor provincial expeditionary forces had the organizational permanence of a regular army, and neither had anything like the discipline or training.

Their fortifications were primitive; their system of supply was rudimentary; and regular linear tactics, combined-arms warfare, and siegecraft were completely beyond their competence. Indeed, colonial forces were little more than unskilled infantry, equipped with handguns and light artillery and capable of fighting only in loose formations. They tried mainly to exhaust their enemies with small skirmishes and the destruction of their food and shelter. But in their own primitive ways colonial forces fought for far higher stakes than the standing armies of Europe. While Europeans waged limited wars to adjust boundaries and settle dynastic disputes, the English colonists of North America fought to conquer a continent.

Anglo-Indian Warfare

The first English colonists to settle permanently in the New World expected to have to fight to sustain themselves; and they did. During the seventeenth century, they were most often at war with American Indians and only occasionally with themselves or other Europeans. They had hoped to take possession of undeveloped lands in America, to trade with or employ Indians, and to spread the Protestant faith. They were prepared to destroy anyone who opposed them. They soon found that some Indians were hostile at first meeting and that many others became so in time. Indians resented being coerced—being forced to provide food for the English or to accept English laws and religious practices. They also resented being disparaged as a primitive people and becoming economically and culturally dependent on the English. Most of all, they resented the steady increase in the number of English colonists and their expansion into land that had traditionally supported Indian agriculture, hunting, and fishing. These resentments were often expressed in isolated acts of defiance and violence. But when the Indians made concerted efforts to stop English expansion—when they launched widespread attacks in Virginia and Massachusetts—they precipitated unrestrained warfare that involved all colonists and Indians living together on the frontiers of North America. The colonists responded with devastating punitive expeditions in the largest and most destructive of seventeenth-century Anglo-Indian wars: the First and Second Tidewater wars (1622–1632, 1644–1646) and Bacon's Rebellion (1675–1676)—both in Virginia—and King Philip's War (1675–1676) in Massachusetts.

Virginia

Virginians were the first English colonists to wage war with the Indians—the first colonists to create and employ armed forces against their elusive neighbors. To protect themselves against potentially hostile Indians living in their midst, the men who settled at Jamestown in 1607 submitted to a succession of military governors who required all men to drill regularly, maintain fortified communities, and campaign occasionally against the natives. In these earliest campaigns the colonists developed tactics to punish the Indians and push them away from English settlements. Finding it extremely difficult to engage the Indians, the colonists concentrated on destroying their villages, crops, and stores in what were called "feed fights." Feed fights together with strict military rule helped the English survive their first years in Virginia.

Indians were an elusive and frustrating enemy because they sought to wage war without costly battles. Before Europeans arrived, Indians fought one another in relatively bloodless and ritualistic wars. In these wars the aim was to take prisoners who might be enslaved or sacrificed; it was rarely to conquer or destroy an opposing nation. Thus Indians attacked mainly when they had superior numbers and could surprise their enemies, when they could conduct an ambush or raid with a good prospect of taking prisoners. They avoided closing with an enemy of equal strength, preferring to remain at a distance exchanging arrows and protecting themselves with wooden body armor. They also relied on fortifications—ditches and palisades (walls of tree trunks and brush rising twelve feet or more above ground)—to secure their towns. But most Indians, valuing lives above property, were reluctant to assault a fortification or even to defend one when threatened by a larger enemy force. Soon after Europeans arrived, Indians began acquiring metal tips for their arrows and matchlock muskets. By the mid-seventeenth century, Indians of both the Chesapeake and New England would have large numbers of muskets and the skill to repair them, if not to manufacture powder. These weapons would make warfare more lethal; and Indians, responding to European provocations, would seek increasingly to kill the colonists and destroy their property. Even then, Indians remained wary of battle. They continued to raid and ambush their enemies and to retire into swamps and forests rather than risk casualties.

But in 1614, when Indians seemed a relatively passive and poorly equipped enemy, a marriage between an English colonist and an Indian princess brought peace to Virginia and a nearly disastrous relaxation of military preparations. The colonists stopped drilling, neglected their fortifications, and spread out across the Virginia countryside to plant tobacco and turn a profit. This sustained expansion of English settlement alarmed the Indians and left the colonists, now living on private plantations among the natives, vulnerable to attack. In March 1622 the Indians struck, bringing war to the people of Virginia as consuming and destructive as any that would be experienced in Europe during the Thirty Years' War. On that March day the Indians killed 347 colonists and drove the remainder into eight crowded communities along the James River where, during the next winter, another 500 died of malnutrition and disease. Virginia barely survived; by 1624 the English population was only 1,275 (of some 5,000 who had been in or come to the colony since 1618).

After the Massacre of 1622, Virginians embarked on more than two decades of efforts to make their colony secure—to raise and employ the forces needed to drive Indians permanently from English settlements. They began by restoring martial law and raising volunteers for expeditions against the Indians. Those expeditions or feed fights, conducted by infantry

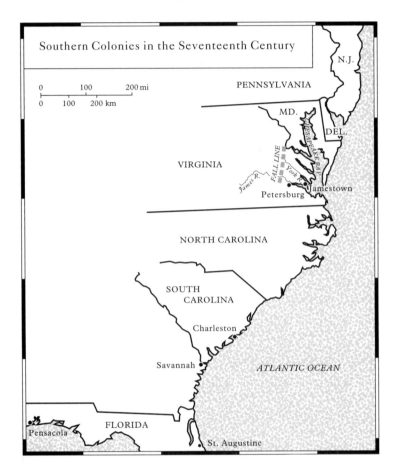

Southern Colonies in the Seventeenth Century

equipped with matchlock muskets, marked the beginning of the First Tidewater War (1622–1632), a war fought to gain the space and time needed to
save the colony. For long-term security the leading men of Virginia relied on
citizens in arms: they distributed weapons to every colonist, required military
service of adult males (1624), and began compensating those on campaign
by working their lands. Beginning in 1629, they also made a determined
effort to clear all Indians from the peninsula between the James and York
rivers, east of Jamestown, and to secure that peninsula by building a six-mile
wall linking the rivers near Jamestown. By the end of the First Tidewater
War in 1632, Virginians had secured the center of their settlements and were
beginning to expand once again.

Over the ensuing fifteen years, Virginians so improved the raising
and use of their forces—so contrived to harness the energy of a growing population—that they greatly increased their security. In 1634 they organized
Virginia into eight counties and made each responsible for maintaining a
militia company. The new companies were to protect the counties when
attacked, provide men for expeditions against the Indians, and support expeditionary forces with food, equipment, and compensatory labor. This system
proved its worth in 1644 when Indians rose again, massacring about 500

colonists. In the Second Tidewater War (1644–1646) Virginia drew men from the county militia to launch coordinated offensives against the Indians—traditional feed fights to destroy villages, crops, and stores and force the Indians farther from English settlements. To keep the Indians at bay, the colonists built four forts (blockhouses with protective palisades) from the head of the York River to what would be Petersburg and imposed a peace that excluded Indians—on pain of death—from all of the lands between the James and York rivers, east of the fall line. Virginia, with a population of more than 8,000 Englishmen, was at last firmly and securely established.

For four decades Virginia's defense had depended on the efforts of nearly all adult male colonists—masters, servants, and slaves. After the Second Tidewater War, defense became the responsibility of only a portion of the white adult male population. Virginia's leaders, feeling relatively secure from the Indians and increasingly apprehensive over arming servants and slaves, decided in 1652 to restrict the militia to "freemen or servants of undoubted Fidelity." This more exclusive militia, still organized by counties, was able to provide adequate security against Indians and servants for more than twenty years.

Then, in 1675, Indians from Maryland attacked the north and west frontiers of Virginia, killing 300 colonists and creating turmoil throughout the colony. Sir William Berkeley, the aging royal governor, persisted in relying on forts and mounted militia ranging between forts to protect the frontiers—on a policy that was wholly inadequate. Frontiersmen with exposed estates and other grievances took matters into their own hands. They joined together under a wealthy young landowner, Nathaniel Bacon, defied Governor Berkeley, and attacked any Indians within reach, friend or foe. Thus fighting Indians blended with rebellion in Bacon's Rebellion of 1675–1676. Not until Bacon died and regulars arrived from England was order restored. But after it was, and after the regulars went home, Virginians reverted to their policy of relying on an exclusive militia to control neighboring Indians and rebellious colonists for the remainder of the seventeenth century.

Massachusetts

The purposes and patterns of settlement, in particular the cultivation of tobacco on scattered plantations, had done much to shape Anglo-Indian warfare in seventeenth-century Virginia. By spreading across the land, Virginians had provoked desperate struggles for territory within fifteen years of their arrival at Jamestown; and living as they did on scattered plantations, they had soon come to rely on county militia, expeditionary forces, and feed fights gradually to clear their lands of Indians. In seventeenth-century New England, where purposes and patterns of settlement were different, Anglo-Indian wars were somewhat delayed, although no less desperate when they came. Because many of the first colonists of New England were intensely religious—more interested in achieving salvation than in turning a profit—they settled in small, covenanted communities and pursued subsistence agriculture, trade, and primitive manufacturing. These early New Englanders

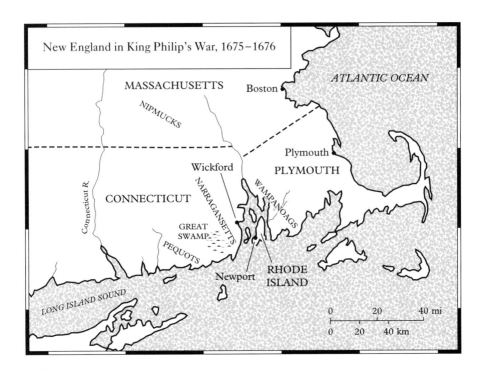

also tended to migrate as small communities, coming within fifty years of the first permanent settlement at Plymouth (1620) to live in villages, interspersed among Indian villages, in each of the four English colonies—Massachusetts, Plymouth, Rhode Island, and Connecticut. With few exceptions, New England communities avoided serious trouble with neighboring Indians until 1675; and when serious trouble arose, as with the Pequots of Connecticut in 1636–1637, the colonists were able to rely on their village militia and expeditionary forces to provide security.

But the rapid growth of the English population eventually made the Indians of New England deeply apprehensive and resentful: by 1675 there were more than 35,000 colonists living among 20,000 Indians in Plymouth, Massachusetts, Rhode Island, and Connecticut. When at last the Indians were provoked to fight, the interspersed character of English and Indian settlements made that fighting unusually destructive and widespread. King Philip's War, which started in June 1675 after Plymouth executed three Wampanoag Indians for murdering a Christian Indian, soon engulfed all of New England. The Wampanoags, led by their supreme ruler, King Philip, began attacking English settlements and gathering Indian allies. In late July, Philip escaped to Massachusetts, brought the powerful Nipmucks into the war, and began battering the Connecticut River Valley. That autumn, after Philip had moved back toward Plymouth, the New England colonies launched a preemptive attack on the Narragansetts of Rhode Island.

The campaign against the Narragansetts, larger and more complex than any of the war, illustrated the difficulty that a loose confederation of colonies had in assembling, supplying, and controlling even a small army of unskilled militiamen. Until the autumn of 1675, the colonies had relied mainly on local militia units to defend their towns and on small expeditionary forces to act against Philip. In November, after learning that the powerful Narragansetts of western Rhode Island were sheltering Wampanoags and preparing for war, commissioners from the United Colonies decided to raise an intercolonial force to attack the Narragansetts. By the second week of December some 650 Massachusetts and Plymouth militiamen (volunteers and conscripts armed with matchlocks, flintlocks, and swords) had assembled at Wickford on the western shore of Narragansett Bay, near the center of Narragansett power and only eleven miles by water from Newport. In destroying nearby Indian villages, the English learned that the Narragansetts had retreated to a secret fortified village in the Great Swamp about ten miles southwest of Wickford. Knowing that 300 Connecticut troops were nearby and that their own supplies would soon be exhausted, the Massachusetts and Plymouth troops decided to join their Connecticut allies and proceed at once to attack the Narragansett village.

On December 19 the intercolonial army of nearly 1,000 men pushed through heavy snow to the northern edge of the Great Swamp. There the Connecticut troops who were in the van exchanged fire with a party of Indians. When the Indians withdrew into the frozen swamp, the Connecticut troops followed, eventually reaching the secret village, five or six acres of high ground surrounded by a palisade and containing shelter and supplies for 1,000 Indians. Without waiting for reinforcements or instructions, the Connecticut troops attacked through the one unfinished portion of the palisade. They succeeded in forcing their way into the village but were met there by such heavy musket fire that they had to withdraw. The remainder of the allied army now arrived, and a second attack by the whole of the intercolonial army succeeded in taking the village and burning the Indians' wigwams and stores. Although the undisciplined and intense fighting had taken a heavy toll of the colonists, about 220 killed or wounded (more than 20 percent of their force), the colonists had inflicted even heavier casualties on the Indians and had destroyed their food and shelter. That evening the colonists retired to Wickford. It would be another month before the intercolonial army could assemble men and supplies to continue their offensive. In late January and early February the colonists made a difficult march of about seventy miles from Wickford, through Rhode Island and Massachusetts, to Boston in a futile effort to overtake and destroy what remained of the Narragansetts. On February 5 the army was disbanded.

The war was by no means over; the Indians were still able to punish the colonists. But it was only a matter of time before the colonists' superior numbers, resources, and organization would destroy the Indians of southeast New England. In February and March 1676 the Indians went on the offensive once again, attacking English communities from the Connecticut River Valley to Rhode Island and forcing many colonists to give up their villages and withdraw to towns around Boston. But just when colonists began to despair of defeating or pacifying the Indians and just when they seemed to be suffering most from the loss of their homes and food supplies, the Indians broke off their offensive. Worn by hunger, disease, and losses in battle, the

Indians began to fish, plant, scavenge for food, and surrender. The colonists mounted a final offensive: surprising Indians along the Connecticut River, tracking down others with dogs, and showing little mercy to any they captured. The war ended in the late summer of 1676 with Philip's death and the destruction or deportation of hostile Indians. The colonists had suffered greatly in King Philip's War, losing more than 5 percent of their population and a dozen towns; but they had permanently broken the power of the Indians of southeast New England.

The Colonial Wars

Although fighting between Englishmen and Indians continued through the remainder of the colonial period, that fighting gradually blended with and became subordinate to wars between the English and other European colonists in North America. During the 1680s, disputes over land, trade, and religion produced clashes between South Carolinians and the Spanish in Florida and between New Englanders and the French in Canada. These clashes soon became part of worldwide conflicts among the principal states of Europe. But if European statesmen considered overseas commerce and colonies valuable assets in their struggles to preserve a balance of power, they did little before 1750 to assist their colonists in wars with one another. In King William's War (1689–1697, which was an extension of the War of the League of Augsburg) the settlers of New England and the French of Canada had mainly Indian allies. Similarly in Queen Anne's War (1702–1713, part of the War of the Spanish Succession) and King George's War (1739–1748, part of the War of the Austrian Succession) English and Spanish colonists bore the brunt of fighting on the southern frontiers while English and French colonists, supported by Indians, did the same in the north. Only rarely, in Queen Anne's and King George's wars—brutal and indecisive conflicts—did regular British forces support the colonists.

For more than a century before King William's War, the English had competed with the Spanish, French, and Dutch for the land and wealth of North America. By right of discovery and papal decree the Spanish had first claimed North America in 1494, and they had been able to sustain that claim through most of the sixteenth century—in part because they had a superior fleet and in part because their rivals were preoccupied with European affairs. But as Spain became mired in the Eighty Years' War with the Dutch (1567–1648) and as the Spanish navy and merchant fleet began to decay, the French, Dutch, and English pushed into North America. The French, who had fished off Newfoundland and traded for furs through most of the sixteenth century, established a permanent settlement at Quebec in 1608, made Canada a royal colony in 1663, and claimed the whole Mississippi Valley in 1682. The Dutch, more interested in commerce than in colonies, established a post at New York in 1624 and, by mid-century, a flourishing trade and fishery in the North Atlantic. But neither the French nor the Dutch were as successful as the English in creating permanent settlements in North America; and Englishmen were tenacious in defending their claims to the land and trade of the New World. The English had explored North America in the late fifteenth century, raided Spanish possessions in the West Indies and Central America in the 1560s and 1570s, and after failures along Albemarle Sound in the 1580s, established colonies in the Chesapeake (1607) and New England (1620). While those colonies were taking hold and becoming sources of tobacco, fish, furs, and timber, English merchants and ministers further asserted their interests in America. In the 1620s merchants invested in privateers that attacked French outposts in Nova Scotia and took Quebec (returned in 1632); and during the Anglo-Spanish and Anglo-Dutch wars of the middle of the century, the English government sent squadrons to capture Nova Scotia and New York. Although the English returned Nova Scotia to France in 1667, they also adopted laws (navigation acts of 1651, 1660, 1663, and 1696) to reap the principal benefits of all trade with their American colonies.

In King William's War (1689–1697) the English colonists of North America found the French and Indians together a far more formidable enemy than either had been alone. Although the total English population was nearly twenty times larger than the French, the population of New York and New England was only four or five times that of Canada; and it was far more difficult for the English to coordinate their efforts—divided as they were in separate colonies—than for the French who lived under one centralized administration. After both sides had begun the war with raids across the frontiers of Canada and New York, and after an expedition from Massachusetts had captured the French privateering base at Port Royal in Acadia, New York and New England joined forces in the summer of 1690 for an invasion of Canada. This was an ambitious operation that required two small armies: one proceeding from Albany across Lake George and Lake Champlain to Montreal, the other from Boston by way of the St. Lawrence River to Quebec. Both forces came down with smallpox, and when the one on the lakes turned back, the other was left alone to face the united forces of New France at Quebec. Outnumbered and suffering from cold wet weather as well as illness, the second English force also turned back in October 1690. The war degenerated into savage frontier encounters and maritime commerce raiding. The French lacked the population for sustained offensives. The English lacked the will; their assemblies were ever slow to vote money for defense and to cooperate with one another. Thus the war fell most heavily on frontier settlements, on local militia units, and on Indian allies. The governments of England and France did little more than send warships to the West Indies and return all conquests and prisoners at the Peace of Ryswick.

Queen Anne's War (1702–1713) began much as King William's War had ended—with fighting across frontiers and commerce raiding at sea. South Carolinians and the Spanish colonists in Florida did do more than

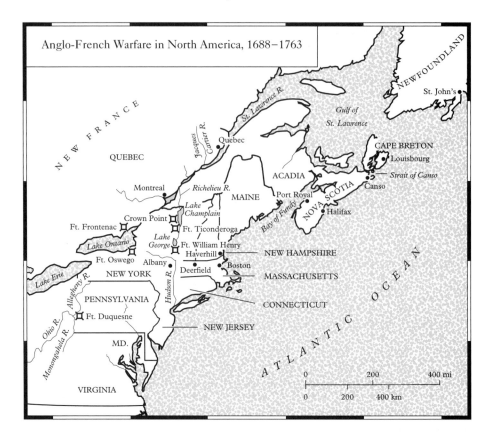

Anglo-French Warfare in North America, 1688–1763

raid frontier settlements: they attacked unsuccessfully St. Augustine, Charleston, and Pensacola in the opening years of the war. But for eight years, New Englanders and French Canadians mainly skirmished in the wilderness and on the high seas. Although the population was growing steadily in the British and French colonies, the French continued to lack the resources for a regular campaign; they hoped that striking at the frontiers of New England would forestall an invasion of Canada or any extension of English settlements. New Englanders began the war without the help of New York and the Iroquois, both of whom preferred to remain neutral. Massachusetts did raise 1,900 men to garrison its frontiers and engage hostile Indians. Yet with money and labor scarce, it was difficult both to garrison frontier posts and to support an invasion of Canada—to raise the volunteers needed for prolonged service away from home. It was also difficult to banish the memory of New England's disastrous expedition to Canada in 1690. Thus until Britain provided direct support in the war, Massachusetts remained mainly on the defensive, absorbing damaging attacks on towns like Deerfield and Haverhill and responding with raids on the coast of what is now Maine and unsuccessful attempts to capture Port Royal.

When Britain did support the colonists, the results were decidedly disappointing. In 1708, New Englanders persuaded the British government to join in conquering Canada. Anticipating the arrival of British forces in 1709, the New Englanders lured New York and the Iroquois from their neutrality and enlisted volunteers for an expedition to Quebec. But the British government, hoping the war would end, delayed sending help until 1710 when a few warships and marines joined the colonists in capturing Port Royal. Only in 1711 did the British provide regular forces enough for an invasion of Canada: 4,300 soldiers, 12 warships, and 40 transports. The colonists responded enthusiastically, if not cooperatively. When in June the British reached Boston, the townspeople raised prices on provisions and obstructed British efforts to recruit seamen and pilots. Thousands of colonists did volunteer to accompany the British to the St. Lawrence and thousands more assembled for a separate colonial expedition across the lakes to Montreal, but the volunteers were not well disciplined or trained. To get the numbers of men required for such operations, the colonists had to recruit many men outside the militia—marginal members of society who saw military service as a chance to improve their fortunes. The British were not pleased with the quality of these provincial volunteers or with Bostonians' efforts in preparing the fleet. And when eight ships went aground on reaching the St. Lawrence, the British promptly canceled the attack on Quebec. The invasion of Canada collapsed amid mutual recriminations.

During King William's and Queen Anne's wars, the British had gradually become superior to the French at sea. Yet they had never vigorously exploited that superiority in North America because they consistently gave priority to war in Europe and because they had considerable difficulty containing a French navy that avoided battle and concentrated on raiding commerce and colonies. Thus during King William's War the French were able not just to batter British merchant shipping in the North Atlantic but also to protect New France while nearly destroying British posts in Newfoundland and Hudson Bay. Until the last years of Queen Anne's War the French continued to have the advantage in North American waters, capturing St. John's, Newfoundland, in 1708, inflicting great damage on British commerce, and holding all of Nova Scotia except Port Royal. Only at the end of Queen Anne's War were the British able to spare ships for expeditions against New France and to surpass the French in commerce raiding. Even then it was not British sea power that won a favorable peace; it was Marlborough and Eugene's success in the Low Countries, the strength of the British economy, and skillful diplomacy that enabled Britain to gain Nova Scotia, Hudson Bay, Newfoundland, and trading privileges in the Spanish Empire at the Peace of Utrecht.

The antagonisms that marred Anglo-American efforts to cooperate in Queen Anne's War reappeared in more virulent form in King George's War (1739–1748). At the beginning of George's war, the colonists were eager to cooperate with British regular forces in attacking neighboring Spanish colonies to make their frontiers permanently secure for settlement and trade. Yet for all their enthusiasm, undisciplined and inexperienced provincials had great trouble working effectively with professional British soldiers and sailors. In 1740 and 1741 Anglo-American expeditions failed to capture Spanish posts at St. Augustine in Florida and at Cartagena on the Spanish Main. Each attempt suffered from disputes between provincials and regulars, and each ended with mutual complaints. Regulars found provincials dirty, ignorant of war, and difficult to manage. Provincials complained of being treated with contempt—of being employed more as laborers than as soldiers, of being pressed into service on British warships, and of being kept under arms well beyond their periods of enlistment.

Even the most successful of Anglo-American operations in George's War created disputes and lingering resentments. In 1744 French forces from Cape Breton Island attacked ports in Nova Scotia and the shipping of New England. Angered by these attacks, the government of Massachusetts organized an expedition against the French base at Louisbourg on Cape Breton—a base established in 1713 on a fine natural harbor and protected by a massive angled-bastion fortress that provided a haven for French warships, privateers, and merchantmen on the eastern approaches to the Gulf of St. Lawrence. Massachusetts raised and funded 2,800 provincial troops. These men, commanded by a prominent colonist, sailed from Boston in March 1745. At Canso in Nova Scotia, they were reinforced by troops from New Hampshire and Connecticut and by British warships from the West Indies. The whole, now under the joint command of a provincial general and a British admiral, proceeded to Cape Breton and took Louisbourg by siege and blockade. The colonists were elated with this victory but dismayed to find their contributions were little appreciated by the British and that they were neither to be fully reimbursed for their expenses nor to be permitted to share in prize money from French ships taken at Louisbourg. The colonists hoped to get British support for an invasion of Canada in 1746 or 1747; instead they were left to garrison Louisbourg and, eventually, to see the British surrender what they had won.

In King George's War, as in their wars against Louis XIV, the British had been superior to the French at sea. But in King George's War their superiority had been so substantial that even while giving priority to the war in Europe—devoting their fleet mainly to protecting their communications with the continent and blockading French and Spanish ports—they were able to gain important advantages over the French in North American waters. The British commitment to America was never very strong. In 1746 they abandoned an attack on Quebec when bad weather and the appearance of a French squadron in the English Channel delayed the sailing of their expedition; and later that year they allowed the same French squadron to reach North America unopposed. (The French might have recaptured Louisbourg had they not lost 8,000 men to illness before the campaign ended.) Even so, the British navy's contribution to the war in America was considerable—in helping capture Louisbourg, in intercepting a convoy bound for Quebec in 1747, and in joining with privateers to gain a clear advantage in commerce raiding in the North Atlantic. At war's end—at the Peace of Aix-la-Chapelle—the British were able to use their successes in North America to offset French gains on the Continent by exchanging

Louisbourg for the territory that Marshal Saxe had taken in the Low Countries. Many colonists were disgusted.

The French and Indian War

In more than a half-century of conflict among English, French, and Spanish colonists of North America, the colonists had been left to do nearly all the fighting. European forces had taken part only fitfully and often ineffectively; and European governments had failed to resolve the disputes over land, trade, and religion that frustrated and alarmed the frontiersmen of each nation. In the final, climactic struggle for the continent—the French and Indian War (1754–1763)—regulars would intervene decisively. British forces and British resources would resolve the long contest for the frontiers of America. But in so doing the British would alienate their colonial allies and awaken a sense of colonial interests and identity that would contribute eventually to the destruction of the British empire in America.

The Beginnings

The British intervened in the French and Indian War primarily to protect their aggressive and uncooperative colonists—not, initially at least, to conquer Canada or Florida. By 1754 the English colonists of North America outnumbered the French 1,042,000 to 55,000 and the Spanish by an even greater margin. But the English were unable to cooperate as effectively as their neighbors, and by 1754 they were everywhere along the frontiers losing contests for land and trade as well as the allegiance of the Indians. In Nova Scotia, French settlements were growing faster than English; in western Pennsylvania the French had defeated the pro-British Miami Indians, built fortresses from Lake Erie to the Allegheny River, and routed all provincial forces that approached them; and on the southern frontiers the French and Spanish were turning the Indians against the English. Delegates from seven English colonies met at Albany in June 1754 to draft a plan of cooperation for defense and Indian affairs. But the Albany Plan was not acceptable to the colonies or to the British government, and the government decided to rely on sending small detachments of regulars to help the colonists secure their frontiers. When the French responded by embarking 3,000 of their own regulars for Canada, the French and Indian War quickly became more than a contest between European colonists and Indian allies. By the summer of 1755, British and French warships had fought off Newfoundland, and Anglo-American forces had both conquered Acadia (deporting most of the French population) and suffered a dramatic defeat along the banks of the Monongahela in western Pennsylvania.

The early appearance of regular British forces in the French and Indian War did not mean that the British government shared the colonists' war aims. By 1755 many leading English colonists had begun to dream of conquering French and Spanish lands in North America. They had learned in more than half a century of conflict to hate their Catholic neighbors and to fear their sudden incursions on frontier settlements. They had also come to see that the French and Spanish and their Indian allies were obstacles to the growing English population—that they restricted access to the rich lands of the Ohio and Mississippi valleys as well as their trade with Indians. To end threats to their frontiers and to open the west to speculators, settlers, and traders, the English colonists needed to do more than haggle with the French and Spanish over existing frontiers; they needed to conquer the French and Spanish colonists and expel them from North America—much as they had conquered and expelled the Indians from the Atlantic seaboard. The British government would be slow to support or even comprehend these war aims. The government would not declare war on France until May 1756 or consider conquering New France until William Pitt became the king's principal minister in December 1756. Until then the British would wage a limited frontier war, while the colonists dreamed of conquest.

Although the colonists had more ambitious war aims than the British government and appealed to the government to help fight their war, they were most uncooperative and ineffective allies. The government did expect the colonists to provide recruits and provisions for British regiments as well as provincial forces to support the regulars. But when in the summer of 1756 British generals arrived to take control of the war, they found the colonists not just unwilling to help recruit men for regular units but also opposed to having provincials serve under regular officers. Colonial assemblies, eager to assert their independence of royal authority, had forbidden provincials to submit to British orders or military justice; and the provincials, having contracted to serve only under their own officers, would have deserted rather than accept British direction. Similarly, the colonists refused to let the British take charge of their systems of supply or to quarter troops at their expense without the approval of the colonial assemblies. To gain the cooperation of the colonists in prosecuting the war, the British commander-in-chief, the Earl of Loudoun, agreed to keep regulars and provincials apart and to let the provincials serve under their own officers who would rank after British majors. Even so, with the exception of New York, the colonies rarely satisfied Loudoun's requests for men, supplies, transportation, and quarters in the campaigns of 1756 and 1757. Those provincials who did come forward were fit mainly for fatigue and garrison duty; they were too poorly trained to be steady under fire and too undisciplined to maintain their health in camp.

Britain Takes Control of the War

In large part because the colonists were such ineffective and difficult allies, Anglo-American forces did not fare well in 1756 or 1757. During the summer and autumn of 1756, while British and colonial officers argued over authority and rank in their combined forces, the French went on the offensive, capturing Fort Oswego and 1,500 provincials on Lake Ontario and ravaging English frontier settlements from New York to the Carolinas. Even after Oswego fell and the French seemed to be preparing to attack Fort William Henry on Lake George, the colonists remained more concerned with establishing the independence of their assemblies than with defending New York. Loudoun concluded that the colonists could not be depended on to win the war and that he would have to rely on regulars, recruited in Britain, to mount the offensives needed to capture Louisbourg and Quebec and end the war in 1757. Yet recruiting an additional 11,000 men in Britain, particularly while the government and its policies were unsettled, took time; and when at last these reinforcements reached Loudoun, it was too late for him to act decisively. By July 1757, the French government had so strengthened its naval forces off Cape Breton as to forestall an attack on Louisbourg or Quebec and to release some troops from Canada for an offensive in New York. On August 9 the French captured Fort William Henry on Lake George and threatened to occupy the upper Hudson. So it was that Anglo-Americans had managed to squander superior resources for two campaigns and to suffer a succession of depressing defeats.

Anglo-American failures in the opening campaigns of the French and Indian War should not be attributed entirely to their difficulties in raising an army. The British also had trouble during these first campaigns in taking advantage of the superiority of their navy—gaining and keeping control of the seas off New England and New France. As in earlier colonial wars, the British were more concerned with establishing their superiority in the English Channel than with protecting their possessions overseas; and establishing themselves in the Channel was not easy because the French had rebuilt their fleet since the War of the Austrian Succession and refused to risk that fleet in a major engagement. Thus to defend the British Isles, to contain commerce raiders, and to protect their colonies from roving French squadrons, the British concentrated on blocking French ports. This strategy was not uniformly successful at the beginning of the war. In 1755 two French fleets eluded British squadrons and reached Canada with a reinforcement of 4,000 men; and by June 1757 the French had collected eighteen ships of the line and three frigates at Louisbourg, giving them temporary control of Canadian waters and frustrating Loudoun's plans for a summer offensive toward Quebec.

Ironically, while the British were struggling to exploit their sea power and were learning not to depend on the colonists to win the war, they were coming to accept colonial war aims. William Pitt, who became the king's principal minister in December 1756, was not to be satisfied with sustaining the boundaries of British North America. Believing that Britain's power depended on trade and colonies, Pitt shared the colonists' enthusiasm for conquering Canada and expanding the British Empire into the Ohio and Mississippi valleys. He was therefore prepared to put greater resources into the war in America than his predecessors, and he pressed Loudoun to use those resources decisively—to take Louisbourg and Quebec and conquer Canada in 1757. When Loudoun failed even to attack Louisbourg, Pitt was determined to take control of the war in 1758: to overcome the colonists'

Jeffery, Lord Amherst commanded British
forces that conquered Canada in 1759–1760.
He was a cautious but very persistent commander who sought victory with few risks.

reluctance to serve by paying for some of the troops they would raise and to encourage his own officers to be more aggressive and obedient by recalling Loudoun and sending two promising young men to commands in America.

Jeffery Amherst was only forty and a colonel when chosen to lead British forces against Louisbourg and Quebec in 1758. Although he had never had an independent command, he had impressed the most influential generals in the British army as an unusually dependable and persistent officer. He had entered the army at fourteen; gone with his regiment to the Low Countries, Germany, and Scotland; won praise for his steadiness under fire at Dettingen and Fontenoy; and served as aide-de-camp to the Duke of Cumberland in the closing campaigns of the War of the Austrian Succession and in the opening campaign of the Seven Years' War. By temperament and experience, Amherst was well equipped to wage the kind of limited war made famous by Marshal Saxe—a war conducted more by sieges, maneuvers, and skirmishes than by general engagements, a war in which commanders sought to minimize casualties even when battle became unavoidable. Amherst was, as his sister described him, "hardly ever in a passion" but "avidly resolute in what he designs." He had the patience, prudence, and persistence not just to prefer, but also to succeed in, a war of sieges and maneuvers. Although he had never commanded, he had had ample opportunity as Cumberland's aide-de-camp during Saxe's conquest of the Austrian Netherlands to study the conduct of armies during the most celebrated campaigns in the history of limited war.

James Wolfe, whom Pitt chose to serve under Amherst at Louisbourg, was also young and without experience in high command; but Wolfe

James Wolfe commanded the British army
that captured Quebec in 1759. Far more
aggressive than most officers in the age of
limited war, he preferred battles to sieges as
the best way of deciding a campaign.

was not so composed or patient as Amherst and not so devoted to the
conventions of limited war. At thirty-two, Wolfe was one of the youngest and
most junior colonels in the army. He had served with his regiment in the
Low Countries, Germany, and Scotland—distinguishing himself not only for
his courage and control of men in battle but also for his ability to discipline
and train men in camp. Like Amherst, he had proved a very knowledgable
and effective aide-de-camp during the Scottish Rebellion and the expedition
against the French port of Rochefort in 1757. But what set Wolfe apart from
Amherst and many of their contemporaries were his extraordinary ambition
and his fascination with battle. Wolfe was desperately eager to succeed in his
profession—to achieve military fame. He studied incessantly to become
worthy of higher command; he put service with his regiment before any personal consideration; and he looked forward to war as the path to preferment.
Above all, he regarded battle as the supreme test of his personal courage and
professional competence; nothing, he thought, was more rewarding than
having the mastery of men under fire—and being recognized for having that
mastery. He acknowledged the importance of fortifications and sieges, but
he preferred the higher risks and greater potential rewards of battle as the
arbiter of wars and reputations.

    In choosing Amherst and Wolfe to provide strong leadership, in
building up a decided superiority in regular units, and in granting large subsidies to encourage the colonists to serve as provincials, William Pitt believed
he was creating Anglo-American forces capable of conquering New France,
perhaps in 1758. Amherst and Wolfe would lead the largest and most important of three, coordinated offensives: an amphibious attack on Louisbourg
and Quebec carried out by more than 13,000 regulars supported by nearly
40 warships, 15,000 sailors, and 110 transports. James Abercromby would
make a secondary attack across Lake Champlain to Montreal with a combined force of more than 20,000 regulars and provincials. And John Forbes

would lead about 6,000 men—mostly provincials—against Fort Duquesne. Although Pitt had not selected Abercromby and Forbes to serve in America and although it was not clear how effective they or their provincial allies might be, Anglo-American forces were everywhere expected to be larger and better supported than the French. It was not just that there would be 23,000 regulars, 21,000 provincials, 40 warships, and 15,000 seamen to oppose 6,800 French regulars, 10 warships, and a few thousand Canadians and Indians; it was also that while the British would benefit from an increasingly effective system of supply and transportation, the French would suffer from a succession of bad harvests, the interruption of their overseas trade and supply, and the defection of their Indian allies.

Quebec, 1758–1759

Notwithstanding the very great advantages they possessed, Anglo-American forces did not conquer New France in 1758. They did take the offensive, but the difficulties of campaigning in a vast primitive country, the inexperience and poor judgment of some of their leaders, the chronic weaknesses of provincials, and the competence of their enemies all worked against them. Amherst and Wolfe had the most success. They left Halifax at the end of May and established a beachhead on Cape Breton Island, four miles west of Louisbourg by June 8. Louisbourg was, however, too strongly fortified to invite an assault, and by the time Amherst had brought up his artillery and conducted a prudent siege—overcoming bad weather, smallpox, and persistent defenders to force a surrender—more than six weeks had passed. It was then the end of July, and although Amherst wanted to press on to Quebec, the British had formidable logistical problems to solve before they could sail. They set about at once preparing transports to send nearly 6,000 French prisoners to Europe, replenishing their own ships for the voyage to Quebec, and reembarking their siege train. These preparations had scarcely begun when news arrived that Abercromby had made a rash and disastrous attack on the French fortress of Ticonderoga on Lake Champlain. This news, together with delays in embarking the French prisoners and his own siege guns, forced Amherst to cancel the attack on Quebec. Instead he sent raiding parties to the Gulf of St. Lawrence and the Bay of Fundy and went himself with 4,000 men to relieve Abercromby. It was early October before Amherst reached Abercromby on Lake George—too late for another attempt on Ticonderoga. The British had taken Louisbourg; they had raided Fort Frontenac at the mouth of Lake Ontario; and in November, they would occupy Fort Duquesne. But the conquest of Canada eluded them in 1758.

Pitt was determined to succeed in 1759 in bringing overwhelming force against the beleaguered defenders of New France. Even before the campaign of 1758 ended, he appointed Amherst to replace Abercromby as commander-in-chief of British forces in North America. He also decided to persist in his strategy of having separate armies converge on the center of French population and power in the St. Lawrence Valley. Wolfe would command an amphibious force proceeding up the St. Lawrence to Quebec:

12,000 regulars supported by a fleet of 22 warships and 150 transports. Amherst would lead an even larger army of regulars and provincials across either Lake Champlain or Lake Ontario to Montreal. To complement these principal offensives, a third and smaller force would advance through western Pennsylvania against French outposts in the Ohio Valley. Knowing that the French had suffered heavy losses at Louisbourg and expecting that the British navy would be able to keep reinforcements from reaching Canada, Pitt assumed that his armies would have the numerical superiority needed to crush an enemy that had the distinct advantage of conducting a defense on interior lines.

Although Pitt was unable to raise all the forces he intended, his forces were far superior to the defenders of New France. To encourage British colonists to support the war, Pitt offered not only to furnish provincials with arms, clothing, and provisions but also to reimburse the colonies for recruiting and paying those provincials. Colonial assemblies responded by voting to raise 20,680 of the 21,000 men that Pitt had requested. But ordinary colonists, having suffered through a succession of disappointing and deadly campaigns, were reluctant to enlist. Only 16,835 provincials served in 1759, and few of them were well disciplined or trained. Neither Wolfe nor Amherst had the numbers of skilled men that Pitt expected. Even so, Wolfe with 9,000 regulars and Amherst with 13,000 regulars and provincials had more powerful armies than their opponents. The French government, placing greater emphasis on the war in Europe than on the defense of its North American colonies, sent only 300 men and small quantities of munitions to Canada. Some twenty vessels with provisions did arrive in the spring of 1759 before the British sealed the St. Lawrence, yet the forces of New France suffered through the ensuing campaign from shortages of men, powder, and provisions.

The French made good use of their meager resources. Louis Joseph, Marquis de Montcalm, commander-in-chief in New France, was an experienced and talented regular officer. Montcalm knew that he could not defend Canada as Frederick was defending Prussia. He had neither the men nor the supplies to conduct an aggressive defense on interior lines—to fight the costly battles and sustain the forced marches that such a strategy required. Nor could he risk losing Quebec while shifting his forces to deal separately with the armies converging on Canada. He could try both to hold Quebec and to trade space for time on Lake Champlain and Lake Ontario in hopes that the war would end before all of New France had been conquered. Thus he posted relatively small forces on the lakes to delay the armies advancing on Montreal, to force them to bring up cannon and to build vessels to gain control of those waterways. And thus he deployed the bulk of his troops around Quebec—possibly as many as 14,000 men, mainly militiamen but also several thousand regulars, a thousand provincials, and a few hundred Indians.

Montcalm's disposition of this mixed force in defense of Quebec was particularly skillful. Although Quebec seemed to occupy a position of great natural strength, built upon a headland rising several hundred feet above the St. Lawrence, the town's defenses were far from complete in 1759. The

Louis Joseph, Marquis de Montcalm,
commanded French forces in North America
during the French and Indian War. His
skillful defense of Canada frustrated British
commanders and significantly postponed
French defeat.

eastern and southern faces of the headland were steep enough to discourage
an attack from the St. Lawrence, but the northern approach to Quebec
across the St. Charles River and the western approaches along the north
bank of the St. Lawrence were more gradual and accessible. And the fortifications covering those northern and western approaches were not yet complete. Montcalm knew that his mixed force could not stand against British
regulars in open country. He also knew that his fortifications and supplies
were not ready to withstand a regular siege of Quebec. He decided, therefore, to spread his forces along the north bank of the St. Lawrence both east
and west of Quebec. He would take up positions, some eight to ten miles in
length, that were too extensive to be besieged and too well protected by the
river, tidal flats, bluffs, and forests to be easily attacked or turned. In these
extensive positions, supplied by water from Montreal, he could hope to survive a short Canadian summer. If the British were rash or frustrated enough
to attack his lines—as Abercromby had attacked them at Ticonderoga in
1758—even his inferior militiamen might prevail. In late May 1759, Montcalm began entrenching the north bank of the St. Lawrence below, at, and
above Quebec; he secured his eastern flank with the Montmorency River, his
western with a roving force of 3,000 men.

James Wolfe soon came to appreciate the quality of Montcalm's dispositions. Arriving off Quebec on June 23, Wolfe saw that it would be hazardous to attack and impossible to besiege Montcalm's extensive positions
on the north bank of the St. Lawrence. Wolfe was one of the most aggressive

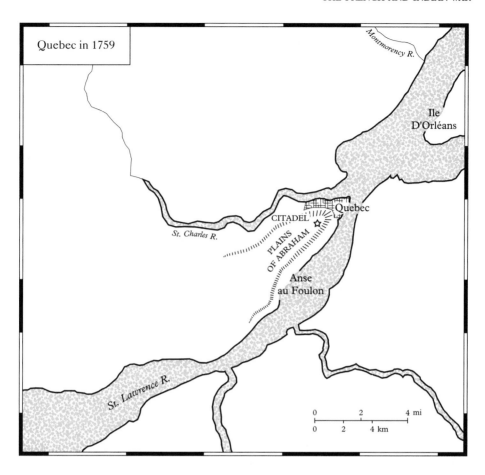

Quebec in 1759

Montmorency R.

Ile
D'Orléans

Quebec

CITADEL

St. Charles R.

PLAINS
OF ABRAHAM

Anse
au Foulon

St. Lawrence R.

0   2   4 mi
0   2   4 km

officers of his era, but he was reluctant to waste lives assaulting well-prepared positions. Thus for more than ten weeks after reaching Quebec, he sought ways to bring Montcalm from his lines or to circumvent him. Wolfe continued to hope that Amherst's advance across the lakes would force the French to divert troops from Quebec—to contract their defenses and retire into the town where they might be taken by siege. He also landed troops on the north bank of the St. Lawrence east of the Montmorency River in hopes of being able to launch an offensive across the Montmorency, striking the flank of the French defenders and driving them across the St. Charles into Quebec. And he tried repeatedly to goad Montcalm into abandoning his lines and risking battle by bombarding Quebec, burning more than 1,500 farmhouses in the surrounding countryside, and sending two expeditions up the St. Lawrence to interdict supplies, destroy ships and magazines, and open a communication with Amherst. Only once did Wolfe yield to his frustrations and try to provoke a general engagement by attacking the French in their lines. That attack, launched across the Montmorency on July 31, failed completely: the British, pinned under heavy fire near the river's edge, lost 440 killed and wounded; the French, 60.

The Plains of Abraham

Wolfe's defeat on the Montmorency—indeed, the failure of all his efforts to dislodge the French—eroded his health and confidence. By the end of August he had become desperate enough to seek the advice of his brigadier generals, to ask how best to defeat the French army. His brigadiers, seeing little chance of attacking successfully between the Montmorency and the St. Charles, recommended approaching Quebec from the west along the north bank of the St. Lawrence. Such an approach would, they thought, force the French to risk battle on British terms (to use their militiamen against regulars in open country) or to let the British take Quebec by siege. Wolfe, who had long been inclined toward an attack from the west, accepted but modified his brigadiers' advice. Rather than put his army ashore well to the west of town where the river's bank was low and the landings might have been expected, he decided to risk a landing within two miles of Quebec where the shore rose steeply and where he stood a much better chance of surprising the French and forcing them to accept battle unprepared. In such a battle he could hope to defeat Montcalm and gain Quebec, if not all of Canada, before winter ended another campaign.

In making and carrying out this decision, Wolfe seemed to recover much of his vigor and confidence. After ten weeks of frustration and inactivity, Wolfe looked forward to battle, not merely as a test of his courage and skill but also as a promising solution to a most vexing tactical problem. He moved swiftly, August 31–September 6, removing his army from the east bank of the Montmorency and reassembling some 3,600 troops on board transports in the St. Lawrence, eight miles west of Quebec. By September 9 he had also taken the crucial decision to land within two miles of the town at Anse au Foulon, where a path led up the face of the bluff to the Plains of Abraham, a grassy plateau just outside the walls of the French citadel. Having made this decision, he arranged elaborate demonstrations to divert attention from the landings at the Anse, now scheduled for September 13. Detachments of British warships and transports would draw French forces four miles to the east and eight to the west of Quebec just before Wolfe's troops were to land. Wolfe would demonstrate against Montcalm's flanks while attacking his center.

The attack, carried out with great secrecy, resolution, and speed, succeeded as well as anyone might have hoped. Chance and French assumptions clearly favored the British, as did the superior discipline of their infantry. In the darkness before dawn on September 13, the British were able to dupe those French sentries who challenged their boats; the French were expecting supplies by water and allowed the British to pass without giving a countersign. The British also managed to disperse sentries guarding the path from Anse au Foulon to the Plains of Abraham without provoking a response in force; Montcalm, expecting an attack east of the St. Charles, assumed that the British were making no more than a demonstration. By the time he understood what they were doing and marched his own forces from east of the St. Charles to Quebec, Wolfe had already drawn up 4,800 British soldiers in line of battle, two ranks deep, on the Plains of Abraham.

Seeing that the British were beginning to dig in, and knowing that if allowed to grow stronger they would eventually take Quebec by siege, Montcalm decided to attack. He formed his militiamen and regulars in columns, flanked by skirmishers, and advanced. Wolfe's disciplined regulars remained in their lines even as the French advancing in columns and firing sporadically bore down on them. When the French came within forty yards, the British fired volleys by platoon that thoroughly disrupted the enemy columns. The British then reloaded, stepped forward beyond the smoke of their own muskets, and fired a second, general volley. At that, the French broke, streaming off the Plains of Abraham, back through Quebec, and across the St. Charles. The Battle of Quebec had ended.

Although the British did not immediately exploit their victory, they soon gained possession of Quebec. By the time the French had begun to retreat, Wolfe was dead, his second in command had been wounded, and 658 of his men were casualties (about 13.5 percent of his force). The interruption in British command together with the casualties they had suffered, a rearguard action by Canadian skirmishers, and a brief appearance of the 3,000 French troops who had been posted west of Quebec all discouraged a vigorous pursuit of the retreating French army. A French garrison continued to hold the citadel of Quebec, and survivors of the battle were able to reassemble east of the St. Charles. Yet the French had suffered about the same number and proportion of casualties as the British; Montcalm had been mortally wounded; and, above all, French morale had been broken temporarily. That night the remnants of the French army began to withdraw to the west, leaving the garrison in the citadel to surrender on September 18. By then the French had decided to take up new defensive positions on the Jacques Cartier River, thirty miles west of Quebec. The British had gained Quebec but advanced no farther up the St. Lawrence in 1759.

The Conquest of Canada

The British had again failed to conquer New France. Their efforts fell short not just because Wolfe was delayed in taking Quebec but especially because Amherst was unable to push his forces across Lakes Champlain and Ontario in time to cooperate with Wolfe's army. Amherst had begun the campaign determined to extinguish French power in Canada. But his prudence, along with the inertia of his allies and competence of his enemies, kept him from reaching the St. Lawrence in 1759. By the beginning of May he had begun to assemble forces at Albany capable of mounting parallel offensives toward Montreal: one of 5,000 men to go by way of Lake Ontario and the St. Lawrence; another of more than 8,000, by way of Lake George and Lake Champlain. Provincials were, however, slow to gather; and it was not until the end of May that he could send troops to Lake Ontario or until June 22 that he reached the south end of Lake George. He then expended another month building boats to carry his siege train across Lake George. He was determined to avoid a repetition of Abercromby's disastrous assault on French fortifications. Although Amherst never had to use his siege train—

the French unexpectedly abandoned their works at Ticonderoga (July 26) and Crown Point (July 31)—he did have to devote another eleven weeks to gaining control of Lake Champlain, building vessels and sweeping aside the French sloops that blocked the way to Montreal. When at last the lake was clear, it was mid-October and too late to go on to the St. Lawrence. Amherst knew that Wolfe's army had taken Quebec. He also knew that his forces on Lake Ontario had stopped short of the St. Lawrence, that winter was fast approaching, and that the provincials under his command were chaffing to go home. On October 19 he returned to Crown Point. The campaign was over.

By October 1759 Anglo-American forces had driven the defenders of New France into narrow corridors along the St. Lawrence and Richelieu rivers and cut their communications with France. William Pitt was impatient to complete the conquest of Canada early in 1760 lest negotiations end the war before the British had established their claim to the rest of Canada. But it would take Anglo-American forces another campaign to conquer Canada. Amherst spent the winter of 1759–1760 enlisting the colonists' support for a decisive, converging offensive against Montreal. He would lead 11,000 regulars and provincials from Albany via Lake Ontario and the St. Lawrence to Montreal. Another Anglo-American force of 3,400 would advance north across Lake Champlain and the Richelieu, and yet a third force of 3,800 British regulars would move southwest along the St. Lawrence from Quebec to Montreal. Although Amherst reached Albany in early May, he was unable to set out for Lake Ontario or to send troops to Lake Champlain until late in June. The colonists, anticipating peace, were slow to join his armies; and it took time to build up magazines on Lake Ontario and Lake Champlain. In the interim the French launched a preemptive attack on Quebec that forced Amherst to reinforce the garrison there. Not until early August were all Anglo-American armies advancing on Montreal. But once in motion, they soon brought overwhelming force against New France. On September 6, Amherst reached Montreal; the next day British forces from Quebec and Lake Champlain arrived; and on September 8 the French surrendered.

The conquest of Canada had been achieved at last by an overwhelming concentration of Anglo-American force—primarily regular and provincial land forces commanded by British officers and subsidized by the British government. But the British navy had also since 1758 played an increasingly important part in isolating and destroying New France. New France had never become self-sufficient; its regular forces had always depended on supplies from Europe and on the timely support of French warships off Cape Breton and in the St. Lawrence. Beginning in 1758, the British navy was so superior to the French that it could both blockade the coast of France and control the approaches to New France. Thus in 1758 British warships hastened the surrender of Louisbourg, first by destroying a convoy off Rochefort that was carrying badly needed supplies to the fortress and later by sealing off the fortress itself while Amherst and Wolfe pressed their siege. Similarly in 1759 and 1760 the British navy was able to shut the St. Lawrence to all except insignificant French reinforcements and to give Anglo-American forces the support they needed to take Quebec and Montreal.

The conquest of Canada helped the British win the Seven Years' War, but it considerably complicated their efforts to make a favorable peace. Once Montreal fell, the British were able to divert thousands of regular and provincial troops for service elsewhere against the French and their allies. In the last two years of the war, the British won victories in Europe, the West Indies, the Far East, and North America. Yet even before negotiators met in Paris in the summer of 1762, Anglo-Americans had begun debating the fate of Canada. Many colonists and some Englishmen argued that Britain should retain Canada to provide for the security of the other British colonies in North America by eliminating the French from their borders. Others— primarily Englishmen concerned with the trade and authority of the mother country—urged that Britain retain Guadeloupe (a French West Indies island taken in 1759) and return Canada to France. Keeping Guadeloupe would give Britain a lucrative source of sugar; returning Canada would encourage British colonists in North America to remain dependent on the mother country for their security and would forestall any movement for American independence. In the end the British government decided to keep Canada, provide for the immediate security of the empire, and accept any longer-term risks of rebellion in America.

The conquest of Canada also left American and British veterans with very mixed feelings about each other. There were many colonists who emerged from the war admiring the British for their courage and discipline and celebrating their contributions to victory over New France. There were also British veterans who liked Americans and chose to remain in the colonies after the war. Yet for all the pleasure that Anglo-Americans took in what they had done together, each had enough unpleasant memories of the other to threaten imperial ties. Americans remembered British officers as haughty and merciless—unwilling to consult provincials, careless of their rights and interests, and contemptuous of them as soldiers. Having gone to war expecting to be instructed rather than coerced into their duties and thinking they were part of a Protestant crusade, provincials were repelled by British military justice and godlessness. The British who had made unprecedented efforts to support the war were deeply offended by the indifference and selfishness of the colonists. It was not just that the colonists made poor soldiers—that they seemed dirty, undisciplined, poorly trained, and cowardly—but also that they refused to provide men and supplies, obstructed recruiting, denied quarters for regulars, engaged in profiteering, and traded with the enemy. Such mutual resentments did more than weaken imperial ties; they made each side more likely to underestimate the other and to resort to force as a way of settling future differences.

☆   ☆   ☆   ☆

Only fleetingly in the French and Indian War had warfare in the British colonies of North America come to resemble that in Europe. For 150 years before Wolfe faced Montcalm on the Plains of Abraham—while Europeans were surviving the Thirty Years' War, developing ever-larger professional armies, and attempting to limit violence—the British colonies of North America were waging primitive wars of conquest against their neighbors. In these destructive wars, the colonists relied mainly on unskilled militiamen to destroy or displace their enemies, on militiamen who were more effective burning crops, stores, and houses than skirmishing with elusive enemies in the wilderness. Although these wars could fall as heavily on civilians as on soldiers, the British colonists were rarely willing to accept the kind of discipline or to bear the costs required to create forces proficient in regular European warfare. Nor were they often willing to cooperate with other colonists or the British government in large-scale operations against the French and Spanish on their frontiers. Even when British regulars brought European military practices to the French and Indian War—to the siege of Louisbourg, the climactic battle on the Plains of Abraham, and the final offensive against Canada—the British had to alter their warfare to suit American conditions and habits. The British simplified their tactics to accommodate the densely wooded and difficult terrain of North America, eliminating cavalry, reducing their infantry from three ranks to two, and developing light infantry. They also adjusted their war aims, methods of raising men and supplies, and campaign plans to gain the help of colonists who wanted to conquer Canada without bearing the costs of or submitting to the regular military discipline required for so formidable a task. By the middle of the eighteenth century, the British colonists of North America were powerfully committed to their own undisciplined and yet decisive way of war.

SUGGESTED READINGS

Anderson, Fred. *A People's Army: Massachusetts Soldiers and Society in the Seven Years' War* (Chapel Hill: University of North Carolina Press, 1984).

Craven, Wesley Frank. *The Colonies in Transition, 1660–1713* (New York: Harper & Row Publishers, 1968).

———. *The Southern Colonies in the Seventeenth Century* (Baton Rouge: Louisiana State University Press, 1949).

Ferling, John E. *A Wilderness of Miseries: War and Warriors in Early America* (Westport: Greenwood Press, 1980).

Frégault, Guy. *Canada: the war of the conquest* (Toronto: Oxford University Press, 1969).

Graham, Gerald S. *Empire of the North Atlantic: The Maritime Struggle for North America* (Toronto: University of Toronto Press, 1950).

Leach, Douglas E. *Arms for Empire: A Military History of the British Colonies in North America, 1607–1763* (New York: Macmillan Co., 1973).

———. *Flintlock and Tomahawk, New England in King Philip's War* (New York: Macmillan Co., 1958).

———. *Roots of Conflict: British Armed Forces and Colonial Americans, 1677–1763* (Chapel Hill: University of North Carolina Press, 1986).

Long, J. C. *Lord Jeffery Amherst* (New York: Macmillan Co., 1933).

Morgan, Edmund S. *American Slavery American Freedom* (New York: W. W. Norton & Co. [1975]).

Pargellis, Stanley M. *Lord Loudoun in North America* (New Haven, Conn.: Yale University Press, 1933).

Richter, Daniel K. *The Ordeal of the Longhouse: The Peoples of the Iroquois League in the Era of European Colonization* (Chapel Hill: University of North Carolina Press, 1992).

Russell, Peter E. "Redcoats in the Wilderness: British Officers and Irregular Warfare in Europe and America, 1740 to 1760," *William and Mary Quarterly* (October 1978), 629–652.

Schutz, John A. *William Shirley: King's Governor of Massachusetts* (Chapel Hill: University of North Carolina Press, 1961).

Shea, William L. *The Virginia Militia in the Seventeenth Century* (Baton Rouge: Louisiana State University Press, 1983).

Shy, John. *A People Numerous and Armed* (New York: Oxford University Press, 1976).

Stacey, C. P. *Quebec 1759: The Siege and the Battle* (New York: Macmillan Co., 1959).

Titus, James. *The Old Dominion at War: Society, Politics, and Warfare in Late Colonial Virginia* (Columbia: University of South Carolina Press, 1991).

Vaughan, Alden T. *American Genesis: Captain John Smith and the Founding of Virginia* (Boston: Little, Brown & Co., 1975).

———. "Pequots and Puritans: The Causes of the War of 1637," *William and Mary Quarterly* (April 1964), 255–269.

Washburn, Wilcomb E. *The Governor and the Rebel: A History of Bacon's Rebellion in Virginia* (Chapel Hill: University of North Carolina Press, 1957).

Waugh, W. T. *James Wolfe: Man and Soldier* (Montreal: L. Carrier & Co., 1928).

Webster, J. Clarence. *The Journal of Jeffery Amherst: 1758 to 1763* (Toronto: Ryerson Press [1931]).

Willson, Beckles. *The Life and Letters of James Wolfe* (London: W. Heinemann, 1909).

5

THE WAR FOR AMERICAN INDEPENDENCE, 1775-1783: THE PEOPLE AT WAR

The Beginnings:
The Militia's War

Strategies for a
Revolutionary War

The Saratoga Campaign:
A Conventional Interlude

A Revolution Within a World
War: Relying on the People
in Arms

The Revolution Preserved:
Unconventional and
Conventional Warfare
in the South, 1780–1783

The War for American Independence was a complex, widespread, and destructive war. It was more than the struggle of thirteen North American colonies for independence from the British Empire, more even than a series of concurrent struggles within those colonies between supporters of the rebellion and of the British government. Once European states intervened on the side of the colonists, the War for American Independence spread throughout the world, from North America to the West Indies and Central America, to the English Channel and the Mediterranean Sea, and to South Africa, India, and the East Indies. In North America, where fighting took place in what would become twenty-seven of the new United States and three Canadian provinces, there were more than 1,500 engagements in eight years. Rebellious colonists, supported at times by their European allies, opposed forces loyal to the British crown—

regular soldiers and seamen, loyal colonists, and Indians—in fighting that claimed the lives of more than 25,000 Americans (0.9 percent of the population in 1780). Indeed, the War for American Independence remains after more than two centuries the second most deadly war per capita in the history of the United States.

Because the War for American Independence was a revolutionary war, it was far different from the limited wars of mid-eighteenth-century Europe. In America both sides understood from the beginning that they were fighting for the allegiance of a people and for the destruction or preservation of one state and the creation of another. Throughout the war, the British argued that they fought to protect loyal colonists from the tyranny of a few ambitious rebels. Thus they tried various strategies: intimidating the rebels with a show of force, combining force and persuasion to break the rebellion without alienating a majority of the colonists, and, eventually, enlisting the support of loyalists in a gradual and cumulative restoration of royal government. The rebels, conversely, had to defeat the British and control the loyalists without losing popular support or destroying the republican principles for which they fought. Hoping to win without having to create the kind of regular army that might deprive them of their liberties, they tried at first to rely on inspired citizen soldiers—unskilled militiamen—to defeat the British and gain a redress of their grievances. But those who had to lead American forces against the British to sustain the revolution and emerging claims to independence, soon saw that unskilled citizen soldiers were rarely a match for regulars. Because the American people remained apprehensive of their own Continental army and unwilling to support it adequately, American commanders had to pursue more evasive and delaying strategies and to rely more on militiamen than they wished—even after the Continental army became a skilled fighting force and France entered the war. Finally, because of their continued dependence on militiamen and partisans, American commanders learned to simplify marching and firing, to command more by persuasion and instruction than by coercion, and to integrate militiamen and regulars—occasionally even riflemen and musketeers—in effective tactical dispositions. By enlisting the support of the people and adopting simplified tactics, both sides in the War for American Independence were departing from the conventions of mid-eighteenth-century European warfare and anticipating changes that would appear more dramatically with the French Revolution.

The Beginnings: The Militia's War

At the beginning of the War for American Independence each side hoped to prevail with minimal force. The British government, assuming that the rebellion in its American colonies was the work of a few ambitious men and that its professional soldiers could easily disperse colonial militiamen, hoped to end the rebellion with little more than a show of force. Leaders of colonial resistance, conversely, believed that inspired patriot militia could successfully resist professional soldiers and persuade the British government to redress American grievances. It was not just that the colonists valued inspiration above discipline but also that they were unwilling to rely on long-serving soldiers to do their fighting, unwilling to create a standing army that might become as destructive of their liberties as any forces of the king. Thus at the beginning of the war, a small army of British regulars stood against American militia and short-term volunteers in circumstances that often favored the unskilled colonists.

From Lexington and Concord to Bunker Hill

In the winter of 1775, after more than a decade of quarreling with its American colonists over taxes and political rights, the British government decided to use force to sustain its authority in Massachusetts, the most disloyal of the colonies. The government ordered its commander-in-chief at Boston, General Thomas Gage, to break the spirit of rebellion by arresting leading colonists, confiscating military stores, and if necessary imposing martial law. Although Gage knew that the colonists had been preparing for months to meet force with force, he decided to assert British authority by sending 800 men to destroy a magazine at Concord, a village seventeen miles west of Boston.

This small force was to achieve far less than Gage had hoped. It marched on the night of April 18–19, exchanged fire early the next morning with seventy militiamen at Lexington, and proceeded to Concord to search for stores and to skirmish with other colonists. About noon the British began their march back to Boston, beset by increasing numbers of militiamen who attacked the flanks of their retiring column. So battered were the regulars by colonists converging on their line of march—by some 3,800 men from more than twenty-four Massachusetts towns—that the British might well have been destroyed had not a relief force of 1,000 men met them near Lexington and escorted them to Boston. Britain's first attempt at intimidating the colonists had clearly failed. Far from demonstrating the overwhelming superiority of British forces, the march to Concord had given the colonists a remarkably favorable opportunity to defeat professional soldiers, to use their inspired but undisciplined and uncoordinated militia with few of the risks that might have been expected in a formal eighteenth-century engagement. At a cost of ninety-five men killed, wounded, and missing (2.5 percent of their total) the colonists had inflicted 286 casualties on the British (16 percent).

Within two months the colonists created a second opportunity to fight on their own terms and to use their militia to their best advantage. News of Lexington and Concord had been received as a call to arms throughout the colonies. By mid-June there were 15,000 New England militia camped around Boston, a loosely organized army under General Artemas Ward of Massachusetts. These New England troops, short on artillery, gunpowder, food, and above all, training, were incapable of storming Boston, now held by about 6,500 regulars. But they were able on the night of June 16 to occupy and fortify positions on Charlestown Neck, which commanded Boston from the north, from across the Charles River. Gage could not ignore what the Americans had done. He had to find a way to force them from Charlestown Neck before they could place artillery there, making Boston untenable. He rejected as too hazardous a plan for trapping the Americans on Charlestown Neck, for putting his troops between the rebels on the Neck and the main body of their forces encamped at Cambridge. He decided instead to land his troops on the easternmost point of the Neck and by advancing to the west drive the rebels back to the mainland. In making this decision, he committed his men to attacking a well-entrenched enemy— to doing precisely what would most likely allow the undisciplined colonists to succeed against his men.

In carrying out Gage's plan, the British did try to avoid a frontal assault on the American works. Major General William Howe, commander of the troops sent to drive the Americans from Charlestown Neck, planned

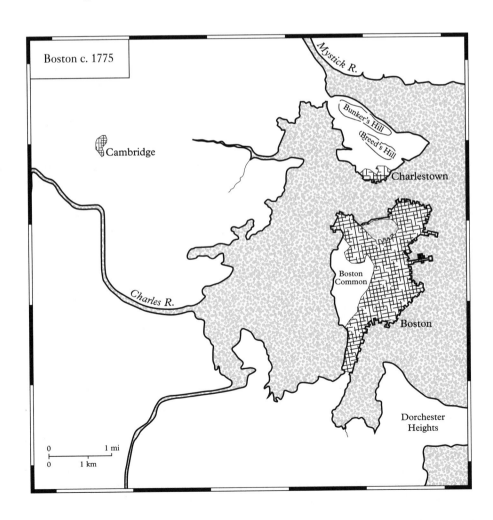

Boston c. 1775

an oblique attack; that is, he planned to land on the east end of the Neck and move against the American lines in echelon, his best troops somewhat advanced on his right flank (along the Mystick River which bounded the Neck on the north) and the remainder, slightly refused, in his center and on his left flank (opposite Breed's Hill, where most of the Americans were dug in). His elite light infantry would attempt to break through the rebel left and take the rest of their forces in flank and rear before the British center and left became heavily engaged. He delayed his attack until mid-afternoon, when he had assembled more than 2,000 men on Charlestown Neck. Then, with his field artillery pushed forward and his infantry in three ranks, he began the attack.

It soon became apparent that Howe's light infantry would be unable to break through the American left on the Mystick shore and that his artillery was ineffective against fieldworks. He might well have reconsidered his plan, but he allowed his attack to continue, to degenerate into a costly frontal assault. His infantry continued to advance across open rising ground toward the center of the American lines. British discipline was no match for the massed fire of the colonists secure in their earthworks. Twice Howe and his men went forward against Breed's Hill; twice they failed. A third bayonet attack succeeded only because Howe had received 400 fresh troops and because the Americans had run out of ammunition and were not properly supported by additional American troops gathered to the west on Bunker's Hill. This engagement, known as the Battle of Bunker Hill, was a nominal British victory. The British did succeed in driving the Americans from Charlestown Neck. Yet they did so at such a cost (the British lost 1,054 killed and wounded or 44 percent of the 2,400 men engaged; the Americans, 441 or 29 percent of their 1,500) as to fail to achieve their strategic purpose. Bunker Hill clearly did not serve to intimidate the rebels, and it left British commanders wary of the costly battles that many would think necessary to end the war quickly and decisively.

Preparing for a Wider War, June 1775 to July 1776

For at least nine months after the Battle of Bunker Hill neither side was able to do more than skirmish with the other. Each knew that it would have to build a larger army and prepare for a more difficult war. However successful the Americans had been relying on untrained militia at Lexington and Concord and Bunker Hill, they realized they would need more and better troops to expel the British from Boston and protect other parts of America. They were not yet ready to consider creating a standing army—one of long-serving professional soldiers who might become as destructive of American liberties as British regulars were seen to be. Americans still wanted to rely on an army of volunteers, serving for six months or a year. Such short-term volunteers would not acquire the discipline and training of regulars. But with simplified tactics and with courage inspired by a religious faith and a sense of America's destiny, they would be able to defeat the British regulars; and they

George Washington commanded the Continental army throughout the War for American Independence. His inspired leadership was essential to preserving the army and winning the independence of the new nation.

would not jeopardize American liberties. The British, for their part, knew that intimidation had failed and that they would need much larger regular forces to destroy the rebel armies, overturn congresses and committees, and restore royal government to North America. They knew as well that the British army had no such forces and that they would have either to expand the army—a costly and lengthy process—or hire foreign troops. They decided to hire foreigners, thereby committing themselves to a measure that would also take time and that would have its own political and military costs.

Even before the Battle of Bunker Hill, the Continental Congress had begun to support and control the militiamen assembled around Boston. As important as any decision that Congress made toward the creation of a Continental army—an army to defend the interests of the thirteen colonies against the British government—was its selection of George Washington as commander-in-chief. Congress saw in Washington—a tall, spare, and impressive man of forty-three—an experienced soldier, a moderate but firm opponent of British taxation, a prominent Virginian who could help bind the

South to New England, and above all, a person whom they could entrust with power. He was, as Congress anticipated, a remarkably good choice. During the Seven Years' War he had commanded militiamen on the frontiers of Virginia, learning not only how to lead his countrymen in battle and to maintain their morale during periods of inactivity but also how to deal with public officials who regularly neglected their soldiers. Although he rose to command Virginia forces and emerged from the war with his reputation intact, Washington failed to satisfy his ambition for military fame and a regular commission in the British army. In the ensuing years of peace he did find increasing contentment as a respected Virginia landowner—as a justice of the peace, vestryman, and member of the House of Burgesses. By 1770 he was also a staunch opponent of British taxation and in 1774–1775 was one of seven Virginia representatives in the Continental Congress. He impressed all who met him in Philadelphia as a man who had the energy, experience, and presence to create an army out of enthusiastic and unruly citizens; the good judgment to preserve that army; and the commitment to republican ideals as well as the control of his own ambitions to keep himself and his army subordinate to the will of Congress.

Washington assumed command of the Continental army at Cambridge, Massachusetts, on July 2, 1775. During the following year he devoted his energies to establishing an effective army, preserving that army against expiring enlistments, and resisting demands that he attack the British before his men were prepared for battle. He began by trying to bring some order and discipline to the 14,000 men camped around Boston: introducing distinctions between officers and men; organizing the army into regiments, brigades, and divisions; and attempting—with little success at first—to provide uniforms for men from different colonies. Although discipline improved, Washington was unable during the summer and fall of 1775 to get enough gunpowder and artillery to attack Boston. Congress, the American people, and even the army became impatient with his refusal to act—to do more than skirmish with the British and cut off their supplies of food and fuel. By December he was struggling to keep even a semblance of an army at Boston. Most enlistments expired on December 31, and Washington found it nearly impossible to persuade men to reenlist while Congress was attempting to create truly continental units (the rank and file did not like serving under officers from other colonies) and while troops at Boston were suffering from shortages of fuel and clothing as well as from inactivity. Not until late February 1776 did Washington have the men, ammunition, and artillery to consider attacking Boston. Even then his officers rejected an assault across the frozen bay, preferring instead to seize Dorchester Heights in hopes of provoking another Bunker Hill. When his troops did succeed in occupying Dorchester Heights, in placing their artillery within range of most of Boston and its harbor, the British decided to give up the town rather than risk a frontal assault on American earthworks. On March 17 the British sailed for Halifax to prepare for a summer offensive against New York. Washington and the Continental army went south to face sterner tests of their military skills.

Strategies for a Revolutionary War

In the campaign of 1776 both sides developed strategies for the unconventional purpose of winning the support of the people. Although the British government was more interested in breaking the rebellion than in cultivating the good will of the colonists, the British commanders-in-chief had different priorities: they shaped their strategies to promote a negotiated settlement and a lasting restoration of the British Empire. Thus they concentrated throughout 1776 on recovering territory so as to minimize casualties, create the impression of British invincibility, and encourage the colonists to accept royal government. Washington too shaped his strategy to gain and keep the support of the American people, to sustain the rebellion even at the risk of losing his army. Thus he defended the middle colonies against greatly superior British forces and used his disintegrating army to attack enemy outposts.

Plans and Preparations for 1776

The British had been forced from Boston sooner than they wished. But they had long intended to begin the restoration of royal government at New York, using it as a base from which to conquer New England and destroy the Continental army. Since news of Bunker Hill reached England in the summer of 1775, the government had intended to shift the war from New England to the middle colonies, from the most disloyal to some of the more loyal of the American colonies. It also agreed to increase its forces significantly and to appoint General William Howe as commander-in-chief. Although Howe received permission in early October to leave Boston, he decided to wait until spring when he would have reinforcements and enough transports to move his army. While he waited—at Boston and then at Halifax—he and the ministry agreed on a plan for ending the rebellion. He would first capture New York City, occupy the Hudson River Valley, take Rhode Island, and send detachments to ravage the coasts from New York to Maine. Then he would push north along the Hudson to join with forces from Canada in completing the encirclement of New England and in attacking the frontiers of Massachusetts. In carrying out these plans, Howe also hoped to lure the Continental army into a decisive battle, which he now thought "the most effectual Means to terminate this expensive War."

Yet before opening the campaign of 1776 at New York, Howe modified his plans. He reached New York from Nova Scotia on June 25, set up his headquarters on Staten Island, and began waiting for the reinforcements needed to attack the rebels entrenched around New York City—on Manhattan, Long Island, and the New Jersey side of the Hudson River. Since it took seven weeks for these reinforcements to straggle in, Howe had many opportunities to reconnoiter American positions and discuss his plans for ending the rebellion with his older brother, Admiral Richard Lord Howe, who arrived on July 12 to command the British navy in American waters. Both

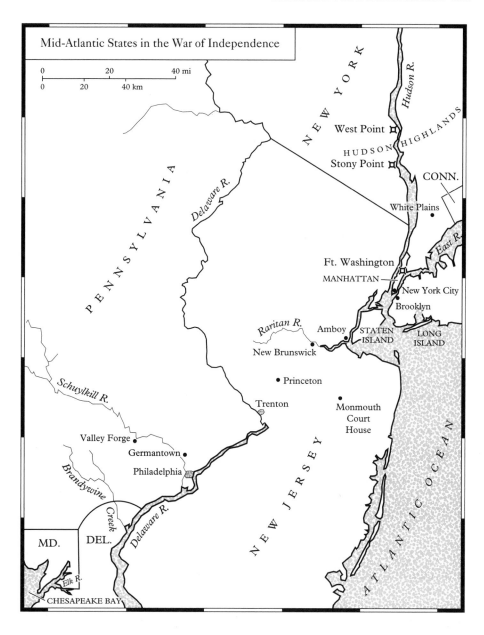

Mid-Atlantic States in the War of Independence

Howes were distinguished officers; both had served in North America during the Seven Years' War; and both, having strong personal ties with the colonies, favored a negotiated settlement of Anglo-American differences. Although they had persuaded the British government to name them peace commissioners as well as commanders-in-chief, they had been unable to get authority to conduct meaningful negotiations, to do more than discuss grievances after the colonies had surrendered. Even so, Lord Howe was determined to try to negotiate or, at least, to avoid the kind of fighting that would permanently alienate the colonists. Failing in his initial efforts to open negotiations (he arrived just after the colonies had declared their independence), he did persuade his brother to modify his strategy. By mid-August General Howe had put aside his hopes of destroying the Continental army in a decisive battle and was concentrating instead on ending the rebellion through a gradual recovery of territory. This new plan promised to create the impression of British invincibility without inflicting heavy casualties on either side—just the use of force that the Howes hoped would encourage the colonists to accept a negotiated settlement and that would spare the British the higher risks and heavier losses of a general engagement.

Like the Howes, George Washington and his generals shaped their strategy to suit political as well as military considerations. Washington felt obligated to defend New York City because Congress and the American people expected him to and because he thought American morale would suffer if he did not. Washington also believed that he should defend New York City to deny the British an ice-free port and to protect American communications along and across the Hudson River, to keep open the main inland routes between the middle colonies and New England. Yet to defend New York City, which occupied the southern tip of Manhattan at the confluence of the Hudson and East rivers, he would have to risk losing his army; he would have to divide his forces among Manhattan, Long Island, and New Jersey in the face of a superior British fleet and army. Thus he worked from mid-April to late August preparing to risk his army defending what many thought indefensible. Assuming the British would strike first on Manhattan, he took particular care in fortifying New York City. He also fortified Brooklyn Heights, which lay across the East River from the city, and the mouths of the Hudson and East rivers. Should the British succeed in taking Brooklyn and placing artillery there, they could make the city untenable; or should they send transports up either the Hudson or East River and land troops on upper Manhattan, they might well capture both the city and its garrison. By August 1776 Washington had over 120 guns and 28,000 men in these separate and vulnerable posts.

Washington's army was remarkably similar in size, composition, organization, and doctrine to the one that was assembling under General Howe. Unlike European armies of the day, both armies at New York in 1776 had been shaped to suit North America and the peculiarities of a revolutionary war. The 28,000 American and 24,000 British troops at New York in August 1776 were primarily infantrymen supported by detachments of light artillery and a few engineers. The basic unit in each army was the infantry regiment (established at 608 men for the Continental army and 477 for the British); and the basic weapons were muskets, bayonets, and light field guns. Because Americans had served with the British in the Seven Years' War and had studied their manuals, books, and histories, both armies intended to fight in much the same way. Americans would use a simplified version of British drill and manual of arms, and both armies would employ what were by European standards relatively simple tactics. Without cavalry to complicate their forces, commanders on both sides would dispense with combined-arms warfare and rely instead on either two or three ranks of infantry supported by light field guns to generate firepower and on columns to gain speed and shock. Neither army had a clear strategic doctrine. Anglo-Americans had no clear preference between the warfare of Saxe and of Frederick the Great—between sieges, skirmishing, and maneuvers on the one hand and decisive engagements on the other. Moreover, commanders in both armies knew that the War for American Independence required strategies that would serve a very unconventional purpose, strategies that would gain the support of the people.

Yet for all the similarities between the opposing forces, the British were much better prepared for war than the Americans. It was not just that the British had the close support of a powerful fleet—30 warships, 400 transports, and thousands of skilled seamen—but especially that the British army was a more experienced, better led, more thoroughly disciplined and trained, and more unified fighting force than the American. British senior officers had seen more of war and had had more opportunities to prove their tactical skills than their American counterparts. Howe knew what his generals had done while commanding regiments in the Seven Years' War; Washington was just beginning to appraise generals imposed on him by Congress and a variety of state governments. Similarly, the British common soldier of 1776 was on average thirty years old with ten years of service in his regiment; the American, twenty years old with less than a year's service. American units varied greatly in quality—from the best disciplined of the Continental and state forces to the rawest militia. Yet even the best of the American troops in 1776 seemed no more than innocent boys by comparison with the regulars of George III.

The Battle of Long Island: Tactics Serving Strategy

By late August 1776 the Howes were at last prepared to use force to end the rebellion. General Howe clearly understood how vulnerable the Americans were at New York, but he rejected a proposal for landing his army on the northern end of Manhattan to trap and destroy the Continental army in New York City. He preferred instead to drive the Americans from the city with as little bloodshed as possible, creating the impression of British invincibility and encouraging the colonists to put down their arms and accept a negotiated settlement. He would shift his army from Staten Island to Long Island, take Brooklyn Heights by siege or intimidation, place his own artillery there, and force Washington to give up New York. He did not seek or expect a general engagement on Long Island. Even after putting 15,000 troops ashore at Gravesend on August 22, and after finding that the Americans were prepared to defend the Heights of Guana which lay across all roads leading from Gravesend to Brooklyn, Howe still hoped to avoid a destructive battle. He ordered another 5,000 men to join him on Long Island and spent five days probing American positions, looking for a way to approach Brooklyn without having to attack the Americans on the densely wooded slopes of the Heights of Guana or at any of the well-defended passes near New York Bay. Finally, he decided to try to turn the extreme left flank of the American army. He would lead 10,000 of his men on a night's march

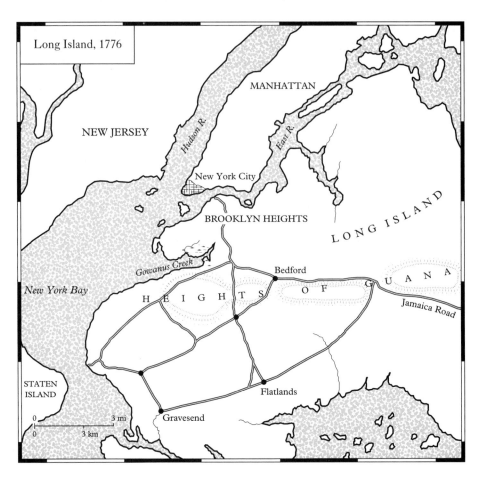

Long Island, 1776

that would take them six miles east of New York Bay, through the Heights of Guana on the Jamaica Road, and into the rear of the American defenders. Thus Howe's efforts to take New York without serious fighting and to avoid a frontal assault on the Heights precipitated the first general engagement of the Revolutionary War.

The British won the ensuing Battle of Long Island because they performed well and because chance, numbers, and, above all, inexperience worked against the Americans. Washington decided to defend the Heights of Guana in hopes of delaying or even defeating the British. He knew he could not hold Brooklyn long against a regular siege; and the Heights, whose overgrown slopes rose from forty to eighty feet above the Long Island plain, offered many strong defensive positions. Yet as the Heights stretched some ten miles to the east of New York Bay, it was naive of Washington to think he could hold such an extensive position with no more than the 3,500 men he deployed there on August 26 (he had another 4,000 at Brooklyn). He was able to put respectable forces at the three passes nearest New York Bay, and he could be fairly confident that Howe would not try to advance through the intervening woods. But he risked the security of his left flank—indeed the safety of all his forces on the Heights of Guana—on five young and inexperienced officers sent to watch the Jamaica Road. Those officers, unwary of Howe's patrols, were captured; and Howe was then able to lead 10,000 men, undetected, through the Jamaica pass at dawn on August 27. Once clear of the pass, Howe rested and fed his men before advancing against the rear of the American units defending the Heights. By 10:00 A.M. his remaining forces had begun diversionary attacks on the front of those same American units. Caught as they were between converging and superior British forces, most Americans surrendered or fled toward Brooklyn. By two in the afternoon the battle had ended. Howe had succeeded in turning the rebels from strong positions without heavy losses (the British suffered 370 casualties, or 1.9 percent of those engaged; the Americans, 1,000, or 28.6 percent). If Howe did not allow his men to exploit their victory—to pursue the Americans into their works at Brooklyn—it was because he was unwilling to risk further losses when he could expect to capture by siege all who remained on Long Island.

That the Battle of Long Island was not more decisive, that it did not destroy more of the Continental army, was in part the result of Howe's intentions; but it was also the result of the nature of the fighting on August 27 and of Washington's subsequent actions and good luck. The north slope of the Heights of Guana with its woods, hedges, small cultivated fields, narrow roads, and rolling terrain clearly favored the Americans, providing cover for men on the defense or in flight and inhibiting those who were attacking or pursuing. Moreover, Howe's insistence that his men use their bayonets to drive the enemy from this difficult country had the effect of tiring and disordering soldiers who had marched all night and who had trouble keeping up with their own units to say nothing of overtaking the fleeing rebels. Finally, because British forces were converging, they had to attack with some caution, taking care not to engage their own men or to mistake Americans for their own; and some Americans did fight well enough to cover the retreat of their comrades. These circumstances as well as Howe's reluctance to press the rebels help to explain why the fighting on August 27 was not more decisive. But it took Howe's continuing interest in conciliation and Washington's considerable leadership and good luck to keep the Americans who remained at Brooklyn on August 28 from becoming prisoners.

Immediately after the battle Howe concentrated on opening a siege of Brooklyn Heights; he took no special measures to prevent the defenders from evacuating their works. Washington at first sent reinforcements to bolster the morale of the garrison at Brooklyn. But seeing that his men were dejected by their defeat and that rain on August 28 and 29 had spoiled their arms and ammunition, he decided to give up Brooklyn to save his army. On the night of August 29–30, he carried out a very skillful and courageous retreat favored by fair winds and a thick morning fog. The British took only three of the nearly 10,000 Americans who had held Brooklyn in the days after the battle.

From Manhattan to Trenton and Princeton: Strategies of Persuasion

Although capturing Long Island did not end the American rebellion, the Howes persisted through the late summer and autumn of 1776 in their strategy of recovering territory to encourage a negotiated peace. Congress did agree after the Battle of Long Island to send representatives to a peace conference with Lord Howe, but when Howe acknowledged that he could offer no concessions until the colonies had surrendered, the conference collapsed. The Howes were disappointed but did not alter their strategy. Rejecting proposals and ignoring opportunities for trapping the Continental army on Manhattan, they executed a series of turning movements, through the East River and Long Island Sound, that forced Washington to abandon New York City and all of Manhattan except Fort Washington at its northern end. In November, after driving the Continental army beyond White Plains, Howe turned south to capture Fort Washington, invade New Jersey, and send an expedition to take Rhode Island. Although he won no decisive battles, his success in limited engagements and in evicting the Americans from New York, New Jersey, and Rhode Island created such an impression of British invincibility, that many Americans considered a reconciliation with the crown. Lord Howe's proclamation of November 30, offering pardon to anyone who within sixty days would swear to obey the king and to remain at peace, attracted some 5,000 subscribers in New York and New Jersey. By mid-December when General Howe sent his troops into winter quarters in villages across New Jersey and at New York City and Newport, the Continental army and the rebellion seemed to be disintegrating. The Howes had missed opportunities for trapping and destroying American forces—the best opportunities that the British would have in the Revolutionary War—yet by mid-December the Howes' strategy of restoring royal government with a minimum of bloodshed and risk seemed close to success.

Washington, thoroughly discouraged by the failure of his army to stand against regulars and by the impending expiration of enlistments for 1776, was considering desperate measures. Congress had tried to help improve the discipline and training of the Continental army, authorizing harsher punishments as well as enlistments for the duration of the war. But these measures, taken in late summer, had as yet done little to make Continentals a match for regulars. By mid-December, defeats and expiring enlistments were threatening to destroy the army and the rebellion. In desperation, Washington decided to act before all his troops had gone home, to attack British outposts in New Jersey. Because the British had scattered their army in small garrisons from the Raritan to the Delaware, Washington hoped he would be able to use surprise and a rapid concentration of force to offset the relative weakness of his troops—to gain a superiority of numbers and firepower that would give his citizen soldiers a chance to defeat Howe's professionals, push them back from the Delaware, and restore American morale.

Although his ensuing attack on the Hessian garrison at Trenton did not go according to plan, Washington was able to create circumstances that clearly favored his men. About dusk on December 25, he led 2,400 men with eighteen cannon across the Delaware some nine miles northwest of Trenton. Two other American detachments were to take part in a complicated attack next morning on the 1,400–man Hessian garrison. Although the weather was so severe that it prevented the other American detachments from crossing the Delaware and kept Washington from reaching Trenton by dawn, he did manage to attack the garrison simultaneously from two sides about 7:45 A.M. The Hessian commander had posted pickets on the roads leading to Trenton, and those pickets did provide a few minutes' warning of the attack. But the Hessians had not taken care to fortify the town or to celebrate Christmas with moderation. By the time they turned out and formed lines of battle across the principal streets, by the time their six field pieces were in action, the town was filled with Americans. The Americans had the advantage of surprise, numbers, and artillery; and when the battle degenerated into a house-to-house struggle, the Americans were able to use initiative and inspiration to overcome their opponents' superior training and discipline. They soon swept the streets and broke Hessian resistance. By 9:00 A.M., Washington's desperate effort had been repaid with a most important victory. At a cost of four men wounded, the Americans had captured 948 Hessians and killed or wounded another 114. A week later Washington again surprised the British, slipping away from 5,500 regulars who threatened to crush his men against the Delaware and defeating the enemy's garrison at Princeton. These victories not only restored Americans' confidence in Washington, the Continental army, and the rebellion but also spoiled the Howes' hopes for a negotiated restoration of royal government. The British now withdrew from all of New Jersey except New Brunswick and Amboy on the Raritan River.

The Saratoga Campaign:
A Conventional Interlude

Washington's victories at Trenton and Princeton disrupted British and American planning for 1777 and helped make a conventional campaign along the Hudson River unusually decisive. Howe, stung by defeats in New Jersey, became preoccupied with invading Pennsylvania. That preoccupation and his continued interest in promoting a negotiated peace not only shaped what Washington would do in 1777 but also left another British army to advance south from Canada, virtually unsupported from New York. The second British army under General John Burgoyne would be conducted in a cautiously conventional way. Much as Saxe had sought to recover the Low Countries in the War of the Austrian Succession, Burgoyne sought to extinguish the rebellion: he would advance along the waterways from Canada to New York, relying on a heavy siege train to overcome American fortifications, avoiding destructive battles, and gaining possession of the principal overland routes across the Hudson so as to isolate and conquer New England. Burgoyne's strategy was not designed to conciliate the colonists, merely to end their resistance. But Burgoyne had the misfortune of being unsupported and of eliciting a cautiously conventional strategic response. The Americans blocked his line of advance, cut off his supplies, and waited for shortages to bring a most decisive end to the campaign.

The Effects of Trenton and Princeton

British failures at the end of 1776 blighted their ensuing campaign. General Howe, who felt acutely responsible for the strategy that had led to defeats at Trenton and Princeton, was eager to show that he had been justified in extending his posts to the Delaware, that the people of Pennsylvania were, as he had assumed, loyal to the crown, and that his efforts toward conciliation were not illusory. He planned, therefore, to invade Pennsylvania in 1777. He would concentrate on recovering territory, giving loyalists a chance to assert themselves and encouraging rebels to accept a restoration of royal government. Although he knew that he would be expected to cooperate with British forces advancing south across Lake Champlain from Canada, he refused to do more to support that offensive than provide a detachment on the lower Hudson—possibly to open the Highlands and act in favor of the Canadian army. But if he refused to be diverted from an invasion of Pennsylvania and if he seemed committed to a strategy of recovering territory so as to encourage a negotiated peace, he also talked repeatedly of needing a decisive victory over the Continental army to end the rebellion.

Just as Howe's plans for 1777 were contradictory, so too was his conduct of the campaign. He remained committed to an invasion of Pennsylvania, but he seemed incapable of acting promptly or of deciding clearly whether destroying the Continental army or recovering territory would best complement his hopes for peace. He stayed in winter quarters through much of the spring, giving a variety of reasons for delaying the opening of the campaign and rejecting all criticisms of his plan for going to Pennsylvania by sea. Yet before he embarked, he spent the last half of June trying without success to lure Washington into a decisive battle in New Jersey. He then reverted to a strategy of recovering territory. Although remaining on the Hudson and cooperating with British forces from Canada would have pleased the ministry and might also have forced Washington into a general engagement, Howe embarked for Pennsylvania in late July. His subsequent decision to proceed by way of the Chesapeake Bay, rather than by the Delaware River, seemed to confirm his renewed preference for recovering territory. But once ashore in Pennsylvania—and discovering that the colonists were not as loyal as he had hoped and that Washington would fight for Philadelphia—Howe again sought a decisive battle. He defeated Washington at Brandywine Creek on September 11, but after failing to exploit his victory, he devoted most of the autumn to taking and securing Philadelphia. Only briefly in December did he seek another battle.

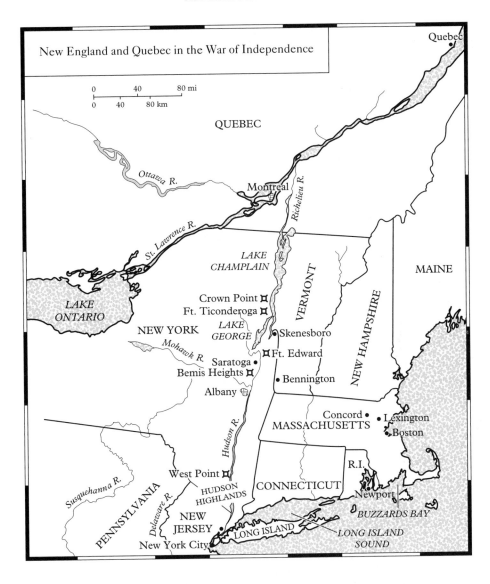

New England and Quebec in the War of Independence

Howe's response to Trenton and Princeton not only blighted his own performance in 1777 but also jeopardized another British army, the army ordered south from Canada under General John Burgoyne. Like Howe, Burgoyne had distinguished himself as a regimental commander in the Seven Years' War and had been sent to Boston in 1775. But when Howe took the army from Boston to New York in 1776, Burgoyne went to Canada to serve as second-in-command to General Guy Carleton. Carleton, who had been expected to proceed across Lake Champlain to join Howe along the Hudson, had been so delayed by shortages and by building boats to clear the lake of rebels that he got no farther than Crown Point in 1776. During the following winter when Burgoyne went to England to discuss plans for

1777, he also managed to blame Carleton for delays in 1776 and to suggest that he, Burgoyne, had the energy needed to force his way across Lake Champlain in time to join Howe for a decisive attack on the frontiers of New England in 1777. King George III and his ministers were persuaded; they ordered Carleton to send Burgoyne with an army of 7,000 regulars supported by Canadians and Indians across Lake Champlain to Albany—to join Howe and to follow his instructions for the remainder of the campaign of 1777. The ministry also told Carleton to send a second force of 675 regulars with Canadians and Indians to join Howe via Lake Ontario, the Mohawk River, and the Hudson. But the ministry, which had already approved Howe's plans for going to Pennsylvania by sea, never did order Howe to co-operate with Burgoyne. It merely sent Howe a copy of its orders to Carleton and told Carleton and Burgoyne to write to Howe for instructions. So it was that the ministry gave Howe the latitude to indulge his preoccupation with Pennsylvania, to destroy any prospect for cooperation between British armies in 1777, and to make Burgoyne's determination to force his way to Albany truly dangerous.

Unlike the British, the Americans clearly benefited from their victories at Trenton and Princeton. But if those victories restored confidence in the Continental army and the revolution, they did not bring Washington the large number of long-term recruits he needed for the campaign of 1777. Immediately after Princeton, Washington was able to use the army and local militia to regain control of New Jersey, to force Americans who had accepted the Howes' offer of pardon to renounce their oaths of allegiance to the king, and to keep the British from drawing food and fodder from the countryside. Whatever their weaknesses in a formal engagement, Continentals and militiamen were quite successful during the winter and spring of 1777 in skirmishing with British foraging parties, inflicting casualties and forcing the British to depend primarily on the British Isles for their supplies. But victories at Trenton and Princeton and success against foragers did not fill the ranks of the Continental army. Americans, knowing that many soldiers had died of illness in 1776 and that bounties for enlistments would probably increase with the demand for men, were reluctant to volunteer. Congress voted to raise an army of 75,760 in 1777; and state and local governments resorted to a variety of measures to fill their quotas: offering bounties in money and land, adopting conscription, and allowing wealthy citizens to hire substitutes. But these measures raised no more than a third of the men Congress wanted, and without large numbers of men serving for three years or for the duration of the war, Washington could not build an effective army. Not until 1778 would he have the substantial training of long-serving men to create a dependable army.

Notwithstanding his difficulties in building an army, Washington's victories at Trenton and Princeton had so raised American expectations of the army as to force him toward a more aggressive strategy than he thought wise. During the winter and spring of 1777, he and his principal aides explained repeatedly to Congress that the Continental army should avoid a general engagement, that it should concentrate instead on controlling loyalists and preventing the British from getting supplies from America. When members of Congress deplored this strategy and encouraged Washington to attack British posts in New Jersey, he replied that he did not have enough disciplined troops to risk an attack; and when in late June 1777 the British tried to draw him into battle, he refused. Not until Howe threatened Philadelphia, the largest city in the United States and an important source of supplies for the Continental army, did he feel compelled to fight to satisfy Congress and preserve American morale. In September he blocked Howe's advance on the city and suffered a nearly disastrous defeat at the Battle of Brandywine. In October, after the city had fallen, he tried to surprise the British camp at Germantown, but his plan was too complicated and the enemy too vigilant for his inexperienced men. Thus Washington was pressed to undertake what he considered imprudent. Those American commanders who opposed the British advancing from Canada were farther from Congress and somewhat freer than Washington to remain on the defensive—to employ the cautious strategy needed to give inexperienced troops a chance to defeat a regular British army.

Toward Saratoga

John Burgoyne reached Quebec on May 6, 1777, to take command of the army that he was to lead from Quebec to Albany. Whatever the Americans might do to resist him on Lake Champlain or along the upper Hudson, Burgoyne knew that he faced a formidable problem in logistics. He proposed to move an army of nearly 9,000 men across more than 350 miles of rivers, lakes, and sparsely settled wilderness. Transporting, feeding, and supplying such a large force in the wilderness and maintaining an ever-lengthening line of communications with Quebec would consume a considerable part of his force. What made his task especially difficult was his insistence on an unusually large artillery and baggage train. The excess baggage was no more than an indulgence to his officers; the 138 guns were an expression of his determination to use firepower rather than men to drive Americans from their entrenchments, for Burgoyne had no intention of repeating the slaughter he had seen at Bunker Hill. Preparing transportation for this heavily equipped force delayed his departure from Quebec for more than a month. He did not embark on Lake Champlain until the third week in June or reach Crown Point (260 miles from Quebec) until July 1. Although he then moved forward rapidly to drive the Americans from Fort Ticonderoga and to reach Skenesboro at the head of Lake Champlain on July 9, he delayed two weeks at Skenesboro while assembling the horses, carts, and artillery he thought necessary to advance the next twenty miles overland to the Hudson. This delay allowed the rebels to regroup and place so many felled trees, broken bridges, and boulders in his way that he did not reach the Hudson at Fort Edward until July 29.

Once on the Hudson, Burgoyne was less than fifty miles from Albany, but he was also more than three hundred from Quebec, his primary source of supply. To go farther, to cross to the west bank of the Hudson and proceed to Albany, would mean giving up communications with Canada. He decided, therefore, to delay his advance until he had gathered the supplies and transportation needed to sustain his march to Albany. That delay would be far longer and more costly than he expected. He not only brought forward food, forage, ammunition, and heavy artillery from Canada by way of Lake Champlain and Lake George but also sent a detachment of 800 men under Lieutenant Colonel Friedrich Baum to collect horses, wagons, cattle, and provisions from a rebel magazine at Bennington, Vermont, some thirty-five miles southeast of Fort Edward. Baum set out on August 11, met resistance and asked for help on August 14, but was overwhelmed two days later at Bennington before help could arrive. Altogether, Baum and the 642 men sent to relieve him lost nearly 1,000 men killed, wounded, and captured in two fierce engagements with 2,000 New Hampshire and Vermont militiamen. (The Americans lost only 70 killed and wounded or 3.5 percent.)

Burgoyne now knew that Howe had embarked for Pennsylvania in late July and could not be expected at Albany. He also knew his army had been reduced to about 5,500 men. He might still have retired safely to Ticonderoga, yet having boasted that he would force his way to Albany and having been ordered to do so by Carleton and Howe, he decided to continue his advance to the south as soon as he had accumulated enough supplies to sustain his army for twenty-five days. On September 13, nearly seven weeks after reaching the Hudson, he left Fort Edward for Albany. Two days later, he crossed to the west bank of the Hudson, giving up his communications with Canada.

Once on the west bank, Burgoyne advanced cautiously. He kept to the main road along the river which gave him access to his supply boats. After three days and only six miles of marching, he learned that an American army was blocking his way to Albany, entrenched across the river road little more than five miles south at a place called Bemis Heights. The American army was at least as numerous as his own and was well dug in on rising ground behind a stream, its right flank on the Hudson and its left extending nearly a mile to the west of the river. Burgoyne was determined to force his way to Albany; he was equally determined to do so without sacrificing his army in a frontal assault on American lines. He decided, therefore, to advance toward the left flank of the American lines to see whether he might turn their position at Bemis Heights or occupy high ground that commanded that position from the west. He organized his army in three divisions: one of 1,100 men under General Riedesel to create a diversion by advancing close along the Hudson, a second of 1,100 under his own command to move against the center and left of the American line, and a third of 2,200 under General Fraser to pass to the west of the enemy works. On September 18 he moved his whole army to within two miles of Bemis Heights. At 10 A.M. the next day his three divisions advanced against the rebels.

The rebels had been preparing their works on Bemis Heights for more than a week before Burgoyne advanced to attack on September 19. They were well aware of his approach that morning, yet they had not agreed on how to meet his attack. Horatio Gates, commander of the northern army, had served as an officer in the British army for twenty-four years before resigning his commission in 1769. He then moved to Virginia, became an ardent patriot, and was appointed a brigadier general in the Continental army in 1775. For all his service in the mid-century wars, Gates was far better at organizing and training soldiers than at leading them in combat. He would have preferred to keep his relatively inexperienced men in their works on Bemis Heights and await Burgoyne's attack. His ambitious and aggressive second, Benedict Arnold, thought those inexperienced men would be more effective if they fought in the woods in front of their works where trees would give them cover and disrupt British linear formations, depriving the British of their advantages in disciplined use of muskets and bayonets. Arnold may also have believed that by advancing he would be able to keep the British from turning the American left flank. If the Americans did fight in front of their fortifications and were defeated, Arnold argued, they might at least fall back on their lines. If they awaited an attack at Bemis Heights and were then defeated, they would probably not be able to keep the British from reaching Albany.

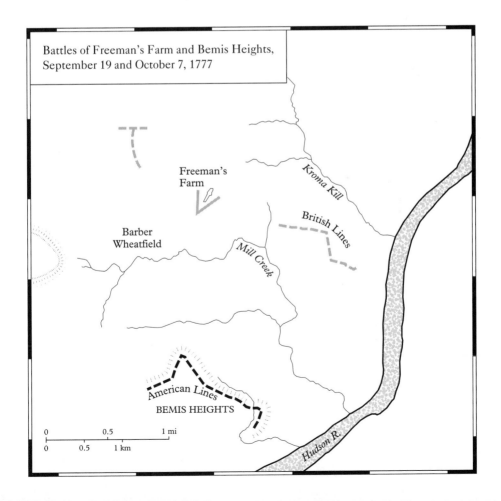

Battles of Freeman's Farm and Bemis Heights, September 19 and October 7, 1777

The Battles of Freeman's Farm and Bemis Heights

These conflicting ideas shaped the ensuing Battle of Freeman's Farm. Gates, commanding the right wing of his army, remained on Bemis Heights to await the British attack. He allowed his half of the army to be almost completely immobilized by General Riedesel's diversionary advance along the Hudson. Gates authorized his left wing to move forward from its lines to meet the British advance. Thus the Battle of Freeman's Farm began in the woods about a mile north of the American left flank when, shortly after noon on September 19, American riflemen encountered a picket from the right of Burgoyne's army. The Americans routed the picket, became disordered while pursuing, and were in turn routed by another British unit. Arnold, commanding on the left, then brought up regiments of Continentals to support the riflemen and became engaged in heavy fighting with the center of the British army around Freeman's Farm. Throughout the afternoon, the battle swept back and forth across the twenty acres of cleared land south of Freeman's house, the Americans relying on combinations of rifle and musket fire, the British on muskets, light artillery, and bayonets. Although Gates refused to support Arnold with more than a brigade, Arnold might well have destroyed the center of the British army had not Riedesel sent artillery and infantry to attack Arnold's right flank and force him to withdraw. The British held the battlefield. But the Battle of Freeman's Farm was an American victory. At a cost of 319 killed, wounded, and captured, the Americans had inflicted 600 casualties on the British and stopped their march to Albany.

For eighteen days after the Battle of Freeman's Farm the opposing armies remained where they had been when the fighting ended. For a brief time Burgoyne considered renewing his attack. But on the morning of September 21 he received a dispatch from Sir Henry Clinton, commander of British forces at New York City, saying that Clinton would support Burgoyne's offensive by attacking American fortresses in the Highlands of the Hudson on September 22. Encouraged by this news, Burgoyne decided to entrench the ground he held and defer any action until Clinton's thrust up the Hudson had had time to draw American forces from Bemis Heights. Gates, unaware of Clinton, was content to remain on the defensive, improving his lines at Bemis Heights, fortifying the high ground that commanded those lines from the west, and waiting for Burgoyne's army to deteriorate. He knew that the British had provisions for only four weeks and that skirmishing would sap their ammunition and morale, eventually forcing Burgoyne either to attack at a disadvantage or retreat. Moreover, Gates's army was growing stronger. Although most of his reinforcements were unskilled militiamen, by early October he had 11,000 men, well entrenched and supplied, to face fewer than 5,000 regulars. By then Burgoyne was becoming desperate because he had heard nothing to confirm that Clinton was—as he had promised—advancing up the Hudson. Burgoyne had put his own army on short rations, and he knew that if he were to withdraw safely to Canada before winter, he would soon have to retreat. But having committed himself to forcing his way to Albany, he refused to retreat until he had made one last offensive effort. Because his generals rejected a full-scale attack, he decided to make a reconnaissance in force. He would take 1,500 men to probe the American left flank to see whether he might use his whole force to seize high ground that would make Bemis Heights untenable or whether he should retreat at once up the Hudson.

Burgoyne's reconnaissance in force proved to be disastrous for his fragile army. Late in the morning of October 7, he emerged from his lines with 1,500 men and marched southwest toward the ridges commanding Bemis Heights from the west. After advancing about three-quarters of a mile, he stopped to forage in a wheat field. He deployed most of his men in line facing south, presumably to cover the remainder who were foraging. With its flanks resting on woods, Burgoyne's detachment was so vulnerable that it tempted Gates to attack. The ensuing attacks on flanks and center of the British line were not perfectly coordinated, but they were carried out with enough determination to shatter Burgoyne's force. In less than an hour his men were retreating to their fortifications. Benedict Arnold was in this, the Battle of Bemis Heights, again in the middle of the fighting. Although he had no formal authority—he had quarreled with Gates and been relieved of command—he not only helped rout Burgoyne's detachment but also organized a counterattack that carried the extreme right flank of the British lines and made the rest of their works untenable. That night Burgoyne, having failed to recover the right of his line and having suffered 600 casualties (to 150 for the Americans), abandoned the rest of his line and withdrew behind Kroma Kill.

The next night Burgoyne started his retreat up the Hudson. Gates followed two days later, overtaking the British seven miles to the north at Saratoga, surrounding them there on October 12, and impelling Burgoyne to begin negotiations on October 13. Too late did Burgoyne learn that Clinton had broken through the Highlands of the Hudson and was pushing toward Albany. On October 17 his men surrendered their weapons and marched into captivity; soon thereafter other British forces withdrew from Lake Champlain and the Hudson. Howe's preoccupation with Pennsylvania, the ministry's assumption that Howe would cooperate with the Canadian army, Burgoyne's preference for a cautiously conventional strategy, his logistical difficulties, and his determination to reach Albany all had worked together with Gates's strategic caution and Arnold's tactical aggressiveness to give the Americans their greatest victory of the war thus far.

A Revolution Within a World War: Relying on the People in Arms

Burgoyne's surrender in October 1777 had a profound effect on the war and the Revolution: it brought French recognition and support for the rebels, disrupted operations in North America, and forced British and American commanders to rely increasingly on the people to do their fighting. The loss of Burgoyne's army and the prospect of having to divert forces from North America to engage the French in Europe, the West Indies, and India greatly reduced Britain's resources. To continue the war in America with any hope of success, the British had to alter their strategy. They had to rely increasingly on their navy and, above all, on the American people—on those loyal colonists who might now be embodied in militia or more permanent units—to support offensives and consolidate gains. Paradoxical as it might seem, Burgoyne's surrender had much the same effect on the Americans. Because France was now an ally and the Continental army was becoming a nearly professional fighting force, the American people—anticipating victory—so relaxed their support of the war as to force Washington to depend increasingly after 1778 on militiamen and other irregular forces to resist the British and the loyalists. The War for American Independence had always been fought for the allegiance of the people; it was now to be fought by the people as well.

Strategic Consequences of Saratoga

The most important and immediate consequence of Burgoyne's surrender—the surrender of nearly one-fifth of the British army in North America—was to demonstrate the vitality of the Revolution and persuade European states to provide the recognition and support that Americans needed to win their independence. France and Spain had long sought opportunities to weaken Britain, to gain revenge for defeats suffered in the Seven Years' War. In the autumn of 1775, France had sent representatives to the Continental Congress offering goodwill and trade. The following year France and Spain agreed to send arms and ammunition to the rebels and, in 1777, to receive American vessels in their ports. This governmental aid as well as private trade brought the Continental army many essential supplies—indeed, 80 percent of all the powder it would use in the first two-and-one-half years of the war. But until Gates received Burgoyne's surrender and the durability of the Revolution was confirmed, European governments were unwilling to recognize the new United States. Even after news of Saratoga arrived in early December 1777 only France was ready to enter formally into treaties and form an alliance with the United States. These agreements, signed February 6 and announced March 13, 1778, guaranteed American independence and virtually assured that France would enter the war against Britain. By the summer of 1778 France and Britain were at war. Spain joined as France's ally in 1779; and by late 1780 the United Provinces, Denmark, Sweden, Russia—eventually Prussia, Austria, Portugal, and the two Sicilies as well—formed a league of armed neutrality against Britain. So it was that Burgoyne's surrender turned the American Revolution into a war that would be fought around the world and that would contribute substantially to the winning of American independence.

Even before France entered the war on the side of the rebels, the British government knew that Burgoyne's surrender would require sweeping changes in the conduct of the war. The loss of Burgoyne's army substantially reduced the number of troops available for operations against the rebels and substantially increased the risk of foreign intervention. To forestall French or Spanish intervention and to encourage a negotiated settlement of the war, the ministry created a second peace commission and authorized it to make concessions on all issues except American independence. To sustain military pressure on the rebels with a smaller army, the ministry sought a more aggressive commander-in-chief and a strategy better suited to limited resources. The ministry appointed Sir Henry Clinton to replace Sir William Howe and ordered Clinton to rely increasingly on the Royal Navy and loyal colonists to end the rebellion. If Clinton were unable to engage the Continental army in a decisive battle, he was to send expeditionary forces to raid and blockade the ports of New England and to assist loyalists in restoring royal government in Georgia, the Carolinas, and Virginia. Once the South had been recovered, the rebellion in the north would, the ministry hoped, wither under a blockade. Although the rebels had always relied on the people—on militiamen—to do much of their fighting, the British adopted a similar strategy only after Burgoyne's surrender left them short of the regular forces needed to carry on the war. Unwilling to ask Parliament for large reinforcements, and thus jeopardize support for the war among British taxpayers, the ministry took the unconventional step of deliberately attempting to involve the American people in the war, of using loyalist militia to supplement British regulars in putting down the rebellion.

The New Strategy Suspended, Spring and Summer 1778

Before Clinton could carry out this unconventional strategy, France openly declared its support for the rebels; and the British government modified its plans for the American war. When the French announced on March 13 that they had signed treaties and entered into an alliance with the United States, the British assumed that a war with France was inevitable and that ending the American rebellion would temporarily be subordinate not only to launching attacks on the French West Indies but also to defending British possessions on both sides of the Atlantic. On March 21, King George III ordered Clinton to send 5,000 men and eleven warships to capture the French West Indian island of St. Lucia and another 3,000 with a naval escort to defend Florida. Once these forces had been dispatched, Clinton was to give up Philadelphia and possibly even New York City to release troops needed to hold Canada, Rhode Island, Nova Scotia, and Newfoundland; and Lord Howe was to send home twenty warships (nearly one-fourth of his squadron) to help defend the British Isles. Although George III and his ministers had already begun to receive reports that France was preparing a powerful expedition to attack British forces in North America, they did not alter their instructions to Sir Henry Clinton or Lord Howe or even send ships to support them.

Just as the British ministry was slow to reinforce Lord Howe, so too were Howe and Clinton slow to carry out the ministry's strategy for a war against France. The dispatches ordering expeditions to St. Lucia and the Floridas reached Philadelphia on May 8. Because Howe's warships were then scattered from Nova Scotia to Antigua, because it would take weeks to assemble those ships and complete their crews, and because the ministry had warned that a French squadron might be en route to America, Howe and Clinton decided to evacuate Philadelphia and concentrate their forces at New York before sending detachments to St. Lucia and the Floridas. They soon found that even evacuating Philadelphia would be a difficult and time-consuming task. Lacking the transports to embark the army, its baggage, and all the loyalists who wished to remain under British protection, they decided to send only the baggage and loyalists by sea and to march the army through New Jersey to New York City. Howe still had to assemble and pre-pare the transports, and Clinton had to keep rebel forces at bay while he readied his army for a fighting withdrawal across New Jersey. (Clinton hoped that by going overland to New York he would lure the Continental army into a general engagement in open country, the kind of battle that might decide the war.) Not until June 18 did Howe and Clinton leave Philadelphia for New York City. They did so believing that the French squadron said to have been en route to America had returned to Brest and that only Washington might contest their passage to New York.

Howe and Clinton were right in thinking Washington might be will-ing to risk battle in New Jersey. His army had emerged from its winter camp at Valley Forge (twenty miles northwest of Philadelphia) larger, healthier, and far better trained than it had been at the end of the previous campaign. The 9,000 men who went to Valley Forge in December 1777 suffered severely during the winter from shortages of food and clothing, from living in dank log huts, and from epidemics of smallpox and typhus. But in March the army had begun to benefit from more food and milder weather and above all, from better training and discipline under the new inspector gen-eral, Baron von Steuben, a forty-seven-year-old soldier of fortune who had been a captain in the army of Frederick the Great and who now volunteered his services to the Revolution. Until Steuben arrived, the Continental army was experienced in war and dedicated to the Revolution; but it was not well organized or trained. It owed its success in battle to circumstances in which enthusiasm and courage could offset superior British discipline—as at Bunker Hill, Trenton, or Freeman's Farm. Steuben now undertook to give the army the standardized organization and instruction it needed to engage the British successfully in open country: to deploy from column to line with-out becoming disordered and to deliver an effective bayonet attack as well as disciplined musket fire. By May 5, when Washington held a grand review to celebrate the Franco-American Alliance, the army was able to march, maneuver, and fire with remarkable skill; and this new skill brought a marked improvement in confidence and morale. The 12,000 Continentals he led out of Valley Forge and across the Delaware were a better army than any that had yet served the United States. Just how much the army had improved became clear when it overtook the British army that was withdrawing through New Jersey. Near Monmouth Court House on June 28, Washington's men did become disordered while attacking the British rear guard. But they were disciplined enough to form a new line of battle under fire, to withstand repeated counterattacks, and to fight veteran, regular troops to a draw. This, the last major engagement of the war in the north, confirmed the effectiveness of Steuben's methods.

Soon after the Battle of Monmouth, a French squadron of twelve ships of the line and four frigates appeared unexpectedly in American waters. This squadron would never justify the fears and hopes that it inspired, but it would thoroughly disrupt the American war for another three months. When the French first arrived at New York on July 11, their ships were more powerful than any that Howe could assemble; and he would have to wait weeks for reinforcements from England. But if Howe and Clinton could do little more than prepare to defend themselves at New York and send troops to Rhode Island, the French soon discovered that their ships were too large—drew too much water—to attack New York safely. They decided, therefore, to accept Washington's proposal for a combined attack on the British garrison at Rhode Island. By August 8 the Americans had landed on Rhode Island and the French were preparing to join them in investing Newport. Although Howe did not have the ships to force his way into Newport, he was able to relieve the British garrison by luring the French to sea where a violent storm dispersed and battered the two squadrons. When on August 20 the French returned to Rhode Island, it was merely to say that they were taking their ships to Boston for repairs. Without French support, the Americans on Rhode Island were vulnerable to attack by the British at New York. The Americans withdrew on August 30 just before Clinton arrived from New York with 5,000 men. Lord Howe, his squadron at last reinforced, went directly to Boston in hopes of engaging the French before they were secure within the harbor. He arrived too late. Except for a British raid in Buzzards Bay the campaign was now over. The first French squadron to reach America had accomplished less than the new allies had hoped or the British feared it would. It had forced a suspension of other operations from late June until late September 1778.

Turning to the People

On October 10 Clinton received instructions to resume the war against the rebellious colonies. After sending expeditions to capture St. Lucia and to reinforce the Floridas, he was to rely once again primarily on the Royal Navy and loyalists to end the rebellion, combining raids and a blockade of New England with a gradual restoration of loyalists to power in the southern colonies. This strategy, set forth on March 8 but suspended after the announcement of the Franco-American alliance, was to be the basic British strategy for the remainder of the American war. Clinton was not optimistic about this strategy, and he knew that it was too late in the year to undertake raids on the coasts of New England. But now that reinforcements had given the British navy control of American waters he decided to give the new strategy a trial. In November after sending 5,000 men to capture St. Lucia, he added 1,000 men to the 2,000–man reinforcement bound for East Florida and ordered the entire force to attack Georgia—to see whether, as the ministry hoped, the loyal colonists would come forward to overthrow the rebels and restore royal government. On December 23, Lieutenant Colonel Archibald Campbell landed near Savannah with 3,000 men and began the reconquest of Georgia.

Campbell was more successful than Clinton expected, but Clinton would not exploit that success for more than a year. By the end of January 1779, Campbell had captured Savannah, gained control of southeast Georgia, and established a post at Augusta. But when he called upon the loyalists of the Georgia backcountry to rise before having crushed the rebels there, he started a civil war that the loyalists could not win. Raw loyalists were no match for veteran rebel militiamen who had controlled Georgia and South Carolina since 1775. Although Campbell remained optimistic that with reinforcements he could recover Georgia and the Carolinas, Clinton refused to be lured from a summer offensive in the middle colonies. Sir Henry hoped to fight a decisive battle with the Continental army or, at least, to restore loyalists to power in parts of New York and New Jersey. As it happened, he raided Virginia and Connecticut and captured two posts on the Hudson River. But Washington refused battle and Clinton did not have the forces to do more. A French fleet kept British troops on St. Lucia from returning to New York for the summer and only 3,300 sickly recruits reached New York from England. Clinton might have gone south in the autumn had not a second French fleet arrived unexpectedly off Savannah. That fleet kept him at New York until December 23. Only then, when he was sure that the French were gone, could he sail with 7,600 men to attack Charleston and begin a full-scale effort to restore loyalists to power in South Carolina and Georgia.

It might seem that the very circumstances that inhibited Clinton throughout 1779 would have encouraged Washington to take the offensive, to hasten an end to the war. They did not—primarily because Washington never had enough men or supplies for a sustained offensive. As the threat of British victory receded, many Americans became preoccupied with their private affairs and were unwilling to take part in or support the war. Without popular support, Congress and the state governments were unable to provide adequately for their forces. Congress, having tried unsuccessfully to pay for the war by issuing paper money, began requisitioning supplies and men from the states. The states were reluctant to impress supplies and often ignored Congress. When the states did adopt conscription, many conscripts evaded service. Thus Washington had to shape his operations to suit scarce resources. During the winter months, he dispersed and even disbanded parts of his army; at other times he pursued a mainly defensive strategy. He avoided general engagements and used small attacks on British outposts (most notably a successful night bayonet attack on Stoney Point, New York, in July 1779) to keep up the morale of revolutionaries through a period of lagging popular support. Indeed, just when his veteran Continentals were gaining in skill and confidence, he had to avoid battle and depend on militiamen supplemented by small detachments of Continentals to oppose the British in the southern states.

The Revolution Preserved: Unconventional and Conventional Warfare in the South, 1780–1783

The War for American Independence was decided at last in the South where each side used combinations of militiamen and regulars in a variety of operations, some unconventional, some remarkably conventional. The British hoped that by capturing Charleston and establishing posts in the interior of South Carolina they would be able to call upon loyalists to restore royal government gradually from south to north. But Americans struck back, using militiamen and partisans to intimidate the loyalists and combinations of militiamen and Continentals to lure the British into destructive battles and debilitating campaigns. The Americans learned to blend unskilled and skilled men, variously armed, in unorthodox but formidable tactical dispositions. They also learned by late 1781 to take their part with the French army in the most orthodox of eighteenth-century military operations—a formal and successful siege. In short, the Americans came to display a remarkable competence in unconventional and conventional warfare.

Charleston to King's Mountain: The British Offensive Arrested

Clinton's invasion of South Carolina began auspiciously. He reached the Carolina coast in February 1780, opened a siege of Charleston on April 1, and captured the town and its garrison on May 12. In capturing the principal American port south of the Delaware with 3,371 men, 300 cannon, and 4 ships of the line, Clinton won one of the most impressive British victories of the war. When he subsequently established posts in the interior of South Carolina, patriot resistance in Georgia collapsed; and South Carolina loyalists came forward in "gratifying numbers" to take oaths of allegiance and enlist in provincial units. Although Clinton's overtures to rebels were unsuccessful, he sailed for New York in June confident that he had broken the rebellion in Georgia and South Carolina and that the regular forces he left behind would be able, with the help of loyalists, to secure North Carolina and advance to the Chesapeake by autumn.

But the rebellion in South Carolina had not been broken, and Clinton's successor, Charles Earl Cornwallis, discovered that organizing loyalists and suppressing rebels was more difficult than either he or Clinton expected. The loss of Charleston had gradually shaken Americans from their complacency, bringing forth a reaffirmation of republican ideals and a greater

The South in the War of Independence

willingness to support the war—at least, to support local militia against loyalists and scattered detachments of regulars. Against such a resurgence of revolutionary feeling, Cornwallis had neither the men nor the supplies to do
what was expected of him. His 8,000 regulars were scarcely adequate to garrison Charleston and posts in the interior, keep open lines of supply, and
repel rebel forces gathering in North Carolina and Virginia. Moreover, his

efforts to augment his regular forces by raising loyalists in the interior of South Carolina failed not just because the people were rallying to the revolution but also because he could not find arms or leaders for the loyalists. And when his supplies of food and fodder ran short and he tried to supplement his dwindling stores with purchases and confiscations, he succeeded mainly in alienating the population. By late July 1780, Cornwallis had clearly failed to restore order to the interior of South Carolina. Attributing his failure to the support that rebels in South Carolina received from North Carolina and Virginia, Cornwallis concluded that he would have to invade North Carolina and destroy rebel forces based there before he could hope to secure South Carolina.

Cornwallis soon destroyed the principal American army in the South and invaded North Carolina, but he was unable to gain control of the South Carolina backcountry, to raise the loyalist support that was now essential to British strategy. On August 9, as he was preparing to march into North Carolina, he learned that General Horatio Gates was advancing on Camden, South Carolina, with an army of 6,000 men. Although Cornwallis had only 2,100 men with him, he decided to attack the Americans rather than retire to Charleston and leave his detachments of regulars and the loyalists of the interior exposed to piecemeal destruction. His army stumbled into Gates's men north of Camden on the night of August 15. Next morning, when the Americans attacked, the British infantry fired a single volley and charged with bayonets fixed, shattering the left and center of the inexperienced rebel forces and winning a "most crushing" victory. At a cost of 324 casualties the British killed, wounded, or captured nearly 1,800 Americans.

To exploit this victory and to secure the interior of South Carolina, Cornwallis decided to proceed with his invasion of North Carolina. On September 8 he marched for Charlotte with the main body of his army, sending a detachment of 1,000 militiamen to sweep west through the mountains of North Carolina and a body of regulars to establish a base on the Cape Fear River. He planned to advance as far as Hillsborough where he would spend the winter raising and training loyalist militia. By early October it was clear that the invasion of North Carolina was not going well. Rebel militia not only succeeded in preventing loyalists from joining Lord Cornwallis but also engaged the British army in a succession of corrosive skirmishes (altogether some thirty-seven small actions in 1780). When on October 7 at King's Mountain the rebels isolated and destroyed the 1,000 loyalist militia who made up the left wing of his army, Cornwallis decided to abandon his invasion of North Carolina. He retired to Winnsboro, South Carolina, to screen the interior of South Carolina and Georgia and await reinforcements.

While Cornwallis struggled to restore royal government in the Carolinas and Georgia, Clinton spent the summer and autumn of 1780 ineffectually at New York. Although he knew that the ministry wanted to emphasize the war in the South, Clinton left only about one-fourth of his troops there. He gathered the remainder at New York—more than 20,000 regulars—to defend New York, seek a decisive battle with Washington, and take advantage of Benedict Arnold's offer to betray the American fortifications guarding the Hudson River at West Point. Clinton had intended to support

British forces in the South by sending a detachment to establish a post in the Chesapeake. But lacking confidence in himself and his plans, he was soon paralyzed by circumstances. When he learned through Arnold that a French fleet and army were bound for Rhode Island (they arrived on July 10), he was unable to persuade the commander of the British squadron at New York to cooperate in occupying Rhode Island or in attacking the French. When a more aggressive British admiral arrived with reinforcements and offered to join in attacking Rhode Island, Clinton lost his enthusiasm for engaging the French. By mid-September he may have been preoccupied with the prospect of recovering West Point or with shortages of provisions for his army. But even after Arnold's conspiracy had been uncovered, Clinton agreed to do no more than send a detachment of 2,500 men to raid the Chesapeake.

Despite the resurgence of revolutionary feeling following the loss of Charleston and the British invasion of the Carolina backcountry, Washington never had the forces he needed for offensive operations in 1780. He had preserved his army through the previous winter by disbanding some regiments and impressing supplies for others. Even so, persistent shortages of food and pay drove two Continental regiments to mutiny in May 1780 and limited the size of the army for the rest of the campaign. Washington was able to continue training his men, and when in July a French army of 5,500 men reached Rhode Island, he did propose a combined attack on Clinton's forces at New York. But the French, observing the weakness of the Continental army and the strength of British forces, rejected Washington's proposals. The French commander, Lieutenant General Rochambeau, preferred to talk of plans for 1781. By autumn, shortages of food, clothing, and money forced Washington to disband and disperse his army; and during the winter of 1780–1781, Continentals again mutinied to express their resentment at being neglected by the people of a prosperous country.

Cowpens to Eutaw Springs: The Attrition of British Power

While Washington struggled with shortages and mutinies, Nathanael Greene and Daniel Morgan brought inspired leadership to American forces in the southern states. Greene, who replaced Horatio Gates as commander-in-chief in the Carolinas and Georgia on December 3, 1780, had to organize the defense of a vast, sparsely populated country with few more than 1,000 Continentals and bands of ill-disciplined militia. His militia were able to intimidate loyalists and skirmish successfully with small detachments of regulars, but unless Greene could create unusually favorable circumstances for a battle, even his Continentals could not hope to defeat any substantial concentration of Cornwallis's 10,000 men. To create such circumstances—at least to make the most of his outnumbered and poorly supplied forces—Greene decided to divide and disperse his army. By creating two divisions of roughly 1,000 men and posting those divisions to the northwest and northeast of Cornwallis's camp at Winnsboro, he could better feed his own men,

Nathanael Greene was the most important of the general officers who served under Washington in the Continental army. He led a small army of Continentals, militia, and partisans in a sprawling, mobile offensive that drove the British from most of their posts in the South.

sustain friendly militia, and harass British detachments. Above all, he could tempt Cornwallis to divide the main body of his army, exposing perhaps a part of that army to defeat.

This strategy, carried out in late December 1780 and early January 1781, had just the effect that Greene intended. When in January Cornwallis decided to leave Winnsboro and advance into North Carolina—to sustain loyalists and crush rebel forces—he also decided to divide his army. He would leave 5,000 men to garrison posts in South Carolina, send 1,100 under Banastre Tarleton against the western division of Greene's army, detach another smaller force to establish a supply depot at Wilmington, and advance with the main portion of his army toward Charlotte and the North Carolina piedmont.

Soon after Cornwallis began his march from Winnsboro, Tarleton's detachment became a victim of Green's strategy and Morgan's tactics. In an effort to overtake and destroy the western division of Greene's army, Tarleton had driven his men across the sodden winter terrain of western South Carolina. On the morning of January 17, 1781, after marching eight miles in predawn darkness, he at last came up with Morgan's division at a place called Cowpens, sixty-five miles northwest of Winnsboro. He found the rebels drawn up in a wooded area, clear of underbrush, with their flanks unprotected and their backs to the Broad River. Without taking time to rest his men or reconnoiter the rebel position, he attacked. His haste, together with Morgan's superb management of his 320 Continentals and 720 militiamen, soon destroyed the 1,100 British regulars. Knowing that his militiamen lacked the discipline to stand against regulars, Morgan deployed the militia in two lines, 300 and 150 yards in front of his Continentals, and asked that each line of militia fire twice before retreating behind the Continentals. A small force of 125 cavalry was posted to the rear to cover his exposed flanks. Thus when Tarleton's men attacked, every rebel knew how the battle was to be fought. The militia in the first lines checked the British cavalry and fired two effective volleys into the British infantry before retreating under cover of their own cavalry and the Continentals. The British infantry then rushed forward against the Continentals who received them with volley after volley of disciplined fire. When the British threatened to outflank the American right, the right retired in good order, faced about, and met the British at fifty yards with another volley and fixed bayonets. The British, who had entered the battle tired and who had become disordered in rushing after the retiring militia and Continentals, disintegrated when the Continentals counterattacked. In about an hour and with a loss of twelve killed and sixty wounded (6.2 percent), the Americans killed, wounded, or captured 90 percent of Tarleton's regulars.

Stung by Tarleton's defeat, Cornwallis now became preoccupied with pursuing and destroying Greene's forces—indeed, so preoccupied as to ignore loyalists and to become vulnerable to Greene's strategy of luring the British far from their sources of supply. Cornwallis had begun his march into North Carolina before he learned of Cowpens. He stopped long enough to burn his baggage—to increase the mobility of the 2,200 men under his command—and then plunged after Morgan who was already retiring toward Salisbury. On February 1, Cornwallis forced his way across the Catawba River; two days later he reached Salisbury, in time to capture some of Morgan's baggage but too late to keep him from escaping over the Yadkin toward Guilford Court House. While Cornwallis rested briefly at Salisbury, Greene brought his whole army together at Guilford on February 6. Because his forces remained decidedly inferior to the British, Greene decided to continue his retreat, to continue north across the Dan River and into Virginia where he could hope to gain reinforcements that would be needed for battle. Thus when Cornwallis resumed his pursuit on February 8, he found the rebels an annoying but elusive enemy that crossed the Dan just ahead of his cavalry on February 15. Not having the boats needed to follow Greene into Virginia, Cornwallis turned back to Hillsborough to rest his army and to begin organizing loyalists. In the month since leaving Winnsboro, he had marched more than 225 miles through a wet, cold, and sparsely populated country without achieving the decisive battle he had sought.

Soon after Cornwallis camped at Hillsborough, Greene returned to North Carolina to harass the British, await reinforcements, and seek a favorable opportunity for battle. His light troops, supported by independent units of partisans, were very effective in keeping the British from raising loyalists and foraging successfully. By February 27 they had forced Cornwallis to march from Hillsborough in search of food and a chance to engage the rebels. Greene continued his harassing tactics and avoided battle until he received substantial reinforcements during the second week in March. Then, with a two-to-one advantage—4,400 men to 1,900—he took up a strong defensive position at Guilford Court House and invited attack. Benefiting from Morgan's advice and Cornwallis's desperation, Greene was able to fight at Guilford on March 15 much as Morgan had fought at Cowpens. He placed his 2,600 militia in two lines well in front of his 1,600 Continentals, used his cavalry and light troops to cover his flanks, and persuaded his militia to fire twice before retreating. Although the British shattered his first two lines, they took heavy casualties and were unable to break his

Continentals. Even so, after three hours of destructive fighting, Greene chose to withdraw rather than risk the disintegration of his own forces in an attempt to destroy the British. His army retired in good order having suffered only 5.9 percent casualties while killing or wounding 28 percent of the British. Cornwallis, his army unfit for further action and unable to feed itself in the piedmont of North Carolina, was forced to retreat at once to Wilmington.

Greene lost no time exploiting Cornwallis's retreat; in the next six months he won no battles, but he so punished the British in battles, skirmishes, and sieges as to force them to abandon the Carolinas and Georgia except portions of the coast around Wilmington, Charleston, and Savannah. He began by securing the piedmont of North Carolina; then in early April 1781 he invaded the backcountry of South Carolina, sending a detachment to capture Fort Watson, and leading some 1,300 troops against the principal British post at Camden. Although he was attacked and narrowly defeated at Hobkirk's Hill just north of Camden on April 25, he kept his army together and continued to exert pressure on British outposts. When on May 10 the British abandoned Camden and retired toward Charleston, Greene and various partisan leaders quickly overran other British garrisons in the hinterlands of South Carolina and Georgia. By early June only one British post remained in the interior (at the settlement called Ninety-Six, 150 miles northwest of Charleston), and that post was under siege. The British subsequently relieved and then abandoned Ninety-Six, pulling back all their forces to the coastal plain by mid-July. In September, Greene resumed his offensive, attacking the British army at Eutaw Springs, some fifty-five miles northwest of Charleston. He did not win this battle, but he did inflict such heavy casualties on the British (36 percent) that they retired to Charleston, leaving the rebels in control of all except the seacoasts of the Carolinas and Georgia.

Yorktown: A Conventional End to an Unconventional War

During the spring and summer of 1781, while Greene recovered the interior of the Carolinas and Georgia, the British concentrated their forces in the Chesapeake. Clinton did not intend such a concentration, but Cornwallis, the British government, and circumstances worked together to frustrate Clinton's plans for an offensive in the middle colonies and make Virginia the seat of the war. By the time Cornwallis reached Wilmington from Guilford Court House on April 7, he had decided that he would have to conquer Virginia to end the rebellion in the Carolinas and Georgia. Having made this decision without consulting Clinton, Cornwallis delayed his march to Virginia only long enough to be sure that he could proceed without being attacked en route (to be sure that Greene had gone to South Carolina) and that there would be British troops in Virginia to support him. Clinton had sent those troops to Virginia in two detachments: the first, to satisfy the British government's desire for a naval base in the Chesapeake, to destroy American magazines, and to favor Cornwallis's offensive in the Carolinas;

the second, to protect and assist the first against Franco-American forces assembling in Virginia. Although Clinton decided in early May to send a third detachment to the Chesapeake—to reinforce troops already there—he never intended to make a principal offensive along the James River. He expected many of the 6,200 men he had sent to Virginia between December 1780 and May 1781 to return to New York for a summer campaign against Philadelphia. He was then furious to learn that Cornwallis had reached Petersburg. But Clinton lacked the self-confidence to take firm control over Cornwallis, particularly when he knew that the British government admired Cornwallis's aggressiveness and favored a strategy of recovering the colonies from south to north. Thus while Cornwallis devoted June and July to plundering Virginia, Clinton tried ineffectually to persuade him to release troops for or join in an offensive against Philadelphia. In mid-July when Cornwallis was at last preparing to send 3,000 men to Philadelphia, Clinton abandoned his plans for an offensive in the middle colonies and ordered Cornwallis to keep all troops needed to take and hold a naval base in the Chesapeake. On August 2, Cornwallis began work fortifying Yorktown.

Soon after Cornwallis reached Yorktown, Washington and Rochambeau began to think of going to the Chesapeake to trap and destroy the British forces assembled there. Although the French had been sending warships and troops to America since 1778, those forces had not as yet been able to cooperate effectively with the Continental army. As recently as the winter of 1781, the French had been reluctant to join forces against the British in Virginia; and French ships had failed in both February and March to trap Benedict Arnold's detachment that was raiding along the James River. In early May, after learning that a powerful French fleet under Admiral de Grasse would come to North America during the summer, Washington proposed that all French and American forces be concentrated against the British at New York. Rochambeau, commanding the French troops already at Rhode Island, not only rejected an attack on New York but also proposed that he and Washington march their armies south to join de Grasse against the British in the Chesapeake. Although Washington at first refused to undertake such a long march, Rochambeau secretly urged de Grasse to proceed from the West Indies to the Chesapeake and took his own troops from Rhode Island to the Hudson to join forces with Washington and be closer to Virginia on the overland route. By late July, Washington, having reconnoitered the defenses of Manhattan, agreed that he and Rochambeau lacked the forces to take New York; and when on August 14 he learned that de Grasse was en route to the Chesapeake with twenty-eight of the line and 3,200 men, he decided at once to march south to try to capture Cornwallis. He and Rochambeau left the Hudson on August 21, passed through Philadelphia on September 2, and brought all of their forces safely to Williamsburg on September 26. De Grasse, who had arrived in the Chesapeake on August 31, had already turned away a British fleet from New York and received a reinforcement of eight French ships of the line from Rhode Island (bringing Rochambeau's siege guns and effectively sealing the Chesapeake against any force the British could then gather). On September 28, Washington and Rochambeau marched from Williamsburg to Yorktown.

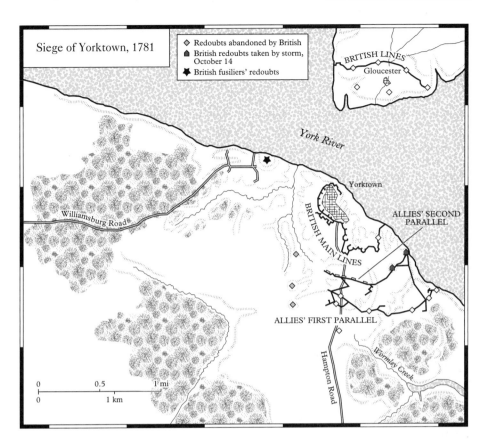

Finding the British too well dug in to invite attack, the allies began a siege that would soon bring them a decisive victory—a victory won by the French navy and by a Franco-American army employing conventional European siegecraft. The siege would be relatively short because the allies had an overwhelming advantage in numbers (16,000 to fewer than 8,000 men) and because the British were isolated in a shallow defensive position against the York River. Cornwallis, lacking the men to hold extensive works, had built a line of entrenchments, redoubts, and batteries close around the village of Yorktown and a similar line across the tip of Gloucester Point just across the York River. He had added another line of works outside the main Yorktown entrenchments but abandoned all except three of those works on September 30 after learning that Clinton intended to sail from New York on October 5 to relieve him.

Once the British withdrew from their outworks, the allies were able to open their first parallel only 600 yards from the main British lines; and once that parallel was completed on October 9, they were able to bring heavy artillery fire against Cornwallis's main line of defense. By October 11, when they began a second parallel 300 yards from the British lines, their guns had silenced nearly all of Cornwallis's artillery and destroyed his ships. Three days later American and French troops took by storm the British redoubts lying along the river east of the town. It was now possible for the allies to extend their second parallel to the river and open a battery that enfiladed the entire British defense. Cornwallis, acknowledging his desperate situation, tried unsuccessfully on October 16 to spike some American guns and to escape across the York. The next day he proposed a meeting to discuss terms of surrender. On October 19, the day Clinton at last sailed from New York, Cornwallis's men put down their arms and marched into captivity. In three weeks and at a cost of 72 killed and 190 wounded (1.6 percent) the allies had won a truly decisive victory.

The siege of Yorktown marked the end of major operations in the War for American Independence. Skirmishing continued for another eighteen months, and Washington had to struggle to keep his army together. But in 1783 peace was at last made and the independence of the new United States was confirmed.

✭   ✭   ✭   ✭

The War for American Independence was far different from the limited wars of mid-eighteenth-century Europe. At a time when most European states relied on highly trained professional armies to settle their differences with the least possible dislocation of civilian life, Anglo-Americans employed combinations of skilled and unskilled soldiers to alter the allegiance of a people. Each side began by trying to gain its political ends with a minimum of force. The British sought to use their small garrison at Boston to intimidate dissidents; the Americans, to use militiamen to resist the garrison and gain a redress of grievances. Each then tried to create and employ more powerful forces without jeopardizing its political goals: the British to end the American rebellion without alienating the people; the Americans, to win their independence without creating a standing army that could deprive them of their liberties. Neither side succeeded. But the Americans fared better than the British, bringing together Continentals and militiamen to capture a British army at Saratoga and gain overt French support. The British, now burdened with a world war as well as a rebellion, turned to loyalists in an effort to continue the war with reduced numbers of regular forces. The Americans, in turn, made the Continental army more professional and used Continentals, militiamen, and partisan bands to keep the British and the loyalists from overrunning the south. By this stage in the war, both sides had become skilled in small-scale, mobile warfare, using simplified methods of fighting suited to citizen-soldiers operating in a vast, sparsely populated, and difficult country. Yet it remained for an army of French regulars, Continentals, and militiamen in cooperation with a French fleet to end the war with a most conventional siege.

Warfare in colonial and revolutionary America was often more modern than that in mid-eighteenth-century Europe; at least, American provincials often came closer than European professionals to anticipating the changes in warfare that would come with the French Revolution. It was not just that Americans waged wars of conquest, that they, like the French revolutionaries, sought to destroy their enemies and permanently alter the boundaries of states; it was also that in North America neither the Indians nor their European allies ever distinguished clearly between soldiers and civilians. War fell on all who lived along the frontiers, and adult freemen were expected to serve in or to support their armed forces. Moreover, because men of every occupation and class served in the militia and provincial forces, and because officers were often appointed by elected governments or elected by their own rank and file, control of American forces depended more on persuasion than on coercion. The citizen-soldiers of British America, like the conscripts of revolutionary France, had to be trained more by instruction and exhortation than by harsh punishment and repetitive training; and they had to be taught relatively simple ways of fighting. Even during the Revolutionary War when Americans tried to create an army capable of standing against British regulars in formal combat—when they tried to give their Continental army professional competence—they were forced to employ persuasion, simplified tactics, and patriotic appeals to turn civilians into soldiers. The Continental army never became truly competent in combined-arms warfare; and all too often Americans had to depend on militiamen and state troops, on the people in arms, to win their independence.

SUGGESTED READINGS

Carp, E. Wayne. *To Starve the Army at Pleasure* (Chapel Hill: University of North Carolina Press, 1984).

Flexner, J. T. *George Washington in the American Revolution (1775–1783)* (Boston: Little, Brown & Co., 1968).

Gross, Robert A. *The Minutemen and Their World* (New York: Hill and Wang, 1976).

Gruber, Ira D. *The Howe Brothers and the American Revolution* (Chapel Hill: University of North Carolina Press, 1974).

Higginbotham, Don. *Reconsiderations on the Revolutionary War* (Westport: Greenwood Press, 1978).

———. *The War of American Independence* (New York: Macmillan Co., 1971).

Mackesy, Piers. *War for America* (Cambridge: Harvard University Press, 1964).

Martin, James Kirby, and Mark Edward Lender. *A Respectable Army: The Military Origins of the Republic, 1763–1789* (Arlington Heights, Ill.: Harlan Davidson, 1982).

Nelson, Paul David. *General Horatio Gates: A Biography* (Baton Rouge: Louisiana State University Press, 1976).

Nickerson, Hoffman. *The Turning Point of the Revolution or Burgoyne in America* (Boston: Houghton Mifflin Co., 1928).

Royster, Charles. *A Revolutionary People at War: The Continental Army and the American Character 1775–1783* (Chapel Hill: University of North Carolina Press, 1979).

Scott, H. M. *British Foreign Policy in the Age of the American Revolution* (Oxford: Clarendon Press, 1990).

Shy, John. *A People Numerous and Armed: Reflections on the Military Struggle for American Independence* (New York: Oxford University Press, 1976).

Smith, Paul H. *Loyalists and Redcoats: A Study in British Revolutionary Policy* (Chapel Hill: University of North Carolina Press, 1964).

Thayer, Theodore. *Nathanael Greene: Strategist of the American Revolution* (New York: Twayne Publishers, 1960).

Wallace, Willard M. *Appeal to Arms: A Military History of the American Revolution* (Chicago: Quadrangle Paperbacks, 1964).

Ward, Christopher. *The War of the Revolution* (New York: Macmillan Co., 1952).

Wickwire, Franklin and Mary. *Cornwallis the American Adventure* (Boston: Houghton Mifflin Co., 1970).

Willcox, William B. *Portrait of a General, Sir Henry Clinton in the War of Independence* (New York: Alfred A. Knopf, 1964).

The Nation in Arms and National Warfare

6

REVOLUTION IN WARFARE DURING THE AGE OF THE FRENCH REVOLUTION

Military Reform and
Revolution, 1763–1792

The Test of War, 1792–1794

The Army and the
Revolution After 1794

In 1789 a revolution began in France; the revolution turned violent on July 14 when a crowd stormed the Bastille, a fortress and prison on the east side of Paris. Many died in that assault on the Bastille, but the greatest casualty was the *ancien régime,* the old order in France, an order dominated by a powerful monarch, a privileged aristocracy, and a rich church. An elected assembly assumed the authority to rule and reform France, stripped the nobility of its privileges, and divested the church of its lands. Revolutionaries proclaimed principles of liberty and equality which reflected those that had inspired American independence. Such a revolutionary government predictably collided with the conservative monarchies of Europe, and in 1792 a war broke out that raged with few pauses for more than twenty years.

Over the course of that long conflict, the French at first fought to preserve their revolution, then to liberate the peoples of neighboring principalities, and finally to dominate Europe. When the French initially took the field they fared badly, and battlefield crisis drove them to revolutionary extremes. Within two years the tide turned, and revolutionary armies advanced beyond the borders of France. Success in war allowed the French to cast aside their most radical leaders, but the expansionist foreign policy remained. In 1796 a young and immensely talented general, Napoleon Bonaparte, received command of a small army in Italy and won victories that still inspire awe. Within a few years this young conqueror overthrew the revolutionary government and in 1804 crowned himself emperor. Napoleon next crushed the armies of Austria, Prussia, and Russia by a series of extraordinary campaigns from 1805 to 1807. As a consequence of his triumphs in battle, Napoleon controlled much of Europe, either directly or as the dominant partner in alliances, but ultimately his greed overreached his own genius. His attempt to force Spain into the French orbit in 1808 set off a war of resistance in which regular forces and guerrillas drained French resources and blood. In 1812, Napoleon committed his greatest blunder when he invaded Russia, where war and weather destroyed the largest army Napoleon ever commanded. After that debacle, even the emperor's military brilliance could not stave off defeat. By 1815 the principal states of Europe had joined to deprive Napoleon of his throne and restore monarchy to France and many of its former satellites.

The era of the French Revolution and Napoleon transformed warfare as Europeans broke with notions of limited conflict. Calling upon revolutionary ideals, the French harnessed the energies of their entire population by conscripting young men into service and by mobilizing the civilian community to equip and supply this new army of unprecedented proportions. These huge forces were driven by a resolve to preserve the Revolution and to serve the nation--new factors in European warfare—and they were led by officers chosen for ability rather than for birth or wealth. France truly became a nation at arms, and while revolutionary fervor eventually subsided, patriotism remained a driving force within the ranks of Napoleon's army. On the battlefield, French forces fought not simply to defeat but to destroy their enemies. Tactical and operational innovations made combat more decisive. Tactically, the French employed flexible combinations that exploited rapid movement, large numbers, and deadly firepower. Operationally, the French increased the scale and speed of operations by employing new organizations and by learning to live off the countryside. Napoleon subdivided his armies into self-sufficient corps that included infantry, cavalry, and artillery. Those corps advanced on parallel routes, thereby disguising Napoleon's intentions and increasing mobility so he could impose battle on unsuspecting or unwilling enemies. To stand against the French, opposing armies learned to either adopt or adapt to French methods, and, as a consequence, French military innovations taught Europeans a new way of war.

Military Reform and Revolution, 1763–1792

Humiliation in the Seven Years' War profoundly shook the French army, particularly its officer corps. With good cause the French had long seen themselves as a preeminent power on the continent of Europe. They boasted a long history of military success beginning with the wars of Louis XIV and extending through the triumphs of Maurice de Saxe in the mid-eighteenth century, and they set political, cultural, and intellectual standards for their age. France also had the largest population of any European state, some 26 million souls by 1789, and the richest continental economy. A state with such a proud history and abundant resources did not accept defeat easily, and the years from the end of the Seven Years' War to the fall of the Bastille witnessed a string of new ideas and reforms designed to reestablish the military primacy of France.

But innovation could not exceed the limitations set by the *ancien régime,* so while efforts at reform provided valuable precedent for military change after 1789, only the political and social transformation achieved during the Revolution could utterly reshape the army. As the soldiers of the Revolution set new standards for military institutions, they benefited from technical advances and theoretical ideas born before 1789; they sifted among them, selecting some and altering others, to create a form of warfare beyond the intentions of the prerevolutionary reformers.

Reform, 1763–1789

Tactical theoreticians had long debated how troops could be most effectively marshaled in battle. For a time after the debacle of the Seven Years' War, French drill regulations aped Prussian methods of the *ordre mince* (thin order), which emphasized a tightly controlled line of three ranks that optimized firepower. But ultimately such imitation gave way to innovation. Many believed that the French were by nature better at an attack with the bayonet than at a defense dependent on disciplined volleys of musketry. One French philosopher of the time even argued "that the French nation attacks with the greatest impetuosity and that it is extremely difficult to resist its shock." Such convictions drove theorists to design a tactical system suited to French capacities by reviving longstanding notions of relying upon rapidly moving columns in the *ordre profond* (deep order). The military intellectual Count Jacques de Guibert realized the advantages to be gained by employing the line for musketry and the column for mobility. In his classic *Essai général de tactique* (1772) he advocated a compromise that exploited both line and column in the *ordre mixte* (mixed order). Guibert won converts to his concepts and strongly influenced the drafting of the drill regulation of August 1791, which served as the basic tactical document of the revolutionary and Napoleonic era. This regulation, however, did not force any one tactical pattern on the French but offered a range of tactical alternatives in line and column that would then be tested in battle to yield the potent methods of the new age.

While the French debated the most effective close-order tactics, they also experimented with light infantry fighting in open order as skirmishers. At mid-century, fear of desertion restrained commanders from dispersing their troops, since once dispersed they might not return to their colors. But eventually the advantages promised by light infantry led all major European armies to employ limited numbers of such troops. This movement was of European origins and was affected only to a modest degree by experience in the New World. The French were at the forefront of innovation in this matter, and by 1789 all French infantry regiments boasted a company of light troops, while the army rolls also included twelve complete battalions of light infantry.

The range of military ideas circulating through France went beyond the confines of infantry tactics to include new ways of employing artillery and organizing armies. Mid-century practice dispersed cannon and frittered their fire away in duels between opposing batteries instead of maximizing that fire by directing it against the main body of enemy troops. In contrast to this, Chevalier Jean du Teil argued that artillery must be concentrated in large batteries and directed against key points in the enemy's lines. Another military author, Pierre de Bourcet, offered new ideas on organizing armies. In his *Principes de la guerre de montagnes,* Bourcet imagined hypothetical mountain campaigns in which the victors broke their forces up into smaller subdivisions that maximized mobility by marching along separate routes but reunited for combat, an operational method the French would later transform from theory to reality. Marshal Victor-François de Broglie had experimented with the notion of grouping his army into divisions during the Seven Years' War, but when peace returned, the divisions ceased to exist. The army, however, later established administrative divisions that grouped regiments together in peacetime. These were not yet combat divisions, but the die was cast. After the wars of the Revolution began, the French organized field forces into divisions that combined infantry, cavalry, and artillery.

The French also forged new tools of war. A new model of "Charleville" musket appeared in 1777. This smoothbore .69-caliber musket did not have the pinpoint accuracy of a rifle, but it was simple, reliable, and capable of firing three times faster than rifled weapons. One contemporary test demonstrated that when fired at large targets, a smoothbore musket hit its mark three out of four times at eighty yards. While other countries would arm some of their light infantry with rifles, the Charleville remained the basic weapon for all French infantry, including skirmishers, throughout the wars of the French Revolution and Napoleon.

About the same time as the Charleville came out, the French also improved their field guns. Through the efforts of Jean Vacquette de Gribeauval, supreme commander of the French artillery after the Seven Years' War, the French armed themselves with lighter, more mobile cannon. The Gribeauval system of 1774 employed a new method to manufacture artillery tubes. Before then the bore was created within the barrel during the casting process. A clay core was affixed within the mold, and the hot metal poured around the core. This method, however, produced pieces with imperfect bores that resulted in such a poor fit of cannon ball to barrel that much of the force of the burning powder was lost. To obtain a better bore, the Gribeauval method cast barrels solid and then drilled out the bores on large machines, harbingers of the industrial age. Because of the much closer tolerances between bore and ball, cannon could be cast much lighter with thinner chamber walls and shorter barrels without sacrificing range or accuracy. Along with the lighter barrels, the Gribeauval system employed new sighting devices and elevation screws to enhance accuracy, while improved carriages

Machine for boring Gribeauval cannon. The whole barrel rotated against a cutting head that advanced steadily by means of weights and cogs. This illustration, produced in 1793–1794 during the Terror, was apparently meant to instruct arms factories in making lighter, more mobile cannon.

and harnessing increased mobility. The more mobile Gribeauval artillery allowed the creation of rapidly moving batteries that could respond to the needs of the battlefield like none before them.

But military reform could make only limited progress in prerevolutionary France because of the political and social restraints that bound military institutions. To take full advantage of the new tactical and technological possibilities, Guibert suggested that the French would need not only new drill and weapons but a new kind of soldier, a citizen who fought with initiative and enthusiasm born of conviction. Such men in the service of a idealistic state would be invincible. A passage in his *Essai* was strangely prophetic:

> Imagine that there arose in Europe a people who united austere virtues with a national militia and a fixed plan of expansion, who did not lose sight of their system, who, knowing how to make war cheaply and live by their victories, were not reduced to putting their arms aside because of financial calculations. One would see this people subjugate its neighbors, and overturn feeble constitutions like the wind bends over fragile reeds.

Others also discussed the glories of the citizen soldier, but this ideal could be realized only through political revolution.

Just as the French could not radically transform their rank and file before 1789, neither could they produce a profoundly different officer corps. Both wealth and aristocratic status determined the fates of officers at midcentury, and while reformers labored to lessen the importance of the former, they strove to retain or even increase the influence of the latter.

Money played a large role in the army because officers required considerable funds to gain and maintain command of units. Many reformers objected to rich men of less prestigious noble families or even from outside the aristocracy gaining an advantage over poorer men from traditional military families. To improve the lot of the impoverished but well-born officer, in 1762 the government relieved company-grade officers of certain expenses they had previously borne. Beyond this, in 1776 the war ministry took the first step in phasing out the purchase system. This archaic practice attached a price tag to the ranks of captain and colonel and required that aspirants to these commands literally buy them from their predecessors. Officers consequently owned their companies and regiments, which represented sizable investments beyond the reach of poorer men. The ministry effectively attacked the purchase system, although remnants of it survived until the Revolution.

The same writers who argued that wealth corrupted the army also insisted that noble birth be a nearly universal prerequisite for command. For generations military observers had argued that officers should have both higher standards of technical competence and greater commitment to the army. Such observers agreed that these goals could best be reached by restricting the officer corps to aristocrats of modest means, men who represented the traditional political and social elite and who would provide dedicated service in exchange for a commission. Typically, Maurice de Saxe contended, "Truly the only good officers are the poor gentlemen who have nothing but their sword and their cape." Viewed from a social perspective, then, what passed as reform was profoundly conservative. For example, officer training schools, which were promoted as devices to raise the level of professional competence, provided instruction primarily or exclusively to the sons of poorer nobles who could trace their lineages back over time.

The capstone of this pattern of aristocratic social-military reform was the Ségur law of 1781. It reserved direct commissions to those young men who could prove four generations of nobility. About the same time, royal decrees reserved regimental command to nobles who had been presented at court—in other words, those from the most privileged and powerful families of France. A reforming administration succeeded in cutting the number of officers carried on the army's rolls shortly before the Revolution, but it had no desire to redefine the privileged character of the officer corps.

Thus while military reform brought positive changes before 1789, reforms occurred only within the conservative assumptions of the *ancien régime* and could go only so far without overturning those assumptions. The Revolution, by destroying the very notion of social and political privilege, promised to change the nature of the army and, eventually, of war itself.

Revolution and the First Stage of Military Change

When government bankruptcy, economic crisis, and social discontent brought on revolutionary upheaval in the summer of 1789, all the great institutions of France were shaken to their foundations, including the royal army. The army could not avoid the watchful eyes of revolutionary politicians for two reasons; first, the officer corps was a bastion of that aristocratic privilege which was anathema to the revolutionaries, and second, the king, Louis XVI, made the army a threat by trying to employ troops against the revolutionaries. In fact, Parisians stormed the Bastille in order to seize ammunition stored there and arm themselves against troops the king had summoned to Versailles in order to intimidate the elected assembly and menace Paris itself.

So it should come as little surprise that throughout the peak years of revolutionary activity, 1789–1794, military policy and reform would always be colored by political overtones.

The government that ran France and restructured the army during the revolutionary era underwent several metamorphoses as the Revolution moved from phase to phase. An elected assembly that changed in name and form several times during these turbulent years held the majority of power. At first the revolutionaries left the king upon his unsteady throne, but in less than four years they condemned the awkward and vacillating Louis XVI to the guillotine, and France became a republic in 1792. At the height of the Revolution, the assembly through its committees exercised executive as well as legislative authority.

When the king first called upon royal troops to intimidate the revolutionary assembly in the summer of 1789, his soldiers often proved reluctant or ineffective. In 1789 the largest regiment in the army, the French Guards, which traditionally garrisoned Paris, simply dissolved as the men in the ranks deserted and merged into the urban masses; some former French Guards even played a conspicuous role fighting alongside civilians in the attack on the Bastille. Desertion soon plagued the entire army, and during the first two years of the Revolution the royal army declined in numbers and cohesion. The condition of the army continued to deteriorate, and in 1790 troops in many regiments mutinied against their aristocratic officers. The worst of these uprisings occurred in Nancy where loyal regiments finally put down the mutiny with bloodshed.

After the fall of the Bastille, Paris and then other towns throughout France created their own citizen militia forces, the National Guard, both to maintain public order and to act as a military counterbalance to the forces of the king. The French municipalities established these militia forces on their own initiative, but the central government later coordinated them. In contrast to the royal army, whose infantry wore Bourbon white uniforms, the National Guard donned the new revolutionary colors, sporting blue coats faced in red with white breaches. France, in a sense, now had two armies.

The revolutionary assembly turned its attention to army reform in 1790. Early that year the assembly abolished the vestiges of the purchase system and then opened officer ranks to all classes; no longer would the commissioned ranks be an aristocratic preserve. In the autumn the assembly proclaimed a new system whereby three quarters of entering second lieutenants would be selected by examination and the remaining quarter would come up from the ranks of the noncommissioned officers.

The reshaping of the army accelerated when Louis XVI attempted to flee France and challenge the Revolution. Although the king and his family were captured at Varennes on June 21, 1791, the assembly viewed the king's attempted escape as evidence that the other monarchs of Europe were ready to attack France in order to restore Louis to power. Fearing war, the assembly voted to increase French military forces; the royal army had shrunk from about 150,000 troops in 1789 to fewer than 130,000 by the end of 1790. But while legislators authorized the army to expand back to its former level, they also called for volunteers from the National Guard, which they regarded as more politically reliable than the old royal army. During the second half of 1791 the government mobilized about 100,000 of these "Volunteers of 1791" who signed on for one year; they were marshaled in their own battalions and served under officers whom they elected. Volunteer battalions, clad in their blue coats, now marched to the front and stood beside the regiments of the royal army.

If the election of commanders by volunteer battalions put a new kind of officer at the head of French troops, so did the turmoil in the old officer corps brought on by the flight of the king. While the legislation of 1790 ushered in a new system by which young men could enter the officer corps at the bottom, it did not purge the existing officer corps of prerevolutionary aristocratic officers. But when the king turned his back on revolution, nobles who felt that their real oath and duty was to the king, not the assembly, began to leave the army in droves, creating large numbers of vacancies. Because the examination system decreed in 1790 proved insufficient to supply enough officers, the only alternative was to commission a great many noncommissioned officers as company-grade officers. Election of commanders and promotion from the ranks began a process that would utterly transform the officer corps until it resembled neither the reality of the old royal army nor the ideals of the aristocratic reformers. From this point on promotion operated in such a way as to realize the revolutionary goal of "careers open to talent"—talent which was not confined to the traditional elite.

The Test of War, 1792–1794

The imagined conspiracy of monarchs so feared by the French did not exist, and war never came in 1791, but it did in 1792. The war resulted as much from the demands of factional politics within France as from any external threat. Radicals who opposed the king expected the revolutionary troops to triumph and felt that a war would make Louis XVI, who had been reinstated in some of his authority after his flight to Varennes, reveal himself as a traitor worthy of being deposed. Reactionary royalists expected the new French armies to crumble before the onslaught of invading forces, who would then reestablish the old order in France and make revolution a thing of the past. With conflicting factions agreeing on nothing except the need for war, the momentum became irresistible, and on April 20 the French declared war on the Austrian monarch, hoping to fight only this one ruler. But soon the Prussians joined forces with the Austrians, and France faced a powerful alliance.

The first campaigns went badly for the French, compelling them to mobilize still more troops to ensure the survival of the Revolution. French attempts to invade the Austrian Netherlands ended in rout, with panicked French troops shouting that they had been betrayed by their generals. Neither royal regiments nor Volunteers of 1791 garnered any glory. As things continued to go from bad to worse, the assembly officially declared that "the country is in danger" in July and resolved to raise an additional 50,000 "Volunteers of 1792." The legislation for this levy set quotas of recruits and authorized that if sufficient volunteers were not found, individuals could be conscripted into service; however, such stern measures were rarely needed because volunteers rushed to the colors. Instead of the mere forty-two battalions anticipated in the legislation, the Volunteers of 1792 formed 275 battalions, which at full strength could have totaled 220,000 men. Whereas the Volunteers of 1791 were supposed to meet the same property qualifications demanded of "active" citizens—those with more political rights—standards were relaxed for the Volunteers of 1792, and as a consequence the levy was more working-class in character. In practice the new levies of 1792 took some time to reach the front and were not trained well enough to play much of a role that year. France was now defended by three different armies, each with a distinct character: the royal army, the Volunteers of 1791, and the Volunteers of 1792.

Volunteers of 1792 march across a Paris bridge on their way to the front. Note the reviewing stand and artillery to the right background. Mothers with small children cheer the passing troops. Married men with children could volunteer but they were not conscripted. One young woman standing to the right center seems to be wearing a female version of military garb.

As the Prussians prepared to invade France, disaster seemed near. The Prussian commander, the Duke of Brunswick, issued a manifesto threatening the French with dire consequences if they dared to harm their king; however, this act of bravado backfired, for Parisian National Guards and an infuriated crowd attacked the Tuilleries palace on August 10 and imprisoned Louis XVI. Although he would not go to the guillotine until January 1793, France was now without a king. The revolutionary left had gained its republic, but could that republic be defended against the invading allies? The army would answer that question at Valmy—against the Prussians who were thought to be the finest soldiers in Europe.

The Valmy Campaign

Before then, the French had to learn through bitter experience. In the spring and early summer of 1792, French troops had run at the mere sight of enemy cavalry, and advances had ended in rout. But time made seasoned soldiers of inexperienced regulars and raw volunteers, and by the process of trial and error the government found better commanders. On the northeastern frontier, for example, General Charles-François Dumouriez replaced the Marquis de Lafayette, who despite the high repute he earned in America was no great success as politician or general in France. For some time, Dumouriez had fought a series of minor actions to acclimate his soldiers to combat, and as autumn approached their performance had much improved.

When the Prussians invaded France, they advanced so slowly that Dumouriez had the time to take up strong defensive positions. Leaving Coblence at the end of July, the Prussians crossed the French frontier on August 19. They took Longwy on August 23 and Verdun on September 2. The Prussians moved in the deliberate fashion dictated by the logistical constraints of the mid-eighteenth century. They halted repeatedly while ovens baked thousands of loaves of bread to replenish their supply trains. The French were not so constrained, and Dumouriez, who counted on the slow pace of Prussian movement, daringly led part of his Army of the North down from Sedan across the eastern face of the Argonne, a very difficult stretch of hills and woods that acted as a natural barrier across the Prussian path. Dumouriez's line of march risked pinning his army between the Prussians and the Argonne, but by taking this brilliant but dangerous course of action, Dumouriez was able to beat the Prussians to the important Argonne passes. Seizing them and concentrating his main army at Ste. Menehould, Dumouriez blocked Brunswick's advance and bought time, while General François-Christophe Kellermann with the French Army of the Center marched to join Dumouriez. Owing to confusion among the French detachments, Brunswick's forces got through a critical Argonne pass north of Ste. Menehould and turned to deal with Dumouriez's forces. By then Kellermann had arrived.

The resulting battle of Valmy pitted 36,000 French troops under Kellermann against 30,000–34,000 Prussians under Brunswick. On the morning of September 20 a massive cannonade shattered the air. Early in

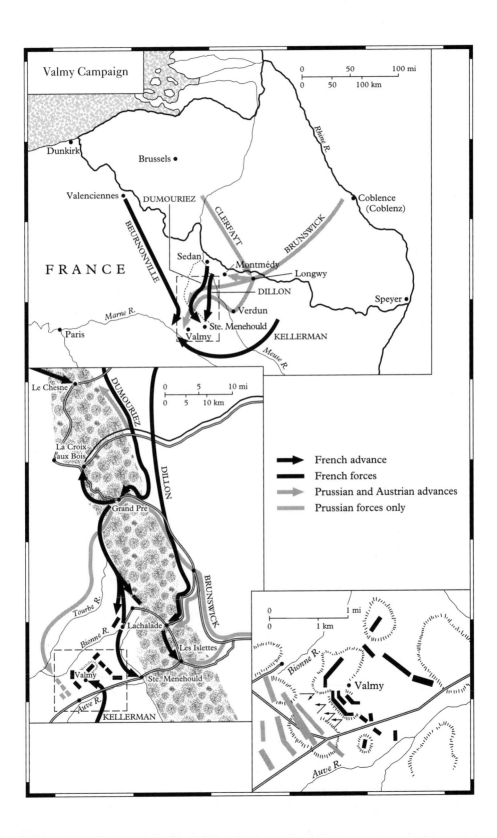

Valmy Campaign

0   50   100 mi
0   50   100 km

Dunkirk

Brussels •

Rhine R.

Valenciennes •

DUMOURIEZ

Coblence
(Coblenz)

CLERFAYT

BRUNSWICK

BEURNONVILLE

Sedan •

FRANCE

Montmédy •

Longwy

DILLON

Speyer •

Marne R.

Verdun •

Paris •

Ste. Menehould •

Valmy

KELLERMAN

Meuse R.

Le Chesne •

DUMOURIEZ

0   5   10 mi
0   5   10 km

La Croix
aux Bois

DILLON

French advance

French forces

Grand Pré •

Prussian and Austrian advances

Prussian forces only

BRUNSWICK

Tourbe R.

Lachalade •

Bionne R.

Les Islettes •

Valmy •

0   1 mi
0   1 km

Ste. Menehould •

Bionne R.

Valmy •

Auve R.

KELLERMAN

Auve R.

the afternoon the Prussians formed for the charge. Brunswick fully expected the French before him to bolt and run as they had so many times before. Instead, the duke beheld a powerful expression of the new spirit of the French troops, who now stood firm to fight for their people and their homeland. Kellermann rode before his soldiers, raised his hat on his sword, and shouted *"Vive la nation!"* (Long live the nation). They thundered back, *"Vive la nation! Vive la France!"* An army of the people declared its patriotism, and at that moment the French won. Faced by murderous artillery fire and unshaken troops, Prussian attacks stalled, and Brunswick conceded the battle. After a week of pointless parleys, the Prussian army began a disastrous retreat. Had the battle of Valmy resulted in a Prussian victory, the course of the Revolution would have changed; Valmy is thus one of history's most important battles. On that field an army of an earlier age was bested by an army of a new one.

As Brunswick's army staggered back into Germany, French forces again went on the offensive in the north and the east. Dumouriez, bent no longer simply on defense but on conquest, took his army north again to the border with the Austrian Netherlands. At the Battle of Jemappes on November 6 he defeated an Austrian army and ensured that the French would occupy the Austrian Netherlands that winter. The French Army of the Rhine also triumphed at Speyer, Mainz, and Frankfurt in the fall. The more radical assembly, voted into office after the fall of the king on August 10, declared that the country was no longer in danger. But even though the Revolution seemed secure, the crisis was far from over.

Extremes in Revolution and Warfare

French victories in the fall of 1792 turned to disaster in the winter and spring of 1793. Volunteers, who believed that their services were no longer needed and who starved in the field because the French logistics system collapsed, drifted back home. In March, Dumouriez lost the Austrian Netherlands, while the allies also pushed back the French in the Rhineland. An attempt to raise still one more levy of troops to replenish French ranks precipitated a horribly bloody rebellion in western France among peasants who refused to volunteer and would not be conscripted. Soon Lyons, Toulon, and Bordeaux also revolted against Paris. In addition to these internal crises, revolutionary France found itself opposed not only by Austria and Prussia but also by England, Spain, Sardinia, and the Dutch Netherlands.

The situation called for extraordinary measures, and the assembly responded by giving extraordinary powers to one of its own committees, the Committee of Public Safety. This committee ruthlessly mobilized France for war by instituting a repressive and dictatorial regime, the Reign of Terror, which demanded sacrifice and revolutionary virtue. In fact the leading spokesman of the Committee of Public Safety, Maximilien Robespierre, styled the regime itself a "Republic of Virtue." Within the committee, one man in particular, Lazare Carnot, stepped forward to direct the war effort. His middle-class origins limited his opportunities during the *ancien régime,*

French general François-Christophe Kellermann, on the white horse at right, directs this battalion of line infantry, as his artillery fires on the Prussian enemy across a shallow valley. National Guard volunteers stand in line by the windmill, the most prominent feature of the featureless Champagne landscape. Ultimately, the Prussians were out-gunned, and their withdrawal from France permitted Revolutionary activities in Paris to continue.

even though he was a talented military engineer, so, not surprisingly, he embraced the Revolution. Carnot, while not a radical in the mold of Robespierre, was very much a republican revolutionary. A man of intellect, energy, and discipline who labored grueling hours on the important work of national defense, he would receive from a grateful France the title "Organizer of Victory."

To meet the challenges on all fronts, the assembly called upon the entire French nation to gird itself for war. In August 1793 the representatives voted the famous *levée en masse* (mass levy) that conscripted young men into the ranks and summoned the rest of the populace to support them.

> Young men will go to battle; married men will forge arms and
> transport supplies; women will make tents, uniforms, and serve in
> the hospitals; children will pick rags; old men will have themselves
> carried to public squares, to inspire the courage of the warriors,
> and to preach the hatred of kings and the unity of the Republic.

New recruits marched off for the front in unprecedented numbers, swelling army rolls by the summer of 1794 to over a million men, of whom about 750,000 were actually present under arms. The Committee of Public Safety grouped these troops in at least eleven distinct armies along the borders of France and in its interior.

Just as the decree promised, civilians also were marshaled for the war effort. In order to equip their expanding armies, the French organized the mass manufacture of weapons. The great gardens of the Tuilleries palace in Paris became a huge outdoor factory producing muskets. Workers from more peaceful pursuits found themselves making firearms: woodworkers fashioned stocks, metal workers made barrels, and watchmakers constructed flintlock mechanisms. So too did seamstresses sew uniforms, cobblers turn out shoes, and harness makers stitch saddles and bridles—all for army consumption. Even prostitutes were drafted into the war effort and forced to make flags, tents, and other essentials as part of their punishment. The French proved so effective at mobilizing manpower that reports from the countryside complained that there were not enough peasants left to work the fields.

The French were creating a radically new army, one that was expected to do more than its predecessors because it represented the whole nation and was inspired by patriotism. In times past, soldiers were regarded as the lowest of the low; a French war minister of the 1770s referred to the men in the ranks as "the slime of the nation." Now, particularly with the *levée en masse*, soldiers represented a true cross-section of French society and included the best young manhood of the nation. Politicians and newspapers repeated that soldiers were "brave warriors" who "flew to the defense of the country." A conscious program of political education involving the distribution of revolutionary newspapers, songs, and tracts among the troops fostered commitment and buttressed the soldier's sense of being the defender of a new society and a great nation. Men who saw themselves as heroes committed to cause and country could be expected to fight with initiative and enthusiasm.

These patriotic soldiers now blended into a single army. In February 1793 the government decreed the end of distinctions between the royal army and volunteer battalions of the National Guard. Through the process known as "amalgamation," it created a new uniform force. In elaborate ceremonies meant to foster a sense of brotherhood within the ranks, battalions of regulars, volunteers, and conscripts were literally mixed together to create new "demi-brigades," three-battalion units which replaced the regiment as the building block of the French army. Demi-brigades of infantry with supporting artillery and cavalry stood together in divisions, for by this point the revolutionary army had adopted the combat division as a standard organization, bringing with it all its potential for improved control and rapidity of movement.

A transformation of the officer corps paralleled the transformation of the rank and file. As new men stepped up to command through trial by fire, aristocrats, who had composed 85 to 90 percent of the corps before the Revolution, sank to a mere 3 percent of the total in 1794. Careers were truly open to talent, and good men rose quickly. In addition to weighing an officer's military capacity, the revolutionary government considered his political reliability. In fact, the government viewed officers with suspicion because generals had betrayed it more than once. Lafayette went over to the enemy in 1792, and Dumouriez deserted to the Austrians after his battlefield defeats of March 1793. To assure the political allegiance of officers in the future, the Committee of Public Safety dispatched Representatives on Mission from the assembly to scrutinize the opinions of the generals. A number of commanders seen as militarily incompetent or as politically unreliable lost their heads to guillotines. The campaign of political education directed at the troops sought to attach their loyalties to the government rather than to their generals.

Building from the base of the August 1791 drill regulation, the revolutionary army erected a new and superior tactical system for infantry. Yet it would be a mistake to see the tactics of revolutionary infantry simply as a product of the military debates that preceded the Revolution, because the actual formations and practices employed by 1794 did not follow exactly the patterns of the reformers or the drill regulation of 1791. Instead, hard experience on the battlefield showed commanders which elements of the official drill failed, which worked, and which could be modified beyond the authors' explicit intentions. The traditional three-deep line still served its purpose of maximizing firepower and troop control, but it was best used only when troops were stationary. For maneuver on the battlefield and for the spirited bayonet assaults that became a trademark of the French, they employed their troops in column twelve ranks deep and some sixty files across. The exact form and use of the attack column was not that prescribed by the drill regulation of 1791 but an adaptation of it found to be more effective through trial and error. To cover the main line of battle and to prepare the way for column assaults, some infantry dispersed into swarms of skirmishers, taking cover where they found it and choosing their own targets, particularly enemy officers and artillery crews. The effectiveness of revolutionary tactics came not from line, column, or skirmishers alone but from the ability to employ them all on the battlefield in flexible combinations that made the most of changing terrain and circumstances.

The troops who used these new flexible tactics were better trained than historians have usually assumed. Certainly the soldiers of the revolutionary army in their tattered uniforms did not look as neat or drill as precisely as did the automatons who fought for the old monarchies, but the French did well enough. Part of the reason that some believe that the French did not fight with any order—that they resorted only to "horde" tactics—derives from a belief that raw recruits went immediately into battle. Except in rare cases this was not the case, and men new to the front drilled relentlessly, usually twice a day, to master basic battlefield skills. Entire new battalions often trained for six months to a year before appearing in the field. During the winter of 1793–1794 infantry even commandeered barns to drill recruits. Napoleon himself later commented that three months sufficed to prepare a recruit for battle if he was with an experienced unit. Revolutionary troops had that kind of time and eventually also that kind of experience.

The French did not take the field with infantry alone; mounted troops and artillery supported the new battalions. During the crisis years 1792–1794 French cavalry did not come up to the standards of revolutionary infantry. Cavalry suffered terribly because of the logistic breakdown during the winter of 1792–1793. By the following spring they were too few in number and could not be increased quickly, since rebuilding the cavalry to appropriate levels would take years. Unlike the cavalry, however, French artillery proved invaluable. As a way of stiffening inexperienced infantry, each battalion received two light artillery pieces, the "battalion guns." Eventually this practice was abandoned, but Napoleon would resurrect it again in 1809 for precisely the same reason. Owing to prerevolutionary reforms, the French enjoyed the technological edge of the Gribeauval system with its lighter and more mobile guns. The army multiplied that advantage by using many of these guns in horse-artillery batteries which moved at the speed of a galloping horse. This great improvement required adding more horses to the artillery teams and mounting the crews as well, so the expense made it impossible to transform all the batteries. In battle the horse-artillery batteries rushed from place to place across the field wherever they were needed. Such mobile guns demonstrated their worth again and again in support of French infantry attacks and in opposing enemy assaults.

Beyond its tactical mobility, the republican army also achieved greater operational mobility by learning to live off the countryside. The armies of the *ancien régime* had been regularly fed from the rear, a process that tied them to lines of supply that limited their speed and range. The logic behind this system assumed that the common soldier was so little committed to cause or country that if sent out to forage for his own food he would take the opportunity to pillage or desert. A ponderous supply system was, therefore, absolutely necessary to maintain army strength and unit integrity. However, the citizen-soldier who knew why he was fighting could be trusted to live off the country without deserting, so when regular logistics broke down or when he outran his supply trains, he was expected to fend for himself. Such independence from slow-moving convoys could give the new army a speed of march that the old armies could not match. Revolutionary generals learned to take advantage of that speed.

Although it would take time for their army to benefit fully from the *levée en masse*, the French were winning victories on their frontiers by the fall of 1793. Luckily, the Austrians and British, who might have driven forward after chasing the French out of the Netherlands, stopped to besiege border fortresses instead of marching on Paris. In September a republican army defeated a force of Hanoverians at Hondschoote, but the French commander was arrested and guillotined for not pursuing the defeated enemy with sufficient vigor. In October his successor, General Jean-Baptiste Jourdan, defeated an Austrian army at Wattignies, the only battle at which Carnot was ever present. When the Committee of Public Safety insisted that Jourdan follow up this victory with a winter campaign, he rightly insisted that the army must stop, reorganize, and train if it were to be ready to fight in 1794. This brave stand cost him his command and nearly his head. But events

proved Jourdan correct, and the French devoted the winter months to completing the amalgamation and to integrating and training the new recruits generated by the *levée en masse*. The army would prove the wisdom of this course of action in the next campaign when revolutionary troops soundly defeated their enemies and secured the survival of the Revolution.

Tourcoing and Fleurus

If Valmy protected the Revolution in 1792, the campaign of 1794 both preserved the French republic from further invasion and expanded its borders, turning the war from one of survival to one of conquest. The most important and illustrative actions came at Tourcoing and Fleurus, victories that challenge certain historical myths. It has been said that the armies of revolutionary France won only by using great numerical advantages to bludgeon their foes through an endless series of mass attacks, that French victories amounted to murder with a blunt instrument. This stereotype holds for Jemappes, but that was 1792, and 1794 was a different case.

After suffering reverses at the beginning of the campaign, the French took advantage of a central position to engage allied forces piecemeal along the northern frontier. At Câteau-Cambrésis in March and at Landrecies in April things went badly, but the revolutionary armies had only been jolted not knocked out. Then came May. The Austrian commanding general, the Prince of Coburg, and the British commander, the Duke of York, agreed upon a grandiose plan to crush the French between six separate bodies of allied troops totaling 73,000 men. To surround the French the six allied columns approached from different points of the compass. The 60,000 republican troops menaced by this maneuver might have been outnumbered, but like Frederick the Great, they soon exploited their central position. Learning that only three of the six columns posed an immediate threat, the French planned to delay one while concentrating against the other two. The resulting battle of Tourcoing was not really a single combat but several distinct engagements fought simultaneously.

The fighting around Tourcoing on May 18 displayed the range of French tactical capabilities and showed how flexible the French could be in using lines, columns, and skirmishers to exploit changing circumstances. That morning, General Dominique-Joseph Vandamme in command of about 10,000 republican troops collided with the largest allied column totaling over 20,000 Austrians. He had the key role, because if he could halt this large enemy column, the remaining French forces could overwhelm other threatening allied forces. Vandamme deployed his men largely as light infantry who took cover on the broken ground. Faced by far superior numbers, Vandamme's men wavered at first, but he rallied them, and they eventually drove the enemy back. At the end of the day his dispersed skirmishers fixed bayonets and successfully assaulted enemy entrenchments. While Vandamme's troops fought their desperate battle, two other French divisions concentrated against two allied columns, one led by the Duke of York. York's column in particular put up a good fight but was eventually compelled to retire. In these struggles the French employed attack columns as well as skirmishers, and in one case even charged in line. Light infantry fought in support of close-order formations. To be sure, the coordination between line, column, and skirmishers was not as smooth as it would be later, but the French were highly effective. In all, the allies lost over 5,500 troops that day and withdrew their encircling tentacles. French troops had triumphed even though outnumbered.

Victory at Tourcoing was soon overshadowed by triumph at Fleurus, where the French were led once more by Jourdan. He had survived his critics to gain command of the Army of the Moselle, which he now led north to the Sambre River. So extreme was the privation endured by his highly motivated citizen soldiers on this march that some men literally died of starvation and exhaustion. On the Sambre, he joined portions of the Army of the North and the Army of the Ardennes which now also fell under his command. When Jourdan besieged the Austrian fortress of Charleroi with 70,000 men, Coburg led an army of 52,000 to relieve the city. On June 26 the two forces collided around Fleurus, where the French had entrenched. Certainly the French enjoyed a substantial numerical advantage that day, but it was the Austrians not the French who threw their regiments forward in costly assaults. Again the Austrians divided their forces into several uncoordinated attacks, and again the French enjoyed the advantage of a central position. Jourdan shifted forces to defeat each separate attack in turn. Already shaken by Tourcoing, Coburg lost heart after his defeat at Fleurus, and he abandoned the Austrian Netherlands, which the French annexed and retained for twenty years.

Paradoxically, one of the casualties of Fleurus was the Reign of Terror. Designed to suppress any hint of counterrevolution, its rigors had been accepted as long as the existence of the revolutionary state seemed to be in the balance. But with internal revolts successfully suppressed and with revolutionary armies now on the offensive after Fleurus, the Terror seemed unnecessary. On July 27, 1794, the assembly condemned the extreme faction of the Committee of Public Safety led by Robespierre. The next day he died on the guillotine, and the Revolution entered a new period.

The Army and the Revolution After 1794

The army of revolutionary France was writing a new chapter in military history; warfare would never be as it was before. However, as the troops in the field redefined the relationship between the soldier and the state, they witnessed an ebbing of fervor and purpose in Paris. More and more remote from the government, the army would eventually back one of its own generals in his bid for political power. That general, Napoleon Bonaparte, would demonstrate as none had before him the tremendous potential of the revolutionary army.

Creation of an Army of Coup d'État

France welcomed the end of the harsh policies and factional strife brought by the Terror, but the passing of the Revolution's most extreme phase hurt the interests of the army. Whatever else it was, the Terror was a government of national defense prepared to pay any price to support the soldiers in the field. But the men who came to power now were not only moderate, they were also corrupt, as intent on aiding their own finances as on advancing the patriotic revolution. Not everyone was corrupt, to be sure—the solid Carnot stayed on in government for a time as a nearly indispensable expert—but all too often revolutionary virtue gave way to mundane vice. More and more, those in government and even the French people shifted their attention away from the army and its needs. From being the favorite child of the radicals, the army became a costly burden to the moderates. When the army declined in size due to death and desertion, no new levies brought it up to strength. From 750,000 men present under arms in 1794, the army shrank to 480,000 in 1795 and 400,000 in 1796, roughly the same size it had been under Louis XIV. Common soldiers, once treated as heroes when they entered cabarets where the patrons bought them drinks and praised their bravery, now sat alone, sipped their wine, and paid their own checks. Civilians no longer seemed to understand how soldiers suffered and sacrificed.

As the revolutionary government seemed to forget its soldiers, the army suffered in the field. Victory eluded the army in 1795, and its already poor logistical support decayed even further. The revolutionary government had never mastered logistics, but now politicians tolerated corrupt contractors who sent shoddy goods to the front, or the authorities in Paris simply left the army to fend for itself in the field. Certainly French soldiers had learned to live off the countryside, but government neglect turned this military strength into a liability, since it justified short-changing the troops.

Yet even as the troops saw the French government abandon virtue, the army still considered itself as embodying the revolutionary ideals of Liberty, Equality, and Fraternity—the defender of Liberty in many battles, the guardian of Equality in careers open to talent, and the repository of Fraternity in the camaraderie of the camp. As the army drifted away from the government, troops became more dependent on generals who led and maintained them. Recoiling from the extreme policies of the Terror, the French government gave regimental officers more authority over their men without sacrificing promotion from the ranks or other characteristics that bound officers and enlisted ranks together. Time redefined the rank and file. They once had been inspired amateurs who had quickly responded to a national emergency, but they had become skilled professionals with long years of experience. Their outlook changed as they came to see the army as their home, although they preserved their dedication to the country. All of these factors helped transform this force of alienated citizen-soldiers into an instrument of coup d'état. The army first meddled in French politics in 1797 when troops marched on Paris to support republican politicians in a successful coup against moderates. But in 1799 that government fell victim to General Bonaparte, who overthrew it and set himself up as ruler in a coup backed by the army's bayonets.

✻   ✻   ✻   ✻

The Parisian crowd that stormed the Bastille on that July afternoon in 1789 faced danger and death to secure the first political and social gains of the Revolution, not to usher in a new age of warfare. But the consequences of their actions had a profound effect on the nature of armed conflict. Perhaps only such a great cataclysm as the French Revolution could have so altered European military concepts and practices.

From 1792 through 1794 the French created an army of national defense to preserve their Revolution and to protect their beloved country from foreign invasion. In the name of such high stakes, the French originated an intense style of war that escaped the bounds that had limited conflict in preceding generations. First through volunteerism and then through the *levée en masse*, the revolutionary government forged the entire population into a nation at arms, into a nation capable of supporting armies of unprecedented size and power. Although ragged in appearance and imprecise in drill, French citizen-soldiers mastered essential military skills and fought with an indomitable spirit rooted in strong patriotism and revolutionary fervor. At the head of these troops stood officers chosen for ability, not wealth or birth. Revolutionary and patriotic motivation formed the basis of a tactical system that combined line, column, and skirmishers to fit terrain and circumstances and that proved remarkably effective. Additionally, the revolutionary troops' reliability and willingness to sacrifice freed them from plodding supply trains and endowed them with the mobility needed to make war decisive.

Whatever its effect on other aspects of European life, the period of 1789 to 1815 clearly transformed military institutions and the practice of warfare. At the most basic level, the limited warfare of the eighteenth century gave way to a far more total warfare calling upon the resources, both material and moral, of entire populations. In his *On War*, Carl von Clausewitz spoke of a triad of warfare that brought together the government, the military, and the people. This triad became complete with the revolutionary and Napoleonic era, as the people were brought into the drama of warfare as never before. In this sense, wars of kings gave way to wars of nations after 1789. The goal of armies became to confront and destroy the major forces of the enemy, not simply to maneuver about to control territory. The French had been the first continental power to appeal directly to nationalism, and the genie of national warfare could not be put back in the bottle once the Revolution had uncorked it.

SUGGESTED READINGS

Bertaud, Jean-Paul. *The Army of the French Revolution: From Citizen-Soldier to Instrument of Power,* trans. R. R. Palmer (Princeton: Princeton University Press, 1988).

Best, Geoffrey. *War and Society in Revolutionary Europe, 1770–1870* (Oxford: Oxford University Press, 1986).

Cobb, Richard. *The People's Armies: The armées révolutionnaires, Instrument of the Terror in the departments April 1793 to Floréal Year II,* trans. Marianne Elliot (New Haven, Conn.: Yale University Press, 1987).

Corvisier, André. *Armies and Societies in Europe, 1494–1789,* trans. Abigail T. Siddall (Bloomington, Ind.: Indiana University Press, 1979).

Forrest, Alan. *Conscripts and Deserters: The Army and French Society During the Revolution and the Empire* (Oxford: Oxford University Press, 1989).

Kennett, Lee. *The French Armies in the Seven Years' War: A Study in Military Organization and Administration* (Durham, N.C.: Duke University Press, 1967).

Lynn, John A. *The Bayonets of the Republic: Motivation and Tactics in the Army of Revolutionary France, 1791–94* (Chicago: University of Illinois Press, 1984).

Palmer, R. R. *Twelve Who Ruled: The Committee of Public Safety During the Terror* (Princeton: Princeton University Press, 1951).

Parker, Geoffrey. *The Military Revolution: Military Innovation and the Rise of the West, 1500–1800* (Cambridge: Cambridge University Press, 1988).

Phipps, Ramsay W. *The Armies of the First French Republic and the Rise of the Marshals of Napoleon I* (Westport, Conn.: Greenwood Press, 1980), 5 vols.

Quimby, Robert S. *The Background of Napoleonic Warfare: The Theory of Military Tactics in Eighteenth-Century France* (New York: Columbia University Press, 1957).

Rothenberg, Gunther E. *The Art of Warfare in the Age of Napoleon* (Bloomington: Indiana University Press, 1978).

Scott, Samuel F. *Response of the Royal Army to the French Revolution: The Role and Development of the Line Army, 1787–93 (Oxford: Clarendon Press, 1978).*

Watson, Sydney J. *Carnot* (London: Bodley Head, 1954).

Wilkinson, Spenser. *The French Army Before Napoleon* (Oxford: Clarendon Press, 1915).

Woloch, Isser. *The French Veteran from the Revolution to the Restoration* (Chapel Hill, N.C.: University of North Carolina Press, 1979).

7

THE RISE OF NAPOLEONIC WARFARE: INCREASING THE SCALE, SPEED, AND DECISIVENESS OF WARFARE

The French Revolution gave many ordinary men a chance to attain prominence through war and politics. Men who would have remained noncommissioned or company-grade officers under Louis XVI now rose to command regiments, divisions, and armies. No one benefited more than Napoleon Bonaparte. In August 1793 he was twenty-four and a captain of artillery; two and a half years later he was the commander of France's Army of Italy. He soon transformed that demoralized army into a force that was able to take the offensive, defeat Piedmont, and in a year of sustained marching and fighting (April 1796 to April 1797) drive Austria from Italy and end the war.

In that remarkable campaign, Bonaparte carried forward changes in warfare that had been introduced prior to and during the French Revolution. He drew freely upon eighteenth-century theorists and republican practices to go completely beyond the operational and tactical conventions of limited war. Relying on the offensive, he drew supplies from the local area, increased the mobility of his units, aggressively confronted his opponents, and forced them to fight at a disadvantage or retreat. When outnumbered and faced with converging enemy forces, he assumed a central position and used detachments to parry one or more of the enemy forces while he concentrated against another. The mobility and flexibility of his divisions enabled him to outmaneuver and overwhelm his opponents.

After becoming First Consul of France, Bonaparte organized the entire French army into self-sufficient corps that included infantry, artillery, and cavalry. By requiring his corps to live off the countryside and operate independently, he gained speed and mobility. In the Marengo campaign of 1800, he used the corps system to defeat the Austrians despite poor intelligence and mistakes on the battlefield. Over the next five years, Napoleon became consul for life and then emperor. He instituted political, economic, and social reforms in France and continued his efforts to improve the army. By 1805 his Grand Army was capable of conducting operations on a greater scale and with more speed and decisiveness than previously thought possible. Unlike his enemies but like Frederick the Great, Napoleon always sought decisive battle as the best way to win a war, and in the campaigns of 1805 and 1806 he defeated Austria at Ulm and Austerlitz and then Prussia at Jena-Auerstädt. In 1807, after failing to achieve a decisive victory at Eylau, he defeated Russia's best army at Friedland. More than anyone in his era, the brilliant, young leader understood how to employ divisions and corps, free his units from the tether of logistical support, use maneuver to gain advantages over his opponents, and make battle decisive. By 1807 he had transformed the European balance of power and shown his opponents a new style of warfare.

The Ascent of Bonaparte

Napoleon Bonaparte's preparation for his rise to power began in the military schools of pre-Revolutionary France. He left his island home of Corsica at nine and, after an intensive four-month course in the French language, entered the Royal Military School at Brienne where he spent five difficult and frustrating years. His schooling shaped many of his views and provided him with a sound education. In addition to his studies, he read voraciously on his own, especially in the classics, history, and geography. Upon graduation in 1784, he gained admission to the *École militaire* in Paris. Anxious to complete his formal education, perhaps because of the penurious condition of his family, young Bonaparte completed the two-year program in one year, ranking forty-two out of fifty-eight students.

Following his graduation in August 1785, Bonaparte, aged sixteen, reported to the renowned *La Fère* artillery regiment, quartered at Valence along the Rhône River. For the first time he had an opportunity to serve as an artilleryman. After completing a probationary period, he received confirmation of his commission and assumed the duties of a second lieutenant. During the next year he familiarized himself with the garrison duties of an artillery officer while he continued his independent studies, concentrating on military history and on the writings of the eighteenth-century military theorists.

In 1788, following his first furlough to Corsica, Bonaparte joined his artillery regiment at Auxonne. There he attended the finest artillery school in France. Under the guidance of its director, Baron Joseph du Teil, he gained valuable insights into the use of the Gribeauval cannon, and he participated in tactical exercises with an experimental artillery battery. He also began to analyze the various military concepts gleaned from his readings. He was impressed with Frederick the Great's emphasis on central position and quest for decisive battle; he was partial to de Broglie's views on creating and using divisions; he saw much wisdom in Guibert's ideas about flexibility and mobility; and he embraced most of Bourcet's concepts on mountain warfare, especially operating with independent columns. Hence by the time Bonaparte had reached the age of nineteen, he had acquired a military education surpassed by few in France.

While he pursued his military studies and developed his professional skills, young Bonaparte became embroiled in the sweeping events of the French Revolution and became a committed republican. During several furloughs to Corsica he participated in the spread of revolutionary ideas and assisted in the formation of a National Guard. After he and his family came under attack by counterrevolutionaries, they fled to France in June 1793. His final departure from Corsica signaled the beginning of a new phase in his life. With an excellent military education, solid technical skills in artillery, and strong republican credentials, he had the potential to make important contributions to revolutionary France.

Toulon: "Men Without Fear"

Bonaparte first served the Revolution at Toulon in 1793. That August royalists seized control of the great port of Toulon on the Mediterranean and opened its harbor to a British fleet and an allied army. About 15,000 allied soldiers (a mixture of British, Spanish, Piedmontese, and Neapolitan troops) manned the fifteen-mile line of fortifications that encircled the harbor and city. The commander of French forces around Toulon launched several ineffective attempts to break the allied lines.

By chance young Captain Bonaparte reached Toulon in September just after the French artillery commander was wounded. Because a "representative on mission" at Toulon was a friend and fellow Corsican, Bonaparte received command of the artillery. After reconnoitering the allies' defenses around Toulon, he proposed bombarding the British ships from a mountainous spur overlooking the harbor and the enemy fleet. The French commander finally gave him permission in late September for an attack, but before a major assault could be launched, the allies recognized the crucial nature of the mountainous spur and built a strong position on it. With twenty-four cannon and two mortars, it became known as Fort Mulgrave. Despite opposition and gross incompetence by his superiors, Bonaparte forged ahead with preparations for an assault, collecting over a hundred guns and necessary munitions. Below Fort Mulgrave, he erected one battery that was pounded unmercifully by British gunners. When French soldiers displayed reluctance to occupy the battered position, Bonaparte placed a sign on it—"Battery of men without fear." He had no more problems obtaining volunteers to man the battery.

A new French commander finally decided to follow Bonaparte's advice and launch an attack against Toulon with Fort Mulgrave as the main objective. Covered by an intense bombardment, the French launched their attack during a sleet storm on December 17, 1793. Because of the allies' strong position, the attackers advanced almost as skirmishers. The assault

Bonaparte's charisma is evident in this portrayal of his crossing the bridge of Arcola during the Italian campaign. His youth, energy, and fresh ideas contributed greatly to his remarkable success in that campaign.

cost the French about 1,000 men. Demonstrating a courage and charisma that would come to characterize his battles in Italy three years later, Bonaparte was wounded in the thick of the fighting. The French captured Fort Mulgrave, and the next day Bonaparte moved a battery of ten guns to the promontory beyond it. On December 19, the guns began pounding the enemy fleet. After burning French ships in the harbor, the British weighed anchor and slipped out of the harbor with their troops and several thousand royalist sympathizers. French troops occupied Toulon and reestablished republican rule.

Bonaparte's technical skills, tenacity, and good fortune at Toulon opened the way to his future rise to power. As a result of the "zeal and intelligence" displayed in the battle, the twenty-four-year-old captain was promoted to the rank of general of brigade. Also sharing in the victory was a small cadre of men who would play a significant role in future campaigns—André Masséna, Auguste Marmont, Jean Junot, Louis Suchet, and Claude Victor—all future generals or marshals of France.

Taking Command of an Army

New opportunities for Bonaparte appeared after Toulon. He soon received command of the artillery of the war-weary Army of Italy which maneuvered in the Alps and along the Mediterranean coast in 1794. In May 1795, Bonaparte received orders to report to an infantry brigade in the Vendée where bloody civil strife had erupted. After traveling to Paris to protest the assignment, he tendered his resignation. Disastrous reverses in Italy, however, compelled the government to restore Bonaparte and attach him to Carnot's topographic bureau, the strategic nerve center of the army. Bonaparte developed a sophisticated plan calling for coordinated operations by three semi-independent divisions that enabled the French to regain the initiative in Italy.

Meanwhile the war ministry struck Bonaparte's name from the list of active general officers on September 15 because he had failed to rejoin his infantry unit in the Vendée. Within three weeks, however, he became the savior of the Republic when—with the famous "whiff of grapeshot"—his cannon turned back a disgruntled mob of 30,000 as they marched on the Tuilieries Palace where the National Convention held its deliberations. Five months later he was named commander-in-chief of the Army of Italy with instructions to implement the operational plans he had proposed for previous commanders.

The First Italian Campaign, 1796–1797

In the spring of 1796, France adopted an aggressive military strategy despite significant domestic difficulties. Four years of war, rebellion, and disorder had caused many hardships and drained France's resources. The revolutionary government's paper currency had collapsed, and many citizens avoided paying taxes and evaded military service. Consequently the army suffered from numerous shortages of food, clothing, shoes, weapons, and munitions. Nevertheless, Carnot, who was again primarily responsible for the overall direction of the war effort, planned a major attack on Austria, France's main enemy on the continent.

Two classic invasion routes from France to Austria existed: north of the Alps, one route went from the Rhine, through central Germany, along the Danube River, to Vienna; south of the Alps, another extended across northern Italy (Piedmont, Lombardy, and Venetia) into Austria. Carnot decided to launch the main attack through Germany with a supporting attack from Italy. As commander of the Army of Italy, Bonaparte was charged with making the supporting attack which would prevent the enemy from shifting forces out of Italy into Germany. His army was the smallest of the three armies that advanced against Austria.

Despite significant odds against success, Bonaparte's first Italian Campaign eventually became one of the most extraordinary campaigns in European military history. In just over ten months and with limited resources, he fought eighteen major battles and forty-seven engagements, defeated Piedmont and Austria, destroyed the First Coalition, and ensured France's territorial integrity under a revolutionary government. He also went well beyond the operational conventions of limited war.

The Army of Italy

In the weeks before Bonaparte left Paris, he struggled in vain to secure logistical support for the Army of Italy. Accompanied by his staff, he bid farewell to Josephine, his wife of two days, and followed the road to Marseille. Arriving at Nice, headquarters of the Army of Italy, on March 27, 1796, he assumed command of a force that had been fighting in the Alps for almost four years.

The army had limited resources, and its soldiers suffered under miserable living conditions. Of the 63,000 men on the rolls, only 37,000 were available for service; the remainder were in hospitals or detached. In a letter to Paris, Bonaparte described his soldiers as being "destitute of everything, without discipline, and in [a state of] perpetual insubordination." Unpaid for months and lacking food, clothing, shoes, and the most basic supplies, many of the men were on the verge of mutiny. Some even lacked muskets and bayonets. Their equipment was in disrepair, and perhaps even more disheartening, the government had long ignored their appeals for support.

Despite its deplorable condition, the army had great potential. Significant tactical, administrative, organizational, and logistical reforms had taken effect. By 1796 the demi-brigades had become relatively homogenous units under highly competent, well-trained officers, noncommissioned officers, and citizen-soldiers who had demonstrated their courage and commitment on the field of battle. With élan infused into the army by social and military reforms, the French units awaited new leadership to unleash their latent power; Bonaparte provided that leadership.

First among the many talented officers in the Army of Italy was General André Masséna. One of Bonaparte's most senior commanders and a future marshal, he had no formal military education but was one of the most experienced and effective infantry commanders in the French army. Of all Bonaparte's subordinates, Masséna was the only commander who functioned successfully at the operational level of warfare (grand tactics). Another able leader and future marshal was General Charles Augereau who commanded one of Bonaparte's divisions. After serving in several foreign armies, he joined the revolutionary army and fought in the Vendée and the Pyrenees before joining the Army of Italy. In six months, he rose from captain to general of division. Though often crude and unpolished, he was a courageous fighter, a natural tactician, and a born leader. The officer on whom Bonaparte relied the most was his chief of staff, Alexandre Berthier. A brilliant staff officer, he coordinated operations and implemented Bonaparte's instructions for moving and sustaining the army. In addition to these men, scores of other dedicated and highly talented officers served with Bonaparte in Italy and would help sustain him for the next fifteen years.

General André Masséna was probably Napoleon's most capable commander. His ability to operate in an independent manner was evident in the battle of Zurich in 1799; his victory in that battle saved France from invasion.

Military Operations

When Bonaparte took command of the Army of Italy, he realized that his forces faced a powerful and well-supplied enemy, but he resolved to launch an offensive and seize the initiative immediately. His primary goal was to divide and defeat the Austro-Piedmontese army and restore the moral and material condition of his own army by gaining access to the vast resources of Piedmont. With France providing little logistical support, he expected to commandeer supplies in the fertile valleys of northern Italy.

In the first phase of the campaign, which lasted from April through June 1796, Bonaparte drove Piedmont out of the war and forced the Austrians from much of northern Italy. He began on April 11 by sending a division to drive back a small Austrian force, while the bulk of his own army swept north through the mountains to split the Austrian and Piedmontese armies at Montenotte on April 12. When the Austrians slowly began massing their forces, he used a secondary force to keep them in the mountains.

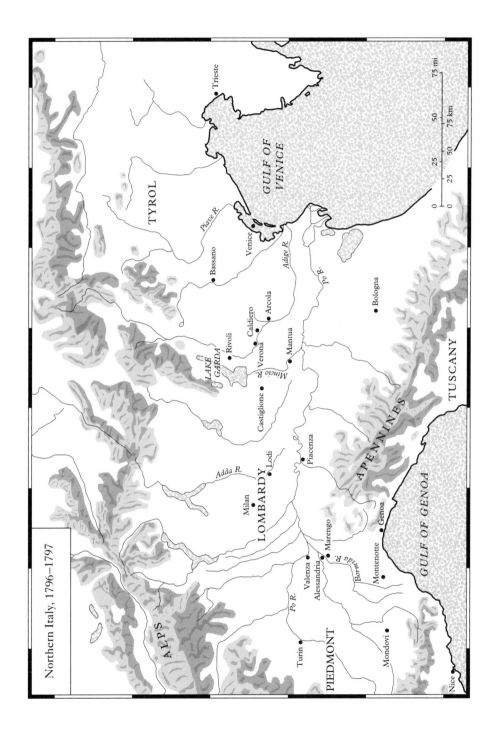

Northern Italy, 1796–1797

TYROL

Piave R.

Trieste

GULF OF
VENICE

Bassano

Venice

Adige R.

Po R.

Bologna

Arcola

Caldiero

Rivoli

Verona

Mantua

LAKE
GARDA

Mincio R.

Castiglione

Piacenza

APENNINES

Adda R.

Lodi

LOMBARDY

Milan

Marengo

Genoa

Bormida R.

GULF OF GENOA

TUSCANY

Po R.

Valenza

Alessandria

Montenotte

Turin

PIEDMONT

Mondovì

Nice

75 mi

75 km

50

50

25

25

0

0

ALPS

Bonaparte then turned on the Piedmontese in the west. Concentrating three of his divisions, he crushed them in a major battle at Mondovi and forced them to accept an armistice on April 27.

Bonaparte then attacked the Austrians who had begun withdrawing on April 25 northeast along the Po River toward Valenza. While sending two divisions toward Valenza in a feint, he led the remainder of the army through the mountains in a sixty-mile forced march toward Piacenza in search of a crossing over the Po. After passing the river on May 8, Bonaparte's forces hurried north to turn the Austrian flank and cut their lines of communication. Recognizing the danger, the Austrians retreated hastily, leaving a rear guard along the Adda River. With chances of a turning movement gone, Bonaparte advanced directly toward the Austrians. On May 10, after a bloody battle, he forced his way across the 180-yard bridge over the Adda at Lodi. While the Austrians withdrew east to the Mincio River, Bonaparte sent forces north to Milan, the capital of Austrian Italy, to raise money and supplies.

On May 28, Bonaparte's forces drove the Austrians north along the Adige River toward Austria. On that same day, French armies crossed the Rhine River far to the north and began their ill-fated attack into central Germany. With the Austrians apparently reeling and French armies advancing rapidly (for the moment) through Germany, the Directory ordered Bonaparte to consolidate his position in northern Italy and expand French control to the south over Genoa, Livorno, Rome, and Naples. This order ended the first phase of Bonaparte's campaign in Italy.

In the second phase, which lasted from July 1796 until January 1797, Bonaparte used his central position to engage and defeat four separate Austrian armies advancing against him in northern Italy. In July he concentrated against the first Austrian army, which approached in three columns from the Tyrol in the north, and finally defeated it at Castiglione on August 5. The Austrians advanced again in September, this time in two columns from the Tyrol. After Bonaparte repulsed the first column at Roveredo, Masséna's and Augereau's divisions raced sixty miles in two days to overtake and crush the enemy rear guard at Bassano. With Masséna and Augereau in pursuit, the remains of the Austrian army fled into the fortress of Mantua, already packed with Austrians. Unwilling to concede the loss of Lombardy or the blockaded garrison at Mantua, the Austrians sent another army, marching in two columns, one from the Tyrol and the other from Trieste in the east, into Italy in mid-November. Decisively outnumbered, Bonaparte first concentrated against the main column coming from Trieste and outflanked it at Arcola on November 15–17. He then turned against the other column and pushed it north. In January the Austrians sent a three-columned army into Italy to crush the French. Operating from a central position, Bonaparte concentrated his forces and defeated the major column at Rivoli; he then marched forty miles south and captured an Austrian column of about 7,000 soldiers, thereby forcing the surrender of Mantua and compelling the other Austrians to withdraw.

In mid-March 1797, Paris gave Bonaparte reinforcements and permission to advance toward Vienna; this began the third phase of the Italian campaign. Archduke Charles, conqueror of French forces in Germany, had assumed command of Austrian forces in northern Italy, but before he could concentrate his forces, Bonaparte attacked. The French drove Charles's army 175 miles through the mountains for five weeks and forced Austria to accept an armistice in mid-April and finally the Peace of Campo Formio in October 1797. Bonaparte's remarkable campaign thus ended in the defeat of Austria and left only Britain as an enemy. During the entire campaign, the French had defeated seven opposing armies and captured over 150,000 soldiers, almost 2,000 cannon, and huge quantities of military supplies.

Ensuring the safety of France and protecting the accomplishments of the Revolution, Bonaparte's victories altered the balance of power in Europe. The creation of two pro-French states in northern Italy (the Cisalpine Republic from Lombardy and neighboring states, and the Ligurian Republic from Genoa) also gave France control of northern Italy.

Operational Methods

Throughout the Italian campaign, Bonaparte demonstrated remarkable gifts as a commander. Many historians have described him as a genius because of his instinctive ability to grasp his enemy's deployment and intentions, appreciate the terrain's characteristics, anticipate the effects of his own movements, and act quickly and decisively. Never one to apply formulas blindly, Bonaparte was a master improviser. He possessed great poise under pressure, and he had a truly charismatic effect on his officers and soldiers. He also had an astonishing ability to recognize and utilize the qualities of his outstanding subordinates.

Against the Piedmontese and Austrians, Bonaparte began to perfect his system of warfare by extrapolating upon the theories propounded by military theorists such as Bourcet and Guibert and adapting them to existing circumstances. French armies had long practiced living off the countryside before the Italian campaign, and divisions had sometimes operated independently, but Bonaparte relied on these capabilities to provide his forces greater mobility, to concentrate his forces on the field of battle, and to gain significant advantages over his enemies. Unlike eighteenth-century commanders who often maneuvered and then fought, Bonaparte made maneuvering an inherent part of fighting and overwhelmed his opponents who relied on traditional methods.

During the Italian campaign, Bonaparte used or attempted to use maneuvers that he would employ again and again in future battles and campaigns. One of his favorites was known as *manoeuvre sur les derrières*, conceptually a simple maneuver. While pressing the enemy front in a feint, Napoleon would outflank the enemy, move into its rear, and thereby sever its lines of communication. This would prevent the arrival of enemy reinforcements, halt logistical support, and often force the enemy into battle under unfavorable circumstances. With much lighter logistical support, with the habit of living off the countryside, and with reliance on speed, the French could operate for a short time in the enemy's rear without fear.

Another favorite maneuver was his use of central position when faced by several large enemy armies. Instead of one climactic battle, Bonaparte fought a series of smaller battles against an enemy's scattered forces. While containing one enemy army with a small French force, he would concentrate against another. One battle that demonstrated Bonaparte's versatility and use of central position occurred at Rivoli where he concentrated his forces rapidly to achieve decisive results.

Rivoli, January 1797

Following unsuccessful attempts to relieve Mantua and defeat Bonaparte's armies in August, September, and November, the Austrians made another major effort in January 1797. General Joseph d'Alvintzi began the offensive on January 7. He approached with 28,000 men down the Adige River valley on the east side of Lake Garda and moved toward General Berthélemy Joubert's division near Rivoli. A second column of 6,000 Austrians advanced from the east against Verona, while a third force of 9,000 men moved south to relieve the Austrians in Mantua.

Anticipating an Austrian attack, Bonaparte posted Joubert's division with 10,300 men above Rivoli on the east side of Lake Garda; he also posted Masséna's division near Verona, and Augereau's to the southeast of Verona. Spreading his forces along possible approaches for the Austrians, he intended to determine the location of the main enemy column and then concentrate against it.

After receiving reports of the Austrian movement, Bonaparte concluded that the largest enemy force was moving along the east side of Lake Garda toward Rivoli. He immediately ordered Masséna to march there. While Augereau's division waited to confront the Austrian columns advancing on Mantua, Masséna marched all night along snow-covered roads, with the first of his units reaching the Rivoli battlefield before dawn. Bonaparte had arrived around two in the morning. Masséna's soldiers moved to the left of Joubert's division, which Bonaparte had pushed forward into better positions. Bonaparte soon saw that the Austrians were sending forces in a wide turning movement around his left flank and attacking in massive columns against his main position. In the crucial phase of the battle, however, one of Masséna's demi-brigades arrived to halt the enemy columns. Despite some momentary reverses, the French turned back the Austrian attacks and captured most of the forces attempting to turn their flank.

Following the collapse of the Austrians at Rivoli, Joubert pursued the enemy as they retreated to the north, while Masséna raced forty miles south in twenty-four hours to intercept the Austrian column marching to the relief of Mantua. Caught in a pincer movement between Masséna and the investing forces, the Austrian column surrendered. In just five days the Austrians had lost 35,000 soldiers. Two weeks later, the 30,000 starving men holed up in Mantua surrendered.

Bonaparte had determined the thrust of the main enemy force, used his central position to concentrate forces rapidly, and gained an important victory. The example of his brilliant campaign in Italy would influence European warfare for the next two centuries.

Consolidation of Napoleon's Power

With the successful conclusion of the War of the First Coalition, Bonaparte returned to France in December 1797 a conquering hero. Anxious to minimize the influence in Paris of their victorious general, officials of the Directory placed him in command of forces preparing for an invasion of the British Isles. After a careful assessment he concluded that landing in England without command of the sea would be impossible. He then proposed an alternative that had long been in his mind—an invasion of Egypt. In March the Directory approved the expedition, and Bonaparte plunged into preparations. If successful, he would destroy British political and economic interests in the region, disrupt their trade, and establish a new French colony. The scheme, however, paid little attention to the fact that Egypt was part of the Ottoman Empire, which was not at war with France, and that Russia had its own designs for the Middle East.

After several months of secret preparations, Bonaparte's army of about 40,000 men sailed from Toulon in May 1798. The French soldiers went to Malta, quickly overran the small island, and then sailed for Egypt. A few weeks after their arrival, they easily defeated the poorly armed and trained Mameluke cavalry and captured Cairo. Shortly thereafter, the British admiral, Horatio Nelson, destroyed the French fleet in the battle of the Nile, cutting off Bonaparte and his army from France.

With Bonaparte and his army now isolated, significant forces began concentrating against France. The Ottoman Empire declared war on France in early September, and in December, Great Britain, Russia, and Naples joined the Ottoman Empire in the Second Coalition. To recoup losses in Italy, Austria joined the coalition about three months later.

Following the Ottoman Empire's declaration of war against France, Bonaparte invaded Syria in February 1799. Successful at first, he failed to capture the key fortress of Acre, which continued to receive supplies and reinforcements from the sea, and he retired to Cairo after the plague broke out in his army. Demonstrating that he had not lost his touch, however, he easily defeated a Turkish invasion of Egypt at the end of July. But the plague had weakened his army, and a British naval blockade cut off supplies and replacements. Concluding that there was little reason for him to remain in Egypt, far from France and the War of the Second Coalition, Bonaparte left his army in Egypt, where it eventually surrendered in September 1801 on the condition that it be returned to France. He sailed for France on August 23, 1799.

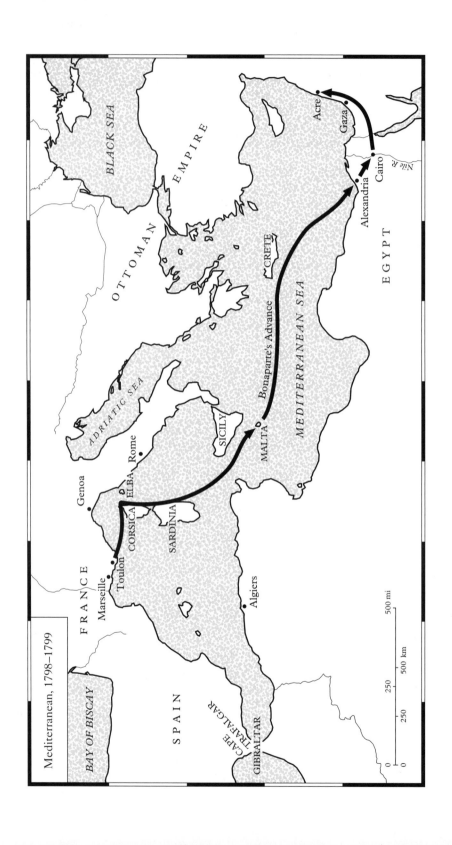

Mediterranean, 1798–1799

In Bonaparte's absence, the armies of the Second Coalition had threatened France from three directions. In Italy the Austrians initially pushed back the French. With the arrival of the Russians, all of Italy, except Genoa, fell to the allies. In Germany, Archduke Charles drove the French toward the Rhine. In Holland, an allied force of British and Russians landed on the coast and advanced slowly. But the abilities of Masséna spared France from invasion. Waging a mobile campaign high in the Alps around Zurich, Masséna launched his divisions in a series of coordinated attacks over a distance of almost one hundred miles, defeated one Austrian and two Russian armies, as well as a royalist army, and halted the allied advance. The victory stabilized the French frontier; Russia withdrew from the Coalition after the disastrous campaign.

Bonaparte as First Consul

The success at Zurich set the stage for Bonaparte's rise to power and his return to Italy. When Bonaparte arrived in France, he was depicted as a crusader, returning from the Holy Land. Failing to recognize the folly of the Egyptian campaign, French citizens embellished his successes and compared them to the Directory's failure to solve the country's political, economic, social, and religious problems. With the government teetering on the edge of bankruptcy, parts of western and southeastern France were in open rebellion, brigandage was common, and corruption was rampant. Members of the government seemed interested only in perpetuating their own power. Indeed only an aggressive foreign policy in Italy, the Low Countries, and Switzerland could provide the necessary funds to sustain the Directory's bankrupt domestic policies and appease the people.

As various factions sought to orchestrate a coup against the ineffective government, Bonaparte joined a faction which included his brother Lucien and was led by one of the civilian leaders of the Directory, Abbé Emmanuel Sieyès. After Bonaparte received command of the garrison of Paris on November 9, 1799, ostensibly to protect the government, he and his fellow conspirators seized power. They established a provisional government and published a new constitution that came into effect on December 25, 1799.

Under the new constitution, the Consulate was formed, with three officials known as consuls exercising the executive power of the government. In reality, the First Consul was the chief administrative official of the new government; Bonaparte held that position. He now directed the boundless energy that typified his activity on the battlefield to domestic affairs. He centralized the administration, instituted electoral and tax reform, reorganized local government, and created a new judicial system to protect the achievements of the Revolution. Although the Consulate was based on the principles of liberty, equality, and fraternity, Bonaparte named the political, administrative, and judicial officials and determined foreign policy. In fact, the republic existed in name only, for Bonaparte soon exercised the authority of a monarch.

The Defeat of the Second Coalition

As First Consul, Bonaparte worked energetically to end civil strife in France and mount an offensive that would bring peace abroad. With Russia out of the Second Coalition and Great Britain safely out of reach, Bonaparte turned toward Austria. In addition to a small army under Augereau in Holland, France had two armies along its eastern frontier, one under General Jean Victor Moreau in the Rhineland and northern Switzerland and another under Masséna along the Italian coast from Nice to Genoa. As civil strife decreased, Bonaparte drew troops from the Vendée and assembled them behind Moreau's army in what came to be known as the Army of the Reserve. With Berthier in nominal command, the Army of the Reserve could move into either southern Germany or Italy where the principal Austrian armies were deployed.

Bonaparte took several steps to improve the readiness of his forces. The government resumed paying its soldiers, provided much-needed supplies, and raised raw conscripts to increase the strength of many undermanned units. Bonaparte also ordered his armies to adopt the *corps d'armée* system. Although first formed on an ad hoc basis as early as 1796, the corps became a formal part of French military organizations in March 1800. Consisting of several divisions, elements of all arms, and a small staff, the corps included fewer than 10,000 soldiers in 1800 (they would be as large as 25,000 men five years later). Capable of operating independently, they enhanced the ability of large French armies to operate in a highly mobile and flexible fashion. Despite these reforms, French forces, particularly those in Italy, did not have enough soldiers or supplies.

The Austrians greatly outnumbered the French in Italy, and in early April they attacked Masséna and split his army. After the Austrians drove Masséna and part of his forces into Genoa and besieged them, Bonaparte decided to concentrate France's main effort against the Austrians in Italy and make a daring crossing of the Alps. No major army had crossed the Alps since the time of Hannibal in 218 B.C. Bonaparte ordered Moreau to push the Austrians back in southern Germany and protect the Army of the Reserve's lines of communication as it advanced through Switzerland. He accompanied the army of some 40,000 men through Geneva and the snow-covered Great St. Bernard Pass while other divisions crossed through different Alpine passes. On May 14, 1800, the French advance guard reached the foot of the Great St. Bernard Pass, and by May 24 most of the Army of the Reserve had passed through the Alps. Bonaparte had achieved the unthinkable—he had led an army across the snow-clogged Alps and was poised for a drive into northern Italy.

Rather than relieve Masséna and his starving forces in Genoa, Bonaparte decided to march fifty miles east to occupy Milan. With a major Austrian force besieging Masséna's troops, he planned a *manoeuvre sur les derrières* that would cut the Austrians' lines of communication and threaten their entire army. Stunned by the French crossing of the Alps, the Austrian commander, General Michael Melas, quickly began concentrating his forces at Alessandria (about thirty miles north of Genoa). After entering Milan on

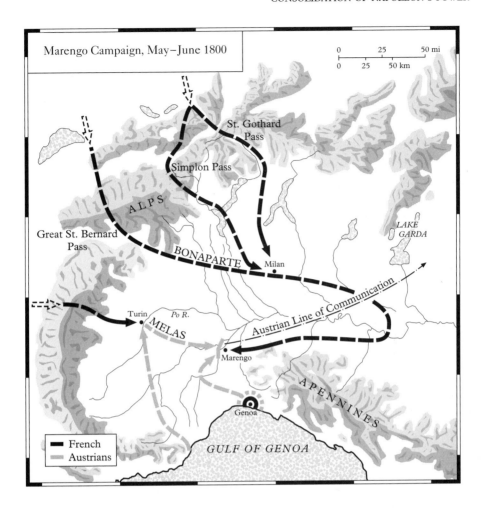

Marengo Campaign, May–June 1800

0   25   50 mi
0   25   50 km

St. Gothard Pass

Simplon Pass

Great St. Bernard Pass

ALPS

BONAPARTE

Milan

LAKE GARDA

Turin

Po R.

MELAS

Austrian Line of Communication

Marengo

APENNINES

Genoa

■ French
■ Austrians

GULF OF GENOA

June 2, Bonaparte marched south and crossed the Po River; he expected to confront the Austrians south of the Po as they attempted to open their lines of communication to the east. Meanwhile the French evacuation of Genoa on June 6 and the arrival of some Austrian troops from the siege allowed Melas to increase the size of his forces. Unaware of the Austrians' concentrating at Alessandria, Bonaparte turned his army toward the west and advanced toward that city. To search for the enemy, he dispersed his forces and sent out several columns to locate them.

On June 13 the French main force bivouacked on the plain of Marengo, across the Bormida River and a few miles east of Alessandria. Early on June 14, 31,000 Austrians poured out of Alessandria, crossed the bridges on the Bormida, and advanced in three huge columns on Marengo. They surprised the French and pushed them back. Hoping to buy time, Bonaparte committed his last reserves, but they did not stop the enemy. Decisively outnumbered and running low on ammunition, the French had clearly lost the first phase of the battle.

When the fighting halted momentarily, Bonaparte withdrew some three miles and met with his subordinate commanders to discuss options. With the support of his generals and the opportune arrival of General Louis Desaix's corps, he began the battle anew. The audacious attack of Desaix's infantry, supported by artillery and cavalry, soon repulsed the enemy. By the end of the day, the French had captured 8,000 men and forty cannon and inflicted some 6,000 casualties; French losses totaled 6,000, including the brave Desaix. Melas, stunned by the reverse, agreed to an armistice to an end of hostilities.

Bonaparte had gained victory despite faulty intelligence, a disregard for the enemy, and poor dispositions; he had committed enough errors to cost him not only his army but also his political position in France. Yet he had seized the initiative, directed a perilous march through the Alps, surprised his enemy, and—thanks to the efforts of his subordinates—achieved victory.

Despite the success at Marengo, the final defeat of the Habsburgs did not come until December 1800 when Moreau's Army of the Rhine defeated the Austrians at Hohenlinden. In February 1801 the Peace of Lunéville ended the war of the Second Coalition and reaffirmed France's domination of northern Italy and the Low Countries. In March 1802 Great Britain, France's last enemy, agreed to the Peace of Amiens, and for the first time in ten years Europe was at peace. In an astonishingly brief period, Bonaparte had gained control of France and a significant portion of western Europe.

The Emperor and the Grand Army

Europe did not long remain at peace. Bonaparte's efforts to resurrect France's colonial empire and to extend his control over Holland, Switzerland, Italy, and Germany created such resentment and anxiety in other states as to drive them to war again. In May 1803 Britain renewed the war against France and in 1805 brought Austria and Russia into the Third Coalition against France.

Between the Peace of Amiens and the Austrian invasion of Germany in September 1805, Bonaparte strengthened his control over France. He packed the French Legislative Corps and the executive branch of government with men who would support his policies. He eliminated political opposition with a combination of repressive and conciliatory actions; and he was elected consul for life in 1802 and then proclaimed emperor in 1804. (He was known thereafter simply as Napoleon.) To gain popular support and ensure the basic reforms of the Revolution, he confirmed the land settlement of the Revolution; protected private property; guaranteed French Catholics, Protestants, and Jews religious toleration subject to state regulation; established a civil code that reformed the legal system and ensured civil equality; and reorganized the French educational system. He also created the Legion of Honor to inspire public and military officials and to reward meritorious service. Finally, to improve the economy and increase public revenues, he not only encouraged industry and agriculture (with subsidies, price controls, a national bank, a stock exchange, and a more stable currency) but also created an equitable tax system and nourished agricultural and industrial reform. These reforms enabled him to marshal the resources of the most populous and advanced state in Europe for war on an unprecedented scale.

Between 1801 and 1805, Napoleon devoted considerable effort to improve his army. He achieved some of his most significant reforms when he organized and prepared 150,000 men for an invasion of the British Isles. Though Napoleon never launched this army (eventually known as the Grand Army) across the Channel, it enhanced France's military capabilities and provided Napoleon with a powerful fighting force. By 1805 the Grand Army included about 450,000 soldiers, including units stationed in Holland, Hanover, and Italy, as well as France. This force was capable of waging war on an entirely new scale and with greater speed and decisiveness than any eighteenth-century army.

As ruler of France and commander-in-chief of the army, Napoleon made all decisions, developed strategy, and determined campaign dispositions; but commanding half a million men over vast distances required a large staff. The emperor asserted control over the army through his personal staff and his general staff, while his intendant general (quartermaster general) obtained, transported, and distributed supplies. The Imperial Headquarters included perhaps 400 officers in 1805 but expanded to about 3,500 officers by 1812. Napoleon's personal staff, the *Maison*, was the operational center of the army; it included Napoleon's chief of staff, Berthier, as well as several officers responsible for household operations, intelligence, daily reports, correspondence, and situation maps. Berthier directed the general staff (*état major*) which had responsibility for transmitting orders, coordinating movements, and securing intelligence, as well as establishing hospitals and managing finances and military justice. Though the general staff enabled Napoleon to control large forces, it never achieved the effectiveness attained by the Prussian general staff in the late nineteenth century and never became a deliberative body that functioned as the brains of the army. It focused on accumulating information and executing Napoleon's orders. Nonetheless, the headquarters staff enabled Napoleon to remain unencumbered and move to any sector of a battlefield, where he could respond to enemy actions, modify orders, encourage his soldiers, and at times, assume command.

Along with obtaining the vast supplies required by any army, the intendant general regulated the collection and distribution of food. In France or in the territory of its allies, requisitions were made through local authorities, paid for in cash or bonds, and distributed directly to the troops. In the enemy's territory, Napoleon's armies continued to live off the countryside. By advancing in widely dispersed corps, the army spread over a large area and encountered greater success in obtaining food and supplies than if it moved along a single route. Marauding and looting soldiers, however, often created bitter antagonisms when they swept through an area. Nevertheless, the army that marched to the Danube in 1805 carried just eight days of rations, which were issued only when the French expected battle or when it was impractical to allow the soldiers to disperse for foraging. The few supply convoys carried primarily munitions.

A major aspect of the Grand Army was its reliance on the army corps, which after the Marengo campaign, had become a permanent feature of the French army. By 1805 the Grand Army had seven corps. Normally ranging in size from 14,000 to 25,000 soldiers but occasionally much larger, the corps included from two to four infantry divisions, usually a brigade of cavalry, several artillery batteries, some engineers, and corps and division staffs. Capable of withstanding attacks from an enemy army, a corps could fight either as an element of a main army or as an independent force. Its ability to operate independently provided great flexibility and mobility to the French army; by moving on parallel and dispersed routes, a corps could live off the countryside and concentrate swiftly with other corps when necessary. The use of the corps also made Napoleon's forces more resilient, for a corps could absorb large casualties without affecting the will to fight or capabilities of other corps. In future campaigns, Napoleon would sometimes group corps together in ad hoc field armies, permitting him to function much like an army group commander.

Between 1801 and 1805 Napoleon made some changes in the weapons and organizations of his Grand Army. The infantry continued to carry the Model 1777 Charleville musket or one of its later versions, but a shortage of muskets forced France to purchase other types of muskets from its satellite states. To ensure greater uniformity in the Grand Army, the emperor organized infantry units in a standard manner. Abandoning the demi-brigade, he placed several infantry battalions in a brigade of approximately 3,600 men and two or three brigades in an infantry division of 6,000–10,000 men. Beginning in 1805, a battalion included six companies, each 140 men strong. He also expanded the size of the Imperial Guard, made entry requirements more selective, and converted it into an elite striking force. Subsequent events, however, sometimes found him reluctant to employ it.

Napoleon made greater changes in the cavalry. Convinced that it was essential for offensive operations, he organized his cavalry into heavy, line, and light units. The cavalry apportioned to each corps in 1804 varied from 450 to 2,000 horsemen, but he kept a large reserve cavalry corps to use in crises. For pursuit, French cavalry were unequaled. He also placed great importance on artillery. The Gribeauval cannon remained standard in the army, but the French also used captured pieces. They distributed between twenty-four and forty-eight guns to each corps for use with infantry divisions and cavalry brigades. An artillery reserve was attached to the army, and even though Napoleon resorted to sieges far less frequently than eighteenth-century armies, the engineers maintained massive artillery trains for siege operations. Thus Napoleon organized his forces for large offensive operations and structured them in a more uniform fashion, resulting in a more flexible and powerful Grand Army.

The Grand Army in 1805 was very different from other European armies. Over a quarter of the army had fought in the revolutionary wars or in the Marengo campaign, and the remainder had been conscripted between 1801 and 1805. Seldom employed as garrison soldiers, Napoleonic troops retained their independence and neglected formal discipline. New recruits spent little more than a week in a training camp; picking up their knowledge and skills by mingling with veterans, they had an outlook and discipline similar to that of the Volunteers of 1792. Napoleon regarded his soldiers as fighters, and his primary concern was their eagerness for battle. Like the soldiers, many officers lacked formal schooling, but almost all officers and noncommissioned officers had experienced combat. Furthermore, most of the higher ranking officers were young and spirited. Of the seven corps commanders of the Grand Army in 1805, only two were over forty; half the division commanders were less than forty. Only one division commander was over fifty. The fervor of the officers and soldiers for battle and their ability to march long distances proved key to Napoleon's success. They recognized, as did Napoleon, that without vast supply trains following them, they had to confront and defeat the enemy quickly.

Thus after the war between France and Austria ended in February 1801, Napoleon devoted considerable energy, time, and resources to reorganizing his army and preparing it to operate in mobile campaigns. By 1805 he had a tightly organized and highly motivated force whose size, speed, and decisiveness would soon astonish the world.

The Ulm and Austerlitz Campaign, 1805

In contrast to the steady improvement of the French military, the Austrians, Russians, and Prussians made few changes. None imitated the French by raising large armies that were motivated by patriotism, for none wished to make the broad political and social changes required to create a national mass army. And very few officers sought to change the eighteenth-century practices upon which their organizations, tactics, and strategy rested.

The Austrians illustrate the reluctance to change. Emperor Francis II reserved the highest positions for his family, and in the 1805 campaign his brothers, Ferdinand, John, and Charles, commanded the three Austrian armies. A few officers came from military academies, but most received direct appointments or transferred from foreign armies. The appointment of officers remained the prerogative of colonels who had complete control over their regiments. Soldiers served for life, and their long-term training produced highly disciplined units despite the great diversity of the Habsburg Empire.

Of those recognizing the need to improve the Habsburg armies, Archduke Charles was the most commited to achieving the necessary reforms. In 1801, Emperor Francis II made him president of the war council and then minister of war and navy. Despite considerable opposition, Charles succeeded in reducing the term of service to ten, twelve, and fourteen years in the infantry, cavalry, and artillery, respectively. He made modest improvements in the training and education of young officers and reorganized the overall administration of the Austrian army. Though limited, the reforms created friction at court between Charles and his critics, as well as the emperor, who rallied around the flamboyant and undistinguished old warrior, General Karl von Mack. In the end, the Austrian army remained wedded to its eighteenth-century organization and methods.

The impulse for war in 1805 came from increasing distrust of Napoleon and his expansionist policies. With Britain, Austria, and Russia as the dominant members, the Third Coalition against France secretly came into existence between April and August 1805. The Habsburg emperor, Francis II, willingly joined the coalition despite Charles's conviction that the army was not ready. The emperor responded to those around the throne clamoring for action against the French, as well as the promised support of at least 50,000 Russian troops, supplemented by British forces in the Mediterranean, and as much as 4 million pounds British Sterling. Members of the Third Coalition planned an offensive to drive France out of the Low Countries and Italy; Austria was to recover northern Italy while Austrian and Russian forces advanced across the Rhine.

Ulm

In early September 1805, the Austrians moved with three armies on line. On the right, Archduke Ferdinand (ultimately superseded by his chief of staff, General Mack) marched with his army into Bavaria. In the center, Archduke John's army began on the defensive in the Tyrol, and on the left, Archduke Charles's army (the largest of the three) occupied Verona, east of the Adige River in northern Italy. The Austrians expected a Russian army to advance and occupy a position on Mack's right. Mack and the Russians were supposed to make a combined attack toward Strasbourg, while John's and Charles's armies moved through Switzerland and Italy toward France. Rather than wait for the Russians, Mack swept triumphantly west through Munich toward Ulm as the Bavarians fell back to await French aid. Expecting the French army to attack from the vicinity of Strasbourg in mid-November, Mack calculated that the Russian army would have ample time to reach Ulm and reinforce him before he met the French.

With the first indication of Austrian intentions to invade Bavaria, Napoleon began preparing for a campaign in southern Germany. On August 26 the Grand Army broke camp along the Channel. Preceded by Marshal Joachim Murat's cavalry, the various corps set out along parallel routes as they marched toward the Rhine. Some units covered well over twenty miles a day and between 120 and 200 miles in two weeks. The first elements of Napoleon's 210,000-man army crossed the Rhine on September 25.

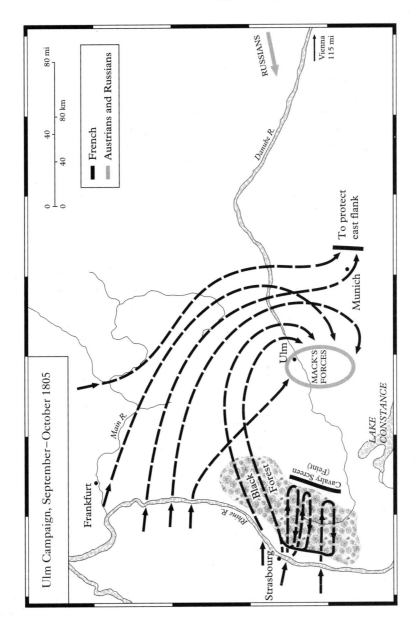

Ulm Campaign, September–October 1805

Napoleon chose a daring campaign strategy, one that would exploit the superior mobility of his corps and the ability of his forces to live off the countryside. While Masséna defended Italy, the Grand Army would drive deep into Germany in a gigantic strategic envelopment to cut off Ferdinand's army. Six corps crossed the Rhine and, reinforced by two Bavarian divisions, marched toward the Danube. Meanwhile, to deceive the Austrians and lure them farther west where they might be enveloped more easily, Murat's cavalry crossed the Rhine River at Strasbourg and advanced into the

Black Forest. On October 6, leading elements of the main French force began crossing the Danube northeast of Ulm. By October 11 the French had two corps in the vicinity of Munich, eighty miles *east* of Mack; they severed his lines of communication and closed his only route of escape. After realizing that the bulk of the Austrian army was still at Ulm, Napoleon quickly marched troops west to encircle the city.

On October 13 the French began closing in on Ulm. The following day Ferdinand abandoned Mack and his forces to avoid capture. As the French encircled the demoralized Austrians, Murat's cavalry chased after those who had escaped. On October 20 a dejected Mack surrendered with 27,000 Austrians.

As for Italy, Archduke Charles had done little despite having more than twice the troops of Masséna. After the French crossed the Adige River and seized Verona, Charles pulled back a few miles to Caldiero where Masséna attacked him ten days later. Though not defeated, Charles continued withdrawing with French forces on his heels. Masséna followed closely to prevent Charles from joining the Austrians near Vienna.

Austerlitz

Three days after the fall of Ulm, Napoleon marched toward Vienna. A Russian army of 36,000 men under General Mikhail Kutusov had occupied a position about sixty miles east of Munich, but the Russians were willing neither to defend Vienna nor risk being destroyed. After withdrawing over the Danube forty miles west of Vienna, they retired into Moravia. Reinforced by the Austrians and by other Russian forces, the allied army increased to some 90,000 men and assembled near Olmütz, one hundred miles northeast of Vienna. When the Russian tsar, Alexander I, arrived, he quickly assumed responsibility for allied operations, despite Francis II of Austria's presence. Although inexperienced and impressionable, Alexander was confident that the allies could defeat Napoleon. Rather than seek the advice of Kutusov or the other senior generals, he turned to his personal aides and the Austrian staff officer who had guided the Russians across Austria.

On November 12 the French advance guard reached Vienna and crossed the Danube while other French forces crossed the Danube to the west. They concentrated seventy-five miles north of Vienna at Brünn. The French had chased the allied armies almost 400 miles, and they now faced critical logistical and strategic problems: their long lines of communication were vulnerable to attack; they were menaced by a much larger enemy and a belligerent population; they faced a cold winter without adequate resources or manpower; and they were uncertain about the intentions of the Prussians. Napoleon recognized that the allies had secure lines of communication running through Poland and Silesia and that he had no chance of a strategic envelopment. He decided to lure Alexander into a decisive engagement and end the campaign with one great battle.

After reconnoitering the area, Napoleon chose the Pratzen heights between Brünn and Austerlitz as the site for the battle. He carefully avoided concentrating his entire army in this position, for he hoped to lure the allies into an attack. He hoped to manipulate their movements so a principal part of their army would attack his southern flank; such an attack would place their line of communication through Olmütz in jeopardy and leave them vulnerable to encirclement and destruction. To deceive his enemy further, Napoleon sent an aide-de-camp to allied headquarters, ostensibly to appeal for an armistice.

Napoleon anchored the left flank of his army on Santon Hill, just north of the Brünn-Olmütz road. A full corps, supported by a detachment of cavalry, straddled the road. He thinly spread a division from Marshal Nicolas Soult's corps for about six miles along the Goldbach stream, south through Sokolnitz to Tellnitz, and supported them with a few artillery batteries. Napoleon expected Marshal Louis-Nicolas Davout's corps, which was approaching from Vienna, to strengthen his right flank when it arrived. The bulk of the French reserves, including additional artillery, the Imperial Guard, and later Marshal Jean-Baptiste Bernadotte's corps, remained hidden behind a hill on the French left wing.

At allied headquarters, the tsar insisted on an immediate battle; the Austrians offered no objections. By November 24, Alexander adopted a plan that in retrospect would place the allies in an extremely awkward position. The allies would move forward from Olmütz; after passing Austerlitz, they would shift to the south and place their forces between Napoleon and Vienna. Then they would crush the French right and drive them north into the mountains toward the vacillating Prussians.

Following three days of preparations, the allied army advanced in five great columns along a five-mile front. On November 30, French troops, feigning disorder, retired from the Pratzen heights. Early on December 1 the Russians and Austrians clambered onto the Pratzen heights. Allied generals had concerns about the complex plans, but the tsar and his advisors believed any shortcomings in their battle plans would be negated by deficiencies in Napoleon's army and dispositions. They had no idea they had been tricked.

On the eve of battle, Napoleon visited French positions and made minor adjustments. He halted occasionally to talk with and encourage his men in the freezing weather. On his return to his headquarters, a soldier recognized him and lit a torch. Soon a line of torches stretched along the entire French line. Reflecting Napoleon's charisma, it was as spontaneous as it was dramatic. Allied soldiers could not have been encouraged by the torchlight parade and the cheers. Before three the next morning, Napoleon examined incoming reports and then issued final battle instructions. As usual, he would make adjustments later, but by dawn of December 2, his army was ready.

The allies planned to make their main attack with three massive infantry columns, totaling almost 34,000 men, against Napoleon's weak right flank. After this attack began, another column, 24,000 strong, would advance from the Pratzen heights toward the French center. Another 30,000 troops would concentrate on the French left, opposite Santon Hill. Alexander had adopted the plan that Napoleon had encouraged by his own deployments.

The torchlight procession at Austerlitz. A member of the Old Guard told Napoleon, "I promise you . . . that tomorrow we will bring you the Russian army's flags and artillery to celebrate the anniversary of your coronation."

With only 50,000 troops initially available, Napoleon had to dispose his troops carefully until Davout arrived from Vienna, almost eighty miles away, and Bernadotte hurried from Iglau, fifty miles to the north. As the allied dispositions became apparent, Napoleon modified his battle plans. He had originally believed the main enemy attack would come near his center about three miles south of the Brünn-Olmütz road, but he soon concluded that the enemy would concentrate their attack about five or six miles south of the road, near Tellnitz. Consequently, when Davout's troops arrived, he shifted them farther to his right to meet the main enemy attack.

The initial fighting proceeded much as the allies had expected. By 8:30 A.M., Russian troops had fought their way into the villages of Tellnitz and Sokolnitz on the French right. The allies appeared to have victory within their grasp until the arrival of Davout's corps. As the fighting intensified in the south, the allied generals weakened their center on the Pratzen heights so they could commit more of their forces to the southern attack.

At the appropriate moment, Napoleon sent two of Soult's divisions into the weakened enemy center. Concealed by thick fog and heavy smoke, they marched out of the murk into the brilliant sun and fought their way up the Pratzen heights to confront the Russians. Atop the heights the fighting

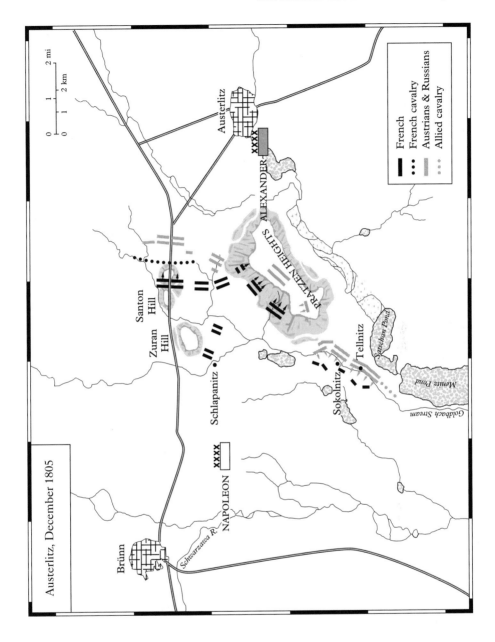

Austerlitz, December 1805

raged fiercely with attacks and counterattacks unfolding in rapid succession. After the commitment of the Russian Imperial Guard in a counterattack, Napoleon reached the heights and ordered the cavalry of the French Imperial Guard forward. A division from Bernadotte's corps also arrived to reinforce the French and throw back the allied counterattack. By two in the afternoon, the allied center had collapsed.

To make matters worse for the allies, Napoleon turned his troops on the Pratzen to the south. Since the allied soldiers on the south flank had the

Satschan and Menitz ponds to their rear, the French movement cut off the escape route of the troops fighting at Tellnitz and Sokolnitz. Hundreds of Russians surrendered, but thousands attempted to escape, some fleeing across the ice of the ponds. Napoleon personally ordered an artillery battery forward to bombard the fugitives. The cannonballs and the weight of fleeing troops broke the ice, and hundreds of allied troops fell into the freezing, waist-deep water. Many surrendered; a few drowned. On the north flank, the right wing of the allied army broke contact and retreated. Darkness soon ended the firing and spared the allied army from further pursuit.

In subsequent years, Napoleon justifiably regarded his victory at Austerlitz as his masterpiece. The allies lost almost one third of their troops, that is, approximately 27,000 men, including almost 13,000 prisoners. The French suffered about 8,000 casualties, of whom 1,305 were killed. On December 3 the tsar decided to withdraw his army toward Hungary, but the Austrian emperor resolved to treat with Napoleon. The next day he met with Napoleon and agreed to an armistice, ending the Third Coalition. France and Austria signed the Treaty of Pressburg on December 26, but its harsh terms ensured Austria's continued enmity. In essence, Austria was completely excluded from Italy and had to give up its influential position in Germany. Although Napoleon expected Russia to seek peace, the defeated and humiliated Russian tsar saw Austerlitz as only the first phase in a continuing struggle.

The Jena Campaign, 1806

During the 1805 campaign, Prussia had remained neutral despite its promise to join Russia in the war against France. Following the battle of Austerlitz on December 2, Prussia meekly renewed its friendly terms with Napoleon. As Napoleon's efforts to transform and control Germany became apparent however, pressure for war increased in Prussia. In Germany, Napoleon elevated Bavaria and Württemberg to kingdoms and Baden to a grand duchy, and after creating the Confederation of the Rhine with himself as its protector, he orchestrated the dissolution of the Holy Roman Empire. In Italy, he took Venetia and added it to his Kingdom of Italy, which combined the former Cisalpine and Italian republics. After invading the Kingdom of Naples he made his brother Joseph the king. Another brother, Louis, was made king of Holland, and his stepson, Eugène de Beauharnais, viceroy of Italy. Naturally these steps greatly expanded French influence over German and Italian affairs.

The spark that brought on war with Prussia, however, came from Napoleon's offer to restore Hanover, the ancestral home of the British kings, to George III in return for peace. Since Napoleon had allowed Prussia to occupy Hanover, Frederick William III was stunned by this revelation and secretly signed a pact with the Russian tsar in July 1806. In early October, Britain would join Prussia and Russia in the Fourth Coalition.

Despite a series of French proposals and counterproposals, the Prussian king began preparing his army in August for war. At the end of September, he demanded that Napoleon evacuate southern Germany or face the Prussian army. Unfortunately for Prussia, its army was a more typical eighteenth-century force than any other army in Europe. Still adhering to the methods of Frederick the Great, and still supported by a system of supply that greatly restricted mobility, it was woefully outdated, a fact that would become all too apparent in the upcoming campaign. As Napoleon prepared to invade Prussia, Frederick William III and his officers debated strategic alternatives and arrogantly predicted victory. Unwilling to wait for promised Russian support, Frederick William occupied Saxony and foolishly dispersed his army over an eighty-five-mile front. Only after the French threatened invasion did he begin concentrating his army on the southwest Saxon frontier behind the Thuringian Forest.

Meanwhile, Napoleon moved as soon as he realized that war was unavoidable. As a precautionary measure, he began to assemble his forces just south of the Saxon frontier during the last weeks of September. He

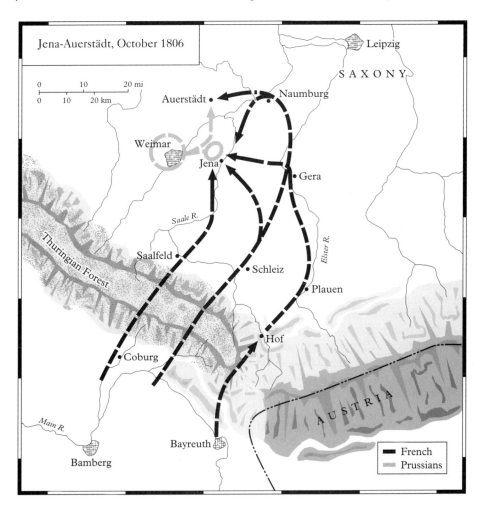

Jena-Auerstädt, October 1806

joined the army on October 2 and organized his 180,000 men into a massive formation known as a *bataillon carré* (square battalion). With seven corps, the reserve cavalry, and the Imperial Guard, supplemented by Bavarian troops, the French formed three massive columns and swept north along parallel routes through the Thuringian Forest into Saxony. Concerned about unpredictable Prussian dispositions and intentions, Napoleon kept his corps within supporting distance of each other so he could concentrate his entire force swiftly and move it in any direction.

The French advance began on October 8, and two days later serious fighting erupted when Marshal Jean Lannes's advance guard struck the Prussians at Saalfeld (fifteen miles north of the Thuringian Forest) and inflicted 3,000 casualties, including Prince Louis Ferdinand of Prussia. The French had fewer than 200 casualties. The defeat had a significant psychological effect on the Prussians, who saw their advance guard almost annihilated and one of the most popular members of the royal family killed.

Jena

Despite this first encounter with the Prussian army, Napoleon remained unaware of the location of the enemy's main force. His army continued moving northeast toward Leipzig. On October 13, Lannes drove enemy pickets out of Jena and moved a battalion up a steep rocky road to the heights of Landgrafenberg. From that position, the French looked down on an enemy force of perhaps 40,000 men. Lannes immediately rushed other elements onto the heights and sent word to Napoleon identifying the enemy's location. Napoleon hurried to the top of the Landgrafenberg and erroneously concluded he had located the main enemy army; by dawn over 45,000 men and seventy cannon were on Landgrafenberg. Meanwhile the corps of Davout and Bernadotte continued marching northeast. Unaware that the main Prussian force was already withdrawing from Jena northeast through Auerstädt, Napoleon expected the two corps to turn and outflank the Prussian army at the appropriate moment.

At dawn on October 14, the first skirmishing began at Jena with Lannes's corps engaging the Prussians. Organized in both line and column and preceded by a cloud of skirmishers, Lannes's corps was supported by Soult's corps on the right and Augereau's on the left. The Prussians, under the command of sixty-one-year-old Prince Frederick Hohenlohe, launched several counterattacks, but the French beat them off and pushed forward. Driven from village to village, the Prussians could not resist the steady French fire despite the arrival of reinforcements.

By 1:00 P.M., Napoleon had concentrated 90,000 men and ordered a general advance. Murat's cavalry poured onto the battlefield, and the French infantry advanced, capturing thousands of prisoners. By mid-afternoon the extent of Napoleon's decisive victory became evident as the Prussians fled before Murat's horsemen. In addition to having 15,000 soldiers taken prisoner, the Prussians suffered at least 10,000 casualties and lost eighty-five cannon. In sharp contrast, the French suffered 6,000 casualties.

Napoleon at Jena. Shortly before the fighting began, Napoleon supposedly rode in front of his troops and said, "Our squares must destroy the famous Prussian cavalry just as we crushed the Russian infantry at Austerlitz."

Auerstädt

While Napoleon fought what he regarded as the main Prussian army, Davout's corps of 26,000 men and forty-four guns, about fifteen miles to the northeast, wheeled around and marched southwest to turn the Prussian flank. Early on October 14, however, Davout encountered a formidable Prussian force near Auerstädt (about thirteen miles from Jena). The arrival of additional units increased the Prussians to almost 64,000 men and 230 guns. Davout's lead division, commanded by General Étienne Gudin, faced the large enemy force while the other divisions of the corps hurried forward. Commanded by the Duke of Brunswick and the King of Prussia, the Prussians struggled to organize an attack but were paralyzed by great disorder and indecision for about two hours. In the interim Davout's second division, commanded by Louis Friant, arrived. Davout's two divisions deployed in squares and held the enemy at bay while awaiting the third division, which was commanded by Charles-Antoine Morand. Outnumbered and under heavy pressure, Davout appealed to Bernadotte nearby for aid, but despite earlier instructions from Napoleon to support Davout, Berna-dotte ignored the pleas.

With no alternatives but to fight or surrender, Davout's corps fought at Auerstädt with a fury and determination that stunned the Prussians. When the Duke of Brunswick was killed and several other senior commanders killed or captured, Frederick William failed to assume command of the army or appoint a new commander. The Prussian fight degenerated into a series of uncoordinated assaults against the French squares. After repelling a Prussian attack, Morand's division advanced and crushed the enemy's right wing. In time, Friant's division overwhelmed the enemy's left wing, and soon the center of the Prussian army collapsed. As the remnants of the enemy scattered north and west, Davout's small cavalry unit pursued the retreating troops but was not large enough to inflict serious damage. Nevertheless, Brunswick's army left 13,000 casualties and prisoners and 115 guns on the battlefield. The French victory was costly, with over 7,000 casualties.

Thanks to Davout, his divisional generals (the "three immortals"), and the rank and file of Davout's corps, the French had achieved a remarkable victory at Auerstädt. Although outnumbered three to two in infantry, six to one in cavalry, and five to one in artillery, they had emerged victorious. Their success proved the efficacy and resiliency of the corps system; one army corps had not only resisted an attack by an entire enemy army but had gained a decisive victory. Napoleon did not learn of Davout's victory against the main Prussian force until after the battle. He considered a court-martial for Bernadotte for refusing to assist Davout, but he eventually did nothing more than publish in an army bulletin a rebuke of Bernadotte's poor performance.

The morning after the Prussian defeat, Napoleon unleashed one of the most determined and sweeping pursuits in military history. Spreading his corps across a one-hundred-mile front, Napoleon chased the Prussians northeast. Crossing the Elbe River, the army raced for Berlin and occupied it on October 24, a mere ten days after the victory at Jena-Auerstädt. Lannes's infantry and Murat's cavalry pursued the remains of Hohenlohe's army more than 200 miles until the Prussian general surrendered sixty-five miles north of Berlin on October 28 with 16,000 infantry, six regiments of cavalry, and sixty-four guns. Soult's and Bernadotte's infantry and Murat's cavalry pursued Prussian forces under General Gebhard von Blücher for more than 300 miles until they cornered and then captured them in the city of Lübeck on November 7. While retreating, Prussian troops surrendered the fortresses of Magdeburg, Stettin, Spandau, and Küstrin. With the loss of almost 140,000 men and 2,000 guns, the Prussian military machine, for all practical purposes, ceased to exist as a fighting force. The extent of the collapse is apparent in the French capture of 250 flags; historically, these unit colors were usually captured only when a unit no longer had the capability to protect them.

The Campaign Against Russia, 1806–1807

Despite the almost complete destruction of the Prussian army, Frederick William III refused to end the war or leave the Fourth Coalition; instead he fled east to Königsberg. He still had one corps under General Anton von Lestocq and garrisons in fortresses along the Baltic seacoast and in Warsaw. As French forces marched across Poland toward Warsaw, Napoleon became concerned about his strategic situation. With Britain providing key financial support to his opponents, Prussia refused to capitulate, Russia remained at war with France, and Austria appeared to be rearming. The threat of Austria's reentering the war caused particular concern because it threatened Napoleon's southern flank. The Austrians, however, were too exhausted to enter the war. On November 28, the French reached Warsaw, 900 miles from Paris.

Hoping to undermine the British economy, which provided subsidies for other members of the Fourth Coalition, Napoleon escalated his economic warfare against "the nation of shopkeepers." In November 1806, while in the Prussian capital, he issued the Berlin Decree which formally established the Continental System, declaring a blockade of the British Isles and closing to British commerce the coastline and ports of all territory controlled by France, directly or indirectly. By cutting off trade with the continent, Napoleon hoped to destroy the British economy so it would cease to be the "paymaster of Europe."

With reports of a Russian army massing for a possible attack, Napoleon pushed 80,000 men deep into Poland. The bitter cold, saturated terrain, impassable roads, and a dearth of the most basic provisions, however, caused acute suffering among the troops and a marked decline in morale. Consequently, Napoleon had no choice but to place his army in winter quarters in late December. Obtaining food and fodder proved to be particularly difficult in the sparsely populated and barren region, so he scattered his forces across a vast area north of Warsaw. He wanted them ready for a spring offensive against Russia.

Several minor confrontations occurred during the following weeks. In late January, Russian General Levin Bennigsen, reinforced by Lestocq's Prussian corp, moved his army west toward the mouth of the Vistula River, where he hoped to take up a strong position for a spring offensive. Napoleon prepared for renewed hostilities, despite the freezing weather and the suffering it caused his men. He expected to surprise the enemy, but a copy of his plan fell into Russian hands and provided Bennigsen sufficient warning to concentrate his forces near Ionkovo (about sixty miles south of Königsberg). On February 3 the French overtook Bennigsen's army, but after a sharp fight, the Russians withdrew during the night. Two days later another engagement occurred at Hoff; both sides lost about 2,000 men.

Eylau

On February 7, Bennigsen's army halted at Eylau (about twenty miles south of Königsberg). Though Napoleon preferred to attack the following day, a minor skirmish quickly grew into a pitched battle, and eight hours of fighting resulted in 4,000 casualties for each army. French troops gained possession of the gutted town while the Russians spent the night in frozen fields nearby.

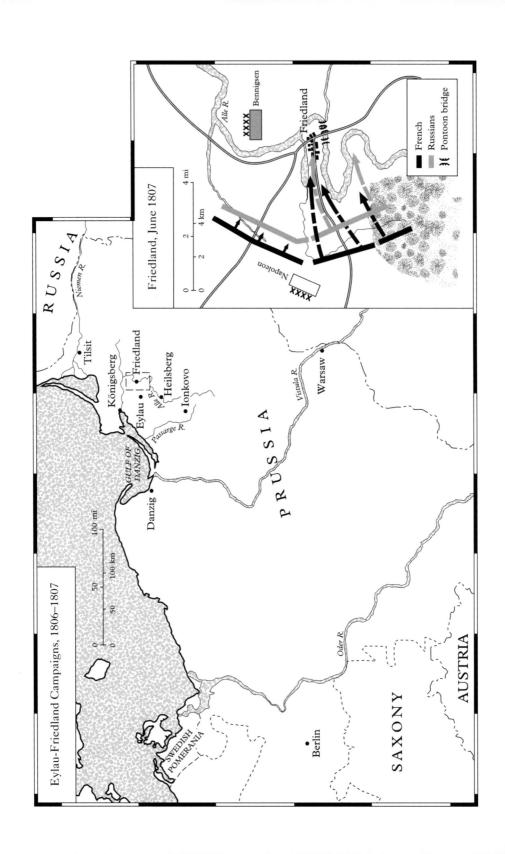

Eylau-Friedland Campaigns, 1806–1807

RUSSIA

Niemen R.

Tilsit

Königsberg

Friedland

Eylau

Heilsberg

Ionkovo

Alle R.

Passarge R.

GULF OF
DANZIG

Danzig

PRUSSIA

Vistula R.

Warsaw

Oder R.

SWEDISH
POMERANIA

Berlin

SAXONY

AUSTRIA

100 mi

0   50   100

0   50   100 km

Friedland, June 1807

Alle R.

Bennigsen

XXXX

Friedland

Napoleon

XXXX

French
Russians
Pontoon bridge

4 mi

0   2   4

0   2   4 km

On February 8, Napoleon found a Russian army of almost 70,000 soldiers deployed before him. Though the French had only 45,000 men at Eylau, Napoleon assumed the corps of Davout and Marshal Michel Ney would arrive soon and planned to launch a double envelopment with Ney striking on the left and Davout on the right. Unaware that the Russians had more than a two-to-one advantage in artillery, Napoleon launched Soult's corps from his left to engage the Russians. A powerful Russian counterattack beat back Soult's attack. When the first of Davout's divisions arrived and attacked on the right, Russian cavalry engaged them.

Surprised by the strength of the Russian resistance, Napoleon prematurely ordered Augereau's corps, supported by a division from Soult's corps, to attack the center of the Russian line. Advancing through a blinding snowstorm, the ailing Augereau and his snow-blinded troops lost all sense of direction. Veering to the left, they fell under the fire of their own guns and then into the withering fire of seventy enemy cannon. The division from Soult's corps emerged from a veritable blizzard at the assigned point, but too weak to attack without Augereau's corps, the soldiers found themselves at the mercy of Russian guns. With Augereau's corps riddled by artillery fire and almost annihilated, a wide gap developed in the French center; Bennigsen immediately launched a counterattack in the gap and crashed into Eylau. Napoleon escaped capture only through the dedication of his personal aides and the prompt action of the Imperial Guard.

On the edge of defeat, the ever-resourceful Napoleon turned to his cavalry. With only part of Davout's corps and none of Ney's on the battlefield, Napoleon ordered Murat to lead the cavalry reserve in a desperate attack directly into the advancing Russian columns. Just before noon, the ground began to tremble as some 10,000 brilliantly attired cavalrymen began their advance of almost half a mile through intermittent snow squalls. Dividing into two massive columns, they swept through the Russian cavalry, rode over the infantry, and penetrated the artillery positions. Reforming into one great column, they rode back through Russian lines to Eylau. Though the French may have lost as many as 1,500 horsemen, this action bought time and extricated the army from a very precarious position.

Since Ney still had not arrived, and the only remaining reserve was the Imperial Guard infantry, Napoleon ordered Davout to press the attack on his right. Davout's attack caused the Russian flank to waver late in the afternoon, but Lestocq's Prussian corps arrived and fell on Davout's open right flank. Before darkness fell momentum seemed to shift to the Russians as they pushed back the French right. Then Ney's corps of 14,500 men finally arrived on the French left around 7:00 P.M. and struck the Russians. Though Ney made only small gains, his arrival convinced Bennigsen to end the battle. Subordinate Russian commanders urged a continuation of the battle the following morning, but the fighting ended at midnight as Bennigsen withdrew his army quietly into the darkness. Badly mauled in the battle, the French were unable to conduct a pursuit.

Eylau was a limited and costly French victory that demonstrated Napoleon was not invincible and that momentarily checked his campaign against Russia. Though the French still held Eylau, they had lost over

Eylau was at best a narrow victory for Napoleon. The bitter struggle occurred in a snowstorm on February 8, 1807.

20,000 men, the Russians somewhat fewer, making Eylau one of the bloodiest battles of the nineteenth century. The French had captured twenty-four guns and sixteen flags, but Bennigsen claimed five French eagles and seven flags. Decisive victory had eluded Napoleon, but in a message to the army, he claimed a triumph. In the final analysis, the French could claim victory only because they held the battlefield, but the Russians could also claim some measure of success for surviving the attacks and inflicting disproportionately heavy casualties on the French.

Friedland

A week after Eylau, the French withdrew to winter quarters west of the Passarge River, and Napoleon began rebuilding his depleted forces. French conscripts and foreign troops soon increased the emperor's forces in Germany and eastern Europe to about 400,000 men, but only 100,000 would participate in the impending summer offensive against Russia. Meanwhile, Napoleon also formed an international corps and made Marshal François-Joseph Lefebvre its commander. Composed of Polish, Italian, German, and French soldiers, the new corps signaled a small but important change in the composition of Napoleon's forces. As early as 1800 the French army had incorporated troops from allied territories, and in subsequent years the proportion of non-French troops increased with each campaign. Because of battlefield losses and the size of the French population, Napoleon simply did not have sufficient French manpower to control his vast empire or achieve his goals. By 1812 less than half the soldiers in the Grand Army would be

French. As the number of veterans decreased and the quality of the infantry declined, French tactics would become less flexible and Napoleon would rely increasingly on artillery.

Beginning in the middle of March, Lefebvre's corps cleared the area on the Baltic Sea coast around Danzig and then besieged a large allied force in the fortress. In early May, when the allies attempted to relieve the city, Napoleon dispatched two additional corps to Danzig. These forces repulsed the allies with heavy losses, and in late May, the city surrendered.

With that threat eliminated, Napoleon turned his attention to the east. Bennigsen attempted to attack across the Passarge River, but when the Grand Army began to move northeast, the Russians fell back toward their fortified positions at Heilsberg. When Napoleon concentrated his forces in front of Heilsberg, Bennigsen successfully beat off a French attack and then withdrew toward the northeast. The Russians halted east of Friedland (about fifteen miles east of Eylau) and sent troops across the Alle River to run some French cavalrymen of Lannes's corps out of the town. With Friedland located on the west bank of the Alle River and with only one bridge on the river, Bennigsen ordered the construction of three pontoon bridges. He slowly sent his army to the west bank of the Alle as Lannes fed more troops into the conflict. Assuming he was confronting only one corps, Bennigsen prepared to unleash a punishing blow against the French.

Unfortunately for the Russians, Lannes's corps managed to engage and hold them until reinforcements arrived. Fighting began around two in the morning on June 14. Reinforced by a cavalry division, Lannes ingeniously deployed his 12,000 men in a thin line to deceive the Russians about his actual strength. The Russians cautiously massed their troops before launching an attack, and by mid-morning the battle had degenerated into a cannonade. This delay played into Napoleon's hands, for it provided him time to concentrate additional forces. By 9:30 A.M., he had 35,000 men on the battlefield.

When Napoleon arrived shortly after noon, he surveyed the battlefield and carefully placed the rapidly arriving French forces in the woods. He was astounded at the poor position of the Russians who had their backs to the steep-banked and deep Alle River. By 4:00 P.M., the French had concentrated some 80,000 troops at Friedland, and an hour later Napoleon began an attack designed to annihilate the Russian army of 60,000 soldiers, most of whom were on the west bank of the Alle. Attacking first on the right along the river with the purpose of cutting off any Russian withdrawal across the Alle and then pressing forward with a frontal attack in the center, the French pushed the Russians toward Friedland. A massed battery of thirty cannon bombarded the Russians as they fell back into the burning town. Pounded by artillery fire and pressed by infantry, the Russians fled for the bridges. Since three of the four bridges had been destroyed, hundreds of Russians had no choice but to swim the Alle, and few could swim. Only the last minute discovery of a ford saved thousands from death or capture. By eleven that evening gunfire ended, and the battle drew to a close.

Napoleon's relatively easy triumph sprang from the great mobility and flexibility of his forces and from the blunders of his opponent.

Bennigsen placed his army in an extremely poor position, and Napoleon showed no reluctance in making the Russians pay for the mistake. French casualty lists totaled fewer than 8,000, while the Russian army lost almost 20,000 men, as well as eighty cannon. Bennigsen's blunder also destroyed the Fourth Coalition.

The Treaty of Tilsit

Five days after the battle, a Russian negotiator arrived at Napoleon's head-quarters to discuss an armistice and arrange a meeting between Napoleon and Tsar Alexander I on a raft anchored in the Niemen River between the two armies. In this dramatic setting, the emperors of France and Russia met privately and discussed the future of Europe while the Prussian king, Frederick William III, waited anxiously on shore. Out of these discussions came the Treaty of Tilsit, which was signed in July 1807.

With this, France and Russia became allies in the effort to subdue Britain. Russia closed its ports to British ships, ended commercial relations with Britain, and entered the Continental System. Additionally, the accords created a rough division of Europe into French and Russian spheres of inter-est. France promised Russia support in its efforts to wrest Finland from Sweden and the Danubian principalities (Wallachia and Moldavia) from the Ottoman Empire. Russia reluctantly agreed to Prussia's losing its posses-sions west of the Elbe, thereby being reduced to half its prewar size. Prus-sia's army was cut to 40,000 men and its ports closed to England. The two emperors agreed to convert Prussia's Polish provinces into the Grand Duchy of Warsaw, which the King of Saxony would rule. They also combined Prussian territory west of the Elbe with territory taken from Hanover and other small German states to form the new Kingdom of Westphalia, which would be ruled by Jérôme Bonaparte, one of Napoleon's brothers. With the Kingdom of Westphalia, the Grand Duchy of Warsaw, and the Confederation of the Rhine, Napoleon in essence had extended French dominance to the Niemen River.

The meeting with Alexander on the Niemen River on June 25, 1807, marked a new level of success for Napoleon; he now dominated most of Europe. Henceforth, France was merely the core of the Grand Empire. Going far beyond the "natural" frontier of the Rhine, the Alps, and the Pyre-nees, the Grand Empire extended from the Baltic, to the Mediterranean, to the Russian border. Surrounded by satellite states, France seemed secure— Prussia had lost much of its territory, Austria had been excluded from Italy and Germany, and Russia was an ally. Only Britain remained at war with France. No French leader expected the British to endure much longer, but no one knew that the battle of Friedland would be the last of Napoleon's truly brilliant victories.

✶   ✶   ✶   ✶

Napoleon Bonaparte took military operations completely beyond the con-ventions of eighteenth-century warfare. As commander of the Army of Italy and then as First Consul, he drew upon the practices of French revolutionary armies and upon the ideas of authorities from Frederick the Great to Bourcet and Guibert. But he went beyond his predecessors—except perhaps Frederick—in his determination to use battle to decide the outcome of a war. On assuming command of the Army of Italy in the spring of 1796, he promptly went on the offensive and after crushing the Piedmontese, he drove Austria from Italy and the war. In the campaigns of 1800 and 1805–1807, he continued to seek climactic battles of annihilation and won them at Austerlitz, Jena-Auerstädt, and Friedland. While showing Europe a new style of warfare, he conducted operations with a greater decisiveness than his predecessors had thought possible.

Napoleon's success often depended on the mobility and flexibility of his divisions and corps. In the Italian campaign, he required his divisions to live off the countryside and operate independently, and he used their enhanced mobility to gain advantages over his opponents and to concentrate his forces for battle. As he expanded his control over France, his reliance on the *corps d'armée* increased. The use of the corps enabled the French in the Marengo campaign of 1800 to defeat the Austrians despite poor intelligence and mistakes on the battlefield. When Napoleon developed the Grand Army, he refined the corps system and the organization of his headquarters; the changes enabled him to move exceptionally large forces rapidly and securely over long distances and to gain the mobility and concentration of forces needed to defeat his enemies.

When Napoleon marched east in 1806 to engage the Russians, however, his corps system was not as effective in sustaining itself as it had been in Germany. In Poland the population was sparser than in Bavaria or Saxony, agricultural production was less, and roads poorer. It was, therefore, more difficult for Napoleon's corps to draw food and fodder from the countryside, to remain within supporting distance of one another, and to move rapidly enough to surprise or overwhelm an enemy. At Eylau in 1807 the corps of Davout and Ney arrived too late to give Napoleon a decisive victory. At Friedland, however, the single corps of Lannes was able to lure the Russian army across the Alle and contain it until the remainder of the French army could assemble and crush it. Thus Napoleon's operations east of the Vistula revealed some of the difficulties of using his corps system in less densely populated and developed regions of Europe. These difficulties would also appear in the Iberian peninsula.

Napoleon nonetheless significantly increased the scale, range, and speed of warfare. Drawing on the resources of France and its satellites and exploiting improvements in military organization, he created field armies of unprecedented size. Armies of the eighteenth century rarely exceeded 100,000 men (Saxe's army of 120,000 on the Meuse in 1747 and the Austro-Russian force of 130,000 in Silesia in 1761 were exceptions). Napoleon was able to lead 210,000 men against Austria in September 1805 and 180,000 against Prussia in October 1806. He was also able to extend the range of his operations well beyond anything that had been possible in the eighteenth century. The most celebrated marches of Marlborough (250 miles from the Low Countries to the Danube in 1704) and of Frederick the

Great (165 miles from Rossbach to Leuthen in 1757) seem modest by comparison with Napoleon's of 1805–1807. Some French corps marched 250 miles to Ulm and another 400 miles to Austerlitz in 1805; others advanced 100 miles to Jena-Auerstädt and then pursued remnants of the Prussian army an additional 200 miles to the Baltic Sea in 1807; and still others continued 300 miles to the east for a campaign in Poland during the winter of 1806–1807. Moreover, Napoleon's armies moved far more rapidly than their predecessors. On his march to the Danube in 1704, Marlborough averaged about seven miles per day, and Frederick averaged slightly better than ten miles per day from Rossbach to Leuthen. By contrast, Napoleon's corps advanced from the Rhine to the Danube in 1805 at more than eighteen miles per day and from Bamberg to Jena-Auerstädt in 1805 at more than sixteen miles per day.

Operations conducted so rapidly and on such a grand scale brought decisive results. Marlborough had won three great battles in four years without ending the War of the Spanish Succession; Frederick had won seven in seven years merely to keep his enemies at bay. In 1805, Napoleon was able to defeat Austria by capturing one army and defeating another in two-and-one-half months; in 1806 he destroyed the Prussian army in just over a month; and the following year he brought Russia to terms after two battles and six months of intermittent campaigning. These victories momentarily concealed the limits of Napoleon's power and his style of warfare.

SUGGESTED READINGS

Chandler, David G. *The Campaigns of Napoleon* (New York: Macmillan, 1966).

———. *Dictionary of the Napoleonic Wars* (New York: Macmillan, 1979).

Chandler, David G., ed. *Napoleon's Marshals* (New York: Macmillan, 1987).

Connelly, Owen. *Blundering to Glory: Napoleon's Military Campaigns* (Wilmington: Scholarly Resources, 1987).

Connelly, Owen, et al., eds. *Historical Dictionary of Napoleonic France* (Westport, Conn.: Greenwood Press, 1985).

Duffy, Christopher J. *Austerlitz, 1805* (Hamden, Conn.: Archon Books, 1977).

Elting, John R., and Vincent J. Esposito. *A Military History and Atlas of the Napoleonic Wars* (New York: Praeger, 1964).

Elting, John R. *Swords Around a Throne: Napoleon's Grand Armée* (New York: The Free Press, 1988).

Gallaher, John G. *The Iron Marshall: A Biography of Louis N. Davout* (Carbondale, Ill.: Southern Illinois University Press, 1976).

Herold, J. Christopher. *Bonaparte in Egypt* (New York: Harper & Row, 1962).

Horward, Donald D. "Napoleon and the Transformation of Warfare," in Robert B. Holtman, ed. *Napoleon and America* (Pensacola, Fla.: Perdido Bay Press, 1988).

Horward, Donald D., ed. *Napoleonic Military History: A Bibliography* (London: Greenhill Books, 1986).

Lachouque, Henry. *Napoleon's Battles: A History of His Campaigns,* trans. Roy Monkcom (New York: Dutton, 1967).

Marshall-Cornwall, James H. *Marshal Massena* (London: Oxford University Press, 1965).

Parker, Harold T. *Three Napoleonic Battles* (Durham, N.C.: Duke University Press, 1983).

Petre, F. Loraine. *Napoleon's Campaign in Poland, 1806–1807* (London: John Lane, 1907).

———. *Napoleon's Conquest of Prussia, 1806* (London: John Lane, 1914).

Phipps, Ramsay W. *The Armies of the First French Republic and the Rise of the Marshals of Napoleon I* (Westport, Conn.: Greenwood Press, 1980), 5 vols.

Ross, Steven T. *Quest for Victory: French Military Strategy, 1792–1799* (South Brunswick: A. S. Barnes, 1973).

Rothenberg, Gunther E. *The Art of Warfare in the Age of Napoleon* (Bloomington, Ind.: Indiana University Press, 1978).

Thompson, J. M. *Napoleon Bonaparte* (New York: Oxford University Press, 1952).

Vachée, Jean B. *Napoleon at Work,* trans. G. Frédéric Lees (London: Adam and Charles Black, 1914).

8

THE LIMITS OF NAPOLEONIC WARFARE

Sea Power in the Napoleonic Era

The Peninsular War

The 1809 Campaign and Wagram

The limits of Napoleon's power and his style of warfare became most apparent after he destroyed the Fourth Coalition in the summer of 1807. In his efforts to defeat Great Britain, he was drawn into a bitter struggle for the Iberian peninsula and a new war with Austria. Having lost any realistic chance of invading the British Isles when his fleet was defeated at Trafalgar in 1805, Napoleon decided to exclude British trade from Europe and ruin their economy. When Portugal refused to support his Continental System, Napoleon joined with Spain to invade Portugal. After the corrupt rulers of Spain revealed their incompetence as rulers and allies, he sent troops into Spain to force the royal family to yield their throne to his brother Joseph. He completely misjudged the Spanish people who rebelled against French rule in the spring of 1808. Napoleon was able to destroy Spanish armies, but civilians and guerrillas, supported by British expeditionary forces based in Portugal, put up fanatical resistance. The beginning of Napoleon's struggle in Spain also encouraged Austria to risk war again with France and try to reverse the humiliating results of the Ulm-Austerlitz campaign. With hundreds of thousands of men committed in Spain, Napoleon found it difficult to raise an army capable of confronting Austria. When he defeated the Austrians at Wagram in July 1809, he insisted once again on imposing harsh terms of peace. His passion for defeating Britain affected most of Europe, and his underestimation of popular feeling kept him at war even after he had again crushed his enemies.

Napoleon's efforts to conquer Portugal, Spain, and Austria not only demonstrated the limitations of his style of warfare but also brought the people into warfare on an unprecedented scale. As in Poland in 1807, the French found it difficult in Spain to employ large forces decisively in sparsely populated and barren regions. As increasing numbers of experienced troops became mired in Spain and Portugal and as casualties mounted, Napoleon had to rely on unwilling conscripts and foreigners to complete his army for the campaign of 1809 against Austria. To increase the effectiveness of these troops, Napoleon reorganized his infantry regiments and equipped them with additional artillery, thereby augmenting their firepower while sacrificing some of the mobility that was essential for decisive offensive action. Moreover, the resistance to Napoleon in Spain and Portugal became more spontaneous, fanatical, and widespread than any that Europeans had known. When popular resistance was stiffened by British forces, it produced an extraordinarily stubborn defense in Spain and Portugal. No wonder that almost 300,000 Frenchmen died in a futile effort to conquer the Iberian Peninsula.

Sea Power in the Napoleonic Era

In the eighteenth century, sea power often expanded conflicts between France and Britain into global clashes. Surrounded by water rather than land, Britain built fleets for extending and protecting its trade, seizing and defending overseas possessions, and attacking enemy fleets. Britain gradually molded a "maritime policy" in which its navy supported its allies in land campaigns on the European continent while also attacking its enemies' sea communications and overseas possessions. France also spent large sums on its navy but gave priority to land operations on which its security depended.

In the Napoleonic era, the British navy dominated the sea while the French army dominated the European continent. British success at sea did not come from advantages in naval architecture, for the design of capital naval vessels had barely changed in the eighteenth century, and French sailing ships often proved faster than those of the British. Moreover, the British did not possess clear numerical superiority in most of the key naval battles of the wars of the French Revolution and Napoleon. British advantages came instead from their fleet's greater aggressiveness and skill. British commanders frequently proved more willing to close with the enemy and more capable of attacking with the wind, and their gunners proved superior to those of their opponents. Their success was the culmination of decades of increasing British proficiency in sea warfare. Their proficiency was also founded on sound public credit, a flourishing maritime trade, and a commitment to maintaining a large, well-equipped fleet.

Early in the French Revolution, the British gained an edge when disorder and economic collapse undermined French naval power. Many noble officers emigrated, leaving the navy with admirals who knew little about fleet warfare. The corps of highly trained naval gunners was disbanded, and the ships suffered from neglect, lacking sails, rigging, and naval stores. With

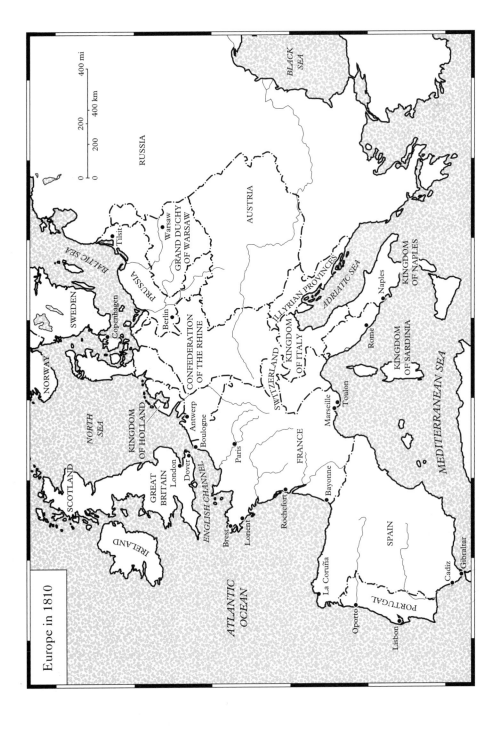

Europe in 1810

crews ill-disciplined and insubordinate, a mutiny broke out in the Atlantic fleet at Brest.

The British proved superior to the French in all aspects of warfare at sea. In the spring of 1794 they seized Guadeloupe and Martinique in the Caribbean, and a few months later on "The Glorious First of June," they defeated a French fleet attempting to protect a convoy of grain being shipped from the United States. In subsequent months, to prevent a French invasion of the British Isles, they concentrated on controlling the coastal waters around Europe, blockading the main French ports (Brest, Rochefort, and Toulon), and engaging warships that eluded their blockade. The British usually posted frigates offshore while more heavily armed ships of the line lay at secure anchorage within striking distance. Such a blockade could be sustained for long periods without exhausting ships and crews, but it permitted French squadrons and individual ships to put to sea occasionally. The British also used their fleet to keep the Mediterranean open, escort convoys, and maintain communications with their allies and their commercial partners. Though their strategy spread the Royal Navy around the globe and exposed ships to many months at sea, it enabled the British to continue their commercial and maritime dominance and use their economic power to subsidize allies on the continent.

Despite the strength of the British navy, French leaders tried repeatedly to invade the British Isles. As early as September 1793, the Committee of Public Safety ordered preparations for an invasion to begin. It was not until late 1796, however, that General Lazare Hoche assembled 13,000 soldiers at Brest and prepared for an invasion of Ireland, which was on the edge of rebellion. Hoche's expedition reached the Irish coast in January 1797, but bad weather prevented a landing and eventually forced the fleet back to Brest.

Recognizing the superiority of the Royal Navy, the French succeeded in gaining the support of the Spanish and Dutch fleets against the British. Shortly after the failure of Hoche's expedition, ships from the Spanish fleet joined the French, but a British fleet defeated them off Cape St. Vincent, Spain, on February 14, 1797. In late 1797 the French pressured the Dutch into sending their fleet into the North Sea against the British. Had the Dutch succeeded in destroying the British squadron, the French would have landed their own forces in England or Scotland. On October 11, however, the British defeated the Dutch fleet at the battle of Camperdown. Although the French landed a demi-brigade in Ireland the following summer, it was quickly cornered and forced to surrender.

Battle of the Nile

In late 1793, the Royal Navy had the opportunity to curtail French naval operations in the Mediterranean when it helped French royalists who had seized Toulon and its important harbor. After French revolutionaries recaptured the city, the British opened another port in Corsica and provided support along the Italian coast to the Austrians during their operations in

Admiral Horatio Nelson joined his first ship
when he was twelve and became captain of a
ship when he was twenty. He managed to
inspire his men and win great victories even
though press gangs had brought many of
them unwillingly into the Royal Navy.

1795–1796. Following Spain's declaration of war on Great Britain in
August 1796 and Bonaparte's occupation of northern Italy, however, the
combined power of the French and Spanish fleets seemed briefly to challenge the Royal Navy for control of the Mediterranean.

Taking advantage of the Franco-Spanish fleets in the Mediterranean,
an army under Bonaparte boarded more than 300 ships and sailed from
Toulon for Egypt in May 1798. Shortly before the French departed, a violent storm disabled a British squadron near Toulon under Rear Admiral Sir
Horatio Nelson. Once refitted, Nelson's squadron could not find the French
even though it combed the Mediterranean for weeks. After landing French
troops near Alexandria, the transports dispersed, but the French admiral
anchored his warships in Aboukir Bay, about fifteen miles to the northeast.
The admiral recognized the inexperience of his men and hoped to nullify
British superiority by remaining at anchor, near shallow water, and fighting a
static battle. On August 1, Nelson's squadron delivered a devastating attack
against the French and destroyed most of their warships. The victory isolated Bonaparte and his army in Egypt, frustrated French efforts to control
the Middle East, and helped spark the emergence of the Second Coalition
against France. It also restored British control of the Mediterranean.

The French had long considered British commerce vulnerable and
had resorted to economic warfare as early as 1793. In one of the earliest

attempts to close European ports to British trade, they encouraged the establishment of the League of Armed Neutrality. In December 1800, Tsar Paul I of Russia established the League with Prussia, Sweden, and Denmark to prevent British warships from restricting their maritime operations. French hopes were dashed, however, by the British who bombarded the Danish fleet at Copenhagen in April 1801 without a declaration of war. The assassination of Paul and the accession of his son, Alexander I, who was pro-British, resulted in Russia's withdrawal from the League.

During the brief period of peace that followed the Treaty of Amiens (March 1802), the French increased the size of their fleet and expanded their maritime and colonial power. After the British accused the French of violating the Amiens treaty and declared war in May 1803, Bonaparte recognized that the only way to defeat Great Britain was to invade and impose a peace. Describing the English Channel as a "mere ditch," he prepared to launch an assault across the narrow Strait of Dover. While building an invasion flotilla of 2,000 craft, primarily flat-bottomed barges, he concentrated and trained thousands of soldiers on the French coast. With French intentions evident, the British used their fleet to block the Channel; they also dramatically expanded the size of their home guard and lined their coast with lookout towers and fortifications.

Battle of Trafalgar

In 1804, Napoleon devised a grand scheme to draw the British fleet away from the Channel. Before the end of the year, he ordered Admiral Pierre de Villeneuve, the new commander of the French fleet at Toulon, to leave port, collect French and Spanish ships along the Mediterranean coast, and sail for the West Indies. There, joined by the Rochefort fleet, already in the Caribbean, and by ships that had escaped from Brest, Villeneuve would attack British possessions and compel the British navy to send reinforcements from the Channel squadrons. With the British diverted to the West Indies, French naval forces would race across the Atlantic, gain momentary control of the Channel, and provide protection for the French crossing.

Villeneuve did escape from Toulon and reach the West Indies in April 1805, but the Rochefort fleet had already returned to France. Nelson's fleet, meanwhile, had pursued Villeneuve across the Atlantic while other British ships remained close to the Channel. When the French admiral learned that Nelson was in the Caribbean, he raced for Spain and managed to brush aside a small British fleet off the northwest coast of Spain. Rather than sail for the Channel as Napoleon ordered, Villeneuve entered Cadiz, northwest of Gibraltar, on August 20. The chance of diverting the British fleet had disappeared, as had the opportunity to invade the British Isles. Almost immediately, Napoleon began planning his campaign in central Europe, which would lead to the victories of Ulm and Austerlitz. In a message to Villeneuve, he ordered him to "dominate" the coast of southern Spain and attack the enemy if the French had superior numbers.

The British victory at Trafalgar in October 1805 destroyed Napoleon's chances of challenging British sea power. Lord Nelson died as he was winning his greatest victory.

Villeneuve set sail for the Straits of Gibraltar on October 20 and on the following morning encountered Nelson's fleet off Cape Trafalgar (on the southern tip of the Spanish coast). Shortly before the fighting began, Nelson signaled his fleet, "England expects that every man will do his duty." With Villeneuve's fleet moving in a single line, the British sailed forward in two large columns; in the *Victory* Nelson led the northern column. The southern column struck first, cutting off sixteen of the French and Spanish ships, and then the northern column struck. Relying on their superior seamanship and gunnery, Nelson's ships fiercely engaged the enemy. Though Nelson was killed by a sniper, the British took or destroyed eighteen of the enemy's thirty-four ships of the line, while losing none of their own. The British victory was one of the most decisive and significant in naval history. The British gained undisputed control of the sea, and the French never again seriously challenged British sea power. Even after Napoleon had defeated the major continental powers in the campaigns of 1805–1807, the British could continue to resist him through peripheral operations in the Iberian Peninsula and in the Mediterranean. While French forces remained land-bound and vulnerable to strikes along the coast, British mobility on the seas enabled them to concentrate forces and provide support wherever they desired along coastal regions.

The Continental System

With Britain safely beyond the reach of his armies, Napoleon turned more energetically to economic warfare. Using his control of European ports, he hoped to close Europe to British commerce and ruin his enemy's trade-based economy by eliminating its chief market. Following the defeats of Austria and Prussia, Napoleon announced the Berlin Decree in November 1806; this decree, which formally established the Continental System, declared a blockade of the British Isles and closed the ports of France and its satellites to ships coming from Britain or its colonies. Following the defeat of Russia, the Treaty of Tilsit in July 1807 brought Russia into the system.

Unfortunately for Napoleon, enforcing the Continental System proved impossible and caused widespread antagonism and illicit trading. Many Europeans had become reliant on inexpensive British products (such as shoes and cotton cloth) and on colonial goods available only through British sources, but they could no longer purchase these goods legally. Restrictions on shipping also hampered export of their own products. To undermine Napoleon's system, British merchants smuggled goods into ports by bribing government officials and using false-bottom vessels. Once Napoleon realized he could not halt the illicit trade completely, he sold licenses to control and profit from it. Ironically, with French commercial shipping curtailed by the blockade, British exports increased dramatically outside Europe, particularly in Latin America which was not under French control; this increase ensured commercial prosperity and saved the British economy despite the existence of the Continental System. Thus, Napoleon's Continental System yielded unintended economic results, and his attempts to enforce its prohibitions eventually drew him into the barren Iberian Peninsula and later into the vast plains of Russia.

Despite the odds, Napoleon did not abandon the possibility of defeating the British fleet. Although the Royal Navy included 113 ships of the line in 1808 and 1809, most suffered from long years at sea. To wrest control of the sea from the British, Napoleon resolved to amass 150 warships. From 1807 until 1813, the French built or collected warships in dockyards throughout the ports of Europe, including Rotterdam, Amsterdam, Antwerp, Toulon, Brest, Genoa, Naples, and Venice. Preparations for the Russian campaign of 1812, however, slowed work in the dockyards as resources, shipbuilders, and sailors were diverted to the army. In the end the French never overcame British mastery of the sea.

The Peninsular War

By the summer of 1807, with Russia as an ally and both Austria and Prussia subservient, Napoleon was master of the European continent. In accordance with the Treaty of Tilsit, Russia joined the Continental System and closed its ports to British commerce. By the fall of 1807, all the nations of continental Europe had signed treaties and joined the system except Portugal and Sweden. When Prince Regent João of Portugal refused to join the Continental System, Napoleon arranged with Spain for an invasion and partition of the recalcitrant country. A small French army, commanded by General Jean Junot, marched through Spain into Portugal in the fall of 1807. The Portuguese did not resist, and on November 30 the French reached Lisbon. A sympathetic Britain could do little but escort the royal family to the Portuguese colony of Brazil while a regency council dealt with the conquering French.

Napoleon now turned on his Spanish allies who had become an uncomfortable liability. He was well aware of the incompetence and corruption of the Spanish royal family and their negotiations with his enemies, and consequently decided to depose them. Under the pretext of reinforcing Junot's army in Portugal, Napoleon sent 127,000 troops into northern Spain to occupy key fortifications in the major towns. When quarrels erupted among the royal family, Napoleon invited them to Bayonne in southern France and offered to mediate the crisis. In the process he forced both the Spanish king and his son, Ferdinand, to abdicate the throne in his favor. Now almost the entire continent of Europe was under French control.

The dramatic events of early 1808, however, stunned the Spanish population, which was already deeply resentful of the French occupation of

After Napoleon issued orders for the arrest of the remaining members of the Spanish royal family, a huge riot erupted in Madrid on May 2, 1808. The French crushed the uprising and then executed those suspected of being its leaders.

their country. When the French attempted to move the remaining members of the royal family to France on May 2, the insurrection of "Dos de Mayo" broke out in Madrid. The French crushed the revolt ruthlessly, executing hundreds of Spaniards, but within the month all of northern Spain was in revolt. Nevertheless, Napoleon named his brother, Joseph, king and sent him to Spain to ascend the throne. As French armies attempted to consolidate their control over Spain, many of the provinces established revolutionary juntas and armies to resist Joseph and the French occupation. Joseph's armies accomplished little; one column that marched toward Cadiz with 18,000 men was trapped in the mountains at Bailen (about 160 miles south of Madrid) and forced to capitulate. Although Joseph was installed in Madrid, he fled into northern Spain in early August after learning of the French surrender at Bailen and the Spanish counteroffensive against other French forces.

To complicate the French position in Spain, early in August 1808 a British expeditionary force of some 15,000 men landed in Portugal to support their insurrection. The British recognized the situation in Iberia would give them an opportunity to intervene on the continent in an area where sea power could provide them advantages in communications and logistics. A young general who had made his reputation fighting in India, Sir Arthur Wellesley (the future Duke of Wellington), received temporary command of the operation. Landing 120 miles north of Lisbon, Wellesley's forces marched south directly on Portugal's capital city. They pushed back a small and hastily deployed rear guard that Junot, commander of the French in Portugal, had sent forward and then defeated the main French forces at Vimeiro on August 21. In a portent of the future, Wellesley deployed his forces deceptively on the reverse slopes of a hill at Vimeiro and turned back the French attacks. Higher-ranking British officers who arrived after the battle ruled out a pursuit, but Junot soon agreed to the evacuation of all French forces from Portugal. The British willingly transported the French and their baggage back to France, thereby ending the first French invasion of Portugal.

Napoleon in Spain

The progression of events in the Iberian Peninsula bewildered Napoleon. He was furious about the capitulation of 18,000 French soldiers at Bailen and disappointed by British success in Portugal. Accustomed to traditional battles, he could not understand how or why an entire population, led by local clergy and minor government officials, could successfully rise up against his armies. He did not understand why his successful methods of fighting could not yield victory in what was to become a "people's war."

Following a meeting with Tsar Alexander I at Erfurt in September 1808, in which the tsar agreed to support France in the event of a war with Austria, Napoleon concentrated on ending the Spanish insurrection and restoring his brother to the throne. He assembled three veteran corps of the Grand Army, the Imperial Guard, and the reserve cavalry, as well as three

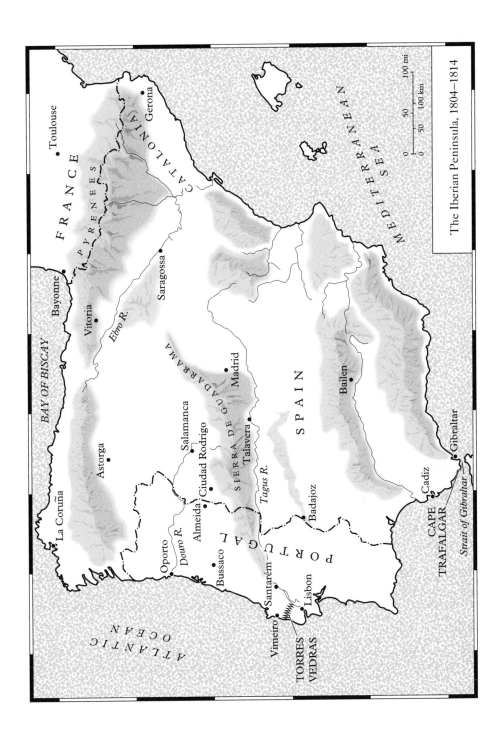

The Iberian Peninsula, 1804–1814

newly formed corps and Junot's repatriated army, for a swift operation in Spain. With almost 140,000 men to reinforce the 150,000 troops already in Spain, success seemed assured. The campaign began in early November, and within three weeks Napoleon's forces had overwhelmed three Spanish armies and regained the capital. Though the French did not quell the insurrection completely, they made significant progress.

After arriving in Madrid, Napoleon intended to march west down the Tagus River valley and drive the small British force at Lisbon into the sea. He received reports, however, of a British army of almost 40,000 men, commanded by Sir John Moore, northwest of Madrid, so he started across the snowcapped Guadarrama Mountains to overtake and destroy the British. Moore had planned on aiding the Spanish armies and cutting the French lines of communication with France. When he learned of Napoleon's approach, however, he rescinded orders for an attack on Soult's isolated corps in north-central Spain and raced for La Coruña on the northwest coast. He expected to rendezvous with the Royal Navy at the city's port. Two French corps and the Imperial Guard, followed by Napoleon, closed in on Moore's army. Not far from Astorga (about one hundred miles from La Coruña and two hundred miles from Madrid), Napoleon received a message about disturbing developments in France and eastern Europe. As he prepared to return to Paris, he ordered the corps of Soult and Ney to continue pursuit of the British forces while he marched for Paris with the Imperial Guard.

While Moore's forces hurried through the rugged mountains of northwestern Spain, Soult's corps remained close behind them. The British finally reached La Coruña, but the entire fleet did not appear until mid-January. A day after the arrival of the British fleet, Soult reached the city and attacked before Moore's forces could be evacuated. Each side lost about a thousand soldiers, but the British forces, who lost Moore in the fighting, escaped destruction. At the cost of almost 7,000 soldiers in the campaign, Moore's forces had diverted Napoleon from his primary objective of capturing Lisbon and driving the small British army there into the sea.

The Iberian campaign should have had a sobering effect on Napoleon and should have revealed the formidable obstacles his forces had to overcome if they were to conquer Spain. He had traveled through some of the most rugged terrain in Spain and had witnessed the isolation of his corps, the hatred with which French troops were regarded, and the effectiveness of Spanish guerrilla forces. He should have recognized the inability of French soldiers to find food and fodder in the desolate countryside. Despite the obvious difficulties confronting his forces, Napoleon left for Paris confident that he would eventually prevail in Spain.

Napoleon might have had a better understanding of the complexity and difficulty facing his forces in Spain had he participated in the siege of Saragossa, which began a few weeks before he departed for Paris. In June 1808 the city had resisted a French army while inflicting 3,500 casualties. Besieged again in the fall of 1808, the city repulsed several attacks. Finally, Marshal Lannes assumed command and breached the walls; he entered the city only to discover that resistance had just begun. Supported by a defiant civilian population, the Spanish garrison had fortified the buildings. For almost four weeks, the French suffered appalling losses as they fought through Saragossa, house by house, block by block, street by street. Losing as many as 20,000 men, they finally forced the city to capitulate by mining and blowing up most of it, but not until some 54,000 Spanish soldiers and civilians had sacrificed their lives in defense of the city.

The fierce fighting at Saragossa was not an isolated incident, for within three months the city of Gerona in Catalonia withstood the continual bombardment and assaults of a six-month siege and inflicted at least 14,000 casualties on the French at the expense of 13,000 civilians and 5,000 soldiers. These sieges were but two in a long series of bloody encounters that occurred throughout the Peninsular War. Such resistance cost the French staggering casualties, much to the dismay of Napoleon who hoped in vain for battlefield victories that would end the struggle. He had greatly underestimated the value of guerrilla bands as they slowly filled the vacuum left by the defeated Spanish armies. Ironically, he was as incapable of dealing with guerrilla warfare as his opponents had been in dealing with his operations in Italy in 1796–1797.

Wellington and the Lines of Torres Vedras

While bloody encounters continued in Spain, the key to the struggle rested with the Portuguese people and the British expeditionary force. Napoleon seemed to recognize this in January 1809 when he ordered Soult to invade Portugal and drive the remaining British troops from Lisbon. Soult marched into northern Portugal before the end of the month, but he halted at Oporto (about 170 miles north of Lisbon) to await the arrival of reinforcements from Spain. Much to his surprise the British arrived before the reinforcements did.

Despite the failure of Sir John Moore's expedition, the British government had sent Wellesley back to the peninsula. In April 1809 he arrived in Lisbon to assume command of 20,000 British troops, while William Carr Beresford, named Marshal of Portugal, began the regeneration of the Portuguese army. With Wellesley's active support, Beresford reformed the Portuguese officer corps, improved administration and logistics, established discipline and order within the ranks, and placed Portuguese units under direct or indirect British command.

Before the reforms were complete, Wellesley moved his forces north to confront Soult at Oporto on May 12. Feinting an attack across the mouth of the broad Douro River at Oporto, Wellesley traveled upstream, slipped across the river, surprised Soult, and forced him to evacuate the city. The withdrawal turned into a headlong retreat as Beresford's Portuguese forces raced to block Soult's route into Spain. Losing most of his baggage, guns, and almost 5,000 men, Soult finally reached the relative safety of Spain. The second invasion of Portugal had come to an ignominious end.

With Portugal now free of enemy troops, Wellesley agreed to march into Spain and support Spanish efforts to expel King Joseph and his armies from Madrid. Wellesley's army, accompanied by about 32,000 Spanish soldiers, marched up the Tagus River valley toward Madrid and encountered a large French force concentrated outside Talavera (about seventy miles west of Madrid). In a savage battle fought in extreme heat, Wellesley turned back several determined French attacks on July 27 and retained control of the battlefield. When he learned that a large French force was moving to cut off his lines of communication to Portugal, however, he withdrew hastily. Wellesley, named Viscount Wellington for his success at Talavera, concentrated for the next year on the defense of Portugal.

Having defeated the Austrians at Wagram, Napoleon turned his attention to Spain in late 1809. He placed three corps under Soult and ordered him to suppress resistance in southern Spain. He united three other corps into the Army of Portugal under Masséna and ordered him to crush resistance in Portugal and drive Wellington into the sea. Masséna joined his new command of 65,000 men in May 1810 at Salamanca (about one hundred miles northwest of Madrid). Instead of permitting Masséna to mask the two frontier fortresses, Ciudad Rodrigo and Almeida, and march directly into Portugal, Napoleon directed that formal sieges be conducted. The subsequent sieges cost almost 2,000 casualties, vast quantities of supplies, and four months of valuable time.

While Masséna's army spent the summer in siege operations, Wellington completed preparations for the defense of Portugal. Frontier fortresses were refurbished, roads cut, militia activated, and all able-bodied males from sixteen to sixty mobilized as *ordenança* to defend the country. In addition, civilians, under pain of death, were ordered to evacuate the area through which the French would march and to take or destroy everything that might be of value to the enemy. The "scored earth" policy transformed the French invasion route into a desert, stripped of both inhabitants and supplies.

Following the battle of Talavera, Wellington had ordered the construction of a series of fortified lines north of Lisbon that became known as the Lines of Torres Vedras. Erected under the direction of British and Portuguese engineers, the Lines consisted of three lines of defensive works across the Lisbon peninsula, stretching almost thirty miles from the ocean to the banks of the Tagus River. As many as 30,000 Portuguese labored for over a year to construct the 165 fortifications on the lines. With a port to its rear, the strongly fortified position provided Wellington a secure, almost impregnable base for operations against the French. If the French managed to breach the Lines of Torres Vedras, he planned to evacuate the entire Anglo-Portuguese army by sea.

After capturing the fortresses of Ciudad Rodrigo and Almeida, Masséna entered Portugal with his army in September 1810. His columns pushed 115 miles in twelve days to the rugged Serra de Bussaco (about twenty-five miles from the coast) where Wellington had concentrated 60,000 men of the Anglo-Portuguese army to bar their advance. On September 27, Wellington's forces turned back the French, but two days later, Masséna discovered a road that enabled him to outflank Wellington's troops and force them to withdraw. The French pursued the allies for over one hundred miles until they reached the Lines of Torres Vedras. After several probes against the allies' position, Masséna deployed his troops before the lines and appealed to Napoleon for reinforcements. The emperor sent orders to Soult whose army was investing the fortress of Badajoz (about one hundred miles east of Lisbon) to accelerate his efforts and advance toward Lisbon. Though Soult eventually captured Badajoz, he did not advance toward Lisbon; instead he turned south toward Cadiz.

After lingering a month before the Lines of Torres Vedras, Masséna's army retired thirty miles to more defensible positions at Santarém where he waited, in vain, for aid. After 108 days, his starving army, now reduced to 40,000 men, disengaged and began to withdraw. The failure of the third invasion of Portugal became the salvation of the allies and the curse of the French. Safely behind the Lines of Torres Vedras, the British had a secure port where they could receive supplies and reinforcements, and Wellington had a secure base of operations from which he could advance into Spain. In addition, the success of the Anglo-Portuguese forces revived the flagging determination of the Spanish. Thus, Masséna's failure before the Lines of Torres Vedras became the turning point of the Peninsular War; the allies gained the initiative and never again relinquished it.

While Masséna attempted to capture Lisbon, other French operations continued in almost every province of Spain. The French had organized the Spanish provinces into military districts under French generals, almost independent of King Joseph. Though they crushed Spanish armies with remarkable regularity, they were utterly incapable of destroying the guerrillas who were fanatically devoted to defending their church, king, and culture. It was becoming increasingly evident to everyone except Napoleon that his forces, totaling well over 300,000 men, controlled only the territory they actually occupied, while Spanish armies and guerrillas dominated the rural areas. The French found themselves torn between having to concentrate their forces to defeat Spanish armies and having to disperse them to pursue guerrillas and search for food.

As the Spanish armies declined in effectiveness, the guerrillas increased their activities. Although some bands of partisans were little more than bandits, others were intensely dedicated to the destruction of the French and the restoration of the monarchy. When elements of the population appeared willing to accept the French, the guerrillas employed terrorist tactics to encourage active resistance. The undisciplined guerrillas and citizens exacted a terrible toll on the French who responded in kind until the struggle became one of extraordinary violence and unspeakable brutality.

The Final Phase

The final phase of the Peninsular War began in late 1811. With the French expelled from Portugal, Wellington attacked the formidable frontier fortress at Badajoz. Masséna's replacement, General Auguste Marmont, marched almost two hundred miles, however, to join Soult in raising the siege. Outnumbered and limited in resources, Wellington wisely retired. At the

Napoleon miscalculated the depth of Spanish hatred for the French. Though poorly armed and equipped, Spanish guerrillas defied all odds to attack French soldiers.

beginning of 1812, Wellington advanced toward the fortress of Ciudad Rodrigo (about 225 miles northeast of Lisbon). Despite the miserable January weather, he besieged and captured the fortress before French relief forces arrived. Wellington then marched south in March and invested and seized Badajoz. By seizing these two fortresses, Ciudad Rodrigo and Badajoz, Wellington had secured the major invasion routes into Spain.

In the spring of 1812, Wellington advanced out of Portugal. Marching northeast from Ciudad Rodrigo, he seized Salamanca and defeated Marmont's army. When the battle finally ended, the French had lost over 13,000 men and twenty guns while the allied losses totaled fewer than 5,000. Rather than pursue the defeated French army, Wellington, aware of the strategic importance of the Spanish capital, advanced east, directly on Madrid. He entered the capital on August 12, thereby forcing Soult's army to raise the two-year siege of Cadiz and evacuate much of southern Spain or risk being cut off.

Despite the capture of Madrid and several Spanish provinces, allied gains were only temporary. Following Wellington's capture of Madrid, 130,000 French troops were available for operations against him. The French managed to concentrate this force despite the extraordinary demands of the 1812 Russian campaign. Wellington's forces soon began the long trek back to Portugal. Pursued by the French, the Anglo-Portuguese army retreated, amid heavy fall rains, in a march reminiscent of Moore's retreat to La Coruña in the winter of 1808–1809.

By the end of 1812, Napoleon, having returned from Russia, began to recall his regiments and generals from Spain for service in Germany. Though the French still had almost 200,000 Imperial troops in the peninsula, many soldiers remained dispersed to deal with the guerrillas. Meanwhile, in addition to 21,000 Spanish troops at Wellington's immediate disposal, reinforcements had increased his Anglo-Portuguese force to about 80,000. In 1813, Wellington, encouraged by Napoleon's disasters in Russia, waged a remarkable campaign to force the French out of Spain. He succeeded in maneuvering the French out of numerous positions and forced them to fall back almost 250 miles to Vitoria where he defeated them on June 21. With this defeat, the French lost Spain and the Peninsular War.

But the defeat came from more than this single battle. From the beginning, Napoleon misunderstood the nature of the war, and he never found the remedy for combating the guerrillas and Wellington's forces simultaneously. So long as the British held Portugal, the guerrillas in Spain had reason for hope and a source of supplies. With the lack of communications and transportation creating insurmountable difficulties, the French never solved their logistical problems in a barren country ravished by six years of war. Napoleon never developed a strategy to end the "bleeding ulcer" that claimed the lives of some 300,000 Frenchmen and became a major factor in the eventual collapse of the Empire.

The 1809 Campaign and Wagram

France's difficulties in Spain raised hopes in 1808 among those Austrians seeking to regain lost territory and to restore and protect their empire. Aware that Austria had been reorganizing its military since Austerlitz, Napoleon sought to defuse the potential crisis by meeting with Tsar Alexander I at Erfurt in September 1808. The tsar agreed to support France in the event of a war with Austria, but at the same time he secretly indicated to the Austrians that his involvement would be minimal. When Prince Clemens von Metternich returned to Vienna from Paris and emphasized the unrest in France and the burden of the Iberian commitment, Austria's leaders decided in late December to attack France in the spring. Learning that Austria was preparing for war, British leaders promised substantial financial support for what would be the Fifth Coalition; they also promised to launch a large diversionary operation.

Napoleon returned from Spain in January 1809. With some of the best units of the Grand Army in Spain, France faced the prospect of a major war against Austria and a diversionary operation by the British in the Low Countries. During the next three months, Napoleon worked hard to increase the number of soldiers in the army. He sought to assemble about 400,000 soldiers for use against Austria, two-thirds of whom would be in Germany and one-third in Italy. Although he accelerated conscription and obtained soldiers from his German allies, by April he could deploy only

275,000 men against Austria. Meanwhile the Austrians, mobilizing since early 1809, had almost 100,000 men in northern Italy and over 200,000 available for an advance into southern Germany.

The Austrians had used the years since Austerlitz to improve the capabilities of their forces. Named as commander of the Austrian forces in 1805, Archduke Charles dismissed incompetent generals, improved logistics and administration, reorganized the cavalry and artillery, increased the number of light infantry units for use as skirmishers, formed corps, and established a national militia. But his reforms were limited by ultraconservative members of the war council. Seniority and birth continued to determine the selection of commanding officers, not merit or experience. Refusing to decentralize and allow lower commanders flexibility, the Austrians maintained a highly centralized command and control system that produced detailed orders for subordinate commanders. Though recognizing the need for greater mobility, the Austrians rejected the idea of living off the countryside, and the army continued to rely on magazines and large supply trains. With subordinate units organized as brigades, rather than divisions, Austrian corps were small. Since corps were adopted at the last moment, high-ranking officers knew little about employing them. As for the national militia, military leaders, including Charles, remained skeptical of their abilities.

While the Austrians had made limited improvements in their forces since 1805, the French army had deteriorated. With many new recruits and foreigners in the ranks and with many of the best officers in Spain or dead, the French could not maneuver as effectively or operate as flexibly as they had in the past. To compensate for this, Napoleon issued a decree in February 1808 to adjust organization, administration, and control within the various infantry regiments. The lack of training and experience, however, led the French to rely heavily on artillery and massive assault columns in the upcoming campaign.

Ratisbon

Although an Austrian invasion seemed imminent in the spring of 1809, Napoleon remained in Paris. Intelligence reports suggested that the main Austrian blow would come along the Danube, an area he knew well from previous campaigns. He expected to halt the Austrian attack and then to advance down the Danube toward Vienna. In his customary fashion, he did not complete a detailed plan, but he located his forces in consonance with the strategy of making a main attack in southern Germany and a supporting attack in Italy.

Napoleon named his chief of staff, Berthier, acting commander of the army in Germany until he arrived. With Napoleon in Paris and Berthier in Germany, the two communicated through the "Military Telegraph Service," which consisted of numerous semaphore signal stations located in lines between Paris and other major cities. After bad weather interrupted transmissions, Berthier, who had not commanded a field army for years, scattered French forces over a seventy-five mile front.

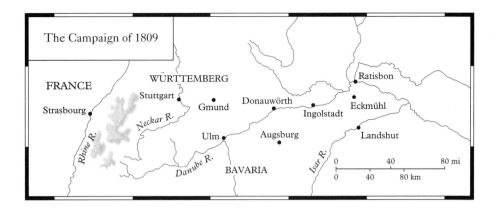

The Austrians attacked in early April with three widely separated armies. Archduke Ferdinand attacked French forces in Poland; Archduke John attacked northern Italy; and Archduke Charles launched the main Austrian attack along the Danube into southern Germany. Early on April 10 about 160,000 Austrians under Charles crossed the Inn River south of the Danube and moved into Bavaria. To the north of the Danube, about 50,000 Austrians marched out of Bohemia. Simultaneously, a revolt against Napoleon's ally, Bavaria, erupted in the Tyrol.

As soon as Napoleon reached his Bavarian headquarters on April 16, he began concentrating his scattered forces to face the main Austrian attack. He had about 170,000 troops in southern Germany, including about 50,000 from the Confederation of the Rhine. To face the other two Austrian attacks, he had about 30,000 troops in Poland and 50,000 in Italy.

Much of the subsequent fighting in what is known as the "Ratisbon cycle" of the 1809 campaign occurred southwest of Ratisbon between the Danube and Isar rivers. Before the army was completely assembled from its widely scattered positions in Bavaria, Napoleon attempted to envelop both flanks of the Austrian army. While he attacked the allied left wing and drove it toward Landshut on the Isar (thirty miles south of Ratisbon), Davout attacked the right wing. Only after seizing Landshut did Napoleon recognize that the bulk of the Austrians were farther north, on the allied right wing, near Ratisbon. Charles had moved forward more rapidly and boldly than he had anticipated; twenty to thirty miles north of Landshut, the main Austrian army of 60,000 men was closing in on Davout.

Departing before daybreak on April 22, Napoleon, accompanied by some 40,000 troops under Masséna and Lannes, began a forced march to the north to rescue Davout and Lefebvre. Early in the afternoon, the French struck the Austrian flank at Eckmühl and, after some sharp fighting, drove them back. Later that night, Charles crossed his forces over the Danube. Shocked by the rapid change in the course of events, he sent Napoleon a letter suggesting the possibility of peace. The Austrians had lost about 30,000 men and vast quantities of matériel.

Defeat at Aspern-Essling

As Napoleon fought the Ratisbon cycle, the Austrian army under Archduke John pushed back the French in northern Italy to the Adige River, and in Poland, the Austrians took Warsaw. Taking count of the strategic situation, Napoleon did not pursue Charles's army northeast into Bohemia. Instead he moved east toward Vienna, since seizure of their capital might force the Austrians to negotiate or seek a major battle. By pushing forward quickly, he placed his forces between the armies of Charles and John, thereby preventing them from uniting.

While Charles and his defeated army retreated into Bohemia north of the Danube, Napoleon's army marched east along the south bank of the river; the first units reached Vienna on May 10 and entered the city three days later after the Austrian defenders capitulated. As in 1805, however, the capture of Vienna did not end Austrian resistance. Concerned about the possibility of Prussian or Russian treachery and the approach of John's army from Italy, Napoleon decided to strike immediately across the Danube. Though he knew little about the location and condition of Charles's army, he did not believe the Austrians could offer strong resistance. After a cursory

Archduke Charles of Austria achieved some
significant reforms in the Austrian army, but he was
nonetheless an eighteenth-century general and
conservative who rejected living off the countryside.
He failed to take advantage of his success at
Aspern-Essling in 1809.

reconnaissance, the French began preparations for a crossing five miles southeast of Vienna. There they built a single, fragile bridge, stretching over two miles, that extended from the river bank, across two sand bars and the large island of Lobau, to the north shore.

Between April 28 and May 16, Charles's army, almost matching the French rate of march, had moved some 200 miles to a position north of Vienna. By the time the French completed their bridge, the Austrians had collected almost 120,000 men just north of the river. Unaware of the large Austrian concentration, Napoleon ordered Masséna's corps to cross the single bridge over the Danube around noon on May 20. Not far from the crossing site one of Masséna's divisions occupied the little village of Aspern; a second held the hamlet of Essling, less than two miles away; and the third remained in reserve. Soon after Masséna occupied Aspern and Essling, the fragile bridge spanning the Danube separated, temporarily halting the flow of soldiers across the river.

After spending most of the night repairing the bridge, the French had three infantry and two cavalry divisions (27,000 troops) on the north bank the following morning. Around 10:00 A.M., the Austrians cut the bridge by floating debris down the fast-moving Danube, and then at 2:30 P.M., in a surprise move, Charles unleashed a massive attack of almost 100,000 men. Napoleon gave little thought of withdrawal, since engineers had finished repairing the bridge about the same time as the enemy launched their attack. With three Austrian corps assaulting Aspern, control of the village changed several times, but the French finally held. At Essling, the French repulsed three fierce enemy attacks while 7,000 cavalrymen defended the line between the two villages. At one point in the battle, Charles personally led a charge against Aspern. At dusk, however, both armies settled down for the night to prepare for the resumption of fighting the next day.

By the following morning, Napoleon had seven additional infantry divisions and parts of two cavalry divisions across the river. Just after 5:00 A.M., Charles unleashed another attack, sweeping in for the kill with 100,000 men and 250 cannon. The French forces, composed of 50,000 infantry, 7,000 cavalry, and 144 guns, held against the onslaught. As the Austrians again concentrated on Aspern and Essling, Napoleon noticed the weakened enemy center and ordered four divisions under Lannes to move forward. The initial attack pierced the enemy line, but a counterattack led personally by Charles halted Lannes's advance. Nonetheless the Austrians were in a precarious position, vulnerable to Napoleon's planned attack by Davout's corps. But Davout did not appear because the Austrians had again cut the bridge. With Lannes's forces running out of ammunition, Napoleon had no alternative but to pull them back to their original position.

Archduke Charles responded by launching a series of attacks, first against Napoleon's center and then against his right at Essling. When these narrowly failed, he massed his artillery and began bombarding the French who had run short of ammunition and had little artillery support. Napoleon finally realized that victory could not be achieved under such circumstances. With Masséna responsible for disengaging and extricating the army from its

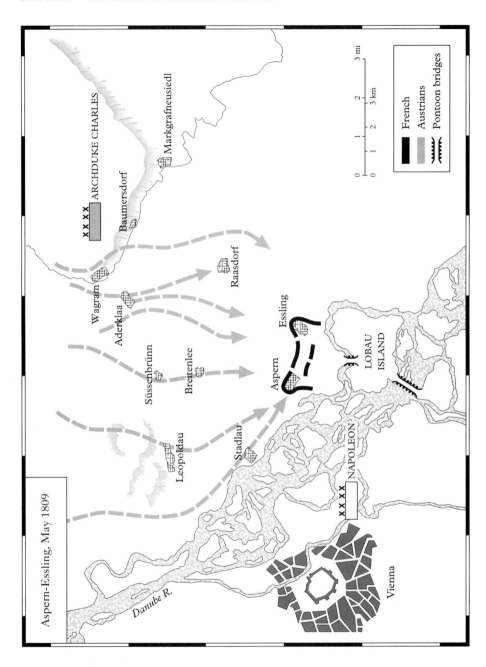

Aspern-Essling, May 1809

untenable position, the French quietly withdrew during the night to the island of Lobau.

Thus ended the bloody battle of Aspern-Essling, Napoleon's first major defeat. Charles acknowledged some 23,000 casualties; the French lost slightly fewer. Napoleon had not performed well; his decision to cross the Danube with little information about the enemy reflected poor judgment, and his occupation of a small bridgehead ruled out any chance of maneuver. Underestimating the Austrians, he tempted fate by erecting only one fragile bridge across the Danube, and when he lost the bridge, he lost the initiative and the ability to send reinforcements across the river. Unlike other opponents in the past, Charles took advantage of these errors and came close to inflicting a fatal defeat on Napoleon. But the French emperor proved capable of reviving his army and learning from his mistakes.

Wagram

Exhausted from the ordeal, Napoleon rested for a day but, refusing to accept defeat, worked energetically for the next six weeks to launch another attack against Charles. To ensure a safe crossing of the Danube, French engineers began building several bridges from the west bank to the island of Lobau; they also erected barriers to protect the bridges and deflect any materials sent down the river to destroy them. Napoleon withdrew all his forces, except for Masséna's corps, from the island and turned it into an armed camp with a battery of 129 guns and redoubts. Great quantities of supplies and bridging materials were then moved forward to the island. To augment firepower and improve confidence, he increased the artillery in his army and added two guns to each infantry regiment. He also pressed into service Austrian guns from local arsenals. With a revolt still boiling in the Tyrol, he took steps to secure his long line of communication along the Danube. Throughout the six weeks additional troops arrived from all over Europe, and by July 1 Napoleon had some 160,000 troops concentrated near Vienna.

During the period of heightened French activity, the Austrians remained inactive in the positions to which they had withdrawn after the battle. Charles did incorporate about 60,000 militia into his army, and he assigned about 200 more guns to the various corps. The Austrians also built fortifications opposite Lobau at Aspern and Essling. Indications of substantial French preparations for a crossing and attack, however, did not induce Charles to produce a coherent plan or operational concept. Perhaps Charles thought negotiations would spare him another confrontation or that Napoleon had lost his appetite for another battle. Whatever the case, he did not prepare his army adequately for another battle.

Though planning to cross the Danube on the east side of Lobau Island, the French built four bridges on the northwest corner of the island, facing Aspern-Essling, to deceive the Austrians. On the night of July 3–4, French troops began concentrating on the island of Lobau. The next night, after feinting a crossing toward Aspern-Essling, they quickly threw several bridges across the Danube on the eastern side of the island and began crossing. By dawn on July 5, Napoleon had most of three corps across the river. As engineers completed more bridges, additional soldiers poured across the river, and the French expanded their bridgehead. By 10:00 A.M. more than 150,000 French soldiers and 450 cannon were on the east bank of the Danube. Anxious to confront the Austrians before they retreated or before Archduke John arrived with 13,000 troops, Napoleon launched a hasty attack against the Austrian center late in the afternoon, but it failed.

French forces crossed the Danube and concentrated on the island of Lobau prior to the Battle of Wagram. The movement required an elaborate and detailed order and enabled Napoleon to face the Austrians with 150,000 soldiers on the first morning of the battle.

At 4:00 A.M. on July 6, Charles launched a massive and bold attack against the French. Two corps were supposed to make the main attack on the French left wing and drive deep into their rear, while three infantry and one cavalry corps attacked and contained the French right and center. Charles's plan required carefully coordinated actions from his corps, but the late arrival of his orders ended any chance of simultaneous attacks. With the Austrian corps attacking at different times, the first action occurred against Davout on Napoleon's right. After receiving reinforcements, Davout halted the Austrians and slowly pushed them back. On the French left, the Austrians' carrying out the main attack succeeded in outflanking the French line. In a crucial moment in the fighting, one of Napoleon's allied units in his center, Saxons under Bernadotte, broke and ran, but the French managed to regain control of the sector. The situation became more desperate later in the morning as the Austrians on the left drove deep into the French rear and threatened to cut them off from their bridges. Fortunately for the French, the grand batteries on the island of Lobau halted the Austrians.

Believing the situation called for desperate action, Napoleon directed Masséna to disengage from the French center, march south across the front of the enemy, and restore the collapsing left flank. As Masséna's forces turned south, Napoleon launched a cavalry charge and organized a massive battery of 112 cannon to cover Masséna's maneuver and fill the gap in the French lines. He then moved General Étienne-Jacques Macdonald's corps into the gap. By midday the crisis had passed, for Masséna had repulsed the Austrians on the left.

When Davout began making progress on the French right, Napoleon decided to break through the enemy's lines. Macdonald organized 8,000 men in a huge hollow square in the left-center of the French line and drove into the Austrians. The thick mass of soldiers made steady progress until the Austrians poured deadly artillery fire into the massive square and desperately closed around it; the square slowed and finally halted. In the meantime, Masséna drove back the Austrians on the extreme left and aggressively moved forward; French and Italian troops finally seized Wagram in the French center, rendering the Austrian position untenable. Not willing to risk his army, despite the imminent arrival of Archduke John's small army, Charles ordered a phased withdrawal.

The French could legitimately claim victory at Wagram, but Napoleon had not destroyed the Austrian army. With more than 320,000 soldiers engaged in the battle (more than in any earlier battle in European history), losses on both sides were huge. Together the participants suffered some 70,000 casualties; of these, the French had more than 32,500 killed, wounded, or captured, and the Austrians 37,000.

Too exhausted to begin an immediate pursuit, the French began moving on July 7. Following a sharp action on July 11, Archduke Charles agreed to an armistice. Initially refusing to admit defeat, the Austrian emperor demoted Charles, reduced his authority, and later accepted his resignation. Ultimately, allied efforts failed to rescue the Austrians. In Spain, Wellesley won the battle of Talavera west of Madrid in late July but abandoned his offensive and withdrew to Portugal. In the Netherlands, the British landed troops in August, but they withdrew most of them in September without achieving any results. And the anticipated revolt in Germany against Napoleon's rear failed to materialize. With discipline deteriorating in the army and without adequate transport or ammunition, the Austrians signed the Treaty of Schönbrunn on October 14, 1809, ending the war of the Fifth Coalition. The Austrians yielded territory to Russia, to the Grand Duchy of Warsaw, and to the new Illyrian Provinces along the Adriatic coast, which the French would rule. They also had to pay an indemnity and reduce their army to 150,000 soldiers.

The battle of Wagram marked a shift in Napoleonic warfare. Though victorious, the French forces at Wagram were clearly not of the same caliber as those who had fought in previous campaigns. While the army in the first Italian campaign had been filled with highly experienced volunteers, motivated by French nationalism and the opportunity to spread the ideals of the republic, the army at Wagram included many poorly trained conscripts, reinforced by large numbers of foreign soldiers. To compensate for the decline in infantry, the French had increased the proportion of artillery from two per 1,000 soldiers in 1804 to 3.5 per 1,000 in 1809. Despite this reinforcement, the French infantry had not performed as well as it had in past battles. In fact the presence of more than 900 cannon from both sides caused horrendous casualties among the infantry. In retrospect, Friedland was Napoleon's last great victory, and Wagram marked the beginning of a more bloody and difficult era of fighting.

Despite the increasingly blunt and unwieldy nature of the French army and the improved performance of its opponents, Napoleon saw no need to seek an accommodation with his potential enemies. The Continental System remained in effect, Great Britain an enemy, and Russia a restless ally. And the Treaty of Schönbrunn ensured Austria's continued discontent. Although it was becoming increasingly evident that France was overextended, Napoleon made little effort to adjust his foreign policy or modify his grand strategy.

☆   ☆   ☆   ☆

Nelson's victory at Trafalgar in 1805 was the clearest evidence of the limits of Napoleon's power. So long as the Royal Navy controlled the seas, Britain lay beyond France's reach. And despite Napoleon's success on the European continent, the British used their control of the seas to support allies and wage a long, bloody campaign in the Iberian Peninsula. Their control of the seas also kept their economy healthy, enabling them to provide substantial subsidies to their allies.

The limitations of Napoleon's operational methods became evident in his efforts to conquer Portugal and Spain and to close the Iberian Peninsula to British trade. Civilians in the peninsula opposed the French in unprecedented numbers and intensity. Even though French armies were able to engage and defeat regular Spanish troops, they were unable to overcome the fanatical resistance of the Spanish and Portuguese people supported by British expeditionary forces based in Portugal and supplied by sea. His efforts to conquer Spain and Portugal piecemeal, to take and hold cities and fortresses, proved extraordinarily costly and, ultimately, ineffective.

While the "Spanish ulcer" tied down French forces and cost an average of 50,000 men a year, Napoleon had to rely on many unwilling conscripts and foreigners to face Austria in 1809. To make such recruits effective, he equipped them with additional artillery, thereby increasing their firepower but reducing their mobility. The army that he took to Vienna in 1809 was more unwieldy than his previous armies and not capable of the kind of rapid offensive action that had made the campaigns of 1805 and 1806 so decisive. Nor was Napoleon as careful or resourceful as he had been in earlier campaigns.

Meanwhile the Austrians had improved the capabilities of their forces, but they still remained less capable than the French. Though Napoleon defeated Austria again, the margin was narrow; weaknesses revealed in the campaign of 1809 and in the peninsula would reemerge all too soon in Russia.

SUGGESTED READINGS

Alexander, Don W. *Rod of Iron: French Counterinsurgency Policy in Aragon During the Peninsular War* (Wilmington, Del.: Scholarly Resources, 1985).

Arnold, James R. *Crisis on the Danube: Napoleon's Austrian Campaign of 1809* (New York: Paragon Books, 1990).

Ellis, Geoffrey J. *Napoleon's Continental Blockade: The Case of Alsace* (Oxford: Clarendon Press, 1981).

Fortescue, John W. *A History of the British Army* (London: Macmillan, 1910–1930), vols. vi–x.

Epstein, Robert M. *Prince Eugene at War, 1809* (Arlington, Tex.: Empire Games, 1984).

Esdaile, Charles. *The Spanish Army in the Peninsular War* (Manchester: Manchester University Press, 1988).

Gill, John H. *With Eagles to Glory: Napoleon and His German Allies in the 1809 Campaign* (London: Greenhill, 1992).

Heckscher, Eli F. *The Continental System: An Economic Interpretation* (Oxford: Clarendon Press, 1922).

Horward, Donald D. *The Battle of Bussaco: Masséna vs. Wellington* (Tallahassee, Fla.: University Presses of Florida, 1965).

———. "British Seapower and its Influence upon the Peninsular War (1808–1814)," *Naval War College Review,* 31 (1978): 34–71.

———. *Napoleon and Iberia: The Twin Sieges of Ciudad Rodrigo and Almeida, 1810* (Gainesville, Fla.: University Presses of Florida, 1984).

———. "Wellington as a Strategist," in *Wellington: Studies in the Military and Political Career of the First Duke of Wellington,* ed., Norman Gash (Manchester: Manchester University Press, 1990).

Marcus, Geoffrey J. *The Age of Nelson: The Royal Navy, 1793–1815* (New York: Viking Press, 1971).

Oman, Charles W. *A History of the Peninsular War* (Oxford: Clarendon Press, 1902–1930), 7 vols.

Pelet, Jean J. *The French Campaign in Portugal, 1810–1811,* trans. and ed. by Donald D. Horward (Minneapolis: University of Minnesota Press, 1973).

Petre, F. Loraine. *Napoleon and the Archduke Charles* (London: J. Lane, 1909).

Rothenberg, Gunther E. *Napoleon's Great Adversaries: The Archduke Charles and the Austrian Army, 1792–1814* (Bloomington: Indiana University Press, 1982).

9

BREAKING NAPOLEON'S POWER:
WARFARE ON A NEW SCALE

The Russian Campaign
of 1812

The Campaigns of
1813–1814

The Belgian Campaign
and Waterloo

Napoleonic Warfare

Although Napoleon had difficulty defeating Austria in 1809 while his forces remained mired in Spain and Portugal, he was determined to maintain France's dominant role in Europe. His insistence on enforcing the Continental System and on crushing anyone who threatened it would soon cost him his throne and destroy his empire. When Tsar Alexander I violated the Continental System and disregarded his alliance with France, Napoleon decided to invade and conquer Russia. His failure to defeat Russia in the campaign of 1812 not only weakened his control over the French empire and his capacity to wage war but also encouraged the principal states of Europe to join against him. He raised other armies and employed them well. But in the campaigns of 1813, 1814, and 1815 he was overwhelmed by superior numbers and by opposing commanders who had learned his methods and were too wary to be drawn into a disastrous battle. As late as November 1813, Napoleon might have been able to keep his throne had he been willing to give up his conquests and make peace, but he was convinced that giving them up would undermine his support in France. Consequently, he continued to fight until he was forced to abdicate, France was reduced to the boundaries of 1792, and the Bourbon family was restored.

In his final campaigns Napoleon increased the scale of warfare dramatically, but he sacrificed much of the speed and decisiveness that had distinguished his earlier campaigns. To conquer Russia, he assembled an army of 600,000. Yet to sustain such an army in a sparsely settled and primitive country, he had to rely on magazines and supply trains, which deprived his army of its mobility. After the Russians drove him out, Russia, Prussia, Austria, Britain, and Sweden, joined by several German states, united in the Sixth Coalition to defeat France. They raised larger forces than Napoleon had faced in any of his earlier campaigns and forced him to assemble another 500,000 men to defend his empire. Indeed, from the summer of 1813 his opponents, after coordinating their efforts, were so numerous and united and his forces so inexperienced that his chances for victory were limited. In 1814 and 1815, when he had barely 100,000 men to defend an exhausted France against half a million invaders, he was able to move rapidly and strike unexpectedly, but with such a small army he could not win decisive battles against massive enemy forces. The size of armies rather than their range, speed, or leadership decided the last campaigns of the Napoleonic Wars.

The Russian Campaign of 1812

Soon after the Treaty of Tilsit in 1807, the alliance between France and Russia became quite tenuous. During the Franco-Austrian war of 1809, Tsar Alexander I did little to assist France but seized some choice Austrian lands when the war ended. He very reluctantly tolerated the existence of the Grand Duchy of Warsaw on his border and was greatly disturbed when Napoleon enlarged it through the Treaty of Schönbrunn in October 1809. When Jean Bernadotte, one of Napoleon's own marshals, became crown prince of Sweden and thus heir to the Swedish throne, the tsar's doubts about Napoleon's motives intensified. Napoleon's decision to marry an Austrian archduchess, Marie Louise, after being rebuffed by the Russian royal family, led the tsar to assume that the French emperor would favor Austrian rather than Russian interests in the Balkans. Napoleon's failure to assist Russia in its war with the Ottoman Empire and to support its claim to Ottoman territory in the Balkans heightened the tsar's distrust of the emperor.

Napoleon's Continental System also proved to be disastrous for Russia's economy. On December 31, 1810, Alexander placed heavy duties on all luxury imports, including those from France. Napoleon considered this action a violation of the Continental System. With his military resources being stretched to their utmost, and with the struggle in the Iberian Peninsula continuing to sap his strength, Napoleon could not tolerate any breaks in the united front against Britain.

By the end of 1810, both Napoleon and Alexander seemed to regard war as their only acceptable option. Napoleon reinforced his troops in northern Germany, and in the spring of 1811 Alexander began to concentrate a force of almost a quarter of a million men in western Russia. Preparations for war had begun.

Strategies and Forces

The Russians introduced several reforms in their army following their defeat at Friedland in June 1807. Building on previous reforms, they improved and increased the number of artillery; by 1812 they had about 1,700 guns. They also adopted new drill regulations, though a large gap existed between doctrine and common practice. Shortly before the 1812 campaign, the Russians introduced the corps system into their First and Second armies. The new corps had two infantry divisions, a cavalry division or brigade, and two artillery brigades. Despite these reforms, Russian forces remained very inefficient and did not have the flexibility or mobility of the French. They had more than two dozen different calibers of muskets, and their soldiers received only minimum training. The officer corps of nobles was also split by cliques and personality clashes.

The fifty-one-year-old Mikhail Bogdanovitch, Baron Barclay de Tolly, was minister of war as well as commander of the First Army, but Alexander determined Russia's strategy and dispositions. Accepting the advice of General Ernst von Phull, a Prussian emigré, he decided to cover the main invasion route to Moscow. Once the French crossed the Niemen River, Russian forces would offer some resistance before retiring about 125 miles to the Dvina River where they would occupy the fortified camp at Drissa. When the French attacked this fortified camp, another Russian army would strike from the south and move deep into their rear. Alexander adopted this strategy despite the opposition of most of the Russian generals and members of his staff, including a young Prussian officer named Carl von Clausewitz.

The Russians had more than 400,000 soldiers available, including more than 225,000 soldiers along the western border. Alexander placed Barclay's First Army of some 127,000 men along the Niemen River in front of Napoleon's most likely avenue of advance. To his south was General Peter Bagration's Second Army with some 48,000 men. South of the Pripet Marshes, General Alexander Tormassov commanded the Third Army of 43,000 men. On the extreme flanks were the Danubian Army in the south and the Army of Finland in the north. The Russians also established large magazines along the presumed invasion route to sustain their armies.

Facing the vast expanse of Russia, Napoleon's strategy called for a rapid advance to overtake and crush the Russian army as quickly as possible. He realized, however, that a campaign in Russia would require magazines and supply trains, reminiscent of eighteenth-century warfare. Because of the vast expanse of land, terrible roads and communications, sparse population, and limited resources, supply trains would have to sustain the army until it could overtake and crush the enemy. Thus, Napoleon's strategy required speed and great mobility for the annihilation of the enemy army, but it also required enormous logistical support which, by its very nature, was slow and not very mobile.

Napoleon collected a huge multinational army for the invasion of Russia. Of the more than 600,000 troops he assembled, including reserves and supporting troops, less than half were French; the rest were German,

Polish, Prussian, Austrian, Italian, Spanish, Portuguese, Lithuanian, Bavarian, Saxon, Dutch, Swiss, Croat, Westphalian, among others. Of these, about 450,000 actually crossed the Niemen River. Napoleon organized his forces into three autonomous field armies that could operate separately or in conjunction with each other. The major force of 225,000 (primarily French troops) would be supported by a second army of 80,000 under his stepson, Viceroy Eugène de Beauharnais; a third army of 70,000 men would march under his brother, King Jérôme of Westphalia. On the extreme flanks of the army, the corps of Marshal Macdonald and Prince Karl Schwarzenberg of Austria were posted. The huge force included more than 1,400 artillery pieces drawn by 30,000 horses and 25,000 supply vehicles drawn by as many as 90,000 horses and thousands of oxen. The French would advance along three different routes carrying twenty-four days' rations in their wagons and knapsacks. Napoleon hoped this would suffice until his massive supply trains and herds of cattle had been replenished or better, until the Russian army had been destroyed.

Thus, Napoleon launched the 1812 campaign under different circumstances than his previous campaigns—with French soldiers a minority, his army was more diverse and less homogeneous than ever before. Its logistical support also exceeded that of any previous Napoleonic army. For an army that derived much of its mobility from its small logistical structure, the presence of huge supply trains would both sustain and constrain future operations. The corps were also more unwieldy; Davout's corps alone included 72,000 men.

Napoleon still retained the command style and personal habits that he had used in the first Italian campaign with a much smaller army. Despite his genius for war, he had failed to develop a system for exerting control over his huge forces or for nurturing commanders capable of independent action. Furthermore, Napoleon failed to comprehend the complex topographical factors, acute variations in weather, or enormous distances involved in a Russian campaign.

The Advance into Russia

Napoleon's troops began to cross the Niemen River on June 23, 1812; they hoped to take advantage of the upcoming summer harvest. Despite the insufferable heat and dust mixed with torrential rains and muddy roads, elements of the French army reached Vilna in three days, an advance of about fifty miles. Napoleon would remain in the city for almost eighteen days to organize a Lithuanian government. Barclay's First Russian Army, concentrated around Vilna, began its withdrawal toward Drissa on June 26 after destroying its magazines. The speed of the French advance not only forced Barclay to retreat, but also increased the distance between his army and Bagration's Second Army in the south. Napoleon attempted to intercept Bagration's army, but the Russians slipped away during the first week of July.

Meanwhile the main French column pushed on toward Drissa only to learn that the Russians had abandoned the armed camp on July 18.

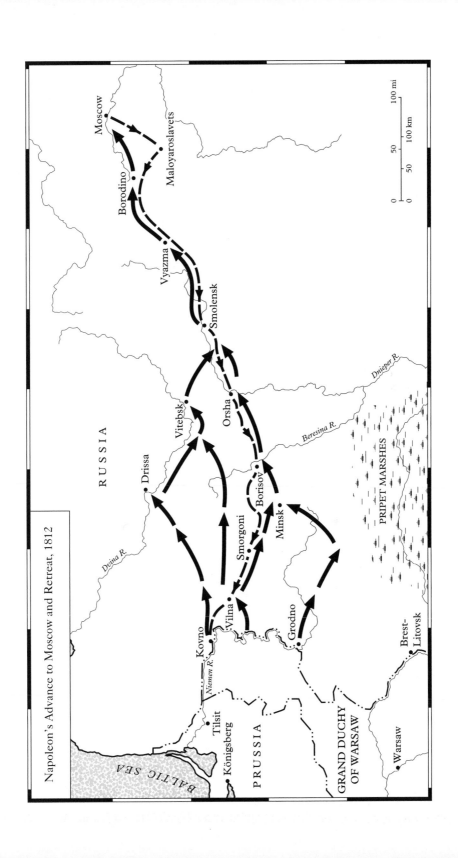

Napoleon's Advance to Moscow and Retreat, 1812

BALTIC SEA

PRUSSIA

GRAND DUCHY
OF WARSAW

RUSSIA

PRIPET MARSHES

Moscow
Borodino
Maloyaroslavets
Vyazma
Smolensk
Vitebsk
Orsha
Drissa
Borisov
Smorgoni
Minsk
Vilna
Kovno
Grodno
Tilsit
Königsberg
Warsaw
Brest-
Litovsk

Dvina R.
Niemen R.
Beresina R.
Dnieper R.

100 mi
50
100 km
50
0
0

Though discouraged, Napoleon was convinced that if he could overtake the Russians, he could bring the campaign to a swift conclusion. For the next one hundred miles weary soldiers marched along the deteriorating roads. Occasionally Russian peasants attempted to resist or destroyed their crops, but Alexander made no concerted effort to enlist the support of the peasants. The memory of earlier peasant revolts haunted the Russian nobles and discouraged them from making such an appeal.

When Napoleon was about thirty miles from Vitebsk, almost 250 miles east of the Niemen River, he learned that the Russians were still in the town. Hoping for a battle but needing time to concentrate his army, he delayed movement for one day, and then on July 28, his forces entered Vitebsk, only to find the Russian army gone.

Establishing his headquarters at Vitebsk, Napoleon provided his exhausted soldiers time to rest and to reorganize their supply trains. With each mile the army advanced, it became smaller—depleted by what is known as "strategic consumption"—as soldiers remained behind to fortify or garrison important points to maintain the lines of communication. While the number of stragglers increased, other soldiers became ill, wagons collapsed, and horses and oxen died. Carcasses of animals and the debris of wagons littered the route of advance. By the time the French forces reached Vitebsk, strategic consumption had reduced their numbers by perhaps 100,000 men. Moreover, 8,000 horses had died between Vilna and Vitebsk, and bread, footgear, and medical supplies were in short supply.

The Maneuver of Smolensk

Meanwhile 125,000 Russians in the First and Second armies finally united on August 4 near Smolensk, north of the Dnieper River. Under great pressure from Alexander, Barclay decided to attack Napoleon, but he encountered opposition from the insubordinate Bagration. The Russians moved forward slowly on August 7. Napoleon concluded on August 12 that the Russians were not going to attack, so he designed the so-called "maneuver of Smolensk" to envelop the southern flank and rear of the Russians, thereby forcing them to fight by cutting their line of retreat to Moscow.

On the night of August 13–14, almost 200,000 troops crossed the Dnieper and headed along its south bank toward Smolensk. On the afternoon of August 16, Napoleon reached the outskirts of the fortified city, most of which sat on the south bank of the Dnieper. Both Bagration and Barclay were concentrated on the north bank of the river but had troops in the city. Instead of continuing east, Napoleon launched limited attacks against the walls of the old city the following day. That night, Barclay, over the objections of his generals, ordered the evacuation of the city.

Napoleon's efforts to bring the Russians to battle had again failed. The French army occupied the gutted ruins of Smolensk, fifteen hundred miles from Paris, with limited supplies and with diminishing chances of overtaking the enemy. Napoleon's thoughts now focused on campaign strategy—should the army winter in Smolensk, or should it drive toward

Moscow? He was confident that Alexander would fight to protect Moscow. He knew the weather would soon turn cold and wet; if the Russians continued to withdraw, the French could face a crippling winter campaign. Yet, if he remained at Smolensk in August (with months of campaigning still ahead), the safety of the Russian army would be assured, and he might face a more formidable Russian force in the future. Recognizing the risks, Napoleon marched farther into Russia with his columns on August 21. Moscow lay 230 miles to their front, the Niemen 330 miles to their rear.

Strategic consumption continued to plague Napoleon's army. By the time he left Smolensk, he had 150,000 men with the army. Hundreds of soldiers deserted daily while thousands suffered from acute dysentery and were incapable of continuing the march. Napoleon himself suffered from a bladder infection (dysuria). He was physically exhausted and emotionally drained from the pressures of the pursuit; the squabbling among his generals, especially Davout and Murat in the advance guard, caused him anxious moments.

As the French neared Moscow, many within the Russian army, as well as the nobles and the tsar, clamored for a battle. They were appalled by the devastation wrought by the invasion, humiliated by the evacuation of Smolensk, and insistent that Barclay be replaced. Hence, on August 20, Kutusov, who nominally commanded the Russian army at Austerlitz, assumed command of the army retiring toward Moscow. As soon as he joined his army, he began developing a plan that would give Napoleon the battle he sought.

Borodino: "The most terrible of all my battles"

On September 5, French forces, totaling 138,000 soldiers and 584 guns, halted within a mile of the Russian army at Borodino, about seventy miles west of Moscow. On the high ground above Borodino, 120,000 Russians and 640 guns occupied a four-mile line on the east bank of the Kalatsha River. The right half of their line extended along the steep banks of the river, and the left extended south across several small hills. In the center and only a few hundred yards from the river, the Russians had constructed the "Great Redoubt." Half a mile to its south, they had fortified the village of Semyonovskaya. Another half mile to the south on a very slight hill were three large flèches, which were arrow-shaped field works with embrasures for more than a battery of artillery. A river and numerous streams crossed the battlefield, several stands of trees obstructed the French advance, the terrain limited the use of cavalry, and Kutusov's troops occupied the high ground above Borodino. Except for the left flank, which was weakly secured by the woods of Utitza, it was a formidable position.

On September 6, after carefully reconnoitering and studying the battlefield, Napoleon decided on a massive frontal attack against the Russian center and left-center, supported by concentrated artillery fire and by minor attacks on the Russian wings. Davout pleaded with Napoleon to launch an envelopment or a *manoeuvre sur les derrières,* but the emperor, apprehensive

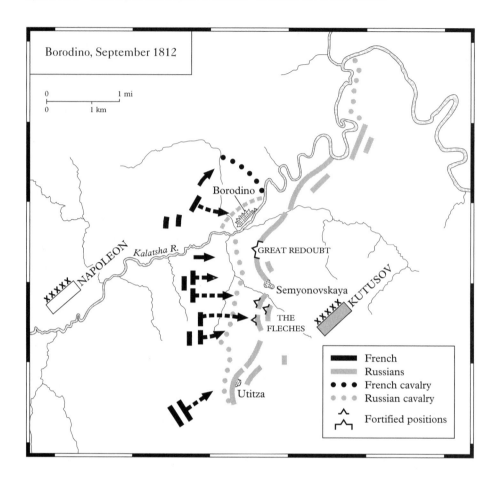

Borodino, September 1812

French
Russians
French cavalry
Russian cavalry
Fortified positions

about the enemy's retreat to avoid battle, ruled out any extensive maneuvers. He was determined to launch a frontal assault directly into the Russian defenses.

Early the next morning after a heavy bombardment from one hundred artillery pieces, Eugène de Beauharnais' corps, reinforced with cavalry, assaulted the village of Borodino on the Russian right, and General Josef A. Poniatowski's corps attacked the extreme left of the Russians near Utitza. At the same time, Davout's corps attacked the flèches in the heart of the Russian left, and Ney's corps attacked the fortified village of Semyonovskaya to the north of the flèches. Despite some momentary gains by the French, the Russians blunted the attacks and then repulsed them with furious counterattacks. Recognizing that the French were concentrating on his center and left, Kutusov shifted one of his corps from his right to his left.

Shortly after 10:00 A.M., Napoleon sent the corps of Ney, Davout, and Junot, plus two cavalry corps, against the middle of the Russian left. He attempted to support the attack with 250 guns, but 300 Russian guns inflicted horrific casualties on the massed infantry columns. The French took the flèches and finally seized the gutted ruins of Semyonovskaya, only to be driven back with heavy losses by a Russian counterattack. Despite appeals from Murat, Davout, and Ney, Napoleon refused to send the Imperial Guard; the French assaulted the village again and eventually recaptured it. By midday, they had driven back the middle of the Russian left.

French attacks now concentrated on the Great Redoubt which had been under attack by Eugène since early morning. Amidst preparations for this attack, some Cossacks swept around the French left and into Borodino, forcing Eugène to divert his forces to regain Borodino. Around 2:00 P.M., his corps and a cavalry corps assaulted the Great Redoubt. Supported by about 400 guns, they finally captured and held the position despite several counterattacks by the Russians. When a breach opened in the Russian lines, Eugène ordered his cavalry forward, but two Russian cavalry corps threw them back. Eugène appealed for the assistance of the Imperial Guard, but Napoleon refused his request, thereby permitting the Russian infantry to withdraw safely to new positions. Eugène brought his artillery forward and began bombarding the Russians. Under the pressure of constant French attacks, Kutusov shifted forces from his flanks into his center and concentrated the Russians along a narrower front. French artillery pounded this massive target unmercifully.

Late in the afternoon the Russians sent a corps toward Semyonovskaya, but the massed fire of French artillery halted them. Shortly thereafter, Napoleon ordered Poniatowski's corps forward against the Russian left and forced it back. By 6:00 P.M., the Russians occupied a new line about one thousand yards behind their original position but showed no signs of collapse. After twelve hours of continuous fighting, the two exhausted armies faced each other. Some of the Russian generals argued for renewing the battle on the following morning, but Kutusov ordered a withdrawal that night. Although the Russians were defeated and driven from the field, the battle of Borodino had ended without their destruction.

Throughout the day, artillery played a key role on both sides. The French fired 90,000 rounds, and the Russians fired 60,000. Never before had such concentrated fire been seen on a European battlefield. The strong reliance on artillery resulted in extremely high casualties. The French sustained some 30,000 casualties, while the Russians suffered approximately 45,000. About one third of all participants in the battle of Borodino were wounded or killed.

During the battle at Borodino, Napoleon suffered from a bladder infection and an acute case of influenza and, for the first time, played a relatively passive role. His overall operational concept, although uninspired, was understandable, considering the condition and international composition of his army. Yet his indecision, inactivity, and failure to capitalize on battlefield opportunities allowed the Russian army to escape with 90,000 men. Moreover, throughout the battle he refused to commit the Imperial Guard. Fortunately for the French, Kutusov had been even less active and decisive than Napoleon.

Within a week the French advance guard occupied the abandoned capital of Moscow, and Napoleon arrived to reside in the Kremlin Palace on

Napoleon entered Moscow on September 15, 1812. His advance guard had entered the previous day after agreeing to let the Russians evacuate the city. Despite appearances in this picture, many of the French suffered from disease and exhaustion.

September 15. Although he expected representatives of the tsar to negotiate with him, none came forward. Then Moscow began to burn. With heavy winds whipping the flames, several fires, some accidental and others deliberately set by Russian arsonists, consumed 80 percent of the city. Nevertheless, French troops found shelter in hundreds of stone buildings that had not burned and discovered considerable food (but no fodder) in the capital. The soldiers systematically looted the remaining houses, undermining what remained of army discipline.

As weeks passed, Napoleon attempted unsuccessfully to open negotiations with the tsar, but Alexander refused to negotiate as long as foreign troops remained on Russian soil. As each day passed, the strategic and logistical predicament facing the French forces became more acute. With winter rapidly approaching, attacks against outlying units increasing, and resources dwindling, Napoleon decided to evacuate the city and withdraw west.

Retreat from Moscow

The French army of 105,000 men marched out of the Russian capital on October 19. After considering a move directly toward St. Petersburg, Napoleon determined to march to Smolensk and occupy winter quarters there. To avoid the devastated invasion route, he decided to withdraw along a route to its south. When the French evacuated the capital, they made a fatal decision to leave food behind so thousands of wagons, piled high with loot, could follow the army. During the next six days, the army moved about seventy miles without major incident until they reached Maloyaroslavets. In a desperate day-long battle, Eugène's Italian soldiers finally drove the Russians out of the town. With some 35,000 men engaged, each side lost about 6,000 men.

Alarmed by the grim state of affairs and unnerved by near capture, Napoleon decided to change the route of march and return to the devastated Moscow-Smolensk route. On October 26, followed by massive trains of loot, the French turned toward Borodino, which still contained the carcasses of tens of thousands of men and horses. The advance guard of the army reached Vyazma on October 31 with the remainder of the army stretching some seventy miles behind it. On November 3 a light snow began to fall. That evening some 30,000 Russians with 120 guns attacked the French rear guard of 20,000 men under Davout eight miles east of Vyazma. Ney, Poniatowski, and Eugène turned back to rescue Davout's men, but soon found themselves in the midst of a major battle of almost 60,000 men. Davout's corps finally escaped, but in considerable disorder, so Ney assumed rear-guard duties with his corps.

Despite persistent attacks by Cossacks, the French columns pushed forward toward Smolensk. On November 9, Napoleon reached Smolensk amid heavy snow storms to find most of the storage magazines depleted. Over the next four days the remaining corps of the army entered the city and plundered the food magazines, leaving little for Ney's starving rear guard. The lack of food and continued pressure from the Russians convinced Napoleon to move west toward Minsk, and on November 14 his forces began marching out of the city. Some thirty miles west of Smolensk, the Russians cut off several French corps. Desperate fighting enabled the French to escape despite severe losses, but others had to slip around the Russians. Ney's rear guard lost 85 percent of its soldiers.

Fully aware that enemy forces could cut the route again, Napoleon marched quickly toward Orsha to secure a passage over the Dnieper. Fortunately for the French, they discovered well-stocked magazines in Orsha. Napoleon reorganized his ravaged forces, rearmed the stragglers, and destroyed surplus vehicles and equipment before he continued the westward march. When Napoleon reached the Beresina River (about seventy-five miles west of Orsha), he found that the Russians had captured the town of Borisov and cut the bridge. With almost 150,000 Russians closing in for the kill, the French managed to build two bridges by dismantling several nearby villages. As many as 30,000 troops crossed the fragile bridges while other troops delayed the advancing Russians. On November 29 the French burned the bridges, abandoning thousands of stragglers and camp followers.

Although well beyond the Beresina and almost 400 miles from Moscow, the French were still not out of danger. Kutusov's troops accelerated their pursuit as Napoleon's army, ravished by the cold and famine, plodded toward Vilna and its well-stocked magazines. On December 5 at

After the French erected two flimsy bridges across the Beresina, most of the army crossed. A break in one of the bridges, however, caused panic and a wild rush to cross. Though order was restored, approaches to the bridges remained piled with corpses and abandoned equipment.

Smorgoni, eighty miles northwest of the crossing site on the Beresina, Napoleon held a final meeting with his generals and announced his departure for Paris. He claimed that the army was out of imminent danger and that the political needs of the empire demanded his attention. That night Napoleon departed for France leaving Murat in command of the battered army. Within thirteen days the emperor was in Paris organizing a new army for the defense of his empire.

Between Smorgoni and Vilna, the French lost thousands of stragglers. In fact, fewer than 15,000 men marched in columns. Despite the vast magazines in Vilna, which included 4 million rations, the army continued its headlong retreat toward Prussia. The last remnants of Napoleon's army crossed the Niemen on December 11.

The campaign of 1812 came to a disastrous end for Napoleon and his army. They could not overcome staggering logistical problems, a tenacious enemy, vast expanses of terrain, and unimaginable weather conditions. The failed campaign damaged Napoleon's reputation as a great commander, and it encouraged his enemies to renew their struggle against France. The Imperial army never recovered from the loss of about 400,000 men, 1,000 cannon, and 200,000 horses. Though the Russians lost approximately 200,000 men, plus many irregulars and civilians, they had driven the French from Russia, ensured their territorial integrity, and secured for Russia a preeminent role in Europe for the next half-century.

The Campaigns of 1813–1814

Despite his losses in Russia, Napoleon remained master over much of Europe when he returned to Paris in December 1812. With Prussia and Austria as allies, he still controlled Italy, the Low Countries, the Illyrian Provinces, and much of Germany. Furthermore, Napoleon recognized that Russia would have difficulty pressing the war farther into central Europe and that Britain's small army remained deeply involved in Portugal and Spain. On the last day of December, Napoleon emphasized to an Austrian emissary the strength of French resources and his resolve to invade Russia again. That strength soon proved illusory.

On the day prior to Napoleon's meeting with the Austrian emissary, the commander of the Prussian corps with French forces, on his own initiative, signed the military Convention of Tauroggen with the Russians and agreed to remain neutral until orders arrived from the King of Prussia; he also agreed to allow Russian forces to march through Prussian territory. Though King Frederick William III initially repudiated the agreement, the Prussian people enthusiastically welcomed the advancing Russians, and the king signed a treaty with Russia in late February by which he agreed to continue the war with the Russians against Napoleon. In the middle of March, Frederick William declared war on Napoleon. During the same period, the commander of the Austrian corps with the French forces signed an armistice with Russia on January 30, and the Austrians quickly offered to mediate between the French and Russians. Napoleon had lost the assistance of the Austrians and now faced the combined forces of Russia and Prussia.

After the Russians crossed the Niemen, Russian and Prussian forces advanced on a broad front against the French. As the situation deteriorated, Murat withdrew 300 miles west of the Niemen, relinquished his command to Eugène, and departed for Naples. The French abandoned Warsaw in the first week of April; by the end of the month they had retreated over 200 miles and halted behind the Elbe and Saale rivers.

The Saxon Campaign

Meanwhile Napoleon struggled to create a new army to protect his empire and allied states. With the conscripts of 1813 and 1814, units of the National Guard, regiments from Spain, the gendarmes, naval personnel, the municipal guard, and some foreign regiments, he collected almost 400,000 men. Needing more troops, he called up individuals from conscript classes of the previous four years who had escaped or avoided conscription. The new army of almost half a million men suffered from numerous shortages, including junior and noncommissioned officers, artillery, and horses. Some of Napoleon's allies also provided troops. Though most members of the Confederation of the Rhine looked forward to the French withdrawal, some feared Russian occupation even more and sent contingents to Napoleon's new army.

In mid-April, Napoleon left Paris and concentrated 150,000 men behind the Elbe. He decided to take the offensive and confront each enemy army in succession. Crossing the Saale on April 30, Napoleon's forces moved into Saxony and advanced east toward Leipzig. On May 2 a combined Russian-Prussian army surprised a detachment of Ney's corps near Lützen. Napoleon quickly concentrated his forces on the battlefield and drove the allies back. Only the lack of French cavalry saved the allies from a devastating defeat. After the allies withdrew to the east and evacuated Dresden, the French crossed the Elbe River and made contact with an allied army at Bautzen on May 16. Napoleon concentrated his forces, and on May 20–21, he again gained a victory, renewing the legend of his invincibility.

With Napoleon poised to drive his enemy back, both sides readily agreed on June 2 to an armistice. Recognizing the possibility of Austrian intervention, Napoleon wanted time to build up his forces in Germany and Italy. He hoped to reinforce his army, secure new mounts for his cavalry, obtain additional ammunition, and—if possible—divide his enemies. Considering the condition of his army in December 1812, he had to be satisfied with its remarkable successes even though no decisive results had been achieved. Agreeing to an armistice, however, proved to be a major error.

Like the French, the allies needed time to recuperate from the rigors of the campaign and to consider a new strategy, but they also used the armistice to convince Austria to enter the war against France. Within a month Austria agreed to join the allies if Napoleon did not agree to dissolve the Duchy of Warsaw, enlarge Prussia, and return the Illyrian Provinces to Austria. Though the allies proposed that France retain its territory west of the Rhine, as well as Belgium and Italy, Napoleon refused, agreeing only to yield part of Poland to Russia. With his confidence momentarily reinforced by his recent victories, he failed to recognize the strength of the gathering coalition and his inability to regain control of Europe.

The armistice ended on August 10, and for the first time France faced four great powers (Russia, Prussia, Austria, and Great Britain) simultaneously. Adding to the allied superiority, Bernadotte, a former marshal of France and now the Crown Prince of Sweden, agreed to send an army into Germany against France. Allied resolve was strengthened by news of Wellington's victory in northern Spain at Vitoria, as well as by the huge subsidies provided by the British.

Before hostilities began, the allies met at Trachenberg and agreed that if Napoleon confronted one of their armies, it would withdraw while other armies moved immediately to attack the French lines of communication. Instead of fighting a single great battle, they intended to wear down Napoleon's army through time and attrition. The allies also agreed to field three combined armies against Napoleon. Bernadotte commanded 120,000 Swedes, Russians, and Prussians near Berlin; Schwarzenberg commanded 240,000 Austrians in Bohemia; and Blücher commanded 100,000 Prussians and Russians in Silesia. While the three armies were poised around

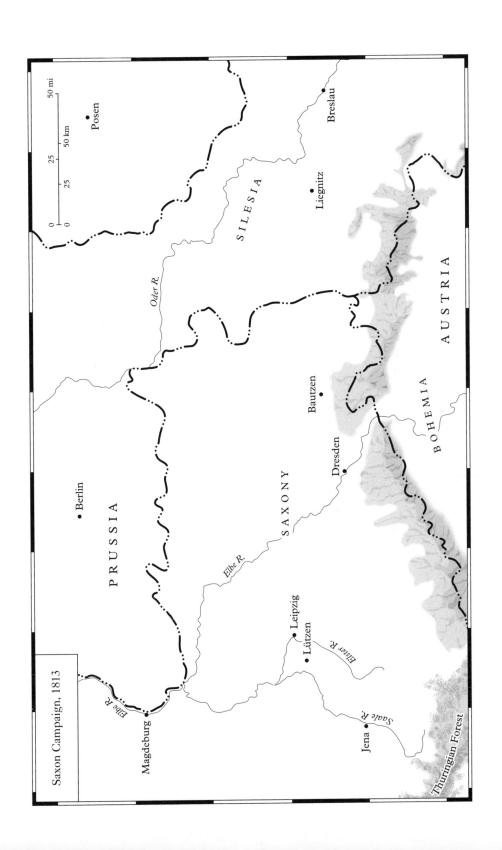

Saxon Campaign, 1813

50 mi

50 km

PRUSSIA

• Berlin

Magdeburg

Elbe R.

Leipzig
• Lützen

Jena

Saale R.

Elster R.

Thuringian Forest

SAXONY

Elbe R.

Dresden •

Bautzen •

SILESIA

Oder R.

• Posen

• Liegnitz

• Breslau

BOHEMIA

AUSTRIA

Napoleon's forces, another Russian army in Poland, 60,000 strong, was preparing to march.

The allies intended for Blücher in Silesia and Bernadotte in Prussia to advance, drawing Napoleon's forces toward them. Schwarzenberg would then attack north from Bohemia toward Dresden and sever Napoleon's lines of communication. Following Austria's declaration of war on August 12, Blücher moved west on August 14. Napoleon immediately advanced east to intercept him, but the Prussian commander retreated in accordance with the "Trachenberg plan."

As Napoleon pursued Blücher's forces, he received an urgent appeal from French forces at Dresden, which were threatened by Schwarzenberg's advance. After initially hesitating, he sent Macdonald to continue the pursuit of Blücher while he marched west to relieve Dresden. Following an extraordinary march of almost 125 miles in four days, Napoleon led 70,000 reinforcements into Dresden on August 26. With the arrival of 50,000 more men the following day, he crushed the flanks of Schwarzenberg's forces and drove in the Austrian center. The stunned Austrians and Russians, having suffered 38,000 casualties, began a headlong retreat. Though the French still lacked cavalry, Napoleon attempted a pursuit. One aggressive corps commander, however, was surrounded and captured with half his troops. A few days prior to this, Blücher had turned on Macdonald's forces in Silesia and had beaten them badly. At the same time, Bernadotte had pushed French forces back from Berlin. Thus despite the French victory at Dresden, the allies remained strong.

After the brilliantly executed but futile victory at Dresden, Napoleon continued making plans to crush the allies, but appeals from his subordinates sent him racing from one direction to the other. As his exhausted troops marched and countermarched across Saxony, he remained so busy reacting to allied actions that he had no time to seize the initiative. By October 11, Napoleon resolved to occupy a central position and concentrate his army in the vicinity of Leipzig "to fight a great battle." Nothing illustrates better his self-confidence and his desire for a single climactic battle than his willingness to face the much larger allied armies at Leipzig in what became known as the "Battle of Nations."

Napoleon occupied Leipzig on October 14 with 171,000 men; three allied armies converged on the city with some 340,000 troops. On October 16 the battle began with an allied assault against Napoleon's forces south of Leipzig. Attacks and counterattacks continued all day. Little occurred on October 17, but on the following day fighting exploded anew. The French repulsed the initial attacks, but arrival of an additional 140,000 allied forces forced Napoleon to withdraw his army shortly after midnight. The withdrawal went smoothly until a terrified French corporal mistakenly blew up the only bridge across the Elster River and trapped most of the rear guard in Leipzig. Hundreds of soldiers tried to swim the river, and many of them drowned in the process. When the battle finally ended, the allies had lost 54,000 men and the French 38,000 in addition to the 30,000 captured in Leipzig. Napoleon's position was weakened further by the defection of his last German allies.

The French retreated across Germany and finally crossed the Rhine River with 80,000 exhausted soldiers and 40,000 stragglers. In search of a decisive victory, Napoleon had wasted an army of almost half a million men for the second time in a year. With Germany lost, he now had to build a new army and defend the frontiers of France.

The Campaign in France, 1814

By the end of 1813, allied forces threatened France from all sides. The armies of Russia, Prussia, Austria, Sweden, and assorted German states advanced toward the Rhine; in the south a victorious Anglo-Portuguese army had crossed the frontier; in northern Italy, the armies of Austria and Naples pressed French forces under Eugène. Despite their overwhelming superiority, the allies' conflicting war aims and their distrust of each other disrupted efforts to defeat Napoleon. They disputed France's postwar boundaries and whether Napoleon, the Bourbons, or Bernadotte should rule France. The clash between Austria and Russia was especially sharp since both desired postwar France to favor them. Other contentious issues, such as the disposition of Poland and Belgium, split the coalition further.

As representatives of the allied powers held several conferences on their war aims, the campaign stalled. So long as Napoleon remained in power, key questions on France's territory and government remained open. The Austrian government instructed its forces to move "cautiously" and to

Napoleon faced overwhelmingly negative odds in the 1814 campaign. Recognizing the odds, he told his chief of staff, "We must repeat the campaign of Italy." Through sheer will he propelled the French army forward but nonetheless lost.

avoid "warlike acts," and at one point it threatened to make a separate peace with Napoleon.

While the allies procrastinated, Napoleon organized a new army composed of conscripts, veterans, units recalled from Spain, and every able-bodied man available. Of the 930,000 men called up, however, fewer than 125,000 joined the colors. In the early months of 1814, Napoleon attempted to incite a popular uprising in France against the invading armies and wage guerrilla warfare on their flanks and rear. Instead, many of the French avoided military service, refused to pay taxes, and initially did little to oppose the foreign troops marching through their villages. Exhausted by twenty years of war, few responded to the idea of defending the empire against the kings of Europe. Not until the allied armies began to plunder France did their attitudes change.

In northeastern France, Napoleon faced three major armies. On December 21 an army of 200,000 Austrians under Schwarzenberg crossed the frontier just north of Switzerland. On January 1 an army of 100,000 men under Blücher crossed the middle Rhine. During the same period, an army of 150,000 Prussians and Russians advanced through the Low Countries. Operating from a central position with Paris as the hub of his operations, Napoleon planned on concentrating against each enemy army as it approached Paris. Though the subsequent campaign of maneuver and rapid concentration proved to be one of his finest, Napoleon could not produce a decisive victory.

Leaving his brother, Joseph, in Paris to administer the government, Napoleon departed to command his small, dispirited forces. Beginning on January 29, Napoleon defeated Blücher at Brienne (about one hundred miles east of Paris) and then on February 1 was beaten by elements of Blücher's and Schwarzenberg's armies at La Rothière (three miles south of Brienne). On the same day as the tactical victory at La Rothière, the allies began six weeks' futile discussions at Châtillon with the French in an attempt to reach a negotiated settlement.

Meanwhile, even though the allies had not yet reached agreement on the terms of a settlement, Blücher attempted to end the war quickly by marching directly on Paris. In the process he created a gap between the allied armies, particularly after the Austrian commander, Schwarzenberg, retired eastward. Recognizing the significance of the gap, Napoleon attacked the scattered elements of Blücher's army and fought four major battles in five days about one hundred miles east of Paris, inflicting about 20,000 casualties on the Prussians. Though greatly outnumbered, Napoleon maneuvered rapidly, marching almost seventy-five miles, to crush his enemy and raise the spirits of his troops. As Napoleon mauled Blücher's forces, Schwarzenberg resumed his advance toward Paris. Napoleon raced south, covering forty-seven miles in thirty-six hours, and with 60,000 men attacked the Austrians near Montereau on February 17–18. Though the Austrians suffered 6,000 casualties, they managed to escape.

On March 1 the allies, after long discussions among themselves, signed the Treaty of Chaumont. They pledged to remain in the Sixth Coalition until Napoleon was defeated and agreed to reduce France to the bound-

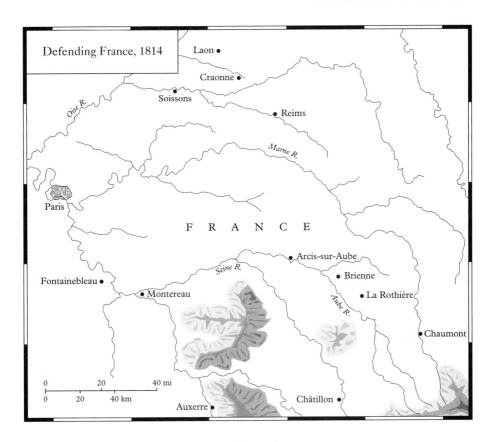

Defending France, 1814

aries of 1792. The coalition would continue for twenty years in the event of future French aggression.

Early in March, Blücher marched north toward Laon to unite with other allied forces. Napoleon followed in hot pursuit. On the plateau of Craonne (about seventy miles northeast of Paris), the two armies clashed, but the Prussians managed to slip away. Near Laon on March 9, Blücher's entire army of 85,000 attacked French forces and drove them to the southeast. Despite the defeat at Laon, Napoleon continued fighting. Following a series of battles culminating in his repulse at Arcis-sur-Aube by 80,000 Austrians, negotiations at Châtillon between the allies and French collapsed. On March 17 the allies announced that they no longer sought a negotiated settlement with Napoleon.

On the night of March 23–24, the allies captured several dispatches destined for Napoleon describing the weakness of Paris's defenses. Tsar Alexander convinced Schwarzenberg to join with Blücher and march directly on Paris. After learning of the allied advance, Napoleon considered attacking and destroying their lines of communication, but his marshals objected to his bold plan. On March 30, after he learned that the allies had seized Paris, he retired to the palace of Fontainebleau to consider his options. With 60,000 troops assembled near Fontainebleau, Napoleon summoned his marshals to receive new orders, but they refused to lead their troops into another battle—ending any hope of continuing the struggle.

After attempting to abdicate his throne in favor of his young son, Napoleon abdicated unconditionally on April 6, 1814. The allies permitted Napoleon to retain his title of emperor, agreed to have the restored Bourbon monarchy provide him a pension of 2 million francs a year, and banished him to the island kingdom of Elba in the Mediterranean.

Napoleon had waged a remarkable campaign against overwhelming odds. Threatened by almost a half-million allied troops along the entire French frontier, Napoleon succeeded in holding them off for three months even though he never had more than 100,000 soldiers at any one time. Lacking cavalry, artillery, bridging equipment, and the basic necessities of war, Napoleon led his old veterans and young conscripts into battle against insurmountable odds. With maneuvers more reminiscent of northern Italy than Russia, he moved his forces quickly and concentrated them at critical points. Unlike his opponents, he struck quickly and effectively, skillfully using the terrain to his advantage. Once the allies finally agreed, however, on the main outlines of a peace settlement, their much larger forces gained the final victory.

The Belgian Campaign and Waterloo

Napoleon spent ten months on the island of Elba reorganizing his tiny kingdom and creating a miniature army of 700 men and a small undermanned navy. Perhaps never abandoning the idea of returning to France, he remained well informed of events in France, particularly of the dissatisfaction in France over the restoration of the Bourbons. The return of the emigrés, who now demanded that their estates be restored, and the retirement of army officers on half pay created much discontent. Napolean was encouraged by many supporters to return, and the refusal of the Bourbons to pay his pension, guaranteed by the Treaty of Fontainebleau in April 1814, encouraged him further.

At the end of February 1815, in a carefully arranged escape from Elba, Napoleon sailed in a small convoy of seven ships with his tiny army of 1,100 men. He arrived on the south coast of France at Fréjus and began his 450-mile trek through central France. The Bourbons sent armies to halt Napoleon, but most of the soldiers and officers including Marshal Ney joined him instead. On March 20 he entered Paris and announced to Europe and the world that he desired only peace. The allies labeled him a "disturber of world order" and began preparing for war.

Without hope of peace or a split among the allies, Napoleon announced mobilization on April 8, but conscription was not instituted until the end of the month. Almost 90,000 volunteers and veterans quickly joined the rapidly expanding army. With the addition of National Guard units, naval personnel, customs officials, and anyone whom the recruiters could induce to join, France had almost 280,000 soldiers in uniform within two months. The allies responded at once by mobilizing their forces. Blücher moved into the Low Countries with 117,000 Prussians where he joined an Anglo-German-Dutch-Belgian force of 110,000 men under the Duke of Wellington. To the east almost 210,000 Austrians under Schwarzenberg advanced toward the east bank of the Rhine, while 150,000 Russians under Barclay marched across central Europe toward the Rhine.

Napoleon decided to strike the allied forces in Belgium before they had time to coordinate their actions or concentrate their armies. He would move immediately, occupy a central position between Blücher and Wellington's armies, and defeat each separately. Then he would seek to split the alliance or defeat the Austrians and Russians.

Frantically, Napoleon labored to create and equip what he called the *Armée du Nord*. France was transformed into an arsenal, reminiscent of the early days of the Revolution. Working day and night, the people of France produced extraordinary quantities of arms and equipment, but they would not provide what Napoleon most desperately needed—men. By June, Napoleon had begun to concentrate his forces secretly for the advance into Belgium. Since some troops remained on the frontier while others suppressed armed insurrection in the Vendée and other royalist sectors of France, he had only 120,000 men available for the campaign.

Quatre Bras and Ligny

On June 12, Napoleon slipped out of Paris and joined his army near the Belgian frontier. While the two allied armies in Belgium remained dispersed, Napoleon began the campaign. On June 15 his army moved north toward Charleroi with hopes of splitting Blücher's and Wellington's armies. Blücher reacted immediately and began concentrating his forces near Ligny, north of Charleroi. Wellington, on the other hand, thought his line of communication to the Channel was being threatened and ordered his forces to move west and southwest of Brussels. This move actually increased the distance between his army and the Prussians.

On June 15 as the French advanced along a route that would take them to Brussels by way of Charleroi, Quatre Bras, and Waterloo, Napoleon appointed Ney to command the left wing of the army and Grouchy to command the right wing. Ney received instructions to advance on Quatre Bras (fourteen miles north of Charleroi), and Grouchy to advance on Ligny (twelve miles northeast of Charleroi). Napoleon kept the Guard in reserve with the intention of committing it to either wing when needed.

Not until the morning of the 16th did Wellington receive accurate information about Napoleon's advance and comprehend that he was moving toward Brussels. On that same day, Napoleon expected the major action of the day to occur on his left against Wellington's army. As French forces advanced, however, it became clear that Blücher had concentrated his own

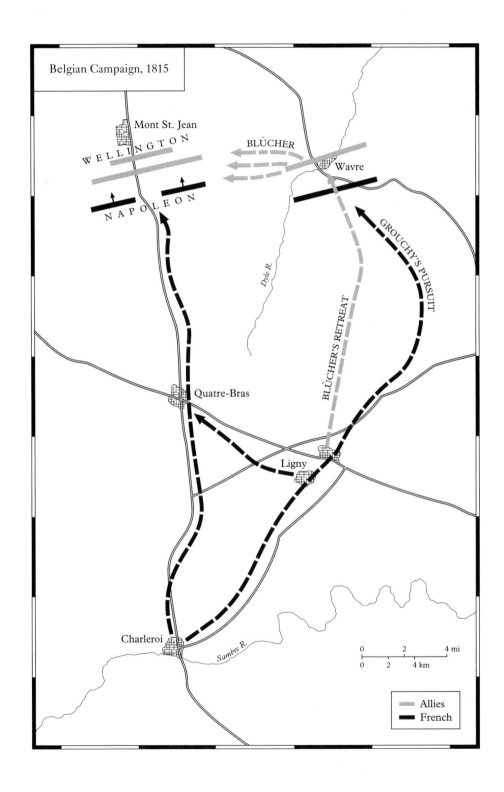

Belgian Campaign, 1815

Mont St. Jean

WELLINGTON

BLÜCHER

Wavre

NAPOLEON

Dyle R.

GROUCHY'S PURSUIT

BLÜCHER'S RETREAT

Quatre-Bras

Ligny

Charleroi

Sambre R.

| 0 | | 2 | | 4 mi |
| 0 | 2 | | 4 km | |

Allies
French

forces on Napoleon's right, near Ligny. Unaware that Wellington's forces were hurrying toward Quatre Bras, Napoleon decided to launch an attack on the Prussians at Ligny. He intended to begin the attack with assaults against the Prussians' center and right. Then Ney would turn at Quatre Bras and strike the Prussian rear, while the Imperial Guard crushed their center. In the course of the battle, however, Ney remained engaged against increasing numbers of Wellington's soldiers at Quatre Bras and never struck Blücher's rear. During the battle, Napoleon diverted 20,000 troops of Ney's command to the fight at Ligny. When Ney, outnumbered by Wellington's forces, learned of the order, he recalled them. Consequently, 20,000 soldiers who could have been used at Ligny or Quatre Bras spent the day marching between the two battles.

At Ligny, the battle raged between the outnumbered French and the Prussians, who were finally driven out of the village after numerous bloody assaults. When Napoleon unleashed the Guard and broke the Prussian line, Blücher personally led an unsuccessful counterattack with cavalry. Under the cover of darkness, the Prussians, having lost 16,000 men and twenty-one guns, fell back about one mile and then, thanks to the lack of French pursuit, retired toward the north. With French losses numbering over 11,000, Napoleon could claim success at Ligny, but not the decisive victory he had sought.

When the Prussians retreated from Ligny, Blücher's chief of staff, General August Neidhardt von Gneisenau, withdrew the army toward Wavre in the north rather than toward its base at Liège in the east. In the fight at Quatre Bras, Wellington had massed 36,000 men, losing 5,000 of them. He remained at Quatre Bras for the night and the following morning learned of the Prussians' defeat and their withdrawal toward the north.

The Battle of Waterloo

Having previously identified a favorable defensive position at the crossroads of Mont St. Jean, just south of Waterloo, Wellington withdrew his army to the north. He told the Prussians that he would stand against Napoleon at Mont St. Jean if they provided support. Fortunately for the allies, Wellington's and Blücher's forces moved in the same direction and remained within supporting distance of each other.

The following morning, Wellington remained at Quatre Bras until about noon when his forces began marching north toward Mont St. Jean. Meanwhile the French did little until Napoleon sent Grouchy with 33,000 men, almost one third of his total force, to pursue and contain the defeated Prussians. About 2:00 P.M., the rest of the French followed after Wellington, but their rate of march slowed when heavy rains began. They spent the night of June 17–18 in a pouring rain a few miles south of Wellington's bivouac at Mont St. Jean.

On the following morning, Sunday, June 18, Napoleon had some 72,000 men and 246 guns facing Wellington's army of 68,000 men and 156 guns at Mont St. Jean. With many of the allied soldiers on the reverse side

Waterloo, June 1815

Braine l'Alleud

WELLINGTON

Mont St. Jean

Papelotte

La Haye-Sainte

Château de Hougoumont

Plancenoit

NAPOLEON

Allies

French

of a slope at Mont St. Jean, where they were partially hidden and received some protection against enemy fire, Wellington concentrated his forces on a front of about 5,000 yards. To break up French attacks, he placed soldiers forward on his right front in the chateau of Hougoumont, on his center in the walled farmhouse of La Haye-Sainte, and on his left in the farmhouses of Papelotte and La Haye. Confident that Grouchy would prevent Blücher's Prussians from joining Wellington's army, Napoleon delayed his attack until the rain-saturated ground had dried enough to improve traction for horses and ensure a more deadly effect from ricocheting cannon balls. Except for the torrential rains, Napoleon would have begun the attack soon after dawn, as was his custom. Unfortunately for the French, this delay provided the Prussians time to reach Mont St. Jean.

Napoleon devised a simple battle plan: while a diversionary attack concentrated on the chateau of Hougoumont on the allied right, the main attack, preceded by heavy artillery fire, would strike their left and center. Napoleon massed more than eighty cannon in front of Wellington's position and began bombarding the enemy around 11:00 A.M. A half-hour later, Napoleon sent a corps in the diversionary attack against Hougoumont on Wellington's right. Though Napoleon hoped to induce Wellington to shift his reserves away from his center, where the main attack would hit, the diversionary attack quickly escalated into a major battle that occupied the attention of a corps for the entire day. Unwilling to commit his reserve to what was apparently a secondary effort, Wellington sent only a brigade to support the defenders at Hougoumont.

At 1:00 P.M., Napoleon instructed Ney, who was entrusted with tactical decisions on the battlefield, to launch the main French attack on La Haye-Sainte, forward of the allied center. At about the same time the leading elements of what proved to be General Friedrich von Bülow's Prussian corps, 30,000 strong, appeared in the distance, on the French right. Nevertheless, Napoleon believed he could defeat Wellington's army before the Prussians could strike his flank. To contain the Prussians, he shifted cavalry and an infantry corps toward his right.

Earlier, Wellington had received a dispatch from Blücher, announcing that he was marching with at least two corps to support him while one corps remained at Wavre to detain Grouchy. Eventually three Prussian corps would reach the battlefield. At Wavre, Grouchy misinterpreted the movements of the Prussians, assumed the small enemy force in front of him was the entire Prussian force, and refused the pleas of his lieutenants to march to the sound of the guns. This mistake resulted in Blücher's having an open road as he rushed toward Waterloo.

For the attack on Wellington's left-center, Ney ordered a heavy bombardment of the allies' position and then sent General Jean-Baptiste d'Erlon's four divisions forward around 1:30 P.M. The divisions advanced in massive formations, each having a front of 160 yards. British artillery knocked down entire rows of soldiers in the massed divisions. With little support from French cavalry, the infantry finally reached Wellington's line, but concentrated fire from the allied infantry beat them back. In the midst of the heaviest fighting, the British cavalry charged into the fray and quickly put the remnants of Erlon's corps to flight. As the French infantry fled, the British cavalry rushed across the field toward the massed French artillery and were met by the thundering roar of French artillery and charging cavalry. They lost 1,000 soldiers in minutes. With the French preoccupied by the cavalry charge, Wellington reinforced La Haye-Sainte and the areas in his line mauled by Erlon's attack.

By 3:00 P.M., knowing Grouchy would not reach the battlefield in time, Napoleon ordered an all-out attempt to seize La Haye-Sainte. Ney led the attack and somehow became convinced the allies were retreating. Though the initial order was for an attack by a brigade of cavalry, more than 5,000 cavalrymen, unsupported by infantry or artillery, charged forward against the allied center, which quickly formed into twenty squares. Ultimately, other horsemen joined in the attack until almost 10,000 were charging across the fields and toward the allied squares. In the melee, the French swept over the allied artillery but failed to spike the pieces. When British cavalry moved forward to support the infantry's squares, the allies repulsed

The failure of the Guard broke the French will to fight. Napoleon attempted to halt the mass of fleeing soldiers, but he, too, soon had to flee.

the French attacks. Shortly after 6:00 P.M. the French launched infantry and cavalry in another attack on La Haye-Sainte and finally captured it. Heavy fire from an artillery battery rushed forward by Ney caused the allied center to waver, but Napoleon refused to commit the Old Guard.

Meanwhile, Blücher's troops poured out of the woods on Napoleon's right at 4:00 P.M., and a savage fight ensued. After the Prussians captured the small village of Plancenoit, Napoleon sent the Young Guard and then the Old Guard, who recaptured Plancenoit with bayonets. By 7:00 P.M., Napoleon's right flank was again stabilized.

With a third Prussian corps approaching, Napoleon decided to unleash his last reserve—nine battalions of the Old Guard. If they could exploit Ney's success at La Haye-Sainte, the British army would be cut in half and beaten; already thousands of allied troops had fled the battlefield. The Guard advanced in two or perhaps three columns. Wellington reinforced his line and deployed his infantry behind defensible terrain. Unsupported by artillery or cavalry, the Guard received heavy allied artillery fire. When they reached Wellington's position, British infantrymen greeted them with concentrated, devastating musket fire. As the men in both armies watched, the Guard broke and began to retreat.

As shock and then panic swept through Napoleon's army, Wellington ordered his line forward; the Prussians also advanced. Though Napoleon tried to quell the spreading disorder, the allies swept the French off the battlefield. The French had suffered some 25,000 casualties and had some 8,000 captured, while the Allies acknowledged 22,000, of whom 7,000 were Prussian, 7,400 Anglo-Hanoverian, and the remainder Dutch, Belgian, and German. Napoleon had fought his last battle.

After Waterloo, Napoleon returned to Paris with every intention of continuing the struggle. But the national legislature refused to support a continuation of the war. Having no real choice, Napoleon abdicated. The allied armies pursued the debris of the French army to Paris where an armistice was concluded in July 1815. No longer willing to accept the boundaries of 1792, the allies reduced French frontiers to those of 1790, and an allied army of occupation remained in the country for three years. Exiled by the allies, Napoleon left at the end of July for the island of St. Helena in the south Atlantic. The Napoleonic era had closed.

Napoleonic Warfare

The wars of the French Revolution and Napoleon brought dramatic changes in warfare. As French revolutionaries fought to defend France and their Revolution against the principal states of Europe and to spread their revolutionary ideology abroad, they rejected the conventions of limited war and thus initiated an era of nearly total war. Seeking goals beyond those of the dynastic and commercial struggles of the eighteenth century, they created national armies of unprecedented size to destroy their enemies, overthrow their governments, and annex their territories. When the armies of the new republic first appeared on the battlefields of Europe, they were, out of necessity, composed of citizen-soldiers committed to the defense of their country and motivated by a spirit of patriotism. As the European powers concentrated against them, the French took drastic measures, as exemplified by the famous *levée en masse,* to mobilize every aspect of their country for its defense. France became a nation in arms and molded its strategy and operations to accommodate its new armies.

The French blended units of regulars, volunteers, and conscripts to combine republican zeal with tactical skills, and they opened their officer corps to men of talent. The commanders of these new revolutionary armies were expected to find and destroy enemy forces; there would be no conventional campaigns of maneuver, skirmish, and siege and no reliance on a magazine supply system. To gain greater flexibility and mobility, French commanders subdivided their armies, enabling them to move by multiple routes, draw supplies more easily from the countryside, and impose battle on an unsuspecting or reluctant enemy. The French also relied on superior numbers, simplified tactics, and improved artillery.

Employed by the most gifted of the revolutionary generals, Napoleon Bonaparte, the new methods increased significantly the scale, speed, and decisiveness of warfare. The young, energetic leader recognized the advantages of divisions and corps, the changing requirements of logistics, the opportunity for maneuver, and the capability for decisive action. While commanding a relatively small army in Italy in 1796–1797, Bonaparte kept his forces divided into divisions so he could feed them more easily and gain speed and deception. He coordinated their actions carefully and destroyed the larger Piedmontese and Austrian forces.

Once Napoleon became First Consul, he organized the entire French army into self-sufficient corps of 14,000 to 25,000 men that included infantry, artillery, and cavalry. These corps lived efficiently off the enemy's countryside; they had the speed and mobility to surprise and outmaneuver the enemy; and they had the resiliency and power to make battle decisive. Particularly in the campaigns of 1805 and 1806, Napoleon used the corps system to transform warfare. No longer dependent on magazines, he increased the size of his forces and more than doubled their rate of advance and range of operations. Thus in his campaign against the Austrians in 1805, when he advanced from the Rhine to the Danube with 210,000 men, he marched more than eighteen miles per day and covered more than 650 miles during the brief autumn campaign. The following year he did much the same against the Prussians; he led 180,000 men one hundred miles from Bamberg to Jena at sixteen miles per day and pursued the remnants of the Prussian army another 200 miles in three weeks. With such exceptionally large forces moving with such unusual speed and deception, he was able to achieve decisive results in relatively brief campaigns. He defeated the Austrian army in two-and-one-half months in 1805 and the Prussian army in just over one month in 1806. After being stymied by the Russians at Eylau in February 1807, he then defeated their best army at Friedland in June. All things considered, Napoleon's Grand Army performed brilliantly at Ulm, Austerlitz, Jena-Auerstädt, and Friedland.

Napoleon's defeat at Aspern-Essling in 1809 and his hard-won victory at Wagram seven weeks later, however, signaled the end of his quick, decisive victories. Economic conditions in the theater of operations contributed to the change in French furtunes. In areas with a dense population, an agricultural surplus, and good roads, Napoleon's corps could draw supplies from the countryside, move rapidly on parallel roads, and remain close enough to be mutually supporting and capable of acting together decisively. In poorly developed or barren areas, such as in Poland or later in Spain, Portugal, and Russia, the corps system had limitations. In Poland and East Prussia, Napoleon dispersed his corps to feed them during the winter and spring of 1807 and had great difficulty concentrating them for decisive action. Nevertheless, he massed enough forces to defeat the Russians at Friedland when they did offer battle. In Spain and Portugal he had even greater difficulty subduing his enemy. Unable to live off the exhausted countryside in the Iberian peninsula, many of his forces had to employ cumbersome supply trains or risk starvation. Finally in Russia, Napoleon reverted to a magazine system to sustain his army of 600,000 men. Together with Russia's poor roads and vast expanse, magazines and supply trains slowed his advance and hampered his ability to engage the Russian army until it had retired nearly 500 miles. Thus as Napoleon's grand ambitions pushed his forces greater distances from France, the limitations of the corps system became most apparent.

Other problems came from the changing nature of Napoleon's army. As mounting casualties among veterans compelled ever-greater reliance on conscripts, French soldiers often lacked the training, experience, and commitment of the highly motivated soldiers who had fought in the first Italian campaign. Similarly, the expansion of the French Empire induced Napoleon to include greater numbers of non-French soldiers in his armies. In June 1807, Friedland became the first Napoleonic battle in which foreign troops formed a significant part of the Grand Army. Over the next few years, armies also became larger and larger until Wagram (July 1809) included almost half a million men and a thousand cannon. By 1812 most of the soldiers who invaded Russia were not French. As the quality of Napoleon's forces declined, he increased the proportion of artillery and thereby decreased the mobility of his units and reduced his capacity to make battles decisive.

Adding to Napoleon's difficulties, his enemies partially reformed their armies and copied elements of his system. Despite the absence of political revolutions in Austria, Prussia, and Russia, mass armies eventually became common, as did the use of corps. Most European military leaders

Wellington and Blücher meet after the Battle of Waterloo. Wellington won the Battle of Waterloo because of the steadfastness of his troops and the arrival of Blücher's Prussian soldiers. Wellington asked for one Prussian corps, and Blücher brought three.

abandoned eighteenth-century tactics and began relying on columns covered by skirmishes and supported by concentrated artillery. During the 1813 Saxon campaign and the 1814 campaign in France, Napoleon's mastery of maneuver and concentration could not overcome the immense armies opposing him. The sheer numbers and resources of the enemy overwhelmed his forces. During the campaigns of 1814 and 1815, Napoleon briefly regained the mobility to surprise and defeat his enemies in a series of limited actions, but he was defeated in the end by the prudent, persistent, and coordinated use of massive allied armies, all of which were sustained by Britain's financial support.

Napoleon's personal limitations also became apparent. Just as other European powers could not come to grips with his system of warfare, he could not adjust to the Spanish guerrillas or negate the advantages provided by British sea power. And in Russia, the swelling of his forces to half a million men created insurmountable logistical problems and constrained his mobility. In the end, food and supply shortages did as much to destroy his army as the Russians. Supremely confident of his own abilities, Napoleon failed to comprehend what happened in Spain or in Russia.

Napoleon's fatal weakness, however, resided in a desire for ever-greater power and influence for himself and France. Intoxicated by his success on the battlefield, he expanded his control over Europe and became increasingly unwilling to compromise. As his yearning for greater glory and power increased, his political objectives moved beyond his military capabilities. In 1802 he might have achieved peace after the British accepted the Treaty of Amiens. He could have retained buffer states beyond the Rhine and the Alps and kept France free and secure behind its natural frontier, but his expansionist policies quickly convinced the British he was using the peace to extend French influence. In 1806 he advanced beyond the buffer region, and with the Treaty of Tilsit the following year he moved into eastern Europe and tied France's destiny to the Continental System. Napoleon's power reached its peak in 1809, following the defeat of Austria, but erosive influences were already at work. Frustrations with the Continental System, uneasiness over the expansion of French influence, discontent among the satellite states, and the corrosive effects of the war in Spain and Portugal guaranteed future problems. Napoleon might have compromised in 1813 and might have retained his position in Paris and the natural frontiers of France, but he was never willing to make the necessary concessions.

Almost two centuries later, Napoleon's brilliance as a leader and campaign strategist remains clear. Always an improviser, he possessed a genius for war that enabled him to measure a situation accurately, assess his alternatives, and act quickly and decisively. Never one to shirk hard work, he used his phenomenal memory and mental ability to master the fundamentals of his profession, and he relied on his strong will and personal charisma to exercise a remarkable influence over his officers and soldiers. Among his many victories, Austerlitz and the torch-lit demonstration the preceding evening most clearly illustrate his extraordinary gifts. In the end, however, his brilliant leadership and capacity as a campaign strategist could not compensate for his failures in grand strategy and foreign policy.

SUGGESTED READINGS

Becke, Archibald F. *Napoleon and Waterloo* (London: Kegan Paul, 1939).

Brett-James, Antony, ed. *1812: Eyewitness Accounts of Napoleon's Defeat in Russia* (New York: Macmillan, 1966).

————. *Europe Against Napoleon: The Leipzig Campaign, 1813* (London: Macmillan, 1970).

————. *The Hundred Days: Napoleon's Last Campaign From Eyewitness Accounts* (New York: St. Martin's Press, 1964).

Chandler, David G. *Waterloo: The Hundred Days* (New York: Macmillan, 1980).

Clausewitz, Carl von. *The Campaign of 1812 in Russia* (Westport, Conn.: Greenwood Press, 1977).

Duffy, Christopher. *Borodino and the War of 1812* (New York: Scribner, 1973).

Howarth, David A. *Waterloo: Day of Battle* (New York: Atheneum, 1968).

Josselson, Michael and Diana. *The Commander: A Life of Barclay de Tolly* (Oxford: Oxford University Press, 1980).

Lachouque, Henry, and Anne K. S. Brown. *The Anatomy of Glory, Napoleon and His Guard* (Providence, R.I.: Brown University Press, 1961).

MacKenzie, Norman. *The Escape from Elba: The Fall and Flight of Napoleon, 1814–1815* (New York: Oxford University Press, 1982).

Olivier, Daria. *The Burning of Moscow, 1812,* trans. Michael Heron (New York: Crowell, 1966).

Palmer, Alan W. *Napoleon in Russia* (New York: Simon & Schuster, 1967).

Parkinson, Roger. *Fox of the North: The Life of Kutuzov, General of War and Peace* (New York: D. McKay Co., 1976).

————. *The Hussar General: The Life of Blücher, Man of Waterloo* (London: Peter Davies, 1975).

Petre, F. Loraine. *Napoleon at Bay, 1814* (London: J. Lane, 1914).

————. *Napoleon's Last Campaign in Germany, 1813* (London: J. Lane, 1912).

de Segur, Philippe-Paul. *Napoleon's Russian Campaign,* trans. J. D. Townsend (Boston: Houghton Mifflin, 1958).

Weller, Jac. *Wellington at Waterloo* (New York: Crowell, 1967).

Professionalism, Industrialization, and Mass Warfare in the Nineteenth Century

10

AMERICAN MILITARY POLICY, 1783–1860: THE BEGINNINGS OF PROFESSIONALISM

Arming the New Nation, 1783–1846

The Mexican War

Technological Adaptation and Strategic Thought

Considering that it was a nation founded in blood, the United States took a notably relaxed attitude toward its military defense during the years between 1783 and 1860. Americans created only a very modest standing army and navy, resented efforts to professionalize the officer corps, and for a long time regarded the permanent armed forces as inimical to sound republican principles. Scornful and suspicious of regular armed forces, they preferred to regard the militia as the chief reliance for defense. Yet in practice, Americans neglected the militia system even more than they did the despised standing army, so that by the mid-nineteenth century the system was practically moribund.

Indeed, in nearly every respect, during its first seventy-five years the United States possessed an uneven military policy and a ramshackle military establishment. Yet during the same period it managed to drive the Native Americans beyond the Mississippi River, hold its own in a second full-scale war with the British, and conquer vast new territories in an amoral but highly successful conflict with Mexico. Judged by results, the new republic turned in a creditable military performance.

Although partly due to circumstance or good fortune, some of America's martial success stemmed from the early emergence of a professional officer corps. Sobered by a brush with disaster during the War of 1812, the army overhauled its bureaucracy, inaugurated an orderly system of officer recruitment, and established professional standards of conduct, particularly through the reform of the U.S. Military Academy. Meanwhile

Congress, despite continuing lip service to the militia, adopted a cadre system that tacitly made the regular army the centerpiece of the nation's land-defense system. Within the new environment, officers increasingly viewed their work as a lifelong calling. Careers grew longer, a distinctive corporate identity emerged, and officers rapidly divorced themselves from partisan politics. By the time of the Civil War, the army officer corps had established an identity, ethos, and outlook that greatly assisted the full flowering of military professionalism in the late nineteenth and early twentieth centuries.

Arming the New Nation, 1783–1846

In its earliest stages, the permanent American military establishment was the product of two factors. First, the political faction known as the Federalists believed the new central government had to develop a significant *national* army and navy. Second, a prolonged period of international upheaval underscored the need for adequate armed forces. Even so, the creation of a permanent military establishment did not occur without significant opposition. Many Americans were unhappy with the idea of creating a standing army. But a significant minority, especially those who had served in the Continental Army, agreed with George Washington, who understood the fear of a standing army but also believed that fear should not be blindly heeded. Unlike European mercenaries who had no stake in the political order, Washington argued, an American army was composed of citizens with common interests—"one people embarked on one cause; acting on the same principle and the same end." Since those interests were the same as that of the larger community, the army logically posed no threat to liberty. Eventually Washington's view triumphed, but it took thirty years, a number of small military incidents, and a major war before that occurred.

The Creation of Permanent Military Forces

After the war with Great Britain ended in 1783, the Confederation turned to the matter of a permanent peacetime military establishment that would be able to police the land and maritime frontier, defend against a full-scale invasion, and help maintain internal order. In 1783 a Congressional committee chaired by Alexander Hamilton asked Washington for his opinion concerning the requirements of such an establishment. Washington responded with "Sentiments on a Peace Establishment," a four-point program that became the basis of the nationalist agenda. First, a small regular army (2,631 officers and men) was required to "overawe" Indians and guard against incursions from Canada and Spanish Florida. Second, a "respectable and well-established Militia" was also needed, preferably under federal as well as state control, with the central government imposing uniformity in training, arms, and organization. It should have two tiers: a volunteer militia to be kept in an advanced state of readiness, and a common militia composed of the remaining male population of military age. Third, the national government must establish arsenals and factories to support the armed forces. And fourth, it must create military academies to foster military science.

The Hamilton Committee greeted Washington's proposals with enthusiasm and modeled its own report along similar lines. But Congress, then predominantly antinationalist in tone, rejected the report. Rather than create a standing army, it elected to disband the Continental Army except for eighty men and a few officers to guard military stores. Instead it created the First American Regiment, composed of 700 militiamen (drawn from four states) to serve one year. This ad hoc arrangement—like the Confederation itself—proved inadequate, and when the Americans scrapped the Articles of Confederation in favor of a new Constitution, they attempted to create a more effective military establishment that would not jeopardize American liberties.

The solution was to divide control of the military establishment. The president would serve as commander-in-chief, but Congress would appropriate money for the armed forces, devise regulations for their government, and hold the authority to declare war. Control of the military establishment was further divided between the national government, which could create a national army and navy, and the states, which maintained control over the militia. A modest system of arsenals and munitions factories also sprang up, and in 1802 Congress authorized creation of a military academy at West Point, New York. (Naval officers continued to be trained aboard warships; Congress would not create the naval academy at Annapolis, Maryland, until 1845.)

Thus by the early years of the nineteenth century the United States possessed a land force roughly corresponding to the model outlined in "Sentiments on a Peace Establishment." The chief departure was the very limited federal control over the militia. Attempts to increase control—for example, to create the sort of volunteer or "federal select" militia favored by Washington—routinely failed. As a result, although in times of emergency the national government could mobilize the militia for a period of ninety days, it had little influence over the peacetime organization, regulation, training and equipment of the militia. Since most state governments were notoriously lax in such matters, the militia—supposedly the nation's chief reliance in wartime—was an uncertain patchwork of units without uniform organization, training, or equipment.

Old World Frictions

These developments occurred against a background of European revolution and war. Less than a year after the American Constitution went into operation, violent political upheaval erupted in France. With their own revolution just recently behind them, Americans watched the unfolding drama in France with more than passing interest. Indeed, as the months rolled on, the

French Revolution exerted an almost tidal pull on American political life. Then, in 1792, the new French republic declared war on Austria, inaugurating twenty-three years of near-continuous war that embroiled not only most of Europe but eventually the United States as well. Moreover, the unfolding French Revolution, as Americans alternately cheered its triumphs and deplored its excesses, deeply influenced the ongoing debate between two emerging factions in American politics: the Federalists, led by Alexander Hamilton, and their Republican opponents, led by Thomas Jefferson.

The Federalists were nationalist in their orientation, comfortable with an active central government, and wary of placing too much power in the hands of the common man. Although at first elated by the events in France, they soon grew to distrust the direction in which the French Revolution was moving. It seemed to have degenerated into radicalism and mob rule. In the burgeoning wars of the French Revolution, therefore, the Federalists usually supported the British, who were fighting against the French. The Republicans, however—more democratic and also suspicious of what seemed the "monarchist" tendencies of the Federalists—were not disillusioned by the excesses of the French Revolution and continued to prefer the French. Officially, the United States was neutral.

The question of whether to back one side or the other had more than academic significance. The wars of the French Revolution were characterized not only by major land battles but also by a long campaign of economic warfare at sea. The British navy blockaded French ports; the French responded by sending out large numbers of privateers and commerce raiders to prowl the world's oceans. Since American merchants traded with both Britain and France, each side freely attacked American vessels bound for enemy ports.

Trouble began first with Great Britain, which routinely seized neutral ships carrying contraband goods to France. The Royal Navy captured 250 American merchant vessels before the Washington administration negotiated a treaty, ratified in 1795, in which the United States essentially accepted the British position on contraband in exchange for a promise that British troops would abandon a number of posts still illegally occupied on American soil. The French, however, interpreted the treaty as an American attempt to aid the British and eventually began seizing American merchant ships on the high seas. In 1798 a two-year undeclared naval war broke out between the United States and France.

These difficulties with Britain and France led to the early growth of the United States Navy. Begun in 1794 with the authorization of six frigates, the new navy at the height of the "Quasi-War" with France boasted fifty-four warships supported by more than a thousand armed merchant vessels. At about the same time Congress created a separate Department of the Navy and authorized construction of the first American ships of the line. American warships not only performed well against the French but also conducted a number of minor but dramatic punitive expeditions against several pirate states in North Africa.

By 1800, however, the Quasi-War had ended. Its main significance was to reinforce the need for adequate American armed forces, so that when the Republican party took power in 1801 with the accession of Thomas Jefferson as president, the Jeffersonians did not dismantle the military establishment created by the Federalists. To be sure, for a time they did reduce the size of the army and navy, mostly in response to a temporary reduction in European tensions. But they basically accepted and, in time, even enhanced the military institutions whose custodianship they inherited. And as a fresh cycle of wars began in 1805, the Jefferson administration found itself sliding into a new and grave crisis with Great Britain.

The War of 1812

Once again the British and French were locked in mortal combat (this time with Napoleon leading France), and once again the navies of both powers seized American and other neutral ships in a bid to throttle each other's commerce. Americans were furious with both nations, but of the two, Britain had the larger navy and thus the greater effect on American shipping. Jefferson and his successor, James Madison, made several efforts to force the British and French to respect American maritime rights, most notably an 1807 Embargo Act that essentially prohibited American exports. Based on the premise that the European powers needed the American trade and could not long do without it, the embargo was intended as an instrument of

Presidents Thomas Jefferson and James Madison tried to use economic coercion to force the British and French to respect U.S. maritime rights, but many Americans resented their policies, as suggested in this contemporary political cartoon. "Ograbme" is "Embargo" spelled backward.

economic coercion. In the short run, however, it hurt American merchants far more than Europeans and generated violent political opposition.

Forced to retreat from outright embargo, the Madison administration struggled to convince Congress to maintain some sort of economic coercion. But increasingly some members of the Republican party demanded that the administration should go farther and declare war on Great Britain. The seizure of American vessels seemed provocation enough, but on top of that the Royal Navy had for years forcibly impressed sailors—some of them U.S. citizens—from American-owned vessels. Further, many Americans living in the South and along the western frontier sought war for other reasons. Many westerners believed the British had been inciting Native American uprisings; they also thought that if war came, it might be possible to grab Canada. Similarly, southerners tended to suspect the British of plotting to seize New Orleans; they also noted that if war broke out they might be able to seize Florida from Spain, whose royal family was then allied with the British.

Madison himself was far from eager for war. But he grew convinced that economic coercion alone would never succeed, because the policy was based on a faulty premise. In earlier years, Britain might have depended on the United States for naval stores crucial to its fleet and seaborne empire. But the growing economic development of Canada gave Britain a viable alternative source and thereby gravely reduced the American bargaining posture. Only a credible threat against Canada could compel the British to respect American maritime rights.

Madison therefore reluctantly asked Congress for a declaration of war. He got one on June 18, 1812, but the margin of the vote was the narrowest for a declaration of war in U.S. history. To a man, the Federalist party rejected the necessity for military action. Deep political divisions persisted throughout the conflict itself, for few on either side tried to create bipartisan support for a struggle against a common foe.

The United States was woefully unprepared in 1812 to take on a major power like Great Britain. Despite recent legislation that authorized an increase to 35,000 men, when war broke out the regular army numbered just 7,000, scattered in various garrisons. A sustained war effort would thus have to be built upon volunteer militia companies backed by the common militia. The naval establishment was no better: just sixteen ships, seven of them frigates, plus swarms of small gunboats. Administrative support had improved little since 1775. Not only was the War Department inadequate to manage a substantial military effort, the federal government had limited ability to finance the war.

Given Canada's importance in Madison's calculations, an invasion of the province was the obvious American strategy. The province was only lightly defended and in theory the Americans should have been able to advance northward in overwhelming strength. Reality proved different. A prompt invasion necessarily depended upon the use of militia forces, yet these were under state control. The best invasion route was north along the Lake Champlain corridor toward Montreal, but the springboard for such an advance—New England—had the least enthusiasm for war of any region in the country.

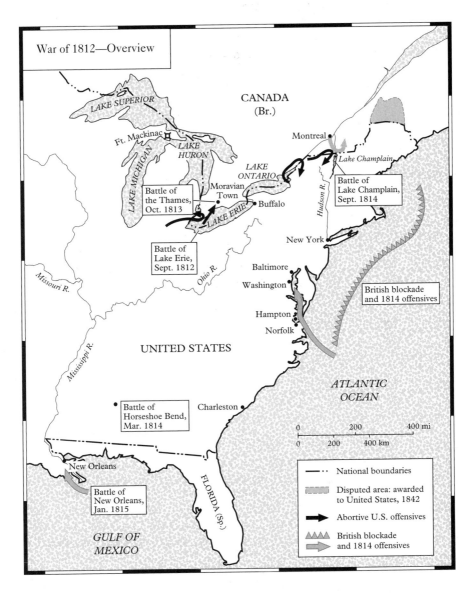

War of 1812—Overview

CANADA (Br.)

LAKE SUPERIOR

Ft. Mackinac

LAKE HURON

LAKE MICHIGAN

Montreal

Lake Champlain

Battle of Lake Champlain, Sept. 1814

LAKE ONTARIO

Battle of the Thames, Oct. 1813

Moravian Town

Buffalo

LAKE ERIE

Hudson R.

Battle of Lake Erie, Sept. 1812

New York

Missouri R.

Ohio R.

Baltimore

Washington

British blockade and 1814 offensives

Hampton

Norfolk

UNITED STATES

Mississippi R.

ATLANTIC OCEAN

Battle of Horseshoe Bend, Mar. 1814

Charleston

0   200   400 mi
0   200   400 km

New Orleans

FLORIDA (Sp.)

Battle of New Orleans, Jan. 1815

——·· National boundaries

Disputed area: awarded to United States, 1842

➤ Abortive U.S. offensives

◢◣◢◣ British blockade

⇨ British blockade and 1814 offensives

GULF OF MEXICO

Asked by Madison to mobilize their militias, the Federalist New England governors flatly refused, objecting that such forces were intended solely for local defense. A volatile political situation in New York further complicated efforts to mount an offensive into Canada. Instead of a rapid, victorious advance, therefore, practically nothing happened in the key Montreal sector.

By contrast, Americans living in the western frontier region were far more eager for war. There the problem was not so much to raise the necessary volunteers and militia as it was to equip, feed, and manage them. But the modest American government could do none of these things effectively. The initial American thrusts were poorly coordinated, understrength—and disastrous. Numerically inferior but better organized British troops repelled them, seized Detroit, and threatened Michigan Territory and Ohio.

In October 1813, Americans under Major General William Henry Harrison defeated a combined force of British and Indians in the Battle of the Thames, fought on the Lake Erie frontier. Coupled with Andrew Jackson's 1814 win at Horseshoe Bend, Harrison's victory broke the back of Native American resistance east of the Mississippi River.

Fortunately for the United States, Britain was too preoccupied with European matters to mount a major effort in North America. Thus in 1813 the United States had a chance to accomplish what it had failed to do in 1812. But again, poor leadership, inadequate administrative support, and disjointed efforts resulted in scant success. This was particularly true on the Niagara front, where a mixed bag of tactical successes and setbacks resulted in stalemate. Somewhat better results were achieved in the western Lake Erie region. Detroit was recaptured, and Commodore Oliver Hazard Perry destroyed a British squadron near Put-In Bay, Ohio. Major General William Henry Harrison entered Canada, won the Battle of the Thames against a combined British and Native American force, and slew Tecumseh, the great Shawnee chieftain. Yet while these successes secured the western U.S. frontier, they contributed little toward ending the war.

At sea the Royal Navy far outnumbered the diminutive U.S. Navy— even though the British had to concentrate on Napoleon until 1814. Consequently the British were able to blockade the American coast at will. Interestingly, for a long time they chose *not* to blockade New England, since they knew New Englanders generally opposed the war. Indeed the U.S. government even allowed a certain amount of trade with the enemy. American vessels sailed to Spain, for example, and supplied grain to Wellington's army. Even so, by 1814 the blockade had reduced merchant trade to 11 percent of prewar levels.

The blockade was loose enough, however, that U.S. warships had little difficulty getting to sea, and although they could scarcely compete for control of the ocean, American vessels performed very well at commerce-raiding and single-ship duels; sloops and 500 privateers seized over 1,300 British merchantmen. Nevertheless, the British still managed to supply forces in Canada and conduct raids against American coasts. These raids, small at first, expanded dramatically in 1814.

A common nineteenth-century saw declared that "God takes care of fools, drunkards, and the United States." In 1814, America needed providential help. After the defeat of Napoleon in the Saxon campaign of 1813, the British for the first time were able to send large forces across the Atlantic. About 40,000 arrived by year's end. These occupied much of Maine and expanded their raids along the coast. Fortunately for the United States, competent leaders had begun to emerge by this time, especially Jacob Brown, Edmund Gaines, Winfield Scott, and Andrew Jackson.

The United States began the year with two new offensives against Canada—one on the Niagara front and one along the Lake Champlain corridor. Neither came to much, but the Americans handled the Niagara operations much better tactically than the one along Lake Champlain. The British launched three offensives of their own: first, south from Canada via Lake Champlain, a thrust blunted in a naval battle on the lake in September; second, along the Chesapeake Bay, which resulted in the capture and burning of Washington but which failed to seize the privateering base of Baltimore, Maryland; and finally, up the Mississippi River against New Orleans. Forces under Andrew Jackson, in the largest battle of the war, decisively halted this last attack on January 15, 1815. But by then the war was officially over. Six weeks earlier the United States and Great Britain had signed the Treaty of Ghent.

Why did the British, who clearly held the advantage, choose to end the war? For one thing, they could not identify a plausible way to win it. After the Lake Champlain offensive was rebuffed, the Duke of Wellington commented that the United States had no vulnerable center of gravity. "I do not know where you could carry on . . . an operation which would be so injurious to the Americans as to force them to sue for peace." Moreover, with the defeat of Napoleon the reasons for war had largely disappeared. Thus, both sides willingly accepted a peace nominally based on the status quo antebellum.

In some respects the United States achieved significant benefits from the conflict. The war had furnished an opportunity to thrash yet again Native Americans, who were the main losers in the contest. Tecumseh's death at the Battle of the Thames forever ended the most significant threat to white America's settlement of the Old Northwest, while in Alabama, at the 1814 Battle of Horseshoe Bend, Andrew Jackson defeated the Creeks and forced them to cede 23 million acres of land.

But for the most part, the poor American showing in the War of 1812 underscored the essential weakness of its military system. Unreflective nationalists might crow over victories like the battles of Lake Erie and New Orleans, but more reflective observers realized that the country had narrowly

The Battle of New Orleans. This idealized postwar engraving captures the War of 1812 as Americans liked to remember it, with homespun heroes fending off the best Great Britain could send against them. But such triumphs were few, and after the war American policy makers made several needed military reforms.

escaped disaster. The militia had proven unequal to its key role in American defense. The regular army had done better but still suffered from leadership problems, particularly in the war's early stages. The serious administrative deficiencies demonstrated that the War Department required substantial reform, and in the years that followed, American policy makers took significant steps to improve the situation.

Early Attempts to Professionalize

After 1815 the United States entered what one historian has called an "era of free security" in which the country faced little external threat to its existence. He meant that the United States did not need seriously to concern itself with threats from abroad and thus did not have to maintain a sizable army and navy. With minimal risk of foreign invasion, the American armed forces functioned mostly as a "frontier constabulary," a kind of national police force to assist western settlement, intervene in disputes between whites and Native Americans, enforce federal authority, and protect maritime commerce.

Strategically, however, the chief mission of the American army and navy was to defend against foreign invasions. Americans, while continuing to reject creation of a large navy that could challenge an enemy fleet for command of the sea, did permit a modest increase in the number of warships. The navy, then, would function as the first line of defense. The second line was an extensive network of coastal defenses that would hamper an invasion.

Work on such a fortification system began before the War of 1812 but really took off afterward. It consisted of a series of casemate forts guarding not only major harbors but also most navigable inlets. Fifty sites were identified at first; the number eventually ran much higher. The coastal forts were not intended as an absolute defense against attack but rather to ward off sudden raids and force an attacker to come ashore in areas distant from important military objectives. That, in turn, would allow sufficient time to mobilize the militia, which would slow the progress of any invader while a large citizen-based force could be built around the regular army.

Policy makers disagreed about how much reliance to place on the militia, however. Some continued to believe it could function effectively in wartime; others, more skeptical, thought the regular army would have to play the principal role even in a conflict's early stages. The key proponent of the second view was John C. Calhoun, a former "War Hawk" congressman from South Carolina, who became secretary of war in October 1817. Obliged by Congress to reduce the size of the army after the war, he sought to do so without destroying its ability to respond quickly in the event of a crisis. To this end he proposed a cadre system (often called an "expansible army" system) whereby a relatively small peacetime army could be rapidly built up in time of war. He proposed an army that would contain just 6,316 men but would have an officer corps and organization sufficient for an army of 11,558 men. Peacetime units would be kept at about 50 percent strength. In wartime the army could be nearly doubled just by filling out units to wartime strength using federal volunteers; and by adding 288 officers, the army could absorb enough additional privates and noncommissioned officers to raise the total to 19,035 officers and men.

The effect of this cadre proposal was subtle but profound. On the one hand, Congress declined to adopt the plan in its original form—it was too advanced for the time. Republicans had become more comfortable with the army's political reliability, but not enough to acknowledge the regular army unambiguously as the nation's main line of defense. Yet the plan eventually adopted was, in fact, a modified version of the cadre system that tacitly acknowledged Calhoun's central point: that in the event of war, the regular army was the most reliable means of national defense. From that point onward, the regular army officer corps suffered none of the wide-ranging shifts in size that characterized its early years. The frequent deep reductions in force had led many young officers to regard military service as a temporary vocation only. Within the more stable environment created by the Calhoun reforms, young officers could now consider military service a viable, lifelong career. As a result they remained officers longer, took their duties more seriously, and became more competent than their pre–War of 1812 counterparts.

Yet another important postwar development was a major revival at the U.S. Military Academy that marked the real beginning of its traditions. The catalyst was Captain Sylvanus Thayer, appointed West Point superintendent in 1817. Thayer established a four-year curriculum, inaugurated a system that ranked cadets according to merit, and introduced the emphasis on engineering and mathematics that would characterize West Point for several decades. Other indications of a budding professionalism included a more efficient military bureau system and two military schools of practice—one for artillery at Fort Monroe, one for infantry at Leavenworth, Kansas—which flourished briefly until fiscal constraints led to their closure in the late 1830s. Finally, a number of officers began to publish in journals devoted to the study of their craft.

Even so, it would be wrong to mistake these developments for the emergence of a fully mature, professionalized army. True professionalism still lay over a half-century in the future. The Indian pacification duties of this period formed a powerful distraction to the U.S. Army's preparations to wage European-style warfare. A second distraction was the nation's insistence that both the army and navy assist the protean economic expansion that dominated the years after the War of 1812. On land, army engineers deepened harbors and surveyed the routes for turnpikes and—a bit later—railroads as well. At sea, naval officers undertook voyages of exploration, mapped the coastline, and created hydrological charts as aids to navigation. Such duties not only diverted officers from the study of warfare but also shaped their ideas concerning what the military profession was all about. For some, overawing the Indians and surveying the wilderness seemed to have become their primary purpose in life.

Further hampering the professionalizing impetus were two powerful contrary forces: continued suspicions of the regular military establishment and a continuing belief that any man of good character was capable of exercising military leadership. Logically, both developments should have meant a continued commitment to a strong militia. But by the 1830s an odd situation had developed. On the one hand, politicians and citizens still praised the

This whimsical, faintly mocking view of a pre–Civil War militia muster reflects the decline of a venerable American military institution. Though the minuteman tradition remained strong in rhetoric, the actual militia began a steep decline after the War of 1812 and by the time of the Civil War was practically moribund.

militia as a bulwark of liberty. On the other, everyone had long since realized that the militia was, in practice, more or less a joke. Musters became less frequent, militiamen received little or no serious training, and their weapons and equipment were antiquated and poorly maintained.

The federal government could not, and the states would not, reform the militia. Indeed, some states abolished compulsory militia service altogether. Fortunately, volunteer companies took up some of the slack and maintained the tradition of the citizen-soldier. These were units that originally existed independently of the statewide militia systems, although many were later incorporated into them. Often they were the only functional part of the militia. Initially most were run as elite social societies. One had to have a modicum of wealth to join since volunteers bought their own uniforms and drill instructors cost money. Members carefully screened new recruits for good moral fiber and gentlemanly qualities. Over time, clerks, artisans, and laborers formed their own volunteer companies. So did immigrant groups, especially the Irish and Germans. After 1840 some states made the volunteer companies their entire "active militia" force.

The military value of these volunteer units was problematic. Although they provided their own uniforms, they often borrowed their weapons from state armories and rented their horses. They were also usually too small to be of great military significance—many contained about forty to fifty men. And they tended to emphasize martial dash and enthusiasm rather than serious tactical training. Still they provided a substantial reservoir of military experience. A number of future Civil War generals, including some very good ones, served in volunteer units.

Thus, by the mid-1840s, the United States had acquired a basic land-force policy characterized by de facto reliance on a small, peacetime regular army, coupled with the realization that the standing forces would have to be supplemented by a substantial contingent of citizen-soldiers. The available pool of citizen-soldiers varied widely in terms of organization, training, and equipment, but the general standard was low. Americans seldom worried about this, however. The absence of a serious foreign threat and a continued belief in the inherent military prowess of patriotic American males further sustained their confidence.

The Mexican War

Expansion was the hallmark of U.S. foreign policy during this period. Many Americans agreed with the newspaperman John L. O'Sullivan when he declaimed that their nation had a "manifest destiny" to possess all of North America. Examples of this conviction were legion. Already the United States had made two unsuccessful grabs for Canada; had acquired the Louisiana territory from France and Florida from Spain; and had briefly courted armed conflict with Great Britain before agreeing to divide the Oregon Country at the 49th Parallel. Then in 1845 Congress annexed Texas,

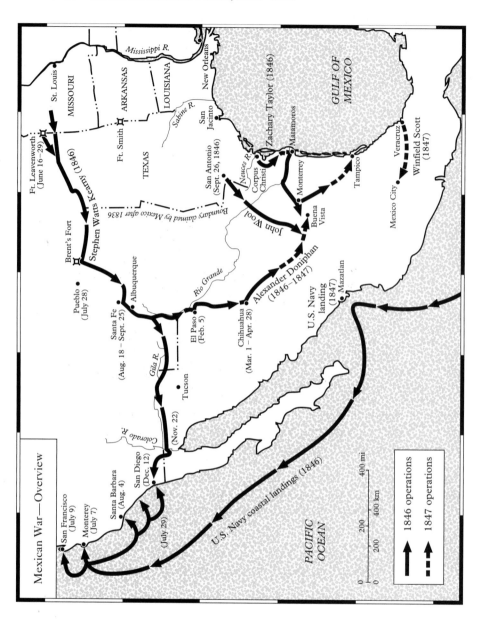

which Mexico still considered a wayward province in revolt, and thereby took a long step toward a major war. The first clashes occurred between U.S. and Mexican forces in 1846; sixteen months later the United States won a resounding triumph and added vast new territories to its already sprawling domain.

Origins and Objectives

Until 1836, Texas had been a province of Mexico. The Mexican government had welcomed American settlement in Texas, only to see a torrent of

Americans flood the province, swamp the ethnic Mexican population, and eventually rise up in an open bid for complete independence. This Texas Revolution culminated in triumph when, after initial setbacks at the Alamo and Goliad, the Texans defeated a Mexican army at the Battle of San Jacinto on April 21, 1836. After ten years as a separate republic, Texas joined the Union in July 1845. Relations between the United States and Mexico rapidly deteriorated, for Mexico had never relinquished its claim to the region.

American ambitions did not end with Texas. A number of Americans were also interested in Upper California and New Mexico, two northern provinces only tenuously under Mexican control. American merchants and politicians especially coveted the magnificent San Francisco harbor, widely regarded as the key to Far Eastern trade. President James K. Polk shared this expansionist vision, and while it is probably not true that he deliberately engineered a military confrontation with Mexico, indisputably he wanted California and New Mexico and was not particular about how he got them. His aggressive policies openly courted war.

Tensions between the United States and Mexico increased when Polk sent an American army into Texas led by Major General Zachary Taylor. After training seven months at Corpus Christi, Taylor's army crossed the Nueces River, the border between Texas and Mexico as the Mexicans understood it, and advanced to the Rio Grande, the border insisted upon by the Texans. For two weeks, Mexican and American forces glared at one another across the disputed boundary. The situation grew more intense, and in April 1846 the Mexicans attacked an American scouting party. "Hostilities," Taylor tersely informed Washington, "may now be considered as commenced."

Like the struggle of 1812–1814, the war was a highly partisan affair for Americans. This time the prowar camp was the Democratic party. Most members of the rival Whig party opposed it on principle, arguing (correctly)

General Zachary Taylor's Mexican War exploits helped make him president, but "Old Rough and Ready," as his soldiers called him, was in many respects a throwback to the amateurism of the War of 1812.

that the United States had no valid claims south of the Nueces. Antislavery Democrats and Whigs also charged that the war's purpose was to spread slavery and thus increase the political power of the southern states. Yet Whig opposition was less united and intransigent than the Federalists had been during the War of 1812. Although Mexico had clearly been provoked, most Whigs believed they could not refuse to support American troops now that they were engaged in combat.

Even so, real enthusiasm for the war tended to be confined politically to the Democratic party and geographically to the South. Because of the conflict's sectional and party overtones, manpower policy was essentially a political question with military implications. Given the soft support for the war, especially in the northeast, the Polk administration decided, by and large, not to use militia. Instead the regular army would double its existing units to 15,000 by filling them up to full strength. Congress also authorized the raising of 50,000 volunteers, most of whom were summoned by Polk from southern states, where support for the war was strongest.

American prewar planning was much better than it had been before the War of 1812. The United States had positioned troops to seize Mexican territory quickly. In addition to Taylor's army along the Texas border, American agents and an "exploring party" under John C. Frémont were in California; there were also naval units off the California shore. Another force under Colonel Stephen Kearny marched against Santa Fe two days after war was declared in May 1846.

American strategists essentially faced two problems. The first was to project U.S. strength into the lands they wanted; this occurred promptly after the declaration of war. The second was to get Mexico to accept an imposed settlement; this proved much trickier. Initially the Polk administration thought it could compel Mexico to the negotiating table by securing California and New Mexico and then holding a few of Mexico's northern provinces as bargaining chips. When that did not work, the Americans finally mounted a remarkable expedition to seize Mexico City itself.

Taylor in Northern Mexico

The Polk administration had entrusted about 4,000 men—most of the regular army—to General Taylor. Dubbed "Old Rough and Ready" by his men, Taylor dressed casually and spoke bluntly. He had as little use for rarefied notions of strategy and tactics as he did for the regulation uniform. In many respects he was a throwback to the amateurish generalship of the War of 1812, but he inspired his troops with confidence. Against a truly capable adversary Taylor might have gotten into serious trouble. As things turned out, however, he compiled a gleaming war record that eventually carried him into the White House.

Although the United States had a larger population than Mexico (17 million as opposed to 7 million) and was far more developed economically, the Mexican government at first believed it held the upper hand. After all, its regular army of 32,000 handily outnumbered the American army of just

In the Battle of Palo Alto, one of the first engagements of the Mexican War, U.S. field artillery proved especially potent at breaking up enemy charges and ensuring an American victory.

8,000. Its foot soldiers were trained in the best Napoleonic tradition and its light cavalry was among the best in the world. Mexican generalship, however, tended to be mediocre and the Mexican supply system was never very good. Fractious political infighting plagued the Mexicans throughout the struggle. And although the American army was usually outnumbered in the field, it was well-equipped and could draw upon a much bigger manpower base. It also possessed superb field artillery, an advantage it drew upon often.

The first major engagements occurred in May 1846, when 4,000 men under General Mariano Arista crossed the Rio Grande near its mouth, intent on thrashing the American upstarts at once. At the Battle of Palo Alto on May 8 he sent his infantry charging into Taylor's lines while his cavalry tried to turn the Americans' flanks. Taylor's artillery, however, crushed these attacks; the American infantry, for the most part, was never seriously engaged. The following day Taylor and Arista clashed again at Resaca de la Palma. Once more the Mexican army was beaten with heavy losses. Mexican casualties in the two battles exceeded 1,600 men; the Americans, by contrast, lost fewer than 200.

Nine days later Taylor crossed the Rio Grande and took possession of Matamoros, where he received substantial reinforcements and awaited instructions from the Polk administration. Eventually it was decided that he should capture Monterrey, the provincial capital of Nuevo León. After restaging his army to Camargo, Taylor began his offensive in August. One month later, having covered the intervening 125 miles, he fought a grueling three-day battle for Monterrey that bled his army heavily. When his opponent offered to yield the town in exchange for an eight-week armistice, Taylor agreed, much to Polk's baffled fury when he learned of the arrangement. The president promptly ordered Taylor to abrogate the truce and resume hostilities. Taylor complied and marched onward to Saltillo, the capital of Coahuila. Meanwhile another American column advanced through the province of Chihuahua. The end of 1846 found the United States firmly in control of much of northern Mexico as well as the coveted regions of California and New Mexico.

The Polk administration had calculated that the Mexican government should sue for peace at this point. It did nothing of the kind. Instead it redoubled its efforts under the charismatic leadership of General Santa Anna, the same man who had conceded Texas independence a decade earlier. Santa Anna was slippery and shrewd. When the war broke out, he had been living in exile in Cuba, a victim of Mexico's near-constant political turmoil. He sent word to Polk that if allowed to return to his homeland he would be willing to negotiate a swift end to the war. Polk therefore instructed the navy to give him safe conduct through its blockade of the Mexican coast. Once ashore, however, Santa Anna trumpeted that he had arrived to save the nation from American imperialism. He soon regained command of Mexico's army and by December 1846 had become president as well.

Early in 1847 it became apparent to Santa Anna that the Americans were planning a new offensive, this one apparently aimed at the coastal port of Veracruz. He also learned that many of Taylor's troops in northern Mexico had been diverted for this new operation. Accordingly, Santa Anna moved north at the head of 20,000 men, hoping to destroy Taylor's force and then swing eastward to defend Veracruz. After a remarkable 200-mile march across desert terrain, Santa Anna confronted the Americans at Buena Vista, just south of Saltillo. Although he had lost a full quarter of his strength in the rapid approach march, he still had 15,000 men to hurl against Taylor's 5,000.

Taylor had assumed the Mexicans could not march an army across such barren country to attack him. But he gamely withdrew a few miles into a naturally strong position near a hacienda called Buena Vista and there awaited the enemy attack. This position—a latticework of hills and ravines—partially nullified the Mexicans' numerical advantage. Even so, Santa Anna hurled his troops forward with great determination. For two days (February 22–23), the battle raged; and on several occasions the American line nearly broke. But Taylor shuttled his troops from one threatened point to another and each time the Americans managed to hold. A particularly crucial ingredient in the American defense was their magnificent field artillery. Without it, one U.S. general remarked, "we could not have maintained our position a single hour." Finally Santa Anna withdrew, having lost 2,000 men killed and wounded. American losses were fewer—about 750—but greater in proportion to the number of troops engaged.

Although Buena Vista sealed "Old Rough and Ready's" reputation and helped vault him into the White House, it was, in many respects, a needless battle. The advanced position held by the Americans was of little strategic value; a better defense could have been made at Monterrey. By electing

General Winfield Scott epitomized the incipient professionalism of the American officer corps in the mid-nineteenth century. His campaign against Mexico City in 1847 was a masterpiece.

to fight at Buena Vista, Taylor risked a disastrous reversal that might have prolonged the war indefinitely.

Scott's 1847 Campaign

While Taylor fought at Buena Vista, a new campaign was beginning along the Mexican coast. Commanded by the U.S. Army's general-in-chief, Winfield Scott, this campaign was aimed at capturing the port of Veracruz on the Gulf of Mexico and then marching inland against Mexico City. With the enemy's capital in American hands, it was believed, Mexican political life would be paralyzed and the Mexicans forced to the conference table.

Thus far, American operations in the war had been characterized by much the same amateurishness as in the War of 1812, notwithstanding their much greater success. Scott's campaign, however, was a masterpiece from beginning to end and displayed considerable thought in planning as well as audacity in execution. A new level of professionalism was on display at Veracruz, where Scott's troops made a well-synchronized landing in surf boats designed expressly for the purpose. Moreover, the fleet of transports had been carefully "combat-loaded," to use a twentieth-century term, so that the items needed first were stored so that they would be the first to be unloaded. The Mexicans chose not to oppose this landing, but even had they done so the Americans would probably still have prevailed, thanks to Scott's meticulous preparations.

Veracruz fell after a brief siege. In April, Scott's army began its advance inland. Ahead of them lay Santa Anna who, with his usual energy, had hustled back from northern Mexico and assembled another army of about 25,000 to confront this new American offensive. Forty miles inland

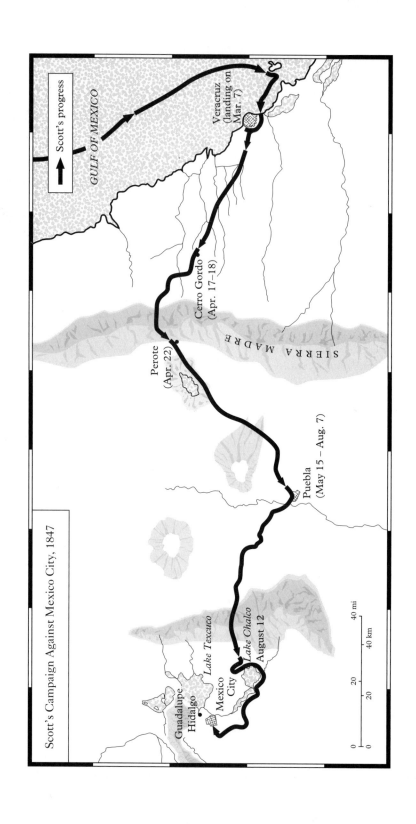

Scott's Campaign Against Mexico City, 1847

GULF OF MEXICO

→ Scott's progress

Veracruz
(landing on
Mar. 7)

Cerro Gordo
(Apr. 17–18)

Perote
(Apr. 22)

SIERRA MADRE

Puebla
(May 15 – Aug. 7)

Lake Texcuco

Lake Chalco
August 12

Guadalupe
Hidalgo

Mexico
City

0   20   40 mi

0   20   40 km

the highway from the coast to Mexico City ascended rapidly into the mountains of the Sierra Madre. At a place called Cerro Gordo the Mexican commander elected to make his stand. The position seemed impassable; Scott, however, sent his engineers to locate a path around it and, when one was found, sent an infantry division on a circuitous march around the Mexican left flank and rear, turning the main line of defense. After a sharp little fight, Santa Anna's army fell back in disorder. Scott continued another twelve miles to Jalapa.

At Jalapa the essentially amateur nature of the American military establishment reasserted itself. Seven regiments of Scott's troops were twelve-month volunteers whose enlistments were about to expire. Most flatly refused to reenlist, and Scott had no choice but to let them march back to the coast and board ships back to the United States. At about the same time, realizing that the yellow-fever season would soon grip the lowlands, he withdrew most of the garrisons linking him with Veracruz. Then in August he continued his advance inland. He was now down to just 11,000 troops and had no dependable line of communication. The venerable Duke of Wellington, told of this development, is supposed to have declared flatly, "Scott is lost. . . . He can't take [Mexico] city, and he can't fall back upon his base."

But Scott proved the duke wrong. Husbanding his troops with great care, he masterfully kept up his offensive through a series of adroit maneuvers. His operations generally followed the pattern set at Cerro Gordo. The Mexicans would establish a seemingly impregnable defensive position, but young American officers would reconnoiter tirelessly until they found an unguarded path through or around the Mexican lines. In this fashion, Scott's army advanced within a few miles of the capital.

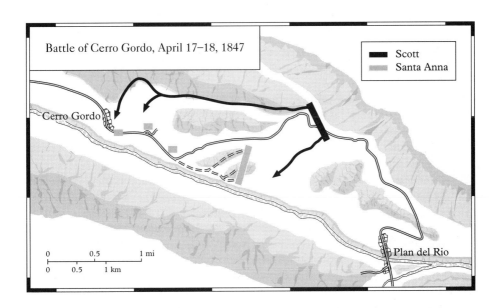

Battle of Cerro Gordo, April 17–18, 1847

Scott
Santa Anna

Cerro Gordo

Plan del Rio

0   0.5   1 mi
0   0.5   1 km

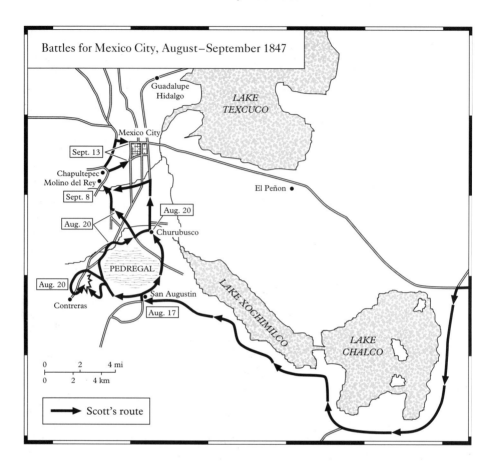

Battles for Mexico City, August–September 1847

        The final assaults on Mexico City displayed the American army at its doughty best. Each operation typically began with a careful reconnaissance by engineer officers who probed the enemy lines for weaknesses and generally found them. The terrain was a rough network of hills, marshes, and rock-strewn fields, but Mexican defenders tended to overestimate its difficulty. When told, for example, that American artillery was picking its way through a solidified lava bed called the Pedregal, one Mexican officer laughed. "No! No! You're dreaming, man. The birds couldn't cross that Pedregal." Only when solid shot began to rain on his position did he realize his error.

        As the anecdote suggests, American cannoneers often placed their light fieldpieces at the forefront of the fighting. Artillery typically opened an offensive engagement, where its fire helped neutralize enemy cannon, demoralize the defenders, and embolden friendly foot soldiers. When the infantrymen attacked, they tended to work their away around the Mexican flank or exploit gaps in the defenses. Only occasionally did they resort to a frontal attack. When they did, however, severe casualties could result. At the Battle of Molino del Rey, for example, the American division that made the assault lost 25 percent of its strength in a few hours of fighting. But the U.S. troops had formed the habit of winning, so that even when good tactical sense was lacking, their self-confidence and élan prevailed. When the formidable castle of Chapultepec—a key to the defense of Mexico City—fell to the Americans, a stunned Santa Anna remarked, "I believe if we were to plant our batteries in Hell the damned Yankees would take them from us." But although impressive, these American triumphs were ultimately misleading, for they occurred where the enemy possessed smoothbore muskets and artillery. They gave American officers an exaggerated view of the frontal assault's potential. During the Civil War to come, such attacks against rifled muskets and artillery often resulted only in expensive failure.

On September 14, 1847, Scott's army entered the Mexican capital. They had achieved a remarkable success. With fewer than 11,000 troops, the Americans had overcome a force of 30,000, well-entrenched and fighting on the defensive, and killed, wounded, or made prisoner a number of Mexican soldiers equal to Scott's entire army. Nominally the Mexican army remained intact. But just as Scott had predicted, the seizure of the capital so paralyzed Mexican political life that within a few weeks, the Mexicans opened negotiations for peace. The resulting Treaty of Guadalupe-Hidalgo was signed in February 1848. Under its terms, the Americans received Texas (with its boundary stipulated as the Rio Grande) and also gained California and New Mexico. In exchange the United States assumed the claims of American citizens against the Mexican government and also paid Mexico $15 million.

The Americans also gained an unexpected political nightmare. The question of whether the newly acquired territories would be slave or free haunted the nation for the next decade; it eventually exploded into civil war. Ulysses S. Grant, who considered the Mexican War "one of the most unjust ever waged by a stronger against a weaker nation," would see in this a bitter justice. "Nations, like individuals, are punished for their transgressions," he would note in his memoirs. "We got our punishment in the most sanguinary and expensive war of modern times."

The Mexican War was the first successful American attempt to project a major force beyond their own boundaries. The navy played a role similar to that of Great Britain's navy in the American Revolution: it permitted U.S. forces to move at will and to remain, for the most part, in continuous supply. By and large, both American regulars and volunteers performed well. The United States proved able to mobilize and maintain forces over a long period and at considerable distance from American soil.

On the American side, about 30,000 regular officers and men served in the war. Of these, 7,700 died—about 900 in battle, the rest from disease. About 73,000 volunteer officers and men enlisted, but many never left the United States. Of those who did, 607 were killed (most in Taylor's dubious battle at Buena Vista); another 6,400 died of disease.

Most senior American officers turned in the same uneven performance characteristic of previous American wars. The young, West Point–trained officers, however, displayed a consistent military competence rarely seen before. They thus bore testimony to a still-underdevoped but growing military professionalism. Winfield Scott, of course, was the outstanding military strategist of the war—one might say the only real strategist. Yet ironically Taylor, not Scott, became the next president, although Scott made his own bid for the White House in 1852.

The Mexican War is often considered a "dress rehearsal" for the Civil War. It certainly gave many future Civil War commanders experience. But it was really more like a well-fought War of 1812. The armies were still quite limited in size—Scott's entire army, by Civil War standards, would scarcely have made a respectable army corps. Both sides used predominantly smoothbore muskets and cannon with ranges and performance little different from those of the eighteenth century. The objectives of the Mexican War and Civil War were also quite dissimilar. While the Civil War was, in most respects, a total war fought for sheer national survival, the Mexican War was essentially a limited war fought in a manner not terribly different from the dynastic wars of eighteenth-century Europe. Limited in geographic setting, limited in allocation of resources, limited in immediate domestic impact and on the enemy's own political and social system, it bore little resemblance to the cataclysm whose origins it inadvertently sowed.

Technological Adaptation and Strategic Thought

That greater catastrophe, however, lay years in the future. In the meantime the American military congratulated itself on its victory, basked in a brief moment of glory, and then returned to its usual work of policing the now greatly expanded frontier. Discouraged by their colorless peacetime duties, a number of American officers left the service during the 1850s and sought more lucrative employment with the railroads, banks, and mining concerns that grew with the booming economy. Those who remained, however, continued the twin tasks of professionalizing the armed forces and trying to keep pace with the fast-moving technological currents of the day. Their achievements would greatly affect the conduct of the massive conflict now looming, unseen and only dimly felt, just beyond the political horizon.

New Technologies

Arriving in New York harbor in 1861, a visiting Frenchman was charmed by a calliope cheerfully piping away from the fantail of a nearby steamboat. That this novel instrument used steam to make music struck the Frenchman as both charming and appropriate. "The grateful Americans," he wrote, "have introduced that powerful agent of their fortune everywhere and even admit it into the realm of art." It was an apt comment, for no technological force exerted a greater effect on nineteenth-century America than that protean brainchild of James Watt, the steam engine.

This "agent of fortune" had two main incarnations. On water, steamboats freed vessels from the tyranny of wind and currents. On land, smoke-belching railroad trains sent dozens of passengers and tons of freight hurtling along at speeds (25 to 50 miles per hour) that seemed to annihilate distance. Taken together, these two forms of steam transportation battered down the geographical barriers to trade and increasingly brought Americans within the orbit of a single, nationwide market. Their economic value was obvious, their military importance scarcely less so. From the 1820s onward, American soldiers and sailors spent a great deal of time pondering the potentialities of steam power.

The steamboat came first. John Fitch constructed a working steam vessel as early as 1789, and by 1807 Robert Fulton's famous *Clermont* was plying the Hudson River. Seven years later, Fulton built the world's first steam warship to defend New York harbor against British attack. The potential military advantages of such a warship were considerable. It could go anywhere, heedless of adverse wind patterns or periods of calm. It could enter harbors and rivers more easily and thus held special promise for inshore operations against forts. The disadvantages, however, initially seemed daunting. Chief among these were the huge cost of the engines; the reduced cruising radius when using engines; the myriad complications from maintenance problems and coal sources; and the decreased working and living space for the crew, made necessary by the sheer bulk of the steam engines.

The drawbacks did not end there. Steam power was at first quite inefficient, requiring huge quantities of fuel in exchange for comparatively

A splendid example of the U.S. Navy's new generation of steam-powered warships, the USS *Merrimac* was also a fully rigged sailing vessel, partly as an economy measure, partly as insurance in case of mechanical failure. Although scuttled at the outbreak of the Civil War, it was salvaged by the Confederates and converted into the ironclad CSS *Virginia*.

little useful work. The development in 1837 of a high-pressure, reciprocal engine eased this problem a bit, but steam vessels remained energy hogs—particularly in comparison with elegant, inexpensive wind-powered sailing ships. There was also the matter of the huge paddlewheel that propelled the steam vessel through the water. Not only did it dramatically reduce the number of cannon that a warship could mount, the paddlewheel was highly vulnerable to enemy fire. The obvious alternative, the screw propeller, raised technological problems that took time to solve. Not until 1843 did the American navy launch its first propeller-driven warship, the *Princeton*. With its introduction the navy at last had a steam-powered warship that could fully compete with its wind-driven counterpart. But even then the problem of greater expense remained.

A major improvement in naval artillery also occurred during the 1850s. Commander John A. Dahlgren—chief of ordnance at the Washington Navy Yard from 1847 to 1861 (when he became its commandant)—tirelessly sought to develop large but safe shell-firing guns. Eventually he hit upon a durable design—an 11-inch muzzle-loading smoothbore weapon with a distinctive "coke bottle" shape to absorb gunpowder blast. It could fire either solid shot or shell. Shells could splinter the hull of a wooden warship in a way solid shot could not, while solid shot remained useful for duels against shore fortifications. Dahlgren's invention became an important intermediate step between the old-style smoothbore cannon from the days of Nelson and the high-velocity rifled artillery of the future.

The Dahlgren gun also signaled a trend toward mounting fewer but larger guns aboard warships, a trend driven in part by the growing use of steam engines aboard warships. The marriage of steam and ordnance involved a major trade-off as increases in engine size forced reductions in the space available for guns. During this period of transition in naval technology, developing an optimal design for warships proved difficult. The notion of protecting warships with iron plates further complicated the problem. Both Great Britain and France experimented with such "ironclad" vessels, but the United States initially held back. Not until the Civil War would Americans construct armored warships.

On land the army also grappled with the implications of steam and improved ordnance. To be sure, the navy's harnessing of steam power had no exact counterpart in the army. The War Department neither constructed special military trains nor commissioned studies—as did the Prussian general staff—to think systematically about the possible use of railroads in national defense. Nevertheless, inspired by its role in the republic as an important surveyor of potential railroad routes, the War Department did sponsor a number of engineering studies that dealt with such technical matters as track gradients, the design of suspension systems, and so on. Although little was directly related to warfare, such studies gave many engineering officers a close acquaintance with the demands and potentialities of the railroad. When the Civil War came, as a result, most commanders possessed a fairly good understanding of railroads and were quick to exploit this new means of transportation.

By 1860, however, steam warships had not replaced the sailing navy, nor had the railroad eclipsed the army wagon. All steam vessels remained fully equipped with masts, sails, and rigging for purposes of fuel economy or the likely event of engine failure. And where railroad tracks ended, men and supplies still had to be transported by water or, more usually, by teams of horses. Civil War armies typically needed about one draft horse for every two or three soldiers.

Technological innovation also occurred in the realm of army ordnance. Two deceptively simple advances in the realm of small arms contributed heavily to the carnage of the Civil War. The first of these was the percussion cap, the latest advance in the continuing quest to touch off a powder charge with greater reliability. Essentially a small brass fitting with a daub of mercury fulminate painted on the inside, it could be fitted snugly over a nipple at the breach of the weapon; the nipple had a small hole that provided access to the powder charge. When the weapon's hammer fell, it struck the percussion cap with enough force to ignite the mercury fulminate, send a spark into the chamber, and ignite the powder charge. The used cap could then be quickly discarded and a new one emplaced for the next firing. The percussion-cap system dispensed with the need to prime the weapon and achieved a much lower rate of misfire than the flintlock system that had been in use since the seventeenth century. During the Mexican War the American regular army largely eschewed the new-fangled percussion cap, but less hide-bound volunteer units used it widely. By the 1850s the army had adopted this system, and it was in general use during the Civil War.

The other significant advance was the creation of the first truly practical rifled musket. For centuries marksmen had understood that a projectile that spiraled in flight went farther and more accurately than a projectile that did not. The trick, of course, was to put spiral grooves in the barrel that would impart the desired spinning motion. For the grooves to achieve their effect, however, the projectile needed to "grip" the barrel snugly, a requirement that created significant military problems.

Model 1855 Rifled Musket. Civil War rifled muskets employed two new technologies: the percussion cap, which reduced the number of misfires; and the Minié ball, a bullet that enabled rifles to be loaded as rapidly as smoothbores. The result was an unprecedented extension in range and accuracy that transformed the battlefield.

With a smoothbore musket one could simply pour some powder down the barrel and then drop in the bullet, a process that took very little time. With a rifled musket, however, one had to pound the bullet down the barrel with a mallet and a long rod. All that pounding took time. Meanwhile, an enemy armed with a smoothbore musket could hurry forward and shoot first. That was why armies in the eighteenth and early nineteenth centuries mainly used smoothbores. Only special troops used rifles.

In the 1840s, however, a French army captain, Claude E. Minié, invented a way to load a rifled musket as easily as a smoothbore. Called the "Minié ball," it was a cylindro-conoidal bullet that could be dropped right down the barrel. One end of it was hollow. When the rifle was fired, the expanding gas made by the gunpowder widened the sides of this hollow end, and the sides of the hollow end gripped the rifling, creating the spinning effect required for good accuracy. Instead of hitting a target at a maximum of one hundred yards, a good marksman could hit a target with a rifled musket at four times that range or better.

Spurred by the energetic Jefferson Davis, who served as secretary of war in the mid-1850s, the army quickly adopted the rifled musket. It also pondered how to modify its infantry tactics to adapt to this innovation. The fruit of these ruminations, however, amounted to little more than an increase in the regulation marching pace of soldiers on the attack. They must reach the enemy line more rapidly, it was understood, to compensate for the increased range and accuracy of the rifled musket. No one yet guessed what thousands of Minié balls—deadly at ranges of 400 yards and beyond—could really do to troops advancing shoulder-to-shoulder in the old Napoleonic style. As is usual (and quite understandable) in such situations, military men expected that this new development would simply modify the existing tactical environment, not overthrow it.

American Military Thought

Few American officers during the 1850s gave extended attention to the problems of conducting a major war. Most were too busy fighting Indians, angling for promotion, or simply enduring a life of monotonous garrison duty. As future Confederate General Richard S. Ewell remarked, before the Civil War he learned everything there was to know about commanding fifty dragoons and forgot about everything else. Still, some officers did think seriously about strategic matters. And since most of these rose to high rank during the Civil War, their efforts leavened the indifference of their peers and, in fact, gave the conduct of that war a surprising degree of coherence. Like soldiers the world over, these more industrious American officers had to grapple with the legacy of Napoleon. But they also had to consider the military realities of defending a nation with only a small standing army and one that was, after all, separated from any major enemy by 3,000 miles of ocean.

The dean of American strategic thinkers was Dennis Hart Mahan, professor of military science at West Point. A deep admirer of Napoleon, Mahan saw this great captain chiefly through the eyes of the Swiss military theorist Antoine Henri, Baron de Jomini. Jomini emphasized the offensive essence of Napoleonic warfare but gave it an orderly, geometric cast. Similarly, Mahan celebrated the aggressive pursuit of offensive victory but lavished even greater attention upon the problems of defense. Recognizing that, in the event of war, many American soldiers would be half-trained volunteers, Mahan dwelled heavily on using field fortifications to steady new troops and reduce casualties. His ideal was the active defense—to weaken and absorb the enemy's blow, then "when he has been cut up, to assume the offensive, and drive him back at the point of the bayonet."

During his many years at West Point, Mahan drilled his ideas into a generation of cadets and presided over a "Napoleon Club" that studied the emperor's campaigns. His principal disciple, Henry Wager Halleck, translated Jomini's principal works into English and also wrote a somewhat derivative study entitled *Elements of Military Art and Science* (1846). Halleck solemnly extolled not only the virtues of field fortification but also the imperative need to keep one's forces well concentrated and vigilant against surprise attack.

Although never adopted as a West Point text, Halleck's book was probably the strategic treatise most widely read by American officers. But that is not really saying a great deal. Few references to Jomini or formal strategic theory appear in Civil War correspondence, and successful Civil War commanders often regarded their strategy as a matter of applied common sense. As Grant remarked of Napoleon, "[M]y impression is that his first success came because he made war in his own way, and not in imitation of others."

After the Mexican War the U.S. War Department sent a number of officers abroad in an effort to keep abreast of recent European military developments. But the results were not impressive. For example, a trio of officers sent to study the armies of Europe returned to make a bulky but uneven report. From their observations of the Crimean War they commented learnedly on the leggings used by Russian soldiers but failed to say anything about the Russian conscription system. American officers did better when they left the higher realms of military policy and pondered more workaday issues instead. A number of them wrote military manuals or prepared articles on technical aspects of the military profession. Some discussed better ways to train infantry, others offered suggestions on the improvement of cannon, saddles, firearms, and other items of equipment. One historian has argued that in this respect, antebellum officers were at least as professionally active as their late-twentieth-century counterparts.

★   ★   ★   ★

By the eve of the Civil War, the United States had created a modest but reasonably proficient military establishment. Although its regular army numbered just 16,000 men in 1860, the limited standing force was adequate to perform the duties of a "frontier constabulary," and, supplemented by short-term volunteers, it had handily prevailed over a numerically larger opponent during the Mexican War. Moreover, Americans had also created a substantial system of permanent fortifications to guard their coastline.

American forces had also kept abreast of technological improvements. On land, army officers understood the importance of railroads and were well prepared to exploit that new means of transportation during the Civil War. They had also adopted the rifled musket and had attempted, however imperfectly, to anticipate its effect on infantry tactics. At sea, the navy possessed steam warships of advanced design and had also deployed new, state-of-the-art naval guns.

Perhaps most impressively, in the years after the War of 1812 the officer corps took the first significant steps toward true professional status. The U.S. Military Academy, although established in 1802, came into its own with the Thayer reforms of the 1820s. Officers increasingly viewed the military profession as a lifelong career, and a sizable number of them thought seriously about the military art. When the vicissitudes of Congress permitted, they even established schools of practice to train more thoroughly in infantry and artillery tactics.

Yet substantial problems lingered. In the years after the War of 1812 the militia system steadily declined. The presence of some peacetime volunteer companies and the enlistment of additional volunteers in wartime only partially offset the endemic shortage of trained military manpower. A strong amateur tradition also persisted. Most Americans continued to believe that an intelligent man of character, imbued with martial enthusiasm and fired by republican ideals, could make not only a good soldier but also a competent officer. Among its many other effects on American society, the Civil War would mortally challenge this belief.

SUGGESTED READINGS

Bauer, K. Jack. *The Mexican War, 1846–1848* (New York: MacMillan, 1974).

Coffman, Edward M. *The Old Army: A Portrait of the American Army in Peacetime, 1784–1898* (New York and London: Oxford University Press, 1986).

Crackel, Theodore. *Mr. Jefferson's Army: Political and Social Reform of the Military Establishment, 1801–1809* (New York and London: New York University Press, 1987).

Cunliffe, Marcus. *Soldiers and Civilians: The Martial Spirit in America, 1775–1865* (New York: Free Press, 1968).

Hickey, Don. *The War of 1812: A Forgotten Conflict* (Urbana: University of Illinois Press, 1989).

Kohn, Richard H. *Eagle and Sword: The Beginnings of the Military Establishment in America* (New York: Free Press, 1975).

McCaffrey, James M. *Army of Manifest Destiny: The American Soldier in the Mexican War, 1846–1848* (New York and London: New York University Press, 1992).

McKee, Christopher. *A Gentlemanly and Honorable Profession: The Creation of the U.S. Naval Officer Corps* (Annapolis: Naval Institute Press, 1991).

Mahon, John D. *History of the Second Seminole War* (Gainesville: University Presses of Florida, 1968).

Morrison, James L., Jr. *"The Best School in the World": West Point, the Pre–Civil War Years, 1835–1866* (Kent, Ohio: Kent State University Press, 1986).

Prucha, Francis P. *The Sword of the Republic: The United States Army on the Frontier, 1783–1846* (New York: MacMillan, 1969).

Skelton, William B. *An American Profession of Arms: The Army Officer Corps, 1784–1861* (Lawrence: University Press of Kansas, 1992).

Smith, Merritt Roe. *Harper's Ferry and the New Technology* (Ithaca, N.Y.: Cornell University Press, 1977).

Stagg, J. C. A. *Mr. Madison's War: Politics, Diplomacy, and Warfare in the Early American Republic, 1783–1830* (Princeton, N.J.: Princeton University Press, 1983).

Utley, Robert M. *Frontiersmen in Blue: The United States Army and the Indian, 1848–1865* (New York: MacMillan, 1967).

11

THE CIVIL WAR, 1861–1862:
THE LETHAL FACE OF BATTLE

Strategic Overview

War for the Borderland

Cracking the Confederate
Frontier

At 4:30 A.M. on April 12, 1861, a dull boom thudded across the tranquil harbor of Charleston, South Carolina. From the city, observers could clearly see the fuse of a mortar shell as it climbed across the soft moonlit sky, then plunged in a graceful arc toward casemated Fort Sumter near the harbor entrance. A moment later the shell exploded directly above the fort, raining fragments on the federal garrison below. The Civil War—the deadliest conflict in American history and, in many respects, the central episode of that history—had begun.

No one had any idea what to expect. Most Americans supposed the war would be decided by one or two major battles. A few even believed it might end without any serious fighting at all. But nearly everyone agreed that, at most, the struggle would be settled within a year. They also assumed that the fundamental patterns of American society would remain unaltered. Indeed, the preservation of those patterns formed the very object for which Americans on both sides were contending. White Southerners expected to maintain an agrarian, slave-holding society that, in their minds at least, corresponded to the republic established by the Founding Fathers. Northerners sought to restore the unbroken alliance of states toasted by President Andrew Jackson nearly three decades before ("Our Federal Union—it must be preserved!").

But instead of a brief contest, the Civil War raged across the central and southern United States for four long years. And instead of conserving the old America—however defined—it steadily and profoundly reshaped the political, economic, and social contours of the nation. By the time it ended, the original American republic was gone forever.

The Civil War was, as one historian has aptly called it, "the Second

American Revolution." Like the War for Independence, it was a revolutionary conflict, combining the mass politics and passions of the wars of the
French Revolution with the technology, productive capacity, and managerial
style of an emergent industrial society. Both the Union and the Confederacy
fielded armies that dwarfed all military formations previously seen in the
New World. They supplied these vast hosts with food, munitions, and equipment shipped by rail and steamship. They connected units hundreds of
miles apart with webs of telegraph lines, and motivated soldiers and civilians
alike with ceaseless barrages of political propaganda. When necessary they
repressed dissent with intimidation and arbitrary arrests. Before the war was
half over, both sides abandoned cherished notions of individual liberty and
conscripted men to serve in the armies. In their quest to finance the struggle they trampled venerable ideas about limited taxation and fiscal recti-
tude. And by the war's third year they had begun to accept attacks upon
enemy civilians and property as necessary and even virtuous. Both sides
mobilized their resources and populations to the utmost limit of their mid-
nineteenth-century ability and, when they reached the end of that ability,
strove for ways to extend it. The Union and the Confederacy, in short,
waged a total war: a war in which both societies pitted their full destructive
energies against each other.

Strategic Overview

To understand the course of the war, one must understand its origins, for
perceptions concerning the roots of the conflict profoundly shaped the
objectives and strategy of both sides. The central issue was slavery, although
many Americans did not accept this at the time (and some still do not
today). One alternative view suggests that the Civil War was a struggle over
"states' rights" versus centralized government—yet most Northerners believed in states' rights as much as most Southerners. Another regards it as
a contest between an agrarian South and an industrialized North, neglecting
to note that the Northern states were also primarily agricultural—in the case
of the midwest, overwhelmingly so. Still another posits a conflict between
two allegedly distinct cultures—overlooking the fact that North and South
shared a common language, a common history, and a common belief in
republican government. Such political, economic, and cultural differences
as did exist could be traced, by and large, to a single source: the fact that the
South was a slaveholding society and the North was not.

Roots of War

By the mid-nineteenth century, slavery had become the South's bedrock
institution. In the 250 years since the first shackled Africans had arrived on
American shores (and especially in the decades following the American

Revolution), white Southerners had evolved a complex set of beliefs about their "peculiar institution." Not only did they consider it vital for the cultivation of the region's major cash crops, they also thought it the only acceptable basis on which whites and blacks could coexist. Slaveholders liked to regard their bondsmen essentially as children incapable of self-improvement and therefore in need of their master's lifelong paternal care. Many believed—or affected to believe—that the blacks themselves preferred a life of slavery and benefited from it. Paradoxically most Southerners also possessed a profound if usually unstated fear of a slave revolt. The need to maintain absolute, unquestioned control over their slave population gave Southerners a strong incentive to preserve an ordered, stable society. As a result, social change of any kind occurred in the South more slowly than in the North. And although only one in four Southern families actually owned slaves, most accepted the proslavery philosophy. They either aspired to ownership or, at a minimum, appreciated the advantages of living in a society whose lowest tier remained permanently reserved for blacks.

Northerners, however, increasingly found the "peculiar institution" distasteful. Comparatively little of this distaste reflected humanitarian concern for the slaves. Perhaps 5 percent of the Northern population entertained "abolitionist" sentiments: that is to say, a belief in both immediate, uncompensated emancipation *and* political and social equality for blacks. The vast majority of antislavery Northerners objected to the "peculiar institution" not because of its effect on black people, but because of its effect on whites. It degraded the value of free labor. It encouraged an agrarian society dominated by a comparative handful of wealthy planters who (many believed) monopolized political power in the South. Conversely it discouraged the creation of new industry and economic diversity. And to the extent that slavery was permitted in the western territories, it meant that white families would be forced to live beside blacks, a prospect that many Northern whites considered repugnant.

Until the late 1840s this tension between pro- and antislavery forces remained largely submerged. It surfaced rapidly when the Mexican War broke out. Many Whigs and some Northern Democrats regarded the conflict as nothing but a naked land grab by Southern slaveholders eager to extend slavery into Mexico. In August 1846 antislavery congressman David Wilmot of Pennsylvania introduced a resolution that formally renounced any intention by the United States to introduce slavery into any lands that might be seized from Mexico during the war. This "Wilmot Proviso" failed to pass both houses of Congress, but it succeeded in reinjecting slavery into national political life. For the next fifteen years the question of slavery in the territories constantly dogged American policy makers.

At bottom, the question dividing Americans might be summarized thus: was the United States a slaveholding republic with pockets of freedom in the North, or was it a free republic with pockets of slavery in the South? The answer had profound implications for the very nature of the American experiment and its future. Proslavery Americans sought to extend slavery into the territories because they considered anything less to be an abridgment of their rights and an implicit query against the legitimacy of their way of life. Antislavery Americans wanted to bar the extension of slavery because they believed the system degraded the dignity of free labor and stifled economic diversity. More darkly, they suspected that the slave system sustained a planter aristocracy that controlled political life in the South and was trying to maintain control over national political life as well.

Throughout the 1850s, both sides saw evidence to support their own beliefs. Political compromise grew more difficult. An attempt to permit western settlers to decide for themselves whether a given territory would be slaveholding or free degenerated into violence when the rival factions in Kansas Territory undermined the democratic process through intimidation, fraud, and murder. Then in 1859 the abolitionist terrorist John Brown raided Harpers Ferry, Virginia, hoping to foment a slave insurrection. The operation was a fiasco; Brown was captured and hanged, as were most of his followers who survived the attack itself. But the Harpers Ferry raid shocked the entire white population of the South, especially when they discovered that a few Northern abolitionists had helped finance Brown's attack. The fact that many in the North considered Brown a martyr only increased the Southerners' sense of anger and alienation.

For thirty years some Southerners had discussed the possibility of secession if the national government ever threatened the continued existence of slavery. The election of Republican candidate Abraham Lincoln seemed to bring that threat uncomfortably near. His party openly opposed the extension of slavery in the territories, and although Lincoln renounced any intention to touch slavery where it already existed, as president he would have power to appoint judges and federal marshals in the South. Such officials, indispensable to maintain the system of law and order on which slavery depended, would now be of dubious loyalty to the "peculiar institution." Perhaps most gallingly, Lincoln won election despite the fact that hardly any Southerners had voted for him. In most slaveholding states he had not even been on the ballot.

Many Southerners now sensed that they had lost control of the national government; they could no longer expect that government to preserve slavery. Honor and self-interest dictated that they must leave the Union if they expected to retain control of their own destinies. The secessionist impulse was particularly strong in South Carolina, a state in which slaves outnumbered whites and which had a long tradition of radicalism on the subject of slavery. On December 20, 1860, a convention of South Carolinians unanimously voted to leave the Union. Six other states followed in the next six weeks: Mississippi, Alabama, Louisiana, Georgia, Florida, and Texas. It was the worst crisis the nation had ever faced.

However, eight slave states—North Carolina, Tennessee, Virginia, Arkansas, Maryland, Kentucky, Missouri, and Delaware—remained loyal to the Union. This suggested that many Southerners did not wish to secede, an impression reinforced by the fact that in most of the states that *did* leave the Union, a substantial minority had voted against secession. For these and other reasons, when the Lincoln administration took office in March 1861, it hoped that some means might be found to undermine the secessionist

Perhaps America's greatest war president, Abraham Lincoln combined political skill with dogged determination and at times even ruthlessness.

movement without bloodshed. Perhaps, as Secretary of State William Seward believed, most Southerners would eventually repudiate disunion if given time to reconsider.

In the meantime, however, delegates from the seceded states formed a new nation, the Confederate States of America. Meeting in Montgomery, Alabama, they drafted a new constitution and established a provisional government to be led by Jefferson Davis, a former U.S. senator and secretary of war. One of the new government's first acts was to assume authority over the artillery batteries erected by South Carolina to threaten the tiny Federal garrison of Fort Sumter.

The Confederate government insisted that the Lincoln administration withdraw the garrison: its claim to sovereignty over the seceded South would be meaningless if a "foreign" power continued to occupy one of the Confederacy's principal ports. The symbolism of Fort Sumter was equally important to Lincoln, since to order its evacuation would be a fatal display of weakness. For weeks the standoff persisted. Finally President Davis gave orders that if the fort refused to surrender it must be bombarded. The firing on Fort Sumter on April 12 ended any chance the sectional rift could be repaired without bloodshed. Undermanned, low on food, and cut off from resupply, Fort Sumter surrendered on April 14. The following day Lincoln requested 75,000 three-month volunteers to suppress the rebellion.

Military Resources and Objectives

Lincoln's call for troops triggered a second wave of secession. The upper tier of southern states—Virginia, Arkansas, North Carolina, and Tennessee—all left the Union rather than support the North in a war against the Confederacy. By June the Confederacy consisted of eleven states, sprawling across a territory the size of western Europe and boasting a population of 9 million. Of these, about 5.5 million were whites. Most of the rest were slaves—a huge potential security problem, to be sure, but also a major economic asset.

The Confederacy's aim at the beginning of the war was simple: hold on to the de facto independence already obtained. It did not need to invade the North or dictate a peace treaty on the steps of the White House. All it had to do was to continue the struggle long enough for the North to tire of the war and accept the fact of secession. In many respects this aim was little different from that of the American colonies during the Revolution, a struggle still close enough in time to be almost a living memory. That earlier conflict had been won largely by attrition. The British had captured the colonies' cities almost at will, traversed American territory as they pleased, and dominated the seas that bathed American shores. But they could neither quench the Americans' will to fight nor prevent foreign intervention once the Americans had shown their capacity for sustained resistance.

Conceivably the Confederates might have adopted a similar strategy: pin their forces to the defense of no fixed area or city, draw the invaders in, and wear out the Federals by a protracted war of attrition. Instead Davis and his advisors decided to fight the battle at the frontier. They would repulse incursions and attempt to hold major concentrations of population and resources. A number of considerations made this the obvious strategy. First, the discrepancy in military strength between North and South, although hardly an even match, was far less forbidding than that between Britain and the American colonies. Second, the political pressures within the Confederacy for a conventional defense were also great—every locality clamored for Southern troops to protect it. Third, a conventional defense would give the Confederacy greater legitimacy in the eyes of its own citizens and in those of the world. And finally, the delicate "peculiar institution" needed the stability of law and order to survive. The mere presence of a hostile political party in the White House had threatened that stability enough to spur the cotton states to secession. Given the enormous sensitivity of this issue, the Confederacy could hardly permit Federal armies to plunge deep into Southern territory. Even if formal Federal policy remained one of noninterference with slave labor, an advancing Union army would surely disrupt slave labor, create a flood of runaways, and perhaps even raise the spectre of a race war of slave against master. The Confederacy, then, had many good reasons to defend itself at the border.

The South would not conduct a passive defense, either. Davis preferred what he called the "offensive-defensive." According to his scheme, Confederate forces would permit a Union thrust to develop, gauge its main axis of advance, wait for an advantageous moment, then concentrate and counterattack at a time and place of their own choosing. General Robert E.

Jefferson Davis was highly qualified to be the Confederacy's president, having been a Mexican War hero, Secretary of War in the Franklin Pierce administration, and a senator from Mississippi.

Lee described this operational concept in an 1863 letter: "It is [as] impossible for [the enemy] to have a large operating army at every assailable point in our territory as it is for us to keep one to defend it. We must move our troops from point to point as required, and by close observation and accurate information the true point of attack can generally be ascertained. . . . Partial encroachments of the enemy we must expect, but they can always be recovered, and any defeat of their large army will reinstitute everything."

Confederates worried comparatively little about the larger size and greater resource base of their opponent, partly from overconfidence, but primarily because of a conviction that the war would be brief and comparatively limited—a contest on the scale, say, of the recent Mexican War. But in a longer struggle the North's advantages were substantial. With a population of 20 million, the Northern states obviously possessed a much larger military manpower base, but their industrial capacity was far greater as well. In 1860 the North had over 110,000 manufacturing establishments, the South just 18,000. The North produced 94 percent of the country's iron, 97 percent of its coal and—not incidentally—97 percent of its firearms. It contained 22,000 miles of railroad to the South's 8,500. The North outperformed the South agriculturally as well. Northerners held 75 percent of the country's farm acreage, produced 60 percent of its livestock, 67 percent of its corn, and 81 percent of its wheat. All in all, they held 75 percent of the nation's total wealth.

The North's advantages did not end there. It controlled the resources of a long-established government, including the 16,000 men of its army and the ninety warships of its navy. It had a much better financial structure. The South, by contrast, had no preexisting armed forces, few banks, and relatively little specie. Its wealth lay primarily in land and slaves—assets difficult to convert to liquid capital. Shortly after the war began, the Confederate government made this deficiency even worse by ordering an embargo on the sale of cotton abroad. The decision, intended to pressure textile-producing nations like Great Britain into supporting the Confederacy, only hurt the South's ability to obtain more hard currency.

Even so, most of the North's advantages were potential rather than real. It would take time for the Union to translate its demographic and economic resources into effective strength, and in the interim the Confederacy would create military forces of impressive size. To be sure, the Federals usually held the edge in manpower and heavy weaponry, but only at the margins. And the South possessed considerable advantages of its own. Although the Union possessed more men, it also had the daunting task of projecting large armies across hundreds of miles of territory, much of it difficult to traverse and sparsely populated. Southern forces could rely upon a largely loyal population, whereas Union forces would have to divert large numbers of troops to guard supply lines and garrison key points against guerrilla incursions. Southern forces could fight on the defensive and exploit interior lines to concentrate against separate Union columns. Then too, the fact that Southerners were fighting to defend their homeland made their cause more concrete and thus more potent. Finally, with millions of slaves to keep the Southern economy running, the South could afford to send a larger percentage of its white manpower to war.

Of further benefit to the South was the fact that the Lincoln administration had to contend with an all-but-insoluble political conundrum. It had to maintain as broad a base of domestic support for the war as possible, despite the fact that some Northerners opposed any attempt to coerce the South, while many others believed the attempt must be made without trampling on the constitutional rights of Southerners—including their right to hold slaves. The administration also had to fight the war hard enough to gain victory but not so violently as to foster deep bitterness among the Southern people. The North's objective, after all, was a reunion of the states. If that were to be accomplished it required that the Southern people must eventually choose—grudgingly, perhaps, but essentially voluntarily—to renew their loyalty to the United States government. The dilemma facing the Lincoln administration was thus one of enormous complexity. It had to find a policy vigorous enough to win the war, but not so vigorous as to forfeit domestic support or alienate the South completely.

War for the Borderland

Nowhere was the Union task more delicate than in the borderland, a region consisting of Missouri, Kentucky, Maryland, and the western counties of

Virginia. These were slaveholding areas, each with considerable secessionist sentiment but also with substantial populations loyal to the Federal government. If the Lincoln administration could hold these areas, it stood a fighting chance of containing the rebellion. If, however, the Confederacy gained control of the borderland, it could isolate Washington, D.C., add another million people to its population, and render a Federal victory all but impossible. As both sides mobilized their field armies, they struggled first for control of the border states between them.

Mobilization

Since they shared an identical military heritage, it was scarcely surprising that the Union and Confederacy organized for war in similar ways. Lincoln, of course, had the advantage of preexisting War and Navy departments as well as small, permanent land and naval forces. But the Davis administration quickly created identical departments. In any event the United States prior to 1860 had no experience with a command structure adequate for the unprecedented size and scope of the conflict, and as a result both Davis and Lincoln had to experiment.

The paper organization Davis created was not bad. It combined a secretary of war with an adjutant and inspector general whom Davis expected would perform as a de facto chief of staff. In reality, however, Davis ran much of the war effort himself. The secretary of war position never amounted to much. The job passed from one man to another until the end of the Confederate government's existence. Davis apparently never sought, and certainly never found, a forceful and able secretary of war.

The Union command structure, although similar, had a few important differences. First, Lincoln wisely chose to invest his secretary of war with very wide powers. His initial choice for the position proved corrupt and inefficient, but in January 1862 Lincoln appointed a new man, Edwin M.

As Lincoln's Secretary of War, Edwin M. Stanton presided over a Union army of over one million men and kept it well supplied with arms and equipment.

Stanton of Pennsylvania, who became one of the most energetic and forceful secretaries of war in American history. "Stanton," Lincoln once remarked, "is the rock upon which are beating the waves of this conflict. . . . I do not see how he survives—why he is not crushed and torn to pieces. Without him, I should be destroyed." Lincoln also insisted—except for one brief interlude—on having a general-in-chief. During the course of the conflict he had four of them (Winfield Scott, George B. McClellan, Henry W. Halleck, and Ulysses S. Grant), and his experiences with all but the last were often frustrating. But by maintaining the post he prevented himself from becoming overwhelmed by detail and also, at least in theory, received the benefit of expert military advice.

Both sides spent the first months of the war feverishly generating armies far larger than any the United States had previously fielded. To do so, each mobilized its limited contingents of existing state militia, but these barely began to furnish the necessary manpower. To augment the militia, volunteer troops were enlisted by tens of thousands. In keeping with the traditional American political philosophy, chief responsibility for raising the volunteers reposed not with the central government but rather with the individual states. The Union and Confederate War departments simply asked each state to raise a certain number of regiments. The state governors, in turn, had the task of actually finding, organizing, and equipping the needed men. To do so they often turned to community leaders—men of established standing who could persuade other men to enlist under their command. Thus a prominent local attorney might announce that he was organizing a company of infantry. Other men, familiar with the attorney's reputation and willing to serve with him, would then enroll in the company until its rosters were filled. Afterward they would elect the key company officers and sergeants. The attorney, of course, would invariably be elected captain. The company would then band with other companies into a regiment, and the regiment's colonel would then be selected. Sometimes the governor would appoint him; sometimes he would be elected, if not by the rank and file then by the various company commanders. In this way the states met their quotas. The exact details varied widely but were always in keeping with the loose-jointed, localistic nature of American society.

In their homespun way, Americans were harnessing the same thing that had fired the French Revolution: popular sovereignty, the notion that the people themselves formed the ultimate source of political authority and legitimacy. Nowhere in the nineteenth-century world was this idea more potent than in the United States, and as a result both Northerners and Southerners felt a profound sense of identification with the cause for which their governments were contending. The gulf between the Civil War soldier and his eighteenth-century counterpart could hardly be more absolute. The old European soldier felt little sense of involvement with his sovereign's cause, nor did the peasants and burghers whose taxes paid for the war. By contrast, the Civil War soldier was a member of one of the most intensely politicized societies on earth. His sense of involvement with his cause—whether the cause of Union or the cause of Southern independence—was profound; the communities that sent him to war were equally so. The explosion of martial energy this produced in 1861 was as powerful as that of the French Revolution.

The consequences of popular sovereignty affected the Union and Confederate war efforts in other ways as well. For one thing, the improvised nature of the mobilization gave the state governors an enormous degree of importance and thus considerable influence. Two governors of particular note were Oliver Perry Morton of Indiana and Joseph G. Brown of Georgia. Morton took an almost proprietary interest in his Hoosier regiments and was known to complain vigorously whenever he believed they were being mishandled. He advanced or undercut the careers of several Union commanders. Brown, for his part, became the gadfly of the Davis administration, damned various administration policies, circumvented the operation of military conscription in his state, and often retained supplies and equipment for the use of Georgia troops alone.

Both sides also found it expedient to offer high military rank to important political figures. The Lincoln administration in particular tried to clinch the support of various Northern constituencies by making generals of favorite politicians. Thus Nathaniel P. Banks, former Speaker of the House, received a major general's commission to make sure that New England Democrats backed the Union war effort. Lincoln also made Franz Sigel a major general in order to secure the support of the German-American community. Students of the Civil War have long poured scorn upon these "political generals." But their derision reflects a fundamental misunderstanding of the military ethos that prevailed in mid-nineteenth-century America. A professional officer corps, in the modern sense of the term, hardly existed, and few Americans understood why it should. In the minds of many, the chief attributes of effective command were character and leadership ability, and surely any widely admired political figure possessed these. Such scorn also overlooks the fact that many of these "political generals" performed at least as well as some of their West Point–trained counterparts, while a few of them displayed genuine gifts.

As soon as these newly formed units could gather—erratically uniformed, gawky, ill-disciplined, but filled with ardor—they began to gravitate toward various points along the military frontier. Few of these movements occurred as the result of comprehensive planning on the part of the Union and Confederate high commands. No such planning had occurred; no overarching strategic vision existed on either side. Often a governor or department commander decided what places must be garrisoned or occupied as bases for subsequent advances. At this early stage, the war efforts of both North and South were very much improvised. Like the armies themselves, strategic decision-making was generally an ad hoc affair.

The Border States

Even so, both sides had evident priorities. The Confederacy positioned substantial forces to block the approaches to Richmond; the North, for its part, exerted almost frantic energies to ensure the safety of Washington. The

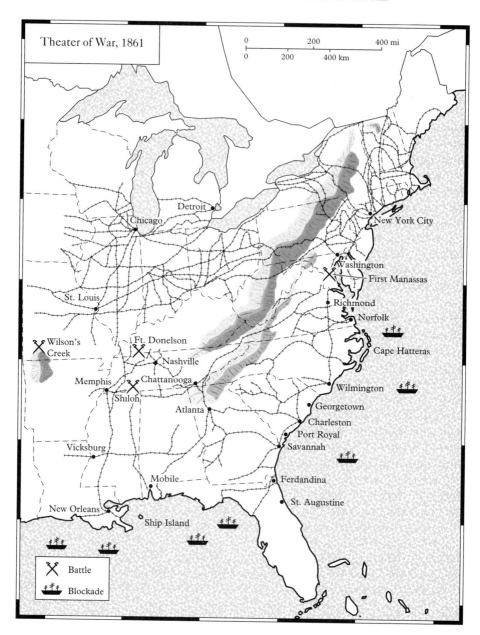

Theater of War, 1861

0   200   400 mi
0   200   400 km

Detroit

Chicago

New York City

Washington

First Manassas

St. Louis

Richmond

Norfolk

Wilson's
Creek

Ft. Donelson

Cape Hatteras

Nashville

Memphis   Chattanooga

Wilmington

Shiloh

Georgetown

Atlanta

Charleston
Port Royal
Savannah

Vicksburg

Mobile

Ferdandina

New Orleans

St. Augustine

Ship Island

⚔ Battle

⛵ Blockade

Federal capital was surrounded by slaveholding territory—Virginia, now part of a hostile power, lay just across the Potomac bridges, while Maryland hemmed in the District of Columbia on its remaining three sides. For a brief but terrifying moment it seemed likely that Maryland might leave the Union as well. Scant days after Fort Sumter, a secessionist mob had pelted Massachusetts troops as they marched through Baltimore en route to Washington; it was also widely rumored that the state legislature would shortly vote to join the Confederacy. The Maryland lawmakers never got the chance, however. Abandoning all concern for constitutional niceties, the

Lincoln administration suspended the writ of habeas corpus, declared martial law, imprisoned suspected persons, and in general clamped on Maryland a military despotism. This development was utterly startling in a nation long-wedded to the concept of limited government. It was also highly effective in keeping Maryland firmly within the Union—whether Marylanders liked it or not.

The Federal government enjoyed similar success in the western counties of Virginia. Economically this mountainous region was more tied to Ohio and Pennsylvania than to tidewater Virginia. It possessed relatively few slaves, a long tradition of resentment toward the more densely populated eastern counties, and considerable Unionist sentiment. In late May, when Federal troops from Ohio first crossed into western Virginia, they were widely received as liberators. The Confederacy had only a few weak units in the region, and those soon departed from the region after a series of minor clashes that nevertheless brought great results. The Federal victories in western Virginia secured Union control over the Baltimore and Ohio Railroad, a strategically invaluable artery between the eastern and western theaters of war. They also paved the way for the creation (in 1863) of the new state of West Virginia.

Kentucky, like western Virginia, was a state settled largely by Southerners but tied geographically and economically to the Ohio River valley. Perhaps not surprisingly, in the sectional squabbles that had preceded the war its citizens had exhibited a strong preference for compromise. The "Great Compromiser" himself, Senator Henry Clay, had been from Kentucky. So was Senator John J. Crittenden, principal proponent of a compromise proposal that had floated briefly during the secession winter. Nowhere was the "war of brothers" image more appropriate than in the Bluegrass State. Sixty percent of white Kentuckians who fought during the conflict wore Union blue; the rest wore gray. And in Kentucky the lines were indeed sometimes drawn within family circles. Crittenden had two sons who became generals on opposite sides.

When war broke out, Kentucky's governor tried in vain to mediate the conflict. When his efforts failed, the legislature voted that the state would maintain "strict neutrality." Lincoln, fearful that a tough policy would push Kentucky into the Confederate fold, gave orders to respect this extralegal neutrality. So did Davis. This anomalous situation lasted only until early September, when Confederate General Leonidas Polk—acting on his own authority—marched into Columbus, Kentucky. The town's position on a high bluff overlooking the Mississippi River gave it strategic value. By seizing Columbus, Polk strengthened the defense of the river, but the political cost was substantial. Although Federal troops (under Major General Ulysses S. Grant) promptly occupied other Kentucky towns at the mouths of the Cumberland and Tennessee rivers, the fact that the Confederacy had violated Kentucky neutrality first made it seem the aggressor. The state legislature embraced the Union; the prosecessionist governor resigned. By the end of the year Federal forces held most of the important points in Kentucky, including Louisville, the largest city, and Frankfort, the capital. The Confederates occupied only a thin strip along the state's southern frontier.

Missouri proved a thornier problem for the Lincoln administration. Although most of its citizens were pro-Union, a substantial minority favored the Confederates, and while Kentuckians adopted a largely neutral stance, the rival factions in Missouri quickly came to blows. Trouble began in mid-May when a mixed force of Union home guards and regulars marched into the camp of prosecessionist state militiamen and disarmed them. The Federal commander, Captain Nathaniel Lyon, had the captured militia herded through the streets of Saint Louis. An angry mob gathered, shouting "Hurrah for Jeff Davis!" and throwing brickbats. Presently someone shot an officer and the Union troops opened fire. At least twenty-eight civilians and two soldiers died in the ensuing melée, and dozens more were wounded.

Although provocative, Lyon's decision to disarm the militia was basically prudent. The prosecessionist militia had already received cannon and ammunition spirited to them from Louisiana; given time they might well have seized control of Saint Louis. Even so, his action and the ensuing riot fueled passions on both sides and promised further violence. To avert the possibility of more internal fighting, Missouri moderates arranged a meeting between Lyon and the prosecessionist governor. But after four hours of negotiation Lyon lost his temper. "Rather than concede to the State of Missouri for one instant the right to dictate to my Government in any matter . . . I would see you . . . and every man, woman, and child in the State, dead and buried. *This means war.*"

In the weeks that followed, Union forces managed to push the secessionist militia—without any major fighting—toward the southwestern part of Missouri. Lyon pursued with about 5,500 men and occupied the town of Springfield. But his forces dangled at the end of a tenuous supply line, he could receive no reinforcements, and soon the 8,000 secessionist militia (led by Major General Sterling Price) were joined by 5,000 Confederate troops under Major General Benjamin McCulloch. Lyon nevertheless refused to retreat and, learning that the Rebels would soon begin an offensive, decided to attack first. On August 10 he struck the enemy at Wilson's Creek, ten miles south of Springfield.

Lyon's attack was an incredible gamble that came amazingly close to success. The rebel troops were poorly trained and equipped, and Lyon managed to achieve surprise with a daring two-pronged attack. A confused, savage battle ensued along the banks of Wilson's Creek. Lyon's men managed to hold their own, despite odds of nearly three-to-one, until Lyon was fatally wounded. With his death the Union forces lost heart. Nearly out of ammunition anyway, they retreated. Eventually they fell back over one hundred miles to Rolla, a railhead town with links to Saint Louis.

Union losses in this battle were 1,300; Southern losses were about the same. The Confederates followed up their victory by marching into the Missouri River valley and capturing the important town of Lexington, Missouri, in mid-September. For a brief period, then, Price's militia controlled half the state. But Price soon discovered he lacked the manpower to hold such a vast region, and in October he withdrew again to the southwest corner of the state. In February 1862 a substantial Union army under Major General Samuel Curtis managed to eject Price from Missouri for good.

Then, in the Battle of Pea Ridge, Arkansas (March 6–8, 1862), Curtis stopped a major Confederate attempt to drive him back.

Almost despite itself, the Union had managed to hold on to Missouri. Its grip was tenuous and remained so. Throughout the war, Missouri was the scene of a continual and vicious guerrilla struggle, particularly in the proslavery Missouri River valley. Still, by early 1862 the Lincoln administration had achieved an important objective—it controlled the borderland.

First Bull Run

From a Union perspective, securing the borderland was a defensive goal. To do so might keep the rebellion within manageable limits, but it did little to defeat the Confederacy. For that the Union needed an offensive plan, and as the spring of 1861 progressed, the Lincoln administration pondered how best to proceed.

Its general-in-chief, the once magnificent but now aging Winfield Scott, proposed a very cautious strategy. Like many Northerners, including Lincoln, Scott believed that popular support for the Confederate regime was shallow; the Southern people, after all, had been until recently loyal citizens of the United States. An adroit approach might detach them from the Davis government and woo their allegiance back to the Union. But how to do this? Scott suggested a three-phase plan. First, blockade the Southern harbors, cutting them off from outside assistance. Second, send a strong column down the Mississippi River to hold that vital artery of commerce and further isolate the Confederate states. Third, wait. If the North did these things, Scott maintained, it "will thus cut off the luxuries to which the people are accustomed; and when they feel the pressure, not having been exasperated by attacks made on them within their respective States, the Union spirit will assert itself; those who are on the fence will descend on the Union side, and I will guarantee that in one year from this time all difficulties will be settled." If, on the other hand, Federal armies invaded the South at any point, "I will guarantee that at the end of a year you will be further from a settlement than you are now." The press, likening the strategy to the coilings of a giant constricting snake, soon dubbed Scott's proposal the "Anaconda Plan."

Some Cabinet members agreed with Scott, but most believed his plan would backfire. The longer the Confederate government functioned, the more legitimacy it would acquire in the minds of the Southern people. For this reason an immediate offensive against Richmond, the capital of that government, seemed imperative. Lincoln concurred with this second view and in late June gave orders that the Union forces assembling around Washington must advance against Richmond. The commander of these troops, Brigadier General Irvin McDowell, objected that his men were as yet too unseasoned for such an operation. Lincoln refused to budge. "You are green, it is true," he said. "But they [the Confederates] are green also. You are all green alike."

On July 16, 1861, McDowell left Washington with about 35,000 men. Twenty-five miles to the southwest lay a smaller Confederate army of

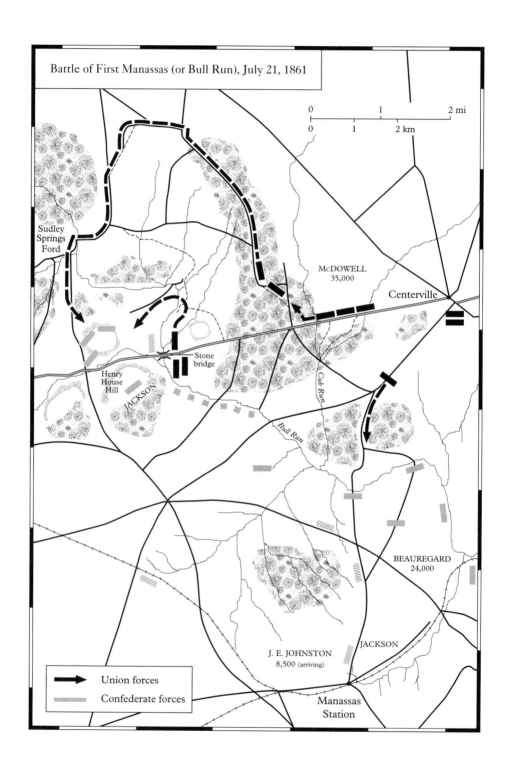

Battle of First Manassas (or Bull Run), July 21, 1861

Sudley
Springs
Ford

McDOWELL
35,000

Centerville

Stone
bridge

Henry
House
Hill

JACKSON

Cub Run

Bull Run

BEAUREGARD
24,000

JACKSON

J. E. JOHNSTON
8,500 (arriving)

Manassas
Station

Union forces
Confederate forces

25,000 men—led by General P. G. T. Beauregard, the victor of Fort Sumter. Beauregard had deployed his brigades along a lengthy stretch of a bramble-choked stream called Bull Run. From this position Beauregard's army held the railroad town of Manassas Junction and blocked the direct overland approach to Richmond.

McDowell outnumbered Beauregard by a considerable margin, and if the Confederates at Manassas had fought unaided he might have won a considerable victory. But fifty miles to the west, 13,000 Rebels under General Joseph E. Johnston guarded the lower Shenandoah Valley. Opposing them was a somewhat larger Union force under an elderly militia general named Robert Patterson. Patterson's mission was to prevent Johnston from reinforcing Beauregard once McDowell advanced; however, he botched the assignment. Leaving a thin screen of cavalry to deceive Patterson, Johnston loaded most of his troops on railcars and sent them rolling down the Manassas Gap Railroad. They reached the Bull Run position on the afternoon of July 21, just as McDowell was pressing home a skillfully prepared attack upon Beauregard's beleaguered men. These reinforcements (coupled with a tenacious defense by Confederate Brigadier General Thomas J. Jackson, who earned the nickname "Stonewall" for his role in the battle) turned the tide against the Federals. Then, just as McDowell had feared, the inexperience of the Union troops transformed a reversal into a rout. The Northerners streamed back toward Washington in a disheveled, uncontrollable mass. It might just as easily have happened to the equally inexperienced Confederates. But it did not, and the Battle of Bull Run became a symbol of Southern prowess and Northern humiliation.

The Union lost about 625 killed in this first major engagement, along with 950 wounded and over 1,200 captured; Confederate casualties numbered 400 killed and about 1,600 wounded. By itself, the battle decided nothing. But in the South it created a sense of dangerous overconfidence, while Northerners regarded it as a stinging summons to greater efforts. From a purely military standpoint its most interesting aspect was the Confederates' use of the railroad to reinforce the threatened Bull Run sector. Without the railroad, Johnston's troops would have reached the battlefield too exhausted for action—if indeed they would have arrived at all.

Cracking the Confederate Frontier

Railroads played a significant role in the struggle for the borderland. The Union thrust into western Virginia was dictated, to a considerable degree, by the need to control the Baltimore & Ohio Railroad, one of the main east-west trunk lines. The Union offensive in Missouri also followed the railroad as far as possible. Meanwhile, along the coast and in the trans-Appalachian west, the Union began to exploit the nineteenth century's other great agent of mechanized power: the steamship. In the months that followed the Bull Run defeat, the Union's edge in sea and riverine power helped it recover from this initial setback. Federal warships began the long, slow process of strangling the South's commerce by blockading its ports, and using Union troops to secure a number of enclaves along the Confederate coast. And in the Mississippi River valley, Union gunboats and transports played a major role in the North's first decisive victories during the winter of 1862.

The Coast, 1861–1862

The seceded states had nearly 3,000 miles of coastline. In part this formed a Confederate asset, because it offered nearly eighty points where Southern blockade runners could find safe harbor. But the long coastline was also a major liability, because it gave Union forces wide opportunity to exploit the North's command of the sea. Defending the long, vulnerable sea frontier diverted many thousands of Confederate troops from duty with the field armies. Even so, Union troops generally had little trouble seizing whatever coastal point they chose. From a Southern perspective, the situation was depressingly like that of the colonists during the American Revolution. The revolutionary general Charles Lee once complained that he felt "like a dog in a dancing school" when confronted by superior British sea mobility. A number of Confederate generals grew familiar with the same sensation.

The first Union beachheads were established primarily as coaling

Union landing at Hatteras Inlet, August 1861. The Union had a formidable edge over the Confederacy in sea power, and troops transported by the U.S. Navy established numerous enclaves along the Southern coast during the course of the Civil War. The enclaves supported the Union blockade and provided springboards for advances inland.

stations for blockaders. In August 1861 a Northern detachment occupied Hatteras Inlet, North Carolina; three months later a larger force seized the magnificent harbor at Port Royal, South Carolina. By March 1862 additional troops had occupied much of eastern North Carolina. Once established, these enclaves provided bases from which Union troops could raid inland. Perhaps as importantly, they acted like magnets for hundreds of slaves who escaped their masters and took refuge within Union lines.

Many of these initial amphibious operations pitted Union warships against the casemated forts that had formed America's principal defensive network since the republic's early years. Conventional wisdom held that in a slugging match between ships and forts, the forts would inevitably prevail, but events challenged this old notion. Armed with the new Columbiad and Dahlgren shell-firing guns, Union warships routinely reduced forts within a few hours. Steam power also made it possible for warships to navigate with greater precision in shallow coastal waters, so that they could perform feats that might have proved fatal for older sailing craft.

The greatest single victory for Union sea power occurred in April 1862, when a Federal fleet engaged the two forts that guarded the Mississippi River below New Orleans. Assisted by a flotilla of mortar boats that rained heavy shells into the forts, the fleet—led by Flag Officer David G. Farragut—managed to steam past the forts and on to nearly defenseless New Orleans. On April 25, Union troops hoisted the Stars and Stripes above the port's customs house. The Confederacy's largest city was gone. Just as bad, Union warships now had access to a long stretch of the lower Mississippi River.

The Emergence of Grant

As the Federal navy prepared to attack New Orleans, a joint force of Northern ground troops and gunboats penetrated the Confederacy's long, vulnerable frontier along the Tennessee-Kentucky border. In the fall of 1861 the rebel general Albert Sidney Johnston—widely considered the South's ablest commander—had constructed a defensive cordon that ran from Columbus, Kentucky, on the Mississippi River to Cumberland Gap in the Appalachian Mountains. Just south of the Tennessee-Kentucky border his troops had also built two major works—Forts Henry and Donelson—to bar Federal navigation on the Tennessee and Cumberland rivers, respectively.

But Johnston had only 43,000 men to hold this 300-mile line. The Federals confronted Johnston with more than twice that many troops, but three factors combined to reduce this numerical edge. First, a significant portion of Union strength had to protect lines of communication once Federal offensive operations began. Second, their massive logistical needs compelled Union armies to move only where railroad or river transportation was available. That, in turn, limited the Federals to just four avenues of approach to the south: down the Mississippi River against Columbus; up the Tennessee River to Fort Henry; up the Cumberland River to Fort Donelson; or along the Louisville & Nashville Railroad to Bowling Green in

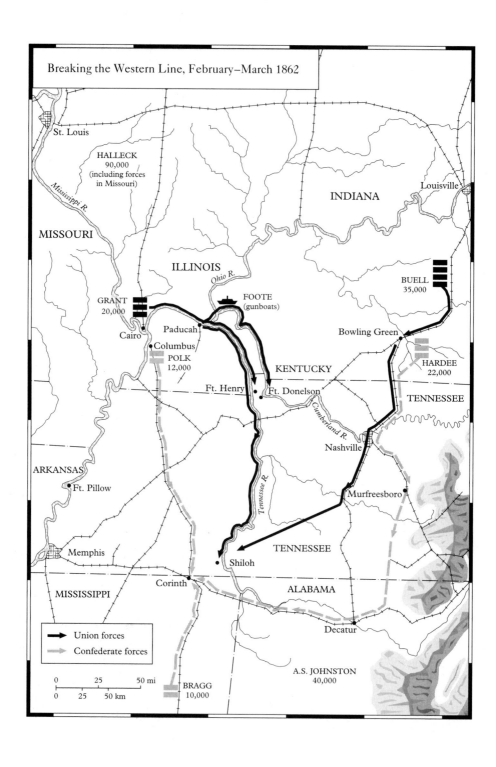

Breaking the Western Line, February–March 1862

St. Louis

HALLECK
90,000
(including forces
in Missouri)

INDIANA

Louisville

Mississippi R.

MISSOURI

ILLINOIS

Ohio R.

BUELL
35,000

GRANT
20,000

FOOTE
(gunboats)

Cairo

Paducah

Bowling Green

Columbus
POLK
12,000

KENTUCKY

HARDEE
22,000

Ft. Henry

Ft. Donelson

TENNESSEE

Cumberland R.

Nashville

ARKANSAS

Ft. Pillow

Tennessee R.

Murfreesboro

Memphis

TENNESSEE

Shiloh

Corinth

ALABAMA

MISSISSIPPI

Decatur

A.S. JOHNSTON
40,000

➤ Union forces
➤ Confederate forces

0	25	50 mi
0	25	50 km

BRAGG
10,000

south-central Kentucky. Johnston could read a map as well as anyone and had placed most of his forces to block these approaches.

The greatest difficulty affecting the Union high command, however, was of its own making. Whereas Johnston enjoyed complete authority within his theater of operations, the Lincoln administration had divided the same region into two parts: the Department of Missouri, commanded by Major General Henry W. Halleck; and the Department of the Ohio, led by Major General Don Carlos Buell. Their operations could be coordinated only by a third party, Major General George B. McClellan in faraway Washington. Complicating this awkward arrangement were the personalities of the three generals themselves. All were cautious by nature, all displayed great sensitivity about their own administrative domains, and all believed that if the enemy possessed interior lines—an advantage the Confederates actually did possess at the moment—then any attacking force must labor at a forbidding disadvantage. Consequently, this timid, touchy triumvirate dawdled over adopting a plan to crack Johnston's line.

Ultimately this delay was overcome less by any decision on the part of these generals than by the initiative of Brigadier General Ulysses S. Grant, a key Halleck subordinate. The chain of events began early in January 1862, when Grant received orders to take a small force up the Tennessee River and make a diversionary demonstration against Fort Henry. He did so, discovered the fort was much less formidable than previously believed, and urged Halleck to let him attack the fort. As soon as he received Halleck's approval, Grant piled about 15,000 troops aboard transports and

The South's many navigable rivers gave Northern forces excellent access to the Confederate interior, and Union gunboats often cooperated effectively with Union land forces. Sometimes they even accomplished important results on their own, as in their unassisted capture of Fort Henry, Tennessee, in February 1862.

headed up the Tennessee River. A flotilla of gunboats, commanded by Flag Officer Andrew H. Foote, steamed along in support of the expedition. On February 6, Grant landed a few miles below Fort Henry while Foote's gunboats steamed upriver to shell the place. To everyone's surprise, the fort surrendered almost at once. Winter rains had raised the Tennessee to flood stage; most of the fort was under six feet of water. The garrison commander had sent most of his 2,500 men to Fort Donelson, twelve miles east, leaving only a handful of artillerists to confront Foote's naval squadron. After a brief bombardment the Confederates ran up the white flag. The boat crew sent to receive the surrender sailed right through the rebel sally port, and the navy, not Grant, captured Fort Henry.

Things then happened very quickly. With no further fortifications blocking navigation of the Tennessee, Foote's gunboats raided upstream as far south as Muscle Shoals, Alabama. Grant notified Halleck that he planned to attack Fort Donelson at once. Johnston, meanwhile, took the defeat at Fort Henry as a signal that his defensive cordon could not hold much longer. He withdrew part of the garrison at Columbus, abandoned Bowling Green, and sent substantial reinforcements to Fort Donelson.

Reinforcing the fort proved a mistake. On February 13, Grant's army—now increased to about 23,000—invested Donelson. The following day Foote's gunboats attacked and tried to repeat their success at Fort Henry. This time a Confederate fort managed to hold its own. Seriously damaged, the Union flotilla had to retire. Even so, the generals inside Fort Donelson believed Grant would soon surround the place. They elected to break out to the south. The attempt succeeded. But then, incredibly, they ordered everyone to return to the Donelson trenches. After a bizarre council of war in which the two senior commanders abdicated their responsibilities and escaped the fort, the number-three man, Brigadier General Simon Bolivar Buckner, sent a flag of truce to Grant and requested terms of surrender.

Grant's response made him an instantaneous celebrity in the North. "No terms except unconditional and immediate surrender can be accepted. I propose to move immediately upon your works." The terse ultimatum miffed Buckner, who thought it ungenerous, but he had little choice save to accept. The next day approximately 12,500 Confederates lay down their arms. It was the first major Union victory of the war.

With Fort Donelson gone, Federal gunboats could now range up the Cumberland River as well. Nashville, Tennessee's capital city and an important supply center, was abandoned by the Confederates without a fight. Johnston's forces were now in full retreat. Grant's army moved up the Tennessee River to within a few miles of the Mississippi state line. Buell's command, meanwhile, occupied Nashville and advanced cautiously toward a junction with Grant.

Grant's army took up position at a stopping point for Tennessee River steamboats known as Pittsburg Landing. Pittsburg Landing possessed only two significant attributes: it had enough level ground nearby to permit an encampment for 40,000 men; and it was only about twenty miles from the little town of Corinth, Mississippi.

Because of two key railroads intersecting there, Corinth formed the main Federal objective point in the west. North and south ran the Mobile and Ohio line. East and west ran the Memphis and Charleston Railroad—a major trunk line and, in effect, the Confederacy's backbone. Union military and political leaders widely believed that if the Union could occupy two points in the South the rebellion would collapse. One of them was Richmond. Corinth was the other.

General Albert Sidney Johnston also concentrated the Confederate forces that had recently abandoned the Kentucky-Tennessee line in the little Mississippi rail town. In addition, President Jefferson Davis saw to it that Johnston got reinforcements from all over the South, so that by the end of March about 40,000 troops had collected around Corinth. On April 3, Johnston placed the entire force on the road to Pittsburg Landing.

Johnston understood that in numerical terms his army was barely equivalent to Grant's. He knew as well that most of his troops had never been in combat and that many of them were armed only with shotguns and old flintlock muskets. But he also recognized that he had only one chance to redress Confederate fortunes in the west. If he could hit Grant's army at once he might achieve surprise, press it back against the Tennsssee River, and destroy it. If he waited more than a few days, Buell's troops would join those of Grant, the numerical odds would become forbidding, and there would be little choice but to concede western and middle Tennessee to the Federals for good.

The roads were bad and the troops unseasoned. It required two full days to negotiate the twenty miles from Corinth to the Union encampment, and along the way the raw Southern troops made so much noise it seemed impossible the Federals could remain unaware of the impending attack. P. G. T. Beauregard, the hero of Manassas and now Johnston's second-in-command, urged that the offensive be abandoned. Johnston would have none of it. "I would fight them if they were a million," he reportedly said, and on the evening of April 5 he deployed his troops for battle.

Shiloh

The terrain around Pittsburg Landing was typical of many Civil War battle-fields. The ground was heavily wooded, cut by ravines, and choked with undergrowth. Two sluggish little creeks enveloped the Union encampment and flowed indolently into the Tennessee River. The roads in the area—hardly more than forest tracks—connected a few widely separated farm lots. Bordering the main road from the landing to Corinth was a little wooden church known as Shiloh Meeting House.

Amazingly the Federals had almost no inkling of the impending Confederate attack. A few Union officers suspected something was afoot, but when they approached the senior general in the area—a grizzled redhead named William Tecumseh Sherman—their fears were brusquely dismissed. Convinced the Confederates remained demoralized after their recent defeats, Sherman refused to entertain even the idea that they might launch a counterstroke. "Take your damn regiment back to Ohio," he snarled at one

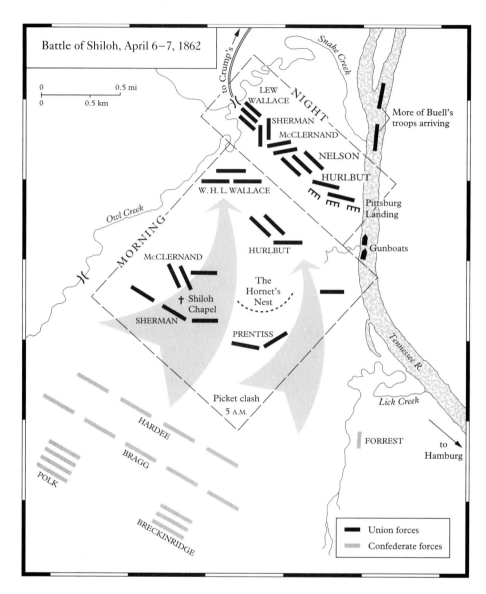

Battle of Shiloh, April 6–7, 1862

0   0.5 mi
0   0.5 km

to Crump's

Snake Creek

LEW WALLACE
NIGHT
SHERMAN
McCLERNAND
NELSON
HURLBUT
W. H. L. WALLACE

More of Buell's troops arriving

Owl Creek
MORNING
McCLERNAND
HURLBUT
Pittsburg Landing
Gunboats

The Hornet's Nest

† Shiloh Chapel
SHERMAN
PRENTISS

Tennessee R.

Picket clash
5 A.M.

Lick Creek

HARDEE
BRAGG
POLK

FORREST
to Hamburg

BRECKINRIDGE

Union forces
Confederate forces

nervous colonel. "There is no enemy nearer than Corinth." Grant shared this view of things, and although he visited the encampment on April 5 he felt assured enough to retain his headquarters at Savannah, a town some ten miles downstream. Neither Grant nor Sherman gave orders for the troops to entrench.

Despite some security precautions the Federals were taken largely by surprise on the morning of Sunday, April 6, when Johnston's army came boiling out of the woods. They came in waves, with each of the four Confederate corps piling in one behind the other. Although this unorthodox formation helped the attack get off to a quicker start—it would have required additional hours to deploy the corps in conventional fashion—it soon created severe problems of command and control. The rebel troops crashed through the Federal encampments shortly after dawn, drove the terrified Unionists back toward Pittsburg Landing, and tried to press home their attack. But units from the various corps soon became intermingled, so that by midday the Confederate brigade and division commanders increasingly found themselves trying to lead nothing more than huge armed mobs. Troops who had never seen each other, much less trained together, were forced to carry out Johnston's demanding all-or-nothing offensive.

The Federals were, in some cases, equally disorganized. Thousands—possibly as many as one-fourth of Grant's army—simply ran for the shelter of the steep bluffs that rose from Pittsburg Landing. The rest stayed with their divisions and fought with determination, only to discover time and again that Confederate troops had lapped around their flanks, forcing them to retreat.

Grant reached the battle around 8:30 A.M. The scene that confronted him was ghastly. The thousands of men who had fled the battle now crowded the bluffs at Pittsburg Landing. Beyond them the woodlands around Shiloh Meeting House shook with the concussion of rifle fire and the screams of men. Grant quickly ordered more ammunition brought up and detailed two regiments to round up stragglers. For the rest of the day he rode back and forth along the battle line, pausing now and then to confer with his division commanders. He could see that the battle had degenerated into a huge slugging match, devoid of tactical finesse. For the Federals the important thing seemed just to hold on long enough for reinforcements to arrive.

Near the Union center, Brigadier General Benjamin M. Prentiss's division withdrew to the cover of a narrow road running parallel to the Confederate front. Grant gave Prentiss an emphatic order to hold the position at all costs. The order was obeyed. Prentiss's men drowned every attempt to dislodge them in a hail of gunfire. Before long, with bitter respect, Southerners attacking the position began calling it the "Hornet's Nest."

Meanwhile the remaining Union forces withdrew slowly, grudgingly, against furious but diminishing thrusts by the rebel army. Exactly as instructed, Prentiss held on grimly to the Hornet's Nest. Only at 5:30 P.M., with the position entirely surrounded, did he reluctantly surrender his men. His stand made it possible for Grant's chief artillerist to plant fifty cannon a quarter-mile from the landing and end the threat of the Confederates pushing on to the river. Sundown brought an end to the day's fighting. During the night, while rainstorms lashed the battlefield and surgeons worked feverishly in improvised hospitals, Wallace's and Buell's forces finally arrived. Numbering about 28,000 men, they more than offset Union losses during the day.

Despite the arrival of reinforcements, most of Grant's officers were extremely discouraged. Many of them, including Sherman, believed retreat might be the best course. During the day, Sherman had fought his division with coolness and determination, but he still believed the army had lost this battle and late that night he sought out Grant to tell him so. He found his commander standing beneath a tree in a downpour, rain dripping from his hat, a cigar smoldering between his teeth. Something in Grant's demeanor made Sherman decide not to discuss retreat. Instead he said simply, "Well,

When Ulysses S. Grant won the Union's first major victory at Fort Donelson in February 1862, his capture of 12,000 Confederates made him a hero in the North. But two months later, criticism of his conduct at Shiloh discouraged him so much that he briefly considered resigning.

Grant, we've had the devil's own day, haven't we?" "Yes," Grant agreed, then added: "Lick 'em in the morning, though." Ultimately his stubborn strength made the difference between victory and defeat at Shiloh.

The following day events went as Grant predicted—the Federals "licked" the Confederates. The Southerners, like their Northern counterparts, were utterly exhausted by Sunday's battle. They had gotten badly disorganized and suffered huge numbers of stragglers. They had even lost their commanding general: the previous afternoon a bullet had clipped one of Sidney Johnston's arteries, causing him to bleed to death within minutes. Worst of all, the Confederates had no fresh units to feed into the struggle. Although they fought grimly throughout Monday, April 7, the strongly reinforced Union army ground them down. At sunset, the Rebels began a sullen retreat to Corinth.

The Battle of Shiloh horrified both North and South. In two days' fighting the Confederate army lost 10,699 men killed, wounded, or missing; Union casualties totaled 13,047. The North American continent had never endured anything like it. Shiloh's cost in human lives far exceeded that of any engagement in previous American experience. Losses were five times those of Bull Run. The battle virtually doubled the year-old war's casualty figures. Northerners who considered this shattering toll found it impossible to regard the battle as a Union victory. It seemed more like an unmitigated disaster, and many who had praised Grant a few weeks earlier now clamored for his removal.

Yet Shiloh *was* a Union victory, and a big one, for it confirmed the previous Federal successes at Forts Henry and Donelson. The Confederacy had lost much of western and middle Tennessee, and the Union's victory at Shiloh ensured that the Rebels would not regain this region. Two additional victories soon consolidated the Union's success. On April 7 a force of 30,000 men under Brigadier General John Pope captured Island No. 10, a

Confederate fortress blocking navigation of the Mississippi River near the Kentucky-Tennessee line. And on June 5 a Union flotilla seized Memphis after a brief but savage naval battle.

✳   ✳   ✳   ✳

The first year of the Civil War saw the conflict assume very wide dimensions that readily eclipsed any previous war on American soil. Both North and South had created and fielded large armies, led by a combination of professional and amateur officers and manned by enthusiastic though as yet unseasoned volunteers. Both sides were performing at a level much better than American forces during the War of 1812, testimony to the leadership exerted at the top by West Point graduates. The Union side in particular had managed some very creditable feats of army-navy cooperation.

By the end of spring 1862, Federal and Confederate armies had also fought a number of battles that demonstrated that the war would be much bloodier than previous American struggles. Part of this heightened lethality owed to the impact of the rifled musket, but most of it was due to the increased size of the rival armies and the earnestness with which both sides fought. The casualty figures were not exceptional by European standards— Shiloh was no worse than some of the battles fought by Frederick the Great. They seemed worse, perhaps, because the men who were killed and wounded were much more representative of their parent societies than professional European forces were of theirs.

The Northern cause had made excellent progress during the war's first year. Despite a serious early reverse at Bull Run, Union troops had managed to retain control of the crucial border states, to accquire a number of enclaves along the Southern coastline, and to impose a naval blockade of the Confederacy. Most promisingly, they had also broken the Confederate defensive cordon in the western theater. Taken together, these victories suggested that it might well be possible to destroy the rebellion and restore the Union without having to address the politically explosive slavery issue or to destroy large amounts of Southern property.

All eyes now turned to McClellan's great campaign against Richmond. The first six months of 1862 had brought a string of victories: Forts Henry and Donelson, the seizure of the North Carolina coast, the battles of Pea Ridge and Shiloh, the capture of New Orleans, Island No. 10, and Memphis. The Confederacy had been bludgeoned along its entire frontier. Everyone now expected the Army of the Potomac to deliver the death blow.

SUGGESTED READINGS

Catton, Bruce. *The Coming Fury.* (Garden City, N.Y.: Doubleday, 1961).

———. *Terrible Swift Sword.* (Garden City, N.Y.: Doubleday, 1964).

Connelly, Thomas L. *Army of the Heartland: The Army of Tennessee, 1861–1862* (Baton Rouge: Louisiana State University Press, 1967).

Connelly, Thomas L., and Archer Jones. *The Politics of Command: Factions and Ideas in Confederate Strategy* (Baton Rouge: Louisiana State University Press, 1973).

Cooling, Benjamin F. *Forts Henry and Donelson: The Key to the Confederate Heartland* (Knoxville: University of Tennessee Press, 1987).

Davis, William C. *Battle at Bull Run* (Garden City, N.Y.: Doubleday, 1977).

Hattaway, Herman, and Archer Jones. *How the North Won: A Military History of the Civil War* (Urbana: University of Illinois Press, 1983).

Linderman, Gerald F. *Embattled Courage: The Experience of Combat in the American Civil War* (New York: Free Press, 1987).

McDonough, James Lee. *Shiloh: In Hell Before Night* (Knoxville: University of Tennessee Press, 1977).

McPherson, James M. *Battle Cry of Freedom: The Civil War Era* (New York: Oxford University Press, 1988).

Nevins, Allan, *The War for the Union*, 4 vols. (New York: Charles Scribner's Sons, 1959–1971).

Potter, David M. *The Impending Crisis, 1848–1861* (New York: Harper, 1976).

Williams, Kenneth P. *Lincoln Finds a General*, 5 vols. (New York: Macmillan, 1949–1956).

Williams, T. Harry. *Lincoln and His Generals* (New York: Alfred A. Knopf, 1952).

Woodworth, Steven E. *Jefferson Davis and His Generals: The Failure of Confederate Command in the West* (Lawrence: University Press of Kansas, 1990).

12

THE CIVIL WAR, 1862:
ENDING THE LIMITED WAR

"A Single Grand Campaign"

The Failure of Limited War

Confederate Counterstrokes

Autumn Stalemate

By early June 1862 the war seemed all but over. The border states, including western Virginia, were solidly in Union hands. Federal units controlled the lower Mississippi River from the delta to New Orleans and also held the middle reaches of the river as far south as Memphis. Halleck's armies had captured western Tennessee, controlled much of middle Tennessee, and pressed into northern Alabama. Most importantly they had seized the strategic railroad junction at Corinth, Mississippi. This last victory had been virtually bloodless. Halleck's huge force—numbering well over 100,000 men—had crept toward the rail town barely a mile per day. At night it dug extensive entrenchments; Halleck wanted no repetition of the damaging surprise attack at Shiloh. By the end of May, Beauregard, who now commanded Sidney Johnston's army, prudently abandoned Corinth and slipped away to Tupelo, some eighty miles south. Some Northerners regretted the Confederate escape but most simply smiled at this latest Yankee triumph.

Then, abruptly, the Union dream of victory was shattered. McClellan's great offensive against Richmond collapsed. Not only did the rebel capital elude capture, but the Confederate army in the east then began a series of aggressive counterstrokes that carried the war, in a matter of weeks, from the shores of the James River to the banks of the Potomac. In the western theater other Confederate armies carried out similar offensives of their own. With sickening swiftness, many in the North realized that the war would not be short or easy and that its conduct had to change. Until then the Lincoln administration had waged a limited war. Its armies had aimed their blows exclusively against rebel military units and had tried, as far as possible, to preserve the constitutional rights of Southern civilians—including the right to hold slaves. Now many in the North clamored that this "kid glove" warfare, as it was derisively called, must end. The Lincoln administration agreed. The reversals of summer 1862 led directly to the collapse of limited war and the advent of new, more severe measures against the South.

Another development that marked this period was the deployment of the *corps d'armée,* a military organization that had not existed at all in previous American wars. Although nominally begun during the early months of 1862—McClellan adopted the corps system in March 1862 and then Sidney Johnston used a similar arrangement at Shiloh—the corps organization was at first mainly an administrative expedient. Not until midsummer did the corps emerge as an operational unit. From then on, the Union and Confederate armies utilized the corps system not only to control large masses of men more effectively but also to maneuver against one another's flank and rear and, when necessary, to fight independently. Civil War armies began to march and fight in the classic Napoleonic style.

"A Single Grand Campaign"

The greatest hope for an early Union victory reposed in the person of Major General George B. McClellan. Just thirty-four years old when the war broke out, McClellan had quickly risen to high command. Although he had left the army in 1856 to become a railroad executive, his West Point training brought him at once to the attention of Ohio's governor, who placed him in charge of the state's volunteer forces. In the early summer of 1861 he had won a series of minor victories in western Virginia that brought him considerable laurels. Newspapers began calling him "the Napoleon of the present war." When, after the debacle at Bull Run, Lincoln looked about for a commander to replace McDowell, he speedily settled on McClellan.

Arriving in Washington on July 27, McClellan was appalled by the confused condition of McDowell's battered troops. But he quickly rebuilt the force around Washington, which he soon dubbed the Army of the Potomac. In early August, at Lincoln's request, he also sent the president a memorandum detailing his conceptions for winning the war. McClellan wanted most Union strength concentrated for a single, overwhelming thrust against Richmond. To achieve this objective the young general sought to create a juggernaut of 273,000 men and 600 cannon. McClellan's rationale for his plan was largely political. Like many Northerners, he believed the common people of the South were lukewarm in their support for the Confederate government. In McClellan's view, only a display of overwhelming military force, coupled with a lenient policy toward Southern civilians, could create the conditions for a restoration of the Union. Implicit in his plan was the conviction that a lengthy struggle would embitter both North and South and make reunion more difficult.

Called the "Young Napoleon" by an admiring public, George B. McClellan was a talented organizer, a charismatic leader, and a good strategic planner, but he was ultimately hamstrung by frictions with the Lincoln administration and an overcaution verging on timidity.

The vigorous style of McClellan's memorandum promised action, but its substance suggested delay. The young commander did not want to go off half-cocked. He needed time to amass and train the huge army he contemplated, and indeed it is difficult to see how McClellan could have begun this great offensive much before the spring of 1862. Unfortunately, from the outset he never made this clear to either the public or his political superiors. Instead he let them believe that he might commence major offensive actions during the autumn of 1861, and when no sign of this offensive materialized, his near-unanimous bipartisan support began to fade. Democrats and conservative Republicans continued to back McClellan, but the radical wing of the Republican party turned sharply against him.

It did not help that McClellan detested Lincoln, whom he termed "the original Gorilla." Lincoln nevertheless displayed amazing patience with McClellan and in November 1861 even appointed him general-in-chief. But as the months slid by without action, Lincoln's confidence in McClellan declined. Mutual distrust between the president and his chief commander characterized every phase of the great Richmond offensive when it finally began.

Genesis of the Peninsula Campaign

After the Bull Run defeat the strategic situation in Virginia looked like this. McClellan's army held the Union capital and a long stretch of the Potomac River both north and south of the city. The Confederate army, under General Joseph E. Johnston, was concentrated at Centreville, just up the road from the old Bull Run battlefield. The Rebels had also erected batteries that interdicted passage of the lower Potomac River and, in effect, placed Washington under a partial blockade.

By September, McClellan had gathered over 100,000 troops into his Army of the Potomac. Johnston, by contrast, had barely 40,000. Had McClellan been so disposed he might well have advanced directly against the Confederates, but instead he did nothing. McClellan defended his inaction by claiming that Johnston had 150,000 troops, the estimate given to him by Allan Pinkerton, his chief of intelligence. If Johnston really did have 150,000 men, of course, an overland offensive stood little chance of success. Thus McClellan always looked for alternatives. By December he had settled on a scheme to convey most of the Army of the Potomac by sea to Urbanna, a small town on the Rappahannock River about fifty miles northeast of Richmond. This would cut in half the overland distance the army must cover; better yet, it would render the Confederate lines at Centreville untenable, force Johnston's army into precipitate retreat, and possibly create advantageous conditions for a Union attack.

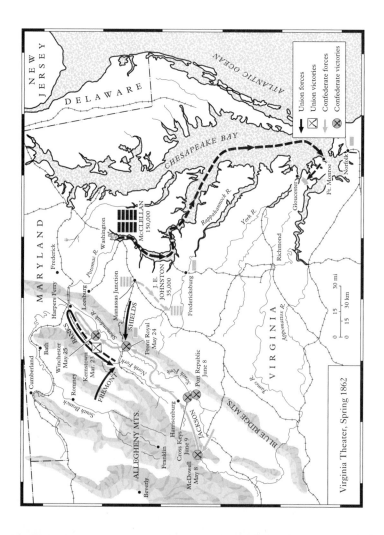

Unfortunately for McClellan, a Confederate redeployment soon rendered his original plan all but impossible. Johnston had long regarded his Centreville position as too exposed. On March 8–9, 1862, the rebel army therefore fell back to a new position behind the Rappahannock in central Virginia. With Johnston's army now much closer to Urbanna and Richmond, the strategic rationale for the Urbanna scheme largely disappeared. Accordingly, McClellan switched to an alternate plan. The Army of the Potomac would still move against Richmond by sea, but instead of landing at Urbanna it would disembark at Fort Monroe. This Union-held outpost lay at the tip of a long peninsula formed by the York and James rivers. It was not so close to Richmond as Urbanna—seventy-five miles as opposed to fifty—and the route to the Confederate capital was blocked by a small force stationed at Yorktown, but it still seemed preferable to an overland advance.

Before beginning the great campaign, McClellan took his army on a brief shakedown march to the abandoned Confederate position at Centreville. This served only to exacerbate his already considerable political difficulties, for it soon became obvious that the lines could not possibly have held 150,000 men. Lincoln's doubts about McClellan increased, and on March 12 the president removed him as general-in-chief. Lincoln explained the change by saying that once McClellan took the field he would be fully occupied with command of the Army of the Potomac. The young commander, however, regarded it as an implied rebuke, as it almost certainly was. McClellan began his great campaign under a cloud.

From Yorktown to Seven Pines

The transfer of McClellan's army to Fort Monroe began on March 17. Since the U.S. government possessed nowhere near enough vessels for so great a task, it chartered every available steamer from Maryland to Maine: 113 in all, as well as an additional 276 smaller vessels. Within three weeks 121,500 men, 14,492 animals, 1,224 wagons, and over 200 cannon had reached the tip of the Virginia peninsula. It was—as one astonished British observer remarked—"the stride of a giant" and it showed the extent of the North's advantage in sea power.

The advance inland began on April 4. But just twenty-four hours later it ceased abruptly when Union troops encountered a belt of Confederate fortifications extending across the peninsula from Yorktown to the James River. The existence of this line, while not altogether unexpected, convinced McClellan that a formal siege would be necessary for its reduction. His decision further strained his already poor relationship with the Lincoln administration. Relations became even worse when the administration discovered that McClellan had left nowhere near enough troops to defend Washington during the Army of the Potomac's absence. As a result it withheld McClellan's I Corps—some 40,000 men—and retained it in northern Virginia.

McClellan, furious, now found that he must "crush the rebellion at a single blow" with a significantly reduced force. Nevertheless, although he refused to believe it, he handily outnumbered the Confederates facing him, even after most of Johnston's army abandoned the Rappahannock line and came down to Yorktown. Well aware of his numerical disadvantage, Johnston remarked, "Nobody but McClellan would have hesitated to attack."

For nearly a month, Federal engineers and artillerists sweated to emplace the mammoth siege guns that would blast the Yorktown defenders into oblivion. Johnston, however, did not wait to be blasted. On May 1 he notified Richmond authorities that the Yorktown position was untenable, that he intended to withdraw, and that all possible reinforcements should be concentrated near the Confederate capital. Two nights later his army left Yorktown.

The retreat had severe strategic costs. It opened the York and James rivers to Federal gunboats, led to the abandonment of Norfolk and its navy yard, and forced the scuttling of the daunting Confederate ironclad warship *Virginia*. For a brief time Confederate authorities even contemplated the evacuation of Richmond, but Jefferson Davis's military advisor, General Robert E. Lee, made a passionate plea for the capital's continued defense.

Fortunately for the South, at that point Confederate defenses began to stiffen. On May 15 several artillery batteries at Drewry's Bluff, below Richmond, rebuffed the Federal navy's lunge up the James River. In the Shenandoah Valley, troops under Major General Thomas J. "Stonewall" Jackson, a dour ex-professor of the Virginia Military Institute, won a series of astonishing small victories over much larger Union forces. And although by the end of May McClellan's massive army had come to within seven miles of Richmond, it advanced gingerly. Moreover, it was clear that McClellan, instead of launching an immediate attack, planned to conduct a siege of Richmond.

McClellan had placed his main supply base at White House Landing on the Pamunkey River. A short rail line from Richmond had its terminus there, which offered a reliable way to transport his heavy siege guns to the front. But his choice of base meant that his army had to straddle the Chickahominy River northeast of Richmond. Heavy spring rains rendered the stream almost impassable, thus dividing the Army of the Potomac. On May 31, Johnston took advantage of this and tried to crush the southern wing of McClellan's army in the Battle of Seven Pines. But nothing went right. Johnston's plans were vague and his management of the battle was terrible. The Confederates lost 6,000 troops; the Union, about 5,000. The most important result of the two-day battle was that on June 1 Johnston was severely wounded. To succeed him, Davis appointed Robert E. Lee.

In June 1862, Lee was still comparatively unknown in the South, and what Southerners did know of him they did not like. Although a well-respected figure in the prewar U.S. Army and one of the highest ranking officers to side with the Confederacy, Lee's wartime career to date had been disappointing. In the autumn of 1861 he had conducted a brief, ineffectual campaign in the western Virginia mountains that earned him the derisive nickname "Granny" Lee. In March 1862, President Davis had appointed him his military advisor, a seemingly imposing assignment but one with little formal authority. Small wonder that many Southerners were dismayed to find Lee in charge of Richmond's defense.

Jackson in the Valley

What few knew, however, was that Lee had pronounced ideas about aggressive action. Indeed he had already tried them out. His partner in this venture was "Stonewall" Jackson. The arena in which they tried out their offensive scheme was the Shenandoah Valley. One of the most productive agricultural regions in North America, the Valley also had qualities that arrested the strategist's eye. Its farms produced much of the Confederacy's grain and many of its horses. The Baltimore & Ohio Railroad ran across its northern reaches; thus any Confederate force in full control of the valley also controlled the Union's single most important east-west communications link. And the sheltering mountains on either side made the Valley a natural avenue of invasion into Maryland and Pennsylvania. For these reasons both Federals and Confederates sought to possess the region.

In the fall of 1861 the defense of the Valley became Jackson's responsibility. With only 4,500 men under his command, Jackson's position was precarious from the outset, and in early March 1862, some 38,000 Federals under Major General Nathaniel Banks entered the northern part of the Valley and drove him away from Winchester, the region's largest town. After a short pursuit, Banks left a single division of 9,000 men at Winchester and withdrew the rest back toward Washington. On March 23, hoping to defeat the lone division at Winchester, Jackson attacked.

He failed, but the bold Confederate attack convinced his opponent that Jackson had either received reinforcements or expected them shortly. As a result, Banks returned to the Valley with a second division of 9,000 men. Then Lincoln detached a 10,000-man division from the Army of the Potomac and ordered it to join Major General John C. Frémont's forces in western Virginia, on the theory that if Jackson were strong enough to attack at Winchester he might threaten Frémont as well. Nor was this all. The fact that Banks was no longer available to cover Washington, D.C., during McClellan's germinating peninsula campaign helped spur Lincoln to withdraw McDowell's 40,000-man corps from McClellan's control (as mentioned earlier) and retain it in northern Virginia. Jackson's battlefield defeat thus turned into strategic success; it tied up the movements of nearly 60,000 Federal troops.

It also set the stage for Lee's first major attempt at an offensive-defensive strategy. By mid-April the Confederates in Virginia faced four main threats, of which McClellan was merely the largest. Banks's corps was advancing and had reached Harrisonburg in the central Valley; McDowell's corps in northern Virginia could march south at any time. Frémont's forces in western Virginia also seemed active, and McClellan of course menaced Richmond itself. In every instance the Federals far outnumbered the rebel forces opposing them. A passive defense could never hope to resist so many pressures.

Lee believed the only solution was to combine against one of the Northern forces, eliminate it, and thus dislocate the remaining Union forces. On April 21 he wrote to Jackson suggesting that Jackson should link up with a division led by Major General Richard S. Ewell. He would then hurl his augmented force against Banks's isolated corps. Jackson, however, replied that even with Ewell's help, he would still need 5,000 more troops to attack with any chance of success. When Lee could not furnish the extra 5,000, Jackson proposed a modified plan. Instead of striking Banks, he would unite with 2,800 troops under Confederate Major General Edward Johnson and hit Frémont's advance guard. Then, using both Ewell and Johnson, he would attack Banks. Lee approved the plan and on May 8, Jackson defeated Frémont at the Battle of McDowell, Virginia.

Jackson's victory inaugurated one of the classic campaigns of military history. Reinforced to about 10,000 men after the Battle of McDowell, Jackson united with Ewell—thereby adding another 7,000 troops to his command—and lunged northward toward Banks. Thoroughly misleading the Union commander, Jackson appeared in front of Banks, then suddenly swung around the Union flank, using cavalry to screen his movement. On May 23 he captured a small Union garrison at Front Royal; Banks now frantically withdrew down the Valley before Jackson could cut off his retreat. At

When a series of major defeats shook the Confederacy in early 1862, the exploits of Major General Thomas J. "Stonewall" Jackson helped bolster Southern morale. His campaign in the Shenandoah Valley is still considered a military masterpiece.

Winchester he attempted to make a stand, but in a battle on May 25 the Confederates had little trouble dislodging the Federals and sending them into headlong retreat. Banks did not stop retreating until he crossed the Potomac the next day, having lost 35 percent of his force.

In Washington, Lincoln and his advisors viewed the situation with alarm, mingled with the shrewd awareness that an opportunity now existed to trap Jackson's entire force. A march of forty miles would place Frémont's 15,000 men at Harrisonburg, eighty miles in Jackson's rear. Lincoln instructed Frémont to make this march. Similarly he ordered McDowell at Fredericksburg to detach 20,000 men and seize Front Royal, a move that would imperil Jackson's line of retreat. The main issue was whether the Union forces could move fast enough to close the trap before Jackson could escape. As Lincoln remarked, it was "a question of legs."

The plan failed. For a variety of reasons, Frémont did not advance into the Valley by the most direct route and instead marched northward for a considerable distance, thereby squandering the best chance to trap Jackson. The Confederate commander managed to elude both Frémont and McDowell. Then he chose a position at Port Republic, a small village where two small streams met to form the south branch of the Shenandoah River.

Spring rains had swollen these streams to the point where they could be crossed only at bridges or rare fords; by controlling the crossings at Port Republic, Jackson could concentrate against either Frémont or McDowell while denying his opponents the opportunity to join forces. Then, in two sharp fights on June 8–9, he bested both rivals. A highly religious man, Jackson exulted to Ewell at the close of the second battle, "General, he who does not see the hand of God in this is blind, sir, blind!"

Whether Ewell viewed it that way is open to question, but military analysts have never had trouble discerning in Jackson's Valley campaign the hand of a master campaign strategist. With an army less than half the size of the forces opposed to him, he had managed to defeat the enemy on five major occasions, hold on to the upper third of the Shenandoah Valley, and above all, force the diversion of thousands of Union troops who might otherwise have joined McClellan's army on the peninsula. His success in the Valley played a crucial role in saving Richmond.

The Failure of Limited War

The modest size of his force notwithstanding, Jackson had already advocated an invasion of the North. He insisted that with 40,000 troops he could do it, and although Lee believed such a venture must await the relief of Richmond, he viewed the idea with interest. Lee reinforced Jackson in hopes that Stonewall might crush the remaining Federals in the Valley. But when no Union forces offered themselves for immediate crushing, Lee changed plans and ordered Jackson to bring most of his troops to Richmond. All possible Confederate forces must be concentrated to defend the capital.

In Lee's mind such a defense could not be passive; a passive defense would allow McClellan the maximum benefit of the powerful artillery in his siege train. Therefore, despite numerical inferiority, the Confederates would have to attack. He knew of Napoleon's successful exploits against larger armies and had witnessed Winfield Scott's triumph over a larger Mexican army. Numbers, in Lee's opinion, were important, but not all-important. Initiative, concentration of force at a decisive point, surprise, and determination counted for at least as much. Good intelligence was also vital. Accordingly, on June 11 he summoned to his headquarters Brigadier General Jeb Stuart, the army's twenty-nine-year-old chief of cavalry. Stuart took 1,200 troopers on a two-day reconnaissance completely around McClellan's army. When he returned he told Lee the Federal right wing was "in the air"—that is, it continued several miles north of the Chickahominy River and then simply ended, anchored to no substantial natural obstacle. Also, McClellan's supplies were still being drawn exclusively from White House Landing on the Pamunkey River. No effort had been made to change the Federal base to a forward point on the James River. Armed with this information, Lee decided to concentrate his army on the exposed Union right flank, break it, then pitch into McClellan's rear and cut his supply line. If successful the Federals would be forced to withdraw the way they had come, back down the peninsula.

The Seven Days

McClellan had five corps east of Richmond—arrayed in a north-south line about five miles east of the city—but only one corps north of the Chickahominy. That force, the V Corps under Brigadier General Fitz John Porter, had the dual mission of screening the Federal base at White House Landing and facilitating a juncture with McDowell's corps should it ever be released by Lincoln from its mission of screening Washington. Lee proposed to use the bulk of his 80,000 available troops to crush Porter and leave only 20,000 to hold the Richmond trenches. It was a daring gamble, but Lee expected McClellan to go on the defensive the moment the Confederate attack opened.

On June 23, 1862, Lee met with his key commanders. Stonewall Jackson was there, having left his troops, then en route to Richmond, and ridden fifty miles to attend the meeting. Lee gave him the vital assignment of turning the right flank of the Union V Corps. Jackson promised to be in position by June 26, and Lee shaped his timetable accordingly. But to everyone's astonishment, Jackson failed to carry out his assignment on time and did not report to headquarters news of his situation or whereabouts. Noon came and went on June 26, and nothing happened. Then at 3 P.M. a division commander, Major General A. P. Hill, decided that the offensive could no longer wait for Jackson. Without asking clearance from Lee, he led his troops straight for the packed cannon of the V Corps. Reluctantly, Lee committed his other divisions to support the charge. Without Jackson to turn the flank, however, his carefully planned offensive degenerated into a brutal frontal assault. Thousands of rebel troops fell to Union rifle and artillery fire

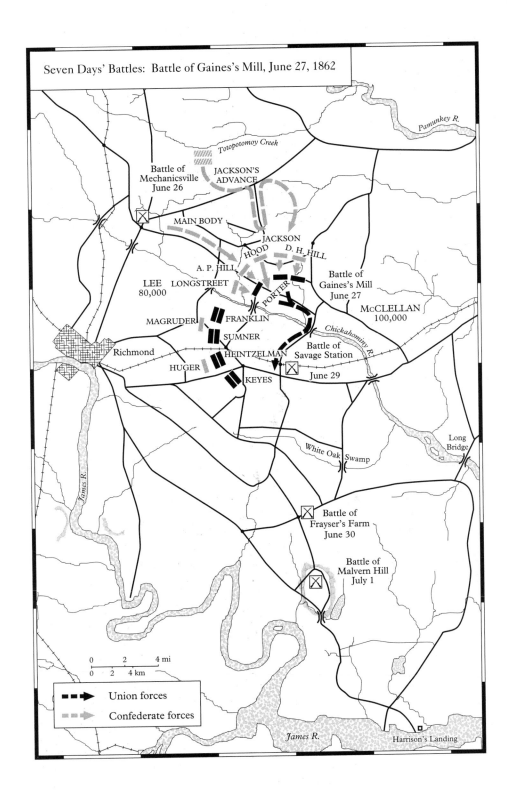

Seven Days' Battles: Battle of Gaines's Mill, June 27, 1862

Pamunkey R.

Totopotomoy Creek

Battle of
Mechanicsville
June 26

JACKSON'S
ADVANCE

MAIN BODY

JACKSON

HOOD   D. H. HILL

A. P. HILL

LEE   LONGSTREET
80,000

Battle of
Gaines's Mill
June 27

PORTER

McCLELLAN
100,000

MAGRUDER   FRANKLIN

SUMNER

Chickahominy R.

Richmond

HEINTZELMAN

Battle of
Savage Station

HUGER

KEYES

June 29

White Oak Swamp

Long
Bridge

James R.

Battle of
Frayser's Farm
June 30

Battle of
Malvern Hill
July 1

0   2   4 mi
0   2   4 km

Union forces

Confederate forces

James R.

Harrison's Landing

without ever piercing the V Corps' formidable positions near Mechanicsville. Worse, the Federals learned of Jackson's belated approach and during the night conducted a skillful withdrawal to even stronger positions at Gaines' Mill, two miles east.

The offensive's second day threatened to be a replay of the first, with much of Lee's force again bludgeoning the Federals in brave but useless charges while Jackson floundered about north of the battlefield. In the afternoon, however, Stonewall finally got his troops into action against the Union right flank, and by dusk the Federals were beaten. Porter successfully withdrew his battered corps south of the Chickahominy. Just as Lee expected, McClellan went over to the defensive. But Lee's own plans never quite worked out. The unfortunate battles at Mechanicsville and Gaines' Mill seemed to set the tone for the entire campaign. Time and again, bad staff work and faulty generalship scuttled spectacular opportunities to maul McClellan's army. Jackson, in strange contrast to his stellar conduct of the Valley campaign, continued to perform poorly—most likely due to the effects of prolonged mental and physical stress.

Still, the victory at Gaines' Mill forced the Federals to abandon their supply base at White House Landing and begin a risky withdrawal south toward a new base along the James River. Lee saw the withdrawal as a chance to demolish McClellan's army completely. But poor intelligence, poor use of artillery, poor tactics and, of course, poor generalship combined to prevent so decisive a result. On June 29 a portion of Lee's army got into a costly but useless fight at Savage Station. The following day saw a botched

The North had good artillery and plenty of it, and when concentrated to deliver massed fire, the results could be devastating. At Malvern Hill on July 1, 1862, Union artillery blasted wave after wave of attacking Confederate infantry. "It was not war," confessed one Southern general, "it was murder."

attempt to envelop the Union army at Frayser's Farm. By July 1, McClellan had nearly made good his withdrawal.

Atop a spacious ridge called Malvern Hill, McClellan deployed much of his field artillery to cover the final stage of his retreat. Swampland on either side of the hill precluded any chance to turn the position, and it appeared much too formidable to be taken by a direct attack. But Lee stubbornly refused to concede McClellan's escape. He ordered a frontal assault. Lines of Confederate soldiers swept forward against the Yankee guns packed along the crest. They were soon shattered as Union artillery tore their ranks to shreds. A Confederate division commander said afterward, "It was not war, it was murder."

But the Seven Days, as the battles between June 26 and July 1 came to be known, resulted in the salvation of Richmond, which was all most Southerners cared about. Lee became a hero. The Army of the Potomac, beaten though not seriously damaged, cowered along the banks of the James at Harrison's Landing. Of the 85,500 Confederates engaged in the battles, 20,141 became casualties, a loss rate of nearly 24 percent. The Federals, by contrast, lost only 15 percent of their own force—15,849 from an army of about 105,000.

A number of historians have since questioned the wisdom of Lee's costly offensive strategy. But the real question is whether he could have saved Richmond in any other way. And the loss of its capital might well have resulted in the Confederacy's political collapse, just as many contemporary observers believed. Even assuming the Confederates were able to relocate their capital and continue the struggle, the loss of Richmond would have opened up the entire eastern Confederacy to further Union attacks. If the South could not successfully defend Virginia, where the gap between sea and mountains was only one hundred miles wide, how could it hope to defend the more open regions farther south?

The End of Conciliation

No sooner did the Army of Northern Virginia dispose of one threat than the Lincoln administration produced another. On June 26, 1862, the Union activated a new "Army of Virginia," composed of three corps under McDowell, Banks, and Frémont, and led by Major General John Pope. Pope came from the war's western theater where he had made a name for himself through the capture of the Mississippi River fortress at Island No. 10. Conceited, pompous, and boastful, he was an easy man to dislike. Soon after assuming command he alienated virtually everyone in his army by issuing a tactless proclamation that seemed a slap in the face to the soldiers who had served in the recent, ill-starred Valley Campaign. The Northern press also derided Pope's broadside.

But Pope soon redeemed himself with a series of draconian orders regarding Virginia civilians. Henceforth, he instructed, the soldiers under his command would live as far as possible off the countryside. They would no longer guard private homes and property. The citizens of occupied territory would be held responsible for guerrilla activity in their midst; the guerrillas themselves would be shot. Persons who refused to take the oath of allegiance would be treated as spies. All in all it seemed clear that Pope intended—as the Northern press put it—to wage war with the kid gloves off.

This sounded a new and increasingly welcome note. Since the beginning of the war most Federal commanders had treated Southern civilians according to the tenets of what was known as the conciliatory policy. This policy assumed that most white Southerners had been hoodwinked into secession by a slaveholding aristocracy, that popular support for the Confederacy was lukewarm at best, and that a program of mild treatment would convince most white Southerners to return to their former allegiance to the United States. As a result, when Union troops first entered Southern territory, they usually promised not to interfere with slavery and to preserve, as far as possible, all constitutional rights. They seldom took food and other supplies from Southern civilians without payment and often furnished guards to protect private homes against intrusion by unruly soldiers.

The Union had no firmer adherent to the conciliatory policy than McClellan. "I am fighting to preserve the Union and uphold its laws," he assured a wealthy Virginia planter, "and for no other purpose." His distaste for the Lincoln administration stemmed, in part, from the conviction that the president was not strong enough to stand up to the pressures for a sterner "war of subjugation" endorsed by the Radical Republicans. When, shortly after the Seven Days' battles, Lincoln came down to Harrison's Landing to visit the Army of the Potomac, McClellan took the occasion to hand the president a letter urging him not to abandon the conciliatory policy. Instead McClellan urged that the government conduct the conflict "upon the highest principles known to Christian Civilization." Private property should be stringently protected and even an "offensive demeanor" by the military toward citizens should receive prompt rebuke. Furthermore, the army should have nothing to do with slavery, "either by supporting or impairing the authority of the master." Lincoln accepted the letter politely. A consummate politician, however, he knew that the time for the limited struggle envisioned by McClellan had run out.

The Drive Toward Emancipation

The war, in any case, had moved beyond conciliation. The major casualty of the shift was slavery. At the war's outset the Lincoln administration had refused to accept any interference with the "peculiar institution," for fear that it would alienate the border states, embitter white Southerners to greater resistance, and alienate many in the North who were willing to support a war for the Union but who rejected fighting to free the slaves. Yet it was clear not only that slavery lay at the root of the struggle but also that the labor of slaves was sustaining the Confederate economy and even being used to construct military fortifications. It was therefore almost impossible for Union troops to battle the Confederacy without disturbing slavery.

Union retreat from Richmond. McClellan's defeat during the Seven Days' battles destroyed the North's hopes for an early victory, scuttled the conciliatory policy, and helped convince Lincoln that the Union could not win the war without attacking slavery.

Indeed, the very presence of Union troops on Southern soil disrupted the stable order on which slavery rested. From the outset, some slaves escaped to Union lines, hoping to gain their freedom. At first—in accordance with orders from Washington—they were returned, but many Northern troops found this policy utterly distasteful. Then, Union Major General Benjamin F. Butler, a former Democratic congressman from Massachusetts, proposed a novel solution to the problem. When a Confederate officer appeared at his headquarters at Fort Monroe, Virginia, demanding the return of several fugitive slaves, Butler rebuffed him. The slaves in question, he said, had been helping to construct Confederate fortifications; as such, he was justified in holding them as "contraband of war." Butler's use of the term was loose, but his argument made excellent practical sense. In early August 1861 the U.S. Congress codified the general principle in its First Confiscation Act, which declared the forfeiture of any slaves used in direct support of the Confederate war effort. The military necessity of such a policy was obvious.

Less obvious was a proclamation issued by Major General John C. Frémont later that month. Then in command of the Department of Missouri and frustrated by the guerrilla warfare in his midst, Frémont decided to free the slaves living in the southern part of the state. Lincoln promptly overruled him. The order was too sweeping, its military purpose unclear. In May 1862, Lincoln overruled Major General David Hunter when Hunter tried the same thing in South Carolina.

Yet by that point Lincoln himself was beginning to move toward a policy of emancipation. In March 1862 he urged Congress to consider a program of compensated emancipation. Six weeks later he signed into law a bill for the compensated emancipation of slaves in the federally regulated District of Columbia. Subsequent legislation ended slavery in the Federal territories—this time without compensation.

Lincoln eagerly waited for the border states to take up his call for compensated emancipation. Their failure to do so profoundly disappointed him. In the meantime, the Peninsula Campaign collapsed and Congress moved toward a harder line, passing a more stringent Second Confiscation Act in July. Lincoln made one final appeal to the congressmen from the border states. When this too failed, Lincoln made his fateful decision to emancipate the slaves by executive order. "We must free the slaves or be ourselves subdued," he told a cabinet member. The slaves were undeniably an element of strength to the Rebels, "and we must decide whether that element should be with us or against us."

On July 22, 1862, Lincoln met with his cabinet and read them a draft of his preliminary Emancipation Proclamation. Most agreed that it was time to issue such a document. The only objection had to do with timing. Secretary of State Seward worried that, given the Union's recent military setbacks, issuing the proclamation immediately would seem like a confession of desperation. Better to wait until a Federal victory. Lincoln saw the logic of this and for the time being put the Emancipation Proclamation aside. In the meantime its existence remained a guarded state secret, while the president waited for a Northern battlefield success.

Confederate Counterstrokes

As it turned out, he had to wait nearly two months. In the meantime McClellan's battered army remained at Harrison's Landing. McClellan asked for 50,000 reinforcements, claiming that with them he could resume

Called "Old Brains," Henry W. Halleck had been a military intellectual in the prewar U.S. Army. As Union general-in-chief from July 1862 to March 1864, he brought greater administrative efficiency to the North's war effort but frustrated Lincoln by his frequent refusal to give field commanders direct orders.

his Richmond offensive. Lincoln considered this pure moonshine. In mid-July he summoned to Washington Major General Henry W. Halleck—his most successful commander to date—and named him general-in-chief. (Since March, when McClellan was relieved of this assignment, the post had been vacant; Lincoln and Stanton had acted, in effect, as the general-in-chief.) Among the first issues Lincoln put to Halleck was what to do with the Army of the Potomac. Although habitually reluctant to make decisions in such matters—he firmly believed that field commanders could best judge their situations—Halleck did little to discourage Lincoln's growing conviction that McClellan's army should be withdrawn. On August 15 the Army of the Potomac began boarding river transports for the return trip. This huge ferrying operation would continue for most of the month.

Meanwhile, in mid-July Pope's new Army of Virginia became active. Pope's mission was threefold: to protect Washington, to ensure Federal control of the Shenandoah Valley, and by operating against the Confederate rail center at Gordonsville, Virginia, to draw Confederate strength from Richmond and thereby divert attention from McClellan. Hindered by the wide dispersion of his forces, his newness to the eastern theater, and his matchless knack for alienating almost everyone, Pope ultimately became the victim of one of Lee's deftest bits of offensive-defensive strategy.

Second Manassas

Lee shaped his planning step by step, constrained by the knowledge that McClellan still lay within striking distance of Richmond. As McClellan's quiescence showed no sign of change, Lee felt assured enough to detach three divisions and send them against Pope's army. These he entrusted to Stonewall Jackson.

On August 9, Jackson fought a preliminary battle against a corps from Pope's army at Cedar Mountain in north-central Virginia. Soon afterward Lee brought most of his army north to join in the struggle against Pope. He knew that McClellan temporarily posed no threat because the Union army had begun its withdrawal from the James River. For nearly two weeks Lee sparred with Pope in the Rappahannock River valley, fruitlessly trying to bring him to bay before McClellan's army reentered the picture.

Lee did not feel strong enough to attack Pope directly, so he elected to maneuver, hoping to cut Pope's communications, threaten Washington, and avoid a general engagement. On August 24 he called Jackson to his headquarters and instructed him to sever the Orange and Alexandria Railroad, Pope's principal line of communications. To accomplish the mission Jackson was given 23,000 troops, leaving Lee with only 32,000 to hold the Rappahannock crossings and fix Pope's attention. Dividing the army violated conventional military wisdom, but Lee saw no alternative. The disparity in numbers between the contending forces rendered the risk unavoidable.

Jackson's execution of the operation gave proof that the military brilliance he displayed in the Shenandoah had not been lost. In a remarkable forced march of fifty-seven miles in two days, Jackson placed his swift

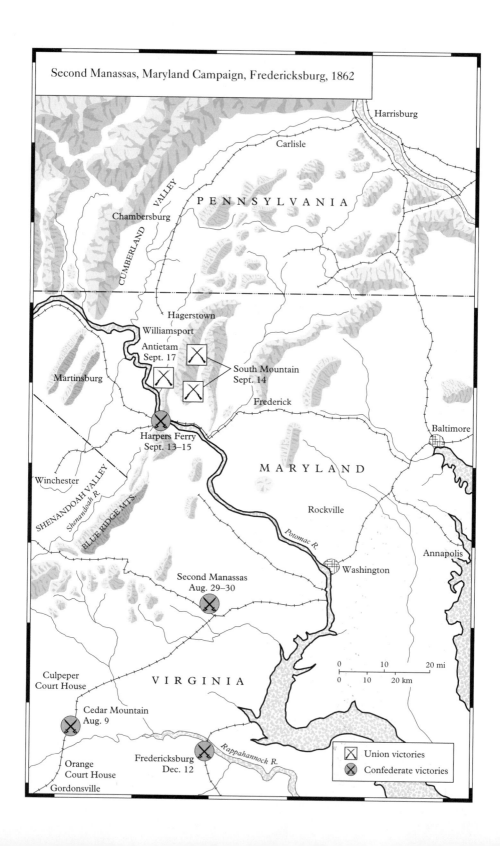

Second Manassas, Maryland Campaign, Fredericksburg, 1862

Harrisburg

Carlisle

CUMBERLAND VALLEY

P E N N S Y L V A N I A

Chambersburg

Hagerstown

Williamsport

Antietam
Sept. 17

South Mountain
Sept. 14

Martinsburg

Frederick

Harpers Ferry
Sept. 13–15

Baltimore

Winchester

M A R Y L A N D

SHENANDOAH VALLEY

Shenandoah R.

BLUE RIDGE MTS.

Rockville

Potomac R.

Annapolis

Second Manassas
Aug. 29–30

Washington

Culpeper
Court House

V I R G I N I A

0   10   20 mi
0   10   20 km

Cedar Mountain
Aug. 9

Orange
Court House

Gordonsville

Fredericksburg
Dec. 12

Rappahannock R.

Union victories

Confederate victories

infantry—jocularly dubbed his "foot cavalry"—squarely upon Pope's line of communications, cut the Orange and Alexandria Railroad, and demolished a gigantic Union supply depot at Manassas Junction. As a finale, he disappeared into a secluded, defensible position a few miles west of Manassas to await developments.

Aware only that Jackson lurked somewhere in his rear, Pope abandoned his defensive line along the upper Rappahannock River and began beating about the countryside in a disorganized attempt to locate Stonewall's forces. Lee, meanwhile, disengaged from the Rappahannock line as well and began a circuitous march aimed at a juncture with Jackson. Around noon on August 29 the Army of Northern Virginia was reunited as Longstreet's divisions assumed positions just southwest of Jackson's line.

Jackson's troops had been in a fierce battle the day before, and Pope assailed them again early on the 29th. But the Federals were unaware that Longstreet was now in the vicinity. On August 30, still blissfully ignorant of Longstreet's presence, Pope struck Jackson yet again. For a time the rebel situation was critical, but then Longstreet's five divisions broke from their cover and smashed the exposed Union left, sending the Federals in wild retreat until their officers could rally them for a stand on the old Bull Run battlefield. There, repeated Confederate attacks failed to dislodge them. It made no difference. Stung by repeated reverses, Pope elected to withdraw his demoralized forces northeast toward Washington. At a cost of 9,500 men, Lee had inflicted 14,500 casualties upon the Federals and cleared northern Virginia of any major Union army. In twelve weeks of campaigning, Lee had reversed the tide of the war in the east.

Antietam

With Pope beaten and McClellan's army withdrawn behind the Washington fortifications, Lee believed it was time to carry the war from Virginia into enemy country. The Union armies were weakened and demoralized, creating the opportunity to seize the initiative. An advance into Union territory might cause Maryland to secede and perhaps even lead Great Britain and France to grant diplomatic recognition to the Confederacy (although Lee doubted either event would ever occur). Most important, entering enemy territory would permit his army to forage in Maryland and give Virginia the chance to harvest its crops unmolested.

An offensive into Maryland would be difficult for even an army of 200,000, much less Lee's ragged, ill-equipped veterans, now reduced to something less than 50,000. But Lee was developing an almost mystical regard for the prowess of his Confederate soldiers. Time and again he asked them for the impossible, and incredibly, they often gave it to him. He grew convinced that there had never been soldiers like them. He also formed a correspondingly dismal picture of the Union forces and, especially, Union leadership. When a subordinate seemed dubious about his offensive plans, for example, Lee blandly explained that McClellan's caution made them quite practical.

Lee's army crossed the Potomac River on September 4–7. The bands played "Maryland, My Maryland" and the ragged soldiers looked in wonderment at the unspoiled countryside around them. From the outset, however, things went badly. To begin with, Lee expected that his thrust northward into Maryland would force the withdrawal of a 12,000-man Union garrison at Harpers Ferry. The garrison blocked the lower Shenandoah Valley, the avenue by which Lee planned to maintain communications with the South. When the garrison stayed in place, Lee had no choice but to reduce it. After a short stay in Frederick, Maryland, he divided his army into four parts. Three of them, under Jackson's overall command, went after Harpers Ferry. The fourth, consisting of Longstreet's corps and a division under General D. H. Hill, proceeded to the town of Boonsboro to await the operation's completion.

At this point additional problems arose. Unfounded reports of Federal units operating around Chambersburg, Pennsylvania, prompted Lee to divide his army further: D. H. Hill remained at Boonsboro while Longstreet shifted northwest to Hagerstown, Maryland. Jackson's forces took longer than anticipated to get into position. Not until September 13—a full day behind schedule—did they surround Harpers Ferry. Although the town's surrender then became a mere matter of time, it turned out that time was something the Confederates did not have.

Lee had miscalculated McClellan's response to the Maryland invasion. The Virginian had believed it would take three or four weeks for McClellan to reorganize the Union armies defeated at Second Manassas. Instead, McClellan did the job in less than seven days. As Jackson's units sewed up Harpers Ferry, the Army of the Potomac arrived at Frederick, Maryland, just one day's hard march from the scattered Confederate army. The situation would become critical if the Union general realized the exposed state of Lee's army. And that is precisely what occurred.

By incredible coincidence, two Federal soldiers found a copy of Lee's plan for the Harpers Ferry operation in a field outside Frederick. This soon-to-be-famous "Lost Order" quickly went to McClellan, who took one look at it and became understandably ecstatic. "Here," he exulted to one of his generals, "is a paper with which if I cannot whip Bobbie Lee, I will be willing to go home." Unfortunately for the Union cause, McClellan lacked the killer instinct required to capitalize on the situation. Instead of an immediate, rapid advance into the center of Lee's widely divided forces, he sent his columns forward at a leisurely pace. He gave Lee just enough time to retrieve the situation.

Lee heard about McClellan's dangerous advance about midnight on September 13. He issued orders for his troops to occupy the passes of South Mountain, a wooded ridge that formed a barrier between the Union army and his own. The next day three Union corps attacked. Lee's forces managed to fend them off for most of the day, but by evening Lee's hopes for a Northern invasion lay in ruins. From then on he was strictly on the defensive.

Lee probably should have withdrawn across the Potomac River as soon as possible. Initially he planned to do so, but word that Harpers Ferry

Union infantrymen charge through a cornfield at Antietam, September 17, 1862, the bloodiest single day of the war. Though McClellan achieved only a drawn-out battle, Lee was nevertheless forced to abandon his invasion of Maryland. Lincoln issued the Emancipation Proclamation five days later.

was about to surrender emboldened him. He chose instead to withdraw about ten miles west of South Mountain and make a stand at Sharpsburg, Maryland, along the banks of Antietam Creek. The wisdom of this decision is questionable—it meant fighting with a wide river directly in his rear—but Lee's conduct of the battle was magnificent. McClellan advanced slowly, cautiously, giving Lee plenty of time to concentrate most of his army. The Union assault did not come until September 17, and then in a piecemeal fashion that allowed Lee to shift his own outnumbered forces from one threatened point to another. The Army of Northern Virginia held its ground, albeit at tremendous cost: 13,700 casualties out of approximately 40,000 engaged. Union losses totaled 12,350 out of about 87,000 present on the field. This Battle of Antietam had the grim distinction of being the bloodiest single day of the Civil War.

It had another significance as well. Although McClellan missed a spectacular chance to destroy Lee's army, the battle looked enough like a Union victory for Lincoln to follow through on the promise he had made in July. On September 22, 1862, he issued the preliminary Emancipation Proclamation. If the South did not abandon the war by January 1, 1863, he warned, the slaves residing in the rebellious areas would become forever free.

The Emancipation Proclamation irretrievably changed the nature of the war. It outraged Southern opinion, the more so since it conjured fears of the race war white Southerners had always feared. Jefferson Davis considered the proclamation "the most execrable measure recorded in the history

Lincoln's decision to issue the Emancipation Proclamation sparked controversy in the North and outraged the South. In this cartoon penned by a Southern sympathizer living in Baltimore, Lincoln is shown writing the proclamation surrounded by demonic images, his foot planted on the U.S. Constitution.

of guilty man" and for a time considered treating captured Federal officers as inciters of servile insurrection. More than ever, the war had become a struggle to the death.

Bragg's Kentucky Raid

Lee's invasion of Maryland was not the only Confederate offensive during this period. At practically the same time as Lee's Maryland campaign, Confederate forces under Major General Earl Van Dorn tried to recapture the important rail center of Corinth, Mississippi, only to be repulsed on October 4. The Confederate offensive that went farthest and lasted longest, however, was the invasion of Kentucky, masterminded by General Braxton Bragg.

Bragg took over the army (soon to be called the Army of Tennessee) at Tupelo, Mississippi, in mid-June, after Beauregard departed abruptly on sick leave. In many respects Bragg was a most capable officer: energetic, determined, aggressive. He possessed a good strategic mind and sound administrative abilities. It would eventually develop, however, that Bragg possessed equally obvious shortcomings. He had an irascible temperament that alienated many around him, including his chief subordinates. And although decisive, even daring at times, during a crisis he often turned cautious, almost as if he no longer grasped the situation. But until these darker qualities manifested themselves, Bragg looked like a remarkable soldier. Indeed, few campaigns of the Civil War were better conceived and—up to a point—better executed, than Bragg's Kentucky raid.

After his bloodless victory at Corinth and before he became general-in-chief, Halleck dispersed his huge army into two main parts. One part—about 31,000 men under Major General Don Carlos Buell—was ordered east toward Chattanooga, Tennessee, another key railroad town and also the gateway into eastern Tennessee, a bastion of Unionist sentiment. The other, consisting of about 67,000 troops, was scattered about in order to consolidate the Federal grip on western Tennessee. Halleck's questionable disposition drained most of the momentum from his western offensive. When, in mid-July, he went east to become general-in-chief, operational control passed to Buell—now in northern Alabama—and Grant, who commanded the dispersed Union troops in western Tennessee.

Grant needed months to reconcentrate sufficient forces to resume offensive operations. In the meantime Buell, advancing toward Chattanooga, ran into a variety of delays from frequent guerrilla incursions, enemy cavalry raids, and the burden of repairing his lines of supply—the railroads leading east from Corinth and south from Nashville.

Grant's immobility and Buell's glacial movements invited some kind of Confederate riposte. Rejecting the option of an advance toward Grant, Bragg decided to shift his army eastward toward Chattanooga, then join forces with Confederate units in eastern Tennessee and embark on an invasion of Kentucky. In so doing he would turn Buell's flank and force him to retreat—perhaps even to abandon middle Tennessee. The move might also encourage Kentucky to join the Confederacy and fill his army's ranks with thousands of Bluegrass volunteers. Leaving a covering force at Tupelo under Major General Earl Van Dorn, Bragg embarked on this new operation in mid-July.

The shift east required over a month to execute. Bragg sent his infantry to Chattanooga via railroad—a long, circuitous journey that carried them as far south as Mobile, Alabama. Meanwhile his slow-moving artillery and wagon trains traveled by road. As Bragg's army completed its concentration, the Confederates in eastern Tennessee, under Lieutenant General Edmund Kirby Smith, began an advance across the Cumberland Plateau into central Kentucky. By the end of August Kirby Smith had reached Lexington. Bragg then rapidly advanced from Chattanooga and within two weeks stood on Kentucky soil.

This gigantic raid terrified the inhabitants of Illinois, Indiana, and Ohio and briefly installed a pro-Confederate governor at Frankfort, the state capital of Kentucky. It also forced Buell's Union army to abandon northern Alabama, relinquish much of central Tennessee except Nashville, and fall back practically to Louisville, Kentucky, before turning east to deal with Bragg's army. By that time it was early October. Bragg then had about 22,500 veteran troops with him, supported by another 10,000 under Kirby

Battle of Munfordville, Kentucky. While Lee advanced into Maryland, a second Confederate army under Braxton Bragg invaded Kentucky. Bragg hoped thousands of Kentucky men would flock to his forces, but few did. "Their hearts are with us," one Confederate general complained, "but their bluegrass and fat cattle are against us."

Smith. Buell had about 60,000 troops, but his imposing numerical advantage was partially offset by the fact that his army contained many unseasoned troops and its organization was largely improvised.

Neither side fully understood the other's dispositions. The Battle of Perryville that ensued began as a meeting engagement when units from both sides stumbled into one another while searching for fresh water in drought-stricken central Kentucky. The main fight commenced at 2 P.M. on October 8 and continued until well into the night. When it was over, the Federals had lost 845 killed, 2,851 wounded, and 515 captured or missing: a total of 4,211. Confederate casualties numbered 510 killed, 2,635 wounded, and 251 captured or missing—3,396 in all. But although the Rebels inflicted greater losses and held most of the battlefield at day's end, Bragg correctly realized he could not capitalize on the victory. Perryville ended his invasion of Kentucky; he withdrew southward to Murfreesboro, Tennessee.

Autumn Stalemate

In many respects the simultaneous Confederate raids into Maryland and Kentucky in the summer and fall of 1862 represented the military high tide of the Southern cause. Never again would a rebel triumph seem so within reach. By the end of August reports from Great Britain had indicated that the British were starved for cotton, impressed by the Confederacy's resilience, and perhaps on the verge of recognizing the Southern nation. A major Confederate victory at that point might have triggered foreign intervention, just as the American triumph at Saratoga had brought about the French alliance during the War for Independence. The population of the South had felt a rising thrill of expectation; Northerners were correspondingly alarmed and depressed. But the moment ended quickly, and autumn brought only a new round of campaigning.

Fredericksburg

After the Battle of Antietam, McClellan, much to the disgust of the Lincoln administration, tamely kept his army in western Maryland until the end of October 1862. Eventually McClellan crossed the Potomac and headed south toward Warrenton, Virginia, but Lincoln had had enough of his excessive caution and on November 7 relieved him of his command.

McClellan's replacement was Major General Ambrose E. Burnside, an amiable, modest soul who had enjoyed success in amphibious operations against the Carolina coast. When offered command of the Army of the Potomac, he tried to decline the job because he felt unequal to the responsibility. Although events would swiftly and amply prove him correct, at the outset he did rather well.

Within a week of assuming command, Burnside started the Union army on a new "On to Richmond" campaign. This one aimed at sliding past Lee's right flank and crossing the Rappahannock River at Fredericksburg, about fifty miles north of the Confederate capital. Lee had to move rapidly to counter the move; initially he even felt he might have to fall back to a position along the North Anna River, about halfway between Fredericksburg and the capital. Burnside, however, soon lost control of the situation and wound up giving Lee the easiest victory of his career.

Burnside's plans required a prompt crossing of the Rappahannock into Fredericksburg before the Confederates could oppose him in force. Unfortunately for him, the necessary pontoon bridges failed to arrive until well into December, giving Lee ample time to concentrate in and around the town. The Army of Northern Virginia took well-nigh impregnable positions on Marye's Heights just west of the city. Burnside foolishly persisted in his now pointless plan of campaign, and on December 11 two Confederate signal guns announced that the Federals were attempting a crossing.

Lee was unfazed. He wanted the Northerners to attack. With his troops posted on Marye's Heights, defeat was out of the question. The only unknown factor was the ultimate size of the Union casualty list. The entire Army of Northern Virginia had the same absolute certainty regarding the battle's outcome. Longstreet asked one of his artillerists about an idle cannon, only to be told that other Confederate guns already covered the ground so well that its use was academic: "A chicken could not live on that field when we open fire on it."

Lee made no serious attempt to keep the Federals from entering Fredericksburg. On December 13, Burnside made six major assaults against

Marye's Heights. All failed. Massed rebel infantry and artillery scythed them down by the hundreds. The Battle of Fredericksburg ended as it was destined to end—in an inexpensive Confederate victory. The Federals lost over 12,500 men; Confederate losses totaled fewer than 5,500. But the constricted battle area offered Lee no scope for a counterattack. He had to content himself with watching the wounded enemy retire to the river's far bank.

Grant's Overland Campaign Against Vicksburg

Meanwhile in Mississippi, Grant had at last gathered enough of an army to inaugurate a late autumn offensive. His objective was Vicksburg, Mississippi. The city stood on high bluffs at a hairpin turn in the Mississippi River, about three hundred miles downstream from Memphis. After the loss of Columbus, Kentucky, and Island No. 10, Vicksburg became the Confederacy's main fortress on the Mississippi; a second bastion was built at Port Hudson, Louisiana, two hundred miles farther south. Between these two points rebel forces still controlled the river. As long as they did, the Confederacy would remain an unbroken nation stretching from Texas to the Virginia capes; as long as they did, midwestern produce could not be shipped down the Mississippi. Capturing Vicksburg thus became a vital Union goal.

In many respects this task was a general's nightmare. The ideal way to attack Vicksburg would have been to move a large army downriver to within striking distance of the city, supply it by river transports, and then maneuver against the city from the northeast. Geography, however, denied Grant so straightforward a solution. Just north of Vicksburg lay the Yazoo River Delta, a vast stretch of woodlands and swamps. The Delta country sprawled along the eastern bank of the Mississippi for about 140 miles; in places it was forty miles across. No army could hope to operate in such a region. There was really only one point north of Vicksburg from which the city could be attacked, albeit with difficulty, and that was at Chickasaw Bluffs immediately above the town. The Chickasaw Bluffs position, however, combined excellent terrain for the defender with scant maneuvering room for the attacker; this unhappy fact, from the Federal point of view, made it an approach of last resort.

South of Vicksburg the ground was less forbidding than the Delta country but almost as inaccessible. The guns of the fortress made it impossible to transport an army there by river, and if Grant tried to march his troops past the city along the west bank, he would find it impossible to keep the army supplied. An attack directly from the west was out of the question: at Vicksburg the Mississippi was a half-mile wide. That left an attack from the east. But in order to get there, Grant would first have to march his army 250 miles; worse, to supply it he would have to depend exclusively on the Mississippi Central Railroad, a conduit that seemed not only inadequate but mortally vulnerable to interdiction by fast-riding Confederate cavalry.

Still, the overland route seemed the least forbidding prospect and in November Grant set forth with his army, now christened the Army of the Tennessee. Initially everything went smoothly. Lieutenant General John C.

Pemberton, the Confederate commander assigned to defend Vicksburg, fell back before Grant's advance and did not stop until he reached Grenada, Mississippi—about one third of the total distance Grant's men would have to cover. Grant got as far as the town of Oxford, after which the roof caved in. Far back in Tennessee, Confederate cavalry raider Nathan Bedford Forrest led a column of horsemen in a lightning stab that wrecked a good portion of the railroad from which Grant received his supplies. Closer to home, a second raid led by Major General Earl Van Dorn struck Grant's advanced supply base at Holly Springs, Mississippi. Grant had no choice but to withdraw his entire force back to Tennessee.

Even so, the loss of Holly Springs afforded Grant an intriguing lesson. With his military foodstuffs destroyed, Grant instructed his troops to live off the countryside. He hoped they could scrounge enough food to keep body and soul together until they could link up with a regular supply line again. Instead the army not only survived but actually *feasted*. It turned out that this part of the country had a huge food surplus; the men found plenty of hams, corn, poultry, and vegetables. Grant was impressed: in the middle of December, a small corner of the state of Mississippi could feed 40,000 extra mouths. It was something he did not forget.

Simultaneously with Grant's abortive drive down the Mississippi Central Railroad, a second force under Sherman embarked at Memphis and steamed down the Mississippi River to Chickasaw Bluffs, just north of Vicksburg itself. The plan called for Grant's army to distract Pemberton's attention while Sherman made a sudden grab for the city. In the wake of Holly Springs the scheme became a fiasco. Grant's precipitous retreat enabled Pemberton to bring one third of his own men back to Vicksburg. They arrived in plenty of time to bolster the lines at Chickasaw Bluffs, and when Sherman attacked on December 29 he received a crisp rebuff. The year ended with Vicksburg looking tougher to crack than ever.

Stone's River

The same might be said of middle Tennessee. After its withdrawal from Kentucky, Bragg's Army of Tennessee took up position at Murfreesboro, astride the railroad that led from Nashville to Chattanooga. Buell's army came south and occupied Nashville. Meanwhile Lincoln, disenchanted with Buell's lack of aggressiveness, replaced him with a new commander, Major General William S. Rosecrans.

Rosecrans had performed capably in previous operations, possessed good administrative abilities, and enjoyed a strong rapport with his troops, who dubbed him "Old Rosy." But like many Union commanders, he did not like to advance until he felt completely ready, and he spent most of November and December gathering tons of supplies at Nashville. Only on December 26 did he move southeast against Bragg's army at Murfreesboro.

The last dawn of 1862 found Rosecrans's army a few miles west of Murfreesboro with the Confederates drawn up in front of them. Rosecrans planned to attack the rebel right flank; Bragg, however, anticipated him and

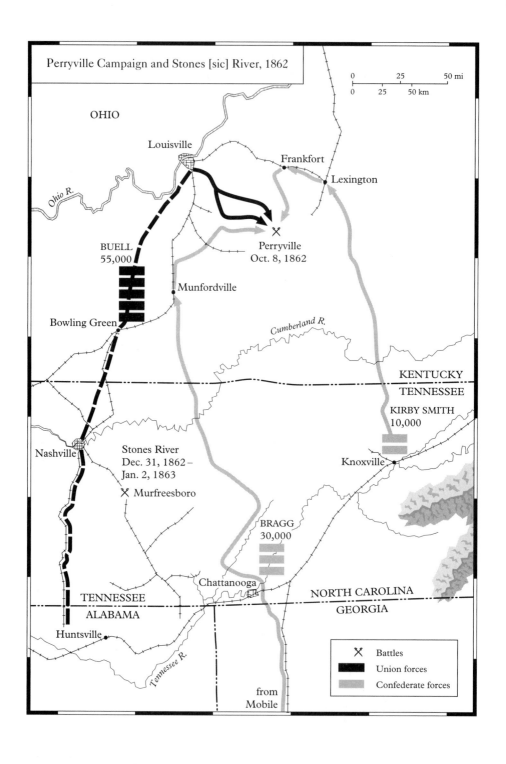

Perryville Campaign and Stones [sic] River, 1862

OHIO

Louisville

Frankfort

Lexington

Ohio R.

BUELL
55,000

Munfordville

Bowling Green

Cumberland R.

KENTUCKY
TENNESSEE

KIRBY SMITH
10,000

Nashville

Stones River
Dec. 31, 1862 –
Jan. 2, 1863

Murfreesboro

Knoxville

Perryville
Oct. 8, 1862

BRAGG
30,000

Chattanooga

NORTH CAROLINA
GEORGIA

TENNESSEE
ALABAMA

Huntsville

Tennessee R.

from
Mobile

0   25   50 mi
0   25   50 km

X   Battles
        Union forces
        Confederate forces

struck the Union right flank instead. Surprised by the suddenness of the attack and shattered by its weight, the right wing of Rosecrans's army collapsed. By early afternoon the Federal position resembled a jackknife with the blade nearly closed. Only the most desperate fighting saved the Northern army from collapse.

That evening Rosecrans held a council of war and asked his chief subordinates if they thought a retreat in order. His senior corps commander, Major General George H. Thomas, gave the obvious reply: "Hell," he boomed, "this army can't retreat." It was true. The Union situation was so precarious, its sole line of retreat so exposed, that any rearward movement would have quickly dissolved into a rout. Recognizing the logic of this, Rosecrans elected to stand.

New Year's Day of 1863 was quiet as both armies recovered from the previous day's ordeal. Bragg believed he could not press his attack on the Union right flank—his troops in that sector were exhausted and decimated by the vicious fighting there—but neither did he want to give up his hard-won advantage. On January 2, therefore, he ordered his remaining fresh troops to strike the Union left in an attack across Stone's River. This assault, however, delayed until late in the day, was torn apart by Union artillery. With his army now completely worn out, Bragg reluctantly decided to fall back some thirty miles southeast to Tullahoma, Tennessee. The Union army, as shattered by its barren victory as by a major defeat, did not pursue.

☆ ☆ ☆ ☆

Thus the year 1862, which had begun with the belief that a quick and relatively bloodless victory was still possible, ended in military stalemate. From a Union perspective, the military problem of defeating the Confederacy loomed greater than ever. Geography was one factor. In Virginia, the constricted, river-choked arena made it difficult even for large armies to bring their strength effectively to bear. Fredericksburg had shown that. In the west, great distances meant that the Federals had to supply their forces over long, vulnerable lines of supply—a point rammed home by the cavalry raids of Forrest and Van Dorn.

The respective fighting power of the two opponents was a second factor. Although the Federals usually enjoyed a substantial numerical advantage, the rival armies had shown themselves too evenly matched in strength and resilience. Battles like Stone's River suggested that even the most determined, well-executed assaults wrecked the attacker as much as the defender, and although at Stone's River the attackers were Confederates, the onus of offensive warfare still lay chiefly with the North.

A third factor—and from the Federal point of view the most surprising—was the psychological strength of Southern resistance. At the beginning of 1862 most Northerners subscribed to the belief that popular support for the Confederacy was shallow at best. Lincoln doubted whether secessionists formed a majority anywhere except South Carolina and thought that a large, latent Unionist sentiment lay just below the surface, awaiting only a Federal victory to emerge and throw off the Confederate yoke. Thousands of

Northerners shared this conviction, including Ulysses S. Grant. Looking back on this period of the war years later, Grant wrote that until the spring of 1862, he had supposed the Southern people were not in earnest and that one or two decisive Federal successes would make them quit the war. "[Forts] Donelson and Henry," he continued, "were such victories." But when they led only to the furious Confederate counterattack at Shiloh, "then, indeed, I gave up all idea of saving the Union except by complete conquest."

Most Northerners took a bit longer to reach the same conclusion. The turning point, for most of them, was the defeat of McClellan's peninsula campaign. The failure of this campaign turned many Northerners sharply against a limited war directed solely against Confederate armies. Until then, Union policy makers had fought the war somewhat in the manner of the "cabinet wars" of the eighteenth century. Severe clashes could and did occur, but an important goal was to prevent severe disruptions in the fabric of society. Increasingly, however, the American Civil War became a struggle with no holds barred, more so than even the French Revolution and Napoleonic Wars. A Union soldier aptly expressed the new outlook: "I am like the fellow that got his house burned by the guerillas," he wrote. "[H]e was in for emancipation subjugation extermination and hell and damnation. We are in war and anything to beat the south."

The issuance of the Emancipation Proclamation signaled this major change in the conflict. The struggle was no longer one to quell rebellion. It had become what Lincoln initially feared it would become—a "remorseless, revolutionary struggle" to overthrow the institution on which the South's social and economic structure depended. As a result, measures unthinkable in the war's first year—the seizure or destruction of crops and livestock, the demolition of factories, even the burning of towns and villages—now seemed not only permissible but necessary. The stakes of the conflict, already great, increased still further. The Civil War was becoming a total war.

SUGGESTED READINGS

Cozzens, Peter. *No Better Place to Die: The Battle of Stone's River* (Urbana and Chicago: University of Illinois Press, 1990).

Freeman, Douglas S. *Robert E. Lee*, 4 vols. (New York: Charles Scribner's Sons, 1934–1935).

———. *Lee's Lieutenants: A Study in Command*, 3 vols. (New York: Charles Scribner's Sons, 1942–1944).

Hennessy, John J. *Return to Bull Run: The Campaign of Second Manassas* (New York: Simon and Schuster, 1993).

Jones, Archer. *Confederate Strategy from Shiloh to Vicksburg* (Baton Rouge: Louisiana State University Press, 1961).

McDonough, James Lee. *War in Kentucky: From Shiloh to Perryville* (Knoxville: University of Tennessee Press, 1994).

McWhiney, Grady. *Braxton Bragg and Confederate Defeat,* Vol. 1, *Field Command* (New York: Columbia University Press, 1969).

Sears, Stephen W. *George B. McClellan: The Young Napoleon* (New York: Ticknor & Fields, 1988).

———. *To the Gates of Richmond: The Peninsula Campaign* (New York: Ticknor & Fields, 1992).

———. *Landscape Turned Red: The Battle of Antietam* (New York: Ticknor & Fields, 1983).

Tanner, Robert G. *Stonewall in the Valley* (Garden City, N.Y.: Doubleday, 1974).

Vandiver, Frank. *Mighty Stonewall* (New York: McGraw-Hill, 1957).

13

THE CIVIL WAR, 1863: MOVING DEMOCRACIES TOWARD TOTAL WAR

The Austerlitz Chimera

Two Societies at War

Vicksburg and Gettysburg

Struggle for the Gateway

The year 1863 saw the conflict's continued evolution into a total war. The North and South had already fielded large armies composed of volunteers, and the South had adopted a conscription law in April 1862. In March 1863 the Union government followed suit with a conscription law of its own. Both sides continued to mobilize their economic resources to support the war and increasingly saw those resources as legitimate military targets. Northern forces in particular began to confiscate or destroy factories, mills, railroads, and agricultural products that might be used to support Southern armies.

The North moved toward such measures in part because breaking the Confederacy's military strength through combat alone had proven impossible. Although slow to recognize it, both sides possessed armies too large and durable to be destroyed in a single great battle—especially when so strongly supported by the full resources of their societies. In this respect the Union and Confederate forces were perhaps even more resilient than their European predecessors. Frederick the Great had tried to apply all the resources of the state to his defense of Prussia, but he had been unwilling to unleash the passions of his people. During the wars of the French Revolution and Napoleon, the French had roused the people, tapped the resources of the entire nation, and raised mass national armies, but they had not gone to the limits of total war. By 1863 both sides in the Civil War were going farther toward total war than Europeans had been willing or able to go. In such a struggle, the larger population and superior economic muscle of the North promised a Union victory—if the political commitment to continue the struggle could be maintained.

It was a big if. When 1863 began, the Confederate leadership still had reason to hope for ultimate victory. The victories at Fredericksburg, Holly Springs, and Chickasaw Bluffs showed the steadiness of Southern valor, while the bloody standoff at Stone's River at least promised continued stalemate. The North, for its part, seemed to be tiring; the autumn elections had resulted in significant gains for the Democrats, many of whom favored a compromise peace. But 1863 proved to be the military turning point of the Civil War; by year's end the tide ran clearly against the South. The Union success occurred in two thunderclaps: first the almost simultaneous triumphs at Gettysburg and Vicksburg in early July, then—after a harrowing ordeal along the Tennessee-Georgia border—a dramatic autumn victory at Chattanooga.

The Austerlitz Chimera

First, however, the Union had to endure a number of humiliations. In January 1863, Burnside tried to redeem himself with a midwinter offensive northwest of Fredericksburg. Torrential rains drowned the operation; soldiers derisively called it Burnside's "Mud March." Then in April a promising cavalry raid in northern Alabama came to grief when pursuing rebel horsemen under Bedford Forrest bagged the entire Union detachment of 2,000 men. The following month the Army of the Potomac—under yet another commander—suffered a major defeat at Chancellorsville, Virginia.

The Quest for Decisive Battle

Perhaps better than any other, the Chancellorsville battle illustrates the mid-nineteenth-century American fixation with the slashing offensive style of Napoleon. Generals commonly issued Napoleonic addresses to their troops and patterned their operations after famous Napoleonic victories. A perennial favorite was the Battle of Austerlitz, fought on December 2, 1805. The reason for the fixation was simple: the name was synonymous with decisive battle. At Austerlitz, Napoleon had routed the Austrian and Russian armies in a single day and secured an armistice from Austria just two days afterward. Austerlitz thus represented the apogee of military art and displayed, as Dennis Hart Mahan, West Point's strategic guru, expressed it, "those grand features of the art [of war], by which an enemy is broken and utterly dispersed by one and the same blow."

To be sure, not every Civil War commander sought an Austerlitz-like victory. On the Union side, Generals Halleck, Buell, McClellan, and Sherman were more concerned with the occupation of strategic places than the destruction of an enemy army in battle. Among Confederates, Joseph E.

Johnston clearly preferred a defensive strategy—his counterstroke at Seven Pines was practically the only major offensive battle of his career. These, however, were exceptional figures. The majority of commanders cherished the vision of a decisive victory over the enemy.

Almost without exception they met disappointment. The possible explanations for this are legion. To begin with, the increased range and fire-power of the rifled musket, especially when combined with field entrenchments (which became an increasingly pronounced feature of Civil War battlefields after 1862), gave defenders a greater edge over their attackers. Then too, Civil War armies typically had a fairly low ratio of cavalry to infantry, and without the combination of speed and power embodied in large formations of heavy cavalry it was almost impossible for a victorious army to catch and destroy a retreating opponent. The heavy woodlands and broken terrain characteristic of Civil War battlefields further limited the utility of cavalry in large engagements. Instead both sides used their horsemen primarily for reconnaissance, screening, and raiding. Thus cavalry charges on a Napoleonic scale occurred only rarely. When they did, however—as at Cedar Creek in 1864—they displayed their traditional ability to overtake retreating infantry, shatter a defeated army, and produce a fairly good approximation of Austerlitz.

Another possible explanation focuses on the organizational limitations of Civil War armies, which were, of course, largely officered by citizen-soldiers. One might also suggest that the failure of Civil War generals to achieve a decisive victory reflected, to a considerable degree, their limited military abilities; after all, it took a Napoleon to win the Battle of Austerlitz.

But perhaps the main reason for the dearth of truly decisive Civil War battles was simply that such battles seldom occurred anywhere, at any time. Although greatly sought-after from the time of Gustavus Adolphus onward, a victory "by which an enemy is broken and utterly dispersed by one and the same blow" occurred, at best, on only a half-dozen occasions each century and required an unusual combination of circumstances to produce. Moreover, even a "decisive" battle was seldom decisive in any ultimate sense. Despite their calamitous defeat at Blenheim, for example, the French fought the War of the Spanish Succession for more than a decade; eventually, indeed, they obtained rather favorable terms for peace. And Austerlitz, of course, was followed ultimately by Leipzig and Waterloo.

Thus to the extent that Civil War commanders quested after decisive battle, they largely pursued a mirage. The Chancellorsville campaign prominently displayed both the seriousness of this quest and its attendant pitfalls and frustrations.

Chancellorsville: Act One

In late January 1863, after his abortive "Mud March," Burnside was replaced as commander of the Army of the Potomac by Major General Joseph Hooker. Although considered an ambitious opportunist, Hooker was also a combative, competent soldier. With astonishing speed and deftness he restored the flagging morale of the Army of the Potomac, largely by improving rations and camp sanitation and by introducing the corps badges that were the prototypes for modern unit patches. Then he prepared for another offensive.

The Army of the Potomac wintered at Falmouth, Virginia, just across the Rappahannock River from Lee's army at Fredericksburg. As the spring of 1863 approached, Hooker formulated an operations plan based largely on the ideas of Montgomery C. Meigs, the Union army's quartermaster general. Meigs had earlier written that "what is needed is a great and overwhelming defeat and destruction of [Lee's] army." His solution was a bold, rapid turning movement around the Confederate left flank—"such a march as Napoleon made at Jena, as Lee made in his campaign against Pope"—with the objective of gaining the Confederate rear. If, Meigs counseled, "you throw your whole army upon his communications, interpose between him and Richmond . . . and he fights, if you are successful, he has no retreat." This was nothing if not the dream of a decisive Napoleonic victory.

Hooker embraced Meigs's plan and also adopted Meigs's additional suggestion to supplement the turning movement by unleashing cavalry against Lee's lines of communication. But he decided to use only a bit more than half his army for the turning movement. The remainder would confront and fix Lee at Fredericksburg. With any luck this second force would distract the Confederates while Hooker made his march. Later, with Union forces established firmly on Lee's flank, Hooker could launch an offensive, and Lee's army could be crushed between the two halves.

Hooker had more than enough troops to do the job: about 110,000 in all. In mid-April a large cavalry force set forth on a major raid against the railroads that linked Lee's army with Richmond. Then on April 28, Hooker placed his great enveloping column in motion. Early next morning Union Major General John Sedgwick, entrusted with the task of fixing Lee, began crossing the Rappahannock River below Fredericksburg under cover of a heavy fog.

Lee's scouts soon brought him word of this latter movement. Word also came from Jeb Stuart of another crossing at Kelly's Ford, some twenty-five miles to the northwest. By evening Lee knew Hooker's main body had forded the Rapidan River and that two large Federal forces threatened him front and rear. Lee had just 59,500 troops with which to oppose an enemy almost twice that size. In effect, Hooker had prepared a gigantic trap for Lee, and conventional wisdom dictated a quick withdrawal before its jaws could spring shut. Lee, however, seldom thought conventionally. He correctly perceived that Sedgwick's thrust was largely a diversion; the situation as a whole was simply his big chance to hit Hooker's army while it was divided.

For the next two days Lee weighed alternatives, finally deciding to concentrate against Hooker's main body. Leaving 10,000 Confederate troops under command of Major General Jubal Early to watch Sedgwick, Lee moved west into the thickets around Chancellorsville, a crossroads eleven miles west of Fredericksburg surrounded by a dense second-growth forest known locally as the Wilderness. Jeb Stuart's cavalry, meanwhile, performed valuable scouting functions and prevented Hooker from finding out much about Lee's forces. By the evening of May 1, Lee knew two important things about the Union army. First, Hooker had stopped advancing. His men were felling trees to reinforce defensive fieldworks, which implied a temporary halt in the Federal offensive. Second, the extreme right of Hooker's army lay "in the air," anchored to no natural obstacle and so inviting attack.

Chancellorsville: Act Two

As a pallid moon rose over the gloomy Wilderness thickets, Lee and Jackson settled down to plot their next move. They conferred for several hours, finally deciding that Jackson would march 28,000 men across Hooker's front and strike that exposed right flank. Lee, meanwhile, would use his 14,000 remaining troops to dupe Hooker into thinking he intended a frontal assault.

As in the Seven Days, if the Union commander realized the true state of affairs, he could turn Lee's gamble into a catastrophe. But in Lee's reckoning Hooker's construction of fieldworks indicated an abdication of the initiative. And whereas Lee had retained his own cavalry to serve as the eyes of the army, Hooker had detached his own to operate against the Confederate supply lines. The Union commander therefore lacked the intelligence-gathering force necessary to grasp sudden changes in the operational picture.

Jackson's flank march did not go off without a hitch. It began three hours late and was not carried off in complete secrecy. Union pickets spotted Jackson's column as early as 9 A.M. By early afternoon scattered musketry betrayed skirmishing between Federals and Confederates along the line of march. Hooker, however, reacted cautiously and Jackson refused to panic. Despite a foray made by a venturesome Union corps against his artillery trains, Jackson continued his advance and by 5:15 P.M. had drawn up his forces astride the Orange Turnpike, west of Chancellorsville, and faced them almost due east. Ahead lay the exposed flank of the Union XI Corps, partially alerted but still largely unprepared.

Jackson gave the order. Suddenly the gnarled thickets filled with the rebel yell and the Confederates went crashing forward in the diminishing light. The XI Corps attempted to make a stand, with units here and there rallying in an attempt to stem the rebel tide, but their tactical situation was hopeless. Jackson pumped additional divisions into the fight as soon as they arrived. Within three hours, the Confederates had driven forward two miles, folding Hooker's lines into a "U" centered upon the large, isolated house called "Chancellorsville," which gave the clearing and battlefield its name. There resistance stiffened, and the Confederate attack lost momentum in the gathering darkness.

Jackson, accompanied by a cavalcade of staff officers, rode forward to reconnoiter. A band of North Carolina troops mistook his party for Union cavalry and opened fire, wounding him dangerously in the left arm. Compounding the mishap, Jackson's senior division commander fell to enemy fire at almost the same moment. Not until midnight did a

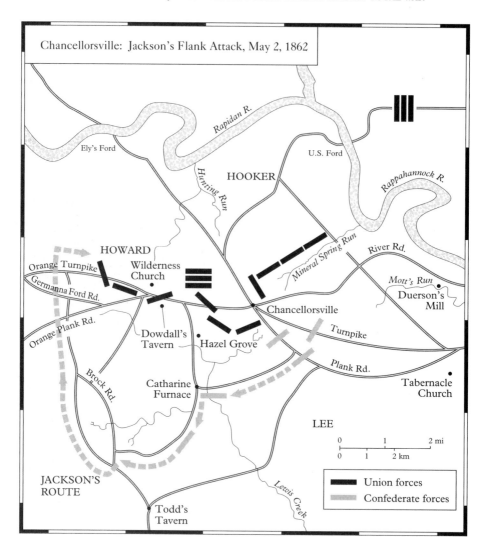

Chancellorsville: Jackson's Flank Attack, May 2, 1862

replacement, Jeb Stuart, assume command of Jackson's corps, and Stuart had almost no idea of Jackson's plans to continue the attack.

Attacks against Hooker's main body continued throughout May 3 without great success. The psychological blow had already been dealt, however. By noon Hooker withdrew his force into an enclave north of Chancellorsville. Meanwhile, Sedgwick's wing at Fredericksburg had shoved aside Early's 10,000 and was moving west at last. But an afternoon counterattack at Salem's Church, about three miles west of Fredericksburg, blunted his advance.

Lee realized he had to turn his full attention to this other threat. Leaving 25,000 troops under Stuart to contain Hooker, the general threw the rest of his army against Sedgwick's two corps. The Confederates, however, could not get into attacking positions until the afternoon of May 4. Sedgwick used the delay to withdraw to safety beyond the Rappahannock.

The Civil War's most famous military partnership was that between Robert E. Lee and Stonewall Jackson. Shown here in a romanticized postwar print, they plan the smashing flank attack that defeated the Union army at Chancellorsville—and cost Jackson his life.

Subsequently, on May 5 Lee again concentrated against Hooker and planned an assault for the following day.

This last decision reflected a tremendous stubborn streak in Lee, for Hooker had plenty of time to prepare his lines against precisely the frontal assault Lee was so determined to make. The implications were stunning: Lee seriously planned to attack an entrenched army numerically superior to his own. He seemed utterly resolved to wreck Hooker's force and blind to the fact that it simply could not be done. Fortunately for the Army of Northern Virginia, the Federals withdrew during the evening. Daybreak found them safely across the Rappahannock. Lee, enraged, vented his wrath against the general who brought the unwelcome news. "Why, General Pender," he said, "That is what you young men always do. You allow those people to get away. I tell you what to do, but you don't do it. Go after them," he added furiously, "and damage them all you can!"

Hooker, however, had long since moved out of reach. It remained only to tally the losses: 13,000 Confederate casualties this time against a total of 17,000 Federals. The Army of Northern Virginia had won again, but had absorbed 20 percent casualties in the process—losses the South could ill-afford. Nor could it replace one loss in particular. On May 10, Stonewall Jackson died of complications following the removal of his wounded arm. For the rest of the war, Lee had to do without the one subordinate who could make his audacious strategies take fire.

At Chancellorsville both commanders had tried—unsuccessfully—to achieve a Napoleonic decisive victory. In the case of Hooker this could be explained simply by a singular failure of nerve. "I just lost confidence in Joe Hooker," the Union general later admitted. The reasons for Lee's failure were obviously more complex. Some historians have maintained that, except for Jackson's tragic wounding, the Confederate counteroffensive would have cut Hooker off from the Rapidan crossings and destroyed that half of the Union army. Such an outcome seems unlikely; it is certainly unprovable. More impressive is the fact that the Federals were able to restore their front fairly rapidly, despite one of the best-executed flank attacks of the war. Rifled muskets and concentrated artillery helped; so did field fortifications. Then too, there was the usual dearth of heavy cavalry: Stuart had plenty of horsemen available for scouting purposes, but nowhere near enough to launch a major attack. The countryside was far too wooded and broken for a mounted charge to succeed anyway. Finally, the Confederate attackers typically suffered heavy casualties and lost cohesion, so that it was difficult to maintain the momentum of attack. In short, despite Hooker's ineptness and Lee's tactical virtuosity, the Confederates failed to achieve anything like an Austerlitz. The Chancellorsville campaign ended with the strategic situation in Virginia virtually unchanged, except that thousands of homes, North and South, had been plunged into mourning.

Two Societies at War

More often than the wars of the French Revolution and Napoleon, the Civil War is called the first total war. In common with the wars from 1792 to 1815, the Civil War encompassed the complete, or near-complete, mobilization of the belligerents' population and resources to fight an enemy. But it went further and also involved the complete, or near-complete, application of violence against that enemy—violence exerted not only against his military force but also against the civilian society that sustained it. Though one could quibble endlessly about whether the North and South mobilized completely, a large percentage of the population and the economy on both sides was bound up in the war effort. And by mid-1863, Federal armies began large-scale operations aimed at the destruction of Southern war resources and, at least to some degree, the demoralization of Southern civilians.

For both sides the problem of mobilization was similar. Each government had to find ways to generate sufficient military manpower, to clothe, equip, and transport its armed forces, and—somehow—to find a way to pay for it all. The magnitude of these tasks was completely unprecedented in American history, but both governments approached them in generally similar ways and, in both cases, with fairly good success.

The Move to Conscription

At first, both the Union and the Confederacy relied upon volunteers to man their armies. This was the traditional American method and politically the only thinkable one in societies that venerated individual liberty and unobtrusive government. Eventually, however, both sides encountered difficulties in securing enough manpower. The South was the first to feel the pinch. By early 1862 volunteering in the Confederacy had fallen off dramatically, while at the same time a string of Federal successes threatened the new nation with early defeat. Spurred by a sense of impending doom, on April 16, 1862, the Confederate Congress passed the first general conscription act in American history (local conscription had been used during the Colonial Wars and the American Revolution). The act made every able-bodied white male between the ages of 18 and 35 liable for military service.

This bill, however, contemplated a very different sort of conscription from the system employed by the French in 1793. Whereas in Europe

A Northern recruiting office. Like the Confederacy, the Union government secured most of its military manpower through volunteers. But by early 1863 voluntary enlistments had dropped off and many Northern communities offered cash rewards, called "bounties," if men agreed to enlist.

governments used conscription to raise new troops, the Confederate Congress invoked it principally as an incentive for veteran troops to reenlist. Since many of them had signed up for only twelve months, their enlistments were expiring and they might return to civilian life. The Confederate conscription act provided that if the men stayed in the army they could remain in their current units, but if they left they could be drafted and assigned to a new, unfamiliar unit.

As the war continued, however, the Confederate government refined the conscription act so that it became a way to raise new troops as well as encourage veteran soldiers to remain in the ranks. And in February 1864 the Confederate Congress passed a new, more stringent conscription act that declared all white males between 17 and 50 subject to the draft.

The Union government also moved toward conscription, albeit more slowly. In July 1862 the U.S. Congress took the first step when it passed a new Militia Act, authorizing the president to set quotas of troops to be raised by each state and giving him power to enforce the quota through conscription if a given state failed to cough up enough volunteers. But not until March 1863 did the Federal government pass a true draft act, making all able-bodied males between 20 and 45 liable for military service.

In both the North and South, conscription was wildly unpopular, partly because it represented an unprecedented extension of government power into the lives of individuals, but also because of the inequitable way in which it was administered. For example, initially the Confederate Congress permitted a conscript to hire someone to serve in his place. The practice was abolished when the price of a substitute soared beyond $5,000; in the meantime, however, hiring substitutes convinced many ordinary Southerners that the Confederacy's struggle was "a rich man's war and a poor man's fight." Even more upsetting was the so-called "Twenty Negro Law" that exempted one white man for every twenty slaves. This meant that the sons of wealthy plantation owners could be exempted, and even if few men actually took advantage of the law, it contributed to the sense of conscription's unfairness. In the North, the conscription act also permitted the hiring of substitutes; moreover, any man who paid a $300 commutation fee could receive exemption from any given draft call. Ironically the commutation fee, designed to keep the cost of hiring a substitute from soaring out of reach, was intended to help the average man. Instead it only fueled a sense that the draft law was rigged in favor of the wealthy.

In the North, well-to-do communities also frequently raised bounty funds to encourage volunteering, so that their own citizens could elude the draft. Under this system, a man willing to enlist received a cash payment totaling hundreds of dollars. As the war went on and volunteers became harder to find, such bounties increased prodigiously. They soon generated a phenomenon called "bounty-jumping," whereby men went from place to place, enlisted, took their bounties, and then absconded at the first opportunity. One bounty jumper claimed to have done this thirty-two times.

The indirect way in which Civil War conscription operated makes it difficult to assess its effectiveness. It almost certainly encouraged enlistments and, particularly in the South, kept veteran soldiers in the ranks; one

Men of the 107th U.S. Colored Troops. Lincoln's emancipation policy paved the way for the North to begin active recruiting of African-American soldiers.

estimate credits the system with augmenting Union troop levels by 750,000. But the number of men actually drafted was surprisingly small. In the North, barely 46,000 conscripts actually served in the armies. Another 116,000 men hired substitutes, while 87,000 others paid the $300 commutation fee. Between conscripts and substitutes, the Union draft furnished only 6 percent of the North's military manpower. The Confederacy did little better. The available evidence, while incomplete, suggests that roughly 82,000 Southerners entered the army through conscription—about 11 percent of total enlistments.

The political costs of conscription, however, were dramatic. Many Southerners eluded the draft and fought off the enrollment agents who came to conscript them. In some states, especially Georgia and North Carolina, governors who opposed the draft used loopholes in the conscription acts to exempt as many of their citizens as possible. In the North, a number of provost officers lost their lives while attempting to enforce the draft. The worst violence occurred in New York City in July 1863 when angry mobs attacked draft offices, roughed up well-dressed passersby ("There goes a $300 man"), and slaughtered dozens of free blacks, whom they blamed for the war and hence for conscription. All in all, at least 105 people died in the New York City Draft Riot, making it the worst such incident in American history.

Fifty years later, when the United States resorted to the draft in order to fight World War I, officials studied the weaknesses of Union conscription. The result was a much more effective and politically palatable system, since they were able to avoid many pitfalls. In sum, although conscription as practiced in the Civil War filled some of the urgent need on both sides for military manpower, it proved to be an almost textbook case in how not to do it.

The War Economies

Both sides did better at managing their economies, although here again the distended nature of mid-nineteenth-century American society limited what they could accomplish. The Confederate government never achieved a realistic fiscal policy. It passed only a very inadequate income tax, amounting to just one-half of one percent. Instead the Southern leadership financed the war largely through borrowing and by printing fiat money, expedients that eventually spawned a whopping 9,000 percent inflation rate. In April 1863 it also initiated a wildly unpopular "tax-in-kind," by which Confederate agents could seize 10 percent of the goods produced by a given farm or business concern.

Of the two adversaries, the Union tended to perform best, partly because it had a greater population and resource base, and partly because its financial management was much superior to that of the Confederacy. The Lincoln administration's fiscal system was created and managed by Secretary of the Treasury Salmon P. Chase. While it too relied primarily on bonds and paper money, it levied a more extensive income tax, and inflation remained under control in the North. Where the Confederacy generated a mere 5 percent of its revenue through direct taxation, the Federal government managed 21 percent. The South underwrote only about 40 percent of its war expenses through bonds, against 67 percent for the North.

The Lincoln administration managed its war economy principally through alliances with the business community. Cooperation, not coercion, was the preferred mode of operation, and usually it worked very well. For example, although Lincoln quickly secured the legal authority to seize railroads and run them directly in support of the war effort, in practice he relied on Northern railroad men voluntarily to "do the right thing." Only on rare occasions did the Federal government assume overt control of the railroads. Similarly, the Union government constructed no munitions or equipage factories of its own, but rather relied upon a wide array of civilian contractors. And it depended on financiers to make its war-bond program a success.

Ironically, given its commitment to limited government, the Confederate government pursued a much more direct, centralized management of the economy. President Jefferson Davis persuaded Congress to assume control of the telegraph network, to construct new railroads for military purposes, and even to assume direct control of the railroads from private hands. He also urged Congress to encourage and engage in the mining and manufacture of certain essential materials. Congress eventually passed a law that offered inducements to potential manufacturers of such strategically important goods as saltpetre, coal, iron, and firearms. The government set up its own salt works in Louisiana, and the Ordnance Department established a large weapons-building empire. By the end of the war, in fact, the Confederate South had become—in theory at least—one of the most relentlessly centralized nations on earth. World War I would force some European nations to do the same. But the Union example of an alliance between business and government would prove an equally viable—and more effective—means to the same end.

Wartime Resentments

Modern wars often begin with a wave of patriotic outpouring that temporarily drowns dissent. Sooner or later, however, the dissent resurfaces, and a wartime government must master it or perish. For the Union and Confederacy, dissent began early and grew steadily worse as the war progressed. Both governments proved up to the challenge. The Lincoln administration suspended the writ of habeas corpus where necessary, held, at one time or another, an estimated 13,000 political prisoners, and occasionally suspended publication of hostile newspapers. The Confederate government also suspended the writ of habeas corpus and waged an unremitting campaign of repression against the Unionist sympathizers in its midst, most notably in east Tennessee. The imperatives of total war thus impinged not only on the battlefield and the economy, but also on personal liberties.

In the North, the main opposition came from a faction known as the Peace Democrats—derisively nicknamed "Copperheads" by their opponents. They believed that the Federal government could never achieve reunion through force; they also argued that the horrors of civil war, coupled with the constitutional abuses of the Lincoln administration, were far worse than permitting the South to go its own way. A second group of Democrats, called "Legitimists," supported the war but balked at the Lincoln administration's handling of it, particularly its decision to make emancipation a war aim. Then too, the lower parts of Illinois, Indiana, Ohio, and Maryland contained many persons of Southern ancestry, some of whom were Confederate sympathizers.

The South had troubles of its own. To begin with, a substantial number of Southerners bitterly despised the Confederate government. The fact that 100,000 white Southerners actually fought for the Union underscores this point. The South also contained a large, restive slave population which might at any moment rise up and attack its masters. Oddly enough, a good many planters also disliked the Confederate experiment, for the war effort required too many sacrifices from them: impressment of livestock, the conscription of slave labor, the confiscation of cotton, and so on.

Finally, the unexpectedly massive degree to which the Confederate government eventually intervened in the economy alienated many

Southerners. By 1864, three years of war had precipitated what one historian has termed a "revolt of the common people." Ordinary Southerners resented the loss of labor manpower, particularly among nonslaveholders, who had no one to work the land once their able-bodied young men went off to fight. They were also antagonized by the frequent impressments and requisitions of crops, forage, and horseflesh. Class resentment also surfaced. Wealthy families did not suffer privation to the same degree as the poor. The paying of substitutes to avoid conscription was not abolished until 1864.

Thus both the Union and the Confederacy contained large cores of dissent, each with the potential to undermine the war effort. In the North, political success by the Peace Democrats could, at best, impede the vigorous prosecution of the war and, at worst, force a compromise peace. In the South, the "revolt of the common people" threatened to create a condition in which disobedience to the Confederate government could become not only respectable but rampant. If that occurred, a hostile population might encourage deserters, shield them from Confederate authorities, and block efforts to secure the supplies needed to feed and sustain Southern armies. The solution, in each case, was military success. Continued stalemate, especially if punctuated by Confederate victories, benefited the South and kept its dissenters in check. The Lincoln administration, for its part, required tangible evidence of military progress; otherwise the pressures for a compromise peace might prove overwhelming. The harnessing of popular sentiment to the state, made possible by the democratic revolutions, thus proved a two-edged sword for policy makers. It enabled them to tap manpower and economic resources in unprecedented ways. But it also forced them to accommodate popular passions. Thus like many other leaders in the age of mass politics, Lincoln and Davis found themselves riding a tiger.

A Destructive War

As each society mobilized ever more thoroughly to carry on the war, it began to seem necessary to strike not only the enemy's armies but also his economic base. Railroads, factories, mills, and cotton gins, as well as crops and livestock, increasingly became the targets of military operations. To some extent both sides embarked on a program of economic destruction, but of the two the North had both the greater need and the greater opportunity to attack the enemy's war resources.

Some Northerners had urged such attacks from the very outset of the war, but the logic of the conciliatory policy had argued persuasively against a campaign of unbridled destruction. The issuance of the Emancipation Proclamation, however, had signaled the demise of conciliation, and by early 1863 Union policy makers increasingly realized that more destructive measures were necessary. As Halleck explained to Grant in March 1863, "The character of the war has now very much changed within the last year.

There is now no possible hope of reconciliation with the rebels. . . . We must conquer the rebels or be conquered by them." Spurred by this grim logic, some Northern commanders began to claim the full extent of the destruction permissible within the existing rules of war. They were driven to this extreme not only by the changed political equation but even more importantly by their need to supply themselves and, by extension, to deny supplies to the enemy.

Attacks on the South's economic base initially arose from the practice of widespread foraging. Such foraging occurred first in the western theater, where Union armies often found themselves operating in areas where suitable rail and water communications were unavailable. When that occurred, normal supply lines proved inadequate, and Union armies had to augment their official rations with crops and livestock taken directly from local farmers. This foraging soon made them very aware that Confederate forces also drew supplies from the countryside, and western armies began a policy of destroying unneeded crops in order to prevent the Confederates from using them.

For a considerable period large-scale foraging and supply-denial policies remained mainly confined to the western theater. Union armies in the east, it turned out, were far slower to adopt similar policies. This was probably because they were much less successful than their western counterparts at capturing Southern territory. Thus their supply lines simply never lengthened. Since eastern armies seldom experienced serious logistical problems, they underestimated the impact supply denial might have on the enemy. It seldom occurred to them to destroy those supplies at their source, despite the fact that the Southern forces in the east drew considerable food and forage from local districts. Western armies, by contrast, had far greater sensitivity to logistical matters.

Extensive foraging, Union commanders recognized, inevitably meant hardship for civilians. Commanders attempted to minimize such hardship by forbidding abuses and by issuing instructions that Southern families should be left enough supplies for their own use. Even so, civilians suffered a great deal. Partly in an attempt to justify the hardship thus inflicted, Union commanders began to see it as a form of punishment. Eventually they deliberately sharpened the effects of foraging in order to produce political effects: for example, by stripping crops as much as possible from the farms of known secessionist sympathizers.

The next logical step in supply denial was to destroy the mills that processed agricultural products and the railroads that transported them, as well as factories that manufactured militarily useful goods. Destruction of this sort had occurred on a modest scale even during the early months of the war. Nevertheless the year 1863 marked a significant watershed, for it was during that year that one can see the emergence of large-scale destruction carried out, in fairly routine fashion, by large bodies of troops. By mid-1863, then, both sides were trying to mobilize fully to prosecute the war, and the North, at least, had embarked on a program of economic warfare. The Civil War had truly become a total war.

Vicksburg and Gettysburg

In April 1863 a mob of housewives, furious that they could not find enough to feed their families, rioted in the streets of Richmond. The incident underscored a serious disturbance in Confederate morale, born of privation and endless casualty lists, that would only grow worse without some decisive victory to offset it. The win at Chancellorsville a few weeks later was encouraging but incomplete. The Federal Army of the Potomac had retired intact to lick its wounds; it would surely resume the offensive within a few months. Out west the situation had grown disquieting: Grant's army had come down the Mississippi River, cast about for a viable means to attack the fortress city of Vicksburg, and discovered one late in April.

Vicksburg

After the failure of his overland campaign in the fall of 1862, Grant had brought most of his army to Milliken's Bend, a bleak piece of bottomland a few miles north of Vicksburg. Although Grant was now much closer geographically to the Confederate fortress, the biggest operational problem remained unsolved: how to get into a position from which the bastion could be attacked successfully. From January through April he tried a number of alternatives. First his engineers attempted to connect a series of creeks, old river channels, and bayous into a waterway that would enable Union vessels to get around Vicksburg to the south, after which Grant would march his army down and have those vessels ferry him across the river to the dry ground on the eastern shore. This scheme became known as the Lake Providence Route, after its central feature, but after weeks of backbreaking labor the project was abandoned. Next, hundreds of troops and escaped slaves attempted to dig a canal across the neck of the great river bend directly opposite Vicksburg in hopes of changing the course of the Mississippi so that its main channel would bypass the city. This project sparked the imagination of many people—Lincoln expressed particular fascination with the idea—but it failed as well. A third attempt—similar in concept to the Lake Providence Route—called for creating a waterway through the Yazoo Delta country via Steele's Bayou. It produced the spectacle of Union gunboats steaming through a narrow channel in what amounted to a huge flooded forest, but constant harassment by Confederate snipers eventually forced its abandonment. A fourth effort aimed at creating a waterway running down from the Yazoo Pass at the northern end of the Delta. This too failed when the Confederates erected a fort to block it.

Four attempts, four failures—yet Grant was not discouraged. Later he would claim that he never expected these efforts to yield results and agreed to them largely in order to occupy his men and create the illusion of action—an illusion necessary to allay his critics in the North while he

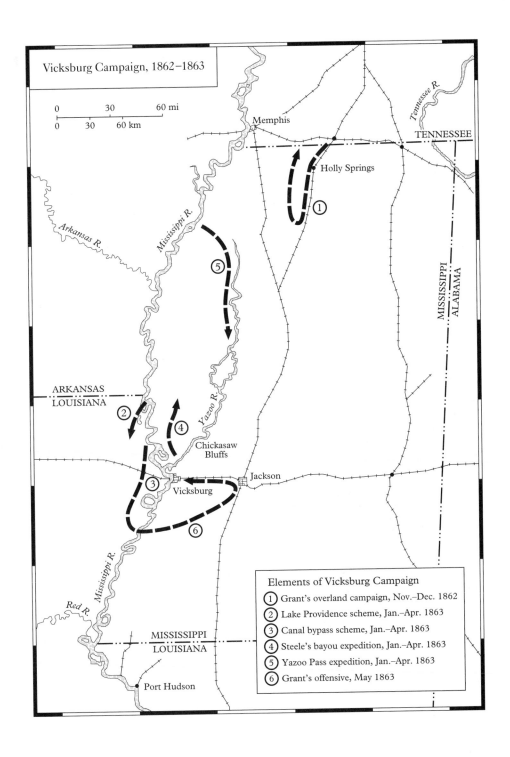

Vicksburg Campaign, 1862–1863

| 0 | 30 | 60 mi |
| 0 | 30 | 60 km |

Memphis

TENNESSEE

Holly Springs

①

Tennessee R.

Arkansas R.

Mississippi R.

⑤

MISSISSIPPI
ALABAMA

Yazoo R.

ARKANSAS
LOUISIANA

②

④

Chickasaw
Bluffs

③

Vicksburg

Jackson

⑥

Mississippi R.

Red R.

MISSISSIPPI
LOUISIANA

Port Hudson

Elements of Vicksburg Campaign

① Grant's overland campaign, Nov.–Dec. 1862
② Lake Providence scheme, Jan.–Apr. 1863
③ Canal bypass scheme, Jan.–Apr. 1863
④ Steele's bayou expedition, Jan.–Apr. 1863
⑤ Yazoo Pass expedition, Jan.–Apr. 1863
⑥ Grant's offensive, May 1863

Grant confers with Admiral David D. Porter during the campaign against Vicksburg, the Confederacy's bastion on the Mississippi River. Close army-navy cooperation was indispensable to the Union victory there in July 1863.

concocted a plan that would work. By early April he had done it. The ensuing campaign sealed his reputation as a great commander.

On the night of April 16, Admiral David Dixon Porter, the naval officer in charge of the riverine flotilla cooperating with Grant's army, led some of his vessels on a midnight run directly past the guns along the Vicksburg bluffs. Darkness shielded Porter's vessels part of the way; even after the Confederates spotted them and opened fire, the Union boats escaped with the loss of only one transport. More steamers made the dash five nights later. Once below the Vicksburg batteries, Porter's fleet awaited the arrival of Grant's army, which took barges and shallow-draft steamers through a series of bayous that wound past Vicksburg on the Louisiana side of the river. That done, Grant's troops began crossing the Mississippi at Bruinsburg, fifty miles south of Vicksburg, on April 30.

The landing at Bruinsburg placed Grant's army squarely between Vicksburg and the secondary river fortress of Port Hudson, Louisiana. Forty miles eastward lay Jackson, the state capital, and a point at which four railroads converged. One of these led to Vicksburg and formed the bastion's main line of supply. If Grant meant to seize Vicksburg, he would first need to choke off those supplies; for that reason Jackson became his first important objective. Yet to march upon Jackson necessarily meant exposing his own line of supply to ruinous interdiction from Pemberton's army at Vicksburg. Consequently, Grant decided to maintain no supply line at all. Just as his troops had done after the disastrous raid upon Holly Springs in December 1862, they would live off the country, except that this time the choice was deliberate.

At the beginning of May his three army corps headed east, hugging the south bank of the Big Black River and guarding the ferries against any attempted crossings by Pemberton's troops. With them rattled along several hundred wagons loaded with ammunition and a few staples like salt and coffee. They fought two minor preliminary battles with detachments from Pemberton's army and by the evening of May 13 had reached the vicinity of Jackson.

Vicksburg fell only after a siege of forty-seven days, much of it under shelling from Union gunboats and field artillery. Confederate civilians huddled in shelters like these. Cut off from the outside world, they were reduced, in some cases, to eating rats.

Ahead of them, a small Confederate force under General Joseph E. Johnston barred entrance to the city. The next day two Union corps attacked the rebels and pushed them north. In weeks to come Johnston would hover to the northeast of Grant's army, gather additional troops, and look for a way to help Pemberton defeat Grant. Grant never gave Johnston the opening.

After burning Jackson's war manufactories, the Union forces swung sharply west and headed for Vicksburg. Pemberton, meanwhile, moved east in search of Grant's nonexistent supply line. On May 16 elements of the two armies clashed at Champion's Hill, a commanding ridgeline about midway between Jackson and Vicksburg. Grant's troops managed to beat Pemberton and send his force in full retreat to the powerful Vicksburg fortifications. After a sharp action along the Big Black River with the Confederate rear-guard, Grant's army reached the outskirts of the river city on May 18. There Grant resumed contact with Porter's gunboats, reestablished a solid line of supply, and began to invest the town.

Once Grant surrounded Vicksburg he made two quick tries to take the city by assault. The first attempt came on May 19, but the Confederates smashed it within minutes. A second, much more determined effort followed three days later. This time most of Grant's army rolled forward against the Confederate trenches that crowned the steep hillsides around Vicksburg, only to be stopped almost at once by a wall of musketry and artillery fire.

Grant suspended the attacks and settled down to a siege. In Washington, General-in-Chief Halleck funneled reinforcements to Grant's army as fast as possible. The Confederate government, meanwhile, met to consider how to avert impending disaster.

Gettysburg

The Confederate high command met in Richmond, weighed alternatives, and struggled to find a solution to the crisis. Secretary of War James Seddon favored dispatching reinforcements from Lee's army to help Pemberton throw Grant back. Then, with the threat to Vicksburg removed, Confederate forces could concentrate to help Bragg win decisively in central Tennessee. Davis agreed; so did James Longstreet, Lee's senior corps commander, although Longstreet reversed the priority: reinforcements should go first to Bragg, then Pemberton. Joe Johnston, P. G. T. Beauregard, and an informal network of other Confederate generals all concurred that some variation on this strategy should be attempted.

Lee, however, did not agree. Troops dispatched to succor Vicksburg, he said, could not reach the city in time to do anything if the fortress were in danger of imminent surrender. In Virginia, on the other hand, the Army of the Potomac could renew its advance at any time. Far from being in a position to donate troops to others, Lee insisted, "[U]nless we can obtain some reinforcements, we may be obliged to withdraw into the defences around Richmond."

The enormous prestige enjoyed by the South's greatest general compelled respect for his views. Davis called Lee to Richmond for a strategy conference on May 15. There, before the president and his assembled cabinet, Lee unveiled his own proposal. He would embark on an invasion of Pennsylvania. Such an offensive would remove the threat to Virginia and open the way to decisive victory on Union soil, with concurrent prospects for foreign recognition and a negotiated peace. At a minimum, he insisted, an invasion of the North would produce such consternation that the Federals would have to relax their grip on Vicksburg.

From anyone else, Lee's scheme would have seemed like the hallucination of an opium addict. But repeated success had given him the reputation of a miracle worker, and Davis saw Lee's point when the Virginian objected that the scheme to reinforce Vicksburg was highly problematic at best. "The answer of General Lee," he decided, "was such as I should have anticipated, and in which I concur."

Lee thus won permission to embark on his invasion of the North. Within three weeks his army was underway; by the end of June his troops had fanned out across southern Pennsylvania, where they courteously but thoroughly plundered the local population. In the meantime, Hooker brought the Army of the Potomac northward in pursuit.

By June 28 the Union army had entered Maryland, always keeping between Washington and Lee's forces. On that date, irritated by a rash of complaints from Hooker, Lincoln relieved him of command and replaced him with Major General George G. Meade, a well-respected but

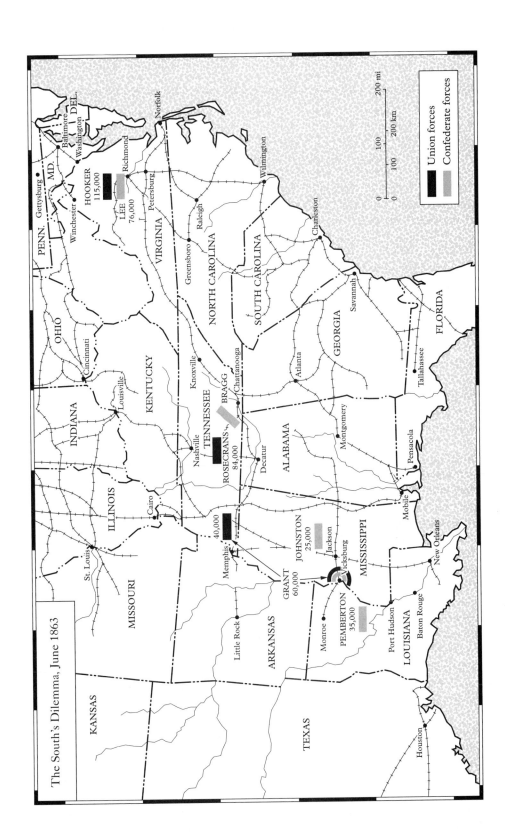

The South's Dilemma, June 1863

Union forces
Confederate forces

200 mi
200 km
100
100
0
0

KANSAS

MISSOURI

St. Louis

ILLINOIS

INDIANA

OHIO

Cincinnati

PENN.
Gettysburg
MD.
Winchester
Baltimore
Washington
DEL.
HOOKER
115,000

VIRGINIA
LEE
76,000
Richmond
Petersburg
Norfolk

KENTUCKY
Louisville

Cairo

Nashville
ROSECRANS
84,000
Knoxville
Chattanooga
BRAGG

TENNESSEE

40,000
Memphis

GRANT
60,000
JOHNSTON
25,000
Jackson
Vicksburg
PEMBERTON
35,000

Decatur

ALABAMA
Montgomery

NORTH CAROLINA
Greensboro
Raleigh

SOUTH CAROLINA
Charleston

GEORGIA
Atlanta
Savannah

Wilmington

Pensacola
Mobile

New Orleans

MISSISSIPPI

Monroe

LOUISIANA
Port Hudson
Baton Rouge

ARKANSAS
Little Rock

TEXAS

Houston

FLORIDA
Tallahassee

comparatively unknown corps commander. Meade thought it bad business to replace an army commander on the eve of battle and tried to decline; Lincoln, however, forced him to accept. Thus the Army of the Potomac approached its greatest battle with an untried leader at the helm.

Lee, meanwhile, did not realize that the Union army was so close to his own. Jeb Stuart—the "eyes" of the rebel army—had taken three brigades on a spectacular but pointless raid around the Union army and was far out of position. Not until June 30 did a spy inform Lee of the Union army's proximity. Lee promptly gave orders to reconcentrate his scattered divisions. The point chosen for the rendezvous was Gettysburg, a small town in south-central Pennsylvania, where a number of good roads converged.

On July 1 the first of Lee's troops approached Gettysburg. Elements of A. P. Hill's Confederate corps ran into Federal cavalry, which already occupied the town. Before long a sizable battle rocked and swelled amid the tidy farm lots north, west, and south of the town. Soon Union infantry came up. Both sides fed additional troops into the fight as soon as they arrived, but the Confederates had the advantage: their troops were closer and came onto the field more rapidly. A second Confederate corps under Lieutenant General Richard S. Ewell happened upon the Union right, north of Gettysburg, and pitched into it furiously. The Federal line cracked under the pressure. By late afternoon the Confederates had routed one corps, pummeled another, and driven the surviving Federals through Gettysburg. Hundreds of Northerners surrendered to closely pursuing rebels while the remaining Union troops withdrew south of the town to Cemetery Ridge.

Lee arrived on the field shortly after noon on July 1 but found the action so fluid and confused that he refrained from giving any orders. As daylight waned, however, he made two fateful decisions. First he elected to fight a general engagement around the fields and hills below Gettysburg, despite earlier doubts that his army was strong enough to fight a pitched battle against the larger Union army. Second, although he instructed Ewell to capture Cemetery Hill "if practicable," he failed to insist upon it. Ewell did not consider the move practicable and therefore did not attack. His reluctance to attack enabled the Federals to use Cemetery Hill, the northernmost point on Cemetery Ridge, as the foundation on which they constructed their entire defensive line.

During the night both sides received reinforcements as additional units took their places in the battle lines. The Union line south of Gettysburg began to take on its famous "fishhook" appearance: the barb at Culp's Hill southeast of the town, the curve at Cemetery Hill, and then a long shank that ran for a mile or so south along Cemetery Ridge. The Confederate II Corps faced Cemetery and Culp's hills while III Corps on its right faced Cemetery Ridge. Behind it lay I Corps under Lieutenant General James Longstreet. Recently arrived on the field and as yet unbloodied, I Corps would make the morrow's main attack. The target would be the Union left flank.

For the Confederates, the attack did not begin auspiciously—it was made without adequate reconnaissance and began only at 4:30 P.M. But the

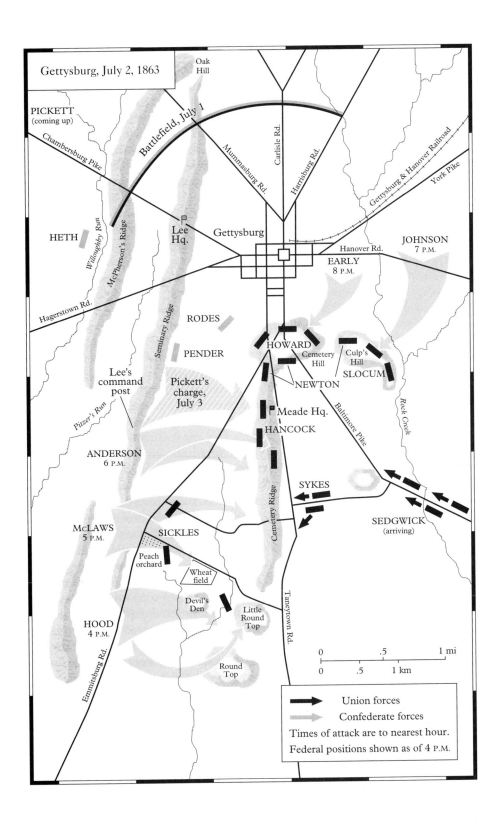

Gettysburg, July 2, 1863

Oak Hill

PICKETT
(coming up)

Battlefield, July 1

Chambersburg Pike

Mummasburg Rd.

Carlisle Rd.

Harrisburg Rd.

Gettysburg & Hanover Railroad

York Pike

HETH

Willoughby Run

McPherson's Ridge

Lee Hq.

Gettysburg

JOHNSON
7 P.M.

Hagerstown Rd.

Seminary Ridge

RODES

PENDER

HOWARD

Hanover Rd.

EARLY
8 P.M.

Cemetery
Hill

Culp's
Hill

SLOCUM

Rock Creek

Lee's
command
post

Pitzer's Run

Pickett's
charge,
July 3

NEWTON

Meade Hq.

HANCOCK

Baltimore Pike

ANDERSON
6 P.M.

SYKES

SEDGWICK
(arriving)

McLAWS
5 P.M.

SICKLES

Cemetery Ridge

Peach
orchard

Wheat
field

Taneytown Rd.

Devil's
Den

Little
Round
Top

HOOD
4 P.M.

Emmitsburg Rd.

Round
Top

0   .5   1 mi

0   .5   1 km

➤ Union forces

➤ Confederate forces

Times of attack are to nearest hour.

Federal positions shown as of 4 P.M.

blow fell like a thunderclap when it came. Afterward, Longstreet would call this attack "the best two hours' fighting done by any troops on any battle-field." It certainly showed both armies at the height of their powers. As such, the engagement well illustrates the dynamics of a Civil War battle.

Longstreet's attack began with massed artillery fire. The cannoneers fired solid shot to disable enemy batteries and shell to strike his foot soldiers. The artillery was still firing when the rebel infantry advanced: two divisions from Longstreet's own corps, supported by a third from another corps. The divisions advanced *en echelon*—that is, one after another, from the right end of the line toward the left—a tactic designed to mislead the enemy as to the actual focus of the assault. The infantry regiments marched steadily, try-ing hard to maintain their two-line, shoulder-to-shoulder battle formation despite the hilly, wooded terrain. Brigade and regimental commanders supervised their units closely. Their main duty was to preserve the troops' linear formation and to prevent their units from crossing in front of one another or spreading out too far.

In severe fighting the Confederates smashed a badly positioned Union corps and plunged up the steep, rocky slopes of Little Round Top, a hill at the end of the Union left flank. Last-minute reinforcements beat back the Confederates there and restored the front; particularly memorable was the famous defense by the 20th Maine Regiment under Colonel Joshua Lawrence Chamberlain. But the fighting swirled back and forth until night-fall. Amid the deafening noise of musketry and cannon fire, each side strug-gled to secure local superiority at several key points. For the commanders the job was mainly to "feed the fight"—finding and throwing in whatever reinforcements became available—while encouraging their soldiers and rally-ing them when a short retreat became necessary. For the individual soldiers, the job was to maintain "touch of elbows" with the man on either side, follow the regimental colors—in the smoke and din the movement of these flags often became a primary means of communication—and fire low. Despite the greatly increased range of the rifled musket, this engagement, like many Civil War battles, was actually fought well within smoothbore range. The two sides were often only a few dozen yards apart. Sometimes they collided; when they did, a desperate close-quarters struggle with clubbed muskets and even bare fists would result.

Several times Longstreet's men came close to victory. But ultimately the combination of rough terrain and tough Union resistance exhausted them, and the attack fell short of success. Things were no better on the bat-tlefield's opposite end. Ewell failed to begin a secondary attack until dusk and won little but casualties for his pains. The Union position had proven too strong, the Confederate thrusts too late or too weak.

Lee remained determined to continue the offensive. The great stub-bornness that had displayed itself at the Seven Days, Antietam, and Chancel-lorsville seemed more entrenched than ever at Gettysburg. Despite the fail-ures on July 2, Lee perceived amid the reports glimmerings of potential success: good artillery positions *had* been seized, charging divisions had *almost* broken through, probing brigades had come *close* to breaching the Union center. Then reinforcements arrived in the form of Stuart's long-lost

The recently invented technique of photography captured the grisly aftermath of Civil War battles. Nearly 620,000 Americans died in the Civil War, far more than in any other conflict.

cavalry and an infantry division under Major General George Pickett. Morale remained good, and Southern valor could still be counted upon. Lee ordered Longstreet to renew the attack the next day.

Longstreet, however, opposed the plan and urged that the Confederate army try an envelopment or a turning movement instead. Lee listened courteously, then instructed Longstreet to attack the Union center with three divisions spearheaded by Pickett's men. After a long preliminary bombardment by Confederate artillery, the climactic attack began on the afternoon of July 3. Fifteen thousand rebel soldiers in battle lines that stretched nearly a mile from flank to flank surged from the wooded crest of Seminary Ridge and headed toward a clump of trees that marked the center of the Union line. The gallant men in whom Lee vested such outsized confidence charged bravely and died bravely but never had a chance. Napoleonic assaults of that sort could no longer win against veteran troops firing rifles that could kill at ranges of 300 yards or more. Nor could they prevail against canister—artillery rounds made up of lead slugs that transformed cannon into huge sawed-off shotguns. Valor was not at issue, for as a general who helped lead the charge claimed, "If the troops I commanded could not take that position, all Hell couldn't take it." What lay at issue were the tactical realities of 1863. By that time, the balance of strength had tilted sharply from the offensive to the defensive.

Pickett's charge illustrated both the lethal effectiveness of artillery on the defensive and a corresponding weakness on the offensive. Although Union cannon scythed down the Confederate attackers in droves, the preliminary Confederate artillery bombardment, although massive and intense, signally failed to create the conditions for a successful infantry assault. In the days of Napoleon, artillery batteries might have advanced to a point just outside smoothbore musket range and battered down the enemy infantry line, but the extended range of the rifled musket—coupled with effective counterbattery fire from the new rifled artillery—made such a tactic impossible. Some Confederate batteries did, in fact, move forward in support of Pickett's attack but nowhere near as far as their Napoleonic counterparts might have gone.

The survivors of what became known as "Pickett's Charge" came streaming back across the field, leaving their dead and dying comrades strewn across the shallow valley that separated the rival positions. Lee rode among the returning troops, shaken, saddened, and moved to a strange, almost wistful tenderness. "It's all my fault," he would tell Longstreet later. "I thought my men were invincible."

Lee lost nearly 20,000 men at Gettysburg. During the retreat he nearly lost his entire army. Summer storms caused the Potomac to rise, barring passage to the retreating Confederate forces. With the fords unusable and the bridges long since destroyed, the beaten Confederates faced annihilation if Meade's Federals caught up with them and launched a determined assault. Meade, however, pursued cautiously. Minor skirmishing ensued, but no major attack. While a jury-rigged ferryboat shipped handfuls of men across, Lee's engineers built a pontoon bridge—a crazy patchwork of planks, scows, and barges completed on July 13. The wagons crept across it, and the infantry waded to safety through chest-high water. The Army of Northern Virginia was saved, scarcely twenty-four hours before Meade planned to launch a belated attack.

Captured during Lee's retreat from Pennsylvania, three rebel soldiers await transportation to a Union prison camp. The Confederate defeats at Gettysburg and Vicksburg occurred within a day of each other and together marked the war's military turning point.

Lincoln was disappointed. He thought Meade had blown a spectacular chance to wreck Lee's army for good. But Meade had probably done as well as was possible. For one thing, at Gettysburg his army had suffered tremendous casualties of its own. For another, the Confederate bridgehead on the Potomac was heavily fortified; an attack against it would most likely have failed. Most important, Meade's successful defense at Gettysburg had inflicted 33 percent casualties on Lee's army and, as it turned out, blunted forever its offensive capability. And coupled with Grant's victory at Vicksburg, Gettysburg offered important new proof that the North was winning the war.

Vicksburg fell on July 4, 1863, after a siege of nearly seven weeks. Inside the town food had grown desperately short; toward the end of the siege, soldiers and civilians started eating horsemeat and rats. Outside, Grant's army bided its time, dined comfortably on the plentitude of supplies arriving at their new river base, and grew steadily stronger as additional troops reinforced those already on the scene. (Grant had conducted his May offensive with about 44,000 men; by the end of the siege he had over 70,000 men in all.)

The capture of Vicksburg reopened the Mississippi River and severed Arkansas, Texas, and much of Louisiana from the rest of the Confederacy, but these results were largely symbolic. The midwestern states had learned to ship their goods by rail, and they continued to do so even after the "Father of Waters" again became an available conduit. The real significance lay in the capture of Pemberton's entire army—nearly 31,000 Confederate troops became prisoners, together with 172 cannon and about 60,000 small arms. The Confederacy could scarcely afford such losses.

Struggle for the Gateway

While Grant was besieging Vicksburg and Lee was advancing and retreating in the East, a third campaign, more prolonged than either of the other two, was underway along the southern fringe of the Appalachian highlands. From June until November 1863 Union and Confederate armies grappled for possession of Chattanooga, a strategic railroad city in southeastern Tennessee. In addition to its significance as the place where three major railroads met, Chattanooga also formed the principal gateway into Unionist Tennessee, whose occupation had been a cherished objective of the Lincoln administration since the war's outset. Even more important, it was the northern end of a corridor that led a hundred miles south to Atlanta, Georgia.

In a real sense, the capture of Chattanooga was more important than that of Vicksburg. With the seizure of the latter city, the Mississippi River was reopened and the strategic purpose of a thrust in that direction reached its logical culmination. But Chattanooga was not only a major objective in its own right; it opened the way to further attacks into the Southern

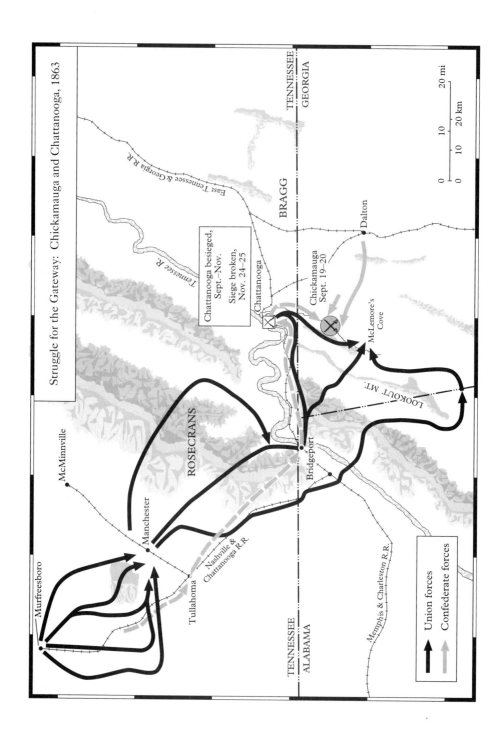

Struggle for the Gateway: Chickamauga and Chattanooga, 1863

McMinnville

Murfreesboro

Manchester

Tullahoma

Nashville &
Chattanooga R.R.

ROSECRANS

Tennessee R.

East Tennessee & Georgia R.R.

Chattanooga besieged,
Sept.–Nov.

Siege broken,
Nov. 24–25

Chattanooga

BRAGG

Bridgeport

LOOKOUT MT.

Chickamauga
Sept. 19–20

McLemore's
Cove

Dalton

Memphis & Charleston R.R.

TENNESSEE
ALABAMA

TENNESSEE
GEORGIA

Union forces

Confederate forces

0   10   20 mi

0   10   20 km

heartland. As events developed, the most fatal blows to the Confederacy would originate from this modest town, hugging a bend in the Tennessee River in the massive shadow of Lookout Mountain. Small wonder that for five months, well over 150,000 men struggled for possession of this city, a struggle in which some 47,000 of them became casualties.

Prologue to Chickamauga

The drive toward Chattanooga did not begin until the year 1863 was almost half over. After the bloody stalemate at Stone's River around New Year's Day, 1863, both the Army of the Cumberland and the Army of Tennessee entered a long period of quiet recuperation. Bragg lacked the numbers to undertake an active campaign. Rosecrans, despite much cajoling from his superiors in Washington, stubbornly refused to begin an advance until he was certain that his army was ready for a sustained offensive that promised decisive results. His subordinates agreed. "We certainly cannot fight the enemy for the mere purpose of whipping him," wrote a division commander. "The time has passed when the fate of armies must be staked because the newspapers have no excitement and do not sell well. I think our people have now comprehended that a battle is a very grave thing."

This was particularly the case if the battle under consideration promised to do no more than push the enemy back a few dozen miles, which was all the carnage at Stone's River the previous winter had done. Instead, Rosecrans hoped that an adroit campaign of maneuver could compel Bragg to fall back all the way to Chattanooga without major fighting. The climactic struggle, when it came, would then be fought for possession of the city itself. Such a thrust, however—effective *and* bloodless—required Rosecrans to place his entire army in Bragg's rear while maintaining his own communications intact. It was one of the most difficult maneuvers in warfare; no Civil War general had managed the feat (although at Second Manassas Lee had come close).

Rosecrans, then, was playing for very high stakes. To win, he believed, required two things. First he must not advance before he was ready. Second, the advance, when made, must be swift and unswerving. It turned out that Rosecrans had a very exacting idea of what it meant to be ready. Not until June 23 did he believe he possessed sufficient cavalry and supply reserves to advance. But when he did he conducted one of the Civil War's most remarkable campaigns. In little more than two weeks of hard marching—punctuated by minor skirmishes in which his army lost just 560 men—Rosecrans seized a key gap in the Cumberland Plateau, turned Bragg's right flank, and forced him to retreat all the way to Chattanooga, a distance of eighty miles. The rough terrain and great difficulty in supplying his army then compelled a pause of several weeks while Rosecrans consolidated his gains. In August he resumed the advance, this time turning Bragg's left flank. While Union artillery kept up a brisk demonstration against Chattanooga, distracting Bragg's attention in that direction, a Union infantry corps crossed the Tennessee River below the town. With his communications now in imminent jeopardy, Bragg abandoned Chattanooga.

The strategic railway city and gateway to the Confederate heartland fell without a fight on September 9.

Predictably, the loss of Chattanooga spurred the Confederate high command to dramatic action. Even before Rosecrans had resumed his advance in August, President Jefferson Davis had considered the possibility of strongly reinforcing Bragg with troops drawn from Joe Johnston in Mississippi. Subsequently Davis conducted a series of conferences with Lee over a two-week period, at the end of which Lee agreed to detach two divisions from his Army of Northern Virginia. These divisions would go by railroad to support Bragg's army; then, with luck and skill, the Army of Tennessee might destroy Rosecrans's force, retrieve Chattanooga, and possibly advance into middle Tennessee.

The most direct line, the Virginia and Tennessee Railroad, was unavailable because of the recent loss of Knoxville, and the two divisions were forced to travel by a circuitous route that doubled the beeline distance. Led by James Longstreet, the reinforcing Confederates rattled along no fewer than ten railroads on dilapidated cars, with frequent transfers and attendant delays. They left Lee's army on September 9, the same day that Chattanooga fell. It took ten days for the first troops to reach Bragg's army. Two-thirds made it in time for the battle then brewing. With their assistance, the Army of Tennessee won its greatest victory.

Chickamauga

The apparent ease with which he had shoved Bragg out of middle Tennessee and Chattanooga made Rosecrans overconfident. Although inordinately careful in his preparations, once on the march Rosecrans tended to be aggressive. As Rosecrans's Union troops swung into northern Georgia in early September, he believed Bragg's Confederates were demoralized and on the defensive. In his judgment, it was important to keep up the pressure and give his opponent no opportunity to sort things out. Bragg, however, was hardly demoralized. Secure in the knowledge that he was about to be reinforced, the Confederate commander kept looking for chances to strike the Federal invaders a resounding blow.

The mountainous Georgia countryside gave Bragg several opportunities, for it forced Rosecrans to send his columns through widely separated gaps. On two occasions the Union commander inadvertently gave the Confederates an excellent chance to concentrate against one or another exposed segment of his army, but on each occasion Bragg's subordinates botched the opportunity. Finally alert to the danger his army was in, Rosecrans ordered his scattered units to concentrate near West Chickamauga Creek about twelve miles south of Chattanooga.

On September 19, Bragg attacked. The two-day battle that ensued was fought in a dense tangle of second-growth timber broken at intervals by small open fields. Both sides had difficulty effectively controlling their units in such terrain; the engagement was really more a series of individual firefights than one concerted battle. The Confederates, for once, had the edge in manpower: about 66,000 rebel effectives against roughly 56,000 Federals. But in the first day's fighting this advantage was largely nullified by Bragg's faulty grasp of the Union dispositions and the confused nature of the fighting, which led to his troops being committed piecemeal. Late in the evening, however, he reorganized his army into two informal wings, placed them under his senior commanders—Lieutenant Generals Longstreet and Leonidas Polk—and made plans to resume the battle next morning.

The fighting on September 20 began about 9:30 A.M. and consisted of a series of sequential attacks made from north to south. None of these charges made much headway, however, and by 11 A.M. Bragg abandoned this *en echelon* approach in favor of a straightforward thrust by his remaining force. Until this moment the Federals had waged a capable defense and by and large had rebuffed every Confederate attack. In the process, however, Rosecrans was forced to shift some of his units from one threatened point to another—much as Lee had done at Antietam. But where Lee had conducted this delicate operation almost flawlessly, Rosecrans—in part confused by the terrain—made a major mistake. Seeking to plug a small hole in his line, he ordered a division shifted from one part of the field to another. That, in turn, created a very large hole: a hole, it turned out, just where four divisions under Longstreet were moving to attack.

The result, of course, was a shattering defeat for the Union army as some 20,000 Confederates poured into the gap. Three entire Union divisions ceased to exist as organized units; two more divisions had to withdraw from the field and could not return to the fray until evening. Rosecrans himself, crestfallen and dispirited, virtually abandoned the field. Two of his corps commanders did the same. Only a magnificent stand by a Union corps under Major General George H. Thomas saved Rosecrans's army from complete disaster. In a masterful defense of Snodgrass Hill in the center of the battlefield, Thomas blunted the momentum of the Confederate attack and enabled the rest of the army to withdraw intact. For that achievement he was known ever after as the "Rock of Chickamauga."

Confederate casualties in the battle totaled 18,454; the Union lost 16,170. Rosecrans's army fell back exhausted into Chattanooga. Bragg refused to pursue vigorously and elected to besiege the Union army by holding the high ground south and east of the town. Despite the victory, most of his subordinates were disgruntled with Bragg's battlefield performance and the way in which he tamely let Rosecrans escape enraged at least one of them. "What does he fight battles for?" growled Confederate cavalry leader Nathan Bedford Forrest. Still, the Army of the Cumberland had suffered a signal defeat, and if it were starved into surrender at Chattanooga, the Union disaster would undo most of what the victories at Vicksburg and Gettysburg had achieved.

Missionary Ridge

In this crisis the Lincoln administration turned to Grant. At the end of September, Secretary of War Edwin M. Stanton arranged an emergency conference with Grant at Louisville, Kentucky. There he gave Grant an order placing him in charge of substantially the entire western theater—everything from the Mississippi River to the Appalachian Mountains except Louisiana. Stanton also asked Grant to decide whether Rosecrans should be relieved. Grant thought he should, and Rosecrans was replaced by Major General George H. Thomas.

The Lincoln administration took one other decisive step as well. It withdrew two entire corps—20,000 men—from Meade's Army of the Potomac and sent them west to reinforce the beleaguered troops in Chattanooga. Railroads had been used throughout the conflict to shuttle troops about, but this September 1863 movement was a logistical tour de force. Within forty hours of the initial decision, the first units were on their way west. Eleven days and 1,200 miles later practically all the detached troops, together with their artillery, horses, and wagons, had reached Bridgeport, Alabama, staging point for the relief of Chattanooga.

Late in October, Grant personally went to Chattanooga to have a closer look at the situation. His party rode on horseback via the only route that remained open into or out of the city—a narrow road, hardly more than a bridle path in spots, that wound about sixty-five miles from Bridgeport to Chattanooga through a desolate stretch of mountains. This road formed the only means by which the besieged Army of the Cumberland could receive supplies. The supplies amounted to hardly more than a trickle, and once at Chattanooga Grant discovered that the horses were starving and the men not far from it.

Efforts to repair the situation got under way as soon as Grant arrived. Within days the Union troops broke out of their encirclement enough to reestablish a solid supply line through the Tennessee River valley—a "Cracker Line," the men called it. Along with a welcome deluge of rations, thousands of reinforcements arrived to help drive away the Confederate army. In addition to the two corps from Virginia, most of Grant's own Army of the Tennessee, now led by red-bearded General Sherman, came up from Mississippi. A new spirit entered the beleaguered army at Chattanooga. "You have no conception of the change in the army when Grant came," one soldier testified. "He opened up the cracker line and got a steamer through. We began to see things move. We felt that everything came from a plan. He came into the army quietly, no splendor, no airs, no staff. He used to go about alone. He began the campaign the moment he reached the field."

By mid-autumn the Union armies were ready to attack, and on November 24–25 they conducted a series of offensives aimed at breaking the Confederate grip on Chattanooga. The unexpected climax of these battles occurred on the second day of fighting, when Thomas's Army of the Cumberland transformed what had been planned as a limited thrust into a wild, hell-for-leather charge up the rugged slopes of Missionary Ridge, smack into the center of the whole Confederate line. It seemed impossible that such a charge could succeed, and Grant, watching the impromptu attack, remarked that if it failed whoever had ordered the assault was going to sweat for it. Yet, incredibly, the Union troops made it to the top and routed the astonished Confederates.

At first glance the victory appeared, if not a "visible interposition of God," as someone remarked, then at least a vindication of continued faith in the frontal assault. In fact it could more accurately be seen as the harvest of sloppy Confederate planning. Most of the Confederate defenders had been placed, not at the military crest of the ridge—the highest point from which a marksman could hit what was below him—but at the topographical crest, where he generally could not hit much of anything. In addition, a good number of rebel soldiers had been deployed at the foot of the ridge, where they were too few to stop the Federal advance, but sufficiently numerous, when they retreated, to force their comrades at the summit to hold their fire. Finally, the Confederates had neglected to cover the numerous ravines that led to the top, so that the assaulting Federal columns found numerous covered avenues as they scrambled up the slope.

Thus through Bragg's failure to pursue Rosecrans after Chickamauga and his mismanaged siege of Chattanooga, the Federals were able to restore the situation, secure permanent control of this gateway city, and win a glittering autumn victory at surprisingly low cost. The Union lost 5,800 men, slightly more than 10 percent of the total engaged. The Confederates lost 6,700 out of 46,000, and embarked on a retreat that did not end until they reached Dalton, Georgia, some twenty-five miles away. The road into the Southern heartland was now open.

Even after the North decided to recruit African Americans as soldiers, fears persisted that blacks would not make effective soldiers. As units like the 54th Massachusetts demonstrated, such fears were misplaced. Its assault at Fort Wagner, South Carolina, in July 1863 was one of the most famous of the war.

* * * *

By the end of 1863 the Confederacy had lost not only two key strategic points—Vicksburg and Chattanooga—it had also lost a great deal of its ability to counterpunch effectively. Lee's great victory at Chancellorsville and his great disaster at Gettysburg had, between them, cost the South about 33,000 men. Roughly the same number went into the bag with Pemberton's capitulation at Vicksburg. The Confederacy simply could not afford to sustain such casualties. It had nearly reached the bottom of its manpower pool, and the losses of 1863 included many of its most experienced and motivated soldiers. The North, by contrast, still had ample manpower reserves. It also had begun to reap one advantage of the Emancipation Proclamation by recruiting and fielding thousands of African-American troops. The first black units had their baptism of fire in 1863 and, to the surprise of white men North and South, performed with courage and élan. Ultimately a full 10 percent of the Union army—180,000 men in all—would be composed of black soldiers.

The reversals of 1863 also began a long-term decline in Confederate morale. The South had endured at least one previous crisis of confidence, during the first six months of 1862, but this second crisis was just as bad. Desertions swelled in the months after Gettysburg and Vicksburg as soldiers decided that "we are done gon up the Spout." A Confederate war department clerk described Chattanooga as an "incalculable disaster," while the wife of a prominent Southern leader wrote that "gloom and unspoken despondency hang like a pall everywhere." As the New Year approached, Southerners knew that the most terrible trial of the war was at hand.

SUGGESTED READINGS

Black, Robert C., III. *The Railroads of the Confederacy* (Chapel Hill: University of North Carolina Press, 1952).

Catton, Bruce. *Grant Moves South* (Boston: Little, Brown, 1960).

———. *Never Call Retreat* (Garden City, N.Y.: Doubleday, 1965).

Coddington, Edwin A. *The Gettysburg Campaign: A Study in Command* (New York: Charles Scribner's Sons, 1968).

Connelly, Thomas L. *Autumn of Glory: The Army of Tennessee, 1863–1865* (Baton Rouge: Louisiana State University Press, 1970).

Cornish, Dudley Taylor. *The Sable Arm: Black Troops in the Union Army, 1861–1865* (New York: Longmans, Green, 1956).

Cozzens, Peter. *This Terrible Sound: The Battle of Chickamauga* (Urbana and Chicago: University of Illinois Press, 1992).

Escott, Paul D. *After Secession: Jefferson Davis and the Failure of Confederate Nationalism* (Baton Rouge: Louisiana State University Press, 1979).

Furgurson, Ernest B. *Chancellorsville 1863: The Souls of the Brave* (New York: Alfred A. Knopf, 1992).

Geary, John. *We Need Men: The Union Draft in the Civil War, 1861–1865* (DeKalb: Northern Illinois University Press, 1990).

Glatthaar, Joseph T. *Forged in Battle: The Civil War Alliance of Black Soldiers and White Officers* (New York: Free Press, 1989).

Griffith, Paddy. *Civil War Battle Tactics* (New Haven, Conn.: Yale University Press, 1989).

Hagerman, Edward. *The American Civil War and the Origins of Modern Warfare* (Bloomington: Indiana University Press, 1988).

McWhiney, Grady, and Perry D. Jamieson. *Attack and Die: Civil War Military Tactics and the Southern Heritage* (University, Ala.: University of Alabama Press, 1982).

Paludan, Philip S. *A People's Contest: The Union and the Civil War, 1861–1865* (New York: Harper & Row, 1988).

Royster, Charles. *The Destructive War: William Tecumseh Sherman, Stonewall Jackson, and the Americans* (New York: Alfred A. Knopf, 1991).

Weber, Thomas. *The Northern Railroads in the Civil War, 1861–1865* (Westport, Conn.: Greenwood Press, 1952).

14

THE CIVIL WAR, 1864–1865:
TOTAL WAR

The Virginia Campaign
To Atlanta and Beyond
The Naval War, 1862–1865
The War Ends

The final year of the Civil War witnessed the full bloom of total war. No western state in centuries had waged a military contest more comprehensively than did the Union and Confederacy. Determined national efforts the world had seen: during the Napoleonic Wars the Spanish and Russian people had fought relentlessly against the French invaders; and in 1813 the Russians had pursued the retreating French for nearly a thousand miles. Yet neither the Spanish nor the Russians had mobilized their populations and economies as systematically as did the North and South. Also, when the allies carried the war into France in 1814, they did not make a sustained effort to destroy the French people's capacity to make war. By 1864, however, the North was not only bringing pressure against the Confederate field armies but was also striking powerfully at the material and psychological resources of the South.

In strictly military terms, the South now had little chance to win the war. With Lee's offensive power blunted, the trans-Mississippi isolated, and Chattanooga in Union hands, the Confederacy's strategic situation was bleak. Moreover, the battles of previous years had bled rebel manpower so heavily that by early 1864 the Confederate Congress was forced to pass a new conscription law that abolished substitutes and "robbed the cradle and the grave" in an effort to secure more troops. Even this did not help. In desperation, a few Confederate leaders began to ponder the previously unthinkable option of using slaves as soldiers—and, in exchange, to emancipate those slaves who agreed to fight for the South.

Most, however, continued to regard this last step as anathema. Instead they pinned their hopes on the fact that in November 1864, Lincoln faced reelection. If the South could only hold out until then, the war weariness of Northerners might result in his losing the White House. "If we can break up the enemy's arrangements early, and throw him back," noted one Confederate general, "he will not be able to recover his position or his morale until the Presidential election is over, and then we shall have a new President to treat with." Presumably this new president would be receptive to a compromise peace.

Lincoln, of course, understood the rebel hope as well as anyone, and he had no intention of permitting a prolonged stalemate. Instead he did what most observers had assumed he would do since the triumph at Chattanooga: he gave Ulysses S. Grant command of all the Union armies. With the new job came the three stars of a lieutenant general, a rank not held by any U.S. officer (except honorifically) since George Washington. In March 1864, Grant came to Washington, met Lincoln for the first time, received his promotion, and settled down to win the war.

The Virginia Campaign

Now installed as general-in-chief (with Halleck retained as army chief of staff), Grant began planning at once for the 1864 campaigns. The content of those plans and the way in which he devised them provide a good lens through which to examine the salient features of his generalship.

To begin with, Grant saw the war as a whole. Until that time most Union generals had viewed the conflict in terms of separate theaters; no one placed much premium on cooperative effort. As a result, the outnumbered Confederate forces had been able to shift troops from one place to another, shoring up one threatened point by diverting strength from quiet sectors. In this way Johnston had gathered over 30,000 soldiers for his vain but bothersome effort to relieve Vicksburg; in this way as well, troops from all over the Confederacy had gathered to administer the near-crippling blow to Rosecrans at Chickamauga. To prevent the Confederates from shifting troops from quiet to threatened sectors, Grant planned for a simultaneous advance along the entire front.

Second, Grant was less interested in occupying "strategic points" than in destroying the enemy's main forces. He believed that when no armies remained to defend them, the strategic points would fall as a matter of course. Important cities like Richmond and Atlanta were useful chiefly because the main Confederate armies would fight for them, and in the course of fighting they could be destroyed. Grant put this concept succinctly in a letter to Major General George Gordon Meade, commander of the Army of the Potomac: "Lee's army is your objective point. Wherever Lee goes, there you will go also."

Third, Grant wanted the 1864 spring offensive to be as strong as possible. He regretted the detachment of so many Union troops on passive occupation duty. Some of this could not be helped—by this period of the

The architect of victory. Appointed to command the Union armies in March 1864, Ulysses S. Grant quickly applied a strategy of maintaining constant military pressure on the Confederacy through coordinated offensives to wear down Southern armies and destroy Southern war resources.

war the Federal armies had to contend with well over 100,000 square miles of captured hostile territory—but it struck Grant that all too often the passive stance was unnecessary. At an April conference with Lincoln, Grant expressed the view that these detachments could do their jobs "just as well by advancing as by remaining still; and by advancing they would compel the enemy to keep detachments to hold them back, or else lay his own territory open to invasion." Lincoln grasped the point at once. "Oh, yes!" he said. "I see that. As we say out West, if a man can't skin he must hold a leg while somebody else does."

Finally, Grant expected to combine destruction of Southern armies with destruction of Southern war resources. Although Sherman would become the general most identified with this policy, Grant had a profound understanding of the fact that Civil War armies had become too large and too powerful to destroy in battle. Their annihilation required not only military defeat but also the elimination of the foodstuffs, forage, ammunition, and equipage necessary to maintain them in the field. His instructions to Sherman reflect this: "You I propose to move against [Joseph E.] Johnston's army, to break it up, and to get into the interior of the enemy's country as far as you can, inflicting all the damage you can against their war resources."

Grant refused to direct operations from Washington and decided to make his headquarters with the Army of the Potomac. He had good reason

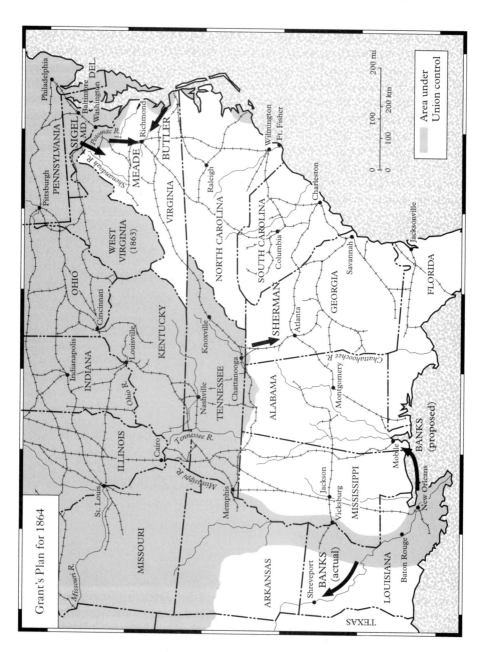

Grant's Plan for 1864

for doing so. That army formed one of the two primary concentrations of Union force; as such it would play a decisive role in the campaign to come. But except for its single defensive victory at Gettysburg, the Army of the Potomac had a depressing record of stalemate or defeat; in its entire existence it had never won a clear-cut offensive victory. Worse, the army had traditionally suffered from its close proximity to Washington, which made it strongly susceptible to political pressures and even to factionalism among the officer corps. In short, the Army of the Potomac seemed to need firsthand attention far more than the other reservoir of Federal striking power—the combined armies of the Cumberland, the Tennessee, and the Ohio—which Sherman had assembled at Chattanooga. Sherman, in any event, enjoyed Grant's entire confidence.

Grant also came to think highly of General Meade, leader of the Army of the Potomac. He had never met Meade before his arrival in Virginia and did not know what to expect, but Meade impressed him by offering to step aside immediately if Grant wished to put someone in his place. Grant declined the offer and Meade remained in command; even so, Grant exerted such close supervision over the Army of the Potomac that it quickly became known, erroneously but enduringly, as "Grant's army."

Grant's final plan for the great 1864 campaign pressed the Confederacy on all sides: in the eastern theater, the Army of the Potomac would advance against General Robert E. Lee's Army of Northern Virginia. Two smaller forces would "hold a leg": Major General Franz Sigel would advance up the Shenandoah Valley while Major General Benjamin F. Butler would conduct an amphibious operation against the Richmond-Petersburg area. Unfortunately, Sigel and Butler were political generals, men of little or no military ability who held important commands exclusively because they had strong influence with constituencies important to the Union war effort. (Sigel was a hero among the German-American community, Butler an important Democrat.) Grant would have been justified in expecting nothing at all from these men. Instead he pinned many of his hopes for the upcoming Virginia campaign on the belief that both would perform capably. Grant gave Butler an especially significant role: he anticipated that Butler's army would be able to seize the important railroad town of Petersburg and perhaps even capture Richmond itself.

Out west, Sherman's three armies would move upon Johnston's Army of Tennessee. Grant had hoped that yet another force, under General Banks, might advance from Louisiana against Mobile, Alabama, but for political reasons Banks marched up the cotton-rich but strategically irrelevant Red River valley. Except for Banks, who had already made—and lost—his campaign by early April, the remaining operations were timed to jump off simultaneously in early May 1864.

The Wilderness and Spotsylvania

Grant, of course, paid closest attention to the offensive against Lee. On May 4 the Army of the Potomac crossed the Rapidan River into the

Wilderness, the same region where Hooker had come to grief the year before. Some miles to the west lay Lee's Army of Northern Virginia. By crossing here, Grant hoped to turn Lee's right flank and compel him to retreat. But that same day Lee got his troops in motion and came thundering east; early the next morning he hurled them into action against two Union corps as they struggled along the narrow lanes of the Wilderness.

Outnumbered nearly two to one (64,000 men against Grant's 119,000), Lee wanted to force a battle in the Wilderness where thick woods would dilute the Union numerical advantage and make it difficult for the Federals to use their numerous and well-trained artillery. During the next two days he savaged the Union army with a sustained intensity Grant had never experienced in his previous campaigns. Those who *had* experienced it were not slow to offer advice. On the second day of the fighting one Union general told him, "General Grant, this is a crisis that cannot be looked upon too seriously. I know Lee's methods well by past experience; he will throw his whole army between us and the Rapidan, and cut us off completely from our communications." Usually phlegmatic, Grant permitted himself a rare show of annoyance. "Oh, I am heartily tired of hearing what Lee is going to do. Some of you always seem to think he is suddenly going to turn a double somersault and land in our rear and on both of our flanks at the same time. Go back to your command," he snapped, "and try to think what we are going to do ourselves, instead of what Lee is going to do."

This kind of thinking brought something new to the Army of the Potomac. The fighting in the Wilderness cost the Union nearly 17,000 casu-

In Virginia, Grant's 1864 campaign began with two bitter days of fighting in the densely wooded Wilderness. Many wounded men on both sides were burned to death when the trees and undergrowth caught fire. Despite harrowing losses, Grant maintained pressure on Lee's army.

alties; Lee, by contrast suffered no more than about 10,000. In earlier days the Army of the Potomac would have retreated after such a battle to lick its wounds. Grant, however, decided simply to disengage and continue his effort to get around Lee's flank. After suffering for years from a chronic sense of inferiority, the Army of the Potomac found itself led by a man who never thought in terms of defeat and who did not lose his will to fight when confronted by casualties.

The army began moving during the evening of May 7, heading for Spotsylvania Court House, an important crossroads, ten miles southeast of the Wilderness, whose swift possession would allow the Union forces to interpose between Richmond and Lee. Confederate troops got there first, however, and in a series of sharp little engagements held the crossroads long enough for Lee's army to arrive in strength. For twelve days (May 9–21), the two armies grappled inconclusively in the fields north and east of Spotsylvania.

Unlike the Wilderness, where Lee had counterattacked early and often, at Spotsylvania the Army of Northern Virginia fought almost entirely behind entrenchments. Grant viewed this as a confession of Confederate weakness. At the same time, however, he found it very difficult to crack the rebel line. On May 10, for example, an imaginative young West Point graduate named Emory Upton managed to break into the Confederate entrenchments using a new tactical scheme of his own devising. His division advanced in column formation, without pausing to fire en route—Upton took the precaution of having his men charge with muskets uncapped except for the leading rank. The attack indeed broke the rebel line, but supporting Federal troops failed to arrive and Upton reluctantly withdrew.

Grant, however, was sufficiently impressed with the new tactic to try it again, this time using an entire corps. Shortly after dawn on May 12 the corps struck a prominent salient in the Confederate position known as the "Mule Shoe." As in Upton's charge, the Federals broke through the enemy trenches, this time capturing more than 4,000 prisoners. Lee was forced to counterattack in a desperate attempt to restore the breach, resulting in some of the most ferocious combat of the entire war. In many places the fighting was hand to hand, and at one point the bullets flew so thick that an oak tree nearly two feet in diameter was completely cut in two. By evening Lee managed to complete a new line of entrenchments across the base of the Mule Shoe, and the surviving Confederates withdrew. In a pattern that would be repeated endlessly during World War I, the defenders had managed to repair a breach in their fortified line faster than the attackers could exploit it.

To the Banks of the James River

Initially Grant was determined to break the Confederates at Spotsylvania— he wired Washington, "I propose to fight it out on this line if it takes all summer." But by mid-May it had become obvious that both secondary offensives in Virginia had failed. A hastily assembled rebel force defeated Sigel on May 15 at the Battle of New Market. Butler landed at the tip of a peninsula

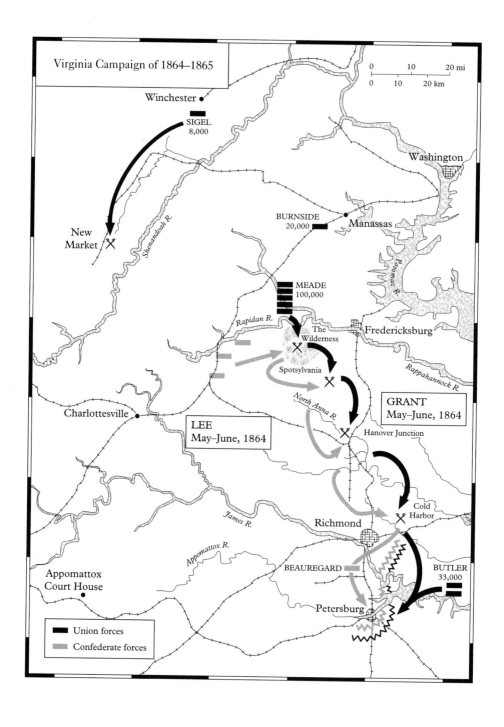

Virginia Campaign of 1864–1865

0   10   20 mi
0   10   20 km

Winchester

SIGEL
8,000

Washington

New
Market ⚔

Shenandoah R.

BURNSIDE
20,000   Manassas

Potomac R.

MEADE
100,000

Rapidan R.

The
Wilderness ⚔   Fredericksburg

Spotsylvania ⚔

Rappahannock R.

North Anna R.

Charlottesville

LEE
May–June, 1864

GRANT
May–June, 1864

Hanover Junction ⚔

James R.

Richmond   Cold
Harbor ⚔

Appomattox
Court House   Appomattox R.   BEAUREGARD   BUTLER
33,000

Petersburg

■ Union forces
▨ Confederate forces

formed by the James and Appomattox rivers, advanced a short distance inland, then stalled. A much smaller Confederate detachment soon sealed off the neck of the peninsula with entrenchments. This left Butler's force, in Grant's scornful words, "as completely shut off from further operations against Richmond as if it had been in a bottle strongly corked." Designed to place additional pressure on Lee and siphon troops from his army, these efforts to "hold a leg" wound up having the opposite effect: with Sigel beaten and Butler neutralized, Lee received 8,500 reinforcements from the forces that had opposed the two Union generals.

Lee's increased strength made "fighting it out" at Spotsylvania no longer such a good idea. Unable to dislodge the Confederate commander, Grant attempted once again to slide past Lee's right flank and continue his advance southward. The formula he had given Meade before the campaign—"Wherever Lee goes, there you will go also"—became reversed: wherever Grant went, Lee went also, and Lee invariably got there first. Yet in every previous campaign, Lee had found a way to wrest the initiative from his opponent. Grant gave him no such opportunity. The Union general-in-chief had both the military strength and the moral determination to keep moving on.

The campaign in progress resembled nothing that had come before. Previous Civil War operations had usually followed a fairly classic pattern: long periods of preliminary maneuver, careful sparring as the opposing forces located one another, then a major battle that ended in clear-cut victory or defeat. Grant's campaign, on the other hand, amounted to a six-week brawl in which the armies seldom broke contact for more than a few hours and from which no clear decision emerged. The losses it generated horrified the Northern population. In the long months since Shiloh the North had grown used to casualty lists on the same scale as those of that bloody struggle; but the fighting in May and early June 1864 produced 55,000 Union dead, wounded, and missing—about five times the cost of Shiloh. Confederate losses exceeded 20,000: much fewer than those of the Federals, but about the same in proportion to the forces engaged.

The campaign differed in one other respect as well. Both sides had learned the value of field fortifications; indeed, the soldiers had gotten so that they would dig in without orders and practically every time they halted for more than a few minutes. "It is a rule," wrote one Union officer, "that when the Rebels halt, the first day gives them a good rifle-pit; the second, a regular infantry parapet with artillery in position; and the third a parapet with abatis [sharpened stakes] in front and entrenched batteries behind. Sometimes they put this three days' work into the first twenty-four hours." These entrenchments had the effect of making it almost impossible to carry a defensive position; those who attempted it generally got slaughtered, while their killers found almost total protection behind rifle pits and earthen parapets.

Though the generals did not quickly grasp the full significance of this, the Battle of Cold Harbor provided a final, chilling lesson. By early June, Grant's army had gotten within seven miles of Richmond, but it had not yet beaten Lee's army and it had nearly run out of room to maneuver:

further efforts to turn the Confederates would run into the tidal estuary of the James River. Partly because of this situation, and partly because Grant thought he discerned a weakness in Lee's line, he ordered a frontal assault against Lee's entrenched defenses. The attack jumped off at about 4:30 A.M. on June 3. It was really nothing more than a succession of charges made along different parts of the line, most of which collapsed within minutes, smashed beneath an annihilating storm of rifle and artillery fire. The abortive and bloody attack cost nearly 7,000 Union casualties. Grant later called it one of two attacks during the war he wished he had not ordered.

With no prospect whatever of breaking through to Richmond, Grant then went forward with an operation he had pondered even while the armies were still fighting at Spotsylvania. He would shift the Army of the Potomac south of the James River, use the river as his line of supply, and try to get at Petersburg, a city about twenty miles south of Richmond through which the Confederate capital—and Lee's army—received most of its supplies. Between June 12 and 16 the Union forces made the crossing, with Grant managing the feat so adroitly that for several days Lee did not know what was being done. As a result the Army of the Potomac almost seized Petersburg before an adequate rebel force could arrive to hold the city. Through misperception and bad management on the part of Meade's subordinates, however, the fleeting opportunity vanished. Lee's army scrambled down to Petersburg, entered fortifications already in place to defend the city, and once again forced a stalemate. The Army of the Potomac settled in for a siege; for the next ten months, Lee and Grant faced one another across a trench-scarred landscape.

The Siege of Petersburg

Militarily the stalemate at Petersburg suited Grant just fine. Although ideally he would have preferred to destroy Lee's army outright, at a minimum he expected the Army of the Potomac's advance to pressure Lee so strongly that the Confederate would be unable to send any troops to support Johnston in his defense against Sherman. This the Army of the Potomac had accomplished. Sherman, meanwhile, was steadily pushing Johnston's army back toward Atlanta, and Grant regarded the Georgia offensive as crucial. Once Sherman had gained control of Atlanta, the entire Southern heartland would lay open, and therein lay the ultimate key to Union victory.

Politically, however, the stalemate in Virginia was sheer poison. Northerners considered it unacceptable that the bloody campaign to reach the Richmond-Petersburg area should have yielded nothing better than a deadlock. War weariness had set in, and although on the map the Union armies had made great gains, none of them seemed to have brought the conclusion of the struggle one whit nearer. Many Northerners began to feel that perhaps the only way to end the war lay in a negotiated, compromise peace. Worse, with the 1864 presidential election approaching, they might well register their discouragement at the polls if the stalemate continued.

Summer brought no reversal in Union fortunes. Grant could not get into Petersburg; Sherman drew nearer to Atlanta but found that the city's fortifications firmly barred entry. Meanwhile Lee managed what looked like a real victory: in June he detached a corps under Lieutenant General Jubal Early and sent him swinging northwest toward the Shenandoah Valley. After clearing the valley of Union troops, Early's men crossed into western Maryland, sliced southeast toward Washington, and by mid-July actually carried their raid to within sight of the Federal Capitol building. Although the Confederates could not penetrate the powerful fortifications that ringed Washington and Union reinforcements soon arrived to drive them away, this seemed less significant than the sheer fact that, in the summer of 1864, a major Confederate force could still successfully threaten the Union capital. Early's raid, coupled with the apparent lack of Union success in Virginia and Georgia, boded ill for the upcoming November election. In August 1864 Northern morale reached its nadir, and Lincoln gloomily predicted that he would shortly lose the presidency.

To Atlanta and Beyond

What saved Lincoln was the capture of Atlanta—another potent demonstration of the close connection between battlefield developments and politics. The chief author of his salvation was Major General William Tecumseh Sherman, Grant's most trusted lieutenant and his choice to head the Military Division of the Mississippi. The triumph came after four months of steady campaigning along the one-hundred-mile corridor that separated Chattanooga and Atlanta. It probably destroyed what remained of the Confederacy's chance to win the Civil War.

Northern Georgia

The Atlanta Campaign pitted Sherman against Joseph E. Johnston, the Confederate general chosen to replace Bragg after the humiliating Chattanooga fiasco. Sherman led approximately 100,000 men, divided into three parts: the Army of the Cumberland, commanded by Major General George H. Thomas; the Army of the Tennessee, led by Major General James B. McPherson; and the corps-sized Army of the Ohio, commanded by Major General John M. Schofield. To oppose the Union forces Johnston had just 50,000 men (although he was shortly reinforced to about 60,000). Although outnumbered, the Confederates had the advantage of fighting on the defensive in rugged mountain country well-suited to the purpose.

Ever since Chattanooga, the Confederate Army of Tennessee had been posted at Dalton, Georgia, and had strongly fortified Rocky Face Ridge just northwest of the town. Sherman called this position "the terrible door of death." A direct attack was out of the question. Instead, in early May he sent McPherson's army on a long swing around the rebel left flank while Thomas and Schofield distracted Johnston. McPherson managed to penetrate into the Confederate rear through a carelessly guarded mountain gap. This penetration forced Johnston to abandon his first line and retreat about ten miles to Resaca. Sherman had taken the first trick, but in retrospect he realized that McPherson had missed a great opportunity. Had he acted more aggressively he might have cut Johnston's line of retreat, but instead McPherson had obeyed the letter of Sherman's orders and avoided this daring but risky move. "Well, Mac," Sherman told his protegé, "you missed the opportunity of your life."

The rival armies lingered three days at Resaca while Sherman vainly searched for a weakness in Johnston's line. Finding none, he sent McPherson on a second wide sweep around the Confederate left flank. This time Johnston withdrew another twenty-five miles until he reached Cassville on May 19. Thus, in twelve days' time the Army of Tennessee had yielded about half the distance from Dalton to Atlanta. President Jefferson Davis was considerably disgruntled by this development, but given the great disparity in troop strength Johnston felt he had little choice.

One of his key subordinates disagreed, however. Lieutenant General John B. Hood, a former division commander in the Army of Northern Virginia, had come west during Longstreet's September 1863 redeployment and had remained with the Army of Tennessee. A gallant fighter—he had lost an arm at Gettysburg and a leg at Chickamauga—Hood had been befriended by President Davis and his wife and had been given command of a corps in the Army of Tennessee. He knew Davis and Johnston despised one another and, as a good Davis ally, sent the president a stream of private letters critical of the army commander. Trained in the offensive school of warfare favored by Lee, Hood considered Johnston far too cautious. Sherman, he believed, should be dealt a whole-souled counterpunch of the sort that had bested McClellan, Pope, and Hooker. Davis agreed and considered relieving Johnston of command if he continued to retreat.

Johnston, however, remained true to his Fabian tactics. (Ironically, on the one occasion when he did plan a counterstroke, Hood proved unready and urged that the attack be called off.) The Army of Tennessee occupied one well-entrenched defensive position after another. Sherman, meanwhile, made yet another swing around the Confederate left flank. The move brought him a few miles closer to Atlanta but no closer to "breaking up" Johnston's army as Grant had instructed.

Unfortunately for Sherman, his three armies relied for supply on a single railroad coming down from Chattanooga. Johnston destroyed the railroad as he withdrew and although Sherman's engineers quickly repaired the damage, Sherman realized the vulnerability of this line. He particularly feared that Confederate cavalry raiders—especially the fearsome Bedford Forrest—might damage his communications in Tennessee, and he diverted thousands of Union troops to forestall them. Consequently, instead of making Confederate raids, Forrest spent the summer of 1864 largely responding to Federal raids into Mississippi. The tactic worked: although Forrest racked

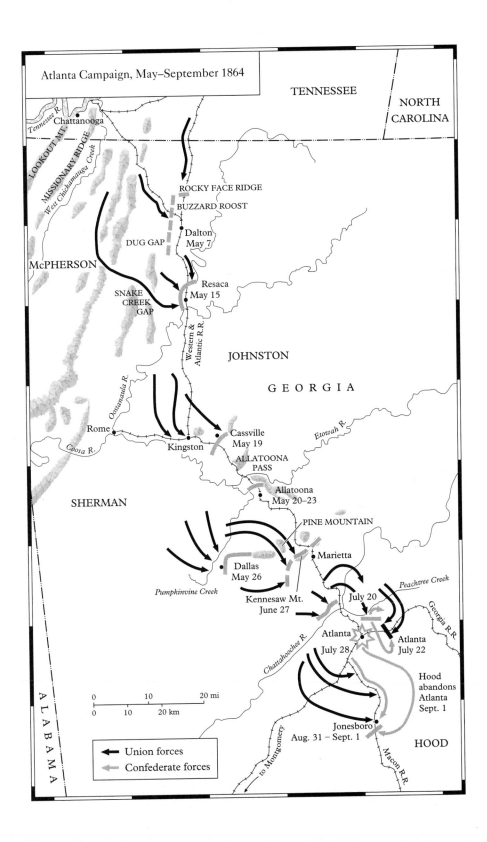

Atlanta Campaign, May–September 1864

TENNESSEE

NORTH CAROLINA

Tennessee R.
Chattanooga

LOOKOUT MT.

MISSIONARY RIDGE

West Chickamauga Creek

ROCKY FACE RIDGE

BUZZARD ROOST

DUG GAP

Dalton
May 7

McPHERSON

SNAKE CREEK GAP

Resaca
May 15

Western & Atlantic R.R.

JOHNSTON

GEORGIA

Oostanaula R.

Rome

Coosa R.

Kingston

Cassville
May 19

Etowah R.

ALLATOONA PASS

Allatoona
May 20–23

SHERMAN

PINE MOUNTAIN

Dallas
May 26

Marietta

Pumpkinvine Creek

Kennesaw Mt.
June 27

July 20

Peachtree Creek

Georgia R.R.

Atlanta
July 28

Atlanta
July 22

Chattahoochee R.

Hood abandons Atlanta Sept. 1

0   10   20 mi
0   10   20 km

Jonesboro
Aug. 31 – Sept. 1

HOOD

A L A B A M A

to Montgomery

Macon R.

Union forces
Confederate forces

up an impressive series of victories against these raiding forces, he was forced to leave Sherman's communications alone.

For the first two months of the Atlanta Campaign neither side risked a major battle. As a result, neither side lost heavily; the Union armies, indeed, suffered casualties only marginally greater than the Confederates. Finally, on June 27, Sherman mounted a major assault upon Johnston's center at Kennesaw Mountain. This part of the Confederate line appeared weak to Sherman, who thought a breakthrough might be possible. Moreover, recent rains had reduced his army's mobility so that the alternative to an attack was delay. Then too, Sherman believed, "The enemy as well as my own army had settled down to the belief that flanking alone was my game." By attacking, he hoped to convince Johnston that he might strike anywhere and thus that Johnston must hold his entire line in strength. He also thought it would restore some aggressiveness to his own troops. They had become so chary of fortifications, he complained, that a "fresh furrow in a plowed field will stop a whole column, and all begin to entrench." But the Battle of Kennesaw Mountain cost his army 2,000 casualties, against just 450 for the Confederates, and gained not an inch of ground.

Sherman then reverted to the flanking game. He made a fourth move around Johnston's left flank, breached the line of the Chattahoochee River—the last real barrier separating him from Atlanta—and followed up with a fifth turning movement, this time around the Confederate right flank. By mid-July, Johnston had withdrawn behind the outer fortifications that ringed the city itself. Although the Army of Tennessee remained intact, it had run out of room to maneuver.

Battles for Atlanta

At about this time a visiting congressional delegation warned Johnston that Davis would surely remove him if he continued his passive defense. Artlessly, one of the congressmen quoted a story that was then making the rounds in Richmond, to the effect that the president had said that "if he were in your place he could whip Sherman now." "Yes," Johnston harrumphed. "I know Mr. Davis thinks he can do a great many things other men would hesitate to attempt. For instance, he tried to do what God failed to do. He tried to make a soldier of Braxton Bragg, and you know the result. It couldn't be done."

Johnston might have heeded the delegation's warning. On July 17, Davis removed him and substituted Hood. He made the change despite misgivings expressed by Lee, who of course had once commanded Hood. Asked for his opinion, Lee was candid: "It is a bad time to release the commander of an army situated as that of Tennessee. We may lose Atlanta and the army too. Hood is a bold fighter. I am doubtful as to other qualities necessary." In perhaps the most controversial military decision Davis made during the war, he went ahead with the replacement anyway. Johnston, despite his excessive caution, had been a canny tactician and frugal with his limited supply of manpower. Hood did exactly what the president wanted:

As this photo attests, the Confederate manufacturing center of Atlanta, Georgia, was one of the most heavily fortified cities in America by mid-1864. Its capture by Sherman's army in September 1864 electrified the North, dismayed the South, and helped ensure Lincoln's reelection two months later.

he fought. The result, as Lee had suspected, was the loss of Atlanta and the crippling of Hood's army.

On July 19, Hood struck the Union Army of the Cumberland while its two sister armies were attempting another of their inevitable turning movements. He achieved little. Two days later he struck again, this time against McPherson's Army of the Tennessee. The attack was adroitly made, but as usual the defending side had the resilience and flexibility to recover and restore the line. A third assault on July 28 resulted in a virtual massacre. Although McPherson was killed in one of these battles (one of only two army commanders to suffer such a fate), Hood's army lost about 15,000 of its 40,000 effectives; Federal casualties numbered just 5,400.

Hood, like his predecessor, now withdrew into the Atlanta fortifications. Sherman inaugurated a quasi-siege, lobbing shells into the beleaguered city, and meanwhile planned to cut the railroads connecting Atlanta with the rest of the South. In late August he carried out this operation. Leaving one corps to distract Hood, he took the rest of his armies on one last turning movement, this time to a point well south of the city. Hood recognized the move and turned to meet it, but he was too late. Sherman had gotten squarely across the Confederate line of communications. When a desperate Confederate counterstroke at Jonesboro failed to dislodge Sherman, Hood had no choice but to abandon the city. It fell on September 2, 1864.

Hood's army, badly weakened, drew off into northern Alabama and tried with limited success to destroy Sherman's extended supply lines.

The fall of Atlanta sealed the fate of the Confederacy. Until then the possibility existed that Lincoln would lose his bid for reelection that year because the North, like the South, had grown increasingly frustrated with a war that seemed to go on interminably. If Lincoln lost, it seemed likely that some sort of negotiated peace might be arranged. But Sherman's victory gave Union morale an enormous boost. The North now was clearly winning.

Union Raids

September brought additional triumphs. In the middle of that month, a Union army under Major General Philip H. Sheridan confronted Early's veterans in the Shenandoah Valley. Badly outnumbered, the Confederates suffered defeat in two sharp battles that forced them to yield the entire valley to Union domination. In October, Sheridan won a third shattering victory that destroyed Early's army for good, but by that time the valley that Early defended had already become "a smoking, barren waste." Its destruction illustrates an important dimension of Grant's strategy.

General Philip H. Sheridan was one of the Union's most implacable "hard war" generals. As commander of Northern forces in the Shenandoah Valley, he defeated the Confederates in two sharp battles, then destroyed the valley's barns and crops to end its days as a source of Confederate supply.

Sometimes called the "breadbasket of the Confederacy," the rich Shenandoah Valley had long served as a major source of supply to Lee's army. Consequently, Grant regarded destruction of the Valley as a legitimate military objective. Once Early's force had been beaten, he believed, the pursuing troops should "eat out Virginia clear and clean as far as they go, so that crows flying over it for the balance of the season will have to carry their provender with them." As he explained to Sheridan, "[N]othing should be left to invite the enemy to return. Take all provisions, forage and stock wanted for the use of your command. Such as cannot be consumed, destroy."

During the early weeks of autumn Sheridan carried out these instructions with grim enthusiasm. By mid-October he could report, "I have destroyed over 2,000 barns filled with wheat, hay and farming implements; over 70 mills, filled with flour and wheat; have driven in front of the army over 4,000 head of stock, and have killed and issued to the troops not less than 3,000 sheep. . . . The people here are getting sick of the war."

The final sentence in Sheridan's dispatch alluded to a new element in the struggle, one that Grant had begun to see as early as 1862 but that had required two more years to reach maturity. The war for the Union had become not only a war against the "slave aristocracy" but against the Southern people as a whole. Typical of this tough new mindset was Sherman's decision, shortly after his capture of Atlanta, to order the evacuation of its entire civilian population. When the city's mayor protested the inhumanity of this action, Sherman responded witheringly: "[M]y orders are not designed to meet the humanities of the case but to prepare for the future struggles. . . . War is cruelty, and you cannot refine it. . . . You might as well appeal against the thunder storm as against these terrible hardships of war." Although Grant never came close to Sherman's desolating eloquence, his own orders as well as his endorsement of Sherman demonstrate that he felt exactly the same way.

For several weeks after the fall of Atlanta, Sherman made no further advances. He was too busy protecting his greatly overextended supply line. No longer obliged to defend Atlanta, Hood had shifted into northwest Georgia and now drew his supplies from neighboring Alabama. With his own lines of communication secure, Hood spent October threatening the vulnerable Western and Atlantic Railroad that was Sherman's lifeline with the North. Sherman's armies spent several frustrating weeks fruitlessly chasing Hood's army as it bedeviled the tenuous Union supply line through the northern part of the state. The Federals, in effect, were having to fight twice for the same real estate.

Clearly some new solution must be found, and Sherman believed he knew what it was. He wanted to cut loose from the Western and Atlantic Railroad entirely, abandon Atlanta, and strike out for a new base on the coast. On October 9 he wrote Grant, "I propose that we break up the railroad from Chattanooga forward, and that we strike out with our wagons for Milledgeville, Macon, and Savannah." The mere occupation of Georgia, he argued, was useless given the hostile population. "[B]ut the utter destruction of its [rail]roads, houses, and people, will cripple their military resources. . . . I can make the march, and make Georgia howl!"

Grant delayed before giving Sherman permission for the operation. Noting that the Confederate leadership might send Hood's army to recover middle Tennessee, he thought it best to eliminate Hood before doing anything else. Lincoln, for his part, confessed that Sherman's idea made him "anxious, if not actually fearful." But Sherman stuck to his guns. He could detach enough troops to protect Tennessee, he argued, and in any event the change of base could accomplish an important purpose in its own right. "If we can march a well-appointed army right through his territory," Sherman argued, "it is a demonstration to the world, foreign and domestic, that we have a power which [Confederate President Jefferson] Davis cannot resist. This may not be war but rather statesmanship; nevertheless it is overwhelming to my mind that there are thousands of people abroad and in the South who reason thus: if the North can march an army right through the South, it is proof positive that the North can prevail. . . ."

Eventually Grant approved Sherman's proposal. Sherman sent about 35,000 troops under General George Thomas to defend Tennessee, then abandoned Atlanta after destroying everything that might support the Confederate war effort. On November 15, advancing against almost no opposition, Sherman and 60,000 veterans began to carve a sixty-mile swath across Georgia. "[W]e had a gay old campaign," declared one of his men. "Destroyed all we could not eat, stole their niggers [sic], burned their cotton & gins, spilled their sorghum, burned & twisted their R. Roads and raised Hell generally."

By Christmas Eve 1864, Sherman had entered the city of Savannah on the Atlantic coast. In February 1865 he headed northward into the Carolinas, repeating on an even grander scale the pattern of his March to the Sea. Ultimately these marches, more than anything else, destroyed the Confederacy. They ruined Southern morale, smashed the remainder of the Confederate rail network, eliminated foodstuffs and war resources, and caused the desertion of thousands of Confederate soldiers who had resisted valiantly for years.

The Naval War, 1862–1865

Shortly after Sherman's army began its march northward into the Carolinas, a Union fleet appeared off Fort Fisher, North Carolina. This sprawling, improvised earthwork commanded the approaches to Wilmington, the last Confederate port open to blockade runners. When, on February 22, 1865, a combined landing party of 6,000 Federal soldiers and sailors successfully stormed the fort, it marked the culmination of a four-year naval campaign aimed at isolating the South from the outside world.

Until 1861, the U.S. Navy had played only a peripheral role in America's wars. During both the War for American Independence and the War of

1812, the Royal Navy had easily predominated; American naval contributions were confined to commerce raiding, a few single-ship encounters, and showing the flag in neutral ports. During the Civil War, however, the U.S. Navy for the first time bore a major strategic responsibility. Not only was it expected to control the open sea—a relatively simple task—it was also required to maintain a close blockade of the Confederate shore, to transport Union military might wherever it was needed, and to fight for control of the Confederate inland waters.

Since the American navy had never before faced such a task, it obviously had to improvise. But at least it had the advantage of existing when the war began. The Confederate navy also had to improvise, but more than that, it also had to create itself and devise a coherent mission under the immediate pressures of war. Although both sides did well with the resources available, the disparity in industrial might between North and South was never more lopsided than in the contest between the two navies. The North had an enormous advantage throughout the conflict. The South was never able to mount a serious challenge to Union seapower.

The Blockade

Sheer numbers convey something of the North's advantage. In April 1861 the Federal government possessed about ninety warships. By December 1864, under the outstanding leadership of Secretary of the Navy Gideon Welles, the North had expanded this total to 671 vessels, including 236 steam-powered ships constructed during the war. Although much of this new navy was used in riverine warfare and to track down commerce raiders, most of it went to enforce the Union blockade.

The blockade served two important functions. First, in economic terms it greatly reduced the South's access to outside markets, making the import and export of goods much more difficult. Second, diplomatically it helped reinforce a sense of the North's iron determination to crush the rebellion and caused European powers to think long and hard before recognizing the Confederacy. But maintaining the blockade was certainly a huge task. The rebellious states had a combined shoreline of roughly 3,000 miles, with 189 inlets and river mouths into which a blockade runner might dart. Blockade duty was dreary. Months might pass without action; during that time the main enemies were discomfort and boredom. One naval officer tried to give his mother some idea of the rigors of blockading duty: "[G]o to the roof on a hot summer day," he advised, "talk to a half-dozen degenerates, descend to the basement, drink tepid water full of iron rust, climb to the roof again, and repeat the process at intervals until [you are] fagged out, then go to bed with everything shut tight."

When a blockade runner was sighted, it enjoyed every advantage. Typically such a vessel would choose a moonless night to make its run, during which time its slate-gray hull would be nearly invisible. Swift and almost silent, the blockade runners would also burn smoke-free anthracite coal to heighten the difficulty of sighting them and would sometimes fire decoy signal flares to mislead the blockaders. Such tactics, coupled with an intimate knowledge of the shoal waters just outside the harbor entrances, resulted in a high rate of success. By one estimate, 84 percent of the runners that attempted the port of Wilmington made it through (1,735 out of 2,054), with a similar ratio prevailing along the rest of the Confederate coastline.

Some historians offer these figures as evidence of the blockade's ineffectiveness. Others, however, maintain that such statistics miss the point. The true measure of comparison, they maintain, should be difference in Southern sea trade before the war and during it. By this criterion the blockade was quite effective. Twenty thousand vessels cleared in or out of Southern ports in the years 1857–1860, compared with just 8,000 during the entire Civil War. Moreover, since blockade runners typically carried less cargo than an average merchantman, the wartime tonnage of goods imported or exported was probably less than one-third of the prewar figure.

That still leaves the question of the role played by the blockade in inflicting Confederate defeat. Here statistics have much less meaning. The issue turns, in part, on such intangibles as the blockade's impact on the Confederacy's morale. A more concrete way to look at the matter is to note the concern (or lack thereof) with which the Confederate government regarded the blockade. Certainly it never saw breaking the blockade as a priority (even if this were in its power, which it was not), and as late as 1864 the government required that only one-half the blockade runners' space be given over to military cargo. Then too, it is difficult to see what the Confederacy required that it could not produce. Food? It had plenty of that; the difficulty there lay in shipping local surpluses to points of need via the Confederacy's inadequate rolling stock. Arms and ammunition? The Confederacy, under the able leadership of ordnance czar Josiah Gorgas, managed to supply these wants to the end of the war.

Ultimately one must concede that the blockade was scarcely decisive in its own right. Still it did have an effect—not just in terms of reducing the South's volume of trade but also in terms of exacerbating high prices for consumer goods that helped fuel a ruinous inflation. But the Confederacy had enough territory to provide for its own needs—and did an ingenious job of exploiting its resources. Perhaps, then, the Union navy's most pronounced contribution to victory came in the support it gave the land forces.

Joint Operations and Riverine Warfare

Throughout the war the Union exploited its great superiority in sea power to throw troops ashore at various points along the Confederate coastline. These operations scarcely resembled the amphibious warfare of World War II, for in the great majority of cases they met little or no opposition directly on the beaches. It was much more usual for the troops to go ashore unopposed, establish a solid, fortified enclave, and only then advance inland. On only two important occasions during the conflict did troops try to fight their way ashore. The first, a Union night attack on Fort Sumter in September 1863, failed miserably. The second, against Fort Fisher in January 1865, was of course a success.

The relative dearth of opposed landings owed mainly to the fact that much of the Confederate coastline was undefended. The rebels maintained troops and artillery only at a few dozen key points. Thus it was easy for Union forces to find places to land without having to fight simply to get ashore. Their troubles came later, for although Union troops had little difficulty establishing a coastal enclave, they found it far more difficult to penetrate very far inland. For one thing, once the Union troops were ashore the Confederates knew exactly where they were and could dispatch sufficient troops to block them. The more important reason, however, was that there were almost never enough Union troops based along the coast to undertake offensive action.

Indeed, for most of the conflict the Lincoln administration neglected to use ocean-based sea power as a major instrument in the land war. McClellan's Peninsula Campaign appears to have permanently soured Lincoln, Stanton, and Halleck on this option. When Grant proposed in January 1864 that 60,000 troops be dispatched to occupied North Carolina, whence to raid the railroads that supplied Richmond, the administration vetoed the plan.

If one excepts the Peninsula Campaign—which functioned, in most respects, like a conventional land campaign—the most sustained joint operation of the war was the siege of Charleston, South Carolina. Although this campaign nominally began as early as November 1861, it did not start in earnest until April 1863, when a Union flotilla composed entirely of ironclads tried to bombard the Charleston forts into submission. The forts pummeled them instead, achieving over 400 direct hits—without, however, doing great injury to the heavily armored vessels. Then throughout the balance of 1863, the army and navy cooperated in a series of attacks upon the forts, but achieved limited success. The geography of Charleston harbor made it an extraordinarily difficult nut to crack. Both the entrance and the approach channel were narrow, so that Union warships had little room to maneuver, while forts protecting the harbor were themselves protected by salt marshes and swamps. Indeed the prolonged campaign was almost certainly a venture not worth the gain, except that Charleston had been the original cockpit of secession and many Northerners ached to see it destroyed. (The city fell only in February 1865, after Sherman's advancing army had cut its communications with the rest of the South.)

In contrast to the relatively limited cooperation between land forces and the bluewater navy, the army and brownwater navy worked hand-in-glove throughout the war. The two services cooperated effectively to reduce Forts Henry and Donelson, Island No. 10, Vicksburg, and a number of lesser Confederate fortresses in the Mississippi valley. Union naval control of the navigable rivers enabled land forces to supply themselves far from their main bases, and the riverine lines of communication proved much more difficult for rebels to disrupt than the highly vulnerable railroads. Moreover Federal gunboats could also interdict long stretches of these rivers, rendering it next to impossible for large Confederate forces to cross. This interdiction significantly impeded Southern mobility, particularly in terms of transferring units across the Mississippi River.

The most striking feature of the coastal and riverine war was the use made of ironclad vessels. When the war broke out the American navy possessed no armored ships of any kind; only Britain and France owned a few experimental ironclads. The Confederacy, however, soon began to construct an ironclad using the hull of the captured frigate USS *Merrimack*, partially scuttled when the Federals abandoned the Norfolk Navy Yard in April 1861. Rechristened the CSS *Virginia*, the new ironclad rode so low in the water that it resembled the roof of a floating barn. It mounted ten 11-inch cannon and, in a throwback to the days of galleys, an iron ram on the bow below the waterline.

Designed to break the Union blockade and protect the James River estuary, the *Virginia* briefly struck terror in Union hearts. During its maiden voyage on March 8, 1862, it steamed from Norfolk into Hampton Roads, rammed one Union frigate, destroyed another with gunfire, and ran a third warship aground before retiring for the night. The next day it steamed forth to wreak further havoc, only to be confronted by an oddly shaped vessel that looked exactly like a cheesebox on a raft. It was in fact the USS *Monitor*, the North's answer to the *Virginia* and a remarkable answer at that. Created by the brilliant naval designer John Ericsson, the heavily armored *Monitor* boasted no fewer than forty patentable inventions, most prominently a rotating turret (the "cheesebox") that mounted two 11-inch smoothbore cannon

In March 1862, the USS *Monitor* clashed with the CSS *Virginia* at Hampton Roads, Virginia, in the world's first battle between ironclad warships. Although the combat ended in a draw, the *Monitor* caused the *Virginia* to return to port, thereby saving Union wooden warships in the area from further damage.

and could fire in any direction. Built in just one hundred days, the Union ironclad managed to wallow down from New York City just in time to save the fleet in Hampton Roads from complete disaster. In a two-hour battle on March 9, the two revolutionary vessels pumped shot after shot at one another, only to see the heavy cannon balls merely dent the enemy's armor and ricochet into the sea. Neither ship was seriously hurt, although the *Virginia* eventually broke off the action and withdrew into Norfolk harbor. Two months later it was scuttled to prevent capture when the Confederates withdrew from the area. (The *Monitor* eventually sank in heavy seas in December 1862.)

Both the *Virginia* and the *Monitor* served as prototypes for further armored vessels. The South ultimately built twenty-one ironclads (and laid the keels for twenty-nine more), mostly patterned after the *Virginia*. The North, which constructed fifty-eight ironclads, tried several designs but concentrated on vessels patterned after the *Monitor*. Every one of these ships was intended either for coastal defense or attack; none fought in the open ocean. Together they confirmed a major technological shift in naval warfare. As the London *Times* remarked shortly after the fight at Hampton Roads, the British navy had suddenly dropped from having 149 first-class warships to exactly two, its twin experimental ironclads. Apart from those two, "[t]here is not now a ship in the English navy . . . that it would not be madness to trust in an engagement with that little *Monitor*."

Commerce Raiders

In addition to its ironclads, the South also built, or purchased, a number of commerce raiders, the perennial resort of weaker maritime powers. It tried privateers as well—privately owned vessels given "letters of marque" and permitted to attack enemy shipping. In older times privateering was a lucrative business, but most European powers had officially disowned the practice by the mid-nineteenth century, and would-be privateers found it too difficult to bring captured prizes into Southern ports. Thus the Confederacy had to use warships manned by regular naval crews and designed primarily to destroy, not capture, enemy merchantmen.

The South deployed only a relative handful of commerce raiders, but they achieved great notoriety and in some respects great effectiveness. They sank a large number of Union merchantmen, forced hundreds more to seek refuge by reregistering under neutral flags, and sent insurance premiums soaring. The CSS *Shenandoah* managed to cripple the New England whaling fleet in the Bering Sea—it did this, incidentally, in June 1865, unaware that the war was over—but the greatest rebel sea raider was the CSS *Alabama*, commanded by the rakish Captain Raphael Semmes.

Like many Confederate commerce raiders, the *Alabama* was built in England, having been covertly commissioned by the tireless Confederate agent, James Bulloch. (Bulloch also tried to get British shipyards to build several ironclads as well, but Her Majesty's government eventually blocked the attempt.) The warship mounted eight guns and could make better than

Although the Confederacy could not begin to match the Union's naval might, it still managed to deploy a number of commerce raiders, including the CSS *Nashville*, shown here burning a captured Northern merchant vessel.

thirteen knots under steam. In its twenty-two-month voyage it destroyed a total of sixty-eight Union vessels—without, however, injuring the crews. Instead the rebel sailors (many of them actually British subjects) boarded the enemy merchantmen, removed whatever they wanted, and took their seamen prisoner. Only then would the enemy vessels be burned or blown up. When the *Alabama* grew too overcrowded with reluctant guests, Semmes would designate the next captured merchantman a "cartel ship," place the prisoners aboard, and let them sail to the nearest port. In that way he accomplished his mission without bloodshed.

The *Alabama* continued its colorful career until June 1864, when the Union frigate USS *Kearsage* cornered the raider while it was in a French harbor for repairs. The *Kearsage* hovered outside the entrance to the port, barring escape. The *Alabama* gamely came forth to do battle, but in a spirited one-hour engagement the Confederate vessel was sunk. Semmes himself went over the side, was picked up by a yacht filled with admiring sightseers, and thus eluded capture.

The commerce raiders exerted a surprising influence on subsequent naval policy. After the war the American navy regarded them as a vindication of its historic emphasis on raiding as opposed to major fleet actions. Despite his own wartime experience with ironclads, Admiral David Dixon Porter led the U.S. Navy throughout the 1870s in its continuing rejection of a battle-fleet orientation. "[O]ne vessel like the *Alabama* roaming the ocean, sinking and destroying," he wrote, "would do more to bring about peace than a dozen unwieldy iron-clads. . . ." Some European navies concurred. Inspired in part by the exploits of Confederate raiders, many French and Italian navalists touted a maritime strategy that emphasized coastal defense and commerce destruction. In any event, not until the 1890s would the United States move decisively toward a naval strategy based unequivocally on the battleship and command of the sea.

All in all, the naval conflict remained a constant and indispensable feature of the Civil War. But the two contending forces compiled very different records. Stephen R. Mallory, the South's highly capable secretary of the navy, certainly did a superb job of creating a navy, yet it must be questioned whether this navy managed to achieve results commensurate even with the relatively slender resources expended on it. The ironclad program produced a number of formidable vessels but usually failed to prevent Union warships from capturing a Southern port when they mounted a major effort to do so. Land fortifications, not armored vessels, seemed the most effective way to defend Southern harbors. The commerce raiders, for their part, did considerable damage but never enough even to deflate the North's will to continue the war. Considering the vast amount of commerce carried by Northern ships, Southern raiders were really little more than a nuisance.

By contrast, the Union navy played a major role in defeating the Confederacy. Union blockaders sharply curtailed the amount of Confederate shipping and may have contributed to a decline in Southern morale. Union gunboats and ironclads vied with their rebel counterparts for control of Southern rivers, sounds, and ports. The Union naval contribution richly deserved Lincoln's wry compliment to Federal seamen in 1863: "At all the watery margins they have been present. Not only on the deep blue sea, the broad bay, the rapid river, but also up the narrow muddy bayou, and wherever the ground was a little damp, they have made their tracks."

The War Ends

Sherman's marches were only the largest of many Union raids that characterized the final six months of the conflict. The Federals, in essence, had abandoned any attempt to hold Southern territory. Instead they simply ravaged it, destroying anything of military use and in the process convincing thousands of white Southerners that the Confederate government could not protect them. The Davis administration, meanwhile, grew increasingly out of touch with the darkening strategic picture. Instead, in the autumn of 1864, Davis made an energetic circuit of the Deep South and argued that if the Southern people would only redouble their efforts, the Confederacy might yet plant its banners on the banks of the Ohio. This visionary thinking actually produced one of the strangest campaigns of the war, Hood's disastrous invasion of Tennessee.

Franklin and Nashville

Conceived in early October 1864, Hood's operation had two main purposes. Strategically it was supposed to recover middle Tennessee and cut off Sherman from the North; Hood even fantasized that he might eventually combine with Lee's army and overwhelm Grant. Politically it was intended to bolster flagging Southern morale; Jefferson Davis hinted on several occasions that Hood's thrust might reach as far as the Ohio River. The fulfillment of either objective was clearly well beyond the reach of Confederate resources.

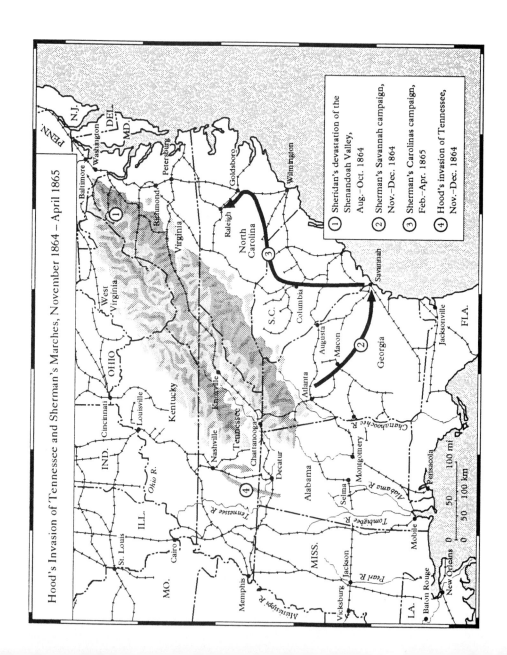

Hood's Invasion of Tennessee and Sherman's Marches, November 1864 – April 1865

① Sheridan's devastation of the Shenandoah Valley, Aug.–Oct. 1864

② Sherman's Savannah campaign, Nov.–Dec. 1864

③ Sherman's Carolinas campaign, Feb.–Apr. 1865

④ Hood's invasion of Tennessee, Nov.–Dec. 1864

For one thing, Hood lacked anywhere near enough troops to do the job. For another, he was not able to begin his campaign until mid-November, by which time his well-advertised invasion had brought thousands of Union troops into position to oppose him.

Even so, the Tennessee gambit gave the Union high command a fairly acute case of heartburn. Grant fretted that Hood's eccentric expedition might somehow disrupt his otherwise promising plans to finish off the Confederacy. Thomas, the Federal commander tapped to oppose Hood, believed the quality of Hood's veterans much superior to that of his own men, many of whom were either recently enlisted or garrison troops with little combat experience. (Thousands of his own veterans had either left the service by this time or had been retained by Sherman for his march to the sea.) Grant wanted Hood stopped as quickly as possible, before he had time to do mischief. Thomas, on the other hand, considered it best simply to delay Hood while he gathered his disparate forces into some kind of cohesive whole.

As a result, Thomas concentrated most of his troops at Nashville. In the meantime he sent Major General John M. Schofield, with 28,000 troops, to delay the Confederate advance. Hood managed to make an end run around Schofield's flank and came close to gobbling up the entire Union force. But somehow his army failed to strike Schofield, and the Federals retreated intact to Franklin, about thirty miles south of Nashville. There Hood caught up with them. Although the obvious move was to turn Schofield's flank again, Hood—enraged by his army's failure—ordered a frontal assault on November 30. In a larger and even more disastrous attack than Pickett's Charge at Gettysburg, 18,000 Confederates lunged into the teeth of Union field entrenchments, artillery, and rapid-fire carbines. More than half of them became casualties. Five Confederate generals lay among the dead.

The Battle of Franklin shattered whatever offensive potential Hood's army retained. Now reduced to about 30,000 men, its remnants continued to the outskirts of Nashville, which after thirty-one months of Union occupation was one of the most heavily fortified places on earth. Behind the scowling entrenchments were about 70,000 Federal troops. Though Hood made a feeble show at "besieging" the city, he had no chance for success.

Despite his formidable numerical advantage, Thomas delayed two full weeks before delivering the counterstroke, largely because of a major ice storm. But on December 15 the weather broke and Thomas attacked. After effectively deceiving Hood about the location of his main thrust, Thomas executed a massive flank attack that by nightfall overwhelmed the Confederate left. The following morning he put Hood's entire army to flight. On both days, massed Federal cavalry played a pivotal role in providing the speed and power necessary to achieve success and pursued Hood tirelessly for several days afterward. Although the casualties were not especially high—the Union forces lost about 3,000 men, the Confederates about 7,000 (three-fourths of them captured)—the Army of Tennessee practically went out of existence, leaving Lee's army as the Confederacy's only substantial remaining military force.

In March 1865, Lincoln met with Sherman, Grant, and Admiral David D. Porter aboard the USS *River Queen* to discuss the closing operations against the Confederacy. Here the president listens as Sherman recounts his destructive marches through Georgia and the Carolinas.

The Collapse of the Confederacy

In the waning months of the war, large columns of swiftly moving Union horsemen slashed through the Confederacy almost at will, crippling what remained of its railroad grid, burning war factories, and spreading despair among the Southern population. Meanwhile the Army of the Potomac patiently maintained its siege of Petersburg. As the long months passed, Grant extended his lines steadily to the west, never quite able to get around Lee's flank but forcing the Confederates to stretch their lines to the breaking point. In March 1865, Sheridan came from the Shenandoah Valley with most of his cavalry. Grant gave him an infantry corps and told him to break Lee's western flank. On April 1, in the Battle of Five Forks, Sheridan did exactly that. As soon as he learned of the victory, Grant ordered a general attack all along the Petersburg front. This final assault forced Lee to abandon the city, which fell on April 3. Union troops entered Richmond the same day.

Lee had only one move remaining: he could try to get his army—now reduced to barely 50,000 men—into central North Carolina, where Joseph E. Johnston with 20,000 troops was fruitlessly attempting to halt Sherman's advance north from Savannah. Grant understood this perfectly, and as he placed the Army of the Potomac in pursuit he made certain that Sheridan's cavalry thwarted every attempt by Lee to turn southward. As a result, Lee was forced to retreat to the west, hoping to reach a Confederate supply dump at Lynchburg, reprovision his famished men, and then somehow get into North Carolina.

On April 6 Union forces caught up with Lee's rear guard and destroyed it, capturing 6,000 prisoners. The following day Grant sent Lee a summons to surrender. Lee declined, but by the evening of April 8, Sheridan managed to get ahead of the beleaguered Confederate army and cut off its retreat. After one last effort to open an escape route—valiantly made but easily repulsed—Lee felt he had no choice but to surrender. On April 9, 1865, Palm Sunday, he requested a conference with Grant. The two commanders met at Appomattox Court House, a small village about eighty miles west of Richmond. There, in the parlor of a modest two-story home, Lee surrendered the Army of Northern Virginia. Early that evening, as word of the surrender spread like wildfire and Union soldiers began to cheer and touch off cannon in salutes to the victory, Grant told his staff officers to put a stop to the celebrations at once. "The war is over," he told them. "The Rebels are our countrymen again."

Although magnanimous, Grant's declaration was also premature. Some rebels continued to resist, among them Jefferson Davis. Not yet ready to submit, Davis had told the Southern people on April 4 that the war had merely entered a "new phase": "Relieved from the necessity of guarding cities and particular points, . . . with our army free to move from point to point, and strike in detail the detachments and garrisons of the enemy, . . . nothing is now needed to render our triumph certain, but the exhibition of our own unquenchable resolve. Let us but will it, and we are free."

Davis and his cabinet fled Richmond and established a new temporary capital at Danville, Virginia. Then, on the afternoon of April 10, he learned that Lee had surrendered at Appomattox Court House the previous day. The news, wrote Secretary of the Navy Stephen Mallory, "fell upon the ears of all like a firebell in the night." Later that evening, Davis and his cabinet left by train for Greensboro, North Carolina. Their famous "flight into oblivion" had begun.

Still determined, Davis met with Beauregard and Johnston and told them that the army could be fleshed out by gathering conscripts and deserters. Both men found this suggestion utterly devoid of realism; in a second meeting the next day, Johnston bluntly informed Davis that "it would be the greatest of human crimes for us to attempt to continue the war." After a prolonged silence, Davis asked for Beauregard's opinion. Beauregard basically agreed with Johnston; so, it turned out, did most of those present.

Afterward the discussion turned to the question of possible surrender terms. Davis still seemed not to grasp the enormity of the occasion, for the terms he suggested substantially failed to acknowledge that the South had lost the war. Realizing that the Federals would not treat with him, however, he authorized Johnston to carry out the negotiations. Yet even so, he obviously thought the contest could be continued and asked Johnston to give his favored line of retreat so that supplies could be stockpiled along the route. The hopelessness of the situation became apparent, however, when a dispatch from Lee arrived, officially announcing his surrender. Until that moment, Davis had seemed at ease and confident. But after reading it, he passed it along and "silently wept bitter tears."

While Johnston opened negotiations with Sherman, Davis and his cabinet made preparations to continue their flight. The president had a vague idea of making it to Alabama, where Confederate troops remained in the field, or possibly to the trans-Mississippi; but his cabinet members were more concerned with getting him safely out of the country. On May 10, 1865, Federal horsemen captured Jefferson Davis near Irwinville, Georgia, about fifty miles from the Florida state line. After a few days he was incarcerated at Fort Monroe, Virginia, where he spent the next two years.

By that time, Johnston had capitulated to Sherman and General Richard Taylor had surrendered most of the remaining Confederate troops east of the Mississippi. On May 26, the last Southern troops laid down their arms when General Edmund Kirby Smith, commanding the trans-Mississippi theater, surrendered his department. The Civil War was over.

The Legacy of the War

In terms of its impact on the United States, the Civil War remains the pivotal episode in American history. Like the near-contemporaneous wars of Italian and German unification, the American conflict took a fairly loose gathering of states and welded them into a nation. Politically it destroyed the concept of extreme states' rights and established the principle that the Union was perpetual. Its impact on American society was no less great. Not only did it result in the emancipation of 3.5 million African-Americans, it also ensured that thenceforward the mainstream of American civilization would be the industrial North, not the agrarian South.

Its significance in the history of warfare was no less great. Even more than the campaigns at the end of the Napoleonic Wars, the Civil War displayed the ascendancy of the defense over the offense, the inability of armies to destroy one another in battle, and the corresponding need to think in terms of a strategy of exhaustion or attrition rather than annihilation. The increased size of armies accounted for part of their enhanced resiliency; so too did the use of the corps, which enabled separate army wings to fight effectively on their own until reinforcements could come to their assistance. Only when Civil War armies allowed themselves to be surrounded and besieged (as at Vicksburg), or when they had previously exhausted themselves through prolonged offensives (as at Nashville) did it prove possible to destroy them.

A second important feature of the conflict was such sociopolitical factors as mass armies, conscription, and the mobilization of entire societies for war. The wars of the French Revolution and Napoleon had also witnessed these developments, but the Civil War carried them to a higher pitch, perhaps because both the Union and the Confederacy were among the most political societies then on earth. Both Northern and Southern soldiers were motivated in no small measure by strongly held beliefs about the causes for which they were fighting. The Western world had seen something like this during the wars of the American and French revolutions and, more recently, the struggles for Greek and Italian liberation. Otherwise one would have to reach back into the sixteenth- and seventeenth-century wars of religion for a parallel.

Third, the Civil War also saw the harnessing of the Industrial Revolution to the emergent forces of popular sovereignty and nationalism. New technologies played an enormous role in the conflict: railroads, rifles, and the telegraph, not to mention such naval innovations as turret-firing guns, iron-clad warships, and so on. Both the Union and the Confederacy worked diligently to exploit their industrial resources to the fullest; the North in particular evolved effective ways to organize and distribute their industrial output to armies in the field. The U.S. Military Railroads under Brigadier General Daniel C. McCallum, for example, achieved a record of energy and efficiency that any European army would have envied.

The Civil War also witnessed the great marches of destruction undertaken by Union forces during the war's final years and highly reminiscent of the English during the Hundred Years' War, numerous armies during the Thirty Years' War, and the French in 1688–1689. Often mistaken for an anticipation of twentieth-century strategic bombing, the Union raids against Southern war resources had much stronger continuities with past experience. The chief difference was that whereas the soldiers of the *ancien régime* in Europe had inflicted much indiscriminate mayhem, the greater political and moral awareness of the Civil War soldier—still thoroughly rooted in the ethical norms of his community—meant that Union armies conducted their attacks on Southern war resources with much greater discrimination. Depredations occurred, but wholesale killing of Southern civilians certainly did not. Private homes were rarely destroyed except in retaliation for guerrilla activity, and rapes—at least of white women—were uncommon. A much larger number of African-American women were assaulted and sexually abused. Taken together, the extensive mobilization of Northern and Southern societies, coupled with the large-scale union attacks on Southern crops and war resources, marked the first appearance of the total war dynamic that would become a pronounced characteristic of many twentieth-century struggles.

Finally, a word is in order about the strategic and operational conduct of the war. In general its quality, on both sides, was quite high. Both governments responded intelligently to the nature of the conflict and adopted realistic strategies. Of the two commanders-in-chief, Lincoln was clearly more able than Jefferson Davis, but then Lincoln was probably one of the three or four greatest statesmen of the past two centuries. Union and Confederate generalship was about equal. If the South had Lee and Jackson, it also had Bragg and Pemberton. Similarly, such lackluster Northern commanders as McClellan and Burnside were more than offset by Grant, Sherman, and Sheridan. Both sides fought according to the Napoleonic model, but both learned to adapt to the rather different logistical conditions of warfare in the vast, largely rural South. Each side eventually grasped the greatly changed tactical environment created by the rifled musket, and each made extensive use of field fortifications. This sound defensive solution, however, was not matched by an equivalent solution on the offensive. Both armies, despite scattered experiments with more open formations and tactics, continued to rely heavily on the traditional, practically shoulder-to-shoulder battle line.

Ultimately, however, the harsh realities of the Civil War battlefield did give a major impetus to the increasing professionalism of officers. It was obvious that largely untrained citizen-officers could not adequately cope with the demands of mid-nineteenth-century warfare, nor could regular officers whose imaginations were geared to skirmishing with Native American war parties. Deeply impressed by the failures of Civil War officership and the attendant waste of manpower, military reformers like Lieutenant Colonel Emory Upton waged a passionate crusade in favor of better professional education and standards. Upton's peers and disciples studied European armies, lobbied for advanced military schools and war colleges, and attempted to drag the United States Army thoroughly into the modern industrialized age. Although it required decades to complete, the result was a new cycle of military reform that prepared American armed forces, albeit imperfectly, to meet the challenges of a violent new century.

SUGGESTED READINGS

Barrett, John G. *Sherman's March Through the Carolinas* (Chapel Hill: University of North Carolina Press, 1956).

Beringer, Richard E., et al. *Why the South Lost the Civil War* (Athens: University of Georgia Press, 1986).

Castel, Albert. *Decision in the West: The Atlanta Campaign, 1864* (Lawrence: University Press of Kansas, 1992).

Catton, Bruce. *Grant Takes Command* (Boston: Little, Brown, 1969).

———. *A Stillness at Appomattox* (New York: Doubleday, 1952).

Donald, David H., ed. *Why the North Won the Civil War* (Baton Rouge: Louisiana State University Press, 1962).

Fowler, William M. *Under Two Flags: The American Navy in the Civil War* (New York: Norton, 1990).

Glatthaar, Joseph T. *The March to the Sea and Beyond: Sherman's Troops in the Savannah and Carolinas Campaigns* (New York: New York University Press, 1985).

Horn, Stanley F. *The Decisive Battle of Nashville* (Baton Rouge: Louisiana State University Press, 1956).

Marszalek, John F. *Sherman: A Soldier's Passion for Order* (New York: Free Press, 1992).

Matter, William D. *"If It Takes All Summer": The Battle of Spotsylvania* (Chapel Hill: University of North Carolina Press, 1988).

Reed, Rowena. *Combined Operations in the Civil War* (Annapolis: Naval Institute Press, 1978).

Rhea, Gordon C. *The Battle of the Wilderness, May 5–6, 1864* (Chapel Hill: University of North Carolina Press, 1994).

Still, William N., Jr. *Iron Afloat: The Story of the Confederate Armorclads* (Baton Rouge: Louisiana State University Press, 1970).

Sword, Wiley. *Embrace An Angry Wind: The Confederacy's Last Hurrah: Spring Hill, Franklin, and Nashville* (New York: HarperCollins, 1992).

Trudeau, Noah Andre. *Bloody Roads South: The Wilderness to Cold Harbor, May–June, 1864* (Boston: Little, Brown, 1989).

———. *The Last Citadel: Petersburg, Virginia, June 1864–April 1865* (Boston: Little, Brown, 1991).

———. *Out of the Storm: The End of the Civil War, April–June 1865* (Boston: Little, Brown, 1994).

Wert, Jeffry D. *From Winchester to Cedar Creek: The Shenandoah Campaign of 1864* (Carlisle, Penn.: South Mountain Press, 1987).

Wise, Steven A. *Lifeline of the Confederacy: The Blockade Runners* (Columbia: University of South Carolina Press, 1987).

15

THE TRANSITION FROM
NAPOLEONIC METHODS TO THE
PRUSSIAN MILITARY SYSTEM,
1815~1871

Continuity and Change

The Crimean War

Reforms in Prussia

The Seven Weeks' War

The Franco-Prussian War

$\mathbb{D}$uring the first half of the nineteenth century, memories of the Napoleonic Wars created a feeling of revulsion against war and helped maintain peace among the major European powers. In 1854, however, France and Britain joined the Ottoman Empire in a war against Russia. With most of the fighting occurring on the Crimean peninsula in the Black Sea, the three allies besieged the Russian naval base at Sevastopol and defeated the Russians. Then in 1866 the Germans quickly defeated the Austrians in the Seven Weeks' War, and in 1870–1871 they defeated the French in the Franco-Prussian War. The latter two wars enabled Prussia to unify Germany and alter the balance in power in Europe.

In the early part of the century, Europe's armies demonstrated little interest in significant innovations; soldiers remained content with the weapons, organizations, and methods that had served them from 1792 to 1815. The middle of the century, however, marked the start of an era of sweeping change. The convergence of new organizational approaches (the Prussian general staff), revolutionary means of mobility (the railway and steamship), and technological improvements (particularly in small arms) altered the nature and speed of campaigns as well as the shape of battle. Changes in the nature of war first appeared in the Crimean War and then became more obvious in the subsequent Seven Weeks' and Franco-Prussian

461

wars. In 1866 and 1870 the Prussians successfully demonstrated how to organize an army on the basis of universal military service, equip it with modern weapons, mobilize it quickly and efficiently, and deploy it with speed. Thus, Prussia led the other European powers in adjusting to changes in warfare and used these adjustments to its advantage in fighting several wars and unifying Germany.

Continuity and Change

The years following 1815 saw a curious mixture of continuity and change. The former resulted from centuries of customary practices, as well as the residual effects of nearly a quarter-century of war. Most European armies had adopted aspects of the French system as a result of disruption or defeat at the hands of Napoleon. In most cases new methods quickly blended with traditional eighteenth-century warfare. Though many reforms of the 1792–1815 period survived, powerful conservative traditions sometimes prevailed. Wars on the periphery, colonial expansion, revolts against the Turks, and even revolutions failed to shake routines or force changes in methods or organizations.

While Europe's militaries settled into somnolent garrison life, important developments occurred that eventually affected the conduct of war and the relationship between political and military authorities. The growth of nationalism, the expansion of industrial and commercial economies, the development of new weapons, and the broad mobilization of peoples and resources in support of the armed forces gradually eroded traditional approaches and relationships and created new ones. By 1871 the notion of military organizations operating in isolation from political authorities no longer reflected changing political, economic, and social realities. Military leaders had to think of war in very different terms from their predecessors of the eighteenth century.

Jomini and Clausewitz

After Waterloo, interpreters of Napoleon dissected his methods and wrote commentaries about his battles and campaigns. Of those who analyzed the wars from 1792–1815, a Swiss officer who served in the French army, Antoine-Henri de Jomini, had the greatest influence in the nineteenth century. Known primarily for his *Summary of the Art of War,* Jomini largely expressed his ideas in eighteenth-century terms. He identified the "one great principle underlying all the operations of war" as "operating with the greatest possible force in a combined effort against the decisive point." He then prescribed four "maxims" that "embraced" the "great principle" and analyzed numerous campaigns in which "the most brilliant successes and the greatest reverses resulted from an adherence" to the "fundamental principle

Baron Antoine-Henri de Jomini spent most of his career in high-level staff positions and emphasized concentration of superior combat power at the decisive point. He saw combat as much more orderly and geometric than Clausewitz.

of war." Military readers appreciated his emphasis on mobility, concentration, and lines of operations. In reality, Jomini's works were "how-to" manuals on campaign strategy and on the operational and tactical levels of war.

Jomini did not ignore the relationship between war and politics; he recognized that governments would seek influence over "the nature and extent of the efforts and operations necessary for the proposed end." Nevertheless, he condemned the "barbarities" of national wars and clearly preferred the "old regular method of war between permanent armies." He explained, "My prejudices are in favor of the good old times when the French and English Guards courteously invited each other to fire first. . . ." Jomini provided a list of twelve "essential conditions" for "making a perfect army" and advocated small armies that made up in quality for what they lacked in numbers. Jomini's clear, uncomplicated writing style and his maxims and geometrical illustrations appealed to officers who sought to understand war by simple, comprehensive concepts. Such officers regarded him as the premier theorist of Napoleonic methods, even though Jomini's writings tended to ignore the complexities, ambiguities, and frictions that have always characterized war.

The Prussian theorist, Carl von Clausewitz, offers a sharp contrast, but he had considerably less influence in the nineteenth century. The complexity of his thought, the depth of his analysis, and his philosophical bent made his writings difficult to understand. Of all the commentators and students of war, Clausewitz was one of the few to raise his commentary from the particular to the general. Even in our century, his writings remain as germane to understanding the processes at work in human conflict as in his own time. Above all, Clausewitz understood that wars are political events, intricately and inextricably linked with the political purposes of the states that wage them.

Though positive about some of Jomini's ideas, Clausewitz particularly criticized Jomini for having emphasized so strongly the pursuit of

Carl von Clausewitz had seen war and combat from the company to the army level and emphasized the friction, fog, and uncertainty of warfare in his theories.

decisive victories; he was also critical of the Swiss theorist's basing general principles of war on the Napoleonic Wars. As Clausewitz explained, "Wars must vary with the nature of their motives and of the situations which give rise to them." He also differed from Jomini in an emphasis on the relationship between war and policy. "War," Clausewitz argued, "should never be thought of as something autonomous but always as an instrument of policy."

According to Clausewitz, war is a phenomenon dominated by popular feeling, chance, and the political aims for which states fight. Since the relationship among the three can vary widely in different wars, ignoring one of them or defining precise relationships among them would "conflict with reality." Thus war is more than a "chameleon that slightly adapts its characteristics" in different situations. Because of the unpredictable and rapidly changing circumstances of war, theory could *not* be a "manual for action" but instead only "a guide to anyone who wants to learn about war from books." Theory could guide officers' self-education but could not provide ready-made solutions for the battlefield.

Much more than Jomini, Clausewitz recognized the fundamental ambiguities and uncertainties that dominate the conduct of war. His discussions focused on the real conditions under which military organizations wage war. Concerned more with analysis than with enduring principles, he believed battle to be the realm of friction, in which many things can go wrong at any time or place and in which the results of actions are often different than expected. "War," he consistently noted, "is a simple thing, but in war the simplest thing is extraordinarily difficult."

But above all, "war is a continuation of politics by other means." This simple but often-quoted aphorism encapsulates Clausewitz's understanding of war's larger context. The stunning success of first the French Revolution and then Napoleon, according to Clausewitz, rested less on military developments than on the French having changed the political context within which Europe waged war. Not until France's opponents responded in comparable terms with mobilization of national spirit and resources did the other powers master the Revolution and its heir, Napoleon. Ironically, most Europeans, including historians, failed to comprehend the nature of this change until the end of the nineteenth century.

Clausewitz's widow published *On War* in 1832, but the first edition did not sell out for twenty years, when a second edition was published. Nonetheless, Helmuth von Moltke, chief of the Prussian general staff after 1857, was a student at the Prussian War College, the *Kriegsakadamie*, when Clausewitz was its director; Moltke later cited *On War* as one of the crucial works that had molded his thinking. German interest in Clausewitz expanded dramatically after 1871, partially because of Moltke's interest but also because Clausewitz had moved away from mechanistic studies of warfare, characteristic of Jomini, to a focus on individuals and their actions in war's unpredictable and uncertain environment.

The Ripples of Change

While theorists and officers grappled with the experiences of 1792–1815, they drifted away from interest in the mass armies of the revolutionary period. Like Jomini, they preferred disciplined, long-term soldiers over the numbers and enthusiasm that short-term conscripts brought to war. Nevertheless, most European states—except for Britain—retained conscription, even though citizen armies had become associated with revolutionary and nationalistic fervor. France reintroduced conscription in 1818 but called to service less than 10 percent of those eligible and required them to serve for six years. Since the rich could hire substitutes, conscription's burden fell on the poor. A similar situation existed in the Austrian Empire. In Russia, military obligations fell on communities, not individuals, for villages and towns supplied men to the army, though individuals could hire substitutes. Nationalism affected many aspects of the nineteenth century, but few military leaders desired to take advantage of patriotic feelings toward the state.

Despite the military's reluctance to change, industrialization had a significant effect on European armies. Of the innovations associated with the Industrial Revolution, railroads significantly enhanced the mobility of armies. The railway era began in 1825 when a small line opened in Britain. The first proposal for military utilization of railroads came in 1833 from a Westphalian industrialist who argued that Prussia could use railways to reinforce its frontiers more quickly. Beginning in 1839, the Prussians utilized railways to transport troops to the fall maneuvers. Following the movement of Prussian troops in 1846 to quell rebellion in Cracow, Europeans made frequent use of railways to transport troops during the tumultuous months of 1848. By 1850 no serious student of military affairs could ignore their potential for military purposes.

Industrialization also affected weapons. In particular, the American system of producing interchangeable parts became common, but the British did not adopt this system until three years after the Crimean War. Having interchangeable parts did away with the laborious and delicate fitting that had accompanied weapons assembly and made mass production of weapons possible. The introduction of rifled barrels had occurred before the American system of manufacture began. Following the patenting of the Minié ball in 1849, most armies gradually converted smoothbore muskets to rifled muskets. The subsequent introduction of breech-loading rifles compelled armies to abandon muskets and equip infantry with new arms. Mass-production techniques permitted European armies to make this transition with unprecedented speed.

Advances also occurred with artillery. Alfred Krupp pressured the Prussian authorities for more than a decade to purchase rifled, cast-steel barrels, and the army ordered 300 in 1859. The barrels provided Prussian artillery greater range and accuracy than older bronze guns. The new Prussian weapons were also breechloaders but could fire no faster than muzzleloaders since their gun carriage recoiled with each shot. Until recoil systems became available in the late nineteenth century, breech-loading rifles were a greater asset than breech-loading, rifled artillery. Thus, by mid-century, the firepower and mobility of armies had significantly increased. Changes occurred slowly and unevenly, however, because of expense and military conservatism.

The Crimean War

At the midpoint of the 1850s the entangled interests of Europe's powers finally resulted in war—the first in nearly forty years between major powers. The issue came from a clash of national interests of Russia on one hand and Britain, France, and the already crumbling Ottoman Empire on the other. The Russians had come through the revolutionary troubles of 1848 largely unscathed, while their army had crushed Hungarian revolutionaries and saved the Habsburg Empire. As the bulwark of conservatism and with an army still basking in the glow of victories over Napoleon, Russia pursued aggressive policies in the Balkans. Among other things, the tsarist state claimed to be the "protector" of Orthodox Christian shrines in the Ottoman Empire, and on June 27, 1853, Tsar Nicholas I ordered his armies to occupy the Danubian principalities of Moldavia and Wallachia, part of the Ottoman Empire. With Britain and France opposing Russian expansion, the Turks sensed they would receive support; in October they declared war on Russia. The French and British dispatched two naval squadrons to the Dardanelles, but in November a Russian naval squadron sank six Turkish frigates and killed 3,000 Turks at Sinope, a port on the southern shore of the Black Sea, 300 miles east of Constantinople.

Since Russia had raised the stakes, Britain and France delivered an ultimatum in February 1854; they demanded that the Russians evacuate the Danubian principalities. In early April, Austria and Prussia joined Britain and France and signed an agreement that opposed dismemberment of the Ottoman Empire. To protect Constantinople, British and French forces disembarked in late April at Varna (on the western shore of the Black Sea), and in June Austria demanded that Russia withdraw from Moldavia and Wal-

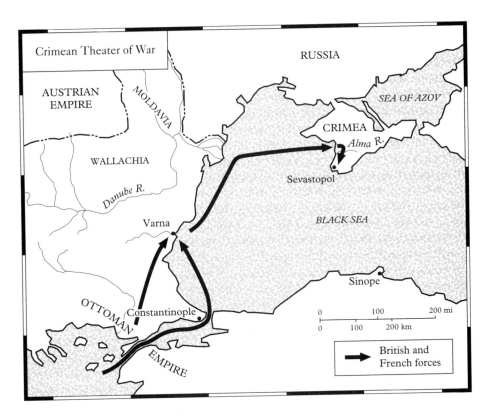

Crimean Theater of War

lachia. Confronted by Austrian threats in the west and Anglo-French military power in the south, the Russians complied. Their decision removed the *casus belli*; it should have brought about an acceptable peace but did not.

The British and French resolved to punish the Russians by attacking their fleet in the Baltic and by seizing the Russian naval base at Sevastopol on the Crimea. A combined British and French fleet moved into the Baltic, while the Russians remained in port. Meanwhile the allies loaded their troops from Varna and transported them across the Black Sea to the Crimea. The allies knew that Russian railroads lagged behind developments in the rest of Europe and that their opponent would find it difficult to support large forces in southern Russia.

In some respects the Crimean War was old-fashioned; in others, it heralded a new age in war. The military forces in Crimea looked, acted, and deployed for battle in much the same fashion as had those of the Napoleonic era. But substantial changes had occurred that affected the entire campaign, the most significant of which were in technology. Using both steam-driven and sailing ships, British and French armies deployed in a few short months to the Dardanelles and then to the Crimea. French and British soldiers possessed rifled muskets and Minié balls, but Russian infantry still possessed smoothbore weapons that placed them at an enormous disadvantage against the longer range and greater accuracy of rifled muskets.

As the campaign unfolded, the telegraph made its appearance. Although the telegraph enabled London and Paris to communicate with army commanders more quickly and over greater distances than in the past, its most significant effect lay in its use by military correspondents. For the first time, journalists could report on a war in a timely fashion. This reporting had a significant effect on public opinion, as well as the conduct of military affairs. In particular, William Russell's dispatches revealed the inadequate logistic support for British forces and caused a national scandal.

Operations in the Crimea

In September 1854, British and French forces landed on the Crimea. A small number of Turks accompanied them. Deciding that a landing near the port of Sevastopol was too risky, the allies came ashore thirty miles north of Sevastopol and then marched south toward the port. After landing at Calamita Bay at dawn on September 14, the allies spent the next four days unloading troops, horses, artillery, supplies, and wagons. Logistical difficulties appeared immediately. British troops had to wait three days before their tents arrived. Amidst poor weather, which alternated between rain and a blistering hot sun, cholera and dysentery soon appeared.

The Russian commander, Prince A. S. Menshikov, chose not to oppose the landing. He sent some observers to watch but prepared to defend on more favorable terrain. Allied naval superiority prevented the Russians from supplying Menshikov's forces by sea, and they soon found themselves struggling to obtain supplies. In subsequent months, more than 125,000 peasant carts carried supplies to the Russian army across the vast plains to the Crimean isthmus. The allies found their long seaborne lines of communication more dependable. The presence of a single Russian railway would have significantly altered the strategic situation.

On September 19 about 60,000 allied troops marched southward along the shores of the Crimea toward Sevastopol, the French along the coast and the British inland. The following day, after marching about fifteen miles, the allies encountered approximately 36,000 Russian troops barring the way on the heights overlooking the Alma River. There the steep hills rose quickly to about 400 feet above the river. In strong positions, the Russians refused their left and expected to throw back an allied assault against their center. Supported by naval gunfire, the French attacked first and easily ascended the lightly defended slope along the coast. Inland, the British advanced through heavy enemy fire and attacked the Russian center. The first British troops to reach the heights were thrown back, but the next attack succeeded. What initially appeared to be an unequal struggle, with the Russians possessing advantages in numbers and terrain, resulted in a slaughter of the tsar's soldiers. More than any army in Europe, the Russians relied on close-order drill and mass tactics; British infantry, equipped with rifled muskets, shredded Russian formations before the enemy's numbers could come into play. The advancing British laid down a murderous fire well out of range of the enemy's muskets and finally forced the Russian infantry to retreat. The British suffered about 2,000 casualties, the Russians about 5,700. The French reported 1,350 casualties.

Though Sevastopol lay open, the allies dallied four days before leaving the Alma. Taking advantage of the delay, the Russians marched toward Sevastopol and arrived at their bivouac site south of the city on September 21. The Russian commander quickly scuttled a line of ships across the harbor mouth north of the city. Then, leaving the city with 18,000 defenders, he moved his army east, where he hoped to attack the allies on their flank or rear.

Sevastopol sat on the northwestern edge of a large pointed peninsula jutting west into the Black Sea. A long harbor (about one mile wide and five miles long) lay on the city's northern side. Fortifications encircled the heights on the northern side of the harbor and much of the city on its south. Upon arrival, the British and French debated whether to launch an immediate assault. The British commander, Lord Raglan, urged such a course; the French commander, General Armand Saint-Arnaud, refused. Instead of seizing the high ground overlooking the harbor and the city, he preferred to move around the harbor and attack from the south. In retrospect an allied attack on the heights north of the harbor might have succeeded because the Russians had not yet set the port's defenses. Hesitancy, however, made a prolonged siege inevitable, for Russian engineers soon made Sevastopol impregnable to direct assault.

The Siege of Sevastopol

Beginning on September 25, the allies marched around the eastern edge of the harbor and fortifications. They positioned themselves south of the city and set up additional defenses to the east for protection in the event of an attack on their flank or rear. This position enabled them to receive supplies from the sea; the French used the port of Kamiesh on the western point of the peninsula, while the British used Balaclava on the south side of the peninsula. After occupying these new positions, the allies began bombarding Sevastopol on October 17, twenty-one days after their arrival.

While the allies shelled Sevastopol, Russian reinforcements arrived in the Crimea. On October 25, the Russians launched an attack on the ill-defended Balaclava position, six miles southeast of Sevastopol. They sought to drive a wedge between the allies and the British base. They attacked from a line of hills, across what was known as the "north valley," over a small hill, toward the "south valley," and then Balaclava. Their attack achieved some initial success; the Russians advanced across the north valley, drove the Turks from redoubts along the top of the small hill, and captured a number of artillery pieces. They then moved into the south valley. Counterattacking from the western edge of the south valley, British heavy cavalry drove the Russians back. As the Russians began pulling some of the captured guns off the small hill, Lord Raglan, who could see the entire position, ordered the commander of the cavalry division, Lord Lucan, to stop the Russians from removing the guns.

Unfortunately, neither Lucan nor Lord Cardigan, commander of the Light Brigade, could see the Russians pulling those guns away. The only

Russian guns in their view lay at the end of the north valley in the heart of the enemy's position. Despite the cavalry commanders' doubts, Lucan ordered Cardigan to attack. The Light Brigade charged straight forward "into the valley of death" against an extraordinarily strong enemy position. Firing from both sides of the valley, the Russians destroyed much of the Light Brigade; of 673 officers and men who began the charge, the Russians killed or wounded 247. Cardigan and some troopers made it to the gun positions and then rode back. A French general observing the attack trenchantly observed, "It is magnificent, but it is not war."

On November 5, 1854, the armies clashed again, this time at Inkerman. The Russians threw some 60,000 soldiers in a desperate attack against the British southeast of Sevastopol. The main attack degenerated into a series of frontal assaults on the lightly held British line, which the British and French reinforced during the battle. Russian artillery provided effective support until a pair of British 18-pound siege guns drove it from the field. The allies' rifled muskets provided the decisive edge. At distances beyond the range of Russian muskets, they blasted advancing columns of enemy infantry to pieces. When the slaughter was over, the Russians had suffered 12,000 casualties, the allies about 3,300. The attempt to relieve Sevastopol had failed, and both sides settled into a prolonged siege.

On November 14, a huge storm struck the Crimean peninsula and destroyed much of the allies' shipping, supplies, and tents. Among the ships lost was the one carrying winter clothing for the British soldiers. A shortage of firewood made life miserable for the allied soldiers. As winter worsened, British logistical support collapsed. But the presence of news reporters made the British public aware of their soldiers' misfortunes. The compla-

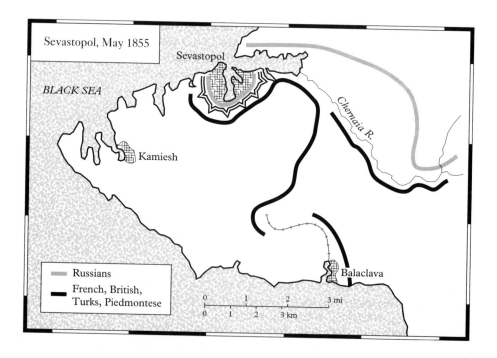

cent disinterest that commanders and governments had all too often displayed toward soldiers in previous eras could no longer survive in the glare of modern publicity. As spring approached, administrative chaos lessened. The British built a railway approximately six miles long from Balaclava into their positions. This was the first railway constructed specifically for a military campaign. With more Turkish labor and boatloads of mules arriving, transport of supplies improved, as did the lives of the soldiers.

In late January 1855, 15,000 Piedmontese joined the allies in front of Sevastopol. The strength of the British army had declined to 34,000, while that of the French had increased to 90,000. The French were now clearly the senior partner in the campaign. Through spring and summer 1855, the allies attempted to drive the Russians from their positions. In Sevastopol, the Russian defenders were increasingly short of rations. In mid-August, the French—supported by their Piedmontese allies—defeated the last Russian attempt to relieve Sevastopol at Chernaia Rechka. During one episode in the battle, the Russians lost 2,000 men in twenty minutes. Altogether, they suffered over 8,000 casualties, while the allies lost fewer than 2,000. Except for Inkerman, this was the most costly battle of the war.

The Capture of Sevastopol

On September 8, 1855, the French launched three separate columns against the Malakhov fortress, a key defensive bastion in the network of fortifications around Sevastopol. For the first time in history, officers leading the separate columns synchronized watches. After fighting that lasted throughout the day, the French captured the position. Following this success, the British attacked Redan, another key defensive point, but failed to capture it. Nevertheless the loss of Malakhov convinced the Russians to abandon Sevastopol; that night they withdrew and occupied new positions on the heights north of the city.

At the end of 1855, the British proposed another campaign against the Russians for 1856, but Napoleon III had accomplished his goals with the fall of Sevastopol. By destroying the Russian Black Sea fleet and capturing Sevastopol, the allies made Constantinople safe against naval attack from the north. In February 1856, the two sides accepted an armistice and in late March signed the final peace treaty in Paris. From the beginning, the allies had little at stake, and in the end they failed to gain much except to protect the Ottoman Empire from further Russian encroachments—at least for the time being. With limited goals, none of the combatants was willing to mobilize either the people or economic resources for total war. In that sense, the Crimean War represents a reversion to the limited wars of the eighteenth century.

There are a number of interesting features about the conflict. It was the first war from which substantial photographic evidence exists, and the first war in which news reporters exercised a significant role. The building of a railway from Balaclava to allied positions was also a first. Additionally, the introduction of rifled muskets had a significant effect on the fighting,

The Crimean War was the first major conflict where the new science of photography provided a pictorial record of soldiers and their life. In this case, members of the British 77th Regiment appear in their winter dress.

providing the allies with a distinct advantage. By the war's end, most modern armies viewed smoothbore muskets as obsolete, but none yet recognized the effect the rifle would ultimately have on their tactics, organization, and equipment. Fought largely by long-service professionals, the war provided few insights into the larger wars of the future. In the long term, the Crimean War may have had a greater effect on naval warfare than on land warfare. The introduction of ironclad ships during the war ushered in the age of naval armor, and by 1860 most navies regarded warships without steam power as obsolete.

Reforms in Prussia

Following the Crimea, Prussia gradually emerged as the greatest military power in Europe, primarily because it was able to raise, equip, deploy, and maneuver a large army effectively. As is often the case, Prussian reform began after a defeat—this time at the hands of Napoleon at Jena-Auerstädt in 1806. Following that battle, a committee under the leadership of General Gerhard von Scharnhorst established the principles under which the reform of the Prussian army took place. One of Scharnhorst's assistants was Captain Carl von Clausewitz. The reforms improved schools for officers, opened avenues of promotion to the middle class, established a simpler and more efficient administrative system, and affirmed universal military service by men. In 1813 the Prussians created the *Landwehr*, a militia designed to fight alongside the standing army, and by 1815 the army had assumed the role of the "chief training school of the whole nation for war." In subsequent years, however, reactionary forces unraveled many of the reforms, and by 1859 when war erupted in northern Italy between France, Austria, and Piedmont, Prussia recognized the dangers of a major war with France and did little more than mobilize its forces.

Efforts had already begun, however, to renew the army. When Prince Wilhelm of Prussia became regent in 1858, his extensive military experience made him more receptive to key reforms. Concerned about military deficiencies that became apparent in the 1859 mobilization, he established a commission under Albrecht von Roon and charged it with devising proposals for the Reichstag's (Prussian assembly) approval. These proposals included creation of a more coherent command structure, increases in the strength and efficiency of the standing army, and establishment of "area commands" to improve training of reserves and militia and ensure an efficient call-up in time of war. With each army corps stationed in the area from which it drew its reserves, the Prussian army had corps, divisions, and regiments in existence in peacetime that it could mobilize quickly in war.

Strong opposition, however, appeared in the Prussian assembly in 1860. Wilhelm demanded maintenance of a three-year term of service for conscripts as well as sufficient funding to ensure that the increasing population in Prussia could serve in the military. The assembly, however, refused additional appropriations unless the monarch granted constitutional reforms. When Otto von Bismarck became chancellor in September 1862, he announced that with a deadlock between the king and assembly, the constitution permitted the king to collect taxes for expenditures necessary to support the state's activities. Amidst increasing discontent, the king dissolved the assembly in late 1863. But within six months the outbreak of war with Denmark over Schleswig-Holstein and a surge of nationalist sentiment derailed attempts to establish responsible constitutional government. Wilhelm implemented the Roon reforms, but not until after the war of 1866 with Austria did the assembly formally approve them.

The General Staff

The establishment of the Prussian general staff proved to be a key step. In most armies staff officers were little more than clerks for commanders, but they became something clearly different in the Prussian military. Following Jena-Auerstädt, improvements in officer education resulted in the formation of the War College, the *Kriegsakademie*. That institution turned out a small number of highly trained, intellectually prepared staff officers to attend to the myriad details confronting military organizations. These officers performed well enough in the "war of liberation" against the French (1813–1815) to keep postwar retrenchment from eliminating the War College.

After 1815 the most talented graduates of the *Kriegsakademie* formed the body of the Prussian general staff. After two years of service on the staff and the successful completion of another examination, candidates became full members of the general staff only if they received the recommendation of their superiors. The final step in a general staff officer's training was participation in a "staff ride," or study of a historical campaign, under the chief of the general staff's personal supervision. Officers who entered the elite group were intensively schooled in operations, staff procedures, and technical matters, but as subsequent events were to demonstrate, they lacked a thorough understanding of strategy and its relationship to policy.

Neither the general staff nor its leader, the chief of the general staff, dominated the army or its officer corps, but the presence throughout the army of specialists trained in the intricacies of military planning ensured that commanders received high-quality advice about the conduct of operations. Ultimately the general staff's administrative and professional skills provided the Prussians with the capacity to mobilize, deploy, and then support large forces in a fashion that no other army could match. Additionally, the general staff provided an alternative chain of command through which the chief of staff could bend the army to his will. Rigorous training of general staff officers ensured that they shared a common vocabulary and approach and that they understood the technical intricacies of managing large military organi-

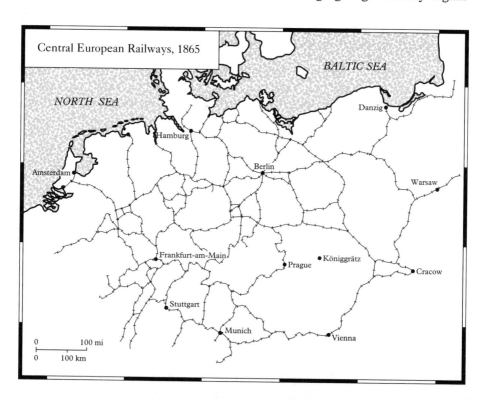

Central European Railways, 1865

zations. In effect, the general staff represented a crucial step in advancing professionalism in European military institutions.

Members of the general staff played a crucial role in preparing the Prussian army for the next war and in adapting its institutions to an increasingly complex and technological world. Among its innovations, the general staff invented war games and used them to delineate operational features and possibilities. As a consequence of war games and technical studies, general staff officers recognized very early the value of railroads to the mobilization and deployment of armies. Given the fact that Prussia had frontiers with three major powers—Russia in the east, France in the west, and Austria in the south—railroads offered the Prussians important advantages. From 1840 to 1860, Germany's railroad systems expanded rapidly. In 1840 the German railroads possessed only 291 miles of track; by 1850 the lines had grown to 3,369 miles, a rate of expansion double that occurring in France; and by 1854 the German Confederation possessed nearly 7,500 miles of railroads. By 1860, Prussia itself possessed 3,500 miles of railroads. The expansion of railways went hand-in-glove with significant input from the Prussian general staff.

But it was not just the utilization of railroads that provided the Prussians an advantage over potential opponents. The Prussian army also quickly recognized the importance of the telegraph for communicating with its forces. It was also the first military force to adopt a breech-loading rifle, the needle gun. That weapon, whatever its defects—and they were considerable—allowed Prussian infantry to load and reload at a rate three to four times faster than soldiers equipped with muzzle-loading weapons. Moreover, Prussians soldiers could now reload while lying down, an obvious advantage.

Despite the willingness to adopt a new rifle, the Prussians were less willing to innovate with artillery. Not until 1859 did the army purchase cast-steel barrels for its artillery. As the Danish War of 1864 drew to a close, the Prussians purchased additional cast-steel barrels. The army would enter the Seven Weeks' War in 1866 with 90 of its 144 artillery batteries supplied with cast-steel, rifled, breech-loading guns and with 54 batteries equipped with bronze, smoothbore muzzleloaders. The greatest flaw with their artillery, however, proved to be in doctrine, for the Prussians habitually placed their guns too far in the rear.

Despite shortcomings in artillery, Prussia possessed a military instrument of great potential. Adding to this potential was the presence of General Helmuth von Moltke, chief of the general staff after 1857. Moltke joined the Prussian army in 1822, attended the *Kriegsakademie,* and in 1833 became a member of the general staff. He spent little time in troop assignments; instead, he served most of his career as a staff officer focusing on the problems of mobilization and on the use of railroads. For a time in the 1840s, he even served on the board of directors of one of the new railroad companies that had sprung up throughout Germany.

As chief of the general staff, Moltke instituted a number of planning exercises and war games to examine how the army might best utilize railroads in potential conflicts. In fact, a general staff exercise on a proposed

After becoming Prussian chief of the general staff in 1857, General Helmuth von Moltke increased the power and prestige of that position. He recognized the operational and strategic implications of railroads.

concentration of the army around Hamburg eventually formed the basis for the deployment against Denmark in 1864. His studies and his participation in these exercises enabled Moltke to become one of the most outstanding campaign strategists in the nineteenth century.

On the eve of war with Austria, Wilhelm had great confidence in the abilities of Moltke and in June 1866 granted him authority to communicate directly with subordinate commanders and to bypass the Ministry of War. Moltke became the *de facto* commander of the Prussian army, his power limited only by the powers of the king. In the middle of 1866, Prussia possessed an army and a chief of the general staff capable of executing the strategic policies of the king and chancellor in brilliant campaigns.

The Seven Weeks' War

Improvements in the Prussian army occurred at the same time that Bismarck became chancellor and assumed the reins of power. Possessing clear foreign policy objectives, he warned the Prussian assembly: "Not by speeches and majority votes are the great questions of the day decided—that was the great mistake of 1848 to 1849—but by blood and iron." At first, Bismarck did not aim at a unified Germany. Rather, he hoped to achieve a *modus vivendi* with the Austrians, in which Prussia would control Protestant north Germany, while Austria dominated the south German Catholic states. But the Austrians displayed no interest in such an agreement; they believed they held the upper hand in Germany. Bismarck, however, understood that the coming contest was not a matter of right or historical tradition; it was a matter of military and economic power, something he would demonstrate conclusively in the Danish War of 1864, the Seven Weeks' War of 1866, and the Franco-Prussian War of 1870–1871.

During the first war, which began in 1864 in a crisis over the fate of Schleswig-Holstein, Bismarck consolidated his internal position in Prussia and set the stage for the conflict with Austria. The provinces of Schleswig-Holstein had traditionally formed a portion of the territories ruled by the king of Denmark. But there was no direct male heir to the late king, and the issue of who would inherit the provinces loomed as a major issue in European politics. The Danes maintained their claim to the provinces; popular opinion in the German states—including Austria—demanded that a German prince rule Schleswig-Holstein. An unequal struggle ensued in which the armies of the German Confederation, led by Prussia and Austria, easily defeated Danish forces and dictated peace in Copenhagen. The Prussian army performed effectively but not brilliantly in this campaign. Its commander, an elderly Prussian field marshal, even complained that the general staff did not make a useful contribution and placed unnecessary administrative requirements on him.

Through the chancellor's manipulations, Prussia and Austria received joint stewardship over Schleswig-Holstein until the German states agreed on a final settlement. The Austrians occupied territory, the lines of communication to which lay entirely under Prussian control. Thus Bismarck could squeeze the Austrians to his heart's desire, while the latter possessed little leverage. Initially Bismarck hoped to turn the situation to Prussia's advantage in negotiations, but Vienna obdurately defended its position as the first state in Germany.

Austrian intransigence encouraged Bismarck to seek a more decisive end to Habsburg interference in north German affairs, and by early 1866 he had laid the groundwork for war with Austria. He promised Napoleon III territorial gains in south Germany if the French remained out of the war. On their part, the French calculated that Prussia was the underdog; they also believed that a struggle between German powers would allow France to make major gains in south Germany. In April 1866, Bismarck concluded a secret agreement with Italy and promised that the Italians could annex Venetia if they fought on Prussia's side. As the crisis intensified, the British displayed general disinterest in central European troubles; the Russians were equally disinterested. Bismarck's greatest problem lay in persuading Wilhelm that a war with Austria was both moral and necessary. The Austrians, fortunately, provided both rationale and argument. By denouncing Prussia in the German Diet in ringing terms, Austrian leaders handed Bismarck the chance to depict them as the aggressors.

On the eve of war, European military experts regarded the Austrian Empire as the strongest power in central Europe. Nevertheless the Austrians suffered from severe deficiencies. Their commander, Field Marshal Ludwig von Benedek, had no experience with maneuvering large forces. Additionally, the Austrians had no reserve organization like the Prussians, no modern mobilization system, no divisions (having only corps and brigades except in the cavalry), no modern staff system akin to the Prussian general staff, and no rigorous professional education for their officers. The Austrians also relied on infantry shock tactics reminiscent of Napoleonic methods. French tactics of 1859, which included an initial advance with skirmishers followed by a mass bayonet charge, had greatly impressed the Austrian generals. But such tactics would prove most vulnerable in 1866 to accurate fire from breech-loading rifles. The Austrians had converted their muskets to rifled muskets, but these were no match for the Prussians' needle guns. About the only advantage they possessed was in their artillery. Since the Austrians believed that victory depended on shock effect from infantry columns, they placed their artillery as far forward as possible, rather than in the rear. They also had more rifled cannon, and their batteries had trained in the areas in which the major battles would occur.

The Initial Moves

With regard to the strategic situation, the Prussians appeared to enjoy few advantages in the summer of 1866. The other German states supported Austria; Prussia's territory spread from the Rhine to Russia, while its western provinces (Rhineland and Westphalia) not only were unreliable but also were separated from the Prussian heartland by the Kingdom of Hanover. Moreover, Austria's control of Bohemia and Moravia—the modern Czech state—provided the Austrians with an advantageous position where they could mobilize and deploy and from which they could strike at Berlin. The Prussians' task was even more difficult because the king was reluctant to appear the aggressor and thus delayed mobilization. Though the Austrians began their mobilization on April 21 and accelerated it on April 27, the Prussians did not begin mobilizing until May 3 and gave the order for complete mobilization only on May 12.

Despite such apparent disadvantages for the Prussians, organization and technological improvements had changed the game. As the Austrians slowly mobilized, the Prussians mobilized in less than half the time and—relying on railways—quickly occupied Hanover; thus they had linked the Rhineland with the center of Prussia at the beginning of the conflict. Meanwhile, Moltke used five railway lines to deploy the major armies around Bohemia and Moravia; the western-most army invaded the Kingdom of Saxony—allied with Austria—and promptly drove the Saxons out of their country, back on the assembling Austrians. Moltke had determined that a skillful use of railroads would allow him to deploy his forces more quickly on the Bohemian frontier than the Austrians. With great mobility, he could then march forward into Bohemia and *concentrate* the Prussian army before the Austrians completed their preparations. The preliminary actions in June 1866 fully met his expectations.

Facing threats from Prussia and Italy, Austria prepared for a two-front war. The southern army easily and quickly defeated the Italians at Custozza on June 28. However, there were problems in the north. With only one railway line available, Field Marshal Benedek began moving the northern army toward Bohemia on June 18. After confirming the direction of the Austrian move, Moltke ordered his forces to advance into Bohemia,

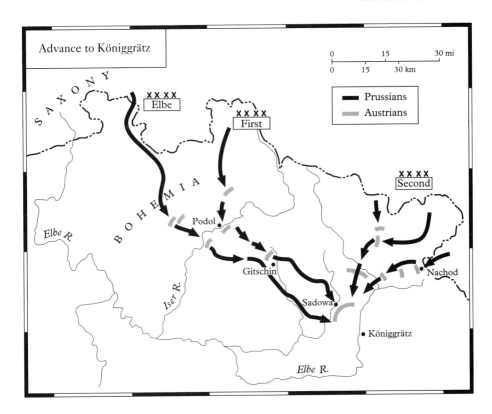

Advance to Königgrätz

0   15   30 mi

0   15   30 km

Prussians

Austrians

SAXONY

XXXX
Elbe

XXXX
First

XXXX
Second

BOHEMIA

Elbe R.

Iser R.

Podol

Gitschin

Nachod

Sadowa

Königgrätz

Elbe R.

and the first Prussian troops crossed the border on June 22. The Prussian campaign strategy was unorthodox, for it planned on three armies advancing on widely separate routes (split by some one hundred miles from the far left to the far right) and converging on the main Austrian forces. The plan did place the Prussian forces at risk, for it offered Benedek the opportunity to use interior lines to defeat each Prussian army in turn. Moltke, nonetheless, believed that his forces could concentrate before the Austrians could react.

The 1866 Campaign

On the Prussian right and center, the Elbe Army and First Army advanced through western and central Bohemia. In one battle on June 26, the Austrians relied on a bayonet charge against Prussian infantry concealed in woods. In another action that day, the Prussians seized a bridge across the Iser River at Podol, but the Austrians drove them back. When the Austrians charged, Prussian fire from accurate, rapid-fire, breech-loading rifles had a devastating effect on their closely packed columns and finally forced them to withdraw. With the loss of 130 men at Podol, the Prussians inflicted more than 1,000 casualties on the Austrians. This battle and the performance of the needle gun set the tone for the remainder of the campaign.

On the Prussian left, the first heavy fighting occurred at Nachod in northeastern Bohemia on June 27. V Corps, which was part of Second

Army, moved forward rapidly and occupied a small plateau in eastern Bohemia. The Austrians attempted to clear the plateau with artillery but soon launched a series of ill-coordinated infantry attacks. In what some have called a "contest between the bayonet and the bullet," breech-loading rifles again inflicted devastating casualties on the Austrians. After some spirited cavalry charges, the Austrians withdrew, having lost 2,200 killed or wounded and 3,400 captured or missing; the Prussian losses were only 1,112. In other battles in eastern Bohemia, the Prussian Second Army pushed back Austrian forces on June 27–28.

On their right in central Bohemia, the Prussians won a sharp fight at Gitschin on June 29 against an Austro-Saxon force. Though achieving some success, the Saxon commander received orders to pull back and attempted to do so while still in heavy contact. In the resulting confusion, the Austrian and Saxon formations disintegrated. The defeat at Gitschin, as well as the other losses, shocked Field Marshal Benedek. Though his troops had bested

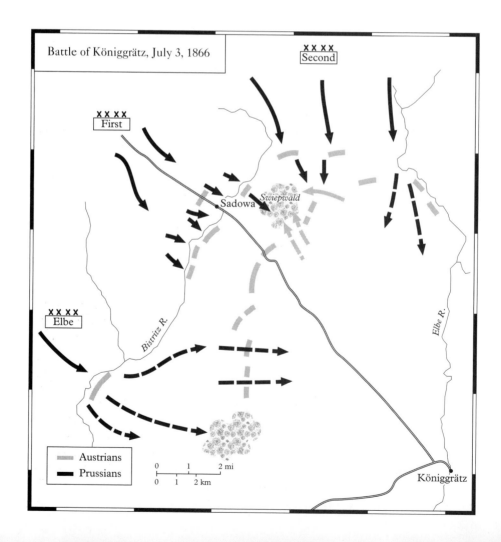

the Prussians in a few encounters, he concluded that they could not win and asked his emperor to make peace. The emperor refused, leaving Benedek no choice but to choose a location for a final fight.

Pulling back, Benedek placed his army in a weak defensive position along a line of hills eight miles northwest of Königgrätz with his back to a river. He planned on wearing the Prussians down with a defensive battle and then counterattacking. The Austrians prepared their position in a lackadaisical fashion and uncharacteristically massed their artillery to the rear. On July 3, Prince Frederick Charles's First Army arrived on the battlefield; it had traveled about seventy miles from the Prussian frontier. It received the first Austrian artillery fire at 7:30 in the morning. The Prussians initially did not recognize that they had encountered the main enemy force, drawn up in a tight defensive position, and Frederick Charles began preparing to smash the Austrian center.

Before his subordinates, Moltke sensed that Prussian forces had hit the main Austrian army. While First Army pressed against the Austrians' center, attacks on the flanks—Moltke believed—would decide the battle. The Elbe Army would press the Austrian left and Second Army would crush their right. With the arrival of Second Army still uncertain, Moltke recognized the risks of First Army suffering heavy losses and being subjected to a major counterattack by Austrian reserves.

In the early morning First Army launched a frontal assault against the Austrian center; it met the massed power of Austrian and Saxon artillery and rifled muskets. While Prussian artillery contributed little to the battle, Austrian artillery proved highly effective. Their rifled muskets also had a greater effect than in earlier encounters, because heavy smoke from black-powder ammunition concealed the Austro-Saxon forces and provided some respite from the needle guns. Despite heavy enemy fire, the Prussian 7th Division seized a small wooded area, the *Swiepwald,* in the center-right part of the Austrian line. It then crushed a counterattacking Austrian brigade.

Instead of defending, the Austrian IV Corps commander determined to regain what his troops had lost. An Austrian brigade attacked with bugles blowing and drums beating and tried to overrun the Prussians. Its attack died before the firepower of breech-loading rifles. Other assaults by brigades in IV Corps and then II Corps followed until the Prussians had mauled eight out of the ten brigades in the two corps. As these attacks continued, the Austrian right flank slowly but inexorably weakened, while the Prussian 7th Division maintained its hold on the woods.

By noon, the Austrians had shown little sign of collapse, and the Prussians worried about the arrival of Second Army. Units from Crown Prince Frederick William's army finally arrived and by two o'clock were decisively engaged. The Crown Prince's army had been approximately fifteen miles from the battlefield in the morning and, hearing heavy fighting near Königgrätz, had marched toward the sound of guns. When it arrived, it found the enemy thoroughly distracted by the attacks of First Army and its right weakened by bloody assaults on the *Swiepwald.*

Though heavy fighting continued, the Austrian right flank eventually collapsed before Second Army. At about the same time, the Elbe Army pushed through the Austrian left flank. Only extraordinary efforts by Benedek prevented the Prussians from destroying his entire army. He launched VI Corps in a desperate attack against the Prussian center and followed up with an attack by I Corps. In this second attack, I Corps lost 10,000 men in barely one hour—half its morning's strength. The final resistance helped the Austrians get some forces back across the river to their rear. In one day's fighting, however, they had lost 41,000 killed or wounded; a further 20,000 were in Prussian hands as prisoners. Total casualties for the Prussians were only 9,000 killed or wounded.

Making Peace

The remaining Austrians were incapable of continuing. Despite victory over the Italians at Custozza on June 28, the army was a broken reed that could not defend Vienna. Moltke urged his king to allow an advance to the gates of Vienna to complete destruction of the Austrian army. Bismarck, however, disagreed, and a frightful row ensued. Using all of his persuasive powers, the chancellor urged the opposite course: immediate peace with Austria, no financial or territorial penalties on the Habsburg monarchy, and Prussia's territorial gains limited to north Germany.

The chancellor recognized that destruction of the Austrians would serve neither Prussia's strategic nor political interests. France and Russia would gain the most from a collapse of Habsburg power. Moreover, continuation of the war might result in France's entry into the conflict. Finally, Bismarck argued that one could not be sure of Russia's continuing disinterest. If, however, Prussia offered Austria generous terms, especially considering the military situation, the enemy would accept a long-term settlement. After all, Austria would lose no territory and pay no financial indemnity; all it had to do was recognize Prussia's hegemony over north Germany and indirect control of south Germany. Prussia's territorial gains would come at the expense of north German states rather than of Austria. In sum, the Austrians would have to swallow only the loss of other people's territory—a relatively easy thing to endure.

Bismarck's settlement represented inspired statesmanship. The peace treaty dissolved the old German Confederation, and Prussia annexed Schleswig-Holstein, Hanover, Nassau, Hesse, and Frankfurt. Austria recognized the North German Confederation, the new union of north German states under Prussia. Prussia also gained a dominant influence over the military and foreign policies of the south German states. Bavaria signed a secret agreement promising to aid Prussia in the event of war with France. While respecting the territorial integrity of Austria, Bismarck had freed Germany from Austria. Few victories in military history have gained such widespread strategic advantages; those gains, however, flowed as much from Bismarck's diplomacy as from the competence of the army and its general staff.

The Franco-Prussian War

In the aftermath, Bismarck was content to consolidate Prussia's gains. He felt no overwhelming desire for a united Germany; to the chancellor the south German states were bastions of Catholicism and liberalism—both anathema to him. Moreover, another major conflict might cause the fragile North German Confederation to fracture.

But French policy made a prolonged period of consolidation impossible; the formation of the North German Confederation had altered the balance of power and created a menacing concentration of power on France's northeastern frontier. In an attempt to redress the balance, Napoleon III demanded compensation from Bismarck in the form of territory on the left bank of the Rhine and in Belgium. Bismarck refused. Public discomfiture over the decline in France's position threatened Napoleon's tenuous political position in Paris. He had ruled France as emperor since 1852, and discontent with his rule and demands for democratic reforms had increased during the 1860s. With Napoleon desperately in need of diplomatic or military triumphs, it was difficult to avoid an international crisis.

While Napoleon III blustered, Bismarck became increasingly concerned about the unstable political situation in southern Germany. As long as the south German states remained semi-independent, they represented an incalculable factor that outside influences—either French or Austrian—could manipulate to Prussia's disadvantage. By 1870, Bismarck had ensured that French efforts to bring Austria and Italy to the French side would fail. His generous terms, as well as the thorough thrashing the Austrians had received, persuaded Vienna to remain outside any Franco-Prussian conflict, unless things went badly for Prussia. Having been soundly beaten by Austria in 1866, Italy had insufficient funds and forces to risk war. The Russians promised neutrality, and the British had no desire to become involved in another war on the continent. Recognizing that a war would come sooner or later, Bismarck believed the situation was ripe.

The Opposing Forces

As had the Austrians, the French appeared to be a capable foe for the Prussians. After all, they had achieved military success in the Crimean War of 1854–1856 and in the Italian War of 1859. The French had failed, however, to adapt their forces to the new demands of warfare; they remained content even though serious deficiencies—particularly in transportation and supply systems—were apparent in the 1859 Italian campaign. France had abandoned the universal military service of the revolution and relied instead on 350,000 professionals and those few who drew "bad numbers" in a national lottery and could not afford to hire substitutes. After 1859, the French attempted to improve their inefficient reserve system, but the reforms remained only partially implemented. Additionally, they had no staff system comparable to the Prussian general staff. Napoleon III, the French emperor, had recognized the effectiveness of the Prussian military system during the Seven Weeks' War, and he attempted to create a similar system. Unfortunately for France, the emperor met substantial opposition across the spectrum of political life. Liberals refused to pass the necessary legislation unless the emperor granted political concessions, while conservative generals displayed little interest in reserve forces. The result was evident in the chaotic mobilization for the war. A telegram sent by a general officer to the Ministry of War in July 1870 underlines the system's failure: "Am in Belfort; can't find brigade; can't find commanding general; what must I do; don't know where my regiments are."

The French also had little experience in maneuvering large units. They maintained few forces above the regimental level in peacetime, and when war came they formed brigades, divisions, corps, and field armies on an ad hoc basis. Training of regiments in peacetime mostly consisted of parades and carefully controlled field maneuvers. Expeditions to northern Africa and other parts of the world against poorly armed opponents further obscured the importance of officers' knowing how to control and supply large formations or how to combine infantry, cavalry, and artillery. Veterans of such campaigns saw no reason for a systematic study of warfare. Except for regimental schools, which primarily taught reading and writing, most officers had no formal military education. In the simplest terms, the French military structure was woefully out of date.

The Prussians had a much better system. As demonstrated during the Seven Weeks' War, they could mobilize, deploy, and maneuver a large army quickly and easily. After 1866 the Prussians expanded their military system throughout the North German Confederation. Though some reluctance to change appeared, the system of "area commands" covered the entire Confederation with an army corps in each area. The Confederation relied on universal military service and the reserves and militia. Conscripts had to spend three years in the active force, four years in the reserves, and five years in the militia. The king of Prussia received complete command over the armies of the states in the Confederation, and Moltke and the general staff—though small in numbers—held great influence because of their superb performance in 1866.

The Prussians made some adjustments to their tactical doctrine between 1866 and 1870. They had begun the 1866 campaign by employing thick skirmish lines ahead of battalions in column. Finding such formations too dense, they modified their tactics and employed skirmish lines ahead of companies in column. This spread their troops and made them less vulnerable to enemy fire. During the course of the 1870–1871 campaign, however, the Germans would discover that even greater dispersion was necessary against rapidly firing, breech-loading rifles.

Though Prussian infantry tactics and weapons were less successful in 1870, the effectiveness of Prussian artillery proved one of the most significant surprises of the war. Shortly after the Seven Weeks' War, the Prussians replaced the last of their bronze, smoothbore guns with cast-steel, rifled breech-loading guns, which outranged those of the French. Napoleon III had personally supervised the production of bronze, muzzle-loading, rifled guns, which had performed well against the Austrians, but they would not perform well against the Prussians.

Ironically the Prussians lost a major tactical advantage they had possessed in the war against Austria. French infantry possessed a rifle, the *chassepot*, superior in every respect to the needle gun. Developed after the French saw the effectiveness of Prussian breechloaders in 1866, the *chassepot* was a rifled breechloader with greater range and rate of fire. The newest, and most impressive, technological advancement, however, found little use on the battlefield. The French had developed a machine gun, the *mitrailleuse*, but since it was about the size of a light field gun, they placed it with the artillery rather than the infantry. In the end, the Prussian victory came less from advantages in weapons than from superior strategy, better operational performance, a more effective command-and-staff system, and a more modern military organization.

The Initial Moves

In hindsight, the incidents precipitating the war were trivial. In early 1870 the Spanish king died without an heir. Impressed by the Prussian victory over Austria, the Spanish offered an obscure Catholic member of the Hohenzollern family their crown. The French immediately objected. Napoleon III felt that the offer represented an insult to France's honor and a significant blow to his weakening political position.

Bismarck, however, was delighted at an opportunity to manipulate the French, especially if he could make them appear the aggressors. But Wilhelm proved unwilling to allow a quarrel over Spanish inheritance to escalate into a conflict between Prussia and France. At this point, the French had won a significant point, but Napoleon III miscalculated. He ordered his ambassador in Berlin to *demand* that the Prussian king agree that no Prussian prince would *ever* consider such an offer. Wilhelm sent Bismarck an account of the meeting in which he (the king) had acted in exemplary fashion. The chancellor then edited the text in such a fashion that the Prussians believed that the French had insulted their ruler, while the French concluded that the Prussian king had mistreated their ambassador. The Ems Dispatch precipitated a crisis between the two powers, as crowds in Berlin and Paris demanded war. On July 19, Napoleon III declared war on Prussia and immediately found himself and his nation isolated. Austria, Italy, Russia, and Britain quickly indicated they would remain out of the war.

After mobilization, Napoleon III planned to invade south Germany as quickly as possible. He expected such an attack to convince the south German states to remain neutral and to encourage the Austrians to join in the war against Prussia. Prior to the outbreak of the conflict, the French had prepared to concentrate their forces in three armies on the northeastern frontier. Concluding that a nephew of the great Napoleon had to lead his armies in the field, Napoleon III announced that he would command the army in person and that it would not be divided into field armies. French forces began concentrating at Metz and Strasbourg under the provisional control of Marshal François Bazaine until the emperor arrived. Amidst the chaotic and poorly planned mobilization, less than half the reservists had reached their regiments three weeks after mobilization, and most lacked key items of uniform and equipment. The assembling armies also lacked crucial supplies, including food, medical stores, and maps.

The Battles Along the Frontier

Despite such shortcomings, six divisions of the French covering force moved into Germany and occupied Saarbrücken on August 2 against little resistance; on the next day, they pulled back three miles from the Saar River to strong positions around Spicheren. Over succeeding days, Napoleon III scattered his corps along the northeastern frontier, so they could block obvious avenues of approach. The distances between them, however, were too great to allow them to be mutually supporting. Notions of striking deep into Germany disappeared under the harsh realization that the French army did not possess the supplies to support such a move. To make command of his

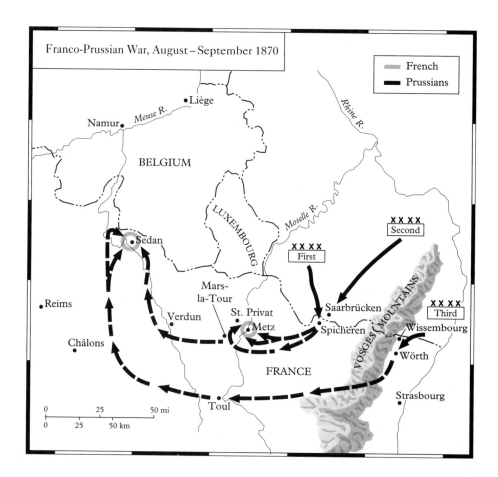

scattered forces easier, Napoleon III placed his right wing under the control of Marshal Patrice MacMahon and his left wing under Marshal Bazaine.

Meanwhile the German mobilization proceeded smoothly, and Moltke soon had three armies under his command. On his right was First Army under General Carl Friedrich von Steinmetz with 50,000 men; in his center was Second Army under Prince Frederick Charles with 134,000; and on his left was Third Army under Crown Prince Frederick William with 125,000. Hoping for another Königgrätz and expecting the French to strike across the Saar River, Moltke planned to receive the attack with his center, First Army, and then to envelop the French with the stronger Second and Third armies on the wings.

After the French pulled back from Saarbrücken, German forces advanced toward the Saar on August 6. When they discovered the French withdrawal, the commanders of the First and Second armies threw aside Moltke's careful plans and advanced; they believed the French were retreating. Discovering the French instead on the heights of Spicheren, and marching to the sound of guns, units from both armies rushed into battle. The French II Corps performed well in its strong defensive positions; the highly accurate and rapid fire from *chassepot* rifles threw back the German frontal assaults against the heights. But Bazaine failed to move reinforcements forward, even though he had four divisions within fifteen miles of the battle. The Germans eventually moved around the French flank in the north and forced them to withdraw.

Fifty miles to the east, Moltke's Third Army moved against Wissembourg (twenty miles west of Karlsruhe) on August 4, easily overwhelming the outnumbered defenders. On August 6 Third Army unexpectedly encountered the French at Wörth and the Froeschwiller heights. What began as a minor shelling of a few French defenders in Wörth ultimately involved more than three German corps. In a bitterly contested battle that Marshal MacMahon personally directed, the French found themselves helpless under devastating artillery fire. French resistance finally collapsed, and MacMahon lost nearly 20,000 men, including 9,000 prisoners, while the Germans lost about 10,500 troops.

The Battles Around Metz and Sedan

The two defeats on August 6 had far-reaching effects on the French. Losing his nerve, Napoleon III abandoned all hopes of invading Germany and ordered his armies to retreat to Châlons, more than one hundred miles to the west. He soon reversed himself and had the four corps on the French left fall back on Metz (about thirty miles to the rear), while the other corps retreated to Châlons, where he intended to form a new army. On August 10, MacMahon began entraining his exhausted men for Châlons, and between August 9 and 13, Bazaine marched four corps to positions ten miles east of Metz. Bazaine eventually ended up with 180,000 soldiers along a twelve-mile front.

As the French withdrew, Moltke's hopes for another Königgrätz evaporated, but he ordered his armies forward. The Germans advanced with the three armies abreast, spread over a front of more than fifty miles. On August 14 the French began a disorganized withdrawal across the Moselle River at Metz just as the enemy's advance guard struck their defensive positions in an impetuous attack. The French beat off the German attack, but in doing so they delayed their crossing of the Moselle River and their withdrawal to the west. Meanwhile, German forces crossed the Moselle south of Metz, turned north, and threatened to cut off the French route of withdrawal. With the Germans threatening to encircle the French, the heaviest fighting occurred along the main road out of Metz at Rezonville, Vionville, and Mars-la-Tour. Despite heavy losses, the Germans finally managed around dark on August 17 to cut the road at Rezonville, leaving the French only one route out of Metz toward Châlons. Instead of trying to break through to the west and regain operational freedom, Bazaine pulled his forces back toward Metz. This allowed the Prussians to continue their drive and placed the entire French force in danger of encirclement.

Moltke, with the First and Second armies west of Metz, moved north the following morning and completed the envelopment of Bazaine's army. The Germans soon discovered that the French had pulled back into strong defensive positions between Gravelotte and St. Privat. Attacking from west to east, the Germans pressed against Gravelotte on their right. After pounding the French position for hours with artillery, the commander of First Army ordered his men forward, but heavy rifle fire threw them back with heavy losses. A series of uncoordinated attacks served only to add to the casualty lists without results. French defenders smashed the last attack so decisively that German attackers almost entirely collapsed. In the north at St. Privat, the French VI Corps of 23,000 men held off attack after attack throughout the day by nearly 100,000 Prussians of Second Army. Though initially cautious, the commander of Second Army inexplicably gave the order around 6 P.M. for a frontal assault without artillery support. The Germans lost more than 8,000 men in about twenty minutes.

Fortunately for Moltke, the French never launched a counterattack. During the heaviest fighting, the Imperial Guard, the elite reserve of the French army, moved to a position between St. Privat and Gravelotte and awaited orders from Bazaine. None came. One brigade commander in the French forces recognized how serious the German position was, but he did nothing. He wrote in his report, "I did not think that I should pursue them [the Prussians], having been ordered to remain on the defensive."

Despite suffering some 20,000 casualties on this day while inflicting only 12,000 on the French, the Germans managed to get around the northern flank of the French at St. Privat. This maneuver forced the French to pull back into the fortress at Metz on August 19. Though Moltke had not won another Königgrätz, the Germans had succeeded in trapping the main Imperial army.

While the Germans encircled Bazaine at Metz, the French assembled some 130,000 soldiers and 423 guns at Châlons. Marshal MacMahon received command of these forces, but the emperor, in thoroughly bad health, accompanied them—seeking to raise the empire's prestige—while the empress remained in Paris to control a rising tide of criticism. MacMahon's advance proved as misshaped in its operational concept as those that had resulted in the surrounding of Bazaine's army. Seeking to break through to Metz, MacMahon moved his forces on August 21 north toward Belgium. He hoped to relieve Metz by advancing east along the frontier. This move, however, robbed his army entirely of its room for maneuver. Denied movement north by Belgian neutrality, MacMahon's forces soon found themselves in the same situation as the troops in Metz.

Leaving screening forces at Metz, Moltke advanced west on a broad front. On August 26, German cavalry located MacMahon's forces, and four days later German infantry made contact with them. After a series of skirmishes, the Germans drove the French north into Sedan, the site of an equally disastrous French defeat seventy years later.

By September 1 the Germans had hemmed the relieving French army in the fortress at Sedan. Two desperate cavalry charges failed to break through the German lines, and heavy artillery fire began smothering every French movement. Despite objections from French commanders, the emperor formally surrendered with 83,000 men and 449 guns on September 2; this was one of the most humiliating defeats French arms have suffered ever.

Besieging Paris and Fighting the French Nation

Destruction of MacMahon's army at Sedan signaled the end of the second Bonapartist empire. Like the encirclement of Bazaine's army, however, it did not end the war. News of the catastrophe at Sedan led to the proclamation in Paris of a republic. Hoping to launch a revolution akin to that of 1789, the leaders of the new regime refused to negotiate. Instead, they declared a *levée en masse* and a mobilization of the economy to fight a total war against the invading Germans. They might have stood some prospect of success had Sedan and Metz not resulted in a loss of virtually all of France's professional officers and noncommissioned officers. Republican leaders set in motion desperate measures to replace the forces the empire had lost; the international arms market stepped in to supply a mixed collection of arms to equip newly mobilized armies that the republic desperately attempted to train. But the problem for France was that it was starting with almost nothing. The new army had no logistics system to support a modern army, no staff system to control its movement, and few professional soldiers to provide the leadership and training to turn raw levies into serious soldiers. Nevertheless, republican leaders hoped that while Paris held out, the provinces could mobilize and deploy forces sufficient to defeat the invader.

By mid-September, German forces had encircled the French capital. Without an effective field army, the French had withdrawn from the area around Paris; but the Parisians had strengthened the city's fortifications and had built up stocks for a prolonged siege. The besieged Parisians used balloons to communicate with the outside world, but the balloons could not offset German military superiority. To Bismarck, continued French resistance created the possibility of Austrian or British intervention. Almost immediately after German forces reached Paris, the chancellor demanded that military commanders bombard the city to force the French to capitulate. Short of heavy guns and ammunition, Moltke refused; his commanders were reluctant to undertake an assault on the city's outer fortifications. Most military leaders preferred to starve the Parisians into submission. Bismarck's efforts to force the army to begin the bombardment infuriated Moltke; the chief of staff regarded the chancellor's actions as the intrusion of politics and interference in the army's sphere. But Bismarck even dragged the German press into the quarrel. As winter approached, squabbling among German leaders intensified.

Meanwhile the war became something other than a contest between regular armies. With the German lines of communication long and vulnerable, the French launched a systematic guerrilla war aimed at breaking up the logistical lines. In response, German forces undertook savage reprisals. As the war assumed an unfamiliar pattern and the distinction between soldier and civilian faded, Moltke complained, "It is all wrong to lead whole peoples against each other. That is not progress, but a return to barbarism." The French Republic also launched its ill-trained armies at the Germans in a series of desperate attempts to relieve Paris. Despite the extraordinary courage and enthusiasm of the French, such attacks had no chance; German forces were well equipped and trained and possessed great confidence because of their earlier victories.

The bombardment of Paris finally began on December 27. However, the chief of staff and the chancellor continued their argument over political and military issues. In the end Wilhelm, soon to become the emperor of the Germans, came down on Bismarck's side. Though the chancellor won the quarrel over political control in the war against France, Moltke continued to argue that operations should remain "independent" from politics. He insisted, "I am concerned only with military matters." His attempt to separate military issues from politics had an unfortunate long-term effect on the German military's thinking about strategy and politics in the twentieth century.

In the end, the bombardment of Paris accelerated the collapse of French resistance. On January 28, 1871, the two sides signed an armistice. In March, however, another revolution broke out in Paris, this time against the newly elected French National Assembly. The second siege of Paris began on April 2, this time by the French army. In some of the most savage fighting of the nineteenth century, the French finally quelled the rebellion at the end of May.

Proclaiming the German Empire

With the armistice, Bismarck confronted the questions of making peace with France and solidifying the new German state. In dealing with these issues, Bismarck arrived at less than satisfactory conclusions, but the crush of events and the intractable nature of the problems limited the paths open to the chancellor. He attempted to turn aside nationalists' demands for punishing

France, but the Prussian military added their voices to demands that Germany acquire Metz as well as Alsace-Lorraine to defend the Rhine. Bismarck recognized that such an acquisition would severely damage future relations between France and Germany, but he eventually yielded to demands to punish France. In contrast to the generous peace accorded Austria, France had to cede the provinces of Alsace and Lorraine and pay an indemnity of 5 billion francs.

In the hall of mirrors in Louis XIV's palace at Versailles, the Prussian military proclaimed the new empire. The circumstances of its *political* declaration in the palace of a defeated enemy, before senior officers of the Prussian and German armies, established an unfortunate path for the new state. Those circumstances distorted political processes and civil-military relations in Germany until the end of World War II. The aura of an invincible army, led by Moltke's general staff, provided the military of the new state with a status and arrogance that held dangerous political consequences for the future. Much of the German nation accepted the uncritical notion of their army's invincibility. They forgot the decisive role that Bismarck's political and strategic genius had played in creating the conditions under which the army had waged its successful wars.

Germany's new constitution also placed the military of the state beyond the control of popularly elected officials. The army would answer only to the emperor. After Bismarck left the scene, the next generation of politicians would have neither constitutional links to the military nor other means to control the military's input into the political and strategic goals of the state. Such constitutional arrangements were exceedingly dangerous, but the newly acquired prestige of the German army, the military's rejection of political control, and the irresponsibility of Kaiser Wilhelm II after 1888 magnified the danger. The result was a recipe for national disaster and continental catastrophe.

✯   ✯   ✯   ✯

Between 1852 and 1871, the conduct of war assumed a different form from that of 1815. The introduction and perfection of the rifled musket and then the breech-loading rifle changed the face of battle. Modifications also occurred with artillery as the cast-steel, rifled, breech-loading gun replaced the smoothbore, muzzleloader. These changes added significantly to firepower and compelled the infantry to modify its tactics. Most armies abandoned massive Napoleonic formations and dispersed their infantry units.

Though these tactical and technological changes are important, more significant changes concerned the mobilization, movement, and support of large armies over great distances. The Prussians achieved success in 1866 and 1871 because their army relied on universal military service of men, possessed an organization of coherent military formations, had equipment from modern industrial factories, and was led by well-trained and schooled professionals. Additionally, the Prussians were organized in more flexible and mobile units than the Austrians and French, and they relied on modern means of communication and transportation. In the broadest sense, the German victories sprang from the Prussian "military system" in which universal military service, reserves and militia, education, training, staff skills, transportation, logistics, and technology had a place. Though the leadership of commanders and the bravery of soldiers remained important, the Germans had adapted to how warfare was changing; the French and Austrians had not.

SUGGESTED READINGS

Adriance, Thomas J. *The Last Gaiter Button: A Study of the Mobilization and Concentration of the French Army in the War of 1870* (New York: Greenwood Press, 1987).

Clausewitz, Carl von. *On War,* trans. by Michael Howard and Peter Paret (Princeton: Princeton University Press, 1976).

Craig, Gordon A. *The Battle of Königgrätz: Prussia's Victory over Austria, 1866* (Philadelphia: J. B. Lippincott, 1964).

———. *The Politics of the Prussian Army, 1640–1945* (London: Oxford University Press, 1955).

Curtiss, John S. *Russia's Crimean War* (Durham, N.C.: Duke University Press, 1979).

Goerlitz, Walter. *History of the German General Staff, 1657–1945,* trans. by Brian Battershaw (New York: Frederick A. Praeger, 1953).

Gooch, Brison D. *The New Bonapartist Generals in the Crimean War: Distrust and Decision-Making in the Anglo-French Alliance* (The Hague, Netherlands: Martinus Nijhoff, 1959).

Hamley, Edward. *The War in the Crimea* (Westport, Conn.: Greenwood Press, 1971).

Howard, Michael. *The Franco-Prussian War: The German Invasion of France, 1870–1871* (New York: Dorset Press, 1961).

Jomini, Antoine-Henri de. *The Art of War,* trans. by G. H. Mendell and W. P. Craighill (Westport, Conn.: Greenwood Press, 1971).

Lambert, Andrew D. *The Crimean War: British Grand Strategy, 1853–56* (Manchester: Manchester University Press, 1990).

Paret, Peter. *Yorck and the Era of the Prussian Reform, 1807–1815* (Princeton: Princeton University Press, 1966).

Porch, Douglas. *Army and Revolution: France, 1815–1848* (London: Routledge, 1974).

Pratt, Edwin A. *The Rise of Rail-Power in War and Conquest, 1893–1914* (London: P. S. King & Son, 1915).

Rothenberg, Gunther E. *The Army of Francis Joseph* (West Lafayette, Ind.: Purdue University Press, 1976).

Showalter, Dennis E. *Railroads and Rifles: Soldiers, Technology, and the Unification of Germany* (Hamden, Conn.: Archon Book, 1975).

PHOTOGRAPH CREDITS

Chapter 1: p. 8, Simon Pepper and Nicolas Adams, *Firearms & Fortifications Military Architecture and Siege Warfare in Sixteenth-Century Siena*, University of Chicago; p. 11, B. P. Hughes, *Firepower Weapons Effectiveness on the Battlefield, 1630–1850* Charles Scribner's Sons/Courtesy of Harvard College Library; p. 13, The National Swedish Art Museums. **Chapter 2:** p. 38, (Sebastien le Prestre de) Vauban, *De L'attaque & de la Defences des Places, La Haya de Hondt*/Courtesy of Harvard College Library; p. 44, National Portrait Gallery, London; p. 45, By permission of the Duke of Marlborough, photo by Jeremy Whittaker; p. 53, *Marlborough as Military Commander*, Charles Scribner's Sons/Courtesy of Harvard College Library; p. 54, British Museum. **Chapter 3:** p. 73, The Board of Trustees of the Royal Armouries; p. 79, Kurpflzisches Museum der Stadt Heidelberg; p. 84, Staatlliche Kuntsammlunden Dresden; p. 92, Christopher Duffy, *The Wild Goose and the Eagles a Life of Marshall von Browne 1705–1757*/Courtesy of Harvard College Library; p. 99, National Maritime Museum. **Chapter 4:** p. 118, National Gallery of Canada, Ottawa; p. 119, McCord Museum of Canadian History; p. 122, National Archives of Canada. **Chapter 5:** p. 136, Pennsylvania Academy of the Fine Arts. Gift of Maria McKean Allen and Phoebe Warren Downes through the bequest of their mother, Elizabeth Wharton McKean; p. 163, Courtesy, Independence National Historic Park. **Chapter 6:** p. 177, By permission of the Houghton Library, Harvard University; p. 181, Giraudon/Art Resource, NY; p. 185, Giraudon/Art Resource, NY. **Chapter 7:** p. 199, Giraudon/Art Resource, NY; p. 202, Art Resource; p. 220, Giraudon/Art Resource, NY; p. 225, Giraudon/Art Resource, NY; p. 230, Giraudon/Art Resource, NY. **Chapter 8:** p. 241, National Maritime Museum; p. 243, National Maritime Museum; p. 245, Art Resource, NY; p. 252, Print Collection. Miriam and Ira D. Wallach Division of Art, Prints and Photographs New York Public Library; p. 256, The Mansell Collection; p. 260, Victoria & Albert Museum. **Chapter 9:** p. 274, Giraudon/Art Resource, NY; p. 276, Giraudon/Art Resource, NY; p. 281, Giraudon/Art Resource, NY; p. 290, Giraudon/Art Resource, NY; p. 293, Hulton Deutsch. **Chapter 10:** p. 303, New York Historical Society; p. 306, Indiana Historical Society; p. 308, Courtesy of the Historic New Orleans Collection, Museum Research Center, Acc. No. 1958.98.6; p. 310, Anne S. K. Brown Military Collection, Brown University Library; p. 313, Library of Congress; p. 315, Library of Congress; p. 317, Library of Congress; p. 323, Beverly R. Robinson Collection, U.S. Naval Academy Museum; p. 325, Courtesy of the West Point Museum, United States Military Academy, West Point, NY. **Chapter 11:** p. 335, Library of Congress; p. 337, Library of Congress; p. 339, National Archives; p. 348, Library of Congress; p. 351, Beverly R. Robinson Collection, U.S. Naval Academy Museum; p. 356, Library of Congress. **Chapter 12:** p. 361, Library of Congress; p. 366, Valentine Museum;

p. 370, Library of Congress; p. 373, Library of Congress; p. 374, Library of Congress; p. 379, American Heritage Picture Collection; p. 380, M. and M. Karolik Collection, Museum of Fine Arts; p. 382, Print Collection. Miriam and Ira D. Wallach Division of Art, Prints and Photographs. The New York Public Library. Astor, Lenox and Tilden Foundations. **Chapter 13:** p. 397, Valentine Museum; p. 399, National Archives; p. 401, Library of Congress; p. 408, U.S. Naval Historical Center; p. 409, Library of Congress; p. 415, Library of Congress; p. 416, National Archives; p. 423, William Gladstone Collection. **Chapter 14:** p. 429, National Archives; p. 432, Library of Congress; p. 441, Library of Congress; p. 442, National Archives; p. 448, National Gallery of Art, Washington, D.C. gift of Edgar William and Bernice Chrysler Garbisch; p. 450, Courtesy, Peabody & Essex Museum, Salem, MA; p. 454, Copyright by White House Historical Association; Photograph by National Geographic Society. **Chapter 15:** p. 463, Hulton Deutsch; p. 464, Hulton Deutsch; p. 472, Hulton Deutsch; p. 476, Library of Congress.

INDEX